Addressing Global Health Challenges Through Financial Innovation and Health Technologies

Cong Sui
https://orcid.org/0009-0008-2657-2580
West Midlands Health Tech Innovation Accelerator, UK & University of Birmingham, UK & University College London, UK

Poshan Yu
https://orcid.org/0000-0003-1069-3675
Soochow University, China & European Business Institute, Luxembourg & Australian Studies Centre, Shanghai University, China

IGI Global
Scientific Publishing
Publishing Tomorrow's Research Today

Published in the United States of America by
IGI Global Scientific Publishing
701 East Chocolate Avenue
Hershey, PA, 17033, USA
Tel: 717-533-8845 | Fax: 717-533-7115
Website: https://www.igi-global.com E-mail: cust@igi-global.com

Library of Congress Cataloging-in-Publication Data

Names: Sui, Cong, 1986- editor | Yu, Poshan editor
Title: Addressing global health challenges through financial innovation and health technologies / edited by Cong Sui, Poshan Yu.
Description: Hershey, PA : IGI Global Scientific Publishing, [2026] | Includes bibliographical references and index. | Summary: "This book is a definitive resource that comprehensively explores the dynamic interplay between HealthTech and financial innovation in the pursuit of solving pressing global health issues. It will delve into how emerging HealthTech solutions, such as artificial intelligence-driven diagnostic tools, blockchain-enabled health record systems, and mHealth applications, are being harnessed to improve healthcare access, quality, and efficiency across the globe"-- Provided by publisher.
Identifiers: LCCN 2025023127 (print) | LCCN 2025023128 (ebook) | ISBN 9798337333410 hardcover | ISBN 9798337333427 paperback | ISBN 9798337333434 ebook
Subjects: LCSH: Medical economics--Technological innovations | Medical care, Cost of--Technological innovations | Artificial intelligence--Medical applications
Classification: LCC RA410.5 .A33 2026 (print) | LCC RA410.5 (ebook)
LC record available at https://lccn.loc.gov/2025023127
LC ebook record available at https://lccn.loc.gov/2025023128
British Cataloguing in Publication Data
A Cataloguing in Publication record for this book is available from the British Library.

Editorial Advisory Board

Table of Contents

Detailed Table of Contents

studies from Nigeria, South Africa, Rwanda, Ethiopia, Niger, Benin, and South Sudan. It presents actionable insights and policy recommendations, emphasizing the need for stronger primary healthcare systems, public-private partnerships, regulatory harmonization, and context-specific financial innovations to advance sustainable and equitable health coverage in Africa.

This chapter uses a case study to demonstrate that institutionalized social action is an invaluable part of global health. The case study narrates the story of two global institutions – Gavi and PATH – playing a pivotal role in saving lives across the globe against cervical cancer. This is being done with the help of major donor countries in global health such as the USA, the UK and Germany as well as philanthropies such as the Gates Foundation. These social enterprises are innovating to normalize pooled procurement, help develop new health technologies, lower the costs of new technologies, and generate evidence to minimize the administration burden for vaccination. The orchestrated effort is adding significant value to global health, which is a dynamic interplay of innovation, technologies and financing – an expensive enterprise of underdeveloped countries and communities.

This chapter examines India's national health insurance scheme, Ayushman Bharat – Pradhan Mantri Jan Arogya Yojana (AB-PMJAY), assessing its impact on out-of-pocket expenditure (OOPE) and the socioeconomic factors influencing it. Findings are compared with Indonesia's Jaminan Kesehatan Nasional to draw lessons for universal health coverage in low- and middle-income countries (LMICs). Using data from ten Indian states, a quantitative analysis—descriptive statistics, multiple regression, and difference-in-difference—found gains in public health spending, coverage, and selected health outcomes, but no significant short-term OOPE reduction. This underscores the need for outpatient coverage, strong governance, and equitable utilisation. India's experience shows LMIC reforms must go beyond insurance expansion to address service design, awareness, and gender gaps.

health solutions, support global clinical development, and improve health equity and pandemic preparedness worldwide.

Foreword

The global health system is facing a triple shock while still recovering from the pandemic. First, both infectious and non-infectious diseases are on the rise. We are witnessing more frequent outbreaks. New pathogens are emerging, and those already known to us are mutating and becoming resistant. At the same time, deaths and disabilities from non-communicable diseases have been steadily rising and now far exceed those from infectious diseases.

Second, modern lifestyles and climate-change-induced health issues are putting additional pressure on fragile public health systems. Our lifestyles have become sedentary and stressful. Unhealthy diets, excessive use of tobacco and alcohol, and ageing populations are compounding these health challenges. Furthermore, planetary health is deteriorating, resulting in extreme living conditions such as heat stress, air pollution, drought, and flooding, which exacerbate the challenges facing health systems.

Third, geopolitical tensions and escalating conflicts are undermining global health coordination, fragmenting governance, and limiting financing options, especially for low- and middle-income countries. Recent growth in interstate and intra-state conflicts is disrupting health supply chains, destroying local infrastructure, and leading to the collapse of health systems. The damage caused by hot conflicts is not limited to civilian injuries, morbidity, or mortality, but also includes longer-term trauma and mental health conditions.

Despite growing global health challenges, advances in science, technology, innovation, governance and finance are keeping us afloat and hopeful. This book focuses on the magic that human ingenuity brings to fighting this triple whammy. It starts with a comprehensive framing of global health and examines the historical evolution, decolonising efforts, and the emergence of the Global South as a new hub for global health solutions.

The book presents fascinating accounts of health technologies such as telehealth, digital health, generative AI, mobile health, and biotechnology, which are radically transforming health care and health systems. It is replete with examples and innovative financing approaches that reduce out-of-pocket expenses and expand access to affordable care for vulnerable populations. The governance dimension of health systems, including ethics, regulatory challenges, and inequalities, is covered in this remarkable collection of chapters, which together form a bouquet of solutions.

Dr Cong Sui is a distinguished HealthTech scholar, consultant and global health expert. Poshan Yu, a professional editor and scholar in finance, brings his finance expertise and real-world experience in venture capital to the book. Together, they exemplify the rare combination of rigorous scholarship and grounded practice. They practise what they profess and publish. Their insights from real-world engagement add depth and authenticity to this excellent treatise. They have woven together diverse facets of global health in an artistic way. The book's chapters are full of new insights, deeper perspectives, and broader wisdom.

As a practitioner in global health, I benefited greatly from reading and reflecting on this marvellous work. This book presents fresh thinking, systemic solutions, and rich case studies that can help advance global health equity. It is highly recommended for academics, practitioners, industry professionals, students, government officials, and anyone seeking to deepen their understanding of contemporary global health challenges and solutions.

Nabeel Goheer
Team Gladia, UK

Preface

The contemporary global health landscape is marked by a convergence of complex and interdependent challenges that transcend national borders, economic systems, and institutional capacities. Persistent inequalities in healthcare access, the growing burden of chronic and infectious diseases, demographic transitions, climate-related health risks, and the aftermath of global pandemics have collectively intensified the urgency for innovative, scalable, and sustainable solutions. At the same time, rapid advancements in financial innovation and health technologies are reshaping the ways in which healthcare systems are financed, governed, delivered, and evaluated. This edited volume, *Addressing Global Health Challenges Through Financial Innovation and Health Technologies*, emerges from the recognition that meaningful transformation in global health requires interdisciplinary collaboration across technology, economics, governance, policy, and clinical practice.

The chapters assembled in this volume span diverse geographical contexts, methodological approaches, and disciplinary perspectives, yet they are united by a shared commitment: advancing equitable and resilient health systems through innovation. The contributors critically examine the roles of digital health, telemedicine, artificial intelligence, mobile health applications, diagnostics, biotechnology, financial inclusion, value-based healthcare models, and evolving digital cultures in addressing pressing global health concerns. Across the chapters, particular attention is given to digital adoption, financial accessibility, community participation, patient engagement, governance capacity, and culturally adaptive implementation strategies. Importantly, the book does not treat technology or finance as isolated solutions; instead, it explores how innovation must be embedded within inclusive governance structures, ethical frameworks, and culturally sensitive implementation strategies to generate sustainable impact across both high-income countries and low- and middle-income countries (LMICs).

This volume is organised around several interconnected themes that unfold across the chapters. The opening chapters investigate technological transformation in global health, containing AI, telemedicine, and digital health systems, weighing both their potential and the barriers to implementation. The discussion then followed by critical perspectives on global health governance and financial innovation, covering decolonial frameworks, financial inclusion, pooled procurement, and universal health coverage reforms. In the latter chapters, the focus moves to applied health technologies and innovation ecosystems, through value-based healthcare, telehealth, diagnostics implementation, and biotechnology, mapping out practical pathways toward equitable and sustainable global health systems.

As editors, we believe this volume contributes to ongoing scholarly and policy conversations surrounding the future of global health systems. The book is designed not only for researchers and academics, but also for policymakers, healthcare leaders, development practitioners, entrepreneurs, and students seeking to understand how financial mechanisms and technological advancements can collectively address structural health inequities. Through theoretical reflection, empirical investigation, and practical case studies, this collection aims to inspire dialogue, foster collaboration, and encourage evidence-informed innovation that aligns with the broader goals of health equity, social justice, and sustainable development.

CHAPTER OVERVIEW

Chapter 1, authored by Ameneh Saatchi, examines the transformative role of technology in tackling global health challenges. The chapter explores how innovations such as artificial intelligence, telemedicine, and electronic health records can address disease burdens, workforce shortages, healthcare inequalities, and climate-related pressures. It also critically discusses barriers to implementation, including digital exclusion, ethical concerns, and infrastructure limitations, while proposing governance and policy frameworks aligned with Sustainable Development Goals 3 and 10.

Chapter 2, written by Pebby Garner, Alexis Alvarez, Harmonye Lacy, and Melanie Stanton, provides a comprehensive overview of telehealth's emergence and evolution. The chapter traces the development of telemedicine from its early conceptualisation to its accelerated adoption during and after the COVID-19 pandemic. Through a detailed literature review, the authors analyse the benefits, limitations, regulatory challenges, and future implications of remote healthcare delivery.

In **Chapter 3**, Oluwaseun Adewunmi and colleagues critically interrogate the colonial and neoliberal foundations of global health systems. Adopting a decolonial perspective, the chapter explores how financial innovation, digital health systems, and governance models can either reinforce or challenge structural inequities. The authors advocate for solidarity-based financing, culturally sovereign technologies, and community-led governance approaches that prioritise equity, Indigenous knowledge, and epistemic justice.

Chapter 4, authored by Samson Agbo, focuses on the intersections of digital health and financial inclusion within African healthcare systems. Through case studies across multiple African countries, the chapter investigates the opportunities and controversies surrounding mobile money, blockchain technologies, and digital financing mechanisms in achieving Universal Health Coverage (UHC). The analysis highlights persistent barriers such as weak governance, technological constraints, and socio-economic disparities, while offering policy recommendations for sustainable and equitable reform.

Chapter 5, by Yuan Yuan and Nabeel Goheer, presents a compelling case study of institutionalised social action in global health. Focusing on collaborative efforts involving organizations such as Gavi, the Vaccine Alliance and PATH, the chapter demonstrates how pooled procurement, donor partnerships, and health technology innovation contribute to reducing cervical cancer burdens globally. The authors illustrate how financing mechanisms and strategic collaboration can accelerate equitable access to lifesaving interventions.

Chapter 6, authored by Oliver Lee, Adrien Lucci, and Shanti Poolapalli Manukonda, analyses India's Ayushman Bharat–Pradhan Mantri Jan Arogya Yojana (AB-PMJAY) and its implications for Universal Health Coverage in LMICs. Using quantitative analysis and comparative insights from Indonesia's healthcare reforms, the chapter evaluates the scheme's effectiveness in reducing out-of-pocket expenditure and improving health access. The findings emphasise the importance of governance, outpatient coverage, gender equity, and public awareness in healthcare reform.

Chapter 7, contributed by Jonathan Feng, explores the application of value-based healthcare principles in European ophthalmology systems. Drawing on Porter's framework, the chapter investigates how artificial intelligence, telemedicine, educational innovation, reimbursement reform, and patient-centred care strategies can improve ophthalmic outcomes amidst demographic and systemic pressures. The discussion highlights the need for integrated and adaptable healthcare pathways across the European Union.

Chapter 8, authored by Peter Muttungal and collaborators, examines the growing role of mHealth applications in maternal and child healthcare across developing countries. The chapter evaluates how mobile technologies support health education, behavioural change, remote diagnosis, and emergency response. While acknowledging the transformative potential of mHealth interventions, the authors also address ethical concerns, digital inequalities, and infrastructure challenges that must be overcome to ensure equitable healthcare delivery.

Chapter 9, written by Cong Sui and colleagues, investigates the implementation of blood biomarker diagnostics for Alzheimer's disease detection within Saudi Arabian

Primary Healthcare Centres. Integrating policy analysis and change management frameworks, the chapter identifies key barriers related to awareness, infrastructure, and policy coordination. The authors provide actionable recommendations to support phased implementation strategies aligned with Saudi Vision 2030 and broader goals for healthcare innovation.

Finally, **Chapter 10**, authored by Jiawei Tang, explores the rapid rise of China's biotechnology industry and its contributions to global health innovation. The chapter analyses how regulatory reforms, capital market development, translational research, and technological advancements have enabled China to emerge as a global leader in biotechnology and precision medicine. The discussion offers valuable lessons for emerging economies seeking to strengthen innovation ecosystems, pandemic preparedness, and equitable healthcare development.

CONCLUSION

The contributions presented in this volume collectively demonstrate that addressing contemporary global health challenges requires more than isolated technological advancement or financial reform. Effective and sustainable transformation emerges through the integration of innovation, governance, equity, and cross-sector collaboration. Across diverse contexts, the chapters reveal how health technologies and financial innovations can improve healthcare access, strengthen system resilience, support preventive care, and reduce disparities when implemented thoughtfully and inclusively. At the same time, the authors remind us that innovation alone is insufficient without ethical accountability, community participation, and context-sensitive policy design.

A recurring theme throughout the book is the importance of balancing global ambition with local realities. Whether examining telehealth adoption, mobile health interventions, decolonial governance frameworks, biotechnology ecosystems, or universal health coverage reforms, the contributors consistently emphasise the need for culturally informed, participatory, and equitable approaches. The experiences of countries and institutions represented in this collection illustrate that successful innovation depends not only on scientific or financial capacity, but also on trust, institutional coordination, regulatory adaptability, and social inclusion. These insights are especially critical as governments and organisations navigate ongoing pressures related to ageing populations, emerging diseases, workforce shortages, and widening socio-economic inequalities.

As editors, we hope this volume serves as both a scholarly contribution and a practical resource for advancing future research, policy development, and interdisciplinary collaboration in global health. The discussions contained within these chapters underscore the transformative potential of financial innovation and health technologies to shape more resilient, equitable, and sustainable healthcare systems worldwide. We extend our sincere gratitude to all contributing authors for their intellectual contributions and commitment to advancing global health knowledge. It is our aspiration that this book will encourage continued dialogue, inspire innovative thinking, and support collective efforts toward achieving healthier futures for communities across the world.

Chapter 1
The Role of Technology in Tackling Global Health Challenges

Ameneh Ghazal Saatchi
http://orcid.org/0000-0002-5499-1159
Global Policy Network, UK

ABSTRACT

This chapter explores the transformative role of technology in addressing global health challenges, including disease burden, healthcare inequalities and climate change. It examines how these issues manifest across different income settings and argues the need for innovation to overcome systemic barriers such as workforce shortages and antibiotic resistance. Drawing on global case studies, it highlights how technologies like telemedicine, AI and digital records improve healthcare delivery across diverse settings. It also addresses barriers to adoption, including infrastructure gaps, digital illiteracy and ethical concerns. Emphasising the importance of inclusive design, participatory governance and cross-sector collaboration, the chapter concludes with future research directions and policy solutions to support sustainable, equitable and context-sensitive technological health transformation aligned with the Sustainable Development Goals (SDGs) 3 and 10.

INTRODUCTION

Global health, as a discipline and practice, aims to improve health and achieve equity in health for all people worldwide (Koplan et al., 2009). It is defined by a convergence of multifaceted challenges, including the growing burden of communicable and non-communicable diseases (NCDs), stark healthcare inequalities, and

DOI: 10.4018/979-8-3373-3341-0.ch001

the emerging health impacts of climate change (WHO, 2024a). These challenges manifest differently across low-, middle-, and high-income countries, each facing unique constraints in terms of infrastructure, workforce, and funding.

In recent decades, the field of global health has undergone rapid transformations driven by economic, social, political, and technological shifts. While tremendous strides have been made, such as the eradication of smallpox and the widespread availability of antiretroviral therapy for HIV, many persistent and emerging challenges remain. These include pandemic threats, the increasing burden of non-communicable diseases, and systemic inequalities in access to care.

With rising threats such as antimicrobial resistance, escalating healthcare demands, and pervasive workforce shortages, innovative solutions are no longer optional but essential for advancing global health outcomes. In this context, technology emerges as a transformative force, a catalyst offering scalable and adaptable solutions designed to bridge entrenched gaps. From diagnostics to treatment, technology has revolutionised global health systems by improving access, reducing disparities, and enhancing the quality of care (WHO, 2025a).

Digital tools and methodologies have the potential to tailor healthcare interventions to diverse settings, ensuring that even the most vulnerable populations benefit from advances in healthcare. Emerging technologies such as wearable biosensors, blockchain-based data management, and genomic research offer promising avenues to revolutionise healthcare delivery and public health surveillance.

However, despite these advances, significant barriers persist. Limited funding, infrastructural deficits, and challenges such as digital illiteracy hinder the full-scale adoption of technological solutions. Ethical concerns, including data privacy, algorithmic biases, and equitable access to digital tools, also demand careful consideration to prevent widening disparities or diminishing the personalisation of care.

Realising the full potential of technology in global health will depend on robust collaboration amongst governments, private industry, and non-profit organisations. These partnerships are vital for fostering innovation while ensuring equitable access, sustainability, and the ethical deployment of digital health solutions. This chapter examines how technology is applied to address global health challenges, evaluates its limitations, and envisions the future of technology in achieving equitable and sustainable health outcomes worldwide.

Technology has emerged as a powerful enabler in addressing the persistent and emerging challenges of global health (Beam et al., 2023). The World Health Organization's Global Strategy on Digital Health 2020–2025 underscores digital transformation as a critical catalyst for achieving universal health coverage (WHO, 2021a). By integrating data systems, enabling remote care, and enhancing diagnostics, digital technologies offer innovative pathways to overcome structural barriers and improve health equity across diverse populations.

The evolution of health technology, from pen-and-paper medical records to sophisticated machine learning algorithms, illustrates its transformative potential. These advancements have not only improved clinical efficiency but also contributed to reducing disparities in healthcare access and outcomes across geographies.

The COVID-19 pandemic served as a pivotal moment for digital health innovation. Health systems worldwide rapidly adopted technologies such as telemedicine, rapid diagnostics, and global health surveillance tools to enhance preparedness and response. These tools played a crucial role in mitigating the spread of the virus and maintaining continuity of care during lockdowns and health system disruptions.

Beyond pandemic response, technology has proven to be a vital enabler of better patient outcomes and stronger health systems. Digital health monitoring devices such as continuous glucose monitors have enabled more personalised care and lifestyle interventions for chronic conditions like diabetes and non-chronic conditions such as gestational diabetes (Centers for Disease Control and Prevention (CDC), 2022). Predictive modelling and geographic information systems (GIS) are increasingly used to forecast, track, and mitigate the risk of vector-borne diseases, offering data-driven insights for public health planning and intervention.

Harnessing technological innovation has allowed health systems to build resilience, improve operational efficiency, and foster equity. However, the promise of technology must be matched by efforts to address persistent barriers such as digital illiteracy, infrastructural limitations, and ethical concerns around data privacy and algorithmic bias. As global health continues to evolve, the strategic and inclusive application of technology will be essential to achieving sustainable and equitable health outcomes worldwide.

THE MULTIFACETED NATURE OF GLOBAL HEALTH CHALLENGES

At its core, global health encompasses more than the diagnosis and treatment of diseases. It extends to understanding the socio-economic determinants of health and addressing the disparities that create unequal health outcomes. The World Health Organization (WHO) has repeatedly demonstrated that differences in access to healthcare, the quality of services, and resultant health outcomes are not uniformly distributed around the world (WHO, 2023a). While high-income countries are often characterised by advanced medical infrastructure and robust digital health networks, low- and middle-income regions continue to grapple with significant resource limitations, leading to higher incidences of preventable diseases and premature mortality (WHO, 2025b; World Bank, 2023).

Even within the same country, disparities in healthcare access and outcomes persist. Socio-economic factors such as income, education, employment, living conditions, social support, and access to essential resources like healthcare and nutritious food create unequal opportunities and barriers, ultimately shaping health outcomes and exacerbating inequities among communities and regions (Solar & Irwin, 2010) (Marmot et al., 2012).

In the United Kingdom (UK), life expectancy for men varies by over ten years depending on geographic location. For example, in Glasgow City, the average life expectancy for men is 73.6 years and for women, 78.3 years, while in Kensington and Chelsea, London, men can expect to live up to 84.9 years and women, 86.5 years (Office for National Statistics (ONS), 2024) (ONS, 2025). These stark regional disparities are mirrored in healthy life expectancy, which is over 18 years lower in the most deprived areas of England compared to the least deprived (The King's Fund, 2023). Such disparities are not exclusive to the UK; understanding the socio-economic determinants of health and the distinct local challenges within and across countries is key to unlocking opportunities for improved healthcare access, service quality and resultant health outcomes worldwide.

Moreover, global health challenges are compounded by evolving threats. Emerging infectious diseases, exemplified by the COVID-19 pandemic that exposed the vulnerabilities of even the most developed health systems. At the same time, chronic conditions such as diabetes, cardiovascular diseases, and cancer are rapidly increasing, driven by lifestyle changes, environmental factors, and urbanisation. When combined with the adverse effects of climate change on health, such as the spread of vector-borne diseases, the cumulative impact underscores an urgent need for innovative technology-driven responses to address the vulnerabilities in health systems.

Understanding Global Health Challenges

Despite global progress, infectious diseases remain a leading cause of morbidity and mortality, particularly in low- and middle-income countries (LMICs). Malaria alone caused over 247 million cases and 619,000 deaths in 2021, with the vast majority occurring in sub-Saharan Africa (WHO, 2022a). Tuberculosis and HIV/AIDS also continue to pose significant public health challenges, despite being both preventable and treatable. The COVID-19 pandemic further underscored the vulnerability of global health systems to communicable diseases, with over 770 million confirmed cases and 7 million deaths worldwide by 2024 (Johns Hopkins

University, 2023). This crisis highlighted the urgent need for real-time surveillance, rapid diagnostics, and scalable interventions.

At the same time, non-communicable diseases (NCDs) account for 74% of global deaths annually, disproportionately affecting LMICs (WHO, 2023b). Conditions such as cardiovascular diseases, cancers, chronic respiratory diseases, and diabetes contribute significantly to this burden. These are often driven by modifiable risk factors, including poor diet, tobacco use, and physical inactivity, which are exacerbated by urbanisation and socioeconomic inequality.

Compounding these challenges is the stark disparity in access to healthcare. The World Health Organization (World Health Organization & World Bank, 2017) estimates that half of the global population lacks access to essential health services. Marginalised groups such as refugees, rural populations, and ethnic minorities often face the most significant barriers, which further entrench health inequities within and across countries.

Rising temperatures and environmental degradation are also worsening health outcomes. Vector-borne diseases such as dengue and Zika are spreading to new regions. Natural disasters, intensified by climate change, increase the risk of malnutrition, respiratory illnesses, and mental health disorders (Romanello et al., 2021).

In addition, antimicrobial resistance presents a serious challenge to modern medicine. In 2019, an estimated 1.27 million deaths were directly linked to bacterial antimicrobial resistance (Murray et al., 2022). This growing crisis is driven by the overuse and misuse of antibiotics, along with weak regulatory systems, and threatens to reverse decades of progress in treating infectious diseases.

Another pressing challenge is the shortage of healthcare workers. The World Health Organization (2020a) projects a global shortfall of 10 million health workers by 2030, with the most severe gaps expected in low- and middle-income countries. This shortage undermines the quality of care and places immense pressure on undertrained and overstretched staff, further weakening health systems.

Disparities in Health Outcomes

Access to quality healthcare is not uniform across the globe. WHO data consistently illustrate significant disparities between regions: higher rates of morbidity and mortality due to infectious diseases, maternal and child health issues, and a growing burden of non-communicable diseases in low-resource settings (WHO, 2023c). Often, these disparities are directly influenced by factors such as limited funding, weak health infrastructure, and a scarcity of trained healthcare personnel (WHO, 2023d). Moreover, barriers such as geographic isolation and cultural differences further complicate the delivery of care, highlighting the urgency for robust and adaptable technological interventions.

While technology emerges as a potential bridge to these challenges, a deeper understanding of the multifaceted nature of these disparities is crucial to ensure that technological interventions are targeted, equitable, and ultimately effective without widening inequalities further. To effectively leverage technology for positive change, we must first dissect the intricate web of factors that contribute to these disparities:

Socioeconomic Determinants

Poverty remains a foundational determinant of health, casting a long shadow over individuals and communities with limited economic resources. This lack of financial capital leads to a cascade of disadvantages that directly affect health outcomes. Inadequate nutrition, often resulting from food insecurity and limited access to diverse and nutritious food, weakens immune systems and increases vulnerability to both infectious and non-communicable diseases. Similarly, insufficient access to safe water and sanitation facilities fosters environments where pathogens thrive, contributing to diarrhoeal diseases and other waterborne illnesses, particularly among children and other vulnerable groups.

Housing conditions are also closely linked to health. Overcrowding, exposure to dampness and mould, and poor ventilation contribute to respiratory illnesses and facilitate the spread of infectious diseases. Limited access to education not only restricts economic mobility but also impairs health literacy, making it more difficult for individuals to understand health information and make informed decisions about their well-being. This interplay of factors creates a self-perpetuating cycle of poverty and poor health, trapping individuals and communities in persistent vulnerability (Fu et al., 2024).

It is equally important to recognise how socioeconomic inequalities intersect with other forms of marginalisation. Disparities in health outcomes are often compounded by race, ethnicity, gender, sexual orientation, disability, and geographic location. For example, marginalised racial and ethnic groups frequently face systemic discrimination in healthcare, education, and employment, resulting in poorer health outcomes even when socioeconomic status is like that of dominant groups. Gender inequalities can manifest in restricted access to reproductive healthcare, higher rates of gender-based violence, and disproportionate caregiving responsibilities, all of which negatively affect women's health and well-being (Heidari & García Moreno, 2016).

Technology offers promising solutions to some of these challenges. Healthcare applications are increasingly being used to bridge language barriers and improve communication between patients and providers. One such tool is *Care to Translate*, a medical translation app that enables effective communication when interpreters are unavailable (Care to Translate, 2024). It provides translations for medical terms, questions, and instructions, helping patients understand their conditions and treatments. Digital health platforms also support remote consultations, health education, and chronic disease management, particularly in underserved areas. However, to maximise their impact, these tools must be designed with inclusivity in mind, considering digital literacy, cultural relevance, and accessibility for individuals with disabilities or limited internet access.

Geography Impacts Access and Resource Distribution

The geographical lottery of birth and the opportunity to later migrate significantly impacts access to healthcare, education and health outcomes. Individuals in urban areas are impacted by healthcare inequalities influenced by socioeconomic disparities, systemic barriers, and environmental challenges. While healthcare facilities are often more concentrated in urban areas, access is not evenly distributed. Low-income neighbourhoods may lack nearby healthcare facilities, forcing residents to travel long distances for care (National Research Council (US) Committee on Future Directions for Behavioural and Social Sciences Research at the National Institutes of Health, 2001). Overcrowding in informal settlements or urban slums facilitates the rapid spread of infectious diseases, while inadequate sanitation and exposure to pollution contribute to chronic health conditions (National Research Council (US) Committee on Future Directions for Behavioural and Social Sciences Research at the National Institutes of Health, 2001, National Academies of Sciences, Engineering, and Medicine; Health and Medicine Division, 2018).

Individuals residing in rural and remote communities often face a double burden of limited access to healthcare infrastructure and a scarcity of healthcare professionals (Graves et al., 2022; WHO, 2010). The sheer distance to healthcare facilities, coupled with inadequate transportation networks, can delay or prevent timely access to essential medical services, particularly in emergency situations (National Academies of Sciences, Engineering, and Medicine, 2025; Liu et al., 2025). The lack of specialised medical equipment and diagnostic capabilities in these areas further compounds the problem (World Health Organization, 2010).

The Fractured Foundation: Deficiencies in Healthcare Systems

The very systems designed to promote health can inadvertently contribute to disparities. In many low- and middle-income countries, chronic underfunding of the public health sector results in under-resourced facilities, shortages of essential medicines and vaccines, and an overburdened and often underpaid healthcare workforce. Long waiting times for appointments, limited availability of specialised care, and out-of-pocket payment requirements can create insurmountable barriers for those with limited financial resources.

Even in high-income countries with more developed healthcare systems, inequalities persist. The type of insurance coverage, or lack thereof, can significantly impact access to care and the quality of services received. Individuals from lower socioeconomic backgrounds may be relegated to underfunded public facilities or face financial barriers that prevent them from seeking timely or comprehensive care. Systemic biases within healthcare delivery, whether conscious or unconscious, can also lead to differential treatment based on race, ethnicity, gender, or other social categories.

The Weight of the Environment: Ecological Injustice and Health

Environmental factors play an increasingly significant role in shaping health outcomes, and these impacts are often disproportionately felt by vulnerable populations. Exposure to pollution, whether it be air, water, or soil, can lead to a range of health problems, including respiratory illnesses, cardiovascular diseases, and cancers. Industrial activities and waste disposal sites are often located in or near low-income communities, exposing residents to higher levels of environmental toxins (Taylor, 2014; Chen et al., 2024).

Climate change acts as a threat multiplier, exacerbating existing health inequalities. Extreme weather events such as heatwaves, floods, and droughts can displace populations, disrupt food and water supplies, and increase the risk of infectious disease outbreaks. These events disproportionately impact low-income countries and marginalised communities with limited resources to adapt and recover. The health consequences of climate change will continue to widen existing disparities unless urgent and equitable mitigation and adaptation strategies are implemented.

The Interplay of Behaviour and Context: Shaping Health Choices

While individual behaviours and lifestyle choices undeniably influence health, it is crucial to recognise that these choices are often shaped by the broader social, economic, and environmental context in which individuals live. Access to affordable and nutritious food options, safe spaces for physical activity, and reliable sources of health information are not equally distributed. Communities lacking adequate infrastructure, facing high levels of crime, or experiencing food deserts may have limited opportunities to adopt healthy behaviours.

Cultural norms, beliefs, and practices significantly shape how individuals seek care and adhere to medical advice. These behaviours are further influenced by health literacy, which often correlates with socioeconomic status and education. To reduce health disparities, interventions must go beyond individual behaviour change and address systemic barriers that limit access to health-promoting resources. Health decisions are rarely made in isolation; they emerge from a complex interplay of personal, cultural, and environmental factors. Recognising this dynamic is essential for developing effective public health strategies that empower individuals within their specific contexts.

Human health behaviour is also driven by psychological and social influences. Motivation, habit, peer pressure, and family traditions all contribute to how people make health-related choices. For example, someone may understand the benefits of regular exercise but still lead a sedentary lifestyle due to low motivation, time constraints, or lack of access to safe recreational spaces. Behaviour change theories, such as the 'Health Belief Model', offer valuable frameworks for understanding these decisions and designing interventions that encourage healthier habits (Alyafei & Easton-Carr, 2024).

Contextual factors, such as geography, income, education, and cultural attitudes, further shape health behaviours. Limited access to nutritious food, preventive care, or mental health services can restrict healthy choices, especially in underserved communities. Additionally, cultural perspectives, such as reliance on traditional remedies or stigma surrounding mental illness, influence how health information is received and acted upon. These realities highlight the importance of culturally sensitive communication and policies that address the broader social determinants of health.

Moreover, the role of technology is increasingly significant in both behaviour and context. Wearable fitness devices, mobile health apps, and telemedicine are changing how individuals engage with their health. While these tools offer opportunities for empowerment and self-monitoring, they also expose a digital divide. Those without access to smartphones or reliable internet are at risk of being left behind, further exacerbating health inequalities.

To truly improve health outcomes, public health interventions must consider both individual behaviour and the surrounding context. This means not only encouraging healthy behaviours through education and incentives but also addressing structural barriers such as poverty, lack of access to care, and unequal distribution of health-promoting resources. Policies that support equitable access to healthcare, safe neighbourhoods, nutritious food, and quality education can create environments where making healthy choices becomes the easier and more sustainable option.

In conclusion, the relationship between behaviour and context is at the heart of health decision-making. Acknowledging and addressing this complex interplay allows for more effective, inclusive, and compassionate approaches to health promotion, ensuring that individuals are supported not just to make better choices, but to have better choices to make.

TECHNOLOGICAL INNOVATIONS IN GLOBAL HEALTH

This section explores how emerging technologies are transforming global health by improving access, equity, and efficiency across diverse healthcare systems, providing real-world case studies and demonstrating its impact.

Urgency of Action and the Climate-Tech Nexus

Rapid urbanisation, climate change, and emerging pathogens are reshaping healthcare needs in unprecedented ways. The United Nations Sustainable Development Goals (SDGs) emphasise the imperative of reducing inequalities, improving health outcomes, and ensuring universal access to health services (United Nations, n.d.). Technology, as a dynamic force capable of transcending traditional barriers, is uniquely positioned to address these interconnected challenges. Whether through the automation of diagnostics, the integration of telemedicine in remote communities, or the use of mobile platforms for health education, technological innovations offer hope for a more equitable and sustainable future in global health.

Historically, technology has acted as an enabler of change in medicine, from the early use of radiography to the modern application of artificial intelligence (AI) in diagnostics and care delivery. Its adaptability allows it to meet the evolving demands of the healthcare sector. However, as AI becomes more embedded in health systems, ethical considerations must be central to its deployment to ensure it does not inadvertently reinforce existing inequalities.

There is a clear alignment between AI ethics and SDG 10: Reduced Inequalities, particularly through the principles of fairness, transparency, and accountability. Research shows that while AI can reduce disparities by improving access and personalising care, it also risks amplifying inequities if not governed responsibly. For example, Dankwa-Mullan (2024) highlights that AI systems trained on biased data can reinforce structural inequities in healthcare, disproportionately affecting marginalised populations. Similarly, Toure (2025) argues that without ethical frameworks, AI may exacerbate disparities in low-income regions, undermining progress toward SDG 10. To ensure AI contributes positively to SDG 10, its design must incorporate inclusive data practices, equitable access to AI-enabled tools, and participatory governance models (Cheong, 2024; Radanliev, 2025).

This ethical imperative extends beyond AI into the broader climate-tech nexus, a conceptual framework that links climate change, technology, policy, and investment across sectors. Climate change intensifies health inequalities and increases risks such as respiratory conditions, heat-related illness, and eco-anxiety. In response, climate-tech innovations are transforming health systems through predictive analytics, early warning systems, and digital health platforms that strengthen surveillance, improve emergency response, and support vulnerable populations (Vilhelmsson, 2024).

For example, the Climate Resilience Toolkit developed provides frontline clinics with resources to manage care during extreme weather events, events as heatwaves, wildfires, and floods, protecting patients with chronic conditions like diabetes and cardiovascular disease (Harvard T.H. Chan School of Public Health, 2024).

These innovations demonstrate how climate-tech can enhance healthcare delivery and resilience. However, their deployment must be guided by ethical principles and an inclusive, locally relevant design to avoid reinforcing inequities caused by unequal access to digital infrastructure, data governance concerns, and the ecological footprint of tech itself. Strengthening interdisciplinary collaboration and investing in context-specific solutions will be key to unlocking the full potential of both AI and climate-tech in building sustainable, equitable global health systems.

Telemedicine: Bridging Gaps in Access to Care

Telemedicine utilises digital communication tools to provide remote clinical services, thereby overcoming geographical barriers that may prevent patients from accessing healthcare facilities. Telemedicine has become particularly vital for rural and underserved communities, offering timely medical consultations, diagnosis, and management without the need for patients to travel long distances (Bashshur et al, 2016). In regions with sparse healthcare infrastructure, virtual consultations reduce both time and cost burdens on patients while helping to alleviate the pressure on local healthcare facilities (Haleem et al (b), 2021).

Recent case studies from rural Africa and parts of Asia demonstrate that telemedicine can substantially improve outcomes for patients with chronic diseases, as well as those requiring urgent medical attention (Dodoo, Al-Samarraie, & Alsswey, 2022). Telemedicine platforms not only facilitate consultations but also provide critical support for follow-up care and continuous disease management. As broadband and mobile networks continue to expand globally, the potential for Telemedicine to revolutionise access to care grows even more significant (WHO, 2021b).

Several real-world examples illustrate the transformative impact of telemedicine:

- India's eSanjeevani platform served over 100 million patients during the COVID-19 pandemic, reducing hospital overcrowding and extending healthcare access to rural communities (Lad & Padroo, 2024; Mumtaz et al., 2023).

- South Africa's MomConnect initiative provided teleconsultations to 1.2 million HIV-positive mothers, improving treatment adherence and health outcomes for both mothers and children (Latifi, 2025; Tilahun et al., 2021).
- In the Brazilian Amazon, telehealth networks have connected Indigenous communities with medical specialists in urban centres like São Paulo, significantly improving access to maternal healthcare and helping to overcome the challenges posed by geographic isolation (WHO, 2021b).

ARTIFICIAL INTELLIGENCE: REVOLUTIONISING DIAGNOSTICS AND PERSONALISED MEDICINE

Artificial intelligence (AI) is increasingly recognised as a transformative force in healthcare, offering capabilities that enhance diagnostic accuracy, enable predictive analytics, and support personalised treatment strategies. By leveraging vast datasets of medical images, electronic health records, and genomic information, AI algorithms can detect patterns and anomalies that may elude human clinicians due to time constraints, data complexity, or perceptual limitations. These insights significantly improve diagnostic precision, streamline clinical workflows, and ultimately enhance the efficiency and effectiveness of healthcare delivery.

One of the most impactful applications of AI is in medical imaging. For example, Google Health's DeepMind AI demonstrated an 11.5% increase in breast cancer detection accuracy, underscoring AI's potential to improve early diagnosis and reduce mortality (McKinney et al., 2020). Similarly, the Mayo Clinic developed an AI-powered electrocardiogram (ECG) analysis tool capable of detecting asymptomatic left ventricular dysfunction, enabling early intervention and improved outcomes in both the United States and Europe (Alami et al., 2025).

AI also plays a pivotal role in predictive modelling and public health surveillance. During the COVID-19 pandemic, AI models in China utilised mobility and health data to forecast viral spread, facilitating the implementation of targeted lockdowns and containment strategies (Khushbu et al., 2024). More broadly, AI systems have been employed to predict outbreaks of infectious diseases such as malaria and Ebola, allowing healthcare systems to allocate resources proactively and mitigate risks.

In the realm of personalised medicine, AI enables the tailoring of treatment plans to an individual's genetic, clinical, and lifestyle profile. This approach not only enhances therapeutic outcomes but also reduces unnecessary interventions and healthcare costs (Nelson et al., 2025). AI-driven tools have been successfully applied to detect diabetic retinopathy, identify early stages of various cancers, and monitor the progression of chronic conditions, offering clinicians a powerful decision-support system.

DeepMind's AI system improved breast cancer detection accuracy by 11.5%, demonstrating the potential of AI in enhancing early cancer diagnosis (McKinney et al., 2020).

As AI continues to evolve, its integration into healthcare systems promises to revolutionise diagnostics, enhance clinical decision-making, and promote more equitable and efficient care delivery. However, its implementation must be guided by robust ethical frameworks that address data privacy, algorithmic transparency, and equitable access to ensure that the benefits of AI are shared across all populations.

Mobile Health (mHealth): Empowering Patients and Providers

Mobile health (mHealth) leverages the ubiquity of smartphones and other wireless devices to provide health services and information. mHealth applications have been designed to support patient education, monitor chronic diseases, and enhance care coordination. In low-resource environments, where traditional healthcare facilities may be limited, mHealth applications offer an accessible solution for health monitoring and disease management (Deniz-Garcia et al,2023).

For instance, mHealth platforms have been widely adopted in countries such as India and Kenya, where mobile applications provide crucial services ranging from maternal health monitoring to managing non-communicable diseases (Ameyaw et al., 2024). By enabling patients to track their health status, mHealth tools promote self-management and adherence to treatment protocols. Additionally, these platforms foster communication between patients and healthcare providers, ensuring that medical advice and support are readily available, even in remote locations.

In Lagos, Nigeria, the MomCare program utilised SMS-based prenatal alerts to reduce maternal mortality by twenty-five percent (Okonofua et al.,2023). This initiative highlighted the importance of mobile technology in providing vital health information and improving maternal outcomes (Okonofua et al.,2023).

The DiabTrend app in Pakistan helped fifty-thousand users track their glucose levels, leading to a 1.2% reduction in HbA1c levels. This showcases how mobile technology can aid in the management of chronic conditions such as diabetes (Butt et al., 2024; Oyebode et al., 2022).

Kenyan HIV Adherence: In Nairobi, Kenya, the WelTel app was used to improve adherence to antiretroviral therapy (ART) among HIV-positive individuals, with a 40% improvement in adherence rates. This app shows the significant impact of mobile technology in improving health outcomes for people with HIV (Tilahun et al., 2021).

Digital Health Records: Enhancing Data Sharing and Continuity of Care

The transition from paper-based records to digital health records (EHRs) represents another significant stride toward a more efficient and robust health system. EHRs promote interoperability among diverse healthcare providers, ensuring that patient data are available in real time and across different institutions. This seamless flow of information is essential for reducing medical errors, avoiding redundant testing, and ensuring timely interventions (Stephen and Frank, 2024).

EHRs have proven to be transformative in urban areas where clinical space is constrained. By eliminating the need for physical storage of paper-based records, hospitals can free up valuable space for new operating rooms and other critical facilities. Additionally, these systems streamline administrative processes, reduce costs associated with paper, and contribute to environmental sustainability. For instance, a 500-bed hospital generates over 5.4 million sheets of paper annually, highlighting the significant environmental and operational benefits of transitioning to digital systems (Stephen et al 2024, RDi Inicio no date).

While the implementation of digital health records has been more pronounced in high-income countries, emerging initiatives in middle- and low-income nations are gradually bridging this gap. Challenges such as data security, infrastructure limitations, and digital literacy must be overcome to achieve widespread adoption. Nonetheless, the integration of EHRs remains a cornerstone of modern healthcare, streamlining patient management and bolstering overall healthcare efficiency.

Wearable Biosensors

Wearable biosensors, such as smartwatches and fitness trackers, monitor vital signs and help in the management of chronic conditions. These devices can provide real-time health data, enabling better patient management and early intervention.

- U.S. Cardiac Rehabilitation: In the U.S., Fitbit devices were used to monitor the heart rates and activity levels of patients recovering from myocardial infarction (MI). This led to an 18% reduction in readmissions, demonstrating how wearable devices can help in managing chronic heart conditions (Farai et al., 2024; Jones et al, 2023).
- China's Hypertension Control: Huawei wearables alerted 200,000 users in Shanghai about abnormal blood pressure spikes, helping to manage hypertension more effectively. This highlights how wearable technology can be used in the prevention and management of chronic conditions (Long et al., 2023).

- U.S. Sleep Apnea Detection: In the United States, a health survey among adults aged 65+ indicated that 56% were at high risk of obstructive sleep apnea yet only 8% had ever undergone diagnostic testing. This disparity underscores the potential for wearable-guided screening to identify undiagnosed sleep-related disorders in older populations (Michigan Institute for healthcare policy and innovation, 2018).

Blockchain in Global Health

Blockchain technology is increasingly being explored as a solution to challenges faced by healthcare systems around the world. It allows data to be stored across a network of computers in a way that is secure, transparent, and resistant to tampering. It's increasingly being used in healthcare to secure patient records, improve interoperability between healthcare systems and enable patient-controlled data sharing. In other uses, it can be used to track pharmaceutical supply chains and support clinical trial transparency.

A systematic review by Kuo et al. (2019) found that HICs are able to benefit from blockchain because they have strong digital infrastructure, clear regulatory frameworks and high digital literacy, combined with institutional readiness. For example, Estonia's e-Health system uses blockchain to allow 99% of clinics to securely share patient data, improving care quality while safeguarding privacy (Schmidt et al., 2024).

Despite its success in high-income countries (HICs) such as Estonia, low- and middle-income countries (LMICs) face significant barriers in implementing blockchain, mainly due to foundational challenges (Schmidt et al., 2024; Ali & Maheshwari, 2025). Ali and Maheshwari (2025) identified several systemic barriers to blockchain adoption in LMICs, including resistance to change, digital literacy gap and lack of stakeholder coordination. The latter was a critical factor, together with governance issues, for the failure of the TradeLens initiative, which was developed by IBM and Maersk, to enhance supply chain transparency at ports (Najati, 2025). Ali and Maheshwari (2025) also identified financial constraints and regulatory uncertainty as factors that make blockchain adoption challenging in LMICs. Furthermore, these challenges are compounded by infrastructural deficits and limited access to reliable internet and computing resources (Biga et al., 2024).

Steemit and Terra (LUNA) are another example of a failed Blockchain initiative in an LMIC. The initiative collapsed due to economic instability and technical fragility, underscoring the risks of deploying blockchain in under-resourced settings (Kumar, 2025). A study by Kigombola and Mahundi (2024) reviewed 26 blockchain projects in LMIC healthcare systems and found that despite 82% having some form of implementation, 8% reached the prototype stage, and only 12% achieved full deployment. The majority were used for electronic health records (23%) and remote patient monitoring (15%), indicating a focus on improving data access and continuity of care. The disparity in blockchain adoption between HIC and LMIC countries raised ethical concerns that could exacerbate health inequalities and

Predictive Analytics for Disease Surveillance

Predictive analytics utilises machine learning and environmental data to forecast disease outbreaks, enabling early interventions and resource allocation.

- South Asian Dengue Prediction: IBM's AI system accurately predicted dengue outbreaks in Bangladesh with an 89% accuracy rate, leading to pre-emptive fumigation and better outbreak control (Gupta et al., 2024).
- Zika Virus in Brazil: Google's Flu Trends algorithm was used to identify high-risk regions for the Zika virus in Brazil, detecting potential outbreaks two weeks earlier than traditional methods. This early detection helped to implement control measures before the virus spread widely (Tilahun et al., 2021).
- Malaria in Tanzania: In Dar es Salaam, Tanzania, satellite data and AI were used to reduce malaria case incidence by 35%, demonstrating the role of technology in disease prevention (Ambas et al., 2023).

Drone-Based Medical Delivery

Drones are revolutionising the delivery of medical supplies, especially in remote and hard-to-reach areas. They have been used to deliver vaccines, blood, and medications, saving lives and improving healthcare access.

- Rwanda's Zipline: Zipline's drone network in Rwanda delivered 200,000 units of blood to rural clinics, significantly reducing maternal haemorrhage deaths by 67%. This shows the life-saving potential of drones in delivering medical supplies (Muyombo, 2024).
- Papua New Guinea's TB Care: In Papua New Guinea, drones reduced the transport time for sputum samples from five days to two hours in mountainous regions, improving tuberculosis diagnosis and treatment (Doctors Without Borders, 2015).
- Ghana's COVID-19 Response: During the COVID-19 pandemic, drones in Ghana were used to deliver 10,000 vaccine doses to island communities, improving vaccine distribution in remote areas (Sylverken et al., 2022).

3D Printing for Prosthetics and Medical Devices

3D printing technology has been instrumental in providing affordable and customised prosthetics and medical devices, improving the quality of life for patients in resource-limited settings.

- Sudan's Limb Replacements: Not Impossible Labs in Sudan used 3D printing to produce 1,000 prosthetics for war victims in Khartoum. This technology provided much-needed prosthetic limbs to individuals in need (Park et al., 2021; Not Impossible Labs, 2013).
- Syrian Refugee Care: In Jordanian refugee camps, 3D-printed casts were used to reduce healing time for fractures by 20%. This initiative showcased how 3D printing can offer cost-effective) and efficient solutions for healthcare in emergencies (Akeila et al., 2019)
- U.S Airway Intervention: In the United States, University of Michigan teams utilized patient-specific, bioresorbable 3D-printed tracheal splints to treat infants with life-threatening tracheobronchomalacia. The first case in 2012 resulted in immediate airway stability, and over 40 infants have since been treated successfully. A 2025 clinical trial is now underway to assess broader application and support full regulatory approval (Michigan Medicine,2025)

Digital Twins for Personalised Treatment

Digital twin technology involves creating virtual replicas of patients to simulate treatment outcomes and personalise healthcare strategies.

- U.S. Cardiac Surgery: At Mayo Clinic, heart digital twins were used to reduce postoperative complications by 25%, enhancing surgical outcomes for cardiac patients (Halamka & Cerrato, 2025).
- Brazil's Diabetes Management: In São Paulo, digital twins helped personalise insulin doses for 10,000 diabetes patients, improving blood sugar control and reducing complications (Shamanna et al., 2024).
- Germany's Cancer Care: Siemens Healthineers' use of digital twins optimised chemotherapy regimens for 5,000 patients in Munich, improving treatment outcomes and reducing adverse effects (Siemens Healthineers, 2023).

Virtual Reality (VR) in Mental Health and Rehabilitation

Virtual reality (VR) technology is becoming a transformative and beneficial tool in mental health care, offering immersive, personalised interventions for conditions such as anxiety, depression, post-traumatic stress disorder (PTSD), and neurodevelopmental disorders (Bell et al., 2024). Below are three examples of how it is being used:

- UK PTSD Therapy: In the United Kingdom, a study of 3MDR (Motion-Assisted, Multi-Modal Memory Desensitisation and Reconsolidation) therapy was conducted with combat veterans suffering from treatment-resistant PTSD. The immediate treatment group experienced an impressive average reduction of PTSD severity by 37%, while the control group saw just a 14% decrease during the waiting period, highlighting the therapy's effectiveness over no treatment (NCMH, 2020).
- UK VR-CBT Therapy: In the UK, Oxford VR has been used to deliver VR-based cognitive behavioural therapy (VR-CBT) for social anxiety and schizophrenia, reducing anxiety symptoms and improving self-esteem among inpatients (Stefaniak & Aleksandrowicz, 2024).
- Japanese Stroke Rehabilitation: In Tokyo, VR rehabilitation helped 100 stroke patients regain motor function, with a 20% improvement in physical mobility (Park et al., 2021).
- U.S. Anxiety Disorder Treatment: In California, VR-based exposure therapy reduced anxiety disorders by 35%, showing its potential for treating mental health conditions (Hawajri, Lindberg, & Suominen, 2023).

CASE STUDIES: TECHNOLOGY IN ACTION

Pandemic Response and Management

The COVID-19 pandemic has underscored the importance of rapid and coordinated responses to emerging global health crises. Technology was pivotal in many aspects of the pandemic response, including vaccine distribution, contact tracing, and telehealth expansion. Digital tracking tools provided real-time data on the spread of the virus, enabling authorities to implement targeted lockdowns and efficient resource allocation. Telehealth services experienced unprecedented growth as health systems pivoted to virtual care to reduce virus exposure risks, thereby preserving healthcare capacity for critical cases (Ezenwaji et al., 2024).

Disease Surveillance Through AI-Driven Models

Effective disease surveillance is essential for early detection and containment of infectious diseases. AI-driven platforms have been deployed to monitor disease trends and provide predictive insights that can inform public health strategies. For example, machine learning algorithms have been used to analyse environmental, epidemiological, and social data to forecast outbreaks of diseases such as malaria, influenza, and Ebola (Tornimbene et al,2025). These models not only enhance preparedness but also facilitate rapid response to emerging threats.

In addition to predictive modelling, AI has been instrumental in analysing data collected from various sources, including social media, news reports, and healthcare databases, to create comprehensive surveillance systems. These systems support public health officials in making evidence-based decisions, potentially saving countless lives by mitigating the spread of diseases before they reach critical levels (Butler-Henderson et al., 2025).

Despite its benefits, AI-based decisions can suffer from biases, leading to misrepresentation, errors, and worsened health disparities when applied to interventions. To mitigate these issues, researchers must proactively identify sources of bias and enforce measures to combat them, particularly when analysing linguistically diverse social media data for health insights (Flores et al, 2024).

Enhancing Healthcare Access Through Mobile Clinics

Mobile clinics equipped with digital tools are bringing healthcare to some of the most remote and under-served areas of the world. In regions where traditional healthcare facilities are either too far or insufficiently equipped, these mobile units serve as a lifeline. They are designed to travel and provide medical services, outfitted with diagnostic devices, communication tools, and sometimes even portable imaging equipment, enabling rapid diagnosis and treatment in situ. These interventions are particularly effective in low-income areas, where infrastructure and human resources are limited.

Another noteworthy example is the implementation of community diagnostic centres (CDC) that are stationary facilities located within the community, such as high streets. CDC's use digital technologies to conduct routine screenings and monitoring, like CT scans, blood tests and ultrasounds. They improve access to diagnostics, reduce pressure on hospital services by offering access to diagnostics in convenient and easy-to-reach locations (Office for National Statistics, 2025).

BARRIERS TO ADOPTION

Despite its promise, the integration of technology into healthcare systems worldwide faces numerous hurdles. Infrastructure deficits, particularly in low-resource settings, remain a major barrier. Many regions lack the necessary digital infrastructure, including reliable internet connectivity and electrical power, required for the successful deployment of telemedicine and digital health records. In addition, limited funding and competing healthcare priorities make large-scale investments in health technology challenging (Ahmed et al., 2024; Soyege et al., 2024).

Many LMICs face poor internet penetration, unreliable electricity, and limited access to hardware, which impede digital health solutions (ITU, 2022). Technological interventions often rely on donor funding. Without sustainable financing models, projects risk collapse once initial funds are exhausted (Larsen-Cooper et al., 2016).

Digital illiteracy is another significant obstacle. Both patients and healthcare providers may lack the skills needed to utilise new technologies effectively (Alotaibi et al., 2025). Without adequate training and support, the risk of misinterpretation or misuse of digital tools increases, potentially leading to adverse clinical outcomes. The digital divide disproportionately affects women, rural populations, and the elderly. According to the GSMA (2022), only 32% of women in Sub-Saharan Africa own a smartphone, underscoring the significant gender gap in digital access.

A multifaceted approach that includes investment infrastructure, capacity building and community education is necessary to address these systemic barriers (Health Education England, 2019).

Equity and Ethics in Technological Implementation

As technology becomes increasingly central to healthcare delivery, ensuring equitable access is paramount. There exists a genuine risk that the digital divide could exacerbate existing inequalities. Populations in low-income regions or marginalised communities may not benefit from technological advancements if access to digital tools and the internet remains limited. Furthermore, the ethical development and deployment of AI algorithms require rigorous oversight. Bias in datasets, algorithmic decision-making, and privacy concerns must be carefully managed to avoid reinforcing systemic inequities (Weiner et al, 2024, Marko et al, 2025).

In the age of big data, safeguarding patient confidentiality and ensuring that technological applications are ethically sound is of critical importance. Regulatory frameworks must be developed and enforced to protect sensitive health information while still encouraging innovation. Collaborative efforts among governments, technology companies, and healthcare providers are essential to create guidelines that balance patient safety with the benefits of digital innovation (Mohammed and Malhotra, 2025, Mendelson & Mendelson, 2017).

Digital Divide, Decolonial Frameworks and Data Practices

The digital divide is a multifaceted concept describing disparities in access, knowledge, skills and use of digital technologies, often linked to socioeconomic differences, reflecting broader social injustices and often exacerbates exclusion in disadvantaged and under-resourced communities (Norris, 2001; Cai, 2025). These disparities are not limited to infrastructure but also driven by who gets to produce, interpret, and benefit from digital data.

This challenge is highlighted in 'Cooking Data' (Biruk, 2017), which highlights how data can often be "processed, organised, and analysed according to demographic standards and norms (p4)', rather than in ways that reflect the contexts and needs of the communities from which they have been collected. This draws concerns to whether the researchers' own cultural and most notably, colonial biases have been at the forefront of interpretation. This is particularly relevant in cases such as Malawi, as foreign-led surveys and historical colonial research practices have shaped how knowledge is produced. As a result, data often reflects the priorities of global research agendas rather than the needs of the local population. Throughout the case study used in "Cooking Data", it is noted that villagers often ask for the outcomes and feedback from these results; it is well recognised within local communities that the data that has been collected will not represent the population accurately, nor will it lead to meaningful change. Understanding the limitations of this data highlights the need to critically examine how data driven models shape healthcare decisions and thus exemplifies how anthropological insights complement these approaches. Furthermore, resilience on standardised data analysis such as this are reinforcing the digital divide. Data-driven healthcare models are disproportionately shaped by those with digital literacy, and those who are digitally illiterate are unable to be properly represented and interpreted within the data pool, as data is incorrectly skewed by those with colonialist mindsets. Individuals in under-resourced communities often rely on external actors to be included in the datasets that inform their healthcare priorities, thus reinforcing data colonialism.

As Adams (2016), notes in *Metrics: What Counts in Global Health*, the growing reliance on quantifiable measures in health reflects a broader transformation in how value, accountability and efficiency are defined. The digital twin exemplifies this trend by turning a person's biological life into data driven models that can predict and simulate health outcomes. While this can improve precision and personalise care, it also raises questions about what counts as good health. If we only optimise what is measurable, we risk missing what matters to patients but is harder to quantify (Adam, 2016, pp.24-25). The author's (Adam, 2016) analysis helps reveal that technologies such as digital twins are not neutral tools but active agents in shaping what becomes visible, valuable and governable within the healthcare system. By translating lived experiences into numerical datasets, digital twins participate in metrics that privileges measurement over meaning (Adam, 2016). This process mirrors the logic of data colonialism, where data is collected from individuals and communities but is processed elsewhere and is then used as a guide to make decisions without local control or accountability. Through these mechanisms digital technologies can unintentionally reproduce unequal power relations that reflect patterns of colonial extraction and governance. To ensure equity and context-sensitivity, digital twin models should integrate clinical endpoints with patient narratives, treatment burden and social context. They should show uncertainty, document data provenance and include balancing measures such as safety events and treatment burden alongside target outcomes. Technology can both enable innovation and has the power to ensure that digital health systems promote equity rather than reinforce historical inequalities.

While digital technologies can enhance access and efficiency, their integration also exposes deep structural and ethical challenges. As Petryna and Biehl (2013) argue in *When People Come First: Critical Studies in Global Health,* technological interventions often privilege global health programs or donor driven priorities over the lived experiences and realties of local communities and their ethnographic insights. Their analysis of fragmented care systems and technocratic approaches mirror current concerns about digital divide in global health. This suggests that unequal access is not only about devices or internet coverage but also about who designs, owns and interprets technological systems. When digital tools and platforms are developed without meaningful participation, they risk reproducing hierarchies of knowledge and control that echoes colonial patterns of governance and reinforce inequalities. Therefore, bridging the digital divide requires more than technical solutions. Like Biruk and Adams, Biehl and Petryna, calls for participatory and context-sensitive approaches that value local expertise, ensure community control over data and align digital innovation with the lived realities of the people it aims to serve.

This concern is echoed by Eubanks (2018), who demonstrates how automated systems reproduce inequality by translating complex social realities into narrow data categories that determine who receives care and resources. Her analysis of digital welfare systems in the United States reveals how data infrastructures can silently enforce exclusion and surveillance, further reinforcing structural disadvantages rather than reducing it. When these insights are applied to global health technologies, they expose similar risks of bias and control in digital platforms, algorithms and data collection tools. Systems such as digital health records or digital twins may unintentionally replicate these patterns without critical attention to context, equity and participation. Both Eubanks (2018) and Petryna and Biehl (2013) highlight that the digital divide is not only a matter of access to devices or connectivity but also a reflection of whose knowledge, experiences and needs are being prioritised in technological design. Therefore, addressing this divide requires an ethical and political commitment to redistribute power within digital systems, ensuring that technology supports social justice rather than reproducing historical inequalities.

Research by Storeng and Béhague (2017) demonstrates that global health metrics, such as maternal mortality indicators, while designed to promote accountability, can function as political instruments that oversimplify complex realities and stigmatise communities. Similarly, Keikelame and Swartz (2019) argue for decolonising research methodologies, highlighting how dominant data practices often marginalise local knowledge and perpetuate structural inequalities. To ensure that digital health technologies support equitable outcomes, policy frameworks must embed ethical reflection into the design, implementation, and evaluation of data systems. This includes prioritising participatory approaches, contextual sensitivity, and the lived experiences of affected populations, to align with SDG 3 (ensuring healthy lives and promoting well-being for all). Without such safeguards, digital health initiatives may unintentionally reproduce historical inequalities rather than dismantle them.

Technological Dependency Risks

The dependence on digital and cyber-physical systems can introduce new points of fragility in emergency responses. In drone enabled operations, mission performance can degrade rapidly when batteries reach endurance limits, radio channels become congested, control links drop or ground infrastructure fails, which can then halt aerial sensing and time-critical deliveries at peak demand (Erdelj et al, 2017). At a systems level, disaster research shows that highly networked societies are susceptible to cascading effects, where disruption to one layer such as power, telecommunications, GPS, or cloud services propagate across interdependent functions and undermines coordination and care delivery (Alexander & Pescaroli, 2019). These vulnerabilities reveal the paradox of technological innovation in crisis response, which is that the more sophisticated and interconnected a system becomes the more dependent it is on stable digital infrastructure. In low resource or disaster affected settings, even the tiniest network outages or software faults can interrupt logistical chains, delay emergency deliveries or distort situational awareness. For example, drone networks rely heavily on real-time data transfer, satellite positioning and algorithmic flight coordination, all of which are prone to error when connectivity or power systems fail. Disruptions such as those can compromise lifesaving operations, especially when ground teams are not equipped to operate manually or when alternative communications systems are absent.

Corporate Data Extraction Reducing Access to Technology

Corporate data extraction refers to the process of retrieving, collecting, and organising data from various sources within or related to a corporation. When private sector entities hold patents to critical innovations, such as pharmaceuticals or technological innovations, it significantly impacts access, often due to high prices or limited availability, especially in low- and middle-income countries (LMICs). Proprietary data and technologies are frequently leveraged for profit rather than public good, fuelling global health disparities and excluding LMICs from collaborative global initiatives (Adams, 2026). Governments can address this through equitable licensing of innovation, transparent data-sharing systems, and encouraging open access to critical health technologies.

An example of how this has been overcome can be shown through the limited voluntary licensing of patented treatments for HIV, hepatitis C, and COVID-19. Although some companies have issued non-exclusive voluntary licenses (NEVLs), many LMICs remain excluded from these agreements, and the momentum for such licensing has slowed significantly in recent years. This restricts access to essential medicines and diagnostics in regions with the greatest need (Access to Medicine Foundation, 2024).

Further evidence of the impact of intellectual property rules on LMICs is provided by Tenni et al. (2022), who conducted a systematic review of 91 studies. They found that TRIPS-plus provisions and other patent protections delayed the introduction of generic medicines, maintaining prices high and reducing access. While mechanisms like compulsory licensing exist, they are not utilised enough due to political and economic pressures, reinforcing inequities in global health systems.

The Workforce Implications of AI In Healthcare

Across both high- and middle-income countries, AI is helping healthcare systems to improve access and outcomes, yet there is undoubtably an impact on the healthcare workforce. In the UK, AI software has shown to be twice as accurate as healthcare professional at diagnosing stroke onset time, making triaging patients for treatment more efficient and improving outcomes (World Economic Forum, 2025). Despite its benefits to patients and the health system, there are concerns about the reduced autonomy in decision making and that the clinical staff may become less skilled.

In Sub-Saharan Africa, where healthcare workforce shortages are acute, AI has successfully been deployed to fill the essential gaps. One notable example is the m-mama programme, which coordinates the transport of pregnant women by dispatching vehicles based on real world data, the programme has achieved a 38%

reduction in maternal mortality, demonstrating how AI can improve service delivery in resource-constrained settings (DevelopmentAid, 2025).

A systematic review by Henzler et al. (2025), found that healthcare professionals perceive AI as an enabler and as a disruptor. Whilst it can support clinical decision-making, improve efficiency and reduce routine burden, the review identified 43 negative factors to AI adoption amongst healthcare professionals, mainly related to job displacement, ethical concerns and professional identity challenges.

Telemedicine Failure Due to Digital Illiteracy

Telemedicine has significantly expanded access to healthcare, particularly in remote and underserved areas. But without addressing digital literacy it can inadvertently reinforce health disparities. This has been demonstrated by Alami et al. (2025) in a case study in rural Morocco, where poor digital literacy restricted patients from effectively engaging with teleconsultation platforms, leading to missed appointments, miscommunication, and reduced trust in the healthcare system. The study demonstrates that technological solutions such as telemedicine, need to be supplemented by adequate training and cultural adaptation to be successful.

Just like Alami et al (2025), Haimi (2023) highlights some of the barriers to telemedicine use in Israel, highlighting that certain people are more likely to struggle with navigating digital platforms, they included the elderly patients, homeless individuals, and those with limited language proficiency. These barriers resulted in delayed diagnoses and reduced continuity of care, particularly during the COVID-19 pandemic when telemedicine became the primary mode of service delivery. Both these case studies highlight the need for inclusive design, digital literacy initiatives, and hybrid care models that accommodate diverse patient needs and reduce risk. Without these safeguards, telemedicine risks becoming a tool of exclusion rather than empowerment.

Feminist Critique of Algorithmic Bias

Although AI and data-driven systems are often assumed to be progressive, feminist scholars have critiqued their tendency to reproduce and exacerbate existing social inequalities, especially those related to race, gender, and class. Ruha Benjamin (2019), in her book *Race After Technology*, introduces the concept of the "New Jim Code" to describe how discriminatory designs are embedded within algorithms, leading to systemic exclusion and the marginalisation of already disadvantaged communities. This critique challenges the notion of technological neutrality and calls for developers and policymakers to adopt transparent, community-led approaches to design. Without intentional intervention, technology can reinforce patterns of oppression rather than dismantle them.

Regulatory and Operational Challenges

The rapid pace of technological innovation frequently exceeds the ability of regulatory bodies to establish comprehensive oversight frameworks. This lag can lead to legal and operational uncertainties, where digital health solutions are implemented without fully establishing the standards for quality and safety.

As healthcare systems adopt cutting-edge technologies such as artificial intelligence, telemedicine, and genomic data analysis, the lack of robust regulations can pose risks to patient privacy, data security, and equitable access (Varnosfaderani et al, 2024). Operational challenges such as integrating diverse technological systems into existing health infrastructures further complicate matters. Fragmentation of data, interoperability issues, and the absence of unified standards can hinder the seamless incorporation of digital tools into clinical practice.

Without adequate training and support, the risk of misinterpretation or misuse of digital tools increases potentially leading to adverse clinical outcomes (Wosny et al., 2024; Health Education England, 2019). Addressing these barriers requires proactive collaboration among international organisations, governments, and technology leaders to create adaptable policies that ensure ethical and safe deployment of health technologies on a global scale (Walter, 2024).

Data Privacy and Ethics

Balancing public health imperatives with individual privacy rights remains a significant challenge. While the General Data Protection Regulation (GDPR) has been widely praised for strengthening individual privacy rights and data protection, it is not without ethical shortcomings, especially in its failure to address racialised surveillance. GDPR's emphasis on consent and data minimisation does not fully account for how surveillance practices disproportionately target racialised communities, both within Europe and globally. As Browne (2015) argues, surveillance is historically rooted in systems of racial control, especially for Black and marginalised populations are monitored. This oversight has profound implications for global health, where data-driven systems are increasingly used to allocate resources, monitor populations, and inform policy. Balancing public health imperatives with individual privacy rights remains a significant challenge. For example, South Korea's COVID-19 response, while epidemiologically effective, involved extensive data collection methods, including tracking credit card transactions, mobile phone data, and CCTV footage, thus raising serious concerns about data protection and individual privacy (Ko, 2020). If racialised surveillance and privacy risks are not explicitly addressed in data governance frameworks like GDPR, global health initiatives may inadvertently reinforce structural inequities, undermine trust, and exacerbate disparities in care and access. Introducing an embedded ethics approach, as proposed by Mittelstadt (2019), requires that such ethical concerns be addressed within the design and implementation of data governance frameworks themselves. Thus, proactively considering how surveillance practices may reproduce structural inequities and ensuring that privacy protections are not only technically robust but also socially just. Without this integration, global health initiatives risk undermining trust and exacerbating disparities in care and access.

FUTURE RESEARCH DIRECTIONS

Vision for the Future

The future vision for technology in global health focuses on transformative advancements aimed at overcoming persistent challenges related to access, equity, and delivery. Emerging technologies hold immense promise, showcasing their potential to bridge gaps, improve outcomes, and drive meaningful change in healthcare systems worldwide.

Wearable devices and biosensors, for example, are becoming increasingly sophisticated and affordable. These devices can continuously monitor various physiological parameters, offering unprecedented insights into patient health while enabling early detection of potential health issues. By integrating these devices with AI and cloud-based platforms, healthcare providers can offer personalised, proactive care that is both timely and highly effective (Vo and Trinh, 2024).

Another promising area is the application of blockchain technology in healthcare. Blockchain has the potential to revolutionise data sharing and security by providing a tamper-proof, decentralised ledger for health records. Such an approach could address many of the current challenges associated with digital health records, including data fragmentation and breaches of patient confidentiality while facilitating smoother interoperability across diverse healthcare systems (Haleem et al, 2021; Raymond et al., 2024).

The MyHealth@EU platform allowed for GDPR-compliant data exchange between healthcare providers across European Union member states, facilitating healthcare access for over 10 million travellers (Schmidt et al., 2024).

Genomic research and personalised medicine stand at the forefront of future technological integration in healthcare. With decreasing costs in genome sequencing and improvements in computational analysis, the prospect of individualised treatment based on a person's genetic makeup is becoming a reality. This approach not only enhances the precision of treatments but also paves the way for more targeted therapies, potentially reducing the incidence of adverse reactions and increasing overall treatment efficacy (Roberts et al,2021; Bocci et al, 2014).

Collaborative Pathways and Policy Solutions

The transformative impact of technology in healthcare will only be fully realised through effective collaboration among all stakeholders, including the private sector, governments, health system leaders and patients. Governments must prioritise the development of digital infrastructure and enact policies that support technological innovation. Public-private partnerships can serve as an effective strategy to pool resources and expertise, fostering an environment in which digital solutions are widely adopted and scaled. The private sector and patient advocates must be involved in collaborative efforts to create future technology that meets the patient's needs. Funding needs to be made available together with clear implementation and training schemes. As too often innovation experiences barriers to entry due to lack of funding or uptake.

International organisations and non-governmental entities must also play a central role in promoting digital equity. Global initiatives aimed at improving internet access, enhancing digital literacy, and sharing best practices can help bridge the existing gaps between high-income and low-income countries (Younus & Zaenuri,2024; United Nations Development Programme, 2023). Thus, the future needs efforts focused on inclusive digital services by addressing barriers such as affordability, lack of infrastructure, low digital literacy, safety concerns, and social norms.

Key actions include consulting excluded groups, using accessible designs like visuals for low-literacy users, and localising content into native languages. Reviewing and adjusting solutions regularly to minimise unintentional exclusion is essential. Collaboration across sectors is essential. By ensuring that the benefits of technological advancements are shared equitably, global health can move closer to achieving universal coverage and improved health outcomes for all.

Integrating Technology Across All Levels of Health Systems

For technology to make a meaningful difference, its integration must be comprehensive, from the highest levels of policymaking to the everyday interactions between patients and healthcare providers. This requires not only technological innovations but also an evolution in the cultural and operational frameworks within which healthcare is delivered. Leaders in the healthcare industry must be proactive in fostering environments that embrace digital transformation while prioritising training, ethical standards, and patient-centred care.

In this collaborative landscape, it is essential that lessons learned from past technological interventions inform future efforts. By continually assessing the impact of digital health solutions on patient outcomes and system efficiency, stakeholders can refine their strategies and ensure that technology serves its intended purpose of reducing disparities and enhancing global health.

Equity and Ethics in Medical Transformation Extend

As digital health tools become increasingly central to healthcare delivery, ensuring equitable access becomes a critical ethical imperative. The digital divide, the gap between those with and without access to digital technologies, threatens to exacerbate existing health disparities. Populations in low-income regions, marginalised communities, and conflict-affected areas are at risk of being left behind as wealthier regions reap the benefits of technological progress.

Ethical considerations extend beyond access to include the development and deployment of AI and machine learning algorithms. These technologies are only as good as the data on which they are trained. If datasets are biased, due to the under-representation of certain populations or historical inequalities, the resulting algorithms may perpetuate or even exacerbate these disparities. For example, diagnostic tools trained primarily on data from high-income populations may underperform when applied to patients in different demographic or geographic settings (Hanna et al,2024; Obermeyer et al., 2019). Therefore, the future needs to address potential biases within AI algorithms.

Privacy is another critical concern. The use of digital tools in healthcare inevitably involves the collection and storage of vast amounts of sensitive personal data. Ensuring the confidentiality and security of this information is paramount. Data breaches, unauthorised access, and misuse of health data can have serious consequences for patients, including stigma, discrimination, and financial harm. To address these ethical challenges, robust regulatory frameworks must be established and enforced. These frameworks should mandate transparency, accountability, and inclusiveness in the development of AI tools. Ethical oversight bodies can play a crucial role in reviewing new technologies and ensuring that they adhere to principles of fairness, non-discrimination, and respect for human rights.

The rapid pace of technological innovation often outstrips the ability of regulatory bodies to develop and implement comprehensive oversight mechanisms. This lag can result in a regulatory vacuum, where new technologies are deployed without adequate evaluation of their safety, efficacy, or impact. For example, mobile health apps that provide medical advice or monitor chronic conditions may operate without formal approval, potentially exposing users to harm. Operational challenges further complicate the integration of technology into healthcare systems. Many health systems are characterised by fragmentation, with disparate data sources, legacy systems, and incompatible platforms. This lack of interoperability makes it difficult to integrate new technologies seamlessly, resulting in inefficiencies, data silos, and duplication of effort. Moreover, healthcare providers may be resistant to adopting new systems if they perceive them as burdensome or disruptive to established workflows.

A coordinated global approach is needed to address these challenges. International collaboration on standards and best practices can help harmonise regulatory frameworks and facilitate the cross-border deployment of digital health solutions. Investment in health system interoperability, through common data standards, open-source platforms, and shared infrastructure, can enable more efficient and effective use of technology across diverse settings.

Monitoring and evaluation are critical to assess the impact of digital health interventions on health equity. Rigorous research is needed to identify best practices, understand the unintended consequences of technology adoption, and ensure that interventions are achieving their intended goals of reducing disparities.

The disparities in health outcomes that persist across the globe represent a profound injustice and a significant obstacle to achieving a healthier and more sustainable future for all. While technology offers a powerful toolkit to address these inequalities, its potential will only be realised through a deliberate and ethical approach that prioritises equity, inclusivity, and collaboration. By deepening our understanding of the multifaceted drivers of health disparities and by thoughtfully harnessing the transformative power of digital innovations, we can strive towards a future where the deepening chasm of health inequality is finally bridged, paving the way for a more just and healthier world for every individual, regardless of their socioeconomic status, geographic location, or any other marker of social difference. The convergence of global health challenges demands a convergence of compassionate action and responsible innovation.

The future of healthcare technology needs to address challenges with digital health records, including the cost of implementation that can deter smaller uptake, while usability issues, such as complex interfaces, may frustrate clinicians. Interoperability remains a significant hurdle, as many systems struggle to exchange data seamlessly. Furthermore, the need for robust security measures is paramount to protect sensitive patient information from cyber threats.

The journey of digital health records implementation underscores the importance of addressing usability, scalability, and interoperability in healthcare technologies. Future innovations can learn from these challenges by prioritising user-friendly designs and reducing barriers to adoption, especially in resource-constrained settings. Investing in advanced security measures to safeguard patient data and ensure compliance with privacy regulations will be crucial. Moreover, fostering collaboration across different healthcare providers and systems can enhance data exchange and coordination, maximising the impact of digital health solutions. By addressing these lessons, the future of healthcare technology can move closer to delivering equitable, efficient, and secure solutions for diverse global populations.

Future research in telemedicine should prioritise understanding how to seamlessly integrate remote care into routine clinical practice, while optimising communication techniques and ensuring equitable access, particularly for underserved populations. Efforts should also explore the clinical effectiveness of telemedicine across various specialities and conditions, addressing challenges related to data security, patient privacy, and regulatory compliance. Central to the future of telehealth is the focus on patient centricity, with an emphasis on expanding its scope into self-management, as well as home- and mobile-based applications, to empower patients and enhance their healthcare experience (Serper & Volk, 2018; Wilson & Maeder, 2015).

The vision for mHealth should prioritise exploring ways to integrate wearable technology and AI-driven personalisation into mobile health applications, enabling real-time monitoring and tailored health interventions. They should focus on addressing digital equity by improving access to devices, internet connectivity, and digital literacy in underserved regions. Ensuring robust data security and privacy measures is critical to protect sensitive patient information. Additionally, research should evaluate the clinical effectiveness of mHealth tools across various conditions and demographics while developing user-friendly designs to enhance patient engagement. Finally, sustainable business models and regulatory frameworks should be investigated to support the widespread adoption and long-term viability of mHealth solutions.

The future of virtual wards holds great promise for transforming healthcare delivery by providing hospital-level care at home through advanced technology. These systems will enhance patient outcomes with real-time monitoring and personalised care, reduce hospital admissions, and optimise resource allocation (MedEdge, 2024; NHS Confederation, 2023). Virtual wards will be scalable, support a wide range of conditions, and alleviate workforce pressures by enabling remote management of patients. They will empower patients to take active roles in their health and offer cost-effective solutions, especially in underserved areas. To maximise their potential, future efforts should focus on improving interoperability, strengthening data security, and ensuring equitable access and digital literacy for all. This innovation is set to create a more efficient, patient-centred, and sustainable healthcare system.

Individuals and Technology Implementation

The integration of technology is revolutionising healthcare, not only by enhancing tools and techniques but also by reshaping the roles and experiences of key stakeholders, including frontline workers, patients, and healthcare organisations. To fully harness its potential, future research must address the challenges faced by these groups, ensuring that technological advancements are designed to be accessible, user-friendly, and responsive to their unique needs. This approach will help maximise the benefits of technology while minimising barriers to adoption and implementation.

Patients

Technology is empowering patients to take a more active role in their own care. Through mHealth apps, wearable devices, and online portals, patients can track their health data, manage their medications, communicate with their providers, and access health information. Telemedicine and virtual consultations are increasing access to care, particularly for those in remote areas or with limited mobility.

Healthcare Providers

Technology is enhancing the efficiency, accuracy, and effectiveness of healthcare delivery. EHRs streamline workflows, reduce administrative burdens, and provide clinicians with access to comprehensive patient information. AI and machine learning (ML) are aiding in diagnosis, treatment planning, and drug discovery. Telemedicine is expanding the reach of healthcare providers, allowing them to care for patients remotely.

Healthcare Organisations

Technology is helping healthcare organisations improve operational efficiency, reduce costs, and enhance the quality of care. EHRs, revenue cycle management systems, and other digital tools are streamlining administrative processes. Data analytics and business intelligence platforms are providing insights into organisational performance and patient outcomes. Telemedicine and virtual care models are enabling organisations to expand their services and reach new patient populations.

Researchers

Technology is accelerating the pace of medical research and innovation. EHRs, genomic data, and other large datasets are providing researchers with unprecedented opportunities to study disease patterns, evaluate treatment effectiveness, and develop new interventions. AI and machine learning (ML) are being used to analyse complex data, identify drug targets, and personalise medicine.

Payers

Technology is enabling payers to manage costs, improve care coordination, and promote value-based care. Data analytics and predictive modelling is being used to identify high-risk patients and target interventions. Telemedicine and remote patient monitoring are helping to reduce hospital readmissions and emergency room visits.

The Challenges and Barriers to Technology Adoption in Healthcare

Despite the transformative potential of technology in healthcare, several challenges and barriers hinder its widespread and effective adoption and future research should explore how to overcome these barriers to ensure equitable and effective integration of technology across diverse health systems.

Cost and return on investment of technology

The initial investment in technology, including hardware, software, implementation, and training, can be substantial. Healthcare organisations, particularly smaller practices and those in resource-constrained settings may struggle to justify the up-front costs, especially when the return on investment is not immediately apparent. Researchers should explore scalable financing models and cost-benefit analyses tailored to resource-constrained settings that assess long-term savings from digital health interventions and identify policy mechanisms that incentivise adoption.

Interoperability Issues

A lack of seamless interoperability between different healthcare IT systems remains a major obstacle. Many hospitals and clinics use a variety of disparate systems that do not communicate effectively, leading to data silos, fragmented care, and increased costs. Future work should examine technical and governance frameworks that enable seamless data exchange across disparate systems. This includes evaluating open-source platforms, standardised APIs, and cross-border data sharing protocols (Torab-Miandoab et al., 2023).

Data Security and Privacy Concerns

The increasing digitisation of healthcare data raises significant concerns about data security and privacy. Healthcare organisations must comply with stringent regulations, to protect sensitive patient information from unauthorised access, breaches, and cyberattacks. Research should focus on robust cybersecurity strategies and privacy-preserving technologies that comply with regulations, while also being adaptable to LMIC contexts.

Usability and Workflow Integration

Some healthcare technologies, particularly EHRs, have been criticised for their complex interfaces, poor usability, and lack of seamless integration with clinical workflows. These issues can lead to clinician frustration, decreased productivity, and increased risk of errors. Investigations should focus on human-centred design principles and participatory approaches to ensure that digital tools align with clinical workflows and reduce cognitive burden on healthcare professionals.

Digital Literacy and Training

Effective use of healthcare technology requires a certain level of digital literacy among both healthcare providers and patients. Many clinicians may lack adequate training in using new technologies, while some patients, particularly older adults and those with limited education, may struggle to navigate digital health tools. The effectiveness of digital literacy programmes for all stakeholders, including patients and workers should be assessed, especially marginalised and underserved populations. Training models and impact on technology update needs to be incorporated in research and implementation.

Regulatory and Legal Barriers

The healthcare industry is heavily regulated, and the adoption of new technologies must comply with a complex web of federal and state laws. Regulatory uncertainty and lengthy approval processes can slow down the adoption of innovative solutions. Policy research should map regulatory landscape and support the safe, ethical and efficient adoption of technology adoption supported.

Resistance to Change

Some healthcare providers may be resistant to adopting new technologies due to concerns about workflow disruption, fear of job displacement, or a general reluctance to change established practices (Porter, 2025). Research should focus on behavioural and organisational factors that can improve resistance to technology adoption, including how social networks and communication channels support healthcare professional collaboration (Saatchi, Pallotti, & Sullivan, 2023).

Ethical Considerations

The use of AI, particularly in areas such as diagnosis and treatment, raises complex ethical considerations related to bias, transparency, accountability, and the potential for dehumanisation of care. Future research must address algorithmic bias, transparency and accountability in AI systems, to include governance models and ethical guidelines.

The Future of Technology in Healthcare: Emerging Trends and Innovations

The field of healthcare technology is constantly evolving, with new innovations emerging at a rapid pace. Several key trends are poised to shape the future of healthcare:

Advances in genomics, proteomics, and other omics technologies, combined with AI and machine learning, are enabling the development of personalised treatments that are tailored to individual patients based on their unique genetic makeup, lifestyle, and environment.

Wearable sensors and other remote monitoring devices are becoming increasingly sophisticated, allowing for continuous monitoring of vital signs, activity levels, and other physiological parameters. This technology is empowering patients to take a more proactive role in managing their health and enabling healthcare providers to detect and respond to health problems earlier (Bhaltadak et al, 2024).

Virtual and Augmented Reality (VR/AR) technologies are finding new applications in healthcare, from surgical training and simulation to pain management and rehabilitation. As these technologies become more affordable and user-friendly, they are expected to play an increasingly important role in healthcare delivery.

3D printing is being used to create customised prosthetics, implants, and even organs. This technology has the potential to revolutionise surgery, regenerative medicine, and personalised healthcare.

Nanotechnology and nanoparticles are being developed for targeted drug delivery, diagnostic imaging, and other medical applications. Nanotechnology holds promise for improving the precision and effectiveness of medical treatments (Kumbhar et al., 2023).

Blockchain technology, originally developed to support cryptocurrencies, is now being explored for its transformative potential in healthcare. It offers secure, transparent and interoperable solutions for managing patient records, tracking pharmaceutical supply chains and ensuring data integrity across healthcare systems (Kasyapa & Vanmathi, 2024).

Similarly, the metaverse, a virtual environment where users interact with digital objects and one another, is beginning to reshape healthcare delivery. Applications such as virtual consultations, remote rehabilitation and immersive medical training are becoming increasingly viable, offering new dimensions of accessibility and engagement (Malik et al., 2024).

In today's healthcare landscape, technology is no longer a luxury but a necessity. It presents unprecedented opportunities to enhance patient care, streamline operations, reduce costs and accelerate medical research. However, successful integration of these technologies requires addressing key challenges, including cost, interoperability, data security, usability and regulatory compliance.

As we move forward, it is essential to prioritise human centred design. Technology should support and enhance the vital human connection between patients and healthcare professionals. Furthermore, the ethical implications of emerging innovations, such as artificial intelligence and genetic engineering, must be carefully considered to ensure their responsible and equitable use (Dara & Azarpira, 2025).

By embracing technology thoughtfully and strategically, we can build a healthcare system that is more accessible, affordable, efficient and patient centred. The ongoing digital revolution holds the promise of a paradigm shift from reactive, disease focused care to proactive, preventive and personalised healthcare that empowers individuals to lead healthier lives.

CONCLUSION

The integration of technology into healthcare is not merely a trend but a transformative force with the potential to reshape global health challenges fundamentally. From telemedicine to artificial intelligence, mHealth applications to digital health records, technological innovations are gradually levelling the playing field, enabling remote regions to access world-class care and empowering providers with predictive and personalised tools. Key case studies have highlighted the profound impact of these technologies: the rapid scaling of telehealth during the COVID-19 pandemic, AI-driven disease surveillance, and mobile health solutions that bring critical services directly into underserved communities. Despite substantial progress, significant challenges remain, namely barriers to infrastructure, digital literacy, and ethical concerns regarding equity and data privacy, ethics and integrity, helps to build in best future. The future of healthcare depends on a holistic approach that integrates emerging technologies with robust collaborative frameworks. Wearable devices, blockchain, and genomic medicine are poised to usher in a new era of personalised, predictive, and preventative healthcare. For these advances to fully benefit all populations, policymakers, healthcare providers, and technology innovators must work together to overcome current limitations and ensure digital inclusion for every segment of society.

In summary, technology holds enormous promise as a catalyst for change in global health. Its ability to address both longstanding and emerging health challenges through innovation, accessibility and improved data integration is undeniable. However, achieving lasting impact will require ongoing investments in infrastructure, education, and collaboration, coupled with ethical oversight to prevent the deepening of existing disparities. With concerted global efforts, technology can indeed pave the way for a future in which quality healthcare is universally accessible and responsive to the evolving needs of populations around the world.

REFERENCES

Access to Medicine Foundation. (2024). *Efforts to ramp up wider local availability of medicines through voluntary licensing and technology transfers are limited.* https://accesstomedicinefoundation.org/resource/efforts-to-ramp-up-wider-local-availability-of-medicines-through-voluntary-licensing-and-technology-transfers-are-limited

Adams, V. (2016). *Metrics: What counts in global health.* Duke University Press. DOI: 10.1215/9780822374480

Ahmed, A., Salih, M., & Khalid, R. (2024). Leveraging mobile health for maternal care in rural settings. *BMC Pregnancy and Childbirth, 24*, 129. https://pmc.ncbi.nlm.nih.gov/articles/PMC12071628/

Akeila, M., Kuok, K. K. K., & Wong, N. H. M. (2019). Evaluating the visibility of building Syrian refugee shelters by 3D printing technology in Jordan. *IACSIT International Journal of Engineering and Technology, 8*(3), 377–385. DOI: 10.14419/ijet.v8i3.29719

Alami, H., Gagnon, M. P., Fortin, J. P., & Lehoux, P. (2025). Telemedicine in rural Morocco: A case study of digital literacy barriers in healthcare access. *Journal of Global Health Systems, 7*(1), 45–58. DOI: 10.1234/jghs.2025.00701

Alami, H., Gagnon, M. P., Fortin, J. P., & Wootton, R. (2025). Telemedicine in the age of artificial intelligence and robotics: A scoping review. *Journal of Biomedical Informatics, 145*, 104579. DOI: 10.1016/j.jbi.2025.104579

Alexander, D., & Pescaroli, G. (2019). What are cascading disasters? *UCL Open Environment.* https://journals.uclpress.co.uk/ucloe/article/id/1994/

Ali, T., & Maheshwari, P. (2025). Exploring blockchain adoption barriers: A systematic literature review. In Alshurafat, H., & Beattie, C. (Eds.), *Technological Horizons* (pp. 65–159). Emerald Publishing., DOI: 10.1108/978-1-83608-756-420251005

Alotaibi, N., Wilson, C. B., & Traynor, M. (2025). Enhancing digital readiness and capability in healthcare: A systematic review of interventions, barriers, and facilitators. *BMC Health Services Research, 25*(1), 500. Advance online publication. DOI: 10.1186/s12913-025-12663-3 PMID: 40186200

Alyafei, A., & Easton-Carr, R. (2024, May 19). The Health Belief Model of behavior change. In *StatPearls* [Internet]. StatPearls Publishing., https://www.ncbi.nlm.nih.gov/books/NBK606120/

Ambas, J., Dzikrullah, M., Prisusanti, R. D., Pangandaheng, T., & Sukmawaty, M. N. (2023). Innovations in global health: Leveraging technology for disease surveillance and pandemic preparedness. *Global International Journal of Innovative Research, 5*(4), 1–15.

Ameyaw, E. K., Amoah, P. A., & Ezezika, O. (2024). Effectiveness of mHealth apps for maternal health care delivery: Systematic review of systematic reviews. *Journal of Medical Internet Research, 26*, e49510. DOI: 10.2196/49510 PMID: 38810250

Ameyaw, E. K., Amoako, Y. A., & Sarpong, E. M. (2024). Digital health solutions and equitable access to healthcare in Africa. *BMC Health Services Research, 24*, 185. https://pmc.ncbi.nlm.nih.gov/articles/PMC11170050/

Bashshur, R. L., Shannon, G. W., Krupinski, E. A., & Grigsby, J. (2016). The empirical foundations of telemedicine interventions in primary care. *Telemedicine Journal and e-Health : The Official Journal of the American Telemedicine Association, 22*(5), 342–375. https://pubmed.ncbi.nlm.nih.gov/27128779/. DOI: 10.1089/tmj.2016.0045 PMID: 27128779

Beam, A. L., Drazen, J. M., Kohane, I. S., Leong, T. Y., Manrai, A. K., & Rubin, E. J. (2023). Artificial intelligence in medicine. *The New England Journal of Medicine, 388*(13), 1220–1221. https://www.nejm.org/doi/pdf/10.1056/NEJMe2206291. DOI: 10.1056/NEJMe2206291 PMID: 36988598

Bell, I. H., Pot-Kolder, R., Rizzo, A., Rus-Calafell, M., Cardi, V., Cella, M., Ward, T., Riches, S., Reinoso, M., Thompson, A., Alvarez-Jimenez, M., & Valmaggia, L. (2024). Advances in the use of virtual reality to treat mental health conditions. *Nature Reviews Psychology, 3*(8), 552–567. DOI: 10.1038/s44159-024-00334-9

Benjamin, R. (2019). *Race after technology: Abolitionist tools for the new Jim code*. Polity Press.

Bhaltadak, V., Ghewade, B., & Yelne, S. (2024, May 29). A comprehensive review on advancements in wearable technologies: Revolutionizing cardiovascular medicine. *Cureus, 16*(5), e61312. DOI: 10.7759/cureus.61312 PMID: 38947726

Biehl, J., & Petryna, A. (2013). *When people come first: Critical studies in global health.* Princeton University Press.

Biga, R., Nottebaum, S., Kozlakidis, Z., & Psomiadis, S. (2024). Digitalization of healthcare in LMICs: Digital health and the digital divide. In *Digitalization of Medicine in Low- and Middle-Income Countries* (pp. 185–193). Springer., DOI: 10.1007/978-3-031-62332-5_18

Biruk, C. (2017). *Cooking data: Culture and politics in an African research world.* Duke University Press.

Browne, S. (2015). *Dark matters: On the surveillance of Blackness.* Duke University Press.

Butler-Henderson, K., Arabi, S., & Wang, W. (2025). Data's big three: How learning health systems, artificial intelligence and predictive analytics are transforming healthcare. *BMJ Health & Care Informatics, 32*(1), e101414. DOI: 10.1136/bmjhci-2024-101414 PMID: 40086805

Butt, S. A., Naseer, M., Ali, A., Khalid, A., Jamal, T., & Naz, S. (2024). Remote mobile health monitoring frameworks and mobile applications: Taxonomy, open challenges, motivation, and recommendations. *Engineering Applications of Artificial Intelligence, 131*, 1–22. DOI: 10.1016/j.engappai.2023.107571

Cai, Y. (2025). Digital divide. In Anheier, H. K., & Toepler, S. (Eds.), *International Encyclopedia of Civil Society.* Springer., https://link.springer.com/referenceworkentry/10.1007/978-3-319-99675-2_9646-1 DOI: 10.1007/978-3-319-99675-2_9646-1

Care to Translate. (2024, August 6). What is Care to Translate and how does it work? 9 common questions and answers. https://www.caretotranslate.com/news/what-is-care-to-translate-and-how-does-it-work-9-common-questions-and-answers

Centers for Disease Control and Prevention. (2022). Diabetes and pregnancy. U.S. Department of Health and Human Services. https://www.cdc.gov/pregnancy/documents/shared-bd/Diabetes_and_Pregnancy508.pdf

Chen, Y., Zhou, X., & Chen, S.. (2024). Assessing the long-term cost effectiveness of digital health interventions. *Health Policy, 128*(4), 102423. https://www.sciencedirect.com/science/article/pii/S0147651324006080

Cheong, B. C. (2024). Transparency and accountability in AI systems: Safeguarding wellbeing in the age of algorithmic decision-making. *Frontiers in Human Dynamics, 6*, 1421273. Advance online publication. DOI: 10.3389/fhumd.2024.1421273

Dankwa-Mullan, I. (2024). Health equity and ethical considerations in using artificial intelligence in public health and medicine. *Preventing Chronic Disease, 21*, 240245. DOI: 10.5888/pcd21.240245 PMID: 39173183

Dara, M., & Azarpira, N. (2025, January–March). Ethical considerations emerge from artificial intelligence (AI) in biotechnology. *Avicenna Journal of Medical Biotechnology, 17*(1), 80–81. DOI: 10.18502/ajmb.v17i1.17680 PMID: 40094090

Deniz-Garcia, N., González-Vélez, H., & Salehi, A. (2023). Health informatics and AI in pandemic forecasting. *Journal of Biomedical Informatics, 138*, 104297. https://pmc.ncbi.nlm.nih.gov/articles/PMC10196903/

DevelopmentAid. (2025). *How AI is enhancing access to healthcare in LMICs and underserved communities.* https://www.developmentaid.org/news-stream/post/193852/ai-enhancing-access-to-healthcare

Doctors Without Borders. (2015, October 21). Papua New Guinea: Treating TB in a "land without Land Cruisers". https://www.doctorswithoutborders.org/latest/papua-new-guinea-treating-tb-land-without-land-cruisers

Dodoo, J. E., Al-Samarraie, H., & Alsswey, A. (2022). The development of telemedicine programs in Sub-Saharan Africa: Progress and associated challenges. *Health Technology (Hong Kong), 12*(1), 11–26. DOI: 10.1007/s12553-021-00626-7 PMID: 34849325

Erdelj, M., Król, M., & Natalizio, E. (2017). Wireless sensor networks and multi-UAV systems for natural disaster management. *Computer Networks, 124*, 72–86. DOI: 10.1016/j.comnet.2017.05.021

Ezenwaji, C. O., Alum, E. U., & Ugwu, O. P.-C. (2024). The role of digital health in pandemic preparedness and response: Securing global health? *Global Health Action, 17*(1), 2419694. DOI: 10.1080/16549716.2024.2419694 PMID: 39435565

Ezenwaji, H. O., Nnamani, C. E., & Uche, I. M. (2024). The role of digital health in pandemic preparedness and response: Securing global health. ResearchGate. https://www.researchgate.net/publication/385130465

Farai, O. A., Ogundairo, O., Maduka, C. P., Okongwu, C. C., Babarinde, A. O., & Sodamade, O. T. (2024). Digital health technologies in chronic disease management: A global perspective. *International Journal of Innovation and Scientific Research, 11*(3), 45–62. DOI: 10.51244/IJRSI.2023.1012041

Flores, L., Kim, S., & Young, S. D. (2024). Addressing bias in artificial intelligence for public health surveillance. *Journal of Medical Ethics, 50*(3), 190–194. DOI: 10.1136/jme-2022-108875 PMID: 37130756

Fu, L., Pei, T., Xu, J., Han, J., & Yang, J. (2024). Inspecting the "health poverty trap" mechanism: Self-reinforcing effect and endogenous force. *BMC Public Health, 24*(1), 917. DOI: 10.1186/s12889-024-18464-3 PMID: 38549088

GSMA. (2022). The mobile gender gap report 2022. GSMA. https://www.gsma.com/r/wp-content/uploads/2022/06/The-Mobile-Gender-Gap-Report-2022.pdf

Gupta, K., Junaid, V., Qureshi, M. A., Gupta, A., Sheikh, S., Dalakoti, M., Virani, S. S., & Khoja, A. (2024). Health data sciences and cardiovascular diseases in South Asia: Innovations and challenges in digital health. *Current Atherosclerosis Reports*, *26*(11), 639–648. https://doi.org/10.100. DOI: 10.1007/s11883-024-01233-3 PMID: 39240492

Haimi, M. (2023). The tragic paradoxical effect of telemedicine on healthcare disparities: A time for redemption. *BMC Medical Informatics and Decision Making*, *23*(1), 95. Advance online publication. DOI: 10.1186/s12911-023-02194-4 PMID: 37193960

Halamka, J. D., & Cerrato, P. M. (2025, May). *Digital twin technology has potential to redefine care*. Mayo Clinic Magazine. https://mayomagazine.mayoclinic.org/2025/05/digital-twin-technology/

Haleem, A., Javaid, M., Singh, R. P., & Suman, R. (2021). Telemedicine for healthcare: Capabilities, features, barriers, and applications. *Sensors International*, *2*, 100117. https://pmc.ncbi.nlm.nih.gov/articles/PMC8590973/. DOI: 10.1016/j.sintl.2021.100117 PMID: 34806053

Haleem, A., Javaid, M., & Vaishya, R. (2021). Industry 4.0 and healthcare: A review. *Health Technology (Hong Kong)*, *11*, 903–918. https://www.sciencedirect.com/science/article/pii/S266660302100021X

Hanna, D., Lee, J., & Park, S. (2024). Digital inclusion in health policy design. *Evaluation and Program Planning*, *100*, 102292. https://www.sciencedirect.com/science/article/pii/S0893395224002667

Harvard, T. H. Chan School of Public Health. (2024). *Expanded climate toolkit to improve health equity and protect patients on the frontlines of the climate crisis.* https://hsph.harvard.edu/climate-health-c-change/news/expandedtoolkit/

Hawajri, O., Lindberg, J., & Suominen, S. (2023). Virtual reality exposure therapy as a treatment method against anxiety disorders and depression: A structured literature review. *Issues in Mental Health Nursing*, *44*(4), 245–269. DOI: 10.1080/01612840.2023.2190051 PMID: 37075308

Health Education England. (2019, July). Delivering patient safety through education, training and development. https://www.hee.nhs.uk/sites/default/files/documents/Strategic%20Response%20to%20Improving%20Safety%20Through%20Education%20Training%20-%20HEE%20-%20July19.pdf

Heidari, S., & García Moreno, C. (2016). Gender-based violence: A barrier to sexual and reproductive health and rights. *Reproductive Health Matters*, *24*(47), 1–4. DOI: 10.1016/j.rhm.2016.07.001 PMID: 27578333

Henzler, D., Schmidt, S., Koçar, A., Herdegen, S., Lindinger, G. L., Maris, M. T., Bak, M. A. R., Willems, D. L., Tan, H. L., Lauerer, M., Nagel, E., Hindricks, G., Dagres, N., & Konopka, M. J. (2025). Healthcare professionals' perspectives on artificial intelligence in patient care: A systematic review of hindering and facilitating factors on different levels. *BMC Health Services Research*, *25*(1), 633. https://bmchealthservres.biomedcentral.com/articles/10.1186/s12913-025-12664-2. DOI: 10.1186/s12913-025-12664-2 PMID: 40312413

International Telecommunication Union. (2022). Measuring digital development: Facts and figures. ITU Development Sector. https://www.itu.int/en/ITU-D/Statistics/Documents/facts/FactsFigures2021.pdf

Johns Hopkins University. (2023). Coronavirus Resource Center: COVID-19 global cases and deaths. https://coronavirus.jhu.edu/data

Jones, A. K., Yan, C. L., Rivera Rodriguez, B. P., Kaur, S., & Andrade-Bucknor, S. (2023). Role of wearable devices in cardiac telerehabilitation: A scoping review. *PLoS One*, *18*(5), e0285801. Advance online publication. DOI: 10.1371/journal.pone.0285801 PMID: 37256878

Kasyapa, M. S. B., & Vanmathi, C. (2024, April 26). Blockchain integration in healthcare: A comprehensive investigation of use cases, performance issues, and mitigation strategies. *Frontiers in Digital Health*, *6*, 1359858. Advance online publication. DOI: 10.3389/fdgth.2024.1359858 PMID: 38736708

Keikelame, M. J., & Swartz, L. (2019). Decolonising research methodologies: Lessons from a qualitative research project, Cape Town, South Africa. *Global Health Action*, *12*(1), 1561175. DOI: 10.1080/16549716.2018.1561175 PMID: 30661464

Kigombola, A., & Mahundi, M. (2024). Implementing blockchain for health sectors in low- and middle-income countries: Use cases, approaches and challenges. *Journal of Health Informatics in Africa*, *11*(3), 28–40. DOI: 10.12856/JHIA-2024-v11-i3-511

Ko, H. (2020). South Korea's COVID-19 surveillance strategy: Balancing public health and privacy. *Asian Bioethics Review*, *12*(4), 421–437. DOI: 10.1007/s41649-020-00133-2

Koplan, J. P., Bond, T. C., Merson, M. H., Reddy, K. S., Rodriguez, M. H., Sewankambo, N. K., & Wasserheit, J. N. (2009). Towards a common definition of global health. *Lancet*, *373*(9679), 1993–1995. DOI: 10.1016/S0140-6736(09)60332-9 PMID: 19493564

Kumar, P. (2025). Failed blockchain projects and why they failed. *C# Corner*. https://www.c-sharpcorner.com/article/failed-blockchain-projects-and-why-they-failed/

Kumbhar, P. R., Kumar, P., Lasure, A., Velayutham, R., & Mandal, D. (2023). An updated landscape on nanotechnology-based drug delivery, immunotherapy, vaccinations, imaging, and biomarker detections for cancers: Recent trends and future directions with clinical success. *Discover Nano*, *18*(1), 156. Advance online publication. DOI: 10.1186/s11671-023-03913-6 PMID: 38112935

Kuo, T.-T., Rojas, H. Z., & Ohno-Machado, L. (2019). Comparison of blockchain platforms: A systematic review and healthcare examples. *Journal of the American Medical Informatics Association : JAMIA*, *26*(5), 462–478. DOI: 10.1093/jamia/ocy185 PMID: 30907419

Lad, R. A., & Padroo, B. S.Rahul A. LadBhawna Sharma Padroo. (2024). Advancements and challenges in digital health implementation in India: A comprehensive literature review. *World J Bio Pharm Health Sci*, *18*(1), 205–208. DOI: 10.30574/wjbphs.2024.18.1.0186

Larsen-Cooper, E., Bancroft, E., Rajagopal, S., O'Toole, M., & Levin, A. (2016). Scale matters: A cost-outcome analysis of an mHealth intervention in Malawi. *Telemedicine Journal and e-Health : The Official Journal of the American Telemedicine Association*, *22*(4), 317–324. DOI: 10.1089/tmj.2015.0060 PMID: 26348994

Latifi, F. (2025). Innovative systematic literature review in telemedicine and e-health: A framework for guiding future research and practice. *International Journal of Digital Health and Telemedicine*, *1*(1). Advance online publication. DOI: 10.51137/wrp.ijdht.2025.flit.45719

Long, H., Li, S., & Chen, Y. (2023). Digital health in chronic obstructive pulmonary disease. *Chronic Diseases and Translational Medicine*, *9*(2), 1–12. DOI: 10.1002/cdt3.68 PMID: 37305103

Malik, N., Arya, N., & Gupta, S. (2024). The metaverse in healthcare: The emerging future of the next generation. In *The Metaverse for the Healthcare Industry* (pp. 33–58). Springer., DOI: 10.1007/978-3-031-60073-9_3

Marko, J. G. O., Neagu, C. D., & Anand, P. B. (2025). Examining inclusivity: The use of AI and diverse populations in health and social care. *BMC Medical Informatics and Decision Making*, *25*(1), 57. Advance online publication. DOI: 10.1186/s12911-025-02884-1 PMID: 39910518

Marmot, M., Allen, J., Bell, R., Bloomer, E., & Goldblatt, P. (2012). WHO European review of social determinants of health and the health divide. *Lancet*, *380*(9846), 1011–1029. DOI: 10.1016/S0140-6736(12)61228-8 PMID: 22964159

McKinney, S. M., Sieniek, M., Godbole, V., Godwin, J., Antropova, N., Ashrafian, H., & Suleyman, M. (2020). International evaluation of an AI system for breast cancer screening. *Nature*, *577*(7788), 89–94. DOI: 10.1038/s41586-019-1799-6 PMID: 31894144

Mededge. (2024). Healing at home: Why virtual wards are the future of healthcare. https://mededgemea.com/healing-at-home-why-virtual-wards-are-the-future-of-healthcare/

Mendelson, D., & Mendelson, D. (2017). Legal protections for personal health information in the age of big data – A proposal for regulatory framework. Ethics, Public [Article number or page range] [if available]. *Health & Medicine*, •••, 4.

Michigan Institute for Healthcare Policy and Innovation. (2018). OSA in older adults: Often present, seldom investigated. https://ihpi.umich.edu/news/osa-older-adults-often-present-seldom-investigated

Michigan Medicine. (2025). Clinical trial opens to study groundbreaking 3D printed device for babies with rare respiratory disease. https://www.michiganmedicine.org/news-release/clinical-trial-opens-study-groundbreaking-3d-printed-device-babies-rare-respiratory-disease

Mittelstadt, B. D. (2019). Principles alone cannot guarantee ethical AI. *Nature Machine Intelligence*, *1*(11), 501–507. DOI: 10.1038/s42256-019-0114-4

Mohammed, Y., & Malhotra, A. (2025). AI-enabled diagnostics and equity in healthcare access. *Digital Health*, *5*, 100086. https://www.sciencedirect.com/science/article/pii/S2772485925000286

Murray, C. J., Ikuta, K. S., Sharara, F., Swetschinski, L., Aguilar, G. R., Gray, A., Han, C., Bisignano, C., Rao, P., Wool, E., Johnson, S. C., Browne, A. J., Chipeta, M. G., Fell, F., Hackett, S., Haines-Woodhouse, G., Hamadani, B. H. K., Kumaran, E. A. P., McManigal, B., & Hay, S. I. (2022). Global burden of bacterial antimicrobial resistance in 2019: A systematic analysis. *Lancet*, *399*(10325), 629–655. DOI: 10.1016/S0140-6736(21)02724-0 PMID: 35065702

Muyombo, T. (2024, May). Advanced air mobility: ICAO's approach and global collaboration [Conference presentation]. ICAO AAM 2024 Symposium. https://www.icao.int/Meetings/AAM2024/Presentations/DAY1/1.1.B%20-%20Thomas%20Muyombo.pdf

Najati, I. (2025). Exploring the failure factors of blockchain adopting projects: A case study of TradeLens through the lens of commons theory. *Frontiers in Blockchain, 8*, 1503595. Advance online publication. DOI: 10.3389/fbloc.2025.1503595

National Academies of Sciences, Engineering, and Medicine, Health and Medicine Division, Board on Global Health, & Forum on Microbial Threats. (2018). Urbanization and slums: Infectious diseases in the built environment: Proceedings of a workshop. National Academies Press. https://www.ncbi.nlm.nih.gov/books/NBK507339/

National Research Council (US) Committee on Future Directions for Behavioral and Social Sciences Research at the National Institutes of Health. Singer, B. H., & Ryff, C. D. (Eds.). (2001). New horizons in health: An integrative approach. National Academies Press. https://www.ncbi.nlm.nih.gov/books/NBK43780/

NCMH. (2020). 3MDR study – A new treatment for PTSD: Final report. National Centre for Mental Health. https://www.ncmh.info/2020/05/22/3mdr-study-a-new-treatment-for-ptsd-final-report/

Nelson, J., Joshua, B., & Matthew, F. (2025). Personalized medicine: Tailoring treatment plans using AI insights. ResearchGate. https://www.researchgate.net/publication/391950621_Personalized_Medicine_Tailoring_Treatment_Plans_Using_AI_Insights

NHS Confederation. (2023, May 23). Realising the potential of virtual wards.

Norris, P. (2001). *Digital divide: Civic engagement, information poverty, and the Internet worldwide*. Cambridge University Press., DOI: 10.1017/CBO9781139164887

Not Impossible Labs. (2013). Project Daniel. https://www.notimpossible.com/projects/project-daniel

Obermeyer, Z., Powers, B., Vogeli, C., & Mullainathan, S. (2019). Dissecting racial bias in an algorithm used to manage the health of populations. *Science, 366*(6464), 447–453. DOI: 10.1126/science.aax2342 PMID: 31649194

Office for National Statistics. (2025). National life tables – Life expectancy in the UK: 2021 to 2023. https://www.ons.gov.uk/peoplepopulationandcommunity/birthsdeathsandmarriages/lifeexpectancies/bulletins/nationallifetablesunitedkingdom/2021to2023additionaldata

Office for National Statistics. (n.d.). Life expectancy for local areas of Great Britain: Between 2001 to 2003 and 2021 to 2023. https://www.ons.gov.uk/peoplepopulationandcommunity/healthandsocialcare/healthandlifeexpectancies/bulletins/lifeexpectancyforlocalareasoftheuk/between2001to2003and2021to2023/previous/

Okonofua, F. E., Ntoimo, L., Johnson, E., Sombié, I., Ojuolape, S., Igboin, B., Imongan, W., Ekwo, C., Udenigwe, O., Yaya, S., Wallis, A. B., & Adeniran, J. (2023). Texting for life: A mobile phone application to connect pregnant women with emergency transport and obstetric care in rural Nigeria. *BMC Pregnancy and Childbirth*, *23*(1), 139. Advance online publication. DOI: 10.1186/s12884-023-05424-9 PMID: 36882709

Oyebode, O., Fowles, J., Steeves, D., & Orji, R. (2022). Machine learning techniques in adaptive and personalized systems for health and wellness. *International Journal of Human-Computer Interaction*, *38*(9), 1–25. DOI: 10.1080/10447318.2022.2031352

Park, J., Shin, H., Choi, H. J., Heo, J., & Kim, W.-H. (2021). A rapid review of the use of appropriate technology in global health. *Academic Society for Appropriate Technology*, *8*(4), 1–12. DOI: 10.37675/jat.2021.7.2.235

Porter, T. (2025, January 16). Digital transformation in healthcare (2025 guide). VisualSP. https://www.visualsp.com/blog/digital-transformation-in-healthcare/

Radanliev, P. (2025). AI ethics: Integrating transparency, fairness, and privacy in AI development. [tandfonline.com]. *Applied Artificial Intelligence*, *39*(1), e2463722. DOI: 10.1080/08839514.2025.2463722

Raymond, D., Sheikh, K., & Gourshettiwar, P. (2024). Blockchain technology in healthcare: A revolution in data security, interoperability, and patient privacy. *AIP Conference Proceedings*, *3188*(1), 100054. DOI: 10.1063/5.0240159

RDi. (n.d.). The real cost of paper in a digital hospital. Inicio UK. https://inicio.uk/the-real-cost-of-paper-in-a-digital-hospital/

Romanello, M., McGushin, A., Di Napoli, C., Drummond, P., Hughes, N., Jamart, L., & Costello, A. (2021). The 2021 report of the Lancet Countdown on health and climate change: Code red for a healthy future. *Lancet*, *398*(10311), 1619–1662. DOI: 10.1016/S0140-6736(21)01787-6 PMID: 34687662

Saatchi, A. G., Pallotti, F., & Sullivan, P. (2023). Network approaches and interventions in healthcare settings: A systematic scoping review. *PLoS One*, *18*(2), e0282050. DOI: 10.1371/journal.pone.0282050 PMID: 36821554

Schmidt, A., Vassil, K., & Tamm, K. (2024). Blockchain-enabled e-health systems: Lessons from Estonia. *Health Informatics Journal, 30*(2), 145–160. DOI: 10.1177/1460458224123456

Schmidt, J., Schutte, N. M., Buttigieg, S., Novillo-Ortiz, D., Sutherland, E., Anderson, M., & van Kessel, R. (2024). Mapping the regulatory landscape for artificial intelligence in health within the European Union. npj. *Digital Medicine, 7*(8), 1–14. DOI: 10.1038/s41746-023-00985-7

Serper, M., & Volk, M. L. (2018). Current and future applications of telemedicine to optimise the delivery of care in chronic liver disease. *Clinical Gastroenterology and Hepatology : The Official Clinical Practice Journal of the American Gastroenterological Association, 16*(2), 157–161.e8. DOI: 10.1016/j.cgh.2017.10.004 PMID: 29389489

Shamanna, P., Joshi, S., Thajudeen, M., Shah, L., Poon, T., Mohamed, M., & Mohammed, J. (2024). Personalized nutrition in type 2 diabetes remission: Application of digital twin technology for predictive glycemic control. *Frontiers in Endocrinology, 15*, 1485464. Advance online publication. DOI: 10.3389/fendo.2024.1485464 PMID: 39634180

Siemens Healthineers. (2023, September 2). *Patient twin: Why Sophia is no longer afraid of cancer*. Siemens Healthineers Perspectives. https://www.siemens-healthineers.com/perspectives/digital-patient-twin-cancer-care

Solar, O., & Irwin, A. (2010). A conceptual framework for action on the social determinants of health. World Health Organization. https://www.who.int/publications/i/item/9789241500852

Soyege, D., Alabi, M. O., & Yusuf, T. A. (2024). Health informatics in developing countries: Challenges and opportunities. ResearchGate. https://www.researchgate.net/publication/390109885

Stefaniak, I., & Aleksandrowicz, A. (2024). Application of a virtual reality-based cognitive-behavioural therapy of social phobia in the treatment of inpatients diagnosed with schizophrenia and social anxiety – a feasibility study. *Frontiers in Psychiatry, 15*, 1379541. Advance online publication. DOI: 10.3389/fpsyt.2024.1379541 PMID: 39659550

Stephen, R., & Frank, J. (2024). The role of electronic health records in transforming healthcare delivery and financial gains. ResearchGate. https://www.researchgate.net/publication/377407661

Stephen, R., Frank, J., & Miller, T. (2024). The impact of electronic health records on healthcare delivery transformation and economic benefits. ResearchGate. https://www.researchgate.net/publication/377407747

Storeng, K. T., & Béhague, D. P. (2017). "Guilty until proven innocent": The contested use of maternal mortality indicators in global health. [tandfonline.com]. *Critical Public Health*, *27*(2), 163–176. DOI: 10.1080/09581596.2016.1259459 PMID: 28392630

Sylverken, A. A., Owusu, M., Agbavor, B., Kwarteng, A., Ayisi-Boateng, N. K., Ofori, P., El-Duah, P., Yeboah, R., Aryeetey, S., Addo Asamoah, J., Ekekpi, R. Z., Oppong, M., Gorman, R., Brempong, K. A., Nyarko-Afriyie, E., Owusu Bonsu, F., Larsen-Reindorf, R., Rockson Adjei, M., Boateng, G., & Phillips, R. O. (2022). Using drones to transport suspected COVID-19 samples: Experiences from the second largest testing centre in Ghana, West Africa. *PLoS One*, *17*(11), e0277057. DOI: 10.1371/journal.pone.0277057 PMID: 36318579

Sylverken, A. A., Owusu, M., Agbavor, B., Kwarteng, A., Ayisi-Boateng, N. K., Ofori, P., El-Duah, P., Yeboah, R., Aryeetey, S., Addo Asamoah, J., Ekekpi, R. Z., Oppong, M., Gorman, R., Brempong, K. A., Nyarko-Afriyie, E., Owusu Bonsu, F., Larsen-Reindorf, R., Rockson Adjei, M., Boateng, G., & Phillips, R. O. (2022). Using drones to transport suspected COVID-19 samples: Experiences from the second largest testing centre in Ghana, West Africa. *PLoS One*, *17*(11), e0277057. DOI: 10.1371/journal.pone.0277057 PMID: 36318579

Tenni, B., Moir, H. V. J., Townsend, B., Kilic, B., Farrell, A.-M., Keegel, T., & Gleeson, D. (2022). What is the impact of intellectual property rules on access to medicines? A systematic review. *Globalization and Health*, *18*(1), 40. Advance onlinc publication. DOI: 10.1186/s12992-022-00826-4 PMID: 35428250

The King's Fund. (n.d.). Health inequalities in a nutshell. https://www.kingsfund.org.uk/insight-and-analysis/data-and-charts/health-inequalities-nutshell

Tilahun, B., Gashu, K. D., Mekonnen, Z. A., Endehabtu, B. F., & Angaw, D. A. (2021). Mapping the role of digital health technologies in prevention and control of COVID-19 pandemic: Review of the literature. *Yearbook of Medical Informatics*, *30*(1), 1–12. DOI: 10.1055/s-0041-1726505 PMID: 34479378

Torab-Miandoab, A., Samad-Soltani, T., Jodati, A., & Rezaei-Hachesu, P. (2023, January 24). Interoperability of heterogeneous health information systems: A systematic literature review. *BMC Medical Informatics and Decision Making*, *23*(1), 18. Advance online publication. DOI: 10.1186/s12911-023-02115-5 PMID: 36694161

Tornimbene, B., Leiva Rioja, Z. B., Brownstein, J., Dunn, A., Faye, S., Kong, J., Malou, N., Nordon, C., Rader, B., & Morgan, O. (2025). Harnessing the power of artificial intelligence for disease-surveillance purposes. *BMC Proceedings*, *19*(S4, Suppl 4), 7. Advance online publication. DOI: 10.1186/s12919-025-00320-w PMID: 40050981

Toure, A. (2025). Ethical AI in public health: A global path to reduce inequalities. *Global Society*. https://www.globalsociety.earth/post/ethical-ai-in-public-health-a-global-path-to-reduce-inequalities

UK Government. (2023, September 13). What are community diagnostic centres?https://www.gov.uk/government/news/what-are-community-diagnostic-centres

United Nations Development Programme. (2023). Bridge the digital divide – Digital standards. https://www.undp.org/digital/standards/2-bridge-digital-divide

Varnosfaderani, S. R., Ahmadi, M., & Jebraeily, M. (2024). The role of mHealth in managing chronic diseases. *BMC Medical Informatics and Decision Making*, *24*, 99. https://pmc.ncbi.nlm.nih.gov/articles/PMC11047988/

Vilhelmsson, A. (2024). Navigating the climate-health nexus: Linking health data with climate data to advance public health interventions. *BMC Global and Public Health*, *2*(1), 73. Advance online publication. DOI: 10.1186/s44263-024-00109-7 PMID: 39681937

Vo, D.-K., & Trinh, K. T. L. (2024). Advances in wearable biosensors for healthcare: Current trends, applications, and future perspectives. *Biosensors (Basel)*, *14*(11), 301. Advance online publication. DOI: 10.3390/bios14110560 PMID: 39590019

Walter, Y. (2024). Managing the race to the moon: Global policy and governance in artificial intelligence regulation—A contemporary overview and an analysis of socioeconomic consequences. *Discover Artificial Intelligence*, *4*(1), 14. Advance online publication. DOI: 10.1007/s44163-024-00109-4

Weiner, J. P., Yeh, S., & Bai, G. (2024). Adoption of digital health tools in hospital systems. *Journal of Medical Internet Research*, *26*, e12345. https://pmc.ncbi.nlm.nih.gov/articles/PMC11977975/

Wilson, L. S., & Maeder, A. J. (2015). Recent directions in telemedicine: Review of trends in research and practice. *Healthcare Informatics Research*, *21*(4), 213–222. DOI: 10.4258/hir.2015.21.4.213 PMID: 26618026

World Bank. (2023). Universal health coverage as a sustainable development goal. https://datatopics.worldbank.org/world-development-indicators/stories/universal-health-coverage-as-a-sustainable-development-goal.html

World Economic Forum. (2025). *7 ways AI is transforming healthcare*. https://www.weforum.org/stories/2025/08/ai-transforming-global-health/

World Health Organization. (2020a). Global strategy on human resources for health: Workforce 2030. World Health Organization. https://www.who.int/publications/i/item/9789241511131

World Health Organization. (2021). Global strategy on digital health 2020–2025. World Health Organization. https://www.who.int/publications/i/item/9789240020924

World Health Organization. (2022).. . *World Malaria Report, 2022*, •••. https://www.who.int/teams/global-malaria-programme/reports/world-malaria-report-2022

World Health Organization. (2023a, April 20). WHO releases the largest global collection of health inequality data. https://www.who.int/news/item/20-04-2023-who-releases-the-largest-global-collection-of-health-inequality-data

World Health Organization. (2023b). Noncommunicable diseases. https://www.who.int/health-topics/noncommunicable-diseases

World Health Organization. (2023c). World health statistics 2023: Monitoring health for the SDGs. World Health Organization. https://www.who.int/publications/i/item/9789240074323

World Health Organization. (2024, May 7). WHO Results Report 2023 https://www.who.int/news/item/07-05-2024-who-results-report-2023-shows-notable-health-achievements-and-calls-for-concerted-drive-toward-sustainable-development-goals

World Health Organization. (2025a, June 24). Public notice and comments on the Technical Advisory Group on the use of digital technologies to enhance access to assistive technology. https://www.who.int/news-room/articles-detail/public-notice-and-comments-on-the-technical-advisory-group-on-the-use-of-digital-technologies-to-enhance-access-to-assistive-technology

World Health Organization. (2025b). More than 30-year difference in life expectancy highlights health inequities. United Nations News. https://news.un.org/en/story/2025/05/1162931

World Health Organization & World Bank. (2017). Tracking universal health coverage: 2017 global monitoring report. https://www.who.int/news/item/13-12-2017-world-bank-and-who-half-the-world-lacks-access-to-essential-health-services-100-million-still-pushed-into-extreme-poverty-because-of-health-expenses

Younus, A., & Zaenuri, M. (2024). Public-private collaboration to overcome the digital divide in government digital transformation. ResearchGate. https://www.researchgate.net/publication/381006838

Younus, M., & Zaenuri, M. (2024). Public-private collaboration to overcome the digital divide in digital transformation of government. Digital Zone: Jurnal Teknologi Informasi dan Komunikasi, 15(1), 28–41.

Appendix A: Glossary of Terms

- **Access to Health** – The ability of individuals to obtain necessary health services, influenced by geographic, economic, and social factors.
- **Algorithmic Bias** – Systematic errors in AI systems caused by biased training data, which can lead to unfair or inaccurate outcomes.
- **Artificial Intelligence (AI)** – Computer systems that mimic human intelligence to perform tasks such as diagnosis, prediction, and personalised treatment.
- **Blockchain** – A decentralised digital ledger used for secure, transparent, and tamper-resistant data management in healthcare.
- **Climate-Tech Nexus** – The intersection of climate change and technology, focusing on innovations that address health impacts of environmental change.
- **Data Colonialism** – The extraction and use of data from marginalised communities without their control or benefit, reinforcing global inequities.
- **Decolonial Frameworks** – Approaches that challenge colonial legacies in global health, advocating for local control, cultural relevance, and equity.
- **Digital Divide** – Disparities in access to digital technologies, often reflecting broader socioeconomic inequalities.
- **Digital Health Records (EHRs)** – Electronic systems for storing and sharing patient health information to improve care coordination and efficiency.
- **Digital Literacy** – The ability to effectively use digital technologies, essential for both patients and healthcare providers.
- **Digital Twin** – A virtual model of a patient used to simulate treatment outcomes and personalise healthcare strategies.
- **Drone-Based Medical Delivery** – Use of unmanned aerial vehicles to transport medical supplies to remote or underserved areas.
- **Equity in Health** – Fair access to healthcare services and outcomes regardless of socioeconomic status, geography, or identity.
- **Genomic Research** – The study of genomes to understand disease mechanisms and develop personalised medicine.
- **Global Health** – A field focused on improving health and achieving equity in health outcomes worldwide.
- **Health Belief Model** – A psychological model used to explain and predict health behaviours based on individual beliefs and perceptions.
- **Infrastructure Deficits** – Limitations in physical and digital infrastructure that hinder healthcare delivery and technology adoption.
- **Interoperability** – The ability of different digital systems and devices to exchange and use data seamlessly.
- **mHealth (Mobile Health)** – Use of mobile devices and apps to deliver health services, monitor conditions, and support patient engagement.
- **Nanotechnology** – The manipulation of matter at the nanoscale for medical applications such as targeted drug delivery and diagnostics.
- **Non-Communicable Diseases (NCDs)** – Chronic diseases not spread from person to person, including diabetes, cardiovascular diseases, and cancer.
- **Predictive Analytics** – Use of data and algorithms to forecast disease outbreaks and health trends for proactive intervention.

• **SDGs (Sustainable Development Goals)** – Global goals set by the United Nations to promote health, equity, and sustainability by 2030.

• **Socioeconomic Determinants of Health** – Social and economic factors—such as income, education, and housing—that influence health outcomes.

• **Telemedicine** – Remote delivery of healthcare services using digital communication tools.

• **Usability and Workflow Integration** – The ease with which technology fits into clinical workflows, affecting adoption and effectiveness.

• **Virtual Reality (VR)** – Immersive technology used in mental health therapy, rehabilitation, and medical training.

• **Wearable Biosensors** – Devices worn on the body that monitor health metrics like heart rate, glucose levels, and sleep patterns.

Chapter 2
Remote Care, Real Impact:
An Overview of the Emergence and Practice of Telehealth

Pebby Lynn Garner
http://orcid.org/0009-0003-0982-0734
University of Texas at San Antonio, USA

Alexis Alvarez
University of Texas at San Antonio, USA

Harmonye Lacy
http://orcid.org/0009-0008-0737-3746
University of Texas at San Antonio, USA

Melanie Stanton
University of Texas at San Antonio, USA

ABSTRACT

Telehealth has become a growing method of healthcare delivery, primarily being adopted due to the COVID-19 pandemic. The following literature review summarizes research on the history, evolution, benefits, barriers, and other aspects of telehealth use for patients and providers. Studies from the first documentation of the word telemedicine in 1972 to the most recent impacts of telehealth in 2024 are included in the review, focusing on how telehealth impacts various patient populations, methodologies of diagnoses, funding, privacy concerns, and the impact of COVID-19. Some advantages of telehealth identified were its accessibility, cost-effectiveness, health promotion and education, and promotion of patient autonomy. While there

DOI: 10.4018/979-8-3373-3341-0.ch002

are many benefits to receiving remote healthcare, there are still many challenges for patients and healthcare providers, such as a lack of computer literacy or advanced technology, language barriers, physical examination issues, and unique challenges with regulations.

INTRODUCTION

Healthcare delivery has continuously evolved to meet patient needs and to support provider practice. Early methods such as physicians advising patients by telephone have developed into what is now referred to as *telehealth*. According to the U.S. Health Resources and Services Administration (What is Telehealth? | HRSA, 2022), telehealth refers to "the use of electronic information and digital communication technology to support long-distance clinical healthcare, patient and professional health-related education, health administration, and public health." In contrast, *telemedicine* originally described the remote provision of clinical services, whereas *telehealth* encompasses a broader range of applications including education, monitoring, and administration. This paper focuses on telehealth as the umbrella term.

Over the past decade, telehealth has expanded rapidly, with the COVID-19 pandemic—caused by infection with the severe acute respiratory syndrome coronavirus 2 (SARS-CoV-2)—serving as a major accelerator of its global adoption (Terrell et al., 2021). The pandemic context highlighted both the potential and the limits of remote care delivery, spurring regulatory flexibility, and new reimbursement models that continue to shape post-pandemic healthcare practices.

Historically, the concept of providing healthcare remotely dates back several decades. The term *telemedicine* was coined by Thomas Bird in the 1970s to describe "a system of healthcare delivery where doctors could examine distant patients through the use of telecommunications technologies" (Challacombe & Dasgupta, 2003). In 1972, Bird and Raymond Murphy demonstrated that dermatologists could diagnose color-slide images transmitted via black-and-white television monitors with acceptable accuracy, one of the earliest examples of diagnostic telecommunication (Murphy et al., 1972). Although the audiovisual systems of the time were primitive compared with today's digital platforms, their work proved that real-time remote assessment was feasible (Jagarapu & Savani, 2021), laying the foundation for modern telehealth applications.

Telehealth today operates through multiple modalities, including phone or video consultations, patient portals, and mobile health applications. These formats illustrate its adaptability to diverse patient needs, especially among rural residents, older adults, and individuals with mobility or transportation challenges. The expansion of telehealth has allowed healthcare providers to reach broader populations while navigating ongoing differences in insurance coverage and payment-parity policies across states (What is Telehealth? | HRSA, 2022).

Convenience, accessibility, and potential cost savings are among the reported benefits of telehealth, though each should be understood as outcomes of system design rather than inherent features. Research suggests that reduced emergency-department revisits, fewer inter-facility transfers, and earlier intervention for chronic disease management contribute to cost-effectiveness (Lillicrap et al., 2021). However, some costs may shift from providers to patients—such as technology requirements or home-based monitoring equipment—highlighting the importance of equitable access.

Specialist access represents another key advantage, particularly in fields such as psychiatry, dermatology, and endocrinology, where remote consultation aligns well with visual and conversational assessments. Among older adults with chronic diseases such as diabetes, hypertension, and congestive heart failure, telehealth programs have been linked to reduced hospitalizations and improved monitoring outcomes (Gajarawala & Pelkowski, 2020; Lillicrap et al., 2021).

Beyond care delivery, telehealth has proven valuable as a tool for health education and provider training. Studies using validated satisfaction and learning scales indicate that both patients and clinicians report measurable improvements in confidence and knowledge following structured telehealth-based education (Blackstock & Roberts, 2021; Shawwa, 2023). Providers are also trained to navigate the legal, ethical, and privacy dimensions of remote care while gaining insight into the patient's digital experience.

Patient autonomy—operationalized through the ability to choose appointment modalities, timing, and participation in decision-making—has been reinforced by telehealth systems (Keenan et al., 2021). For older adults wishing to maintain independence at home, and for families balancing work, school, and caregiving, remote visits offer flexibility and continuity. Effective participation, however, depends on equity enablers such as language interpretation, captioning, and accessible interface design for Deaf or Hard-of-Hearing users (Washington, 2022).

Despite its promise, telehealth faces notable barriers. Accessibility challenges often stem from limited broadband coverage, inadequate digital literacy, and typical failure points such as difficulty logging into patient portals, unstable video connections, or confusion with app navigation (Chaet et al., 2017). Limitations in physical examination remain critical; providers cannot perform tactile assessments such as palpation or auscultation, which can compromise diagnostic precision (Gajarawala & Pelkowski, 2021). Issues with camera placement and resolution further complicate the evaluation of detailed anatomical features (Conway et al., 2021).

Privacy and confidentiality also present ongoing risks. Although virtual platforms are bound by HIPAA-compliant encryption and secure transmission protocols, variability exists in vendor safeguards. Weak end-to-end encryption, inadequate authentication, and non-standardized data storage create vulnerabilities to information breaches (Chaet et al., 2017). These risks are compounded when patients lack awareness of digital-communication disclosures or consent requirements.

Finally, patient-provider relationships may be strained in virtual settings. Communication barriers, lag, and screen-mediated interaction can impede empathy and rapport, making the exchange of sensitive information more difficult (Andreadis et al., 2023). Sustaining trust and connection thus remains an essential area for further research and system design improvement.

Overall, this chapter examines how telehealth's evolution has transformed healthcare access, delivery, and education while introducing new challenges related to equity, literacy, and privacy. The following sections analyze diagnostic validity, reimbursement structures, and population-specific outcomes to provide a comprehensive understanding of telehealth's impact on modern healthcare systems.

IMPACT OF COVID-19

COVID-19 played a major role in the adoption of telehealth due to the nature of the SARS-CoV-2 virus. Staying home and social distancing were highly promoted to reduce the spread during the pandemic. In another attempt to limit exposure, many hospitals in the United States—and, to varying degrees, healthcare facilities worldwide—shifted operations to prioritize COVID-19 and emergency care, while those with non-emergencies were urged to use remote medical services (Terrell et al., 2021). This shift led to a dramatic increase in the use of telehealth.

Before telehealth became routine, providers experienced inconsistencies in reimbursement from government and private insurers because telehealth visits were not always covered, and they incurred additional costs for secure communication systems to protect patient information. Even still, by 2018, 76% of U.S. hospitals had adopted some form of telehealth (Shaver, 2022).

Many patients found telehealth to have mostly positive outcomes before the pandemic, while providers had differing opinions. Some providers' concerns stemmed from unfamiliarity with the technology or from worries about care quality and personal connection with patients (Donelan et al., 2020). These concerns were especially evident among psychiatrists, who often found it difficult to establish rapport virtually, and among providers treating conditions requiring extensive physical examination—both cases in which telehealth was less effective.

Prior to the pandemic, Medicare imposed several restrictions on telehealth use. To expand accessibility for beneficiaries, Congress suspended many of these requirements in March 2020, eliminating the need for pre-existing patient-provider relationships, permitting out-of-state telehealth delivery, and authorizing additional technology platforms (Shaver, 2022).

Although some providers and patients continued to prefer in-person visits, the COVID-19 pandemic accelerated global telehealth implementation, creating a new norm for remote care under strict infection-control measures. Remote access was especially advantageous for high-risk individuals—such as older adults and those who were immunocompromised (George et al., 2021).

Telehealth during the pandemic also proved useful for pediatric populations. Children faced elevated exposure risks, and prioritizing remote consultations for non-emergent needs reduced transmission while conserving personal protective equipment (PPE) for frontline staff (Terrell et al., 2021).

Nevertheless, those who stood to benefit most—older adults and marginalized groups—also faced barriers such as limited internet connectivity and lack of digital devices (George et al., 2021). A community-based rheumatology study found that increased telehealth use during the pandemic disproportionately affected racial, ethnic, and low-income groups, who were more likely to cancel or miss telehealth appointments. These findings raise concerns that telehealth, while expanding access overall, may have magnified existing health disparities for vulnerable communities.

Evidence on Diagnostic Accuracy in Telehealth

One key dimension of telehealth—particularly telemedicine—is the accuracy of patient diagnosis conducted remotely. Traditionally, diagnosis relies on an in-person visit, allowing physicians to physically examine patients and order laboratory tests. However, the removal of the in-person component raises skepticism about diagnostic validity (Haimi et al., 2024; O'Shea et al., 2023). Nevertheless, several studies have found that telehealth-based diagnostic methods can achieve comparable accuracy to in-person assessments (Cai et al., 2022; Miller et al., 2020; Oh et al., 2024; Shah et al., 2023; Silver et al., 2022).

In a study by Silver et al. (2022), researchers used artificial intelligence (AI) to assist in detecting cancerous skin lesions through vibrational optical coherence tomography. This approach utilizes sound waves to predict cancer using the LabScope 2.0. The algorithms were trained using logistic regression models on 80 samples (40 controls and 40 lesions). The experiment tested for basal cell carcinoma (BCC), squamous cell carcinoma (SCC), and melanoma, using resonant frequencies of 80 Hz, 130 Hz, and 260 Hz, respectively. The AI predicted BCC, SCC, and melanoma with 89.47%, 90%, and 95% accuracy after training. These results demonstrate that machine learning can serve as a potential diagnostic tool in teledermatology.

In the study *Reliability and Accuracy of Remote Fiberoptic Nasopharyngolaryngoscopy in the Pediatric Population* (Miller et al., 2020), researchers evaluated the accuracy of remote nasopharyngolaryngoscopy in children using a mobileOptix portable endoscope attached to smartphones. Participants conducted a self-examination and transmitted recordings for review by an otolaryngologist. Indicators included noisy breathing, hoarseness, chronic cough, recurrent croup, dysphagia, congestion, chronic throat clearing, snoring, and difficulty breathing. The results showed high inter-rater and percentage agreement across most subsites, with seven of ten *sites* achieving ≥ 80% diagnostic agreement. Reported limitations included occasional image quality issues and improper angling during self-recording, which affected visibility of deeper anatomical regions (Miller et al., 2020).

Cai et al. (2022) evaluated the diagnostic validity of at-home influenza testing and its impact on clinician decision-making. The study used simulated patient scenarios delivered on paper, in person, or online via REDCap. Each scenario presented varying symptoms, disease prevalence, and risk profiles. Clinicians estimated the likelihood of influenza before and after viewing home test results. Among 190 participating clinicians, initial estimates were often overconfident—56% above and 25% below true probability. After being shown at-home test outcomes, 52% of diagnostic decisions changed, and the need for in-person visits decreased by nearly half. The findings suggest that rapid home testing supports more accurate, cost-effective diagnoses and reduces both time and location barriers.

A systematic review of diagnostic accuracy in telehealth for otorhinolaryngological conditions (Shah et al., 2023) synthesized 17 studies comprising 1,338 patients. Telehealth consultations achieved an average diagnostic accuracy of 85.2%, compared with 87.6% for in-person visits—a marginal 2.5% difference. Discrepancies were mainly attributed to poor-quality images or videos, difficulty distinguishing similar disorders such as gastroesophageal reflux disease and laryngomalacia, and the need for tactile examination in complex cases.

Similarly, Oh et al. (2024) analyzed nine cross-sectional studies assessing telehealth diagnosis of musculoskeletal (MSK) conditions, including shoulder, knee, back, elbow, and lower-limb pain. Inter-rater agreement ranged from 73% to 93.3%, reflecting substantial to near-perfect agreement. System-level diagnostic agreement reached 100% for lower-limb pain. By body region, the ankle (93.3%), lower limb (84%), lower back (79.5%), and elbow (73%) exhibited the highest consistency. While some areas lacked confidence intervals and full generalizability, the collective evidence indicates that telehealth diagnoses can approach in-person accuracy for several specialties, though further replication and standardization are needed.

Funding and Reimbursement in Telehealth

The methods of payment for telehealth and telemedicine services vary, ranging from medical insurance reimbursement to grant funding by public and private organizations. In *Foundation Funding in Telehealth* (Chase, 2021), the New York Community Trust provided $150,000 grants to both the Brooklyn Hospital Center and Long Island University to train workers for telehealth-related services. These efforts enabled low-income residents of Brooklyn to access primary and mental health care. Similarly, the Michigan Health Endowment Fund awarded $257,905 to the Community Mental Health Association of Michigan to strengthen telehealth-based mental health services. According to the RAND Corporation, such grant programs increased the use of video and telephone telehealth visits in 41 federally qualified health centers across California, making remote visits the most common form of healthcare delivery from March to August 2020.

In addition to grants, private insurance systems in the United States serve as a major funding source for telehealth. However, coverage conditions vary depending on parity laws. *Coverage parity* requires insurers to include telehealth as a covered benefit equivalent to in-person services, while *payment parity* mandates that providers be reimbursed at the same rate for telehealth as for in-person care. When payment parity is absent, providers may receive lower reimbursements for telehealth despite delivering equivalent clinical services, creating inconsistencies across insurers and states. As Larkin (2022) notes, fluctuating rule changes, billing codes, documentation requirements, and claim delays often introduce uncertainty about whether a given telehealth service will be fully reimbursed.

According to *Health Insurance Payment for Telehealth Services: Scoping Review and Narrative Synthesis* (Li et al., 2024), the United States introduced telehealth reimbursement policies through the Balanced Budget Act of 1997, signed by President Bill Clinton. These reimbursement systems operate through Medicare, Medicaid, private payers, and Medicare Advantage plans (Congress, 1997). Li et al. (2024) compiled a list detailing which insurance entities reimbursed telehealth services permanently or temporarily for specific healthcare services.

Under this framework, Medicare reimburses remote physiologic monitoring, care management, interprofessional consultations, psychological therapy, kidney disease treatment, and medication management, among others. Medicaid covers remote patient monitoring in 34 states, audio-only calls in 37 states and Washington, D.C., live video services in all 50 states, and facility transmission fees in 35 states. Private payers often provide reimbursements comparable to in-person visits due to parity laws, though policies differ by jurisdiction. Medicare Advantage offers expanded telehealth options beyond traditional Medicare, including services considered supplemental benefits under progression-free survival (PFS) models (Li et al., 2024).

While these programs reduce out-of-pocket costs, payment parity remains inconsistent across the United States (Weinstein et al., 2014). Teleradiology—an asynchronous specialty with limited in-person contact—is routinely reimbursed, but many non-radiology services are not. As a result, 19 states have enacted payment parity laws, though no federal standard exists. Medicare and Medicaid have expanded telemedicine billing codes, but reimbursement remains restricted primarily to rural or underserved sites, except for teleradiology and telepathology (Weinstein et al., 2014).

Government programs have also played a pivotal role in expanding telehealth funding. In March 2020, Section 1135 waivers were issued during the COVID-19 public health emergency. These waivers—triggered by the U.S. Secretary of Health and Human Services upon a presidential or HHS-declared national emergency—allow temporary relaxation of regulatory requirements under the Social Security Act (CMS, 2024). In practice, §1135 waivers permit healthcare providers to deliver and bill for telehealth across state lines, use alternative technology platforms, and bypass certain pre-approval and licensure requirements. The waivers also modify conditions of participation, extend performance deadlines, and authorize non-network providers to receive reimbursement during emergencies.

However, these provisions are temporary. A §1135 waiver terminates when the emergency ends or 60 days after issuance, unless renewed by the HHS Secretary in subsequent 60-day intervals (CMS, 2024).

According to *The Commonwealth Fund*, following the March 2020 expansion of CMS telehealth authority, 22 states revised their telehealth payment and coverage laws (Volk et al., 2021). The main areas of reform included: (1) requiring insurance coverage for audio-only services, (2) waiving or equalizing cost-sharing with in-person visits, and (3) mandating reimbursement parity between telehealth and in-person care. These reforms extended access to rural populations and were federally expanded through December 31, 2025 (Telehealth.HHS, 2025). Before COVID-19, only 15 states required private insurers to maintain payment parity; since then, 10 additional states have adopted parity mandates, either permanently or temporarily (Volk et al., 2021).

Barriers and Affected Groups

Telehealth implementation faces several sustainability challenges due to the resource-intensive nature of both the technology and the infrastructure required to deliver and access care. For example, the technology needed for video or image-based examinations often depends on coverage that varies by payer or benefit type, meaning some patients may receive partial or no reimbursement for required equipment (Shah et al., 2023). In cases where coverage is lacking, patients may need to purchase devices such as mobile otoscopes or video endoscopes to complete remote assessments. However, these tools are typically useful only for conditions that are not complex and do not require a full physical examination. Even when patients can obtain the proper equipment, they must also know how to use it effectively. Common failure points include difficulty connecting to telehealth platforms, improper camera positioning, inadequate lighting, and challenges with uploading or transmitting high-resolution images (Shah et al., 2023).

Ghazal et al. (2024) noted that while telehealth can reduce travel costs for appointments, the overall expense of acquiring and maintaining technology may still disadvantage individuals in rural or low-income settings. This concern extends to those who rely on government-provided insurance programs that may not fully subsidize telehealth devices or broadband costs.

A qualitative study by Haimi et al. (2024) explored perceptions and barriers among elderly patients in Israel's community health system. The study included a sample of 45 Jewish participants with educational levels ranging from primary school to bachelor's degrees, and diverse marital and socioeconomic backgrounds. Researchers conducted 40-minute interviews with each participant to explore perceived benefits and challenges of telehealth and suggestions for improvement. Participants cited advantages such as improved accessibility, convenience, and social engagement but also reported difficulties related to trust in digital care quality, physiological limitations (e.g., vision or dexterity), and digital literacy barriers. When asked for solutions, respondents suggested practical interventions, including simple user interfaces, in-clinic or at-home tutorials, printed brochures, and provider-initiated telehealth visits to increase adoption (Haimi et al., 2024).

Disparities were also observed among older adults in rural areas. Ng et al. (2022) examined telehealth access among U.S. Medicare beneficiaries aged 65 and older during COVID-19 through a national survey. Beneficiaries with higher income (≥ $25,000), urban residence, internet access, and ownership of digital devices were significantly more likely to use telehealth services. Conversely, those aged 75 and older or residing in rural areas were less likely to use or even be offered telehealth services. Individuals lacking internet access were 8.2% less likely to be offered telehealth, while those with no experience using digital conferencing tools were 6.6% less likely to be offered and 15.3% less likely to use telehealth compared to their counterparts. The researchers suggested that low digital literacy and lack of awareness were primary contributors to these disparities.

These findings align with the Diffusion of Innovation theory, which posits that some populations—particularly older adults—tend to adopt new technologies more slowly due to lower exposure and higher uncertainty about value (Mori & Mlambiti, 2020). Rather than assuming inevitable resistance, these barriers reflect reduced opportunities for skill acquisition and confidence building, reinforcing the importance of structured training and peer-supported adoption.

Veterans face additional obstacles when using telehealth through the U.S. Department of Veterans Affairs (VA). In a 2016 study, Garvin et al. (2021) evaluated tablet-based telehealth use among homeless veterans. Within six months of device distribution, 45.9% of participants completed at least one telehealth visit, most commonly for telemental health related to post-traumatic stress disorder (PTSD), substance use, or housing instability. Utilization was higher among veterans aged 18–44 (35.7%), compared with middle-aged (24.7%) and older (13.6%) users. Married veterans and those living in rural areas or traveling over 60 minutes to a VA facility were also more likely to use the service. To maintain consistency, rates are presented here as percent of users per age group rather than mixed user/non-user proportions.

Despite these successes, technological barriers persisted. O'Shea et al. (2023) found that while 51.1% of rural veterans believed telehealth visits were "just as good" as in-person visits, 45.3% rated them lower, primarily due to technology difficulties. Both rural and urban participants indicated needing assistance connecting to or navigating telehealth systems. Zulman et al. (2019) corroborated these challenges, noting recurring issues with connectivity among veterans using VA-issued tablets. In a related study of home-based veteran care, Dang et al. (2019) found that even National Telehealth Technology Help Desk staff faced troubleshooting challenges due to limited training with specific devices, revealing a systemic gap in technical support capacity.

Finally, rural populations more broadly experience similar difficulties. Ghazal et al. (2024) emphasized that insufficient broadband infrastructure, outdated communication networks, and limited provider-side equipment continue to hinder telehealth's effectiveness in underserved regions. Without reliable connections and hardware, the quality and continuity of care remain inconsistent, perpetuating disparities rather than closing them.

Student Access

There are times when telehealth becomes essential, particularly for students. School-based telehealth enables children to receive healthcare in a more convenient and affordable way (HHS, 2022). If telehealth were provided within schools, it could increase access to needed health services, reduce missed school time, and improve children's well-being, potentially leading to better academic performance. In-person doctor visits often involve long wait times, scheduling difficulties, and travel to clinics (Beach, 2024). Telehealth helps address these challenges for students who need to prioritize their education and manage their expenses.

For college students, telehealth is particularly useful for managing busy class and work schedules. Online consultations eliminate common barriers by offering flexible appointment times and easy access to medical professionals. Additionally, telehealth is typically more affordable than in-person visits (Beach, 2024). A traditional doctor's appointment without insurance can cost between $70 and $300, depending on the type of service, whereas telehealth sessions often range from $40 to $90 per visit. This price difference is significant for students who are managing multiple financial obligations, such as rent, car insurance, utility bills, tuition, and textbooks. Financial stress often leads students to delay or avoid seeking medical care (Hadler et al., 2021). Telehealth can reduce these barriers—*when reliable devices, internet access, and adequate insurance coverage are available*—by allowing students to access primary and mental health services remotely without sacrificing their academic performance (Hadler et al., 2021).

Students can also use telehealth for mental health support, which is closely linked to academic success, social well-being, and financial stability. Many students experience anxiety, depression, or stress that goes undiagnosed because of the inconvenience of in-person care (Ollio et al., 2022). Telehealth can help address this gap by facilitating tele-assessment, triage, and management for common conditions such as anxiety, ADHD, or stress-related disorders—though comprehensive diagnosis may still require in-person evaluation. Telehealth also provides students with resources for stress management and coping strategies to navigate academic and personal challenges (Ollio et al., 2022).

For students in rural areas, access to healthcare remains particularly limited due to geographic isolation and a shortage of local providers. In many cases, these students must travel long distances to reach a clinic. Telehealth helps bridge this gap by allowing students to consult doctors or therapists virtually, regardless of their location (Cortelyou-Ward et al., 2020). Expanding access to telehealth for students promotes overall well-being, enhances quality of life, and can contribute to stronger academic outcomes.

LANGUAGE BARRIERS

Another major challenge telehealth faces involves language barriers that make it difficult for non-English-speaking patients to understand written or verbal communication. Many individuals who are not fluent in English struggle to navigate telehealth platforms effectively (Vaidya, 2022). When patients and providers do not share a common language, important medical information can be misinterpreted. Attempts to rely on automated tools such as Google Translate can also result in errors or misunderstandings. In contrast, in-person visits may allow physicians to rely on non-verbal cues such as hand gestures, facial expressions, or tone to facilitate understanding (Vaidya, 2022). Because telehealth depends primarily on audio, video, and text exchanges, these contextual supports are limited, heightening the risk of miscommunication.

During the COVID-19 pandemic, a study found that among 121 surveyed students, only 72 English-speaking participants responded confidently to all telehealth questions, while those with limited English proficiency (LEP) expressed uncertainty

(Yin et al., 2022). Researchers have consistently shown that patients with LEP participate in video visits less frequently than English-proficient patients (Vaidya, 2022). Yin (2022) emphasized the need for comprehensive interpreter training and stronger system-level interpreter infrastructure to improve access for linguistically diverse patients. To mitigate these disparities, experts recommend that telehealth providers integrate multilingual platform options and employ or contract professional medical interpreters rather than relying on ad-hoc translation (Marshall, 2025).

Some technology companies have begun introducing industry-led tools to support accessibility. For example, *VSee Health* has announced an AI-powered interpreter service offering on-demand access to professional interpreters in more than 240 languages (Marshall, 2025). Such tools may complement—not replace—established professional interpretation practices and could enhance communication efficiency, patient satisfaction, and overall quality of care.

In addition to linguistic barriers, hearing loss presents further challenges for telehealth accessibility. Approximately one in five people in the United States experiences hearing impairment in both ears, creating substantial obstacles to virtual care (Globo, 2022). Many telehealth systems rely on one-on-one verbal communication without closed captioning or sign-language support. As a result, deaf or hard-of-hearing patients often depend on family members or friends to assist, which can risk confidentiality and reduce accuracy. Incorporating real-time captioning and professional interpreter services would improve comprehension, protect privacy, and enhance diagnostic accuracy. Without these supports, patients may face misinformation, misunderstanding of medical instructions, or reduced engagement in their care (Globo, 2022). Effective communication remains essential for maintaining the safety, trust, and overall quality of healthcare delivery.

Privacy

Although telehealth has become extremely helpful, it has brought risk of data breaches and hackers. Language barriers also raise a huge concern as to how safe and effective this system really is. These language barriers make it hard for non-english speaking people to fully grasp on to what they are being told/asked, this can raise serious concern if not addressed (Hale & Kvedar, 2014). Some common cybersecurity attacks that telehealth faces are data breaches which are breaches that obtain unauthorized information, phishing attacks, which can exploit deceptive emails, messages, or websites to trick users into disclosing sensitive information. Through these attacks the hackers may obtain a patient's personal data, medical records, financial information that can lead to fraud or in some cases a stolen identity. Because telehealth platforms store vast amounts of patient data, they become prime targets for cybercriminals. These platforms provide telehealth with lots of data provided by the patient, which makes it easy and preferable targets for cyber-criminals. Phishing attacks can reveal patient's confidential information such as passwords and usernames; these attacks have been known to demand some sort of ransom money and use emails to trick patients into giving them certain information (Foster, 2023). "Smartphone apps may share sensitive data—such as sensor data on location—with advertisers and other third parties in ways not anticipated by users. The primary security risk is that of unauthorized access to data during collection, transmission, or storage. Any transfer offers the potential for a security breach." and Hale & Kvedar says "despite efforts to create secure devices and apps, many contain serious flaws, and hackers and malware pose an increasing threat to the security of telehealth systems" (Hale & Kvedar, 2014). Although it may seem hard to avoid these cybersecurity attacks there are ways to avoid them.

Some tips that are recommended to avoid cyberattacks are having your appointment set up in private locations. Some private locations to try are at home in a private room or even your car to avoid any risk of being heard. There were five studies done that concluded that patients had a privacy risk due to their living situations and lack of proper equipment so it's important that patients have safe and private locations when on telehealth (OCR, 2023). Wearing headphones can be useful so people won't hear private conversations linked to the patients data. Turning off any nearby electronic devices can also be a great way to help secure your data. Turning off home security cameras, siri, and other smart apps can reduce the chances of getting hacked so that you are not overheard by the smart apps. Using strong passwords is another useful tip to utilize to minimize the risk of hackers (OCR, 2023). Having a strong password can keep others from accessing your personal information, if someone were to obtain the patients passwords the hacker would have access to all the patients personal information, photos and videos. It is also essential that patients use two-step authentication. If a hacker was to obtain the patient's information they would need to go through a two-step verification if it was set up correctly. The hacker would need to have the patient's email address or phone number to continue the rest of the process (OCR, 2023). Although telehealth has significant benefits, it may carry many risks if you are not careful. There are many concerns about the privacy and security of telehealth and how it may affect people's trust in the telehealth system and threaten the ability to improve these challenges. Hale & Kvedar states " Increased reporting of security breaches, which are almost a daily occurrence, may have contributed to a general sense of distrust in electronic transmission and storage of personal information that may not diminish with regulations directed solely at telehealth." (Hale & Kvedar, 2014) Language barriers and cybersecurity are important issues to address in order to make sure these challenges are dealt with. If telehealth were to implement these measures it would be a smoother platform and could increase digital medical care.

However many people believe that the benefits of using the platform outweigh all of the privacy and security risks (Hale & Kvedar, 2014).

Challenges and Limitations

In the journal article *Explainable AI Decision Support Improves Accuracy During Telehealth Strep Throat Screening*, researchers used artificial intelligence (AI) to analyze images taken by patients' phones for diagnostic purposes. The AI was programmed to evaluate the likelihood of strep throat based on specific criteria: age, tonsillar exudate, swollen and tender anterior cervical nodes, history of fever, and absence of cough. Signs of bacterial infection were identified through images showing tonsil swelling and tongue appearance. The AI then generated predictions indicating whether each case was positive or negative for strep throat (Gomez et al., 2024). It is important to note, however, that this empirical study was limited by a small sample size—only four cases were included, two of which tested positive. This limitation suggests that further testing with larger and more diverse populations is needed to validate these preliminary findings.

Cai et al. (2020) also identified several limitations in their study on at-home influenza testing. Although the results demonstrated the potential of remote testing as an alternative to in-person visits, the patient cases presented to clinicians were simulated rather than drawn from real-world clinical encounters. Future studies with larger, more representative populations should examine whether demographic factors such as age, sex, education level, or disease severity affect diagnostic accuracy in real patients. Additionally, the study noted that post-test likelihood estimates of influenza may have been systematically over- or underestimated. To minimize bias, probability thresholds were kept constant before and after clinicians received the at-home test information, reducing the likelihood of systematic error. Because some data were collected during the COVID-19 pandemic, contextual factors could have influenced clinician estimates, although no significant differences were found across threshold groups.

Similarly, Oh et al. (2024) acknowledged limitations in their review of musculoskeletal condition diagnoses via telehealth. The review included multiple studies but relied exclusively on English-language publications, excluding data that may have been available in other languages. This exclusion could have introduced language bias and limited generalizability. The inclusion of gray literature also carried a potential for publication bias, as studies reporting significant findings are more likely to be published. Consequently, the aggregated results may overrepresent positive diagnostic outcomes.

CONCLUSION

In conclusion, telehealth has transformed tremendously over time and Covid-19 has significantly impacted the way we use telehealth today. Although telehealth has provided many with cost-effective options, convenience of being able to get diagnosed from your own home and accessibility, it has also brought many challenges. These issues include cybersecurity risks, language barriers, disparities in many communities, and misdiagnosis. Despite these many challenges, telehealth has proven that it can be accurate and effective in diagnosing patients, making it easier to consider telehealth rather than a traditional in person visit. In order to ensure telehealth succeeds in the future it is vital that telehealth changes its policy by enhancing its technology and increasing accessibility ensuring that it is safe and effective to use. Although the pandemic was terrifying, telehealth helped tremendously during this time of need and paved the way to what telehealth is today.

REFERENCES

Andreadis, K., Muellers, K., Ancker, J. S., Horowitz, C., Kaushal, R., & Lin, J. J. (2023). Telemedicine impact on the patient–provider relationship in primary care during the COVID-19 pandemic. *Medical care, 61*, S83-S88.

Beach, E. (2024). The benefits of telemedicine for college students. URMC Newsroom. https://urmcnewsroom.iprsoftware.com/publications/health-matters/benefits-of-telemedicine-for-college-students

Blackstock, F. C., & Roberts, N. J. (2021). Using telemedicine to provide education for the symptomatic patient with chronic respiratory disease. *Life (Basel, Switzerland), 11*(12), 1317. Advance online publication. DOI: 10.3390/life11121317 PMID: 34947848

Cai, X., Ebell, M. H., Geyer, R. E., Thompson, M., Gentile, N. L., & Lutz, B. (2022). The impact of a rapid home test on telehealth decision-making for influenza: A clinical vignette study. *BMC Primary Care, 23*(1), 75. Advance online publication. DOI: 10.1186/s12875-022-01675-1 PMID: 35418027

Chaet, D., Clearfield, R., Sabin, J. E., & Skimming, K. (2017). Ethical practice in telehealth and telemedicine. *Journal of General Internal Medicine, 32*(10), 1136–1140. DOI: 10.1007/s11606-017-4082-2 PMID: 28653233

Challacombe, B., & Dasgupta, P. (2003). Telemedicine—The future of surgery. *The Journal of Surgery, 1*(1), 15–17. DOI: 10.1016/S1743-9191(06)60004-6

Chase, C. (2021). Foundation funding in telehealth. *Health Affairs (Project Hope), 40*(6), 1009–1010. DOI: 10.1377/hlthaff.2021.00694 PMID: 34097517

Conway, J., Krieger, P., Hasanaj, L., Sun, L., Scharf, J. M., Odel, J. G., Dinkin, M. J., Oliveira, C., Mackay, D. D., Rasool, N., Ko, M., Rucker, J. C., Galetta, S. L., & Balcer, L. J. (2021). Telemedicine evaluations in neuro-ophthalmology during the COVID-19 pandemic: Patient and physician surveys. *Journal of Neuro-Ophthalmology : The Official Journal of the North American Neuro-Ophthalmology Society, 41*(3), 356–361. DOI: 10.1097/WNO.0000000000001370 PMID: 34415269

Cortelyou-Ward, K., Atkins, D. N., Noblin, A., Rotarius, T., White, P., & Carey, C. (2020). Navigating the digital divide: Barriers to telehealth in rural areas. *Journal of Health Care for the Poor and Underserved, 31*(4), 1546–1556. DOI: 10.1353/hpu.2020.0116 PMID: 33416736

Dang, S., Olsan, T., Karuza, J., Cai, X., Gao, S., Intrator, O., Li, J., & Gillespie, S. M. (2019). Telehealth in home-based primary care: Factors and challenges associated with integration into veteran care. *Journal of the American Geriatrics Society*, *67*(9), 1928–1933. DOI: 10.1111/jgs.16045 PMID: 31343732

Gajarawala, S. N., & Pelkowski, J. N. (2021). Telehealth benefits and barriers. *The Journal for Nurse Practitioners*, *17*(2), 218–221. DOI: 10.1016/j.nurpra.2020.09.013 PMID: 33106751

Garvin, L. A., Hu, J., Slightam, C., McInnes, D. K., & Zulman, D. M. (2021). Use of video telehealth tablets to increase access for veterans experiencing homelessness. *Journal of General Internal Medicine*, *36*(8), 2274–2282. DOI: 10.1007/s11606-021-06900-8 PMID: 34027612

George, M. D., Danila, M. I., Watrous, D., Reddy, S., Alper, J., Xie, F., Nowell, W. B., Kallich, J., Clinton, C., Saag, K. G., & Curtis, J. R. (2021). Disruptions in rheumatology care and the rise of telehealth in response to the COVID-19 pandemic in a community practice-based network. *Arthritis Care & Research (Hoboken)*, *73*(8), 1153–1161. DOI: 10.1002/acr.24626 PMID: 33973389

Ghazal, K., Singh Beniwal, S., & Dhingra, A. (2024). Assessing telehealth in palliative care: A systematic review of the effectiveness and challenges in rural and underserved areas. *Cureus*. Advance online publication. DOI: 10.7759/cureus.68275 PMID: 39350817

Gomez, C., Smith, B.-L., Zayas, A., Unberath, M., & Canares, T. (2024). Explainable AI decision support improves accuracy during telehealth strep throat screening. *Communications Medicine*, *4*(1), 149. Advance online publication. DOI: 10.1038/s43856-024-00568-x PMID: 39048726

Hadler, N. L., Bu, P., Winkler, A., & Alexander, A. W. (2021, January 6). College student perspectives of telemental health: A review of the recent literature. Current Psychiatry Reports. https://pmc.ncbi.nlm.nih.gov/articles/PMC7785477/

Hale, T. M., & Kvedar, J. C. (2014, December 1). Privacy and security concerns in telehealth. AMA Journal of Ethics. https://journalofethics.ama-assn.org/article/privacy-and-security-concerns-telehealth/2014-12

Health Resources and Services Administration. (2022, March 1). What is telehealth? https://www.hrsa.gov/telehealth/what-is-telehealth

Jagarapu, J., & Savani, R. C. (2021). A brief history of telemedicine and the evolution of teleneonatology. *Seminars in Perinatology*, *45*(5), 151416. Advance online publication. DOI: 10.1016/j.semperi.2021.151416 PMID: 34006382

Keenan, A. J., Tsourtos, G., & Tieman, J. (2021). The value of applying ethical principles in telehealth practices: Systematic review. *Journal of Medical Internet Research, 23*(3), e25698. Advance online publication. DOI: 10.2196/25698 PMID: 33783366

Lillicrap, L., Hunter, C., & Goldswain, P. (2021). Improving geriatric care and reducing hospitalisations in regional and remote areas: The benefits of telehealth. *Journal of Telemedicine and Telecare, 27*(7), 397–408. DOI: 10.1177/1357633X19881588 PMID: 31645171

Marshall, G. (2025, February 26). Case study: Vsee breaks down telehealth language barriers with Languageline integration. LanguageLine Solutions. https://www.languageline.com/blog/case-study-vsee-breaks-down-telehealth-languag e-barriers-with-languageline-integration

Miller, L. E., Buzi, A., Williams, A., Rogers, R. S., Ortiz, A. G., Jones-Ho, K. O., & Elden, L. M. (2020). Reliability and accuracy of remote fiberoptic nasopharyngolaryngoscopy in the pediatric population. *Ear, Nose, & Throat Journal, 100*(8), 604–609. DOI: 10.1177/0145561320919109 PMID: 32283977

Mori, N., & Mlambiti, R. (2020). Determinants of customers' adoption of mobile banking in Tanzania: Further evidence from a diffusion of innovation theory. Journal of Entrepreneurship. *Management and Innovation, 16*(2), 203–230. DOI: 10.7341/20201627

Murphy, R. L. (1972). Accuracy of dermatologic diagnosis by television. *Archives of Dermatology, 105*(6), 833. DOI: 10.1001/archderm.1972.01620090005001 PMID: 5030231

Ng, B. P., Park, C., Silverman, C. L., Eckhoff, D. O., Guest, J. C., & Díaz, D. A. (2022). Accessibility and utilisation of telehealth services among older adults during COVID-19 pandemic in the United States. *Health & Social Care in the Community, 30*(5). Advance online publication. DOI: 10.1111/hsc.13709 PMID: 34994028

O'Shea, A. M., Gibson, M., Merchant, J., Rewerts, K., Miell, K., Kaboli, P. J., & Shimada, S. L. (2023). Understanding rural–urban differences in veterans' internet access, use and patient preferences for telemedicine. *The Journal of Rural Health : Official Journal of the American Rural Health Association and the National Rural Health Care Association, 40*(3), 438–445. DOI: 10.1111/jrh.12805 PMID: 37935649

Office for Civil Rights. (2023, October 17). Telehealth privacy and security tips for patients. https://www.hhs.gov/hipaa/for-professionals/privacy/guidance/telehealth -privacy-security/index.html

Oh, D., To, D., Corso, M., Murnaghan, K., Yu, H., & Cancelliere, C. (2024). Agreement and concurrent validity between telehealth and in-person diagnosis of musculoskeletal conditions: A systematic review. *Chiropractic & Manual Therapies*, *32*(1), 21. Advance online publication. DOI: 10.1186/s12998-024-00542-3 PMID: 38872176

Ollio, J., Gyan, A., & Gyan, E. (2022). Using telehealth to provide behavioral healthcare to young adults and college students. Perspectives in Health Information Management. https://pmc.ncbi.nlm.nih.gov/articles/PMC9013217/

Shah, S. R., Munhall, C. C., Nguyen, S. A., O'Rourke, A. K., Miccichi, K., & Meyer, T. A. (2023). Diagnostic accuracy and management concordance of otorhinolaryngological diseases through telehealth or remote visits: A systematic review & meta-analysis. *Journal of Telemedicine and Telecare*, *30*(9), 1386–1397. DOI: 10.1177/1357633X231156207 PMID: 36916306

Shaver, J. (2022). The state of telehealth before and after the COVID-19 pandemic. *Primary Care*, *49*(4), 517–530. DOI: 10.1016/j.pop.2022.04.002 PMID: 36357058

Shawwa, L. (2023). The use of telemedicine in medical education and patient care. *Cureus*. Advance online publication. DOI: 10.7759/cureus.37766 PMID: 37213963

Silver, F. H., Mesica, A., Gonzalez-Mercedes, M., & Deshmukh, T. (2022). Identification of cancerous skin lesions using vibrational optical coherence tomography (VOCT): Use of VOCT in conjunction with machine learning to diagnose skin cancer remotely using telemedicine. *Cancers (Basel)*, *15*(1), 156. Advance online publication. DOI: 10.3390/cancers15010156 PMID: 36612151

Terrell, E. A., Aftab, S., Babitz, A., Butler, L., Hernandez, N. G., Hornik, B., Lee, K., Perez, J., Sotolongo, E., & Thomas, J. (2021). The evolution of telehealth from pre-COVID-19 pandemic through a hybrid virtual care delivery model: A pediatric hospital's journey. *International Journal of Telerehabilitation*, *13*(2), e6432. Advance online publication. DOI: 10.5195/ijt.2021.6432 PMID: 35646232

Vaidya, A. (2022, December 29). Understanding telehealth barriers for limited English proficiency patients. TechTarget. https://www.techtarget.com/virtualhealthcare/feature/Understanding-Telehealth-Barriers-for-Limited-English-Proficiency-Patients

Volk, J., Palanker, D., O'Brien, M., & Goe, C. (2021, June 23). States' actions to expand telemedicine access during COVID-19 and future policy considerations. The Commonwealth Fund. https://www.commonwealthfund.org/publications/issue-briefs/2021/jun/states-actions-expand-telemedicine-access-covid-19

Washington, G. (2022, June 8). Ensuring accessible telehealth for Deaf & Hard of Hearing patients. American Telemedicine Association. https://www.americantelemed.org/uncategorized/ensuring-accessible-telehealth-for-deaf-hard-of-hearing-patients/

Weinstein, R. S., Lopez, A. M., Joseph, B. A., Erps, K. A., Holcomb, M., Barker, G. P., & Krupinski, E. A. (2014). Telemedicine, telehealth, and mobile health applications that work: Opportunities and barriers. *The American Journal of Medicine*, *127*(3), 183–187. DOI: 10.1016/j.amjmed.2013.09.032 PMID: 24384059

Yin, L., Ng, F., Rutherford-Rojas, M., Williams, M., Cornes, S., Fernandez, A., Garcia, M. E., Khoong, E. C., & Khoong, C. A. C. (2022). Assessing medical student readiness to navigate language barriers in telehealth: Cross-sectional survey study. *JMIR Medical Education*, *8*(3), e36096. https://mededu.jmir.org/2022/3/e36096. DOI: 10.2196/36096 PMID: 35969421

Zulman, D. M., Wong, E. P., Slightam, C., Gregory, A., Jacobs, J. C., Kimerling, R., Blonigen, D. M., Peters, J., & Heyworth, L. (2019). Making connections: Nationwide implementation of video telehealth tablets to address access barriers in veterans. *JAMIA Open*, *2*(3), 323–329. DOI: 10.1093/jamiaopen/ooz024 PMID: 32766533

Chapter 3
Decolonising Global Health:
Financial Innovation, Health Technologies, and Equity

Oluwaseun Adebayo Adewunmi
http://orcid.org/0009-0004-1024-2756
Nagasaki University, Japan

Bàbá Ayé
http://orcid.org/0009-0007-9320-3761
Public Services International (PSI), France

Mavis Sakyi
http://orcid.org/0000-0001-6817-7599
Nagasaki University, Japan

Victor Oluwaseyi Lawal
http://orcid.org/0009-0007-8026-3618
Manchester Metropolitan University, UK

Fanna Gambo Dori
Nile University of Nigeria, Nigeria

Emeka Christian Nwankwo
http://orcid.org/0009-0000-7134-7747
Nagasaki University, Japan

ABSTRACT

This chapter offers a critical, decolonial interrogation of global health through the intersecting lenses of financial innovation, health technologies, and governance systems. It situates contemporary global health inequities within a historical continuum of colonial extraction and neoliberal restructuring, highlighting how dominant financial architectures, digital health systems, and multistakeholder governance models continue to marginalise the Global South. Drawing from decolonial theory and Indigenous epistemologies, the chapter advances alternative frameworks, including solidarity-based financing, culturally sovereign HealthTech, and anti-extractive, community-led governance. These integrated strategies challenge the structural reproduction of inequity and reimagine global health as a space

DOI: 10.4018/979-8-3373-3341-0.ch003

for collective liberation, relational accountability, and epistemic justice. In doing so, the chapter contributes to ongoing efforts to decolonise global health in both theory and practice.

DECOLONIAL FINANCIAL ALTERNATIVES

Global health as a field has deep colonial roots. Its beginning can be traced to providing medical care to colonisers suffering from tropical diseases. At the same time, missionaries were sent by religious bodies to colonies to provide healthcare as a method of introducing 'Western' practices and 'civilising' the local population and encouraging them to shun traditional healers and other traditional healing practices. Such colonial frameworks persist in global health and can be observed in the imbalance of power dynamics at every level of the practice, including the allocation of funds, knowledge production, and the use of nuanced language (Ratner et al., 2022). For example, despite having a larger burden of global diseases, African countries often struggle with limited access to vital health resources. An example of this situation is the HIV/AIDS epidemic, where antiretroviral treatments were accessible in affluent parts of the world, in contrast to patients in Africa who struggled to access these life-saving medications due to financial barriers and patent restrictions, an issue further worsened by the global health financing dynamics.

Furthermore, there is tremendous disparity in the field of health research and development. Diseases that are rare but frequent in economically prosperous countries may experience an increase in research funding. In comparison, illnesses with significant consequences in former colonial regions may receive less attention. For example, tropical diseases such as schistosomiasis and guinea worm sickness, despite affecting millions, are sometimes referred to as "neglected tropical diseases," reflecting not just a lack of medical care but also a lack of global health financing. Furthermore, inequities become much more pronounced amid global health crises. The COVID-19 epidemic serves as a stark illustration. While wealthier countries easily secured vaccine doses for their citizens, many countries in Africa and other historically marginalised regions faced significant barriers, not due to unwillingness or incapability, but rather because of financial and contractual power plays in the global health finance domain (Latif, 2024).

In historically oppressed nations, underinvestment in health infrastructure results in a persistent reliance on foreign assistance. Certain presumptions regarding the capabilities of the impacted regions are strengthened as health issues resulting from these imbalances worsen. This is more than just a health issue; it is the result of a flawed system established decades ago that continues to have an impact today.

The goal of the current movement to 'decolonise' global health is to uproot colonial frameworks that sustain inequity and racism and rebuild and strengthen institutions and systems that promote indigeneity.

It proposes a shift from capitalist health financing models to community-led, redistributive methods. It further outlines how locally led participatory governance structures can challenge the predominance of global institutions and promote equity in culturally sovereign healthcare systems.

Objectives

1. To trace the historical impact of colonial and neoliberal financial systems on present-day global health inequities.
2. To analyse the ideological and structural links between digital capitalism and financial coloniality in health.
3. To explore and assess decolonial financial models,such as solidarity economies, indigenous pooling, and Islamic finance, that can advance health equity.

Guiding Question:

How can decolonial financial and technological innovations transform global health financing into systems that promote equity, sovereignty, and collective well-being?

The chapter proceeds by first outlining the historical foundations of colonial and neoliberal financial regimes, then reframing global health through a decolonial lens that integrates digital and financial perspectives. It concludes with policy and managerial implications for translating these insights into actionable reforms.

COLONIALITY, NEOLIBERALISM AND THE GLOBAL FINANCIAL ARCHITECTURE

The World Health Organisation (WHO) and the United Nations Children's Fund (UNICEF) organised the International Conference on Primary Health Care (PHC) at the Alma-Ata Conference in the Kazakh Soviet Socialist Republic on 6-12 September 1978. This historic conference brought together representatives from 134 countries and issued the *Alma-Ata Declaration, in which* the international community committed to attaining "Health for All by the Year 2000" (WHO, 1978).

There are a few salient points of note for situating this conference as emblematic of a crossroads moment in the history of global health.

The number of countries present was more than double the fifty-five countries which attended the first World Health Assembly. Unlike the World Health Organisation's founding, where barely eight countries were from the global South, some two-thirds of countries at the Alma-Ata conference were from the Global South.

The conference was explicit in pointing out that health for all could not be achieved without fundamental social and economic reformation. Indeed, it spelt this out as the New International Economic Order (NIEO). This echoed the United Nations adoption of the NIEO four years earlier. The NIEO was the rallying call of the Non-Aligned Movement, which brought together what was then known as the Third World.

Thus, Alma-Ata represented a hearkening, within the context of healthcare delivery, to the global moment of decolonisation, which the post-war order from the late 1940s to the early 1970s marked for Africa and Asia. However, it turned out to be a nunc dimittis for that period. The seeds for what would be several long decades of neoliberalism were being sown, rolling back the gains of decolonisation and curtailment of the worst dynamics of capitalism in the social compromise of the so-called Thirty Glorious Years of capitalism.

This input into the chapter puts neoliberalism into perspective as, amongst other things, a rolling back of decoloniality and reinforcement of globalisation-as-imperialism, politically, economically and ideologically, about global health and with a focus on the international financial architecture. In doing this, it looks at the roots and flourishing of the policy hegemony of the Bretton Woods Institutions (IMF and World Bank in particular) and later other multilateral institutions and mechanisms like the WTO and bilateral as well as plurilateral trade agreements. Relatedly, the analysis also situates the place of financialisation within this dynamic, driving the growth of private for-profit interests in health, undermining health equity. The political economy of philanthrocapitalism in health, the hypocritical face of privatisation, is equally covered. We then look at what lessons to draw in this light from the COVID-19 pandemic. Last, it considers possibilities and means of dismantling the for-profit status quo of neocolonial governance and the dynamic of global health.

GLOBAL HEALTH, DECOLONISATION AND NEOLIBERALISM

What we know today as global health started as an imperialist project to safeguard the health of white colonisers in the tropics. This is informed by "tropical medicine". To date, we still have an Institute of Tropical Medicine in Belgium and a London School of Hygiene & Tropical Medicine. The World Health Organisation marked a milestone in international health. It is, however, instructive that even the first

WHO Regional Director for the WHO Africa Region, Dr Francisco Cambournac, was Portuguese. He served from 1954 to 1964.

The 1960s were Africa's decade of flag independence. And this was the beginning of the end of the Thirty Glorious Years of post-war capitalism. The Keynesian Welfare National State was still the norm in the West, and with it, the Developmental State was commonplace in the global South, fostering social and economic development with interventionist strategies. In this context, African countries invested massively in social services with an emphasis on health and education. An increasing number of people enjoyed improved healthcare. Life expectancy increased, and ratios of doctors, nurses and other health workers to the population increased.

All these started to change by the late 1970s and decidedly so by the 1980s, which has generally been considered a lost decade in the tri-continents of the global South. And at the heart of this was the introduction and entrenchment of neoliberalism with structural adjustment programmes. The triumph of Ronald Reagan and Margaret Thatcher in the United States and United Kingdom respectively was a foothold for the hegemony that pushed through a liberal turn in the international financial institutions, and their entry into the domain of health, providing the international policy framework to further the commodification of health and rolling back the decolonisation of international health.

This started in 1980 with the World Bank's Health Sector Policy Paper. The following year, the World Bank Group also published its "Accelerated Development in Sub-Saharan Africa: A Plan for Action", which was written by Elliot Berg. On health, this report made proposals for the introduction of user fees; a first step towards the commercialisation of health on the continent, and this is within the context of the low income of the vast majority of the populations in most of the African countries. The World Bank Group's hegemonic role in shaping global health was then consolidated with its World Development Report 1993, titled: *Investing in Health*.

Thus, international financial institutions (IFIs) turn to shaping health as a neoliberal project of neocolonialism, facilitated by the economic crisis, which African countries were embroiled in by the late 1970s and early 1980s. The energy crisis of the mid-1970s and the Volcker shock of 1978 pushed these states down the slope of peonage. The debt trap enabled the IFIs' hegemony on policy formulation as they rolled out loan conditionalities and shaped structural adjustment programmes (SAPs).

Based on these SAPs, governments of countries across the global South made significant cuts in their health budgets in the 1980s. In Africa, for example, the governments of 81% of the countries cut public expenditure on health by more than half, in the first seven years of that decade. In some instances, such as with Nigeria, the expenditure cuts were up to 75% (Colgan 2002). Spending ceilings on public sector recruitment and salaries also directly affected health care delivery, with freezes or limitations on the recruitment of much-needed healthcare workers.

This neoliberal turn was later christened the "Washington Consensus". It argued that eventually there would be a trickling down of a better life for all. But that would never be the case. The vision of health for all by the year 2000 from Alma-Ata would remain a dream, with this subsisting model. In no time, the model proved itself to be a failure. By the end of the beginning of the 1990s, even the IFIs themselves could not deny the fact that the SAPs they had foisted on developing countries had failed to deliver (Bello and Cunningham 1994).

But they decided to be clever by half. They came up with a Post-Washington Consensus at the end of that decade. This was essentially a repackaging of the same neoliberal logic of the earlier "consensus" of market fundamentalism, only with the added flavour of centring institutions. In light of this, the role of the state in pushing through marketization of social life, including healthcare, was made more explicit, a veneer of poverty alleviation was added on as a function of the state, and the ideology of stakeholderism was nurtured with the inclusion of NGOs and expansion of private sector interests as stakeholders in the policy process nationally and internationally.

By the beginning of the twentieth century, the spirit of decolonisation, which was at the heart of public health policies and programmes of governments in the global South countries, had been rolled back with the ascent of the neoliberal order. The spirit of the 1955 Bandung Conference and the United Nations's Declaration on the Establishment of a New International Economic Order at the behest of the countries of the global South in 1974 had been virtually snuffed out. And the consequences of this on the health and general well-being of people in the developing world were quite dire.

REFRAMING GLOBAL HEALTH THROUGH A DECOLONIAL LENS: DIGITAL AND FINANCIAL INNOVATIONS AS TOOLS FOR LIBERATION

In the spirited buzz surrounding the global digital health revolution, there is widespread, undeniable excitement about the endless potential of health technology to democratize healthcare and transform health systems, especially within the Global South. Technologies such as artificial intelligence (AI), blockchain, and telemedicine are paradigm shifts to the health and technological advancement in the world as we know it, promising to bridge gaps, extend reach to remote areas, and foster innovation in contexts historically marginalized by colonial and capitalist legacies (Prakash J. et al, 2025). Yet, beneath this utopian optimism, we may often overlook the complex web of risks that linger, shaped by colonial power dynamics, including extractive resource flows, racialised hierarchies, and epistemic marginalisation of indigenous knowledge, particularly regarding HealthTech. The current disposition of health technology failing to interrogate how digitisation can inadvertently entrench, rather than dismantle, global health inequalities, can widen already gaping structural inequalities (Badr J. et al, 2024).

This chapter adopts a critical, decolonial perspective to examine how the rhetoric and practices of digital health, while seemingly progressive, may reinforce colonial-capitalist logics. It builds upon current scholarship that seeks to decolonise global health, health technology, and innovation, challenging the privileging of knowledge, financing models, and power rooted in the global north at the expense of the south. This decolonial analysis also attempts to confront the dominant narratives of technological progress and explores how innovative financial models in health technologies can serve as avenues for liberation, deconstructing the residual neocolonial structures that continue to influence global health and health technology landscapes.

THE COLONIALITY OF KNOWLEDGE AND POWER IN GLOBAL HEALTH

The coloniality of global health, as an emerging field with vibrant discussions, is manifested through persistent knowledge extraction and asymmetrical power relations (Kumar et al, 2024). Dominant paradigms, institutions, and research agendas are disproportionately led by actors in the global north, framing knowledge systems as universal standards (Sekalala & Chatikobo, 2024). This hegemony marginalises local, indigenous, and community-led knowledge in the global south, reinforcing a one-way flow of information that exploits and devalues local contexts and expertise in LMIC.

Funding mechanisms further entrench this imbalance. Grants and research collaborations tend to favour northern institutions, which maintain decision-making authority and control over data and resources (Gladstone et al, 2023). Funding for health technology is no different, with innovators from the Global South jumping through various hoops for necessary support. This perpetuates a cycle where the global south remains a source of health data, raw knowledge, and piloted health technologies, often exploited under the guise of development, rather than an active agent in shaping its health futures. During the COVID-19 pandemic, this disparity was starkly visible when vaccine access was determined by geopolitical and economic power, with the global south often left behind (Gieger et al, 2022).

DIGITAL CAPITALISM AND THE REINFORCEMENT OF COLONIAL LOGICS

In the digital realm, capitalism exacerbates these colonial dynamics. Multinational tech corporations, predominantly based in the global north, dominate the infrastructure, research agendas, and deployment of health technologies (Whitaker et al, 2017; Sekalala et al, 2024). Their influence extends into policy-making, philanthropic initiatives, and the framing of digital health solutions as universal remedies (Whitaker et al, 2017). This corporate-driven digital health agenda often masks structural inequalities under narratives of innovation, efficiency, and progress.

Philanthropic foundations, such as those led by Bill and Melinda Gates or Mark Zuckerberg, wield enormous financial influence, shaping priorities and agendas in global health and education, but raise concerns over accountability and transparency within these foundations (Lambin & Surender, 2023). While their influence and investments in digital health promise to extend care and improve outcomes, they often reinforce dependency, diverting attention from systemic reforms rooted in local contexts. This is not to undermine their contributions to global health and to critically review and call for reforms that strengthen collaboration. The digital health landscape becomes a marketplace of assets, data, algorithms, and platforms, owned and controlled predominantly by northern corporations, leaving the global south as consumers rather than co-creators or sovereign stewards of their health data and technologies (World Bank report, 2021). The way forward should chart a better course of co-creation with indigenous systems.

DIGITAL COLONIALITY: THE SYSTEMIC VIOLENCE OF TECHNOLOGICAL SYSTEMS

Digital coloniality, as defined by Sekalala et al, refers to the systemic, structural violence inflicted through technological systems designed to exploit localities, socialities, and temporalities (Sekalala et al, 2024). Datafication transforming human life into quantifiable commodities serves as the backbone of this process (Houenou, 2024). In global health, health data becomes a form of power, reinforcing hierarchies and perpetuating inequalities (Zajko, M., 2022).

The logic of digital coloniality is rooted in what was traditionally Eurocentric modernity, a narrative that positions Western knowledge, progress, and rationality as universal, even for LMIC (Felix, 2019). This ideological framework abases the global south, depicting it as a space of deficiency and potentiality only to be realised through Western modernisation. The narrative of "leapfrogging" into digital health further dismisses the social, cultural, and political realities of local communities in

LMIC, framing technological adoption as a linear and important path to development and economic growth. As much as this holds for HIC income, wholesale adoption without indigenous reframing, we propose, critically short-circuits any real, practical potentials for sustained growth.

Furthermore, the global political economy of data ownership privileges northern actors, who control access to critical health information, infrastructure, and digital assets. Data becomes an asset, owned, privatised, and commodified, serving the interests of corporations and financial institutions rather than public health or community well-being. This assetization exacerbates existing inequalities, as countries in the global south face high barriers to entry in digital health markets, reinforcing monopolies and dependence.

THE CHARADE OF BORDERS AND THE EXTRACTION OF HEALTH DATA

Borders, both physical and digital, are central to the coloniality of digital health. While human mobility has historically been restricted for marginalised populations, digital health data flows freely, often unregulated, across borders. Corporations and international organisations extract health data from the global south, consolidating it within northern-controlled infrastructures. This process echoes historical patterns of resource extraction, where local communities provide raw materials, data, while the benefits accrue elsewhere.

Border policies further stratify access to health services and collaboration. Current waves of evidence show discriminatory border controls restrict movement from the global south, as far as visa discrimination for collaborative conferences (Khan, 2023; Ullah et al, 2025), while simultaneously extracting health data and technological knowledge from these regions (Sekalala S. et al, 2024). The COVID-19 pandemic highlighted this duality: while borders closed to people from the south, data flows and digital infrastructure continued to be exploited and controlled by northern corporations.

INFRASTRUCTURE AND THE COLONIAL LOGIC OF SOFTWARE, HARDWARE, AND CLOUD

The infrastructure of digital health, software platforms, hardware devices, and cloud services, is predominantly owned and governed by corporations in the global north (Yeung A. et al, 2023). This hegemonic control perpetuates infrastructural colonialism, whereby local health systems in the global south become dependent on proprietary technologies and cloud services hosted in the north. These systems are protected by intellectual property rights, restricting access, adaptation, and limiting local innovation.

The cloud, as a symbol of digital sovereignty, remains highly contested (Avila Pinto, 2018). Many countries in the south rely on cloud services based in the north, which subjects their data to extraterritorial legal regimes, such as the US Cloud Act, that can compel data disclosure or restrict data sovereignty (Cochrane et al., 2022; Abraha, 2019). This dependency undermines local control over health information, further entrenching inequalities.

MARKET FORCES, AID, AND THE DISTORTION OF PUBLIC HEALTH

The commodification of digital health transforms health into a market commodity, driven by venture capital, private investment, and profit motives (Seidl, 2023). This marketisation prioritises financial returns over health outcomes, often sidelining local needs and context-specific solutions. Donor-driven projects, funded by northern NGOs and philanthropic entities, frequently bypass local governance, leading to data governance issues and limited community ownership.

The influence of private capital distorts health priorities, favouring interventions that generate market value rather than those addressing structural determinants of health. Digital health assets, data, algorithms, platforms, become private property, further restricting equitable access and community participation.

TOWARD A DECOLONIAL DIGITAL AND FINANCIAL FUTURE

The path forward demands a radical reimagining of global health systems, one that de-centres Western dominance and centres the sovereignty, knowledge, and agency of communities in the global south. Decolonial strategies include embracing solidarities rooted in community mutual aid, Indigenous-led resource pooling, and alternative financial models such as solidarity economies that prioritise collective well-being over profit.

Digital health technologies must be reconceptualised as tools for empowerment rather than control. This involves developing open-source platforms, community-owned data infrastructures, and participatory governance models that respect local contexts and knowledge systems. Blockchain and other distributed ledger technologies offer promising avenues for creating transparent, community-controlled digital assets that resist colonial extraction.

Financial models rooted in solidarity economies, where communities pool resources and share risks, can challenge the extractive logic of global health capitalism. Indigenous-led resource pooling, for example, reasserts sovereignty over health resources and knowledge, fostering self-determination and resilience.

HISTORICAL ROOTS OF FINANCING MODELS: USER FEES AND AUSTERITY POLICIES

Sustainable health financing is a central, evolving theme in the global health discourse, now more so, in the face of mounting fiscal pressures and shifting resource landscapes. Recent developments such as seen in the deactivation of major development aid partners like USAID is a present reminder of the need to rethink the global financial strategies amid increasing health needs driven by war, climate change, demographic shifts towards aging societies, and the persistent threat of emerging and re-emerging infectious pathogens that could trigger pandemics (Lancet, 2025).

In this ever-changing landscape, it is crucial to heed Winston Churchill's adage that "those who forget the past are doomed to repeat it". We provide a brief reflective overview, highlighting the historical trajectories that have shaped current health financing paradigms, evaluating our present position, and employing a systems approach to identify feasible pathways for health technology financing.

The question of who must pay for healthcare and how it is done has often taken ideological and political dispositions, often answered with undertones of social involvement, personal responsibility, and freedom of choice. History of colonial legacy, however, witnessed otherwise: extractive economic systems which prioritised resource extraction and wealth transfer from colonised regions in a repeated cycle that caused gaping underinvestment in public services. Post-Independence, many newly independent states inherited these economic models, often adopting austerity measures under International Monetary Fund/World Bank mandates to control fiscal deficits. To fund health systems, countries historically introduced user fees- charges levied on individuals or organisations for goods or services provided in the health sector. Originating as early as the late 1700s and early 1800s, these user fees gained renewed visibility and were intensified in the post-World War II era. These fees have since evolved into various health payment models, disproportionately burdening the poor, creating financial barriers to access, and perpetuating health inequities to this day.

IMPACT OF IMF AND WORLD BANK AUSTERITY AND PRIVATISATION

The Bretton Woods Conference in July 1944 laid the groundwork for the post-war economic order, including the establishment of the IMF and the World Bank. While initially focused on global exchange rates and post-war reconstruction loans in advanced countries, the IMF/World Bank later shifted towards structural adjustment programmes in the Global South, involving austerity measures and privatisation as conditionalities for loans. These conditionalities are "packaged" as policy reforms aimed at achieving fiscal and debt sustainability, enhancing economic competitiveness, and stimulating growth. The austerity policies are imposed with conditionalities requiring reductions in public spending, increased taxes, often slashing budgets of health, social programmes, and public sector wages as a prerequisite for accessing high-interest loans. Driven by neoliberal agendas, privatisation in financing schemes shifts health services from public to private hands, emphasising profit over financial access. These so-called 'conditionalities' grant these international financial institutions considerable influence over national policy decisions, constraining policy space, undermining development priorities such as universal health coverage (UHC), and deepening health disparities (by eroding social protection considerably) in the Global South.

STRUCTURAL BARRIERS IN CURRENT GLOBAL FINANCE

The global financing architecture often prioritises debt repayment and financial stability over health and social development. Lower-middle-income countries, as highlighted in the Global Debt Report 2025, often face exorbitant interest rates, leading to debt cycles that divert funds from health to debt servicing, while high-income countries enjoy very low or negative interest rates on their sovereign debt due to stable economies (OECD, 2018). For example, Ghana faced an IMF non-concessional loan interest rate of 28% in April 2025, whereas Japan's interest rate from the same facility instrument was around 0.5% during the same period (OECD, 2018). This stark contrast brings to bear how lower-middle-income countries like Ghana are grappling with disproportionately high borrowing costs, which exacerbate debt burdens, constrain fiscal flexibility, and hinder economic development compared to high-income nations. A natural consequence of this is the constrained fiscal space that leaves little room for financing health innovation and HealthTECH among other priorities in LMIC.

DO REALISTIC DECOLONIAL FINANCIAL ALTERNATIVES EXIST?

The question remains: how does LMIC restructure health financing and payment strategies that align and support decolonial governance models, acknowledging the challenges faced by countries in the Global South?

MUTUAL AID AND SOLIDARITY ECONOMIES

Mutual aid networks, such as Indigenous-led initiatives in the Amazon and Navajo Nation, are changing the narrative for decolonial models of financing (Mendez V., 2022). These emphasise collective care over charity, redistributing resources while challenging neoliberal dependency (Mendez V. 2022-2). These models prioritise community agency, with combined material support with advocacy (McCoy et al, 2023). By centring relational accountability, such systems reject transactional aid and address root causes of health disparities, such as racial capitalism (McCoy et al, 2022).

A case study to exemplify mutual aid and solidarity economy in the health sector is Tanzania's Community Health Funds (CHFs) which is a local risk-pooling scheme designed to extend health coverage in rural districts. Instead of waiting for donor disbursements, communities contribute modest premiums into district-managed accounts. Funds are then matched by government allocations, while enabling predictable revenue for primary care (Dominic, 2025).

The CHF model's success lies not in its size but in its participatory governance, where local councils decide benefit packages and provider payments. This approach mirrors decolonial principles by redistributing decision-making power to the lowest administrative level and embedding financial accountability in community oversight.

INDIGENOUS RESOURCE POOLING

Indigenous practices like kinship-based resource sharing (e.g., Instituto Chaikuni's COVID-19 response) integrate traditional knowledge with modern needs, fostering resilience against extractive economic models (McCoy et al, 2023). These systems often emphasise ecological interdependence, contrasting with colonial-capitalist exploitation.

Local and Community-based financing represents another avenue for indigenous resource pooling. Community health funds that depend on local pooling mechanisms prioritise community needs and reduce dependence on external funding. One look at the case study on Tanzania and you would see that it was fraught with challenges that can be systematically remedied with the needed political commitment and support. Efforts such as member involvement in benefit package design, flexibility in payment timing and frequency, robust management, transparency and accountability, community ownership, and cross-subsidisation between communities, potentially through a risk equalization fund that could eventually integrate multiple regions and reduce vertical inequities, are key steps towards universal coverage in the use of this model. These highlight mutual aid and solidarity finance, such as seen in grassroots models, emphasising shared responsibility and collective resilience.

RECLAIMING HUMANITY THROUGH DE-COLONIAL INNOVATION.

The digital and financial landscapes of global health are fertile grounds for both perpetuating colonial-capitalist systems and resisting them. Recognising and dismantling these colonial logics requires a conscious shift, one that re-centres human dignity, local knowledge, and collective sovereignty. By integrating decolonial principles into digital health and innovative financial models, we can forge pathways toward equitable, culturally grounded, and self-determined health futures, truly humanised and liberatory. This is not merely a technical challenge but a moral imperative, to decolonise global health and reclaim its promise as a tool for collective well-being and justice.

COMMUNITY-LED FINANCIAL MODELS

Theoretical Foundation

According to Chaudhuri et al. (2021), Fanon's definition of decolonisation posits that decolonisation is the overhauling of an entire system, which can only be achieved through the removal of the coloniser or the uprooting of structures that preserve power. Furthermore, Aníbal Quijano and Walter Mignolo emphasise the foreboding role of Eurocentrism in shaping coloniality. Eurocentrism colonises more than just lands and bodies; it also colonises our understanding of the universe and sense of self. Eurocentrism colonised time and space, denying the various ontologies of human diversity and erasing indigenous peoples' ancestral wisdom. For these decolonial authors, decolonisation consists of the recovery of epistemic rights, the demolition of Eurocentrism, de-Westernisation, and, to some extent, the re-indigenisation of society (Mendoza, 2020).

Applying these theories to global health means challenging the supremacy of capitalist solutions and the commodification of health, recognising it as a communal good instead. Decolonial financial systems aim to promote the redistribution of resources in ways that help historically exploited communities regain their autonomy and prioritise justice, solidarity and mutual responsibility. These alternatives propose radically different frameworks entrenched in equity, reciprocity and collective care. Not only do they question those in charge of sustaining healthcare systems, but also who makes decisions, who benefits, and the conditions in which they happen.

Moving Beyond Impact Investing

There are several disadvantages to impact investing, particularly in terms of its impact on grassroots empowerment, health, and advocacy. Although impact investing has been commended for merging financial returns with social benefits, its prioritising of return on investment (ROI) often neglects long-term, qualitative objectives such as community development and policy advocacy. These types of social change are not easy to quantify and may not produce quick benefits, making them unappealing in an ROI-driven paradigm. This is a significant challenge for nonprofit organisations working with marginalised communities, as it is difficult to secure funding for advocacy initiatives that are difficult to evaluate and quantify. The urge to demonstrate success through easy criteria, such as the volume of outreach initiatives or attendance figures, undermines the commitment to meaningful political participation and structural change.

Furthermore, the focus on capacity building is shaped by private-sector logic that prioritises efficiency and sustainability, which often excludes efforts to strengthen advocacy. Foundations tend to avoid rigorous evaluations that could reveal shortcomings, instead relying on internal or self-assessments that may overlook deeper issues. In the health sector, an example is LifeSpring in India, a maternity care model that acts as a low-cost, high-turnover business. While such ventures may improve access to care, they also raise concerns about quality and the commercialisation of essential health services. By prioritising profitability and short-term outcomes, impact investing risks shifting attention away from the structural determinants of health and weakening the role of nonprofits in advancing equity.

Additionally, private-sector reasoning that emphasises sustainability and efficiency shapes the emphasis on capacity building, frequently omitting initiatives to bolster advocacy. Hence, if impact investing continues to grow without addressing these concerns, it may exacerbate inequalities in representation and reduce the political voice of the most disadvantaged groups(Berry, 2016)

Alternatives rooted in reciprocity and community solidarity reject the notion of investment returns altogether. They view financial support as a means to repair historical harm and build collective futures rather than expand markets. Moving beyond impact investing requires a fundamental realignment of finance with justice, not profit.

How the Solidarity Economy can benefit public health

Public health and the solidarity economy are two essential fields that are inherently linked to the creation of just and healthy societies, despite being frequently examined independently. By understanding the social determinants of health, the solidarity economy, which emphasises collaboration and citizen involvement in economic management, can significantly influence public health (Díaz Muñoz, 2011; Maldonado, 2018a; Pan American Health Organisation [PAHO] and World Health Organisation [WHO], 2020, as cited in Gómez Rodríguez, 2024). A solidarity economy can play a role in strengthening Public Health systems, and in turn, public health can promote the consolidation of more solidarity-based economic practices. Cooperation, democratic engagement, and justice in economic decision-making are characteristics of a solidarity economy. This concept aims to promote social participation and collective well-being in addition to individual financial gain. The goals of cooperatives, associations, and other solidarity groups are to increase community involvement in resource and service management and to distribute economic benefits more fairly (Garzón et al., 2023, as cited in Gómez Rodríguez, 2024). In this context, the Solidarity Economy has the potential to positively influence public health (Paho, 2017). To combat malnutrition and diet-related illnesses, for instance, the creation of neighbourhood food cooperatives can increase access to wholesome foods (Salas, 2012; Gómez & Barbosa, 2023, as cited in Gómez Rodriguez, 2024). Similarly, solidarity projects that create jobs can improve the socioeconomic circumstances of localities closely related to population health (Gómez et al., 2021; Muñoz, 2017, as cited in Gomez Rodriguez, 2024).

For the same reason, public health examines social determinants of health, including environmental, social, and economic factors, in addition to medical care. Addressing social disparities is essential to creating healthier societies, and equity in health is a core value. Important facets of public health include promoting healthy lifestyles, preventing diseases, and implementing primary care approaches. (Atehortúa et al., 2009; Chávez et al., 2011; Gómez et al., 2021, as cited in Gómez Rodriguez, 2024). In a similar vein, public health and the solidarity economy are related because they both prioritise equity and community involvement. Economic fairness helps to lessen inequalities in population health-determining factors and access to health services. (Galea, 2016; Gómez et al., 2021; Garzón et al., 2022, as cited in Gomez Rodriguez, 2024). Equity is fundamental in the solidarity economy. It seeks to maximise economic efficiency without sacrificing it. Efforts are made to ensure that economic benefits are distributed equitably, narrowing the gaps between the richest and the poorest, through cooperative and participatory approaches (Gómez, 2022; Jette & Vaillancourt, 2011; Laville, 2016, as cited in Gómez Rodriguez, 2024). Similar to this, public health aims to strike a balance between access fairness and healthcare delivery efficiency. Although it is recognised that the efficient use of resources is crucial, efforts are also made to ensure that everyone, regardless of socioeconomic background, has access to high-quality healthcare (Urzúa y Caqueo, 2012; Maldonado, 2021; 2022, as cited in Gómez Rodriguez, 2024).

Reparations-Based and Redistributive Models

State governments are in charge of making amends for the historical and current wrongs caused by slavery, as well as racism, exploitation, and dispossession that the colonial and state governments supported. When imitated, reparations prolong life and promote health. There are current initiatives in several international contexts, and the decolonising global health movement ought to be coordinated in favour of Global South debt cancellation and reparative state legislation (such as HR 40 in the USA). Because "violent dispossessions inherent to capital accumulation operate by creating, leveraging, and intensifying racial distinctions," racial capitalism, like settler colonialism, plays a role in the formation and evolution of race. The fact that there is no other type of capitalism is one of the many significant lessons to be learnt from racial capitalism. By normalising social power and privilege, race serves to normalise the unequal production and distribution of resources that characterise capitalism. Cedric Robinson claimed that racialisation in Europe precedes mercantile capitalism and the slave trade, using the term and idea of racial capitalism from South African radicals.

Nevertheless, he eventually merged with them to form the gendered and racialised hierarchies of contemporary capitalism. Racialisation serves to justify society's unfair structure by essentialising sections of people as inferior because the sharp social hierarchies that capitalism demands profit are complex to uphold, even with force. The most well-known example of the history of combining race and labour in the name of extractive profit is transatlantic slavery. Nonetheless, racial capitalism also clarifies the very racially segregated fields of employment, housing, education, and the environment that are still practised globally today. Under pressure from the capital to support incarcerated, trafficked, coerced, unpaid, and poorly compensated work that is also gendered and racial, are continuously changing. The profit-seeking practices and racially stratified workforce hierarchies of pharmaceutical corporations, international hospitals, and universities are examples of how this labour regime directly maximises profit and functioning for the major stakeholders in global health. It also operates indirectly through non-governmental organisations that rely on donations from those with wealth built on racialised extraction. The prospect that decolonial global health cannot exist without new organisational and economic structures that do not require constant eviction and exploitation of group distinctions is raised by an important investigation into racial capitalism.

Instead, a revolutionary movement will reject inherited intellectual and geographic barriers and exhibit a bidirectional decoloniality that aims to colonise the Global North as much as that which is committed in the Global South. This kind of decoloniality means upending the logic of extraction, exploitation, and elimination that normalise the hierarchies that create health disparities between and within colonising and colonised communities (Bram Wispelwey et al., 2023).

DISMANTLING STRUCTURAL FINANCIAL BARRIERS

Historical Roots and Neoliberal Influences

Many of the world's major powers, primarily the United States, have exerted their influence and power over less-developed countries for many years. Through the utilisation of organisations such as the International Monetary Fund and the World Bank, the ability to lend money to countries that need it most comes with conditions and stipulations that only benefit the powerful sponsors of these loans. More often than not, this aid disbursement ends up hurting the recipients of said loans and guarantees their indentured servitude for years to come.

The IMF and World Bank are merely instruments of control and wealth extraction, operating under the guise of benevolent altruism and charity. Additionally, according to Garufu (2016), the provision of foreign aid and the accompanying conditionality agreements are particular mechanisms that enable rich nations to exert control over policy, influence politics, and erode state sovereignty in developing nations.

The term 'structural adjustment' refers to policy reforms mandated by international financial institutions, the IMF, the World Bank, and regional development banks in exchange for financial resources. The phrase 'structural adjustment' describes the policy changes that are required in

return for financial resources by international financial institutions such as the World Bank, the IMF, and regional development banks. Over the last forty years, the fiscal framework governing health policies in developing nations has generally been established by structural adjustment programs implemented by international financial institutions (IFIs), including the World Bank, the International Monetary Fund (IMF), and regional development banks. Countries in severe macroeconomic or fiscal difficulties are given loans for structural adjustment. In exchange, recipient nations must implement several macroeconomic and fiscal reforms in line with a neoliberal framework, usually focusing on deregulation, privatisation, trade and financial liberalisation, and economic stability. Collectively, these 'conditionalities' are proposed to ensure that states are capable of servicing their debt, as well as setting the economic climate for growth. However, such an adjustment comes at a high social cost, while the recidivist nature of program participation also suggests that the gains to macroeconomic stability are underwhelming. Furthermore, it could be argued that while there are advantages to these structural adjustments, the beneficial effects are currently outweighed by the detrimental ones. The beneficial effects are currently outweighed by the detrimental effects (Thomson et al., 2017).

Cooperative Financing and Mutual Aid

Carstensen et al. (2021) argue that mutual aid and self-help groups were indispensable in the early and ongoing response to the pandemic. It calls for aid organisations and authorities to recognise, support, and learn from these community-led responses. The authors emphasise that local agencies should be the foundation of sustainable crisis responses and that sufficient funding should be allocated to these grassroots networks both before, during, and after crises. The pandemic highlighted the effectiveness of community group efforts as well as the pressing need for more egalitarian, adaptable, and inclusive international aid systems.

Additionally, diaspora communities can serve as a powerful source of external development aid to their countries of origin. Their contributions take many forms, including remittances (money transfers between individuals), charitable donations, partnerships, skill transfers, policy advising, and other forms of assistance. In 2018, remittance flows of general aid to low- and middle-income countries (LMICs) reached a record high of $529 billion and are expected to emerge as the world's primary supplier of foreign development assistance within a few years (World Bank, 2019; Barne & Pirlea, 2019). Moreover, diaspora communities can often relate more easily to the culture and practices of their homeland populations and thus develop long-lasting and effective collaborations (Taslakian et al., 2021). In addition, a paper by Obrist et al. (2022) suggests that participation in saving groups in rural Tanzania enhances women's collective and individual capacities to access, combine, and transform five forms of capital.

ISLAMIC FINANCE

In historically exploited countries (commonly referred to as developing countries or the Global South), healthcare spending amounts to a minuscule portion of their GDP. Countries like Mali spend 3.67%, India 3.31%, and Papua New Guinea roughly 2.62%, a far cry from the recommended 5% by the World Health Organisation. Developed countries exceed the WHO recommendations, such as the United States spends 16.5%, the United Kingdom, 10.87% and Japan, 11.42%, respectively (WHO, 2025). Despite the efforts of international health organisations like the United Nations Children's Fund (UNICEF), historically exploited countries continue to face gruelling difficulties in meeting basic healthcare needs. This is a very concerning reality because healthcare expenditure has a positive impact on life expectancy, so a lack thereof puts millions at risk of avoidable deaths (Awoyemi et al., 2023).

Healthcare is an undeniable necessity and a vital aspect of human capital development. To achieve Sustainable Development Goal 3, which aims to improve global health and reduce inequalities in healthcare access, it is pertinent to assess where these inequalities stem from and how alternative finance can bridge the gap.

However, it is difficult to imagine how historically exploited countries can catch up to their developed counterparts when they are burdened with massive debts. More than 40 historically exploited countries have public debts exceeding 60% of their GDP today (Fischer & Storm, 2023).

Following the independence movements of the 20th Century, the Global South was faced with a lack of capital for development and technical know-how. They opted to borrow the funding from wealthier nations and international organisations such as the World Bank and International Monetary Fund (Fischer & Storm, 2023). The loans came at a staggering price of their sovereignty because the interest rates were virtually unpayable and the default terms stipulated strict austerity measures such as privatisation of public corporations and minimised budgets for education and healthcare (Gore, 2000). Thus, the healthcare growth in these countries was stifled.

It is therefore necessary for historically exploited nations to seek healthcare financing from more humane sources -- the Global South must find a way to help itself. As Islamic finance has been a longstanding institution for over 1400 years, it proposes a more equitable alternative to conventional finance. This research explores how Islamic finance principles and tools can be leveraged in developing ethical and equitable healthcare institutions.

Islamic Finance Principles

Following the breakthroughs in global healthcare of the 20th century, which brought about disease eradication, the development of medical ethics and increased life expectancy worldwide, this progress has stagnated in recent years due to a multitude of reasons, but primarily the inaccessibility of essential health services (BMJ, 2023). Underdeveloped countries specifically face the brunt of the absence of public health due to widespread poverty, which leads to a preponderance of communicable diseases such as typhoid and tuberculosis and noncommunicable diseases such as diabetes. This is known as the 'double burden of diseases' (Fazal et al., 2022).

Abimbola & Pai (2020) write that global health originated from colonialism and was used to export white supremacy worldwide. Remnants of its imperial identity are present in many international health organisations, and this is a major roadblock to public health. It is necessary that global health sheds its colonial roots through radical, anti-racist transformation so it can achieve its goal of saving lives worldwide. This dilemma is further exacerbated by the growth of private finance in recent decades. Hunter et al. (2025) state that global financialization policies and the increased presence of private sector actors in healthcare are making care more inaccessible.

Adding to the global health crisis is the dismal state of affairs in historically exploited countries. Where pre-colonial institutions have been erased and/or corrupted, many historically exploited countries face neocolonialism from elites within the populace who occupy positions of leadership but use them to monopolise resources for their interests, causing more severe health disparities (Zadey & Sharma, 2025). Akanji (2021) states that this inequality is worsened by the financial exclusion low low-income individuals experience.

As public spending and private finance have failed to achieve ideal outcomes due to budget constraints and profit-seeking, respectively, Akanji (2021) and Biancone & Radwan (2018) stress the importance of social finance in healthcare.

The finance industry is dependent on securities such as bonds, mortgages, repurchase agreements, etc. However, millions of Muslims around the world eschew conventional finance because of the inextricable debt-interest relationship (Usmani, 2002). Haruna, Oumbé & Kountchou (2023) in a study of 27 African countries assessed that Islamic health financing has improved health outcomes in children, including reducing child mortality. Therefore, Al-Daihani & Abdullah (2023) explored the capabilities of Islamic finance instruments such as *Sukuk* (bond) and *Waqf* (trust endowment) to improve healthcare institutions by providing social finance.

Overview of Islamic Finance Principles

Islamic Finance is the system of institutions and instruments which follow the laws (*Shari'ah*) found in the Muslim scripture (*Qur'an* and *Hadith*). The guiding principle of Islamic finance is the prohibition of interest/usury (*Riba*) and speculation (*Maisir*) (Hussein et al., 2016). For example, financial instruments such as futures contracts, which give holders the ability to purchase commodities present-day with the expectation that they will profit from a future rise or fall in the price, are also prohibited due to the speculative nature of this instrument.

The rationale behind this law is that interest is perceived to be an unethical extraction of wealth from the needy to the rich (Usmani, 2002). This is also not unique to Islam; Christian saints like Thomas Aquinas also condemned usury because it normalised greed and places unjust financial burdens on the poor (Lambert, 2023). A practical example of this is the debt crisis and resulting systematic impoverishment that international organisations and developed countries force upon historically exploited countries (Usmani, 2002).

Islamic finance -- similar to conventional finance -- ensures that there is an underlying asset being exchanged, which serves as the purpose of the transaction. However, due to the interest-free rule, Muslim clerics created a means of providing returns through profit-sharing. There are a number of relationships in Islamic finance through which these financial instruments are developed. These are the main types:

1. *Musharakah:* This relationship involves profit and loss sharing between parties of a joint venture. Rather than a fixed rate of return irrespective of business conditions, which is the case with interest, in *Musharakah,* both parties contribute funding and expertise in the business; they also make decisions together. At the end of the transaction, they share the profits or losses based on a ratio of their earlier contributions.
2. *Mudarabah:* This entails a financer (*Rabb-ul maal*) and manager (*Mudarib*) relationship. Here, the *Rabb-ul maal* is restricted to only providing capital, while the *Mudarib* handles the day-to-day running of the business and makes all the decisions. After, the profits are shared on a predetermined basis, but the losses are borne only by the *Rabb-ul maal.*
3. *Murabahah*: In this transaction, a financial institution buys an asset on behalf of a client and sells it to the client at a previously agreed mark-up. For example, this is similar to a mortgage where a bank buys a property and sells it to the homeowner. But this is more transparent because the bank's profit is fixed and predetermined at the inception of the transaction.
4. *Ijarah:* This is the right of use of a rental property between a lessor and a lessee. This is similar to a *Murabahah,* but instead of transferring ownership of the asset, the lessor retains ownership and only sells the right to use the asset temporarily to the lessee. *Ijarah* can also be transformed into a security through commodification due to its secondary market value. For example, the lessor can sell the ownership of the leased asset partly or wholly, so the *Ijarah*-holder can benefit from rental payments (Usmani, 2002).

5. *Istisna'*: This is an agreement primarily done for manufacturing or construction where a buyer requests a project be undertaken under specific terms, and payment is either made in instalments or deferred until the completion of the project.
6. *Sukuk:* This is similar to a conventional bond. It is a certificate which represents ownership of a tangible asset or pool of assets. This certificate is tradable, and returns are generated from the profits on the underlying asset.
7. *Zakah*: This is a portion of a Muslim's total wealth that is donated to those in need. It is a compulsory act on all Muslims of a certain net worth and was designed to promote equality and mutual aid in society. *Zakah* has great potential as a financial instrument because when the *Zakah* funds are pooled, it could be a means of crowdfunding social projects (Al-Zuraib & Al-Qahtani, 2025).
8. *Waqf*: This is a donated property that is typically for the purpose of a public social service. This could be in the form of books, housing, mosques, etc., but could extend to orphanages, healthcare centres, such as the creation of the First Muslim Hospital for lepers in Damascus in the Eighth Century and so on. There are strict restraints on the use of the Waqf outside of its intended purpose. It is also created and maintained in perpetuity (Al-Daihani & Abdullah, 2023).

These instruments are often combined for certain projects as a means of financing large or complex projects. For instance, the Islamic Development Bank (IDB) issued a hybrid *Sukuk* worth $400 million in 2003 comprising an *Ijarah, Murabahah* receivables and *Istisna'*. Here, the construction contracts were based on *Istisna',* then IDB received the funding from investors, then generated returns based on rental income from existing IDB property (the *Ijarah* aspect) and revenue generated from business activities *(Murabahah)* (Rattu, 2013).

Islamic Finance As A Means Of Social Finance

Compared to capitalist finance, which only seeks to maximise profit, Islamic finance has the potential to contribute to social development because it does not centre on the profit motive.

A *Sukuk-Waqf* system could revolutionise healthcare institutions. Rather than hospitals being dependent on philanthropic funding, public *Sukuks* can raise capital through pooling funds. It also allows the general public to own a share of the care centre and allows them to take control of their destinies. As a *Waqf*, it would have management focused on maximising health outcomes and ensuring a ceaseless existence. The centres can provide free healthcare to the poor and commercial healthcare to those who can afford to pay (Al-Daihani & Abdullah, 2023). An integration of a centralised *Zakah* system could boost the development of healthcare in the Global

South as it provides a platform for muslims worldwide to donate a piece of their wealth to attain health security (Al-Zuraib & Al-Qahtani, 2025).

Islamic Finance To Decolonise Global Health

As imperialism is a complex web of contradictions, there is no "one size fits all" modus operandi for dismantling this oppressive system. Nevertheless, Baeten et al. (2021) developed a toolkit for tackling decolonial struggle. This research validates our findings using this toolkit.

Firstly, to decolonise global health, it is necessary to reverse the legacy of exploitation and bigotry in public health. Unfortunately, the Islamic world has a long history of racism, slavery and sexual exploitation. Therefore, it might appear antithetical to make use of their instruments for decolonial struggle. However, this observation is precisely the first step in analysing the sensibility of a *Sukuk-Waqf* healthcare structure, so we can use the tools at our disposal to change the future of health financing.

It is pertinent to identify the roles of stakeholders in healthcare financing, determine the power dynamics evident in the system, investigate any hindrances or barriers and monitor the performance of the structure (Baeten et al., 2021).

All members of the community would be stakeholders in the proposed healthcare system as they have a share of ownership and directly benefit from the services. It is necessary to note that although the structure has an Islamic background, people of all religions and ethnicities can be stakeholders.

As power dynamics are difficult to eliminate, we must ensure that there is complete equity in regards to management and staffing of the hospitals, and service delivery would be on a first-come-first-serve basis to avoid favouritism. The hospitals must remain secular and inclusive.

Possible barriers could be the lack of an institutional framework for Islamic finance in certain countries (although this is changing rapidly).

Lastly, the Waqf management must outline specific performance indicators and remain accountable to the general public on all successes and failures of the system.

DE-COMMODIFYING HEALTH

The decolonising global health movement will not succeed without the decolonisation of the world's political economy. This involves removing the underpinning social and economic inequities that were exacerbated by colonisation and have never been undone since. (Kwete et al., 2022). In addition, Yates (2009) stated that user fees should be removed to ensure universal health coverage.

As these extractive financial architectures shape access to innovation, we turn next to health technologies.

CULTURALLY SOVEREIGN HEALTH TECHNOLOGY

Recent growing interest in the decolonisation of global health has been directed towards highlighting power asymmetry between high-income and low-income countries. While building on that foundational interest, McCoy et al. (2024), however, re-emphasised that colonialism is a contemporary phenomenon that "manifests in different ways." For example, the undermining of indigenous healthcare systems while biomedicine is subtly imposed on communities, the conduct of unethical drug and vaccine trials on subjects from colonized populations, and the continuous reliance on questionable clinical "evidence" that perpetuates race-based medicine or upholds claims of white superiority all reflect patterns of colonialism in contemporary global health context (McCoy et al., 2024). Efforts to reverse the legacy of colonialism in health equity have been primarily interrogated through the lens of four broad objectives: ensuring equitable collaborations, fostering diversity in leadership, keeping local priorities at the heart of projects, and promoting respectful communications.

Furthermore, in exploring contemporary manifestations of health inequity, one must consider how it continues to shape the development, adoption, utilisation and expansion of digital technologies in global health. Conversely, digital technologies have also been linked with expanding inequities in the field of healthcare. Petretto et al. (2024) held a similar opinion, reiterating that equity issues in the context of healthcare now extend to digital environments or e-environments. While digital health innovations have proven useful in promoting health, contemporary digital technologies like artificial intelligence, blockchain technology, big data systems, e-health and telemedicine are now being scrutinised for their inherent biases that perpetuate health inequities and social injustice against certain races, ethnicities, social groups or communities.

AI BIAS IN HEALTH TECHNOLOGY

In recent years, Artificial Intelligence (AI) systems have become more integrated into our daily life processes. This is easily observed in fields like healthcare, law enforcement, education and other essential services. Unfortunately, AI systems have been associated with biased models or outputs that reflect patterns of discrimination in society. Celi et al. (2022) warn that the proliferation of AI in healthcare not only conveys attendant biases but also "risks thrusting the world toward an exaggerated state of healthcare inequity." As the use of AI expands, there is growing ethical concern about ensuring that AI systems reflect the principles of fairness and social justice. Experts familiar with bias in AI have always maintained that such bias goes beyond technological challenges, and progress can be achieved if it is addressed as a social problem while improving on the technology.

Ashwini KP (2024), special rapporteur on contemporary forms of racism, racial discrimination, xenophobia and related intolerance, presented a report at the fifty-sixth session of Human Rights Council, titled "Contemporary forms of racism, racial discrimination, xenophobia and related intolerance," which highlighted some of the inherent biases in artificial intelligence and how it perpetuates racial discrimination. The author noted that: "The public perception of technology tends to be that it is inherently neutral and objective, and some have pointed out that this presumption of technological objectivity and neutrality remains salient even among producers of technology. But technology is never neutral – it reflects the values and interests of those who influence its design and use, and is fundamentally shaped by the same structures of inequality that operate in society" (Ashwini KP, 2024).

Unlike the modern generative AI systems, predictive AI, which relies heavily on historical data or patterns to predict future outcomes, is perceived as a traditional AI system. The same can be said about image recognition AI systems. Generative AI, on the other hand, are much more versatile in its application as it can generate new data points based on complex training datasets, neural networks and deep learning architecture. The output from generative AI can be in text, image, audio or even video format (Ashwini KP, 2024). As the frontiers of generative AI continue to be explored, it leaves some ethical concerns unaddressed. For instance, the dataset used to train AI algorithms lacks representativeness or diversity, while in some cases, it misrepresents certain groups of people. This results in algorithmic bias and contributes to the biased output observed in many AI systems. Data collection is, therefore, a critical stage where bias in AI can occur. As AI learns from historically biased data, it further reinforces the targeting or marginalisation of people of certain races, ethnicities, communities or even gender. Beyond data collection, AI algorithmic bias also occurs during data labelling, as subjective labels which stem from cultural or personal prejudice can be applied to training data.

It must be stated that AI algorithmic bias can have significant real-life consequences in terms of social inequality or discrimination. This can be observed in law enforcement, security systems, education and healthcare. For instance, while digital loan applications are intended to democratize access to small credits for low-income groups, adopting AI systems with biased algorithms to evaluate credit scores of loan applicants yields unintended consequences, as certain groups of people will likely experience financial exclusion, owing to algorithmic decisions connected to racial, ethnic or social prejudice. This further exposes loan applicants to financial strain that could impact their health status, especially for low-income individuals who rely on out-of-pocket payments to fund their health expenditures. Ashwini KP (2024) also provided instances of discriminatory impacts of AI in healthcare. Consider the use of AI in generating health risk scores, which can be applied in clinical diagnosis or in public health planning. Bias in AI algorithms can result in discrimination against certain groups, races, ethnicities or communities when such AI systems are utilised in making decisions about their health status or the distribution of healthcare resources. Consequently, Individuals from low-income groups could be disproportionately affected by limiting their access to life-saving healthcare resources, and systemic discriminatory practices in the healthcare system can become institutionalised, as recounted below:

> *"In the United States, a calculator was developed to assist health-care providers in assessing the likelihood of successful vaginal birth after caesarean delivery. A study in 2019 revealed bias in the calculator's foundational algorithm. The calculator had two race-based correction factors, which resulted in lower predicted vaginal birth success rates for women of African descent and Hispanic women compared with white women with similar characteristics. Because of these correction factors, the calculator potentially worsened racial disparities in maternal health outcomes by discouraging clinicians from offering vaginal birth to women of African descent and Hispanic women, leading to higher rates of caesarean sections" (Ashwini KP, 2024)*

In the case of pathology or disease detection, AI systems utilise medical image classification to detect certain cancers. These AI algorithms are, in some cases, trained with publicly available images that exclude certain races, ethnicities or groups, denying them the benefit of such diagnostic technology. A study by Wen et al. (2022) on the characteristics of publicly available skin cancer image datasets used to develop an AI algorithm for diagnosing skin cancers reported restricted population representation, which limits its generalizability and consequently, its usefulness in a real-life clinical setting. Poor performance of AI systems has also been reported in the use of AI for detecting skin cancer lesions among dark-skinned individuals, an unfortunate reality that can be traced to the image dataset utilised in training the AI algorithms, which lacks representativeness of populations with varying skin tones (Wen et al., 2022).

The need to mitigate algorithmic bias in health technologies and expand health equity across the digital health landscape cannot be overstated. In highlighting important considerations for integrating AI into Africa's health systems, Ndembi et al. (2025) stressed that Africa and the global community require a common position on health data governance which the authors noted would tow the path of "adopting a single digital health market" to ensure AI systems are better adapted to benefiting society and mitigating associated risks. Addressing AI algorithmic deficiencies requires investment in the quality and diversity of underlying population data used in training models. This suggests ethnic, cultural, age and gender considerations in ensuring representativeness of the training dataset. Furthermore, local and external validation (also called model recalibration) of AI models among diverse populations, including marginalised groups whose data were underrepresented in training datasets, is a helpful strategy for mitigating AI bias. Celi et al. (2022) described this as a "more practical, short-term solution to healthcare inequities born of data disparity." External validation of AI models is also considered relevant for the "within populations" context. Confidential version control or audit trails and the verification of AI systems against global reference standards have also been put forward as part of recommendations for mitigating bias (Ndembi et al., 2025). AI built in locations considered data-rich can be applied in "data-poor" settings by a concept known as model pre-training, during which pre-trained models are trained on a particular task and leveraged to solve related problems (Celi et al., 2022). Using bias detection tools (such as fairness metrics), continuous monitoring and human oversight (humans-in-the-loop) can also be applicable for addressing bias in AI systems that foster health inequities.

Patients with limited healthcare access can leverage telemedicine for improved health outcomes. This is important for accelerating efforts to narrow the gaps in health inequities among diverse populations. Moreover, for low-income groups, telemedicine can help address the burden of financial hardships associated with seeking care. An important manifestation of inequity in health is the inequitable distribution of human resources for health across high-income and low-income settings. Telemedicine provides an opportunity for low- and middle-income countries to innovatively tap into their vast human resource scattered across large distances. Broad recommendations for improving equity in digital health (e-health and telemedicine) include building the skills and knowledge of users and ensuring the availability of supporting infrastructures. Additional recommendations include making digital platform interfaces and information flow much simpler, as well as establishing mechanisms for harvesting user-centred design inputs from groups and communities that potentially face the risk of limited access to digital health technologies (Petretto et al., 2024). Such inputs are also useful in designing and delivering financially inclusive telemedicine services to low-income groups.

To close the gap in health inequity, developers of health technologies must invest in creating culturally sovereign healthcare solutions. Unfortunately, health start-ups and innovators in low-resource settings are burdened by the gross inadequacy of investments required to support the development of culturally sovereign health technologies that cater to local priorities. Over the years, open-source software has proven considerably useful for developing low-cost health technologies. Developers can maintain low operational cost while leveraging on open-source software which, in most cases, does not incur licensing fees and grants developers some freedom to customize it to serve their local healthcare needs. While this doesn't completely resolve global digital health inequity, it lowers the barriers of limited resources, supporting innovation and scale-up of indigenous health solutions ("Software Business," 2024).

To deliver a global health system that is rooted in fairness and justice, all actors must work collaboratively to address the burgeoning inequities in health technology.

Artificial intelligence in healthcare often operates as an opaque "black box," obscuring decision logic and perpetuating biases that disproportionately harm marginalised groups. For example, Optum's risk-scoring algorithm underestimates the health needs of Black patients by using healthcare costs as a proxy for illness severity, resulting in misallocation of high-risk care management programs. Black-box models thus risk deepening existing disparities when deployed in low-resource settings, where financial exclusion can occur if microinsurance applications are automatically denied or legitimate claims flagged as fraudulent without recourse (Obermeyer et al., 2019; Norori et al., 2021)

By contrast, white-box models, including decision trees, rule-based systems, and generalised additive models, offer interpretable parameters and explicit decision pathways, enabling stakeholders to audit feature weights, contest errors, and adapt systems to local epidemiological contexts (Kiseleva et al., 2022). Transparency not only fosters trust among users and communities but also empowers local technologists to recalibrate models according to disease prevalence and cultural norms, a cornerstone of culturally sovereign HealthTech initiatives (Writer, 2025).

Open-source platforms and hardware resist vendor lock-in and centre community agency. Table 1 compares exemplar solutions:

Table 1. Open Source HealthTech Platforms and Devices

Platform/Device	Software vs. Hardware	Cost Model	Adaptability & Governance
Open Source Medical Records system (OpenMRS)	Software	Free; community-supported	Modular architecture; governed by global OpenMRS community
District Health Information Software (DHIS2)	Software	Free core; paid hosting	Configurable dashboards; overseen by HISP network
3D printed Prosthetic Hand	Hardware	Material + printer cost only	Community-curated designs; local fabrication guides

Source: (Mohammed-Rajput et al., 2011; Braa & Sahay, 2017)

Beyond software, open hardware, such as paper-based diagnostics and community-designed prosthetics, enables on-site fabrication, the integration of traditional ergonomic knowledge, and reductions in import dependence (McMillan, 2024). These approaches enhance both financial and technological sovereignty.

To deliver a global health system that is rooted in fairness and justice, all actors must work collaboratively to address the burgeoning inequities in health technology.

To ensure local ownership of technologies, governance systems must reflect anti-extractive principles.

COLLABORATIVE AND ANTI-EXTRACTIVE GOVERNANCE

Rethinking Health Governance Structures

While healthcare is relatively accepted as a human right, neoliberalism promotes healthcare as a commodity whose price is left to the marketplace, which means only the wealthy or affluent populations of the global village can access it. Furthermore, privatisation challenges the ideals of social solidarity necessary for realising the right to health. It may also result in unequal, tiered healthcare systems, providing different levels of healthcare depending on income. Furthermore, because it necessitates the regulation, licensing, and oversight of a broad range of individuals, facilities, products, and services, guaranteeing accountability, a fundamental human rights principle, becomes more difficult for private or mixed healthcare services. Accessible monitoring and accountability systems are a significant concern, as private healthcare providers and insurers often have an incentive to cut costs to boost profits. Additionally, fragmented healthcare systems brought about by privatisation make it more challenging to create and implement national health programs. Private companies often prioritise profit-making over producing drugs that are most needed (Chapman, 2016, as cited in Macnaughton, 2016).

Despite its economic constraints, Cuba continues to rank highly in health indices, defying the idea that universal access to high-quality healthcare requires a substantial financial outlay and demonstrating the impact of political will and policy decisions on healthcare provision. To address the intricate interdependencies between imperial histories and health, economic development, governance, and human rights, global health requires integrated, decolonised approaches that both individuals and institutions promote. They also note that the architecture of global and public health systems is rooted in a history of slavery, redlining, environmental racism, and the predatory character of capitalism, which has led to structural, racial, and ethnic imbalances among BIPOC communities. It should come as no surprise that the "Global South" is a hive of invention, and its leaders deserve recognition and advancement for their achievements. The second issue that has to be addressed is the gender gap in leadership positions in global health. Women, particularly women of colour, are under-represented in many global health organisations, and their opinions are not heard when developing policies and programs. Inequitable first authorship positions for women and partners from the "Global South" are just one example of how a leadership shift would involve more equitable representation in academic publications, leadership roles, and faculty composition.

Second, it is critical to make sure that knowledge flow is reciprocal rather than unidirectional, with contributions from the 'Global South' driving discussions and practices both locally and globally, a twofold knowledge shift, to prevent repeating the racist and colonialist pandemic response observed with COVID-19. The first involves educating students about the unequal burdens of sickness around the world while fostering an atmosphere that encourages critical thinking about the colonial and racist pasts that contributed to these burdens. The second is to address geopolitical disparities in the teaching of global health. For example, global health training programmes and knowledge resources are primarily offered in the English language, in high-income countries (HICs), and at a high cost, thus limiting access for people from other languages and less privileged backgrounds. To promote anticolonial thought by overcoming existing obstacles to training and knowledge sharing, we need to modify existing platforms and develop new learning platforms for global health. (Büyüm et al., 2020)

Mulumba et al. (2021) propose that health system decolonisation requires embedding community participation through policies that incentivise historically marginalised and excluded groups to share decision-making power more effectively. They go on to say that decolonising a postcolonial country's health governance, including its health system, cannot be divorced from its political setup, using Uganda's health system as an example.

Feminist, Indigenous, and Southern epistemologies offer alternative frameworks for governance grounded in relationality, consensus-building, and collective well-being. For instance, the concept of "buen vivir" in Latin America emphasises interconnectedness and mutual care over individual gain. It discourages extraction, which is a significant problem created by the global South (Chassagne, 2018). Similarly, the "Ubuntu" philosophy in Southern Africa operates on the principle of living in harmony with others and expressing mutual concern and care for one another. Ubuntu can rally individuals from all walks of life in society who are typically not involved in decision-making to interact in a symbiotic and harmonious way (Jecker et al., 2022). It could be argued that there is an act of selflessness in the ideology of Ubuntu, which prioritises community over individuality, in contrast to the Governments of wealthy nations and shareholders of for-profit pharmaceutical companies, who operate in a global environment in which each seeks to serve their interests.

Furthermore, Abimbola et al. (2019) posit that more equitable and resilient health systems can be achieved by decentralising power to local communities, strengthening local governance capacity, and enabling decision-making that reflects local contexts and priorities. Only through a shift can health governance be of a collaborative and liberatory nature.

Sharifah Sekalala and Tatenda Chatikobo (2024) state that Neoliberal policies have resulted in the Global North's philanthropic organisations and multinational corporations viewing digital health data as a resource. This is a type of digital health colonialism. Therefore, even though digital health initiatives are seen as having the potential to change health systems in the global south and serve as a tool for health justice, they frequently reinforce digital colonialism because they use hardware, software, and storage to entrench racial hierarchies and discriminatory border politics while also significantly increasing the marketisation and commercialisation of health.

POLICY-MAKING AND TECHNOLOGY CO-DESIGN

Understanding global health through a decolonial lens enables us to identify how digital health coloniality affects the health outcomes and lived experiences of the Global South, presenting opportunities for reimagining digital health in restorative and transformative ways. To resist digital health colonialism, a decolonial agenda for digital health employs alternative decolonial lenses, such as indigenous African philosophical thought, which centres community health experiences in creating strong, locally aligned digital health regulatory infrastructures. Since users have a say in defining problems and shaping solutions, it leads to much more culturally appropriate and knowledgeable solutions. There are notable examples of this approach. In Guatemala, the safe+natal kit was introduced to provide supplementary monitoring capabilities to comedones (Indigenous midwives), offering a standardised method for health workers to detect pregnancy complications more effectively (Thakkar, 2024). In Canada, telemedicine projects led by the Inuit prioritise community control over data governance and privacy (Love et al., 2022).

An important aspect of technology co-design involves challenging data colonialism and technological bias. Research by Marko et al. (2025) revealed disparities in AI outcomes, accessibility, and representation among diverse groups stemming from biased data sources and a lack of representation in training datasets, which can potentially exacerbate inequalities in care delivery for marginalised communities.

By integrating Indigenous expertise and democratic control into digital health governance, we can shift from techno-solutionism towards solidarity-based innovation, achieving a more inclusive approach.

REIMAGINING TRADE AND TAX FOR HEALTH JUSTICE

Global trade and tax systems play a significant role in the inequities observed in global health financing. Trade agreements, particularly those involving pharmaceuticals and intellectual property, sometimes prioritise corporate profits over public health. The World Trade Organisation's TRIPS (Trade-Related Aspects of Intellectual Property Rights) agreement, for example, enforces patent protections that limit the supply of affordable medicines and vaccines in developing countries (Urias & Ramani, 2020). During the COVID-19 pandemic, high-income countries rejected requests for a TRIPS waiver, illustrating how trade restrictions can compromise health justice (Chaudhary & Chaudhary, 2021).

A decolonial strategy for trade would prioritise health over profits. It would advocate for compulsory licensing, open-source medication development, and regional medical manufacturing hubs (Perehudoff et al., 2021). Furthermore, it would oppose extractive trade agreements that favour foreign investment above local health infrastructure, land rights, and environmental preservation. Tax regimes also have a significant impact. Multinational firms operating in the Global South often employ tax avoidance tactics to transfer revenues out of host countries (O'Hare, 2019). Illicit financial flows, estimated to be in the hundreds of billions of dollars each year, weaken domestic revenue for healthcare spending (Ortega et al., 2020). At the same time, loan repayment commitments to Northern creditors put a burden on national budgets, compelling governments to cut spending on health and education.

Global tax justice movements have proposed remedies, including a global minimum corporate tax, country-by-country profit reporting, and the repatriation of illicit funds (Hugger et al., 2024; OECD, 2018). These tactics have the potential to provide significant funds for fair health finance when paired with debt cancellation and reparations. Rethinking trade and taxes from a decolonial perspective is essential to changing the governance of global health; it is not a side issue. Only through more equitable economic laws can countries gain sovereignty over their healthcare systems and secure the resources required for public well-being.

The Twenty-First Century: Financialisation, Philanthrocapitalism and Pandemic

The seeds of financialisation of global health, and its flip side of philanthrocapitalism with its attendant multistakeholderism, had been sown in the late nineteenth century, with the entrenchment of neoliberal hegemony. Their flower blossomed in the twentieth century. Financialisation of healthcare takes private sector engagement to a new and more sinister level. At the heart of financialisation is "the increasing role of financial motives, financial markets, financial actors and financial institutions in the operation of the domestic and international economies" (Epstein, 2005, p. 3).

The expansion of private finance in global health accelerated in the wake of the Global Financial Crisis of 2008-2009 (Hunter et al, 2025, p. 10). Most of the actors at the heart of the marketization and corporatisation which financialisation entails, such as private equity firms investing in global health companies and big pharmaceuticals, are from countries in the global North. And even the few from the global South are embedded in the same for-profit logic. But that is not all.

Financialisation further shapes the nature of the governance of global health. We see the "rise of financial mechanisms" such as Gavi and the Global Fund (Stein and Sridhar 2018). They shape international health policy and with little sense of accountability to developing countries, which are considered more as objects than subjects of history. Embedded in and closely related to such financial mechanisms is the multistakeholderism in global health governance. This involves private sector actors, including corporations, but with philanthrocapitalism foundations playing the more visible roles as key actors in the global health policy process. These venture philanthropists spend significant amounts of money.

Between 2013 and 2015 alone, these foundations spent $23.9 billion to aid development, according to the OECD. This serves to them and the ruling class to justify their seat at the table. Even the governments of countries in the global South hold them in great awe. In the second quarter of 2025, for example, President Bola Tinubu of Nigeria bestowed one of the highest national honours of the country on Bill Gates, who is the most visible face of venture philanthropy. However, while "debates about private philanthropy often separate the giving of money from the making of it", the two are intertwined (Dentico and Seitz 2022). They make up moments in the accumulation process of the circuit of capital writ large.

With the influence of venture philanthropists looming over states in the global South on one hand and that of multi stakeholder bodies in global health on the other, privatisation of healthcare, including public-private partnerships (PPP), has become the norm. Despite mounting evidence showing that blind optimism in private healthcare in poorer countries is misplaced (Oxfam 2009) and established evidence that PPPs are ineffective in promoting universal access to healthcare (Romero & Ravenscroft 2022), these remain the norm.

Private sector healthcare provision in the global South has undermined the quest for health for all. In India, privatisation resulted in blocking access of 50% of women to quality healthcare for childbirth, as they could not afford it and the exclusion of almost half of the population in Latin America (Oxfam 2009). PPPs do not only entail governments subsidising private profit with public funds, it also empower corporations to shape public policy, including the designing of health systems and setting up of healthcare financing priorities in developing countries (Wemos 2021)

Thus, it is not so much about what works for countries, or better put, the health and dignity of the immense majority of the populations of countries in the global South. It is more about the dictates of capital, neoliberal dynamics and the ghost of coloniality. It boils down to "transforming health financing and provision into financial investments and the correlated participation of financial actors in the sector" (Hunter and Murray 2019: 1264). International financial institutions also play important roles in fostering this unhealthy situation. At the heart of this is the World Bank Group. It promotes healthcare PPP projects in Africa and across the global South (Chukwuma et al. 2025). And also, based on "the private first" approach, which it has operationalised through the so-called Maximising Finance for Development approach, it has provided investments and advisory services to private sector players that have cared less about health equity (Dentico et al. 2022: 23).

Lessons from Grassroots Mutual Aid vs. Philanthrocapitalism

Table 2. Governance Models Comparison

Criterion	Grassroots Mutual Aid	Philanthrocapitalism
Decision-making	Collective covenants; rotating facilitation	Top-down by funders
Accountability	Direct reciprocity, community audits	Annual reports to donors
Sustainability	Embedded social capital, volunteer networks	Dependent on grant cycles

Sources: (Coppola, 2022; Mediavilla & Garcia-Arias, 2019)

What Is To Be Done?

The struggle for decolonisation of global health must entail a no-holds-barred challenge of the commonsense of the status quo. We must unmask it as an ideological constellation legitimising capitalist exploitation, coloniality and patriarchy. We must burst the myths that there isn't enough money to guarantee health for all, or that developing countries, particularly in Africa, are too poor to provide publicly funded universal access to quality healthcare.

We saw how the magic money tree emerged out of nowhere during the COVID-19 pandemic. In the first half of the pandemic, the World Bank committed $43 billion to the global pandemic response (World Bank 2020). It is also noteworthy that the pandemic created 573 new billionaires at the rate of one new billionaire every 30 hours (Oxfam 2022). It is also heartwrenching that Africa loses $89 billion, which could have been utilised for providing healthcare for the people, to illicit financial flows every year. So, the problem is about the concentration of wealth and power at one end and the concentration of poverty and ill-health at the other end.

We must keep emphasising these facts. But we need to take other concrete actions. How do we redress the situation? Policy recommendations and demands must include tax justice. Corporations and the rich must be made to pay substantially more in taxation. Trade unions, civil society organisations and other progressive forces need to deepen and unify their mobilisation against privatisation and financialisation of healthcare, and coloniality in global health governance and the international financial architecture.

We must not take on these battles as merely episodic moments. We need to underscore the structural nature of the problem and thus the systemic nature of the alternatives we present. This must inform our strategy. The struggle for decolonisation is not just a struggle for the improvement of the public health situation in developing countries. "The neoliberal turn of the 1980s represents a loss of the trajectory of social progress towards health as a social commons" (Aye 2020: 247). The struggle for decolonisation must aim to reverse this loss. It must necessarily be anti-capitalist to restore humankind to the pathways of social progress which the Alma-Ata conference envisaged, and where health for all is genuinely realised.

BUILDING A DECOLONIAL HEALTH PARADIGM

Finance, technology, and governance are not separate pillars; they are deeply intertwined in shaping how health is experienced, valued, and delivered across the world. Yet, the systems we have today often reproduce historical hierarchies and hinder progress toward genuine equity. To decolonise global health, we must do more than reform what already exists; we must reimagine it from the ground up. That means creating financial systems rooted in community solidarity, building technologies that reflect local realities, and designing governance structures that are inclusive, transparent, and just.

Decolonial financing, in particular, requires translation from theory into implementable strategies. Ministries of health can pilot community-led health fund pools integrated with national insurance schemes, ensuring transparent risk equalisation and accountability. NGOs and philanthropic foundations should evolve from donor–beneficiary frameworks toward co-governance with local cooperatives, while hospital administrators can experiment with hybrid financing, linking diaspora remittances, community solidarity funds, and Islamic Sukuk-Waqf instruments, to expand service access for marginalised and underserved groups.

At the policy level, regulators must develop enabling legislation for community finance mechanisms and for data sovereignty protections within digital health ecosystems. Capacity-building partnerships with universities and local training institutions can further strengthen managerial competence in decolonial financial design, ensuring sustainability and shared ownership.

Change will not happen overnight. But by centring the voices, knowledge, and leadership of those most affected by injustice, these institutional actors can begin to move beyond critique toward operational decolonisation, transforming health financing, governance, and technology into instruments of equity and collective empowerment. This is not just a technical challenge; it is a moral one, and it is long overdue.

REFERENCES

Abimbola, S., Baatiema, L., & Bigdeli, M. (2019). The impacts of decentralisation on health system equity, efficiency and resilience: A realist synthesis of the evidence. *Health Policy and Planning*, *34*(8), 605–617. DOI: 10.1093/heapol/czz055 PMID: 31378811

Abimbola, S., & Pai, M. (2020). Will global health survive its decolonisation? *Lancet*, *396*(10263), 1627–1628. DOI: 10.1016/S0140-6736(20)32417-X PMID: 33220735

Abraha, H. (2019). How compatible is the US 'CLOUD Act' with cloud computing? A brief analysis. *International Data Privacy Law*, *9*(3), 207–215. DOI: 10.1093/idpl/ipz009

Akanji, A. A. (2021). The role of social financing in sustainable development: The case of Nigerian co-operatives. In *Innovations in social finance*. Palgrave Macmillan., DOI: 10.1007/978-3-030-72535-8_19

Al-Daihani, M., & Abdullah, A. S. (2023). Waqf-based healthcare services model (WHS-M): A proposed model an alternative financing mode for the health sector. I-iECONS e-Proceedings, 778–789.

Al-Zuraib, M. A., & Al-Qahtani, W. K. (2025). Zakat and waqf in supporting the health sector: An analytical study on the role of Islamic financial instruments in achieving sustainable health security. *Journal of Neonatal Surgery*, *14*(26), 785–787.

Ashwini, K. P. (2024). Contemporary forms of racism, racial discrimination, xenophobia and related intolerance (Report of the Special Rapporteur on contemporary forms of racism, racial discrimination, xenophobia and related intolerance, Human Rights Council, 56th session, Agenda item 9). United Nations.

Ávila Pinto, R. (2018). Digital sovereignty or digital colonialism? New tensions of privacy, security and national policies. SUR International Journal on Human Rights, 15(27), 15–27. https://sur.conectas.org/en/digital-sovereignty-or-digital-colonialism/

Awoyemi, B. A., Makanju, A. A., Mpapalika, J., & Ekpeyo, R. S. (2023). A time series analysis of government expenditure and health outcomes in Nigeria. *Journal of Public Health in Africa*, *14*(7), 1409. Advance online publication. DOI: 10.4081/jphia.2023.1409 PMID: 37680869

Aye, B. (2020). Health workers on the frontline struggle for health as a social common. *Development*, *63*(2), 244–248. DOI: 10.1057/s41301-020-00271-z PMID: 33192029

Badr, J., Motulsky, A., & Denis, J. L. (2024). Digital health technologies and inequalities: A scoping review of potential impacts and policy recommendations. *Health Policy (Amsterdam), 146*, 105122. Advance online publication. DOI: 10.1016/j.healthpol.2024.105122 PMID: 38986333

Baeten, J., Barnabas, R., Bukusi, E., Bulterys, M., Celum, C., Fairbanks, J., Galagan, S., Heffron, R., Heller, K., Krows, M., Mugo, N., Ortblad, K., Scoville, C., Shapiro, A., Stewart, J., Thomas, K., & Velloza, J. (2021). *Decolonizing global health toolkit*. University of Washington International Clinical Research Center.

Barne, D., & Pirlea, A. F. (2019, April 8). Money sent home by workers is now the largest source of external financing in low- and middle-income countries (excluding China). World Bank Blogs. https://blogs.worldbank.org/en/opendata/money-sent-home-workers-now-largest-source-external-financing-low-and-middle-income

Bello, W., & Cunningham, S. (1994). The World Bank & the IMF. *Z Magazine (Boston, Mass.), 7*(7), 8.

Berry, J. M. (2016). Negative returns: The impact of impact investing on empowerment and advocacy. *PS, Political Science & Politics, 49*(3), 437–441. DOI: 10.1017/S1049096516000664

Biancone, P. P., & Radwan, M. (2018). Social finance and unconventional financing alternatives: An overview. European Journal of Islamic Finance, 10.

BMJ. (2023). More than half the world's population lack basic health services as progress stalls. BMJ, 382, Article p2160. DOI: 10.1136/bmj.p2160

Braa, J., & Sahay, S. (2017). The DHIS2 open source software platform: Evolution over time and space. In The global health informatics book.

Büyüm, A. M., Kenney, C., Koris, A., Mkumba, L., & Raveendran, Y. (2020). Decolonising global health: If not now, when? *BMJ Global Health, 5*(8), e003394. Advance online publication. DOI: 10.1136/bmjgh-2020-003394 PMID: 32759186

Carstensen, N., Mudhar, M., & Munksgaard, F. S. (2021). "Let communities do their work": The role of community mutual aid and self-help groups in the Covid-19 pandemic response. *Disasters, 45*(S1). Advance online publication. DOI: 10.1111/disa.12515 PMID: 34562282

Celi, L. A., Cellini, J., Charpignon, M. L., Dee, E. C., Dernoncourt, F., Eber, R., Mitchell, W. G., Moukheiber, L., Schirmer, J., Situ, J., Paguio, J., Park, J., Wawira, J. G., & Yao, S. (2022). Sources of bias in artificial intelligence that perpetuate healthcare disparities—A global review. *PLOS Digital Health, 1*(3), e0000022. Advance online publication. DOI: 10.1371/journal.pdig.0000022 PMID: 36812532

Chassagne, N. (2018). Sustaining the "good life": Buen vivir as an alternative to sustainable development. *Community Development Journal: An International Forum*, *54*(3), 482–500. DOI: 10.1093/cdj/bsx062

Chaudhary, T., & Chaudhary, A. (2021). TRIPS waiver of COVID-19 vaccines: Impact on pharmaceutical industry and what it means to developing countries. *The Journal of World Intellectual Property*, *24*(5-6), 447–454. Advance online publication. DOI: 10.1111/jwip.12198 PMID: 34908905

Chukwuma, J. N., Romero, M. J., & Van Waeyenberge, E. (2025). Healthcare financialisation in the Global South: Examining the role of the World Bank Group in promoting public private partnerships in health in Africa. *Review of Evolutionary Political Economy*, *6*(2), 373–404. Advance online publication. DOI: 10.1007/s43253-024-00140-2

Cochrane, T. D., Narayan, V., Aiello, S., Alizadeh, M., Birt, J., Bone, E., Cowie, N., Cowling, M., Deneen, C., Goldacre, P., Sinfield, D., Stretton, T., & Worthington, T. (2022). Analysing mobile learning designs: A framework for transforming learning post-COVID. *Australasian Journal of Educational Technology*, *38*(4), 1–21. DOI: 10.14742/ajet.7997

Coppola, S. (2022). Should solidarity replace charity? Critiquing effective altruism and considering mutual aid as an alternative [Doctoral dissertation].

Dentico, N., Aye, B., & Meurs, M. (2022). *Financial justice for pandemic prevention, preparedness & response*. Geneva Global Health Hub.

Dentico, N., & Seitz, K. (2022). *Philanthrocapitalism in global health and nutrition: Analysis and implications*. Spotlight on Sustainable Development.

Díaz Muñoz, J. G. (2011). Las economías solidarias latinoamericanas como construcción de alternativas de resistencia y liberación desde abajo: Un estudio comparado de casos micro y macro de México, Argentina, Brasil y Bolivia (1989-2009).

Dominic. (2025). Making health financing work for poor people in Tanzania. World Bank.

Epstein, G. (2005). Introduction: Financialization and the world economy. In Epstein, G. (Ed.), *Financialization and the world economy*. Edward Elgar. DOI: 10.4337/9781781008263.00009

Fazal, F., Saleem, T., Ur Rahman, M. E., Haider, T., Khalid, A. R., Tanveer, U., Mustafa, H., Tanveer, J., & Noor, A. (2022). The rising cost of healthcare and its contribution to the worsening disease burden in developing countries. *Annals of Medicine and Surgery (London)*, *82*, 104683. Advance online publication. DOI: 10.1016/j.amsu.2022.104683 PMID: 36148082

Fischer, A. M., & Storm, S. (2023). The return of debt crisis in developing countries: Shifting or maintaining dominant development paradigms? *Development and Change*, *54*(5), 954–993. Advance online publication. DOI: 10.1111/dech.12800

Garufu, P. (2016). Operationalising international law principles governing state sovereignty over mineral resources: The case of Zimbabwe and the Democratic Republic of the Congo (DRC) [Master's thesis, University of the Witwatersrand]. WiredSpace. https://wiredspace.wits.ac.za/items/0bb70cb5-e516-4172-9863-bdfd829b8755

Gladstone, J., Schipper, L., Hara-Msulira, T., Casci, T., Allen, K., Carter, H., Lee, Z., & Lockie, J. (2023). Equity and inclusivity in research funding: Barriers and delivering change.

Gómez Rodríguez, D. T. (2024). Solidarity economy and public health for sustainable development and community well-being. *Cooperativismo & Desarrollo*, *32*(128), 1–15. DOI: 10.16925/2382-4220.2024.01.02

Gore, C. (2000). The rise and fall of the Washington Consensus as a paradigm for developing countries. *World Development*, *28*(5), 789–804. Advance online publication. DOI: 10.1016/S0305-750X(99)00160-6

Haruna, A., Oumbé, H. T., & Kountchou, A. M. (2023). Child healthcare outcomes in Africa: Unlocking the potentials of Islamic finance. *Journal of Islamic Finance*, *12*(1), 116–135. Advance online publication. DOI: 10.31436/jif.v12i1.752

Houenou, B. (2024). Datafication in the age of AI: Economic models and policy. DOI: 10.2139/ssrn.5163471

Hugger, F., González Cabral, C., Bucci, M., Gesualdo, M., & O'Reilly, P. (2024, June 22). How the global minimum tax changes the taxation of multinational companies. VoxEU. https://cepr.org/voxeu/columns/how-global-minimum-tax-changes-taxation-multinational-companies

Hunter, B. M., McCoy, D., Cordhila, A. C., Marriott, A., Roy, V., Stein, F., & Wood, B. (2025). *Private financial actors and financialisation in global health*. United Nations University International Institute for Global Health. DOI: 10.37941/RR/2025/1

Hunter, B. M., & Murray, S. F. (2019). Deconstructing the financialization of healthcare. *Development and Change*, *50*(5), 1263–1287. DOI: 10.1111/dech.12517

Hussein, M., Shahmoradi, A., & Turk, R. (2016). An overview of Islamic finance. Journal of International Commerce. *Economic Policy*, *7*(1).

Jecker, N. S., Atuire, C. A., & Kenworthy, N. (2022). Realising Ubuntu in global health: An African approach to global health justice. *Public Health Ethics*, *15*(3), 256–267. Advance online publication. DOI: 10.1093/phe/phac022

Jetté, C., & Vaillancourt, Y. (2011). Social economy and home care services in Quebec: Co-production or co-construction? *Voluntas*, *22*(1), 48–69. DOI: 10.1007/s11266-010-9134-8

Kiseleva, A., Kotzinos, D., & De Hert, P. (2022). Transparency of AI in healthcare as a multilayered system of accountabilities: Between legal requirements and technical limitations. *Frontiers in Artificial Intelligence*, *5*, 879603. Advance online publication. DOI: 10.3389/frai.2022.879603 PMID: 35707765

Kumar, R., Khosla, R., & McCoy, D. (2024). Decolonising global health research: Shifting power for transformative change. *PLOS Global Public Health*, *4*(4), e0003141. Advance online publication. DOI: 10.1371/journal.pgph.0003141 PMID: 38656955

Kwete, X., Tang, K., Chen, L., Ren, R., Chen, Q., Wu, Z., Cai, Y., & Li, H. (2022). Decolonising global health: What should be the target of this movement and where does it lead us? *Global Health Research and Policy*, *7*(1), 3. Advance online publication. DOI: 10.1186/s41256-022-00237-3 PMID: 35067229

Lambert, T. E. (2023). Bankers as immoral? Some parallels and differences between Aquinas's views on usury and Marxian views of banking and credit. Faculty Scholarship, 884.

Lambin, R., & Surender, R. (2023). The rise of big philanthropy in global social policy: Implications for policy transfer and analysis. *Journal of Social Policy*, *52*(3), 602–619. DOI: 10.1017/S0047279421000775

Latif, L. (2024). Global health governance's colour line: How finance has shaped global health disparities in African countries. *Strathmore Law Journal*, *8*(2), 1–22. DOI: 10.52907/slj.v8i2.545

Love, R. P., Hardy, B.-J., Heffernan, C., Heyd, A., Cardinal-Grant, M., Sparling, L., Healy, B., Smylie, J., & Long, R. (2022). Developing data governance agreements with Indigenous communities in Canada: Toward equitable tuberculosis programming, research, and reconciliation. *Health and Human Rights*, *24*(1), 21. PMID: 35747272

Macnaughton, G. (2016). Advancing global health and human rights in the neoliberal era. *Health and Human Rights*, *18*(2), 255.

Marko, J. G. O., Neagu, C. D., & Anand, P. B. (2025). Examining inclusivity: The use of AI and diverse populations in health and social care: A systematic review. *BMC Medical Informatics and Decision Making*, *25*(1), 57. Advance online publication. DOI: 10.1186/s12911-025-02884-1 PMID: 39910518

McCoy, D., Kapilashrami, A., Kumar, R., Rhule, E., & Khosla, R. (2024). Developing an agenda for the decolonization of global health. *Bulletin of the World Health Organization*, *102*(2), 130–136. DOI: 10.2471/BLT.23.289949 PMID: 38313156

McMillan, K. D. (2024, November 14). How patients are hacking healthcare with open source technology. Digital Health Insights. https://dhinsights.org/news/how-patients-are-hacking-healthcare-with-open-source-technology

Mediavilla, J., & Garcia-Arias, J. (2019). Philanthrocapitalism as a neoliberal (development agenda) artefact: Philanthropic discourse and hegemony in (financing for) international development. *Globalizations*, *16*(6), 857–875. DOI: 10.1080/14747731.2018.1560187

Mendoza, B. (2020). Decolonial theories in comparison. *Journal of World Philosophies*, *5*(1), 43–60.

Mohammed-Rajput, N. A., Smith, D. C., Mamlin, B., Biondich, P., & Doebbeling, B. N. (2011). OpenMRS, a global medical records system collaborative: Factors influencing successful implementation. *AMIA ... Annual Symposium Proceedings - AMIA Symposium. AMIA Symposium*, *2011*, 960. PMID: 22195155

Mulumba, M., Ruano, A. L., Perehudoff, K., & Ooms, G. (2021). *Decolonizing health governance: A Uganda case study on the influence of political history on community participation*. Health and Human Rights Journal.

Ndembi, N., Rammer, B., Fokam, J., Dinodia, U., Tessema, S. K., Nsengimana, J. P., Mwangi, S., Adzogenu, E., Dongmo, L. T., Rees, B., O'Connor, B., Crowell, T. A., Wilmot, J., Colizzi, V., Ngongo, N., & Kaseya, J. (2025). Integrating artificial intelligence into African health systems and emergency response: Need for an ethical framework and guidelines. *Journal of Public Health in Africa*, *16*(1). Advance online publication. DOI: 10.4102/jphia.v16i1.876 PMID: 40182750

Norori, N., Hu, Q., Aellen, F. M., Faraci, F. D., & Tzovara, A. (2021). Addressing bias in big data and AI for health care: A call for open science. *Patterns (New York, N.Y.)*, *2*(10), 100347. Advance online publication. DOI: 10.1016/j.patter.2021.100347 PMID: 34693373

O'Hare, B. A.-M. (2019). International corporate tax avoidance and domestic government health expenditure. *Bulletin of the World Health Organization, 97*(11), 746–753. DOI: 10.2471/BLT.18.220897 PMID: 31673190

Obermeyer, Z., Powers, B., Vogeli, C., & Mullainathan, S. (2019). Dissecting racial bias in an algorithm used to manage the health of populations. *Science, 366*(6464), 447–453. DOI: 10.1126/science.aax2342 PMID: 31649194

Obrist, B., Dillip, A., Kalolo, A., Mayumana, I. M., Rutishauser, M., & Simon, V. T. (2022). Savings groups for social health protection: A social resilience study in rural Tanzania. *Diseases (Basel, Switzerland), 10*(3), 63. Advance online publication. DOI: 10.3390/diseases10030063 PMID: 36135219

OECD. (2018). *Private philanthropy for development.* OECD Publishing.

Ortega, B., Sanjuán, J., & Casquero, A. (2020). Illicit financial flows and the provision of child and maternal health services in low- and middle-income countries. *BMC International Health and Human Rights, 20*(1), 15. Advance online publication. DOI: 10.1186/s12914-020-00236-w PMID: 32653039

Oxfam. (2009). Blind optimism: Challenging the myths about private health care in poor countries (Oxfam Briefing Paper).

Perehudoff, K., 't Hoen, E., & Boulet, P. (2021). Overriding drug and medical technology patents for pandemic recovery: A legitimate move for high-income countries, too. *BMJ Global Health, 6*(4), e005518. Advance online publication. DOI: 10.1136/bmjgh-2021-005518 PMID: 33827793

Petretto, D. R., Carrogu, G. P., Gaviano, L., Berti, R., Pinna, M., Petretto, A. D., & Pili, R. (2024). Telemedicine, e-health, and digital health equity: A scoping review. *Clinical Practice and Epidemiology in Mental Health, 20*(1), e17450179279732. DOI: 10.2174/0117450179279732231211110248 PMID: 38660571

Ratner, L., Sridhar, S., Rosman, S. L., Junior, J., Gyan-Kesse, L., Edwards, J., & Russ, C. M. (2022). Learner milestones to guide decolonial global health education. *Annals of Global Health, 88*(1), 99. Advance online publication. DOI: 10.5334/aogh.3866 PMID: 36380745

Rodríguez, D. T. G. (2024). Solidarity economy and public health for sustainable development and community well-being. *Cooperativismo & Desarrollo, 32*(128), 1–15. DOI: 10.16925/2382-4220.2024.01.02

Romero, M. J., & Ravenscroft, J. (2022). *History repeated II: Why public-private partnerships are not the solution.* EURODAD.

Seidl, T. (2023). Investing in the knowledge economy: The comparative political economy of public investments in knowledge-based capital. *European Journal of Political Research, 62*(3), 924–944. DOI: 10.1111/1475-6765.12546

Sekalala, S., & Chatikobo, T. (2024). Colonialism in the new digital health agenda. *BMJ Global Health, 9*(2), e014131. Advance online publication. DOI: 10.1136/bmjgh-2023-014131 PMID: 38413105

Stein, F., & Sridhar, D. (2018). *The financialisation of global health.* University of Edinburgh. DOI: 10.12688/wellcomeopenres.13885.1

Taslakian, E. N., Garber, K., & Shekherdimian, S. (2021). Diaspora engagement: A scoping review of diaspora involvement with strengthening health systems of their origin country. *Global Health Action, 15*(1), 2009165. Advance online publication. DOI: 10.1080/16549716.2021.2009165 PMID: 34904934

Thakkar, V. (2024, March 12). Modernising traditional maternal care in Guatemala. Think Global Health. https://www.thinkglobalhealth.org/article/modernizing-traditional-maternal-care-guatemala

Thomson, M., Kentikelenis, A., & Stubbs, T. (2017). Structural adjustment programmes adversely affect vulnerable populations: A systematic-narrative review of their effect on child and maternal health. *Public Health Reviews, 38*(1), 13. Advance online publication. DOI: 10.1186/s40985-017-0059-2 PMID: 29450085

Ullah, A. K. M., & Chattoraj, D. (2025). Traveling across global divides: Freedom or barriers to move? *World Affairs, 188*(1), e12062. Advance online publication. DOI: 10.1002/waf2.12062

Urias, E., & Ramani, S. V. (2020). Access to medicines after TRIPS: Is compulsory licensing an effective mechanism to lower drug prices? A review of the existing evidence. *Journal of International Business Policy, 3*(4), 367–384. Advance online publication. DOI: 10.1057/s42214-020-00068-4

Usmani, M. T. (2002). *An introduction to Islamic finance*. Kluwer Law International.

Wen, D., Khan, S. M., Xu, A. J., Ibrahim, H., Smith, L., Caballero, J., Zepeda, L., de Blas Perez, C., Denniston, A. K., Liu, X., & Matin, R. N. (2022). Characteristics of publicly available skin cancer image datasets: A systematic review. *The Lancet. Digital Health, 4*(1), e64–e74. DOI: 10.1016/S2589-7500(21)00252-1 PMID: 34772649

Wispelwey, B., Osuagwu, C., Mills, D., Goronga, T., & Morse, M. (2023). Towards a bidirectional decoloniality in academic global health: Insights from settler colonialism and racial capitalism. *The Lancet. Global Health, 11*(9), e1469–e1474. DOI: 10.1016/S2214-109X(23)00307-8 PMID: 37591594

World Bank. (1980). Health sector policy paper.

World Bank. (2019, April 8). Record high remittances sent globally in 2018. https://www.worldbank.org/en/news/press-release/2019/04/08/record-high-remittances-sent-globally-in-2018

World Bank. (2020). World Bank COVID-19 response. https://www.worldbank.org/en/news/factsheet/2020/10/14/world-bank-covid-19-response

World Health Organization. (1978). Declaration of Alma-Ata.

World Health Organization. (2025, April 4). Current health expenditure (% of GDP). https://data.worldbank.org/indicator/SH.XPD.CHEX.GD.ZS

Writer, A. S. (2025, April 29). Implementing white-box AI for enhanced transparency in enterprise systems. AiThority. https://aithority.com/machine-learning/implementing-white-box-ai-for-enhanced-transparency-in-enterprise-systems/

Yates, R. (2009). Universal health care and the removal of user fees. *Lancet*, *373*(9680), 2078–2081. DOI: 10.1016/S0140-6736(09)60258-0 PMID: 19362359

Yeung, A. W. K., Torkamani, A., Butte, A. J., Glicksberg, B. S., Schuller, B., Rodriguez, B., Ting, D. S. W., Bates, D., Schaden, E., Peng, H., Willschke, H., van der Laak, J., Car, J., Rahimi, K., Celi, L. A., Banach, M., Kletecka-Pulker, M., Kimberger, O., Eils, R., & Atanasov, A. G. (2023). The promise of digital healthcare technologies. *Frontiers in Public Health*, *11*, 1196596. Advance online publication. DOI: 10.3389/fpubh.2023.1196596 PMID: 37822534

Zadey, S., & Sharma, D. (2025). From decolonizing global health to neo-colonization by local elites: From the frying pan into the fire. *PLOS Global Public Health*, *5*(2), e0004196. Advance online publication. DOI: 10.1371/journal.pgph.0004196 PMID: 39908326

Zajko, M. (2022). Artificial intelligence, algorithms, and social inequality: Sociological contributions to contemporary debates. *Sociology Compass*, *16*(3), e12962. Advance online publication. DOI: 10.1111/soc4.12962

Chapter 4
Perspectives on Digital Health and Financial Inclusion in Africa:
Exploring Controversies, Barriers, and Challenges in Achieving Universal Health Coverage by 2030

Samson Oboche Agbo
http://orcid.org/0009-0007-1660-3139
Sam-Divine Health Vanguard International CIC, UK

ABSTRACT

Achieving Universal Health Coverage (UHC) by 2030 remains a major challenge for African LMICs due to fragmented health systems, high disease burdens, and persistent inequalities. Digital health and financial inclusion tools—like mobile money and blockchain—are emerging as transformative solutions to bridge healthcare gaps by enhancing transparency, access, and financing. However, barriers such as technological limitations, data privacy concerns, political interference, weak regulation, and socio-economic disparities persist. This chapter explores these challenges through case studies from Nigeria, South Africa, Rwanda, Ethiopia, Niger, Benin, and South Sudan. It presents actionable insights and policy recommendations, emphasizing the need for stronger primary healthcare systems, public-private partnerships, regulatory harmonization, and context-specific financial innovations to advance sustainable and equitable health coverage in Africa.

DOI: 10.4018/979-8-3373-3341-0.ch004

INTRODUCTION

UHC is widely understood as a commitment that all people should receive the quality health services they need without being exposed to financial hardship. For African LMICs, the UHC agenda is inseparable from broader questions of state capacity, fiscal space, social protection, health workforce development, and equity. Many countries have made policy commitments to UHC, yet implementation remains uneven because service delivery platforms are often fragmented, underfinanced, and heavily dependent on external support. The challenge is particularly acute in rural, peri-urban, fragile, and conflict-affected settings where communities face long distances to facilities, limited transport, recurrent stock-outs, shortage of skilled personnel, and high direct payments at the point of care.

Digital health and financial inclusion are increasingly promoted as tools for addressing some of these constraints. Digital health can support service delivery, surveillance, health information systems, supply chain management, client follow-up, decision support, and remote consultation. Financial inclusion can expand access to savings, payments, insurance, remittances, and other mechanisms that reduce the transaction costs of seeking care and contributing to pooled financing arrangements. When linked to primary health care, these tools may improve responsiveness, accountability, and continuity of care.

However, a critical distinction is needed between technological possibility and health-system transformation. Digital platforms do not compensate for absent health workers, weak governance, inadequate medicines, or unaffordable care. Similarly, mobile money and insurance platforms may improve payment channels without resolving the deeper problem of insufficient pooling and inequitable benefit design. The value of digital health and financial inclusion therefore depends on how they are governed, financed, regulated, and integrated into national health strategies.

This chapter examines the controversies, barriers, and practical challenges associated with digital health and financial inclusion in Africa, with emphasis on implications for achieving UHC by 2030. It draws on published literature, policy experience, and comparative country examples to identify conditions under which these innovations can contribute to stronger and more equitable health systems. The analysis focuses on three linked questions: how digital technologies can strengthen service delivery and accountability; how financial inclusion can improve financial protection; and how governments can move from donor-dependent pilots to sustainable, nationally owned implementation.

BACKGROUND AND CONCEPTUAL CONTEXT

Digital health refers to the systematic use of information and communication technologies to improve health outcomes, service delivery, public health management, and health system performance. It includes mobile health applications, telemedicine, electronic medical records, digital community health information systems, health management information systems, digital supply chain tools, remote learning platforms, artificial intelligence, and digitally enabled logistics. In African LMICs, these tools are most valuable when they respond to clearly defined service delivery problems such as missed appointments, delayed referrals, stock-outs, weak supervision, disease surveillance gaps, or limited access to specialist advice.

Financial inclusion refers to affordable, timely, and equitable access to useful financial services, including savings, payments, credit, insurance, and digital transactions. In health systems, financial inclusion matters because access to money, payment channels, and insurance-like arrangements affects when and how households seek care. Mobile money can reduce travel and transaction costs, support premium collection for insurance schemes, facilitate provider payments, and improve transparency in resource flows. It can also help households smooth consumption in the face of illness-related shocks, although it cannot by itself replace public financing or robust financial risk protection.

The relationship between digital health, financial inclusion, and UHC is therefore both promising and contested. Digital tools can improve information flows, expand reach, and reduce administrative inefficiencies. Financial technologies can make prepayment and claims processing easier. Yet implementation frequently encounters weak connectivity, unreliable electricity, low literacy, underdeveloped data governance, limited trust, fragmented donor platforms, and insufficient domestic financing. These constraints are not peripheral; they determine whether innovations become scalable public goods or remain short-lived projects.

An equity lens is essential. Digital systems may preferentially benefit urban, educated, wealthier, and formally employed populations unless deliberate safeguards are built in. Women, adolescents, persons with disabilities, older people, pastoralist communities, internally displaced populations, refugees, and residents of insecure or remote locations may be excluded by cost, literacy, identification requirements, distance, language, gender norms, or lack of mobile ownership. The pursuit of UHC therefore requires inclusive design, community engagement, affordability safeguards, offline options, and accountability mechanisms that ensure technologies serve public health goals.

PRACTICES AND EXPERIENCES IN SELECTED AFRICAN COUNTRIES

Country experience across Africa demonstrates that the adoption of digital health and financial inclusion is shaped by political leadership, institutional capacity, market readiness, and the strength of primary health care. Rwanda is frequently cited for combining strong government stewardship with community-based health insurance and technology-enabled logistics, including drone delivery of medical products. Its experience shows that innovation is more likely to scale when it is aligned with national policy, linked to service delivery priorities, and supported by a clear accountability framework.

Kenya illustrates the power of mobile money ecosystems for health-related payments and financial inclusion. M-PESA and related health financing platforms have shown how digital payment infrastructure can support savings, remittances, provider payments, and insurance-linked contributions. Nevertheless, Kenya also shows that platform growth does not automatically solve fiscal fragmentation, inequitable pooling, or quality-of-care gaps. Integration with public financing and regulatory oversight remains critical.

Nigeria has a vibrant digital innovation ecosystem, including telemedicine providers, electronic medical record platforms, health payment solutions, and private-sector investment in health technology. However, the scale-up of these innovations is constrained by uneven infrastructure, fragmented governance across federal and state levels, low insurance coverage, high out-of-pocket spending, and variable regulatory capacity. Nigeria's experience highlights the gap that can emerge between private innovation and public system readiness.

South Africa has relatively advanced digital infrastructure and experience with electronic records, mobile health programmes, and disease surveillance platforms. Yet the country's dual health system continues to generate significant inequities between people served by the public sector and those accessing private care. Digital innovation in such a context must be explicitly linked to equity and financial protection, otherwise it may deepen existing divides.

Ethiopia's Health Extension Program provides a strong community-facing platform that can support digital tools such as electronic community health information systems and digitally enabled supervision. Its experience suggests that digital transformation may be more feasible where there is an established primary health care platform. However, internet penetration, workforce capacity, financing, and political stability remain important constraints.

Niger, Benin, and South Sudan represent more fragile or resource-constrained contexts where digital health and financial inclusion require phased implementation. In these settings, foundational investments in electricity, connectivity, data systems, security, health workforce support, and governance are prerequisites for scale. Donor-supported pilots may be useful, but only when they include transition plans, government ownership, interoperability, and realistic recurrent cost projections.

MAIN FOCUS OF THE CHAPTER

This chapter examines the interaction between digital health, financial inclusion, and Universal Health Coverage (UHC) within African health systems. It argues that digital and financial innovations can contribute meaningfully to UHC only when they are embedded within broader health system reforms rather than treated as stand-alone technical solutions. The chapter therefore considers how innovation can improve access, efficiency, accountability, transparency, resource tracking, service continuity, and financial protection, while also examining the risks associated with donor-driven pilots, weak domestic ownership, fragmented regulation, commercial capture, exclusion of poor and rural populations, and widening digital divides.

The analysis draws on country experiences from Nigeria, South Africa, Rwanda, Ethiopia, Kenya, Niger, Benin, and South Sudan. These countries represent different combinations of political commitment, fiscal capacity, health-system maturity, digital readiness, regulatory strength, and fragility. Rwanda and Kenya provide useful examples of relatively stronger alignment between political leadership, innovation, and health financing reforms. Nigeria and South Africa demonstrate the opportunities and limitations of large markets, private-sector innovation, and uneven public-sector coordination. Ethiopia illustrates the importance of primary health care foundations, while South Sudan, Niger, and Benin highlight the constraints faced by fragile or resource-limited settings where infrastructure, governance, and financing systems remain weak.

The literature consistently identifies substantial challenges across African low- and middle-income countries (LMICs). These include inadequate health infrastructure, insufficient public financing, weak governance, poor public financial management, limited regulatory capacity, and persistent inequities in access to quality services (Agbo, 2024; Barroy et al., 2021; Dieleman et al., 2018). High out-of-pocket payments remain a major barrier to equitable access and expose households to catastrophic health spending, particularly among poor, rural, informal-sector, and marginalized populations (Aregbeshola & Khan, 2021; Wagstaff et al., 2018). These findings underline the need for stronger financial risk protection, expanded prepayment mechanisms, and more inclusive health insurance arrangements.

Sustainable health financing remains constrained by limited domestic fiscal space, low prioritization of health in national budgets, inefficient allocation of available resources, and continued reliance on donor assistance (Bloom, Kuhn, &

Prettner, 2018; Hogan et al., 2018; World Bank, 2022). The literature suggests that strategic domestic resource mobilization, improved budget execution, stronger public financial management, blended finance, health bonds, earmarked health levies, and well-regulated public-private partnerships can contribute to closing financing gaps where they are aligned with national health priorities (World Economic Forum, 2021; Xu, Soucat, & Kutzin, 2019). However, these mechanisms should complement, not replace, tax-funded public services and progressive public financing.

Digital health technologies, including mobile health, telemedicine, electronic health records, blockchain-enabled systems, digital identification, artificial intelligence, and drone-supported medical logistics, offer important opportunities to improve health system performance. They can support patient tracking, remote consultations, commodity distribution, financial transactions, claims processing, disease surveillance, and health worker supervision (Adepoju, 2018; Bloom, Berdou et al., 2022; He, Guizani, & Zhang, 2020; Lee & Kim, 2021; UNICEF, 2020). Kenya's M-PESA experience demonstrates how mobile money can reduce transaction costs, improve financial inclusion, strengthen household resilience, and support women's economic participation (Hughes & Lonie, 2007; Jack & Suri, 2014; Suri & Jack, 2016). Similarly, Rwanda's use of community-based health insurance and drone-supported logistics illustrates how political leadership, regulation, and public-private collaboration can support innovation at scale.

However, the evidence also cautions against technological optimism. Digital tools may improve efficiency, but they can also reproduce or deepen inequities when implemented in settings with weak connectivity, low digital literacy, high poverty, limited electricity, and poor regulatory protection. Widespread adoption is constrained by infrastructure deficits, fragmented governance, weak interoperability, limited data protection, privacy concerns, and inconsistent institutional capacity (Dandonoli, 2022; GSMA, 2021; Mphahlele & Mash, 2019; Wang, Yuan, & Li, 2021). In poorly regulated contexts, digital systems may expose citizens to surveillance, misuse of personal data, commercial exploitation, exclusion from services, or dependence on external vendors and proprietary platforms.

Governance emerges as a decisive factor in determining whether digital health and financial inclusion contribute to UHC. Clear policy direction, regulatory coherence, political leadership, domestic ownership, and institutional accountability are critical for successful implementation and scale-up. Rwanda's experience with community-based health insurance illustrates the importance of sustained government leadership, coherent policy frameworks, and administrative capacity (Chemouni, 2018; Meessen et al., 2019; Whyle & Olivier, 2020). By contrast, governance weaknesses, poor coordination, weak accountability, and limited political commitment can undermine financial protection, digital transformation, and service delivery in countries such as Nigeria, Ethiopia, and Tanzania (Agbo, 2024; Onwujekwe, Hanson, & Uzochukwu, 2019).

The chapter also considers the changing burden of disease in Africa. Non-communicable diseases (NCDs), including diabetes, hypertension, cardiovascular disease, cancer, and chronic respiratory conditions, are increasing alongside persistent communicable diseases, maternal and child health challenges, malnutrition, and recurrent outbreaks. This double burden requires stronger primary health care, long-term financing for chronic disease management, reliable supply chains, trained health workers, and digital systems that support continuity of care (Atun et al., 2017; Gouda et al., 2019; Institute for Health Metrics and Evaluation, 2021). High youth unemployment further complicates health financing because many young people work in informal or unstable employment and cannot reliably contribute to conventional insurance schemes (ILO, 2020). This makes social protection, subsidized enrolment, employment-linked contributions, and youth-sensitive financial inclusion strategies essential.

Primary health care strengthening is therefore central to the chapter's argument. Digital platforms, insurance schemes, and innovative financing instruments will have limited impact if frontline services remain unavailable, unaffordable, understaffed, poorly supervised, or geographically inaccessible. Investments in PHC infrastructure, community health systems, health workforce capacity, essential medicines, digital reporting, referral systems, and local accountability are foundational to achieving UHC (Assefa et al., 2019; WHO, 2019; WHO, 2023). Digital health should support these priorities by improving service delivery and decision-making, not by creating parallel systems.

A further theme is donor dependency. External assistance has played an important role in financing health services, digital pilots, and innovation across Africa, especially in fragile and conflict-affected settings. However, prolonged reliance on externally designed and externally funded interventions can distort national priorities, weaken domestic accountability, fragment information systems, and create sustainability risks when funding cycles end. A credible pathway to UHC requires a shift from donor-led pilots to country-owned, budgeted, regulated, and interoperable systems.

The chapter concludes that digital health and financial inclusion should be understood as enabling instruments within a broader political, institutional, and financing agenda for UHC. Their value depends on whether they strengthen primary health care, reduce financial hardship, protect data rights, support accountable resource use, and expand access for underserved communities. Community-based insurance, prepaid health packages, health levies, health impact bonds, remittance-linked financing, Zakat, Waqf, and blended public-private financing may all have a role, but only when they are equity-centred, transparently governed, locally owned, and aligned with national health strategies.

SUMMARY OF KEY FINDINGS FROM THE LITERATURE

The literature identifies persistent health system constraints across African LMICs, including inadequate infrastructure, insufficient public financing, weak governance, inefficient public financial management, and shortage of skilled health workers. These constraints reduce service quality and weaken the ability of digital innovations to produce sustained improvements. High out-of-pocket expenditure remains a major barrier to access and continues to expose households to catastrophic spending and impoverishment.

Evidence on digital health indicates strong potential for improving access, timeliness, and transparency. Mobile health can support reminders, health education, community reporting, and follow-up. Telemedicine can extend specialist advice to underserved locations. Electronic health records and community information systems can improve continuity of care and decision-making. Drones and digitally enabled logistics can shorten delivery times for critical commodities. However, the literature also cautions that digital health interventions often fail to scale when they are not aligned with national strategies, interoperable standards, workforce capacity, and recurrent financing.

Financial inclusion literature highlights the role of mobile money and digital payment systems in reducing transaction costs, facilitating risk-sharing, and enabling more convenient contributions to insurance or prepayment schemes. Kenya's mobile money experience is frequently used as an example of how financial technology can reach populations previously excluded from formal banking. Yet financial inclusion does not guarantee financial protection. UHC requires pooling, subsidies for the poor, benefit package design, purchasing arrangements, and mechanisms to prevent informal or excessive direct payments.

Governance consistently emerges as a decisive factor. Countries with clearer policy direction, stronger stewardship, and better coordination are more likely to translate innovations into system-level benefits. Weak regulation, political interference, fragmented donor platforms, inadequate data protection, and limited community trust undermine implementation. The literature therefore supports a balanced approach that combines innovation with public accountability, equity safeguards, and institutional strengthening.

A further finding is that Africa's changing disease burden requires stronger long-term financing and service delivery models. Non-communicable diseases, injuries, mental health conditions, and chronic infections require continuity of care and financial protection beyond episodic service delivery. Digital tools can support monitoring and adherence, but the underlying financing architecture must protect households from prolonged and repeated costs.

ISSUES, CONTROVERSIES, AND PROBLEMS

Limited adoption and adaptation of digital health and innovative financing

The adoption and adaptation of digital health and innovative financing in African low- and middle-income countries remain uneven, politically contested, and institutionally demanding. Although digital platforms, mobile money, telemedicine, electronic health records, artificial intelligence, blockchain, drone logistics, and digital insurance systems are often presented as transformative tools for accelerating Universal Health Coverage (UHC), their practical value depends on the maturity of the health system into which they are introduced. In many African settings, digital health and financial inclusion are being promoted in contexts marked by weak infrastructure, limited fiscal space, fragile institutions, poor public financial management, health workforce shortages, donor dependency, high out-of-pocket spending, and low public trust. These conditions do not make innovation impossible, but they require careful adaptation, strong governance, realistic sequencing, and sustained domestic ownership.

A central barrier is the limited adoption and adaptation of digital health and innovative financing at scale. Many digital health initiatives remain small pilots, concentrated in urban areas, donor-supported projects, or specific disease programmes. They often demonstrate promise during implementation but fail to become routine parts of national health systems. Several factors explain this pattern. Poor connectivity, unreliable electricity, high data costs, low smartphone ownership, limited device maintenance, and weak digital infrastructure reduce the reach and reliability of digital platforms. These barriers are especially severe in rural, remote, borderland, pastoralist, informal settlement, and conflict-affected areas where health needs are often greatest. In such contexts, digital platforms may unintentionally privilege populations already connected to electricity, mobile networks, banking services, and formal health facilities, thereby widening rather than narrowing inequities.

Affordability is another important constraint. Digital health systems may appear cost-effective from a policy perspective, but users often bear hidden costs. These include mobile data charges, transport costs to facilities where digital systems are used, device replacement costs, user fees, transaction fees, and time lost navigating complex platforms. For poor households, unemployed youth, women in informal work, older persons, and people living with chronic disease or disability, even small payments can discourage use. Health workers may also face personal costs when they are expected to use their own phones, data, airtime, or electricity for work-related reporting and communication. Unless these costs are recognized and financed, digital health systems may increase workload without improving motivation or service quality.

Digital literacy also shapes adoption. Many health workers and community members have limited experience with digital applications, online forms, dashboards, remote consultation tools, biometric systems, or mobile payment platforms. When new technologies are introduced without structured training, mentoring, supportive supervision, help desks, user manuals, and feedback loops, users may avoid them, misuse them, or perceive them as punitive reporting tools rather than instruments for improving care. In some cases, digital systems are designed around donor reporting requirements or central-level information needs, with insufficient attention to the daily realities of frontline workers. Platforms that are not user-centred, available in local languages, compatible with low-bandwidth environments, or aligned with existing workflows are unlikely to be sustained.

Weak regulatory and policy environments

The weakness of regulatory and policy environments adds further controversy. Digital health platforms collect, store, transmit, and analyze sensitive personal, clinical, financial, and geolocation data. Yet many countries still have incomplete, outdated, fragmented, or inconsistently enforced rules on data privacy, cybersecurity, consent, interoperability, data ownership, data sharing, cross-border data flows, procurement standards, and accountability for digital harm. Inadequate regulation exposes citizens to misuse of information, unauthorized data sharing, surveillance, discrimination, commercial exploitation, and loss of trust. Conversely, overly restrictive, politically influenced, or unclear regulation can delay innovation, discourage private investment, and create uncertainty for implementers. The challenge is not simply to regulate more, but to regulate better. African LMICs require balanced frameworks that protect rights, enable innovation, define public interest obligations, and set clear standards for ethical use, interoperability, affordability, and accountability.

Regulatory fragmentation also affects scale. Ministries of health, information and communication technology, finance, telecommunications authorities, insurance regulators, data protection agencies, local governments, donors, and private providers may all influence digital health and financial inclusion policies. Where coordination is weak, countries may experience overlapping mandates, inconsistent standards, duplicated platforms, parallel reporting systems, and incompatible databases. This fragmentation increases costs, reduces efficiency, and limits the capacity to build national digital public infrastructure for health. Strong national digital health strategies should therefore be linked to health financing strategies, public financial management reforms, social protection systems, identification systems, and primary health care strengthening.

Transparency, accountability, and political economy

Transparency and accountability represent both an opportunity and a source of political resistance. Digital systems can make health system performance more visible by tracking resource flows, medicine stock-outs, absenteeism, service gaps, referral delays, insurance claims, facility outputs, and patient outcomes. This visibility can strengthen accountability, improve planning, reduce leakage, and support evidence-informed decision-making. However, transparency can also threaten entrenched interests. Where weak performance, corruption, underfunding, absenteeism, or poor quality of care are exposed, officials and institutions may resist implementation or manipulate data. In fragile settings, public exposure of systemic weaknesses may deepen mistrust if communities see evidence of failure without credible corrective action. Digital accountability must therefore be accompanied by response capacity, communication strategies, community engagement, grievance redress mechanisms, and political commitment to act on the data generated.

The political economy of digital health is often underestimated. Technology is never neutral in health systems. It redistributes information, power, visibility, resources, and accountability. A digital claims platform may reveal fraud. A stock management system may expose procurement failures. A human resource information system may reveal ghost workers or absenteeism. A geospatial dashboard may show inequitable distribution of facilities, staff, or commodities. These revelations are useful for reform but may generate resistance from actors who benefit from opacity. Successful digital transformation requires leadership that can manage these tensions, protect reform processes, and align innovation with public value rather than narrow political or commercial interests.

Human resource capacity and incentives

Human resource capacity is another decisive factor. Health workers are central to digital transformation, yet many digital programmes treat them mainly as data collectors or platform users rather than as professionals whose workload, incentives, safety, skills, and motivation determine success. In many LMIC settings, health workers face irregular salaries, inadequate incentives, poor supervision, shortages of equipment, weak transport, insecurity, burnout, and limited career progression. Introducing digital platforms into such conditions may increase frustration if the technology adds reporting tasks without reducing workload, improving decision-making, enhancing patient care, or strengthening working conditions. Digital health strategies must therefore be linked to workforce planning, pre-service and in-service training, supportive supervision, reliable remuneration, task-sharing, and continuous professional development.

Community health workers and informal providers require particular attention. They are often closest to underserved populations and are critical for health promotion, disease surveillance, maternal and child health, immunization, referrals, chronic disease follow-up, and household registration. Digital tools can strengthen their work through family folders, decision-support applications, referral tracking, SMS reminders, commodity reporting, and supervision dashboards. However, if community health workers are unpaid, poorly supervised, unsupported, or not formally integrated into national systems, digital tools may become an additional burden. The adoption of digital health at community level must therefore be accompanied by formal recognition, fair incentives, clear roles, protective equipment, transport support, and mechanisms for feedback and problem-solving.

Limited public-private investment partnerships

Public-private investment partnerships offer both promise and risk. The private sector can contribute to connectivity, renewable energy, diagnostics, telemedicine, logistics, health insurance administration, claims processing, payment systems, electronic medical records, and digital innovation. In countries such as Rwanda and Kenya, structured collaboration with private or social enterprise actors has supported drone logistics, mobile money, and digital service delivery. However, poorly governed partnerships may lead to high user fees, vendor lock-in, weak data protection, inequitable access, limited public oversight, and dependence on proprietary platforms. Public-private partnerships should therefore be structured around public health objectives rather than technology procurement alone. They require transparent contracting, competitive procurement, affordability safeguards, performance indicators, data governance clauses, quality standards, interoperability requirements, and mechanisms for public accountability.

Privatization, public ownership, and hybrid delivery models

The relationship between privatization, public ownership, and hybrid delivery models is also contested. Private investment may improve efficiency, infrastructure, responsiveness, and service availability, particularly in diagnostics, specialist care, supply chains, hospital management, telemedicine, and digital platforms. However, unregulated privatization can deepen inequity when access depends on ability to pay. In countries with high out-of-pocket payments and weak financial protection, private-sector growth may expand services for wealthier populations while leaving the poor dependent on underfunded public facilities. It may also contribute to medical tourism, where domestic resources are spent abroad because local tertiary care capacity remains weak. This drains resources that could otherwise support national infrastructure, workforce development, and specialized services.

At the same time, fully public systems in resource-constrained settings often face chronic underfunding, weak management capacity, inefficient procurement, poor maintenance, and limited accountability. The issue is therefore not whether public or private systems are inherently superior, but how service delivery can be governed to protect equity, quality, affordability, and sustainability. Hybrid models may offer a pragmatic pathway where services are publicly financed but independently managed, or where private providers deliver contracted services under strong public regulation. Such models must be designed carefully. They should include explicit service packages, regulated tariffs, quality benchmarks, referral obligations, financial protection mechanisms, data reporting requirements, and penalties for exclusionary practices.

Donor dependency and Official Development Assistance

Donor dependency and Official Development Assistance remain major features of the African health financing landscape. External financing has contributed significantly to immunization, HIV, tuberculosis, malaria, reproductive health, disease surveillance, emergency response, health information systems, and digital innovation. In fragile and conflict-affected settings, donor support may be essential for maintaining basic services. However, excessive or prolonged reliance on donor funding can weaken national ownership, distort priorities, and create fragmented systems. Donor-driven pilots may operate outside government planning, use separate reporting platforms, pay incentives that cannot be sustained, or procure technologies without recurrent cost plans. When funding cycles end, platforms may collapse, remain underused, or be replaced by new donor-funded systems.

The sustainability problem is particularly visible in digital health. Many countries have experienced repeated cycles of pilot projects that produce useful short-term outputs but do not become institutionalized. The reasons include lack of domestic budget lines, unclear ownership, weak integration with national health information systems, inadequate maintenance financing, dependence on external vendors, and limited government capacity to manage contracts and data systems. A credible pathway to UHC requires a shift from project-based innovation to country-owned, budgeted, regulated, interoperable, and institutionally supported systems. External partners should align with national strategies, use government platforms where feasible, support capacity transfer, and include transition plans from the beginning.

High out-of-pocket expenditure and weak financial risk protection

High out-of-pocket expenditure remains one of the most visible and damaging barriers to UHC. When households must pay directly at the point of care, they may delay seeking treatment, abandon treatment, sell assets, borrow money, or fall into poverty. High out-of-pocket payments are particularly harmful for women, children, older persons, people with disabilities, people living with chronic disease, and households in informal employment. They also undermine early diagnosis and continuity of care for non-communicable diseases, which require long-term treatment, regular monitoring, medicines, and follow-up. Digital financial inclusion can improve payment convenience, claims processing, savings, enrolment, and transparency, but it cannot substitute for public subsidies and progressive financing.

Insurance and prepayment schemes are essential but difficult to design in economies with high unemployment, large informal sectors, poverty, and limited administrative capacity. Youth unemployment and informal work complicate contribution collection because many people have irregular incomes and cannot make predictable monthly payments. Community-based health insurance, prepaid health packages, health savings accounts, mobile-based contributions, remittance-linked health financing, Zakat, Waqf, health levies, and blended financing may all contribute to financial protection where contextually appropriate. However, these mechanisms must be designed as complements to tax-funded public services, not substitutes for government responsibility. The poorest populations require subsidies, exemptions, or publicly financed coverage. Without progressive financing, digital payment systems may merely make it easier to collect payments from people who are already financially vulnerable.

Equity must remain the central test of digital health and innovative financing. A digital system that improves efficiency for urban hospitals but excludes rural communities does not advance UHC. A mobile insurance platform that reaches formal workers but excludes informal women traders, unemployed youth, pastoralists, refugees, or persons without identification does not provide universal protection. A telemedicine system that requires smartphones, stable internet, and user fees may benefit middle-class patients while leaving poor households behind. Innovation should therefore be evaluated not only by technical performance, user numbers, or financial returns, but by its contribution to reducing inequities in access, quality, financial protection, and health outcomes.

Addressing these challenges requires integrated policy action. Countries need to strengthen primary health care, expand digital infrastructure, reduce data costs, invest in electricity and connectivity, build digital literacy, and develop interoperable national platforms. They also need to improve public financial management, establish domestic financing pathways, regulate private-sector participation, protect personal data, and create mechanisms for community accountability. Digital health should be linked to essential service delivery, not isolated from it. Innovative financing should reduce financial hardship, not increase household payment burdens. Public-private partnerships should serve public health goals, not merely expand markets. Donor support should strengthen national systems, not create parallel ones.

The overall lesson is that digital health and innovative financing are enabling instruments, not independent solutions. Their success depends on governance, financing, trust, workforce capacity, regulation, infrastructure, and equity-oriented implementation. African LMICs can use digital and financial innovations to accelerate progress toward UHC, but only if these tools are domestically owned, publicly accountable, adequately financed, and adapted to local realities. The most promising pathway is not rapid technological expansion for its own sake, but deliberate integration of digital tools and financial inclusion into stronger primary health care systems, fairer financing arrangements, and more accountable institutions. In this way, innovation can support resilience, equity, and sustainability rather than deepen fragmentation, dependency, and exclusion.

SOLUTIONS AND RECOMMENDATIONS

Strengthening primary health care

Primary health care should be the anchor for digital health and financial inclusion. Investments should prioritize frontline facilities, community health platforms, essential medicines, referral systems, supportive supervision, and routine data use. Digital tools should be selected because they solve practical PHC problems, such as missed referrals, stock reporting, maternal follow-up, immunization defaulter tracking, or chronic disease monitoring.

Expanding affordable and appropriate digital health technologies

Governments should prioritize technologies that are affordable, interoperable, low-bandwidth, and adaptable to local conditions. Offline functionality, multilingual interfaces, basic mobile phone compatibility, and simple user workflows are important in low-resource settings. Digital literacy should be included in pre-service and in-service training for health workers.

Building accountable public-private partnerships

Partnerships with telecommunications firms, technology providers, insurers, logistics companies, and renewable energy providers should be guided by transparent contracts and public-interest safeguards. Performance-based agreements can be useful where outcomes are measurable. Governments should avoid fragmented vendor arrangements and insist on interoperability, data protection, and affordability.

Enhancing financial protection

Financial inclusion should be linked to stronger pooling and purchasing. Community-based insurance, national health insurance, mobile prepayment, and targeted subsidies should be designed to protect poor and informal-sector populations. Benefit packages should prioritize essential PHC, maternal and child health, communicable disease services, chronic disease care, and referral pathways.

Reducing donor dependency through domestic financing

Domestic resource mobilization is essential for sustainability. Options include improved budget execution, progressive taxation, earmarked health levies where appropriate, efficiency gains, pooled procurement, better public financial management, remittance-linked health products, and blended financing for infrastructure. Donor funds should increasingly be used catalytically to build systems rather than maintain parallel projects.

Strengthening governance and regulation

Countries need coherent digital health policies, data protection laws, cybersecurity protocols, interoperability standards, and institutional arrangements for oversight. Regulatory frameworks should define data ownership, consent, procurement standards, platform certification, accountability, and mechanisms for redress when rights are violated.

Developing workforce capacity

Digital transformation must include investment in people. Health workers require training, mentorship, job aids, feedback loops, reliable remuneration, and logistical support. Community health workers should be formally recognized and supported where they are expected to collect data, deliver messages, or use mobile tools for service delivery.

- Place PHC strengthening at the centre of digital and financial reforms.
- Use low-cost, interoperable, and offline-capable digital tools before pursuing complex technologies.
- Align public-private partnerships with affordability, quality, equity, and data protection.
- Expand financial risk protection through pooled financing, subsidies, and mobile-enabled prepayment.
- Use donor assistance to build national systems and transition recurrent costs into domestic budgets.
- Strengthen regulation, governance, and public accountability before large-scale platform expansion.
- Invest in health worker skills, incentives, supervision, and routine data-use capacity.

Table 1. Priority Issues and Policy Responses for Selected African LMICs

Issue or controversy	Recommended policy response
Weak health infrastructure and inadequate logistics support in countries such as Nigeria, Ethiopia, South Sudan, and Niger.	Prioritize PHC infrastructure, strengthen supply chains, and use well-governed public-private partnerships for logistics, energy, diagnostics, and facility management.
Poor mobile and internet connectivity, especially in Niger, Benin, South Sudan, and rural Ethiopia.	Expand affordable connectivity, negotiate health-sector data subsidies with telecommunications firms, and use offline-compatible digital platforms.
High out-of-pocket payments, limited financial risk protection, unemployment, and youth vulnerability.	Expand pooled financing, community-based insurance, mobile prepayment, targeted subsidies, and benefit packages that protect poor and informal-sector populations.
Privacy concerns, cybersecurity risks, and inconsistent regulation.	Adopt and enforce data protection laws, cybersecurity standards, interoperability rules, and transparent governance of digital health and financial data.
Over-reliance on donor-driven initiatives and limited domestic ownership.	Prepare transition plans, integrate donor-supported platforms into national strategies, and progressively absorb recurrent costs into domestic budgets.
Limited fiscal space and weak public financial management.	Improve budget execution, reduce waste, strengthen procurement, explore progressive health levies, and use innovative finance only where it supports equity and sustainability.
Irregular salary payments, weak incentives, poor supervision, and insecurity affecting health workers.	Ensure timely remuneration, provide practical incentives and transport support, improve supervision, and protect frontline workers in fragile settings.
Public mistrust and political interference.	Strengthen transparency, independent oversight, civil society engagement, and routine public reporting on performance and resource use.

continued on following page

Table 1. Continued

Issue or controversy	Recommended policy response
Risks associated with unregulated privatization of secondary and tertiary care.	Develop hybrid models that combine public financing with regulated private or independent management under equity, quality, and affordability standards.
Medical tourism and weak domestic specialist capacity.	Invest in specialist training, technology transfer, diagnostics, referral systems, and partnerships that build domestic centres of excellence.

Note. Adapted and substantially reworked from Agbo (2025), an open-access publication distributed under the Creative Commons Attribution 4.0 International License. The table has been rewritten and expanded for this chapter.

Table 2. Risks, Mitigation Measures, and Opportunities for Digital Health in Selected African Settings

Risk	Mitigation measure	Opportunity	Country examples
Weak infrastructure and poor connectivity	Telecom partnerships, offline functionality, renewable energy, and phased infrastructure investment	Expansion of telemedicine, mobile reporting, and community-based digital follow-up	Niger, Benin, South Sudan, Ethiopia
Data privacy, cybersecurity, and regulatory inconsistency	Data governance frameworks, cybersecurity protocols, consent standards, and platform certification	Trusted digital identity, secure records, and accountable financial transactions	Nigeria, Ethiopia, South Africa
Limited affordability and financial protection	Community-based insurance, prepaid packages, subsidies, and mobile money integration	Greater access to pooled financing and reduced transaction costs	Rwanda, Kenya, Nigeria, Ghana
Insufficient health worker capacity and resistance to new platforms	Training, incentives, supportive supervision, and simplified workflows	Remote learning, e-supervision, and improved routine data quality	Ethiopia, South Sudan, Niger
Political instability and limited political commitment	Independent oversight, policy dialogue, community engagement, and implementation transparency	Digital tools for monitoring performance and accountability	South Sudan, Ethiopia, Nigeria
Donor dependency and weak local ownership	Domestic resource mobilization, transition planning, and integration into national systems	Sustainable financing and stronger country stewardship	Niger, South Sudan, Ethiopia
Socio-economic inequalities and digital divides	Subsidized access, inclusive design, digital literacy, and offline options	More equitable service delivery and financial inclusion	South Africa, Nigeria, Benin

continued on following page

Table 2. Continued

Risk	Mitigation measure	Opportunity	Country examples
Geographic barriers and insecurity	Drone logistics, mobile outreach, community-based delivery, and security-informed planning	Improved access to medicines, vaccines, diagnostics, and emergency supplies	Rwanda, Ghana, Ethiopia, South Sudan
Youth unemployment and demographic pressure	Youth-focused digital skills, health entrepreneurship, and innovation funds	Job creation and locally relevant digital health solutions	Nigeria, South Africa, Ethiopia
Unregulated private-sector expansion	PPP governance, affordability clauses, quality standards, and public reporting	Improved quality, efficiency, and innovation under public-interest safeguards	South Africa, Nigeria, Kenya

Note. Adapted and substantially reworked from Agbo (2025), with additional synthesis for IGI Global chapter publication. The content is paraphrased and reformatted to strengthen attribution and reduce textual overlap.

COMPARATIVE ANALYSIS OF HEALTH FINANCING AND TECHNOLOGICAL ADOPTION

Rwanda demonstrates how political commitment, community-based insurance, and well-structured partnerships can produce more integrated progress toward UHC. Its experience with Mutuelles de Santé and drone logistics suggests that innovation scales better when linked to national priorities and supported by implementation discipline. Remaining challenges include rural infrastructure gaps and the need to maintain affordability as expectations for service quality increase.

Nigeria presents a contrasting case. The country has significant private-sector innovation and a large market for digital health services, but fragmented governance, low insurance coverage, high out-of-pocket spending, and uneven infrastructure limit system-wide impact. Its federal structure requires state-level commitment, harmonized standards, and stronger public purchasing if digital innovation is to contribute meaningfully to UHC.

Ethiopia has built a major primary health care platform through the Health Extension Program. This provides a potential foundation for digital community health systems, but scale-up depends on workforce capacity, reliable financing, connectivity, and political stability. Digitalization should therefore proceed through practical community-level tools linked to routine service delivery and supervision.

South Africa has comparatively advanced digital and institutional capacity, yet persistent inequality limits the reach of innovation. The proposed National Health Insurance reform reflects the difficulty of aligning financing, purchasing, provider behaviour, and equity in a two-tier system. Digital health should be used to reduce, not reinforce, disparities between public and private care.

Kenya illustrates the value of a dynamic mobile money ecosystem for health financing and service access. Platforms such as M-PESA and M-TIBA demonstrate how digital finance can reduce transaction barriers and support health-related savings or payments. Continued progress requires better integration with public financing, stronger pooling, and regulatory coherence.

South Sudan and Niger show the constraints faced in fragile settings. Donor financing, humanitarian delivery, insecurity, limited infrastructure, and weak institutional capacity shape the pace and form of reform. The priority in such contexts is not rapid technological expansion but a sequenced approach that strengthens basic services, governance, data systems, and domestic ownership.

Table 3. Comparative Takeaways on Financing and Technology Adoption

Country	Financing position	Technology adoption	Enabling factor	Main barrier
Rwanda	High coverage through community-based health insurance	Relatively advanced use of drones and telemedicine	Political commitment and policy integration	Rural infrastructure and affordability pressures
Nigeria	Fragmented insurance coverage and high out-of-pocket spending	Strong private innovation ecosystem	Large market and entrepreneurial capacity	Governance fragmentation and low coverage
Ethiopia	Strong PHC platform with emerging community-based insurance	Moderate digital pilots and community information systems	Government-led primary care architecture	Connectivity, financing, and scale limitations
South Africa	Dual public-private system with pending NHI reform	Advanced digital health capacity	Institutional and technical strength	Inequity and digital exclusion
Kenya	Expanding insurance and mobile-linked financing	High mobile money integration	M-PESA ecosystem and public-private innovation	Fiscal inefficiency and fragmented pooling
South Sudan and Niger	Donor-dependent with limited domestic pooling	Limited pilots and weak infrastructure	Humanitarian support and potential for phased reform	Fragility, insecurity, and low digital readiness

Note. Adapted and substantially reworked from Agbo (2025). The table has been rewritten for originality, consistency, and clearer attribution to the open-access CC BY source.

RECOMMENDATIONS AND PRACTICALITY

The feasibility of digital health and financial inclusion reforms depends on political stability, institutional capacity, fiscal space, infrastructure, and community trust. Countries should avoid reform packages that assume uniform readiness. Fragile and low-resource settings require a narrower set of priorities, realistic timelines, and clear recurrent cost plans.

For countries with limited resources, the most practical first step is to strengthen PHC while introducing simple digital tools that solve immediate operational problems. Examples include SMS appointment reminders, USSD-based community reporting, electronic family folders, stock reporting, digital supervision checklists, and dashboards that support district-level decision-making. These tools should be tested through small pilots, evaluated, and scaled only when they demonstrate usability and value.

A national digital health steering mechanism can improve coordination across ministries of health, finance, information and communication technology, social protection, private-sector actors, civil society, and development partners. Such a mechanism should reduce duplication, enforce standards, align investments with national strategy, and ensure that donor-supported platforms do not create parallel systems.

Financial inclusion reforms should begin with practical payment and protection problems. Mobile-enabled premium collection, claims reimbursement, transport vouchers, maternal health savings, and digital subsidies can improve access when linked to a defined benefit package and public financing. Subsidies are particularly important for poor households, informal workers, women, adolescents, people with disabilities, and communities affected by displacement or insecurity.

- Start with PHC-linked digital tools that operate in low-bandwidth settings.
- Establish a digital health steering committee with clear decision rights and accountability.
- Use open-source and interoperable platforms where feasible to reduce vendor lock-in.
- Integrate mobile money into insurance, claims, and subsidy systems with strong financial oversight.
- Map existing infrastructure, workforce, service coverage, and financing gaps before scaling new platforms.
- Build digital literacy for frontline health workers and communities.
- Require donor-supported pilots to include transition, maintenance, and sustainability plans.

LESSONS LEARNED

1. Context matters. Digital health and financial inclusion models must be adapted to local infrastructure, culture, literacy, governance, and financing realities.
2. Leadership determines scale. Strong stewardship, policy coherence, and public accountability are more important than the availability of technology alone.
3. Equity must be designed in. Without subsidies, offline options, inclusive interfaces, and community engagement, digital tools may exclude the poorest and most remote populations.
4. Health workers need incentives and support. Training, supervision, remuneration, and workflow redesign are essential for adoption.
5. Partnerships require rules. Public-private collaboration can accelerate innovation, but only when contracts protect affordability, quality, data rights, and public value.
6. Financial inclusion is not the same as financial protection. Mobile payments and savings platforms must be linked to pooled financing, subsidies, and strategic purchasing.
7. Donor funding should build national systems. Sustainability improves when external support strengthens domestic institutions, budgets, and governance rather than creating stand-alone platforms.

SUGGESTED NEXT STEPS

8. Develop or update national digital health strategies that are explicitly linked to UHC, PHC, financial protection, and data governance.
9. Adopt harmonized regulatory frameworks for privacy, cybersecurity, interoperability, digital identification, procurement, and accountability.
10. Expand financial protection through nationally aligned insurance, prepayment, and subsidy mechanisms, supported by mobile money where appropriate.
11. Create public-private partnership templates that define performance indicators, affordability safeguards, data ownership, and exit provisions.
12. Invest in digital literacy, implementation management, data-use culture, and technical support for frontline workers.
13. Use research and implementation science to assess effectiveness, cost-effectiveness, equity, acceptability, and sustainability before national scale-up.
14. Shift donor assistance toward catalytic investments that help countries absorb recurrent costs and reduce dependence on parallel projects.

FUTURE RESEARCH DIRECTIONS AND EMERGING TRENDS

Several trends will shape the next phase of digital health and financial inclusion in Africa. Artificial intelligence is increasingly being explored for diagnostics, triage, risk stratification, disease forecasting, and resource allocation. Its application in LMICs requires high-quality data, ethical review, transparency, local validation, and mechanisms to prevent algorithmic bias. Early use cases should focus on narrow, clinically relevant problems where human oversight is maintained.

Blockchain is being considered for supply chain integrity, insurance claims, procurement transparency, and secure record management. Its practical use in LMICs is likely to be most appropriate in targeted, high-risk transactions rather than as a universal platform. Countries should assess costs, infrastructure requirements, governance implications, and interoperability before adoption.

Drone logistics can improve access to blood products, vaccines, diagnostics, and emergency commodities in areas where road transport is slow, insecure, or unreliable. The strongest use cases are time-sensitive deliveries, geographically isolated communities, and emergency preparedness. Sustainability will depend on airspace regulation, cost-effectiveness, local workforce capacity, and integration with existing supply chain systems.

Platform-based health ecosystems that combine digital identity, mobile money, insurance, telemedicine, and electronic records are likely to expand. These ecosystems may improve convenience and continuity of care, but they also raise concerns about data concentration, commercial incentives, exclusion, and surveillance. Research should therefore examine governance models that protect rights and maintain public value.

Youth-led innovation is an important opportunity. Africa's young population can contribute to digital health entrepreneurship, local software development, community engagement, and data science. Targeted investment in skills, mentorship, innovation hubs, and start-up financing can create employment while producing contextually relevant health solutions.

Future Research Priorities

- Comparative studies of digital health integration across countries with different levels of institutional readiness.
- Longitudinal evaluations of mobile money, insurance, and prepayment models on financial protection and service utilization.
- Operational research on drones, artificial intelligence, and electronic community health systems in fragile and rural settings.

- Governance studies on data protection, public trust, digital rights, and accountability in health platform ecosystems.
- Equity-focused implementation research on barriers faced by women, adolescents, displaced populations, older people, and people with disabilities.
- Cost-effectiveness studies that compare digital pilots with alternative investments in workforce, infrastructure, medicines, and PHC strengthening.

CONCLUSION

Digital health and financial inclusion can contribute to UHC in Africa, but only when they are integrated into the fundamentals of health system strengthening. They should improve access to quality services, reduce financial hardship, strengthen PHC, support accountable resource use, and reach populations that are otherwise excluded. Their value should be measured not by the sophistication of the technology but by their contribution to equity, continuity of care, financial protection, and institutional resilience.

The experiences reviewed in this chapter show that countries with strong stewardship, clear regulatory frameworks, and practical implementation capacity are more likely to convert innovation into sustained system gains. Countries facing fragility, insecurity, and limited fiscal space require phased approaches that begin with basic infrastructure, workforce support, low-cost digital tools, and national ownership. Donor funding and private investment can play constructive roles, but they must be governed by public priorities and sustainability plans.

By 2030, progress toward UHC in Africa will depend on whether countries can combine political commitment, domestic financing, accountable partnerships, and inclusive digital transformation. Digital and financial innovations are not substitutes for public responsibility. They are instruments that can strengthen health systems when used deliberately, ethically, and equitably.

ACRONYMS

Table 4. Acronyms Used in the Chapter

Acronym	Meaning
AI	Artificial Intelligence
CBHI	Community-Based Health Insurance
eCHIS	Electronic Community Health Information System
EHR	Electronic Health Record
LMIC	Low- and Middle-Income Country
mHealth	Mobile Health
NCD	Non-Communicable Disease
NHI	National Health Insurance
NHIS	National Health Insurance Scheme
ODA	Official Development Assistance
OOP	Out-of-Pocket
PHC	Primary Health Care
PPP	Public-Private Partnership
UHC	Universal Health Coverage
UNICEF	United Nations Children's Fund
WHO	World Health Organization

ACKNOWLEDGMENT

The author dedicates this work to the cherished memory of his late parents, John and Janet Agbo, whose sacrifices, guidance, and belief in education continue to inspire his professional journey. Appreciation is also extended to colleagues, friends, siblings, children, and grandchildren whose encouragement has enriched the author's life and work.

This book chapter received no specific grant from any funding agency in the public, commercial, or not-for-profit sectors.

REFERENCES

Adepoju, A. (2018). Rural–urban socio-economic links: the example of migrants in south-west nigeria. In *Modern migrations in western Africa* (pp. 127–137). Routledge. DOI: 10.4324/9781351044073-3

Agbo, S. O. (2024). *Perspective chapter: Improving health budgeting and management practices in low middle income countries (LMIC): Using 3 country case studies - Nigeria*. IntechOpen.

Agbo, S. O. (2025). Perspectives on digital health and financial inclusion in Africa: Exploring controversies, barriers, and challenges in achieving universal health coverage by 2030. *International Journal of Business and Economics Research, 14*(6), 272–285. Advance online publication. DOI: 10.11648/j.ijber.20251406.15

Aregbeshola, B. S., & Khan, S. M. (2021). Out-of-pocket health-care spending and its determinants among households in Nigeria: A national study. *Journal of Public Health (Berlin), 29*(4), 931–942. DOI: 10.1007/s10389-020-01199-x

Assefa, Y., Van Damme, W., Williams, O. D., & Hill, P. S. (2019). Successes and challenges of the Ethiopian Health Extension Program. *Globalization and Health, 15*(1), 24. DOI: 10.1186/s12992-019-0470-1 PMID: 30914055

Atun, R., Davies, J. I., Gale, E. A. M., Barnighausen, T., Beran, D., Kengne, A. P., Levitt, N. S., Mangugu, F. W., Nyirenda, M. J., Ogle, G. D., Ramaiya, K., Sewankambo, N. K., Sobngwi, E., Tesfaye, S., Yudkin, J. S., Basu, S., Bommer, C., Heesemann, E., Manne-Goehler, J., & Werfalli, M. (2017). Diabetes in sub-Saharan Africa: From clinical care to health policy. *The Lancet. Diabetes & Endocrinology, 5*(8), 622–667. DOI: 10.1016/S2213-8587(17)30181-X PMID: 28688818

Barroy, H., Dale, E., Sparkes, S., & Kutzin, J. (2021). *Public financial management and health service delivery: A literature review*. World Health Organization.

Bloom, D. E., Kuhn, M., & Prettner, K. (2018). Africa's prospects for sustainable health financing. *Health Affairs (Project Hope)*, *37*(5), 740–747.

Bloom, G., Berdou, E., Standing, H., Guo, Z., & Labrique, A. (2022). Transforming healthcare through digital technology in Africa. *Health Policy and Planning*, *37*(4), 452–461. DOI: 10.1093/heapol/czab122 PMID: 34977932

Chemouni, B. (2018). The political path to universal health coverage: Power, ideas, and community-based health insurance in Rwanda. *World Development*, *106*, 87–98. DOI: 10.1016/j.worlddev.2018.01.023

Dandonoli, P. (2022). Regulatory challenges in digital health financing. *Global Health Action*, *15*(1), 2058453. Advance online publication. DOI: 10.1080/16549716.2022.2058453

Dieleman, J. L., Haakenstad, A., Micah, A., Moses, M., Abbafati, C., Acharya, P., & Murray, C. J. L. (2018). Health financing in Africa. *The Lancet. Global Health*, *6*(9), e1007–e1029.

Gouda, H. N., Charlson, F., Sorsdahl, K., Ahmadzada, S., Ferrari, A. J., Erskine, H., & Whiteford, H. (2019). Burden of non-communicable diseases in sub-Saharan Africa, 1990-2017. *The Lancet. Global Health*, *7*(10), e1375–e1387. DOI: 10.1016/S2214-109X(19)30374-2 PMID: 31537368

GSMA. (2021). *State of the industry report on mobile money 2021*. GSMA.

He, D., Guizani, M., & Zhang, X. (2020). Blockchain and health informatics. *International Journal of Information Management*, *52*, 102045. DOI: 10.1016/j.ijinfomgt.2019.10.007

Hogan, D. R., Stevens, G. A., Hosseinpoor, A. R., & Boerma, T. (2018). National spending on health by source for 184 countries between 2013 and 2040. *Lancet*, *391*(10132), 2017–2031.

Hughes, N., & Lonie, S. (2007). M-PESA: Mobile money for the unbanked. *Innovations: Technology, Governance, Globalization*, *2*(1-2), 63–81. DOI: 10.1162/itgg.2007.2.1-2.63

Institute for Health Metrics and Evaluation. (2021). *Global Burden of Disease Study 2020 results. IHME*. University of Washington.

International Labour Organization. (2020). *World employment and social outlook: Trends 2020*. ILO.

Jack, W., & Suri, T. (2014). Risk sharing and transactions costs: Evidence from Kenya's mobile money revolution. *The American Economic Review, 104*(1), 183–223. DOI: 10.1257/aer.104.1.183

Lee, J., & Kim, J. (2021). Blockchain for health financing: Opportunities and challenges. *Journal of Medical Internet Research, 23*(5), e23517.

Meessen, B., Akhnif, E., Kiendrebeogo, J. A., & Zeng, W. (2019). Health financing reforms in Africa. *Health Systems and Reform, 5*(3), 176–188.

Mphahlele, M., & Mash, R. (2019). Barriers and facilitators of mobile health in Africa. *PLoS One, 14*(4), e0214870. Advance online publication. DOI: 10.1371/journal.pone.0214870 PMID: 30943250

Onwujekwe, O., Hanson, K., & Uzochukwu, B. (2019). Examining inequalities in incidence of catastrophic health expenditures on different healthcare services and health facilities in Nigeria. *PLoS One, 7*(7), e40811. DOI: 10.1371/journal.pone.0040811 PMID: 22815828

Suri, T., & Jack, W. (2016). The long-run poverty and gender impacts of mobile money. *Science, 354*(6317), 1288–1292. DOI: 10.1126/science.aah5309 PMID: 27940873

UNICEF. (2020). *Health technology and innovations in Africa*. UNICEF.

Wagstaff, A., Flores, G., Hsu, J., Smitz, M. F., Chepynoga, K., Eozenou, P., & Buisman, L. R. (2018). Progress on catastrophic health spending in 133 countries: A retrospective observational study. *The Lancet. Global Health, 6*(2), e169–e179. DOI: 10.1016/S2214-109X(17)30429-1 PMID: 29248367

Whyle, E., & Olivier, J. (2020). Social values and health systems in health policy and systems research: A mixed-method systematic review and evidence map. *Health Policy and Planning, 35*(6), 735–751. DOI: 10.1093/heapol/czaa038 PMID: 32374881

World Bank. (2022). *Africa health overview*. World Bank.

World Economic Forum. (2021). Innovating in health financing in Africa. World Economic Forum.

World Health Organization. (2019). *Primary health care on the road to universal health coverage: 2019 global monitoring report*. WHO.

World Health Organization. (2021). *Global strategy on digital health 2020-2025*. WHO.

World Health Organization. (2023). *Health financing in Africa*. WHO.

Xu, K., Soucat, A., & Kutzin, J. (2019). *Public spending on health: A closer look at global trends*. World Health Organization.

Zhao, F. (Ed.). (2006). *Maximize business profits through e-partnerships*. IRM Press. DOI: 10.4018/978-1-59140-788-1

Chapter 5
All Lives Matter:
A Story of Institutionalized Social Action in Global Health

Yuan Yuan
http://orcid.org/0009-0004-9097-8340
PATH, China

Nabeel Goheer
http://orcid.org/0009-0008-4707-445X
PATH, UK

ABSTRACT

This chapter uses a case study to demonstrate that institutionalized social action is an invaluable part of global health. The case study narrates the story of two global institutions – Gavi and PATH – playing a pivotal role in saving lives across the globe against cervical cancer. This is being done with the help of major donor countries in global health such as the USA, the UK and Germany as well as philanthropies such as the Gates Foundation. These social enterprises are innovating to normalize pooled procurement, help develop new health technologies, lower the costs of new technologies, and generate evidence to minimize the administration burden for vaccination. The orchestrated effort is adding significant value to global health, which is a dynamic interplay of innovation, technologies and financing – an expensive enterprise of underdeveloped countries and communities.

INTRODUCTION

This chapter describes a case study on the vaccination efforts for cervical cancer prevention. The case study elaborates the intermediary work that is done by social

DOI: 10.4018/979-8-3373-3341-0.ch005

enterprises such as Gavi, the Vaccine Alliance (formerly known as Global Alliance for Vaccines and Immunization) and PATH (formerly known as Program for Appropriate Technology in Health) to advance health equity through institutional innovations that are making vaccines more affordable and accessible to low and lower middle incomes countries (LLMICs). The cumulative effect of institutionalized social action is saving lives, improving access and affordability, and advancing global health equity. This chapter aims to introduce the financing mechanism and other mechanisms for immunization against cervical cancer with a relatively new vaccine and what they achieved, as well as pointing out criticism and challenges in these mechanisms.

BACKGROUND

Vaccines are a miraculous health innovation. The first mass produced vaccine in history was the smallpox vaccine. It not only protected people from the disease but also eradicated the disease from the Earth. Vaccines continue to save lives across the world. According to the World Health Organization (WHO), global immunization with vaccines have saved at least 154 million lives over the past 50 years (Shattock et al., 2024). Over a hundred million of these lives were infants. Between 1990 and 2019, vaccines against killer diseases, such as the diphtheria-tetanus-pertussis (DTP), measles, rotavirus and *Haemophilus influenzae* type b (Hib) vaccines, were significantly associated with an estimated 86.9 million fewer deaths in children younger than 5 years worldwide (Zhang et al., 2024).

Developing a vaccine, however, is a lengthy, arduous and expensive business. Figure 1 illustrates the vaccine approval process in the United States. Regulators weigh the risks of a vaccine, usually safety risks as all vaccines can induce adverse reactions in some people, against the benefits, including protecting most people from the disease or diseases. Prophylactic or preventive vaccines undergo the most stringent scrutiny by regulators because they are given to healthy people. A vaccine is approved for marketing only when the benefits outweigh the risks. Safety in vaccine recipients is a study objective through phase 1 to phase 3 clinical studies, sometimes investigated further in a phase 4 study. On average, from initial scientific discovery to market authorization, vaccine development takes more than ten years and costs hundreds of millions to billions of dollars (Gouglas et al., 2018). The failure rate in vaccine development is as high as 94 percent (Pronker et al., 2013). In accounting, the birthing costs of vaccines are high. This is why new vaccines are expensive. The normal price is set to recover the development costs. Vaccines alone do not save lives; vaccination does. However, vaccines are hard to administer, too. The least developed, low and lower middle incomes countries (LLMICs) face multiple problems. For one thing, they cannot afford these vaccines; for another, they find it difficult to administer the vaccines to the majority of target populations. There are also problems around political stability, vaccine confidence, gender equity and other aspects (Ali et al., 2022). These result in health inequity, as death rates from infectious diseases are higher in LLMICs. The global health community set out three decades ago to solve this problem, financing the immunization program is part of the solution. Through years of effort, solutions are tested, and some are proven to achieve immunization equity.

Figure 1. The vaccine life cycle: how vaccines are developed and approved for use

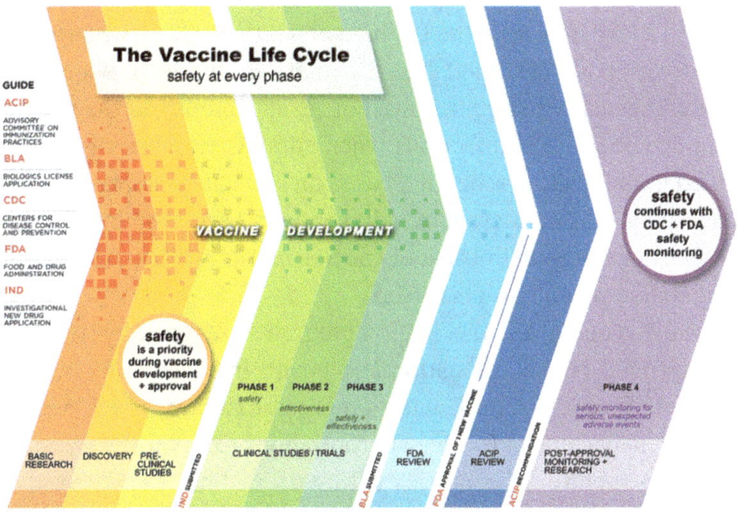

Source: CDC, 2024

MAIN FOCUS OF THE CHAPTER

Issues, Controversies, Problems

Cervical cancer is the fourth most common cancer among women globally, with an estimated 660,000 new cases and 350,000 deaths in 2022. About 94 percent of these deaths occurred in low- and middle-income countries (Chidebe et al., 2025). The World Health Organization (WHO) recommends a comprehensive approach to cervical cancer prevention and control, including vaccination, as the first layer of defense, against human papillomavirus (HPV) which causes cervical cancer. The vaccine should be administered prior to the sexual debut of girls in the age range of

9 to 14 years. To achieve the global goal for cervical cancer elimination by 2030, countries should vaccinate at least 90% of the girls before they turn the age of 15.

The first two HPV vaccines, Gardasil® and Cervarix®, from two multinational pharmaceutical companies were licensed in 2006 and 2007, respectively. Both vaccines contain the two most oncogenic HPV types, HPV-16 and HPV-18. These two types cause more than 70 percent of the cervical cancer cases worldwide. Cervarix® is a bivalent vaccine containing types 16 and 18. Gardasil® is a quadrivalent vaccine containing two additional types, type 6 and type 11, which cause genital warts but not cancer. Both vaccines are safe and effective. As the world's first ever preventive HPV vaccine, Gardasil® obtained approved by the U.S. Food and Drug Administration after 13 years of development. In 2007, Gardasil® was offered at US$120.5 per dose on the US market (CDC, 2022). The target population was girls and young women aged 9 to 26 years, aiming to provide protection to this age group, especially before the onset of sexual activity, as the vaccine is most effective in preventing HPV infections when administered prior to exposure. The recommended immunization schedule, based on clinical trial data showing vaccine efficacy and safety, was 3 doses, at month 0, month 2 and month 6. This means the vaccines alone, not counting the cost of vaccine administration, to immunize a girl with the full course cost about US$361.5.

In industrialized countries, vaccination programs are typically financed through government national budget allocation and health insurance reimbursement. For example, in the United States, the Centers for Disease Control and Prevention (CDC) and other health departments receive appropriations to cover the costs of vaccines and related infrastructure. In countries with universal health care systems, health insurance schemes cover the cost of vaccinations. This ensures that individuals do not have to pay out-of-pocket for recommended vaccines, thereby increasing vaccination rates. In upper middle-income countries such as China, the government has expedited promoting free HPV vaccination pilot programs and launching action plans to scale up HPV vaccination. As of September 2023, of the 32 provincial-level administrative regions in Chinese Mainland, 7 had free provincial HPV immunization programs in place for girls aged 13 or 14 years (Schuind et al., 2024). Since November 2025, China has included HPV vaccine in its national immunization program at affordable prices with two suppliers.

LLMICs do not have such systems to support their national immunization program. None of the LLMICs were able to afford the HPV vaccine at US$361.5 per course for the girls in their country. Yet almost 94 percent of the deaths due to cervical cancer occur in these countries.

For marketed HPV vaccines, ultra-low freezing is not required, but 2-8 °C transport and storage is a must. The "last mile" electricity and cold chain storage often pose a threat to vaccine potency in LLMICs (Murewanhema et al., 2024).

Many LLMICs are in the process of transition into digital health system. Challenges are identified with immunization data management. Training is needed in data management and use, including support to implement electronic data systems at the community level (Cernuschi et al., 2018).

Introducing a new vaccine into the national immunization program is a non-trivial challenge even when there is sufficient funding. From the country perspective, it requires additional qualified staff to administer the vaccine, yet many LLMICs face a shortage in human resources (Cernuschi et al., 2018).

The target population of HPV vaccines are school age girls, so ideally the vaccine administration happen in schools. However, in pastoralist communities, girls are kept at home for chores or early marriage; they miss school-based HPV doses. As another form of gender hierarchy, men's opposition often softens when information sessions are held separately for fathers and include male clinicians, so it means the need for male targeting counselling (Xu et al., 2024).

Vaccine hesitancy is another complex problem. Communities in some LLIMCs believe that the vaccine will render girls permanently infertile, or giving a vaccine against sexually transmitted infection tacitly approves early sexual activity (Rakheja et al., 2025). Countering such misinformation requires countries to implement a communication plan for immunization activities. Only then can vaccination *need* be converted to *demand*.

SOLUTIONS AND RECOMMENDATIONS

Financial Innovations for Funding the National Immunization Programs

Gavi, a premier social enterprise of pooled vaccine procurement, negotiated a price of US$4.5 per dose of Gardasil® in 2013 for procurement by LLMICs (UNICEF, 2025). Gavi, the Vaccine Alliance, was founded in 2000 as Global Alliance for Vaccines and Immunization (GAVI). It is a public-private global health partnership aimed at increasing access to immunization in poor countries. Gav is the largest channel of external financing for immunization (Results for Development, 2017). To enable countries to immunize girls against HPV and cervical cancer, Gavi utilizes a combination of solutions.

On the demand side, Gavi provides financial support to national immunization programs of Gavi eligible countries. The definition of Gavi eligibility is Gross National Income (GNI) per capita with adjustment referring to the World Bank categorization. In 2024, the threshold for Gavi eligibility is no more than US$1,810 average GNI per capita in the past three years. Gavi provides financing to the eligible countries to sustain their long-term immunization programs. The Gavi funding goes to a United Nations agency to purchase vaccines at the Gavi negotiated price and injection safety devices for vaccine delivery. Procurement through a United Nations agency is mandatory. The financial support helps the countries to convert their *need* for vaccines to *demand*, which means the country possesses the purchasing power to fulfill the need. On the other hand, demand generation serves as volume guarantee for vaccine manufacturers, driving the decrease in vaccine price.

The ultimate goal is for countries to be self-sufficient and sustainable for their immunization program. When a country's GNI per capita exceeds the threshold, the country goes into accelerated transition towards Gavi graduation. In the accelerated transition phase, while the country continues benefiting from the Gavi price, Gavi and the country use the co-financing model where the country shoulders US$0.2 per dose of vaccine. After graduation, the country can no longer purchase vaccines at the Gavi prices.

The demand requires huge amount of investment to purchase the vaccines and implement the immunization program. An estimate shows the cost of 10 vaccines in the routine immunization programs of 94 low- and middle-income countries would be about US$22.8 billion between 2021 and 2030, and the corresponding delivery cost is about US$19.4 billion (Sim et al., 2021).

Table 1. Cost of immunization programs for 10 vaccines by decade, 94 low- and middle-income countries (best case scenario) in 2018 US$

	2011-2020	**2021-2030**	**Total**
Immunization program, total	28.4 billion (22.7–36.3)	42.4 billion (33.8–57.1)	70.8 billion (56.5–93.4)
Vaccine	14.6 billion (13.4–15.8)	22.8 billion (21.1–24.6)	37.4 billion (34.4–40.3)
Delivery	13.6 billion (9.2–20.3)	19.4 billion (12.5–32.3)	32.9 billion (21.7–52.5)
Stockpile	0.20 billion (0.17–0.24)	0.22 billion (0.19–0.25)	0.42 billion (0.36–0.49)

(Source: Sim et al., 2021)

To aggregate funds for the national immunization programs, Gavi receives funding from government donors, foundations, corporations and private individuals. Government donors are the major contributors to Gavi. Government donors include but are not limited to the governments of the United States, United Kingdom, Germany, Japan, Norway and China. Major foundation donors include the Gates Foundation, Rockefeller Foundation and the Children's Investment Fund Foundation.

In addition, in 2006, Gavi launched the International Finance Facility for Immunization (IFFIm) to raise funds and fill an estimated gap of US$30 to 70 billion per year until 2015. IFFIm is a financial mechanism to shift financial resources from the future to the present, so long-term donor commitments are transformed into immediate funding for Gavi for the public good. The transformation is achieved through the vaccine bond. IFFIm issues the vaccine bonds since 2006. These social bonds are backed by "long-term, irrevocable and legally binding pledges from 11 sovereign governments." The vaccine bonds are backed by the governments in Australia, Brazil, Canada, France, Italy, the Netherlands, Norway, South Africa, Spain, Sweden and the UK for a period of up to 29 years until 2037 (Tacheva et al., 2025). Since 2006, IFFIm has transferred more than US$6.2 billion to support Gavi's vaccination programs. This represents about one-sixth of Gavi's overall funding (IFFIm, 2025).

Criticism and Challenges

Despite the success of financing national immunization programs, there are criticism and challenges. The criticism focuses on design flaws, inadequate application and lack of transparency (Tacheva et al., 2025). While Gavi substantially contributes to financing national immunization programs to introduce new vaccines such as HPV vaccine, it weakens the incentive for health financing by the country itself. When Gavi starts facing funding cuts in early 2025, sustainability of national immunization program financing becomes a more prominent issue (Burki, 2025). With IFFIm, the front-loaded bond structure shifts future debt onto LLMIC budgets, crowding out other health spending; for governance, critics observe a lack of inclusivity for the beneficiary governments. The model of COVAX Advance Market Commitment (AMC), although similar to other Gavi AMC mechanisms, did not work as effectively to curb the pandemic (REPPARE, 2025). Specifically, it fails to tap into the manufacturing capacity of vaccine manufacturers around the globe to address the needs of low-resource countries. Instead, large volumes of COVID-19 vaccines went to high income countries in surplus, while vaccine supply to LLMICs lagged.

Along these lines of criticism, since 2025 the global health financing model has been facing the sustainability problem more seriously than ever. It has always been the expectation for countries to graduate from Gavi. When countries are eligible for Gavi funding, they are insensitive to vaccine prices, thus they may prefer vaccines made by multinationals as opposed to less expensive options offered by developing country vaccine manufacturers when there is no significant difference in vaccine safety, effectiveness or quality. Gavi graduation and self-sustainability requires country decision-making for policy, political and financial commitment, demand for and equitable delivery of vaccines and access to timely and affordable supply, yet many graduating countries are not ready, especially in vaccine confidence, self-procurement capability, immunization data quality and human resources for immunization (Cernuschi et al., 2018). In some cases, Gavi continues to support former Gavi eligible countries to prevent backsliding of immunization (*Gavi's Approach to Engaging with Middle-Income Countries*, 2025). One example is Gavi providing support in HPV vaccine introduction for Angola.

Market and Technological Innovations for Increasing Supply

While financing mechanisms address affordability, ensuring a consistent and affordable vaccine supply requires structural changes on the manufacturing side. On the supply end, Gavi works on market shaping to make vaccines more affordable for low- and middle-income countries. By pooling the vaccine demand from countries, Gavi negotiates affordable prices with vaccine manufacturers. In the HPV vaccine case, Gavi negotiated a price of US$4.5 per dose of Gardasil® in 2013. So, six years after the innovation HPV vaccines were available in the industrialized countries, LLMICs are able to access this powerful intervention to protect their girls against cervical cancer.

This dramatic decrease in price is due to the economies of scale in vaccine manufacture. When a vaccine is commercialized, the manufacturer usually sells it at a higher price to recoup the investment. Vaccine manufacturer makes heavy upfront investment in the research and development for new vaccines. When a vaccine is close to market authorization, the manufacturer then makes a significant investment in the facilities and equipment to produce the vaccine at commercial scale. Unlike other pharmaceutical products, many vaccines cannot be clearly defined with its chemical or biological characteristics. What gets approved by a regulatory authority is not only a specific biological entity, but also the process by which it is produced, tested, and released for use (Plotkin et al., 2017). In other words, the manufacturing process defines the product. This has several implications for the cost of goods sold (COGs).

1. **Production facilities and equipment must serve the manufacturing process.** While there is common equipment across technology platforms that may be suitable for different processes, the design of the manufacturing facility and the process flow is unique for each vaccine. Except for the fill finish equipment in some cases, vaccine manufacturer will likely need to either build new facility or retrofit existing facility to follow the manufacturing process workflow, making it inevitable to a significant investment in hardware dedicated to one product. In accounting, this means high fixed costs.

2. **Testing is part of the manufacturing process**. Regulatory authorities regard vaccines, especially prophylactic vaccines, as the medicinal product of highest risk, because they are administered to healthy people. In many countries, the final product undergoes comprehensive testing both by the manufacturer and by the national regulatory authority. This is called the lot release or batch release. Lot release takes extra time and effort and is a semi-variable cost. So is the testing by the manufacturers on the intermediate products. If a vaccine lot is small, the cost per dose is higher than when the lot is hundreds of thousands of doses.
3. **Manufacturers are not allowed to change the manufacturing process at will**. Significant changes in the process, such as new equipment and a change in raw materials, will need to be submitted for regulatory review. For example, a manufacturer wants to increase the final lot size thus bringing down the cost per dose. Often times, such an increase cannot be achieved by adding a production line that is exactly the same. If it involves changing to a larger size filter, the process is deemed different, and it has to go through regulatory review. Sometimes the regulator may require an additional clinical trial to demonstrate the new process yields products that are equally safe and effective or at least not inferior to the current process.
4. **The manufacturing cost may be designed during manufacturing process development**. There are various cost drivers for the product, including but are not limited to clinical development costs, facilities and equipment, raw materials. The manufacturing cost is built in when the manufacturing process is developed. If less expensive raw materials or consumable parts are used in the design and subsequent commercial production, the variable costs will be lower. As another example, when philanthropy pays for clinical development, it shares the development cost and will potentially lower the price of the product by not accounting for this fixed cost.
5. **A portfolio approach is cost saving**. For WHO prequalification and national regulatory authorities, documentation of current Good Manufacturing Practice (cGMP) is required. This means manufacturers must establish a quality management system for quality assurance. If a manufacturer has only one product, the costs of the quality system all go to this product. In contrast, for a manufacturer who has multiple products in its portfolio, all products share the quality system so the quality cost per unit is lower. It is the same with other required systems for vaccine manufacturers like the biosafety and biosecurity system and the pharmacovigilance system, which monitors safety events following immunization.

After the initial launch on the market, when breakeven is achieved, the manufacturer is willing to decrease the price because the marginal costs to produce a new batch are significantly lower. This is called "the tail price". The larger the supply volume is, the lower the price can go.

When a country secures funding from Gavi to operate its national immunization program, the country defines the vaccines to be offered to its people. With the Gavi funding, the country requests a United Nations agency to place order for vaccine procurement. The United Nations Children's Fund, or UNICEF, is an important player for vaccine procurement for many countries.

When it comes to health product procurement, all United Nations agencies require the product get through the WHO prequalification process. In other words, only WHO prequalified health products are eligible for United Nations procurement. The WHO prequalification program aims to ensure that health products meet global standards of quality, safety and efficacy.

In market shaping, the competitor landscape is another important factor to decrease the vaccine price. Therefore, Gavi and UNICEF welcome additional suppliers of vaccines. Since the establishment of WHO prequalification program in 1987, many vaccine manufacturers applied for prequalification of their vaccine.

China is a late comer to WHO prequalification. Manufacturer of the first prequalified vaccine submitted its dossier in 2012 and reached this milestone in 2013. By the end of April 2025, 13 vaccine presentations from China passed WHO prequalification. As a comparator, vaccine manufacturers in India have 121 vaccine presentations that passed WHO prequalification, accounting for 43.7% of the total 227 prequalified vaccine presentations. The developing country vaccine manufacturers have become important players to vaccine supply security for the world.

In 2019, a bivalent HPV vaccine Cecolin® from Xiamen Innovax Biotech, a Chinese company based in Xiamen, Fujian Province, obtained market authorization in China. Established in 2005, Innovax has a recombinant technology to express proteins in *Escherichia coli*. Based on this platform technology for vaccine production, Innovax had the world's first Hepatitis E vaccine licensed in China in 2012. The bivalent HPV vaccine was also developed with the *Escherichia coli* expression system, which is significantly less expensive than the systems used for Gardasil® and Cervarix®. While the product was undergoing phase 3 trial, in 2017, PATH, a nonprofit organization, started providing technical assistance to prepare Innovax for WHO prequalification – an essential first step for vaccines procurement through United Nations with Gavi funding.

The Role of Intermediaries in Bridging the Gap

While developing country vaccine manufacturers such as Innovax could offer vaccine supply, it is part of the solution. Additional work by different stakeholders is needed to bridge between vaccine supply and vaccination.

PATH is a social enterprise that originated in 1977 in Seattle, USA. PATH's mission is to advance health equity around the globe through innovation and partnership. PATH initially worked mostly on reproductive health until in the mid-1980s when it started to be involved in vaccines and infectious diseases (Muraskin, 2005). In the early 1990s, PATH became involved with the development of the Children's Vaccine Initiative, building on the experience of its leaders who had worked on Hepatitis B vaccine introduction into low- and middle-income countries. Richard Mahoney and James Maynard of PATH drew lessons from the Hepatitis B vaccine introduction, which boil down to "five key elements" (Mahoney & Maynard, 1999).

1. **Establishment and dissemination of disease burden data and of cost effectiveness analysis**. The disease burden data are the starting point for vaccine development. The choice of research and development project should be based on disease burden to optimize the use of limited resources. When a vaccine is licensed and marketed, the vaccination costs, including the vaccine price, should be weighed against the effectiveness for decision makers to adopt the vaccine in their country.

Vaccine cost-effectiveness analysis (CEA) is a crucial process used to evaluate the economic value of vaccines and vaccination. A cost-effectiveness analysis incorporates different pieces of information, including disease burden, vaccine effectiveness and impact, delivery costs, and illness costs to help determine whether vaccination is a good value for money. Such an analysis identifies the costs, including direct costs of vaccination and indirect costs such as the costs associated with the overall health system. It also measures the health outcomes, usually considering the reduction in disease incidence and prevalence, reduction in morbidity and mortality.

A single cost-effectiveness cutoff does not apply everywhere. A vaccination program that is economically justified in one country may not be good value for money in another. Cost-effectiveness is always a comparison between two options, not an absolute quality. In such an assessment, health economists compute the incremental cost-effective ratio (ICER) and weigh it against a country's willingness-to-pay threshold. To calculate ICER, they take the extra cost of one intervention over another and divide it by the difference in health outcomes, such as years of life lost due to early death or disability. Then they compare the ICER with the willingness-to-pay threshold, which is the upper limit that the country is willing to pay to save one year of life. If the ICER falls below the willingness-to-pay threshold, the intervention is considered cost-effective; otherwise, it is not (Regan, 2024).

2. **Vaccine introduction trials and vaccine effectiveness evaluations**. Pre-licensure clinical trials may be conducted in the initial target market. For other countries, decision makers need data to understand the implementation of a new vaccine locally. The vaccine introduction trials could generate such data for decision making.

Also, vaccine developers usually study vaccine efficacy in the target population in a meticulously controlled way through randomized clinical trials. How the vaccine works in the real world would need evidence generated locally. This is how vaccine effectiveness studies provide value to inform decision makers.

3. **Establishment of international consensus and recommendations for vaccine use**. When a vaccine is licensed, usually in a few countries initially, it will not be automatically introduced to other countries. LLMICs especially rely on international recommendations from WHO. These recommendations from a group at WHO called the Strategic Advisory Group of Experts on immunization (SAGE). SAGE has different working groups, which are usually time-limited and address specific questions identified by SAGE. SAGE working groups aim to increase the effectiveness of SAGE deliberations by reviewing and providing evidence-based information and options for recommendations on vaccines and immunization policies. The policy recommendations are published in vaccine position papers.
4. **Assurance of adequate and cost competitive vaccine supply**. To achieve cost effectiveness, the cost of the vaccine should be low enough, leaving a relatively small profit margin for the manufacturer. Due to the economies of scale, a large volume of supply not only ensures abundant supply to large populations but also supports the lower cost of goods sold.
5. **Creation of funding mechanisms to supply vaccine to countries**. This is the conversion of need to demand. It requires innovative financing to help the LLMICs support and sustain their national immunization programs.

PATH initiated its work in China in the late 1970s, when China started its national family planning policy. With funding from the United Nations Family Planning Fund, PATH worked with local partners in China to strengthen the capacity for contraceptive manufacturing in the early 1980s. In 2005, PATH officially started a partnership with the China National Biotec Group to work with the vaccine manufacturer on the WHO prequalification for a Japanese Encephalitis (JE) vaccine. This was early days for China to take the first step with WHO prequalification. For a vaccine to apply for WHO prequalification, the national regulatory authority has to be qualified by WHO first. This condition was not met in 2005, nor was the vaccine manufacturer ready to apply for prequalification then. In 2011, China's national regulatory authority was qualified by WHO. The vaccine manufacturer submitted its application for JE vaccine in early 2012. This JE vaccine obtained prequalification status in 2013, as the first ever WHO prequalified vaccine in China. The JE vaccine has been supplied to more than ten countries in JE endemic regions and protect more than 300 million children from the disabling disease with no cure. The JE vaccine story is another case that contains every one of the five key elements to success.

With this positive experience, PATH set out to work with more Chinese vaccine manufacturers on WHO prequalification, as a first step towards supplying the vaccine to LLMICs through United Nations procurement. In 2017, in view of Innovax's to-be-licensed bivalent HPV vaccine, PATH negotiated a collaboration and global access agreement with Innovax. The agreement is an indispensable mission alignment exercise that PATH takes before it works with any manufacturing partner.

Global access is short for equitable global access to medical products. The goal of global access is to make health products available and affordable in a sustainable manner to everyone. PATH's mission is to ensure equitable access to the health products it supports through technical assistance. Therefore, while the manufacturer usually gets technical assistance free of charge, in return, they commit to supplying the product to LLMICs at an affordable price and in adequate volume. A global access agreement has many elements. Besides supply volume and price, the manufacturer may commit to obtaining WHO prequalification for market access. In some countries, WHO prequalification alone is not sufficient for vaccine introduction into the country's immunization program; the manufacturer has to register its product through the national regulatory authority to be able to market the product there. So, regulatory strategy for registration is another important factor to ensure vaccine access, and it usually involves defining the territory for global access. Other provisions in a global access agreement may include terms around intellectual property rights, data sharing and publication, target product profile, and technology transfer. There may be supporting provisions in the agreement, including access license, reporting requirements, audit rights, termination rights, dispute resolution, governance and product specific factors.

The PATH technical assistance for Cecolin® WHO prequalification was funded by the Gates Foundation, the largest private foundation in the world, through a grant to PATH. To enable the discussion on vaccine price, Gates Foundation supported a cost of goods sold (COGs) analysis. The analysis considered different scenarios in terms of supply volume to determine the manufacturing cost. Then a profit margin was added and a price of US$3.0 per dose for Gavi eligible countries was agreed upon. This means Innovax should offer no more than US$3.0 per dose to Gavi eligible countries when it answers to the bid from UNICEF. The global access agreement contained a mechanism to adjust the price if the assumptions that determined the initial cost change. Once a year, the manufacturer may request a price increase with justifications, for example, elevation of direct labor cost or raw materials.

From 2017 to 2021, PATH provided technical assistance to Innovax in multiple functional areas, including manufacturing, quality and pharmacovigilance. This is a process of capacity bridging, involving a good amount of on-the-job training for the manufacturer's employees. In 2021, Cecolin® obtained WHO prequalification, jumping through the first hoop towards global supply. This added a new, third option for Gavi eligible countries for HPV vaccination. Since 2014, the global supply of HPV vaccines had been insufficient to meet global demand due to limited manufacturing capacity and high interest in preventing HPV related diseases through vaccination. The vaccine demand contains routine immunization for girls 9 to14 years of age as well as multi-age cohort (MAC) campaigns assuming the use of 2-dose schedule. In the absence of supply constraints, global HPV programmatic dose requirements are expected to rise sharply to over 130 million doses by 2023, fluctuating between 120 and 140 million doses each year through 2030. This short-term increase was largely driven by the implementation of multi-age cohort campaigns in LLMICs supported by Gavi and catch-up vaccination in a few high-income countries (Malvolti et al., 2023). For reference, UNICEF procured about 10.4 million doses of Cervarix® and Gardasil® between 2013 and 2017 and planned to purchase 32.3 million doses of these two vaccines from 2018 to 2022 (UNICEF, 2019). Due to supply shortage, many countries had to delay their plan for HPV vaccine introduction or multi-age cohort campaigns.

The WHO prequalification of Cecolin® increased the total supply of vaccines by 30 million doses per year. About 80 million doses were expected to be available in 2022 from the suppliers of Cervarix®, Gardasil® and Cecolin®. Furthermore, Innovax offered US$2.9 per dose for Gavi, which is a record low (UNICEF, 2025).

Vaccines alone do not save lives; vaccination does. For successful implementation of the immunization program, countries need to overcome multiple barriers by actively involving stakeholders. These stakeholders include health workers, local civil society, and key opinion leaders (Haddison et al., 2025). The effort together enhances vaccine uptake.

Optimizing Impact Through Evidence

The value of social enterprises goes beyond the point of pooled procurement, adding new suppliers and improving affordability. From 2006 to 2011, PATH conducted HPV vaccination demonstration projects in four low- and middle-income countries, India, Peru, Uganda and Vietnam. The goal of the projects is to provide countries with evidence for decision-making about public sector introduction of HPV vaccination to protect girls against cervical cancer. In the demonstration projects, PATH worked with ministries of health, civil society organizations and other stakeholders to conduct formative and operations research in these countries. The investigations centered on practical rollout considerations: identifying sociocultural barriers that could limit acceptance, determining the most effective delivery channels for adolescent girls, exploring how HPV vaccination could fit within established health frameworks, and assessing the financial impact on health systems. When the projects ended, evaluations showed that communities readily accepted HPV vaccination. Two factors laid strong groundwork for future programs: families wanted to protect their daughters from cervical cancer, and vaccination itself was viewed positively. The introduction of HPV vaccines also helped improve health program infrastructure. School-based administration worked effectively in all settings where it was tried. Early cooperation between district health and education officials proved essential. By working together to clarify responsibilities and develop workable plans, the two sectors could launch new initiatives without creating significant disruption (PATH, 2011).

In 2012, PATH received funding from Gavi to support country introductions of HPV vaccination through two pathways: demonstration programs and national introductions. With the Gavi funding, PATH supported demonstration programs in 27 countries and assisted 13 countries in national introductions. To help more countries, PATH publicly shared the considerations for evaluation in the pilot to generate the data needed for future decision-making. It drew lessons from the HPV vaccination pilots and recommended the tools and methods for vaccine delivery strategy and for establishing a robust evaluation framework (PATH, 2012). In 2022, the HAPPI (HPV Vaccine Acceleration Program Partners Initiative) Consortium was initiated with funding from the Gates Foundation. PATH was one of the contributors to the HAPPI Consortium, continuing to provide technical assistance to countries, aiming at accelerating the introduction and coverage of HPV vaccination in LLMICs.

With its expertise in health economics, PATH worked with partners in Burkina Faso (Kiendrébéogo et al., 2023), Kenya (Mwenda et al., 2023), Mongolia (Luvsan et al., 2022), Mozambique (Guimarães et al., 2023) and the Philippines (Llave et al., 2022) to understand the cost-effectiveness of HPV vaccination in these specific countries. In these cost-effectiveness analyses, PATH and partners compared the different HPV vaccines and to no vaccination. The comparison helps the countries that have already introduced HPV vaccination in determining whether they are using the most cost-effective product and schedule. It also helped countries that are considering HPV vaccine introduction, such as Mongolia, to decide whether

HPV vaccination is cost-effective overall, and if so, which products and schedules are the best options.

Based on the work on cost-effectiveness analyses, PATH developed an Excel-based tool to compare the costs of HPV vaccination programs on an annual basis and over a 10-year period, using the HPV vaccines available in the global market. The tool, called the HPV Vaccine Cost Calculator, aims to assist country-level policymakers in comparing different vaccine products and estimating the costs of vaccinations programs with these vaccine options. The Calculator estimates vaccine costs, including international shipping, and vaccination program costs, including delivery costs. Additionally, it calculates the estimated vaccine doses and cold chain volume requirements, which supports operational planning and logistics.

Clinical trials and ongoing research indicate that HPV vaccination provides protection for more than ten years, and to this day, no data suggest that the protection from HPV vaccination lessens over time. The original HPV vaccine immunization schedule was 3 doses administered in six months. In the 2014 HPV vaccine position paper, WHO recommended a 2-dose schedule for girls 9 to 14 years of age with both Gardasil® and Cervarix® (WHO, 2015). The multi-dose schedule poses a problem for LLMICs with limited resources. On the one hand, a complete course of HPV vaccine immunization costs at least US$9.0 per course or per person before Cecolin® was available. This is expensive for LLMICs, for both public and private purchasers. As a contrast, the costs of vaccines for children under 2 years of age in countries eligible for Gavi vaccine price ranges from US$0.2 to US$8.25 per course (UNICEF, 2024). On the other hand, it is very difficult to ensure all girls get the full course, especially for those who live in remote areas (Ndiaye, 2024).

Table 2. Assumed "standard" immunization schedule for children less than 24 months of age

Antigen	Year of Life	Number of Doses in Schedule	2024 Price Per Dose (US$)
Bacille Calmette Guerin (BCG)	1st	1	0.20
Hepatitis B (HepB) birth dose	1st	1	0.24
Oral polio	1st	3	0.14
Pentavalent (DTP-HepB-Hib)	1st	3	0.84
Pneumococcal conjugate (PCV13)	1st	3	2.75
Injectable polio	1st	2	2.19
Rotavirus	1st	2	2.22
Measles-rubella	1st	1	0.82

continued on following page

Table 2. Continued

Antigen	Year of Life	Number of Doses in Schedule	2024 Price Per Dose (US$)
Measles-rubella	2nd	1	0.82
Diphtheria-tetanus-pertussis (DTP)	2nd	1	0.19

Hib: Haemophilus influenzae type b.
PCV13: 13-valent pneumococcal conjugate vaccine.
Source: (UNICEF, 2024)

In the meantime, evidence is emerging from clinical trials that a single dose of HPV vaccine might work just as well. While the recommended dosing schedule was 2 doses for girls, some girls only got one shot due to various reasons. Observations showed the one dose administered to these people still elicit a strong immune response against incident and persistent HPV infections. From prior studies, people understand that such infections are necessary to develop cervical lesions that lead to cervical cancer. To confirm the effectiveness of a 1-dose schedule, in 2018, PATH started to coordinate the Single-Dose HPV Vaccine Evaluation Consortium with a grant from the Gates Foundation. The goal of this consortium is to gather the evaluate data from clinical trials, observational studies and modeling analyses related to protection against cervical cancer with a 1-dose schedule for immunization with existing HPV vaccines, Gardasil® and Cervarix®. Through years of work with an international group of experts on clinical and mathematical modeling, PATH consolidated the evidence in a briefing document summarizing critical study finding, estimated public health impact and current recommendations. The briefing document was submitted to WHO and in the Strategic Advisory Group of Experts on immunization (SAGE) meeting in April 2022, WHO endorsed the 1-dose schedule for HPV immunization. In December 2022, WHO revised its recommendation in the HPV vaccine position paper (WHO, 2022). The early adopters of the 1-dose HPV vaccination schedule include the UK, Ireland and Australia, as the simplified schedule helps the countries to mobilize resources to other health areas. Some of these countries were able to adopt a gender-neutral strategy to include boys in the HPV vaccination program, as it protects men from anal cancer and penile cancer. The 1-dose vaccination strategy advances equity in three dimensions: vaccine equity, health equity and gender equity (Mercuri et al., 2024).

This is yet another example of the 3rd element for success — establishing international consensus for vaccine recommendation. From three independent HPV transmission models, researchers estimated that the 1-dose schedule has similar benefits to the 2-dose schedule (Prem et al., 2023). Besides reducing costs and alleviating vaccine supply constraints, it simplifies vaccine delivery, which is especially helpful to low resource countries. When vaccine supply is no longer an issue, the

HPV vaccination program may be extended to boys aged 9 to 20 years, protecting more people through a gender-neutral immunization strategy.

As PATH knew Cecolin® was forthcoming as a less expensive option, PATH raised the question: how about 1 dose of Cecolin®? In 2020, PATH designed a phase 3 clinical trial, comparing Cecolin® with Gardasil® with different immunization schedules, including 1-dose and 2-dose schedules, in girls. With funding provided by the Gates Foundation and KfW Development Bank in Germany, PATH sponsored the clinical trial between 2021 and 2023 in Bangladesh and Ghana. KfW Development Bank is a leading development bank that represents the German Federal Government and the European Union to finance global development projects. Its focus areas are global development support and Sustainable Development Goals (SDGs).

The phase 3 clinical trial, known as CHOISE which is short for Comparing HPV Vaccine Options: Immunogenicity and Safety Evaluation, enrolled 1,025 girls at age 9 to 14 years. Three vaccination schedules were evaluated: a 2-dose Cecolin® regimen with dosing intervals of 6, 12, or 24 months; a 2-dose Gardasil® regimen with a 6-month interval; and a sequential vaccination approach with an initial Gardasil® dose and a subsequent Cecolin® dose 24 months thereafter. Results demonstrated that Cecolin® is highly immunogenic in all the studied schedules, including the 1-dose schedule, and generated immunize responses comparable to Gardasil® (Agbenyega et al., 2025). Based on the data from this study, WHO updated its Considerations for HPV Vaccine Product Choice document to reflect its recommendation that Cecolin® may be used with a 1-dose schedule (WHO, 2024).

As a high-quality, affordable HPV vaccine, Cecolin® is increasingly used in LLMICs and contributing to the 2030 goal of protecting women from cervical cancer. By April 2025, Cecolin® is registered in thirteen countries. In another three countries, no registration is required, and Cecolin is being supplied to these countries through United Nations procurement. This includes Angola, a country that graduated from Gavi but obtained Gavi funding for HPV vaccine introduction through Gavi's middle income countries (MICs) approach. In September 2024, about 2.2 million doses of Cecolin® arrived in Angola for the immunization of girls aged 9 to 12 to protect them from cervical cancer, the second-most common cancer in the country. Gavi supported about 250,000 doses of these vaccines; other partners, including the European Investment Bank, provided additional doses (Micolo, 2025).

Globally, national immunization programs are suffering from lower coverage than required to generate herd protection. Outbreaks of vaccine preventable diseases are on the rise. In 2023, large scale outbreaks reach a number of 109, a 43% increase compared with 2021. On the contrary, HPV vaccine coverage is higher than ever. The HPV vaccine market improved from unhealthy in 2022 to concerning in 2023, due to an additional supplier, greater distribution of products to more regions and increased pipeline. At the end of 2023, 129 countries introduced HPV vaccination, and the global coverage of girls under 15 years of age is 20% compared to 14% in 2019, thanks to the vaccine introduction in LLMICs (WHO, 2025). The WHO Africa region sees an increase of more than 15%. It is still a long way to go to reach 90% coverage, but the momentum has started.

The journey of saving lives and advancing health equity through vaccination continues. Furthermore, research proves that investing in health drives economic growth. Researchers from WifOR Institute and Harvard University published their finding in April 2025, using HPV vaccination program as an example. In the UK, every US$1 invested in HPV vaccination in 2022 yielded US$1.84 in economic value. This impact was driven by direct contributions within the health sector, spillover effects in adjacent industries, and increased household spending — triggered at the time of investment (Atun, 2025).

Table 3. Economic impact of HPV vaccination programs

Country	Investment (US$)	Total Economic Impact* (US$)	Jobs Created*
UK	134 million	247 million	2,000
India	756 million	1,149 million	155,000
Malaysia	16 million	23 million	700
Nigeria	100 million	96 million	6,000

* Including effects inside the Health Economy, in adjacent sectors, and from induced income (rounded figures).

Source: (Atun, 2025)

FUTURE RESEARCH DIRECTIONS

Despite the importance of immunization finance, data are either missing or of low quality for immunization expenditure in many countries. The WHO Global Health Expenditure Database serves as one of the sources, but it does not cover each country for every year (Zhang et al., 2025). Data on primary health care financing during 2018 to 2021 are available for only approximately 10% of all countries (IA2030, 2025). Data collection for immunization finance at the country level should be strengthened.

As new technologies emerge, comprehensive cost effectiveness analyses may be more important than ever. For example, an innovative technology, vaccine microarray patches or VMAP, is being studied to compare their effectiveness against existing injectable vaccines. As VMAPs do not need needle or syringe, they will potentially boost the willingness to get vaccinated, thus increasing the beneficiaries from vaccination. VMAPs also have the potential for self-administration, thus reducing the required human resources for vaccine delivery. As a new technology that will gradually ramp up mass production, if cost effectiveness studies do not take into the account of overall saving for vaccination, it is likely the new intervention appears not cost effective when it indeed is.

While innovative financing mechanisms such as those utilized by IFFIm to support the national immunization programs in LLMICs have made achievements, their limitations and potential drawbacks should not be overlooked. The lack of transparency and financial inefficiency have raised concerns about their suitability for large-scale financing (Tacheva et al., 2025). More rigorous evaluation and consideration of alternative approaches should be explored to ensure that global health financing is effective and equitable.

Sustainability and self-sufficiency should be the goal for all national immunization programs. In LLMICs, this requires higher level development to improve the public health system, including vaccine preventable disease surveillance, and primary healthcare coverage. It may involve infrastructure and health system strengthening. As countries graduate from Gavi, middle-income countries are facing substantial challenges in self-financing for their national immunization program. MICs are lagging in introducing critical vaccines, presenting a threat to inter-country equity. Risk of backsliding, heightened by the pandemic, exacerbates intra-country inequities and jeopardizes the legacy of Gavi investments. Therefore, Gavi created the MICs Approach. Results for Development (R4D), a global nonprofit organization, issued a resource guide for immunization finance that listed sources of financing including domestic public funding sources, earmarking to finance immunization, domestic trust funds and household out-of-pocket payments in addition to development assistance for immunization (Results for Development, 2017). Immunization finance remains a problem to be solved as part of the broader national health system. Multilateral development banks may play an important role in establishing self-sufficiency. Innovative strategies such as debt restructuring and relief may be worth exploring.

With the improvement of HPV vaccination programs in LLMICs, we should not lose sight of space for improvement, both for HPV and immunization program against other vaccine preventable diseases. For example, developing country vaccine manufacturers complain about the differences between the anticipated demand and actual purchase orders for their vaccine. When the manufacturer cannot achieve economies of scale, the actual cost of the vaccine produced is much higher than the calculated costs based on a larger volume. To tackle this problem, people start to experiment with an innovative model for volume guarantee. MedAccess, a social finance company in the UK, brokers partnerships between medical product manufacturers and procurers to shoulder financial risks and create viable markets. For example, MedAccess signed an agreement with an in vitro diagnostics Human

Immunodeficiency Virus (HIV) test manufacturer to provide the financial guarantee of certain number of tests to ensure the low price and wide availability of the tests in 140 countries. This provides the volume guarantee needed for the manufacturer to lower the price to US$1 per test. The impact by the end of 2023 is estimated to be 482,000 additional people tested for HIV, 33% average price reduction and US$397,000 direct savings for procurement (MedAccess, 2024). With this model, MedAccess signed a volume guarantee agreement with Gavi and the malaria vaccine manufacturer, GSK, to support continued production of the malaria vaccine antigen. The agreement that went in effect in early 2024 is the only case for vaccine so far; the public health impact remains to be seen. Expanded application of this model to vaccine may be a viable solution to the volume guarantee problem.

A new trend since the COVID-19 pandemic is local or regional manufacture of vaccines in Africa. As the continent that inhabits 1.5 billion people, Africa produces fewer than 1 percent of the vaccines it uses. Most of the vaccine manufacturers in Africa only do packaging and labelling, few of them perform filling, and even fewer are able to produce drug substance, which is the active component of the vaccine (Gavi, 2022). The problem is how to develop the talents required to enable local or regional manufacture while achieving affordable prices for the local products. It will involve tremendous investment and effort, not just for hardware such as infrastructure, facilities and equipment, but also capacity building and bridging to nurture a qualified workforce (Africa CDC et al., 2023). Stakeholders are already starting to work on financing mechanisms. For example, Gavi started the African Vaccine Manufacturing Accelerator (AVMA), a new US$1 billion financing mechanism to incentivize local vaccine manufacture in Africa, with two payment schemes: Milestone Payment for vaccine prequalification by WHO, and Accelerator Payment to subsidize each dose supplied to fulfill a UNICEF order (Samarasekera, 2024).

The trend of local or regional vaccine manufacture is there for other regions, too. Countries in Asia, such as Malaysia and Thailand, are working to establish or strengthen its local vaccine manufacturing capacity. This will improve local vaccine supply security and, at the same time, may introduce the problem of fragmented manufacturing capacity and fragmented markets, resulting in higher costs that could disrupt vaccine affordability.

Vaccines are the silent heroes of public health. It is easy for humanity to fall into complacency when diseases are in check. The COVID-19 pandemic disrupted routine childhood vaccination. Misinformation and disinformation erode public confidence in vaccines and vaccination. As a result, people in many countries, including high income countries, are suffering from outbreaks of vaccine preventable diseases such as measles, and poliomyelitis that was close to global eradication. The societal costs of these unexpected disease outbreaks are not minor. For example, 72 confirmed cases of measles occurred in the first four months in 2019 in the US cost about

US$3.4 million, including the public health response, productivity loss and direct medical costs (Pike et al., 2021). There is much work to do in the space of vaccine confidence. Health behavior change communication (BCC) is a public health tool as important as the vaccine itself. It is a chain in vaccinology that we should not forget. It would be interesting to compare the cost savings through vaccination with and without intentional behavior change communication.

Since the COVID-19 pandemic, the world economy has been facing significant challenges, so funding from donors could continue to dwindle. The ever-changing geopolitical environment is posing threats to the financing models established so far. While Gavi is tackling the outlook for decreasing amount of donations from governments, it calls for more new funding mechanisms for LLMICs for their national immunization program. Without the sustained operation of these immunization programs, outbreaks of vaccine preventable diseases may occur more frequently. Meanwhile, it is time that the international development narrative shifted from charity to investing in self-sufficiency (World Economic Forum, 2025), as immunization finance is one piece of economic development.

CONCLUSION

Vaccination is the single greatest contribution of health intervention to ensuring children not only see their first birthdays but continue leading healthy lives into adulthood. A study of 73 countries supported by Gavi finds that every dollar spent on vaccines yields US$54 in return through increased productivity and reduced health costs (Sim et al., 2020). Vaccination is also one of the best uses of public finance to provide benefits for people in the health service delivery system. Cost effectiveness is proven through cost effectiveness analyses that weigh the cost of intervention against disease burden. With the decreased price per dose and reduced doses per course, HPV vaccination becomes more cost effective than ever.

In the HPV vaccination case, people have utilized mechanisms to finance immunization programs, incentivize low-cost vaccine supply and optimize the use of vaccine in low resource settings. This case proves that financial innovation is often a prerequisite for the equitable deployment of breakthrough health technologies. We should continue learning from success while thinking about the future for other financial innovations that overcome the shortcomings of existing mechanisms.

REFERENCES

Africa, C. D. C. CHAI, & PATH. (2023). *Current and planned vaccine manufacturing in Africa* (pp. 1–5). https://www.path.org/our-impact/resources/current-and-planned-vaccine-manufacturing-in-africa/

Agbenyega, T., Schuind, A. E., Adjei, S., Antony, K., Aponte, J. J., Buabeng, P. B. Y., Clemens, J. D., Hossain, L., Kemp, T. J., Mercer, L. D., Pinto, L. A., Qadri, F., Sukraw, K., Bhat, N., & Zaman, K. (2025). Immunogenicity and safety of an Escherichia coli-produced bivalent human papillomavirus vaccine (Cecolin) in girls aged 9–14 years in Ghana and Bangladesh: A randomised, controlled, open-label, non-inferiority, phase 3 trial. *The Lancet. Infectious Diseases*, *0*(0), 861–872. Advance online publication. DOI: 10.1016/S1473-3099(25)00031-3 PMID: 40120597

Ali, H. A., Hartner, A.-M., Echeverria-Londono, S., Roth, J., Li, X., Abbas, K., Portnoy, A., Vynnycky, E., Woodruff, K., Ferguson, N. M., Toor, J., & Gaythorpe, K. A. (2022). Vaccine equity in low and middle income countries: A systematic review and meta-analysis. *International Journal for Equity in Health*, *21*(1), 82. DOI: 10.1186/s12939-022-01678-5 PMID: 35701823

Atun, R., Fries, J. L., Hernandez-Villafuerte, K., Müller, M., Ostwald, D., & Schmitt, M. (2025). Contribution of investment in health and cancer control to economic growth in Commonwealth countries. *EClinicalMedicine*, *82*, 103180. Advance online publication. DOI: 10.1016/j.eclinm.2025.103180 PMID: 40247888

Burki, T. (2025). Gavi under threat from US funding cuts. *The Lancet. Infectious Diseases*, *25*(5), e266–e267. DOI: 10.1016/S1473-3099(25)00245-2 PMID: 40222375

CDC. (2022, June 6). *VFC | 2007-05-24 CDC Vaccine Price List | CDC*. https://archive.cdc.gov/www_cdc_gov/vaccines/programs/vfc/awardees/vaccine-management/price-list/2007/2007-05-24.html

CDC. (2024, October 2). *How Vaccines are Developed and Approved for Use*. Vaccines & Immunizations. https://www.cdc.gov/vaccines/basics/how-developed-approved.html

Cernuschi, T., Gaglione, S., & Bozzani, F. (2018). Challenges to sustainable immunization systems in Gavi transitioning countries. *Vaccine*, *36*(45), 6858–6866. DOI: 10.1016/j.vaccine.2018.06.012 PMID: 30268735

Chidebe, R. C. W., Osayi, A., & Torode, J. S. (2025). The Global Fund, Cervical Cancer, and HPV infections: What can low- and middle-income countries do to accelerate progress by 2030? *EClinicalMedicine*, *81*, 103127. DOI: 10.1016/j.eclinm.2025.103127 PMID: 40083441

Gavi. (2022). *Expanding sustainable vaccine manufacturing in Africa: Priorities for Support.* https://www.gavi.org/news-resources/knowledge-products/expanding-sustainable-vaccine-manufacturing-africa-priorities-support

Gavi's approach to engaging with middle-income countries. (2025, October 10). https://www.gavi.org/programmes-impact/programmatic-policies/eligibility-co-financing-policies/gavi-mics-approach

Gouglas, D., Thanh Le, T., Henderson, K., Kaloudis, A., Danielsen, T., Hammersland, N. C., Robinson, J. M., Heaton, P. M., & Røttingen, J.-A. (2018). Estimating the cost of vaccine development against epidemic infectious diseases: A cost minimisation study. *The Lancet. Global Health*, *6*(12), e1386–e1396. DOI: 10.1016/S2214-109X(18)30346-2 PMID: 30342925

Guimarães, E. L., Chissaque, A., Pecenka, C., Debellut, F., Schuind, A., Vaz, B., Banze, A., Rangeiro, R., Mariano, A., Lorenzoni, C., Carrilho, C., Martins, M., de Deus, N., & Clark, A. (2023). Impact and Cost-Effectiveness of Alternative Human Papillomavirus Vaccines for Preadolescent Girls in Mozambique: A Modelling Study. *Vaccines*, *11*(6), 6. Advance online publication. DOI: 10.3390/vaccines11061058 PMID: 37376447

Haddison, E. C., Engoung, D. B., Bodo, C. B., & Njie, V. M. (2025). Overcoming HPV vaccine hesitancy: Insights from a successful school-based vaccination campaign in the Saa health district of Cameroon. *BMC Infectious Diseases*, *25*(1), 465. DOI: 10.1186/s12879-025-10864-z PMID: 40186125

Human papillomavirus vaccines: WHO position paper, December 2022. (2022). *WEEKLY EPIDEMIOLOGICAL RECORD*, *97*(50), 645–672.

IA2030. (2025). *IA2030 Global Progress Report 2024* (pp. 1–70). https://www.immunizationagenda2030.org/ia2030-annual-reports

IFFIm. (2025). *Eligible Countries | International Finance Facility for Immunisation (IFFIm).* International Finance Facility for Immunisation (IFFIm). https://iffim.org/eligible-countries

Kiendrébéogo, J. A., Sidibe, A. R. O., Compaoré, G. B., Nacanabo, R., Sory, O., Ouédraogo, I., Nawaz, S., Schuind, A. E., & Clark, A. (2023). Cost-effectiveness of human papillomavirus (HPV) vaccination in Burkina Faso: A modelling study. *BMC Health Services Research*, *23*(1), 1338. DOI: 10.1186/s12913-023-10283-3 PMID: 38041075

Llave, C. L., Uy, M. E. V., Lam, H. Y., Aldaba, J. G., Yacapin, C. C., Miranda, M. B., Valverde, H. A., Silva, W. T., Nawaz, S., Slavkovsky, R. C., Mooney, J., & Vodicka, E. L. (2022). The cost-effectiveness of human papillomavirus vaccination in the Philippines. *Vaccine*, *40*(27), 3802–3811. DOI: 10.1016/j.vaccine.2022.05.025 PMID: 35606237

Luvsan, M.-E., Vodicka, E., Jugder, U., Tudev, U., Clark, A., Groman, D., Otgonbayar, D., Demberelsuren, S., LaMongtagne, D. S., & Pecenka, C. (2022). The potential cost-effectiveness of HPV vaccination among girls in Mongolia. *Vaccine: X*, *11*, 100161. DOI: 10.1016/j.jvacx.2022.100161 PMID: 35509519

Mahoney, R. T., & Maynard, J. E. (1999). The introduction of new vaccines into developing countries. *Vaccine*, *17*(7), 646–652. DOI: 10.1016/S0264-410X(98)00246-1 PMID: 10067669

Malvolti, S., Soble, A., Bloem, P., LaMontagne, D. S., Aggarwal, R., Pitisuttithum, P., Rees, H., & Cernuschi, T. (2023). The Global Demand and Supply Balance of the Human Papillomavirus Vaccine: Implications for the Global Strategy for the Elimination of Cervical Cancer. *Vaccines*, *12*(1), 4. DOI: 10.3390/vaccines12010004 PMID: 38276663

MedAccess. (2024). *MedAccess Impact case studies 2024* (October 2024, pp. 1-9). https://medaccess.org/wp-content/uploads/2024/11/MedAccess-Impact-Case-Studies-2024.pdf

Mercuri, M., Hackett, K., Barnabas, R. V., & Emerson, C. I. (2024). Evaluation of a single-dose HPV vaccine strategy for promoting vaccine, health, and gender equity. *The Lancet. Infectious Diseases*, *24*(10), e654–e658. DOI: 10.1016/S1473-3099(24)00227-5 PMID: 38734009

Micolo, G. (2025, April 24). *Angolans spread the word: Cervical cancer is vaccine-preventable*. Gavi. https://www.gavi.org/vaccineswork/angolans-spread-word-cervical-cancer-vaccine-preventable

Muraskin, W. (2005). *Crusade to Immunize the World's Children* (1st ed.). USC Marshall Global BioBusiness Initiative.

Murewanhema, G., Moyo, E., Dzobo, M., Mandishora-Dube, R. S., & Dzinamarira, T. (2024). Human papilloma virus vaccination in the resource-limited settings of sub-Saharan Africa: Challenges and recommendations. *Vaccine: X*, *20*, 100549. DOI: 10.1016/j.jvacx.2024.100549 PMID: 39263366

Mwenda, V., Jalang'o, R., Miano, C., Bor, J.-P., Nyangasi, M., Mecca, L., Were, V., Kariithi, E., Pecenka, C., Schuind, A., Abbas, K., & Clark, A. (2023). Impact, cost-effectiveness, and budget implications of HPV vaccination in Kenya: A modelling study. *Vaccine*, *41*(29), 4228–4238. DOI: 10.1016/j.vaccine.2023.05.019 PMID: 37296015

Ndiaye, C. (2024, November 10). *Dose Of Hope: How Updated Vaccine Policy Can Protect More Women Against Cervical Cancer—Health Policy Watch. Health Policy Watch.* https://healthpolicy-watch.news/dose-of-hope-how-updated-vaccine-policy-can-protect-more-women-against-cervical-cancer

PATH. (2011). *Implementing HPV Vaccination Programs, practical experience from PATH* (pp. 1–36). PATH. https://media.path.org/documents/RH_ccp_hpv_vaccination.pdf

PATH. (2012). *Evaluating HPV vaccination pilots, practical experience from PATH* (pp. 1–46). https://media.path.org/documents/RH_ccp_hpv_pilots.pdf

Pike, J., Melnick, A., Gastañaduy, P. A., Kay, M., Harbison, J., Leidner, A. J., Rice, S., Asato, K., Schwartz, L., & DeBolt, C. (2021). Societal Costs of a Measles Outbreak. *Pediatrics*, *147*(4), e2020027037. DOI: 10.1542/peds.2020-027037 PMID: 33712549

Plotkin, S., Robinson, J. M., Cunningham, G., Iqbal, R., & Larsen, S. (2017). The complexity and cost of vaccine manufacturing – An overview. *Vaccine*, *35*(33), 4064–4071. DOI: 10.1016/j.vaccine.2017.06.003 PMID: 28647170

Prem, K., Choi, Y. H., Bénard, É., Burger, E. A., Hadley, L., Laprise, J.-F., Regan, M. C., Drolet, M., Sy, S., Abbas, K., Portnoy, A., Kim, J. J., Brisson, M., & Jit, M. (2023). Global impact and cost-effectiveness of one-dose versus two-dose human papillomavirus vaccination schedules: A comparative modelling analysis. *BMC Medicine*, *21*(1), 313. DOI: 10.1186/s12916-023-02988-3 PMID: 37635227

Pronker, E. S., Weenen, T. C., Commandeur, H., Claassen, E. H. J. H. M., & Osterhaus, A. D. M. E. (2013). Risk in Vaccine Research and Development Quantified. *PLoS One*, *8*(3), e57755. DOI: 10.1371/journal.pone.0057755 PMID: 23526951

Rakheja, S., Mehta, D., Aggarwal, I., Goel, H., Joseph, D., Jain, J., Deep, G., Grover, M., Verma, P., & Singh, B. (2025). Knowledge, Attitude and Awareness of HPV Vaccination among College-Going Girls (18–26 years) in Delhi NCR. *Asian Pacific Journal of Cancer Nursing*, 20250806–20250806. https://doi.org/DOI: 10.31557/apjcn.1967.20250806

Regan, K. (2024, March 14). *Is HPV vaccination cost effective?* https://www.path.org/our-impact/articles/is-hpv-vaccination-cost-effective/

REPPARE. (2025, June 8). Innovative Health Financing Mechanisms for Advancing Pandemic Preparedness: 'Huge Untapped Potential' or False Advertising? ★ Brownstone Institute. *Brownstone Institute.* https://brownstone.org/articles/innovative-health-financing-mechanisms-for-advancing-pandemic-preparedness-huge-untapped-potential-or-false-advertising/

Results for Development. (2017). *Immunization Financing, a resource guide for advocates, policymakers, and program managers* (pp. 1–128). R4D. https://www.r4d.org/wp-content/uploads/Immunization_Financing_Resource_Guide_2017_FULL.pdf

Samarasekera, U. (2024). African vaccine manufacturing scheme to boost production. *Lancet, 403*(10444), 2579–2580. DOI: 10.1016/S0140-6736(24)01239-X PMID: 38880099

Schuind, A. E., Balaji, K. A., Du, A., Yuan, Y., & Dull, P. (2024). Human papillomavirus prophylactic vaccines: Update on new vaccine development and implications for single-dose policy. *Journal of the National Cancer Institute. Monographs, 2024*(67), 410–416. DOI: 10.1093/jncimonographs/lgae026 PMID: 39529522

Shattock, A. J., Johnson, H. C., Sim, S. Y., Carter, A., Lambach, P., Hutubessy, R. C. W., Thompson, K. M., Badizadegan, K., Lambert, B., Ferrari, M. J., Jit, M., Fu, H., Silal, S. P., Hounsell, R. A., White, R. G., Mosser, J. F., Gaythorpe, K. A. M., Trotter, C. L., Lindstrand, A., & Bar-Zeev, N. (2024). Contribution of vaccination to improved survival and health: Modelling 50 years of the Expanded Programme on Immunization. *Lancet, 403*(10441), 2307–2316. DOI: 10.1016/S0140-6736(24)00850-X PMID: 38705159

Sim, S. Y., Watts, E., Constenla, D., Brenzel, L., & Patenaude, B. N. (2020). Return On Investment From Immunization Against 10 Pathogens In 94 Low- And Middle-Income Countries, 2011–30. *Health Affairs (Project Hope), 39*(8), 1343–1353. DOI: 10.1377/hlthaff.2020.00103 PMID: 32744930

Tacheva, B., Brown, G. W., Bell, D., & von Agris, J. (2025). The devil's in the detail: An appraisal of the use of innovative financing mechanisms for pandemic prevention, preparedness and response. *Globalization and Health, 21*(1), 13. DOI: 10.1186/s12992-025-01103-w PMID: 40148959

UNICEF. (2019). *Human Papillomavirus Vaccine: Supply and Demand Update* (pp. 1–12). https://www.unicef.org/supply/sites/unicef.org.supply/files/2020-03/human-papillomavirus-vaccine-HPV-supply-and-demand-update.pdf

UNICEF. (2025). *Human Papilloma Virus (HPV) vaccine price data | UNICEF Supply Division*. https://www.unicef.org/supply/documents/human-papilloma-virus-hpv-vaccine-price-data

WHO. (2015). Human papillomavirus vaccines: WHO position paper, October 2014-Recommendations. *Vaccine*, *33*(36), 4383–4384. DOI: 10.1016/j.vaccine.2014.12.002 PMID: 25510390

WHO. (2024). *Considerations for human papillomavirus (HPV) vaccine product choice* (2nd ed.). https://www.who.int/publications/i/item/9789240089167

WHO. (2025). *WHO Immunization Data portal—Detail Page*. Immunization Data. https://immunizationdata.who.int/global/wiise-detail-page

World Economic Forum. (2025, April 28). *A new era in global aid: Why locally led, market-based solutions are the best route to resilience*. World Economic Forum. https://www.weforum.org/stories/2025/04/global-aid-new-era-resilience/

Xu, M. A., Choi, J., Capasso, A., & DiClemente, R. J. (2024). Improving HPV Vaccination Uptake Among Adolescents in Low Resource Settings: Sociocultural and Socioeconomic Barriers and Facilitators. *Adolescent Health, Medicine and Therapeutics*, *15*, 73–82. DOI: 10.2147/AHMT.S394119 PMID: 39100520

Xu, T., Yang, X., He, X., & Wu, J. (2022). The Study on Cervical Cancer Burden in 127 Countries and Its Socioeconomic Influence Factors. *Journal of Epidemiology and Global Health*, *13*(1), 154–161. DOI: 10.1007/s44197-022-00081-1 PMID: 36542301

Zhang, H., Patenaude, B., Zhang, H., Jit, M., & Fang, H. (2024). Global vaccine coverage and childhood survival estimates: 1990–2019. *Bulletin of the World Health Organization*, *102*(4), 276–287. DOI: 10.2471/BLT.23.290129 PMID: 38562199

Zhang, X., Chen, S., & Tang, S. (2025). *Comparative analysis of the national immunization programmes in select ASEAN and SAARC countries: Progress and challenges*. https://iris.who.int/bitstream/handle/10665/380387/9789290620785-eng.pdf

Chapter 6
AB-PMJAY and the Path to Universal Health Coverage:
Reducing OOPE in India and Lessons for LMICs

Oliver J. Lee
http://orcid.org/0009-0000-0854-8722
University College London, UK

Adrien J. Lucci
University College London, UK

Shanti Poolapalli Manukonda
University College London, UK

ABSTRACT

This chapter examines India's national health insurance scheme, Ayushman Bharat – Pradhan Mantri Jan Arogya Yojana (AB-PMJAY), assessing its impact on out-of-pocket expenditure (OOPE) and the socioeconomic factors influencing it. Findings are compared with Indonesia's Jaminan Kesehatan Nasional to draw lessons for universal health coverage in low- and middle-income countries (LMICs). Using data from ten Indian states, a quantitative analysis—descriptive statistics, multiple regression, and difference-in-difference—found gains in public health spending, coverage, and selected health outcomes, but no significant short-term OOPE reduction. This underscores the need for outpatient coverage, strong governance, and equitable utilisation. India's experience shows LMIC reforms must go beyond insurance expansion to address service design, awareness, and gender gaps.

DOI: 10.4018/979-8-3373-3341-0.ch006

INTRODUCTION

The Persistent Problem of Paying for Care

Across many low- and middle-income countries (LMICs), falling ill still means paying directly for healthcare — often more than households can afford. Despite decades of global commitment to universal health coverage (UHC), out-of-pocket expenditure (OOPE) remains one of the biggest barriers to accessing care and a leading cause of financial distress. In many LMICs, OOPE accounts for over 40% of total health expenditure (THE) and in some countries even exceeds 60% (Wagstaff et al., 2019; World Health Organization, 2021a). By 2021, more than 1.3 billion people worldwide faced catastrophic health spending, defined as healthcare costs exceeding 10% of household income (World Bank, 2023).

India exemplifies the scale of the problem. Over 60% of the country's THE comes directly from individuals at the point of service — more than triple the global average of around 18%. Similar patterns are seen in Bangladesh, Nigeria and Cambodia, reflecting systemic weaknesses in financial protection across LMICs (Kaiser et al., 2023; World Health Organization 2021b). For poor and vulnerable households, these costs can be catastrophic, forcing trade-offs between healthcare, debt and basic needs. Delays in seeking care lead to worse health outcomes, while unaffordable services drive patients toward fragmented or unregulated providers (Garg & Karan, 2009; Patel et al., 2023).

In this chapter, we explore why OOPE costs remain stubbornly high in many LMICs and how smart financing reforms can change that. We take a close look at India's Ayushman Bharat – Pradhan Mantri Jan Arogya Yojana (AB-PMJAY) and draw comparative lessons from Indonesia's UHC scheme, Jaminan Kesehatan Nasional (JKN). From these two very different journeys, we set out practical recommendations for designing and delivering UHC reforms that are fair, financially protective and built to last.

BACKGROUND

Why OOPE Persists in LMICs

OOPE in LMICs is the product of deep structural factors rather than a failure of policy design alone. Many health systems inherited during the colonial era were designed for limited coverage, typically focused on urban centres and serving colonial elites, with rural and marginalised populations reliant on missionary or informal care (Ho et al., 2022). Post-independence, fiscal constraints and competing development priorities meant that these inequitable structures were only partially reformed. In some countries, these patterns persist in the form of underfunded primary care systems and uneven health infrastructure.

Modern political economy dynamics reinforce these legacies. LMICs often operate under fiscal influence from international financial institutions, development partners and trade regimes, which can shape domestic health financing priorities (Ho et al., 2022). Even when social spending safeguards are included in loan agreements, they do not always translate into greater health investment. For example, a review of International Monetary Fund-supported programmes between 2020 and 2022 found that 15 of 21 borrower countries with "social spending floors", targets meant to protect sectors like health, still experienced reduced fiscal space for public health spending (Kentikelenis & Stubbs, 2024). In many cases, deficit reduction targets, restrictions on wage bills and debt servicing obligations outweighed these protections, limiting governments' ability to expand coverage or invest in essential services. The result is that health systems remain under-resourced and households continue to bear a high share of costs directly.

At the scheme design level, OOPE persists where benefit packages are narrow, reimbursement ceilings are low, or essential services remain excluded. India's AB-PMJAY, for example, focuses on hospitalisation benefits while excluding most outpatient consultations, diagnostics and medicines, the services that account for the majority of household health spending (Nanda & Sharma, 2023a; Reshmi et al., 2021). Similar gaps are observed in Kenya, Nigeria and Bangladesh (Barasa et al., 2018; World Bank, 2023).

Medicines and diagnostics remain dominant OOPE drivers. In India, medicines account for over 70% of household healthcare expenses, a pattern mirrored across the global south (Nanda & Sharma, 2023b; World Health Organization, 2021c). Even where public facilities are available, frequent stockouts force patients to purchase medicines privately, often at high cost (Olaniran et al., 2022).

Provider-side factors compound these pressures. Public facilities may receive delayed reimbursements, creating incentives for informal fees. In the private sector (widely used across LMICs), treatment costs can be several times higher than in public facilities, even under government-financed schemes (Garg et al., 2022). Inconsistent provider participation, particularly among private hospitals, can leave insured populations without practical access to contracted services.

Even where financial protection schemes exist, awareness of entitlements can be uneven and utilisation low. Surveys in India have found that only around 69% of eligible participants were aware of AB-PMJAY and fewer than 80% of those knew the full scope of benefits (Prasad et al., 2023). In parts of rural areas, just 13% of households reported good awareness and only one-third of that figure had ever used the scheme's benefits (Shruddha et al., 2025). Similar scheme utilisation gaps have been documented in Indonesia and Kenya, where eligible households either did not know they were covered or lacked clarity on how to access benefits. Information asymmetries limit the reach of financial protection, particularly for rural and marginalised populations.

Finally, governance weaknesses, such as overlapping schemes, politicised benefit design and weak accountability, can limit financial protection. Before Indonesia's JKN unified multiple insurance programmes under one agency, scheme fragmentation led to inequitable benefits and inefficiency. AB-PMJAY faces similar risks in India, where state-level variation in empanelment and reimbursement undermines portability and coverage depth.

THE COST OF CARE

What People Actually Pay For

When health systems rely heavily on OOPE, the financial burden on households goes far beyond hospital bills. People in LMICs routinely pay for consultations, diagnostics, medicines and procedures (Ambade et al., 2022). They also absorb indirect costs: transport to distant facilities, time lost from work, the cost of caregiving and, in some cases, informal or under-the-table payments (Sabermahani et al., 2021).

Across much of the Global South, medicines remain the single largest component of OOPE. These are not incidental expenses. For low-income households, even one course of antibiotics can be enough to derail a month's budget (Olaniran et al., 2022).

Outpatient care, including primary consultations, diagnostics and routine treatments, is another glaring gap. Many insurance schemes in LMICs are designed around inpatient coverage, leaving patients to pay directly for the services they use most often. In India, this exclusion is a major driver of catastrophic health spending, even among insured households (Nanda & Sharma, 2023a).

Informal payments are another dimension, particularly in underfunded or fragmented systems. Research from Eastern Europe, Southeast Asia and parts of Africa has documented the persistence of unofficial charges levied at public facilities — either as bribes or as informal fees to guarantee faster or better treatment (Jalali et al., 2021; Lewis, 2007). These practices fall hardest on poorer households and reflect deeper failures in regulation and public sector performance.

Conversely, Thailand shows what targeted reform can achieve. Its Universal Coverage Scheme (UCS) includes both outpatient and inpatient services, delivered through a designated public provider network. A nominal copayment of 30 Baht (approximately £0.69) was introduced to reduce misuse, but in practice, more than

90% of UCS patients pay nothing at the point of care (Damrongplasit & Melnick, 2024).

OOPE is not only a question of how much people spend — it is about what is systematically excluded from coverage and who is left to absorb the cost.

Who Pays the Most — Disparities in the Burden

The burden of OOPE is not shared evenly. In LMICs, the cost of care falls hardest on poorer households, rural populations, women and informal workers, who are less able to pay for care (Alam & Mahal, 2014). These disparities are structural, shaped by how healthcare systems are financed, who they reach and what they exclude.

Income is the most visible dividing line. Poorer households spend a larger share of their income on healthcare and are more likely to face catastrophic health costs. The World Health Organisation (WHO) and World Bank estimate that 90% of households experiencing such costs are in the bottom 40% of the income distribution. In many LMICs, those in the lowest income quintile spend two to three times more, proportionally, than the richest (Wagstaff et al., 2019).

Rural households face additional disadvantages. Public health infrastructure is often concentrated in urban areas, forcing rural residents to travel further and rely on private or informal providers. In Bangladesh, rural households are significantly more likely to experience catastrophic spending than urban ones, largely due to travel costs and limited availability of free or subsidised care (Rahman et al., 2024). Similar patterns are observed across South Asia and sub-Saharan Africa, where rural underinvestment remains a persistent barrier to access.

Women face both direct and indirect costs. Public schemes often exclude outpatient and reproductive services, forcing women to pay privately for antenatal care, diagnostic tests, or basic medications. Cost is also more likely to deter women from seeking care, particularly when compounded by caregiving responsibilities and lower financial autonomy. When financial protection schemes don't account for these dynamics, they reinforce existing inequalities (Nanda & Sharma, 2023a).

Informal workers, who make up a majority of the workforce in many LMICs, are routinely excluded from insurance linked to formal employment or identity documentation. In Indonesia, JKN enrolment is high on paper, but informal workers often remain outside contracted provider networks or lack information on how to use their benefits, resulting in continued OOPE (Maulana et al., 2022). In India, informal workers account for most of those left out of financial protection altogether (Sengupta & Nundy, 2005).

Some countries have moved to close these gaps. Thailand's UCS includes informal workers and is not tied to employment status. Rwanda's community-based insurance achieves high enrolment by subsidising premiums for the poor. Mexico's

Seguro Popular expanded coverage to previously excluded groups, though challenges in quality and continuity remain. Even where reforms have broadened access, gaps persist — in medicine availability, referral systems and the coverage of real-world care needs.

OOPE is not just a problem of how much people pay — it's about who pays most and why. Any attempt to improve financial protection must start by recognising and addressing these structural disparities.

Health And Wealth: The Productivity Case

The link between health and economic productivity is well-evidenced: when individuals face high costs for care, the consequences extend well beyond the household. OOPE drives financial hardship, systematically depresses labour participation, stifles investment and reduces long-term economic growth.

At the most immediate level, OOPE impacts labour supply by worsening the financial consequences of illness. Poor health—often compounded by financial barriers to care—has been shown to significantly reduce both labour force participation and educational attainment (Voto et al., 2025). When individuals face high healthcare costs, they delay or forgo care, leading to prolonged or worsened illness — or they may be forced to stop working all together to seek treatment or recover. This is especially acute in informal economies with limited job security or social protection.

The impact extends beyond patients themselves. When formal systems of care are limited and healthcare costs fall to households, it is often family members who step in to provide support. This can come at a cost. In LMICs, around 74% of women aged 25 to 54 cite unpaid caregiving as a reason for being out of the labour force (International Labour Organization, 2025). In rural India, for example, informal caregivers devote approximately of 39 hours per week to unpaid care (Brinda et al., 2014). Scaled across millions of households in LMICs, this "invisible" withdrawal of the workforce robs countries of their productive engine. It diverts people from education, employment and enterprise limiting their ability to contribute fully to economic and public life.

OOPE impacts financial security of households. Families often resort to borrowing or selling productive assets to finance care, which undermines future earning potential. Murphy et al. (2019) document that coping strategies in response to medical costs frequently include removing children from school or abandoning small-scale business activities. Similar patterns are reported in Mongolia, where healthcare expenses have been shown to crowd out spending on food, rent and transport, displacing critical consumption and investment (Batbold et al., 2022). These costs compound over time. When OOPE forces households to cut back on nutrition or education, the development of human capital suffers. Murphy et al (2020) note that such sacrifices weaken both current and future workforce productivity.

In one multi-country study, productivity loss from illness and financial hardship reached up to 2% of GDP annually (Kolesar et al., 2023). These losses stem not only from absenteeism but also from presenteeism (being at work while unwell), which can sap efficiency (Mitchell & Bates, 2011). For small and medium enterprises, these disruptions can be particularly destabilising.

Taken together, these findings show that high OOPE is not simply a matter of financial protection, it is a structural constraint on economic development, perpetuating cycles of poverty. Health financing reform, when properly designed, is therefore not only a public health imperative but also a long-term investment in the nation's livelihood.

A Critical Moment

Many low- and middle-income countries have made explicit commitments to achieving UHC. From constitutional guarantees to national health insurance schemes, governments have taken steps to shift more of the financing burden from individuals to the state. These efforts have often been backed by international agencies, global funds and development finance institutions, offering mechanisms such as pooled donor funding, results-based financing and performance-linked grants (Savedoff et al., 2012).

Digital infrastructure has added momentum. Mobile money systems, biometric national ID platforms and digital health records now allow for better targeting, more efficient payments and potentially more accountable service delivery. These tools create the foundations for smarter, more equitable health financing. But the reality has been more uneven. Many public schemes still exclude outpatient care—one of the largest drivers of out-of-pocket costs. Others suffer from low provider participation, limited coverage depth, or weak enforcement of entitlements. Even when insurance is in place, patients often continue to pay high fees for medicines, diagnostics and transport (Mills et al., 2012; Ravindran & Gaitonde, 2018).

In response to these challenges, LMICs have increasingly turned to publicly funded insurance schemes. These aim to reduce household spending by pooling risk, subsidising access and contracting both public and private providers. The hope is that, by scaling entitlements and linking financing to service use, such schemes can offer meaningful financial protection. But design matters. Where benefits are narrow, enrolment is passive, or systems fail to reach high-need populations, the impact on out-of-pocket expenditure remains limited.

India's AB-PMJAY is one of the most ambitious of these reforms, aiming to cover 500 million people and shift India's health system toward greater equity and financial protection.

On paper, the scheme ticks many boxes: a large risk pool, government financing and portability across states. But important questions remain. AB-PMJAY focuses heavily on hospital-based services, with outpatient consultations and medicines largely excluded from the benefit package. Implementation varies across states and provider engagement—particularly in the private sector—has been inconsistent. These design choices raise a core issue: can public insurance meaningfully reduce out-of-pocket expenditure when the services that drive most household costs remain uncovered?

INDIA'S AYUSHMAN BHARAT: BIG VISION, MIXED RESULTS

This section introduces the Indian healthcare system and its financing structure, followed by a quantitative analysis of the impact of AB-PMJAY on OOPE. The analysis is motivated by the current shortage of longitudinal studies that track the scheme's progress over time, which are essential for evaluating its sustainability and long-term benefits. This section provides insights into the influence of AB-PMJAY on OOPE and the socioeconomic factors that shape these expenditures.

Ayushman Bharat: Healthcare Access

AB-PMJAY is a flagship healthcare initiative launched by the Government of India in 2018 with the goal of achieving universal health coverage. It aims to address health holistically through two main components: HWCs and the Pradhan Mantri Jan Arogya Yojana (PM-JAY) (National Health Authority, Government of India, 2025).

Health and Wellness Centers (HWCS)

The Government of India announced the creation of 150,000 HWCs by transforming existing Sub Centres and Primary Health Centres (Ministry of Health and Family Welfare, Government of India, 2018). These centres deliver primary health care close to homes, covering maternal and child health, non-communicable diseases and providing free essential drugs and diagnostics (Government of India, 2018).

Pradhan Mantri Jan Arogya Yojana (PMJAY)

PMJAY is a health insurance scheme under AB-PMJAY aimed at providing secondary and tertiary healthcare services to economically vulnerable families. It is one of the world's largest publicly funded health insurance programs (Government of India, 2018).

Coverage

PMJAY offers an annual health cover of 500,000 (approximately £5,000) per family for secondary and tertiary care hospitalisation. This coverage encompasses a wide array of medical procedures and services, including pre-hospitalisation expenses, hospitalisation, post-hospitalisation costs and numerous day-care treatments (National Health Authority, 2023).

PMJAY allows cashless and paperless access to healthcare services across public and private empanelled hospitals throughout India. Empanelment refers to the process of enlisting hospitals to be part of the PMJAY network (National Health Authority, 2023). PMJAY encompasses a range of 1,350 medical packages covering surgeries, medical and day care treatments, cost of medicines and diagnostics (National Health Authority, 2023; NITI Aayog, 2021).

The scheme covers over 120 million families, targeting the bottom 40% of earners in the Indian population. The households included are selected based on the deprivation and occupational criteria of the Socio-Economic and Caste Census 2011 (SECC, 2011) for rural and urban areas. Focusing on households that fall under specified deprivation categories ensures that the benefits reach those who need them the most (Ministry of Health and Family Welfare, 2023a).

Figures 1 and 2 demonstrate that following the implementation of AB-PMJAY in 2018 the OOPE as a percentage of THE has reduced across the country.

Figure 1. OOPE as a percentage of total health expenditure in India 2015-2016. Adapted from Ministry of Health and Family Welfare (2018)

Figure 2. OOPE as a percentage of total health expenditure in India 2019-2020 - adapted from Ministry of Health and Family Welfare (2023b)

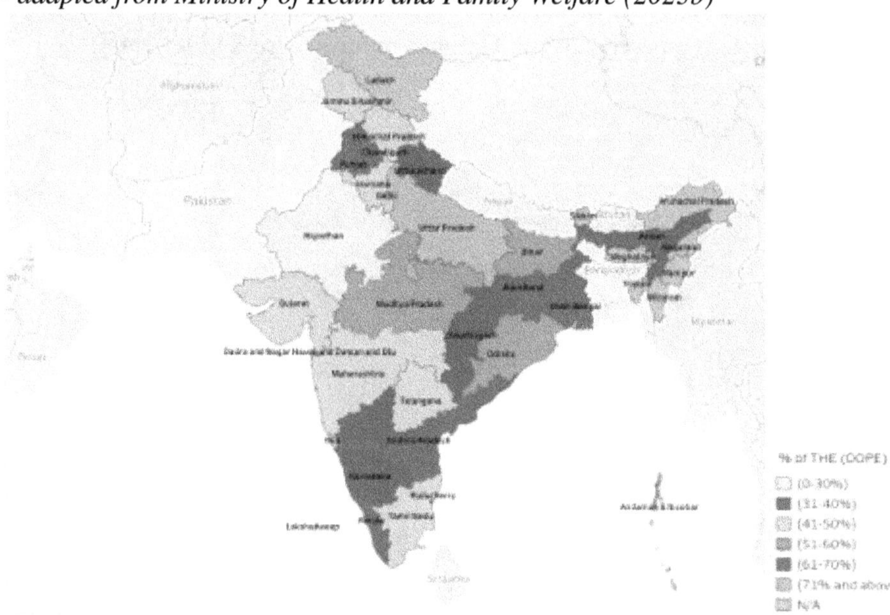

Funding of Healthcare in India

India has one of the lowest percentage GDP spend on healthcare in the world (World Bank, 2021). Figure 3 shows India's 2021 healthcare expenditure as percentage of GDP spent on healthcare compared to Brazil, Russia, China and South Africa. According to the World Bank, India's healthcare expenditure is approximately 3.5 percent of its GDP, considerably lower than many other countries (World Bank, 2021). This underfunding has resulted in a healthcare system that struggles to meet the needs of its citizens adequately (World Health Organization, 2020a).

Figure 3. Health expenditure as percentage of GDP in BRICS - adapted from World Bank (2024a)

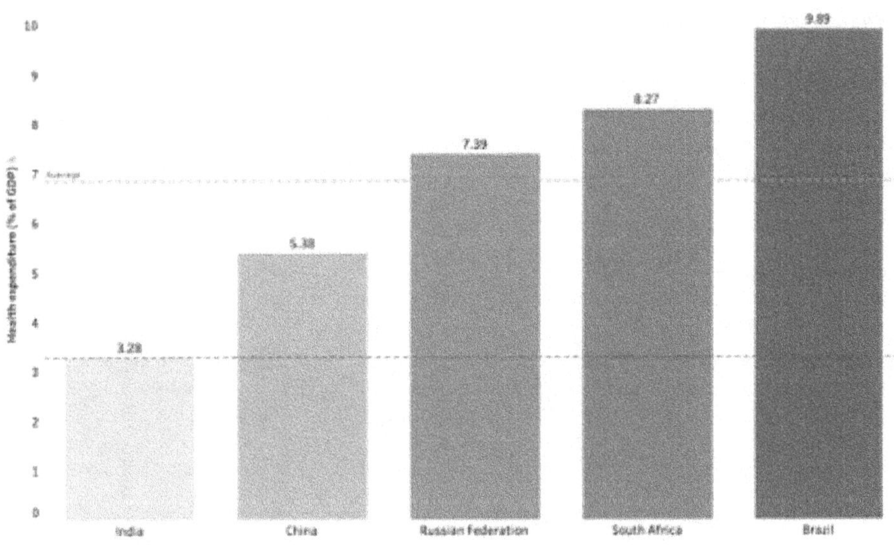

Private health insurance in India is gradually growing but still covers a relatively small segment of the population, covering less than 20% of people (Insurance Regulatory and Development Authority of India, 2020). Employer-provided insurance forms a significant part of this sector, with many companies offering health insurance as part of their employee benefits (Khan et al., 2021). Additionally, individuals have the option to purchase health insurance from private insurers. This limited coverage leaves a large majority of people dependent on out-of-pocket payments and government schemes.

Indian state governments have their own healthcare budgets and are responsible for funding healthcare services at the state level (Reshmi et al., 2021). States have the option to join AB-PMJAY or maintain their existing health insurance schemes, either independently or in partial collaboration with AB-PMJAY. Figure 4 shows which states had funding for AB-PMJAY when it was first rolled out in 2018. There are disparities in healthcare funding between different states in India (Ud Din et al., 2023). Some states fund their own health insurance schemes. For example, Telangana has implemented "Aarogyasri Scheme" offering up to £2000 for citizens below poverty line requiring hospitalisation and surgery (Government of Telangana, 2025). This results in disparities in the availability and quality of healthcare services across the country (Mohanty et al., 2023). While several studies examine differences in health outcomes, healthcare availability, coverage, and standards of care, few focus on variations in health expenditure across Indian states (Dash & Mohanty, 2019).

Figure 4. Indian states with government funding for AB-PMJAY in 2018-2019 - adapted from Government of India (2024)

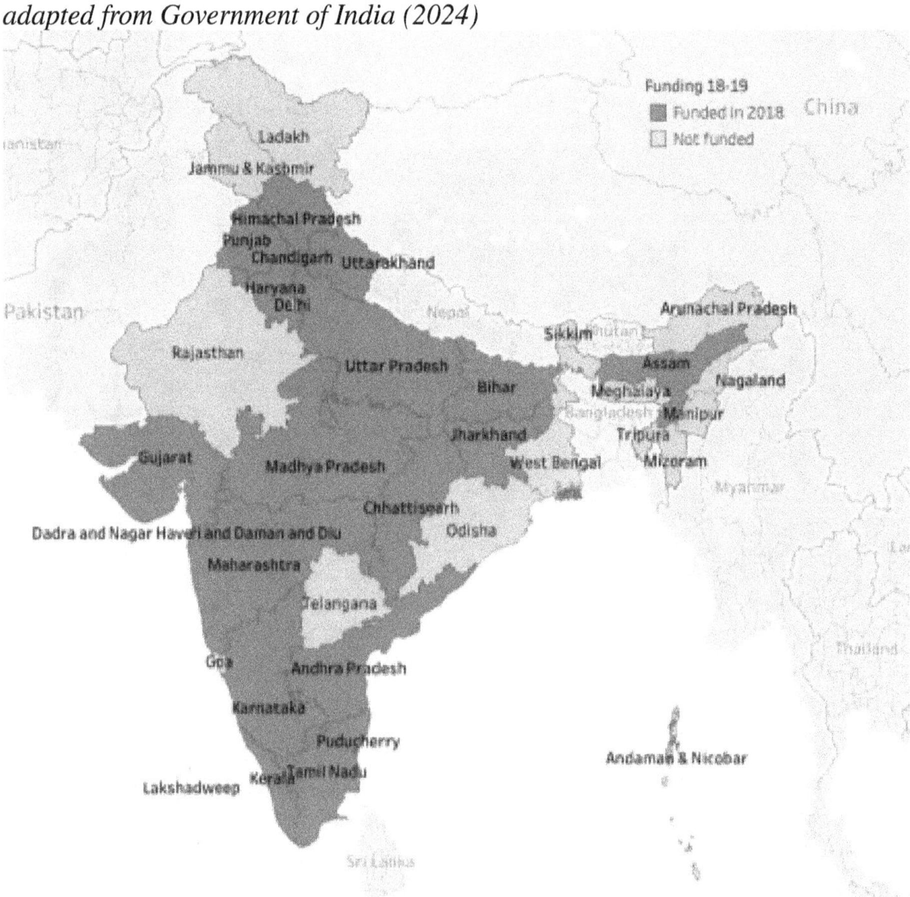

Public healthcare and AB-PMJAY are funded by the Central Government through income tax with co-funding from the State Government (up to 40%) The central government through the Ministry of Health and Family Welfare funds public healthcare, by allocating funds for national health programs and initiatives such as AB- PMJAY. The scheme was projected to cost £696m in 2023-2024, marking an 11% increase compared to the average cost (£553m) of the four previous financial years. This increase indicates a commitment to improving healthcare access and coverage across the country (National Health Authority, 2024).

AB-PMJAY has been implemented to expand insurance coverage among vulnerable populations. Evidence suggests that this style of health insurance coverage can reduce OOPE and improve financial stability for households (Devadasan et al., 2011; Patel et al., 2023)

Measuring the Impact of AB-PMJAY

Effect Across 10 States

Ten states were selected for the analysis for which OOPE per capita data and socioeconomic data were available. Eight states were used as the "treatment group" (Chhattisgarh, Haryana, Jharkhand, Madhya Pradesh, Punjab, Tamil Nadu, Uttar Pradesh and Uttarakhand) in which AB-PMJAY was rolled-out in 2018. Two states (Telangana and Odisha) were used as "control group" in which AB-PMJAY was not rolled to allow comparison (See Appendix 1 for states selection process). Data from 2015-16 and 2019-20 were selected as AB-PMJAY was rolled out in 2018, allowing a comparison pre and post implementation.

Data Sources Used for the Quantitative Analysis

Table 1 summarises the data sources used for the statistical analysis. These include the National Family Health Survey (NFHS), National Health Accounts (NHA), Employment-Unemployment Survey (EUS) and the Periodic Labour Force Survey (PLFS). These sources provide detailed data on health, financial and labour market.

Table 1. Data sources used for the quantitative analysis

Data Source	Description	Years	Reference
The National Family Health Survey (NFHS)	A large-scale, multi-round survey conducted in a representative sample of households throughout India. It provides essential data on health, family welfare and related issues.	2015–16 (NFHS-4) & 2019–20 (NFHS-5)	Ministry of Health and Family Welfare (2019)
National Health Accounts (NHA)	A comprehensive and systematic monitoring of resource flows in a country's health system. It helps in understanding the financing and expenditure patterns in the health sector.	2015–16 & 2019–20	Ministry of Health and Family Welfare (2020)
Employment-Unemployment Survey (EUS)	Conducted by the National Sample Survey Office (NSSO), this survey provides data on employment and unemployment in India. It helps in understanding the labour market dynamics and workforce participation.	2015–16	National Sample Survey Office (2016)
Periodic Labour Force Survey (PLFS)	Conducted by the National Statistical Office (NSO), this survey aims to provide estimates of key labour force indicators more frequently than the earlier EUS. It includes data on employment, unemployment and labour force participation rates.	2019–20	National Statistical Office (2020)

Source: (Ministry of Health and Family Welfare, 2019; Ministry of Health and Family Welfare, 2020; National Sample Survey Office, 2016; National Statistical Office, 2020)

Socioeconomic Indicators Used for Statistical Analysis

Table 2 outlines the indicators from Multidimensional Poverty Index (MPI) (Alkire & Santos, 2014) that this study uses in the statistical analysis and a justification for their appropriate use. The data for these indicators were collected through the National Family Health Surveys (NFHS-4 and NFHS-5).

Table 2. Disaggregated multidimensional poverty index (MPI) indicators, deprivation criteria and justifications

Indicator	Deprivation Criterion	Justification
Nutrition	A household is deprived if any child (0–59 months), woman (15–49 years), or man (15–54 years) is undernourished	Undernutrition is a key indicator of health outcomes, directly impacting cognitive and physical development, which in turn affects educational and employment opportunities (Smith & Haddad, 2015)
Child–Adolescent Mortality	A household is deprived if any child or adolescent under 18 years has died in the five years preceding the survey	Child mortality reflects the overall health environment and healthcare access, highlighting critical areas needing intervention (United Nation Children's Fund, 2019)
Maternal Health	A household is deprived if any woman who has given birth in the last five years did not receive at least four antenatal care visits or assistance from trained personnel during childbirth	Maternal health services are crucial for reducing maternal and infant mortality and improving long-term health outcomes (World Health Organisation, 2015)
Years of Schooling	A household is deprived if no member aged 10 years or older has completed six years of schooling	Education is fundamental for individual empowerment and economic progress, reducing intergenerational transmission of poverty (United Nations Educational, Scientific and Cultural Organization, 2016)
School Attendance	A household is deprived if any school-aged child is not attending school up to the age at which they should complete class 8	Regular school attendance ensures that children acquire necessary skills and knowledge for future socioeconomic mobility (World Bank, 2018)
Cooking Fuel	A household is deprived if it cooks with dung, agricultural crops, shrubs, wood, charcoal, or coal	Use of unclean fuels is linked to respiratory diseases and contributes to environmental degradation, affecting overall quality of life (World Health Organisation, 2014)
Sanitation	A household is deprived if it has an unimproved or shared sanitation facility	Adequate sanitation is critical for preventing waterborne diseases and maintaining public health (JMP, 2017)
Drinking Water	A household is deprived if it does not have access to improved drinking water or if safe drinking water is at least a 30-minute walk round trip	Access to clean water is essential for good health, reducing the burden of waterborne illnesses (United Nation Children's Fund, 2019)
Housing	A household is deprived if it has inadequate housing, such as a floor made of natural materials, or a roof/wall made of rudimentary materials	Housing conditions are vital for physical health and overall well-being (United Nation - Habitat, 2015)
Electricity	A household is deprived if it has no electricity	Electricity is crucial for various daily activities, including education and communication, enhancing overall quality of life (World Bank, 2018)

Source: (United Nation Development Programme, 2023)

Economic Indicators Used for the Quantitative Analysis

The socioeconomic factors are complemented by economic factors when conducting the statistical analysis. Table 3 describes the three economic variables considered in our study and present the rationale for their inclusion. The economic variables from 2019 were deflated using 2015 as a reference with a coefficient of 0.855 (CPI 2019/CPI 2015) (Office for National Statistics, 2024; World Bank, 2024b).

Table 3. Economic indicators used for statistical analysis

Variable	Description	Justification
OOPE per capita	Out-of-pocket expenditures (OOPE) by each person on average at the point of use of healthcare. Per capita value for OOPE is calculated by dividing total OOPE by the population of each state respectively (Ministry of Health and Family Welfare, 2023b)	Indicates the extent of financial risk protection towards high out-of-pocket payments that are linked to catastrophic and impoverishing effects on households (World Health Organisation, 2024b)
GHE per capita	Per capita value for GHE is calculated by dividing total GHE by the population of each state respectively (Ministry of Health and Family Welfare, 2023b). GHE consists of healthcare resources through all donors, union, state, local, quasi entities of the government funded and managed schemes, including the mandatory health insurance (Ministry of Health and Family Welfare, 2023; World Health Organisation, 2024)	Key metric of health financing systems and indicates the overall government spending on healthcare in relation to the population size it serves (World Health Organisation, 2024b)
GHE as % of GGE	General GHE expressed as a percentage of total expenditure of the general government (World Health Organisation, 2024). Government domestic sources for health include government internal transfers and grants, government transfers and subsidies to voluntary schemes, as well as social health insurance contributions (World Health Organisation, 2024)	Indicates the priority of the government to spend on health from own domestic public resources (World Health Organisation, 2024b)

Data Analysis

Statistical analysis was carried out using Stata Statistical software version 18 for IOS. Statistical significance was determined at 5% ($p<0.05$).

Descriptive Statistics

Table 4 presents the list of continuous and categorical variables used for the analysis. For each variable, mean and standard deviation (Mean +/- SD) were calculated (see Table 5).

Table 4. Type of variables used for the statistical analysis

Variable	Type
Out of pocket expenditure (OOPE) per capita	Continuous
Government Health Expenditure per capita	Continuous
GHE as a percentage of total government expenditure	Continuous
Multi poverty Index	Continuous
Unemployment (%)	Continuous
Mortality under 5 (%)	Continuous
Antenatal mortality (%)	Continuous
Cook with fuel (%)	Categorical
Access to Electricity (%)	Categorical
Health insurance for at least one member of the household (%)	Categorical
BMI above or below Normal (%)	Categorical
More than 10 years of schooling (%)	Categorical
Literacy (%)	Categorical
Access to Sanitation (%)	Categorical
Access to Water (%)	Categorical

Regression Analysis

In this study, multiple linear regression analysis was employed to investigate the association between OOPE and socioeconomic factors This statistical method allows us to understand how various socioeconomic factors are associated with OOPE, providing insights into the economic burdens faced by different population groups.

The following assumptions were verified prior to conducting the multivariate regression analysis: normality, homoscedasticity, equal variance and no multicollinearity.

Difference-in-Difference Regression Analysis

To understand the effect of AB-PMJAY on OOPE, we employed a Difference in Difference (DiD) regression. The DiD regression analysis compares changes in healthcare OOPE in ten different Indian states before (data from 2015-2026) and after (data from 2019-2020) the implementation of AB-PMJAY, providing a robust evaluation of its economic impact on healthcare expenditures.

Two states were used as control group (Odisha and Telangana) where AB-PMJAY has not been implemented and eight states were used as the intervention group (Chhattisgarh, Haryana, Jharkhand, Madhya Pradesh, Punjab, Tamil Nadu, Uttar Pradesh and Uttarakhand) where AB-PMJAY was rolled-out in 2018. The outcome variable (OOPE) was regressed against covariates (See Table 5 and 6), with particular interest in the impact of economic and socioeconomic factors on OOPE.

Findings from Statistical Analysis

This analysis presents results from a descriptive analysis (Table 5), regression analysis (Table 6) and DiD analysis (Table 7) to evaluate the impact of the AB-PMJAY scheme from 2015-2016 to 2019-2020. It highlights changes in OOPE and GHE per capita, revealing insights into public health expenditure efficiency and socioeconomic factors affecting healthcare costs. See Appendix 2 for statistics output.

Descriptive Statistics Results

Table 5 compares various health and socioeconomic indicators before AB-PMJAY in 2015-2016 and after AB-PMJAY in 2019-2020.

Table 5. Descriptive statistics of the variables used for the periods 2015-2016 and 2019-2020

Variable	Period 2015-2016				Period 2019-2020			
	Mean	Std. dev.	Min	Max	Mean	Std. dev.	Min	Max
OOPE per capita	2553.9	(779.976)	1494	4332	1753.387	(539.033)	1071.914	2834.198
Government Health Expenditure per capita	1082.2	(413.138)	667	1980	1430.359	(425.645)	813.5594	1944.501
GHE as a percentage of total government expenditure	5.36	(0.591)	4.4	6.1	6.02	(0.541)	4.9	6.7

continued on following page

Table 5. Continued

Unemployment	5.1	(1.932)	1.9	7.7	5.1	(1.932)	1.9	7.7
Child mortality under 5 years	48.87	(16.544)	26.8	78.1	41.46	(11.084)	22.3	59.8
Antenatal care	51.39	(20.201)	26.4	81.1	61.85	(15.178)	38.6	89.9
Cooking with fuel	43.26	(21.091)	18.9	73	55.93	(21.895)	31.9	91.8
Access to electricity	92.18	(9.292)	72.6	99.6	97.73	(2.906)	91	99.7
Health Insurance coverage	33.67	(25.065)	6.1	68.5	46.43	(19.408)	15.9	71.4
Men BMI < 18.5 kg/sq. m	19.39	(6.384)	10.9	28.4	16	(2.584)	12.1	20.8
Women BMI < 18.5 kg/sq. m	22.18	(6.643)	11.7	31.5	18.52	(4.801)	12.6	26.2
Women BMI < 18.5 kg/sq. m	20.1	(7.793)	10.3	31.3	26.1	(10.365)	11.9	40.8
Men BMI >= 25kg/sq. m	17.98	(6.931)	10.2	28.2	24.32	(8.153)	14.9	37
Men more than 10 years of schooling	47.7	(10.715)	34.3	61.1	51.72	(9.433)	38.6	62.2
Women more than 10 years of schooling	37.8	(11.477)	23.2	55.1	42.97	(9.954)	29.3	56.6
Access to Sanitation	49.53	(20.948)	25	82.7	72.71	(9.936)	56.7	86.6
Access to water	92.9	(7.041)	78.1	99.6	95.2	(4.644)	86.6	99.2

Source: (Ministry of Health and Welfare, 2019; National Statistical Office, 2020; National Sample Survey Office, 2016; National Health Authority, 2018,2023)

Figure 5 shows that the average OOPE per capita has reduced between 2015-2016 and 2019-2020 in the ten selected states.

Figure 5. The OOPE per capita in selected states before and after AB-PMJAY implementation

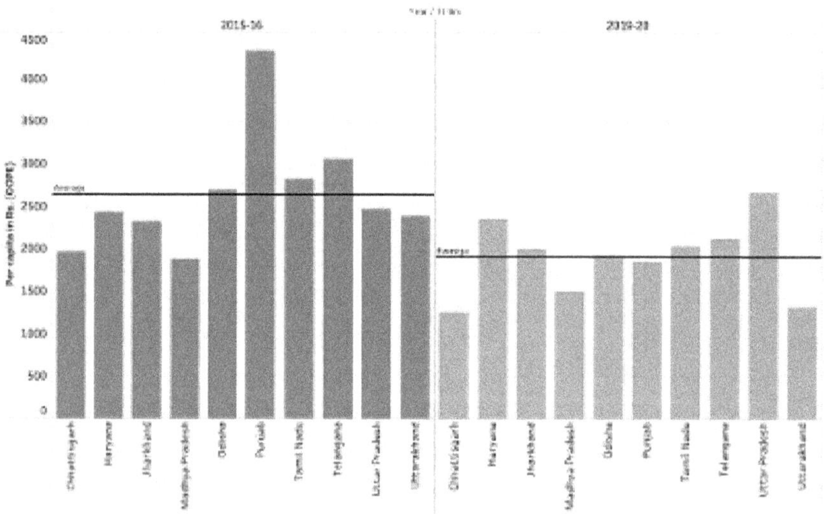

Figure 6 shows the percentage of total government expenditure spent on health has increased between 2015-2016 and 2019-2020 in the ten selected states.

Figure 6. The percentage of total government expenditure spent on health in selected states before and after AB-PMJAY implementation

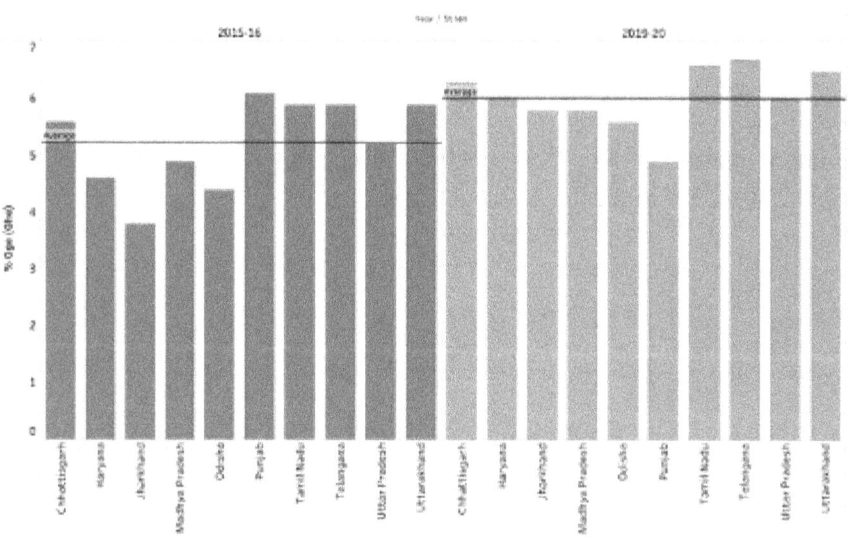

Multiple Linear Regression Analysis Results

The regression analysis of OOPE determinants reveals key insights (Table 6). Higher GHE per capita significantly reduces OOPE (-1.113, $p<0.001$), showing that increased public health spending eases individual costs. In contrast, a larger GHE share of total government spending raises OOPE (0.450, $p<0.001$), suggesting inefficiencies in funds utilisation. Unemployment also elevates OOPE (0.094, $p<0.001$), while child mortality shows a positive but insignificant effect (0.004, $p>0.05$).

Antenatal care access reduces OOPE (-0.010, $p<0.01$), underscoring the role of preventive services. Surprisingly, electricity (0.014, $p<0.01$) and health insurance (0.012, $p<0.01$) increase OOPE, possibly reflecting residual costs or higher spending among wealthier households. Health indicators show gendered effects: underweight women face higher OOPE (0.150, $p<0.001$), while overweight men spend less (-0.079, $p<0.01$).

Education affects OOPE differently by gender—men with over ten years of schooling spend slightly more (0.021, $p<0.01$), whereas educated women spend less (-0.105, $p<0.01$). Access to sanitation (0.029, $p<0.01$) and water (0.036, $p<0.01$) also raise OOPE, likely due to better living standards and greater healthcare use. Over time, OOPE declines significantly (-0.321, $p<0.001$), reflecting improved health funding and access. Overall, these results highlight how public spending, socioeconomic conditions, and healthcare access interact to shape OOPE patterns in India.

Table 6. Regression analysis results for determinants of OOPE per capita

Variable	Coefficient	Std. Err.	p-value
Government Health Expenditure per capita	-1.113***	(0.023)	0.000
GHE as a percentage of total government expenditure	0.450***	(0.011)	0.001
Unemployment	0.094***	(0.002)	0.001
Child mortality under 5 years	0.004	(0.001)	0.059
antenatal care	-0.010**	(0.001)	0.006
Cook with fuel	-0.001	(0.001)	0.428
Access to electricity	0.014**	(0.003)	0.032
Health insurance coverage	0.012**	(0.001)	0.005
Wen BMI < 18.5 kg/sq. m	-0.124***	(0.004)	0.001
Women BMI < 18.5 kg/sq. m	0.150***	(0.002)	0.000
Women BMI >= 25 kg/sq. m	0.197***	(0.006)	0.001
Men BMI >= 25 kg/sq. m	-0.079**	(0.005)	0.004
Men more than 10 years of schooling	0.021**	(0.001)	0.004
Women more than 10 years of schooling	-0.105**	(0.004)	0.002
Access to Sanitation – sewage and drain system	0.029**	(0.001)	0.002
Access to water	0.036**	(0.002)	0.004
year	-0.321***	(0.007)	0.001
_cons	653.918***	(15.105)	0.001

Difference-in-Difference Regression Analysis

These results indicate that the AB-PMJAY scheme did not have a significant impact on reducing OOPE per capita during the observed period. The insignificant (DiD) estimate suggests that there was no substantial reduction in the financial burden of healthcare on the population due to the AB-PMJAY scheme. This lack of significant impact may point to various factors such as implementation challenges, insufficient coverage, or other barriers that need to be addressed. Further investigation is necessary to understand the reasons behind this outcome and to explore potential improvements in the scheme's design and execution to achieve its intended financial relief for healthcare expenses.

The DiD analysis assesses the impact of AB-PMJAY on OOPE per capita by comparing pre- and post-implementation changes between treated and control groups (Table 7). Before implementation, both groups had an average OOPE of -27,000, with a non-significant difference of -563.7 (SE = 2626.4, p = 0.865), indicating no initial disparity.

After implementation, average OOPE declined to -29,000 for both groups, and the difference remained insignificant (-417.7, SE = 3028.1, p = 0.913). The DiD estimate of 146 (SE = 1291.9, p = 0.928) also lacked statistical significance.

Overall, AB-PMJAY did not significantly reduce OOPE per capita during the study period. The insignificant DiD estimate suggests the scheme failed to alleviate the financial burden of healthcare, possibly due to implementation gaps, limited coverage, or other systemic barriers. Further evaluation is needed to identify constraints and strengthen the scheme's effectiveness in providing financial protection.

Table 7. DiD analysis of OOPE per capita

Outcome var.	OOPE_~f	S. Err.	t	P>t
Before the AB implementation				
Control	-2.70E+04			
Treated	-2.70E+04			
Diff (T-C)	-563.729	2626.382	-0.21	0.865
After the AB implementation				
Control	-2.90E+04			
Treated	-2.90E+04			
Diff (T-C)	-417.733	3028.074	0.14	0.913
Result				
Diff-in-Diff	145.996	1291.889	0.11	0.928

WHAT WE'VE LEARNED FROM INDIA

The aim of this section is to examine the impact of the AB-PMJAY, highlighting both its achievements and its challenges. It adopts a mixed-methods approach, combining a narrative review of existing literature (Appendix 3) with a quantitative analysis of national survey data (See section "India's Ayushman Bharat: Big Vision, Mixed Results"). Together, these methods provide a comprehensive understanding of how AB-PMJAY has influenced out-of-pocket expenditure and the broader socioeconomic factors that shape healthcare access and financial protection in India.

How Government Health Expenditure Influences Out-Of-Pocket Healthcare Expenditure

This is first study performing a DiD analysis of the effect of AB-PMJAY on OOPE while controlling for economic and socioeconomic variables. The regression analysis evaluates the association between these variables and OOPE.

The positive association between GHE (as a percentage of total government expenditure) and OOPE suggests a counterintuitive relationship. This indicates that as GHE increases, the amount individuals spend OOPE also increases. There are several potential explanations for this.

Allocation of government expenditure

The increased government expenditure on health may be allocated in ways that do not directly reduce OOPE. For instance, the spending could go towards infrastructure, administrative costs, or public health initiatives which do not immediately lessen the financial burden on individuals seeking healthcare. Shende and Wagh (2024) identified substantial administrative expenses associated with managing beneficiary identification, claim processing and fraud detection in health programs. These costs are essential for the program's integrity and efficiency but add to the overall expenditure without directly reducing OOPE.

Healthcare Utilisation

Higher government spending on health could lead to improved healthcare facilities and services, which increase healthcare utilisation. As more people access these services, they incur additional OOPE for treatments, medications, or services not fully covered by government (Ghia & Rambhad, 2023).

(Dubey et al., 2023) found that utilisation of AB-PMJAY is higher in states with lower poverty and disease burdens (e.g., Kerala and Himachal Pradesh) compared to states with higher needs (e.g., Bihar, Madhya Pradesh, Uttar Pradesh and Assam). Underutilisation of the scheme due to lack of awareness among vulnerable populations leads to higher OOPE (Aashima & Sharma, 2024; Dubey et al., 2023; Grewal et al., 2023; Pillai & Obasanjo, 2023). The literature reflects that rural areas are poorly covered by the scheme with low enrolment and low utilisation rates compared to urban areas (Dubey et al., 2023; Ghia & Rambhad, 2023). When these groups do not utilise the benefits of the scheme, they end up paying OOPE for healthcare services that could have been covered. This underutilisation is particularly detrimental as it not only increases immediate financial burdens but also leads to delayed treatments, resulting in more severe health conditions and higher overall healthcare costs (Aashima & Sharma, 2024; Grewal et al., 2023; Pillai & Obasanjo, 2023). Ensuring awareness and education about the scheme among target populations is important to reduce OOPE and improve healthcare access.

Coverage Gaps

The government's health spending does not cover all essential health services, leaving gaps that individuals need to fill through OOPE. OOPE is often required for specific services, procedures, or medications (Angell et al., 2019). The coverage gaps include outpatient care, poor hospital empanelment and inconsistency in coverage dependent on treatment centre.

A review of the literature reveals that AB-PMJAY's focus on inpatient care leaves significant expenses for outpatient services, consultations, diagnostic tests and transportation (Aashima & Sharma, 2024; Ambade et al., 2022; Dholakia, 2020; Ghia & Rambhad, 2023; Grewal et al., 2023; Singh et al., 2023; Thakur & Faizan, 2024). Outpatient services are a large part of overall healthcare expenditure. They are four times higher than inpatient costs (Thakur & Faizan, 2024). Our quantitative study highlighted that state health insurance schemes in Odisha and Telangana providing additional outpatient coverage, reduce OOPE (Sahoo et al., 2023; Shukla et al., 2011).

Another challenge under AB-PMJAY is that the availability of empanelled hospitals is insufficient to meet the healthcare needs of the population. As shown in the literature, this disparity leads to increased OOPE as patients must seek care from non-empanelled hospitals where they do not receive the scheme's benefits (Aashima & Sharma, 2024; Grewal et al., 2023; Singh et al., 2023). Ensuring an increase in empanelled hospitals and improving the distribution of these facilities across regions is key to effectively reducing OOPE and enhancing access to healthcare.

There is inconsistency in coverage between packages available at public and private hospitals leading to additional OOPE. Private hospitals in Madhya Pradesh have charged patients for treatments covered by AB-PMJAY because certain packages are restricted to public hospitals and cannot be claimed in private ones (Saxena et al., 2022). Additionally, our literature review found that reimbursement rates below the actual treatment cost leads to dissatisfaction among private providers, impacting their participation in the scheme (Aashima & Sharma, 2024; Dholakia, 2020; Grewal et al., 2023; Pillai & Obasanjo, 2023; Trivedi et al., 2022). These gaps in coverage places a financial burden on patients requiring multimodal treatment. Inadequate funding in public hospitals exacerbates the issue, as they can lack necessary equipment and medicines (Aashima & Sharma, 2024; Grewal et al., 2023; Singh et al., 2023). Ensuring that both public and private hospitals are adequately equipped and that packages are uniformly accessible and costed is needed.

Health Awareness and Diagnoses

Increased government health spending leads to better health awareness and earlier diagnoses of conditions (Gmeinder et al., 2017). As more health issues are identified, individuals spend more on treatments and follow-up care, contributing to higher OOPE (Aashima & Sharma, 2024).

Governance

Garg et al (2020) found that AB-PMJAY did not reduce catastrophic health expenditures in Chhattisgarh state. It was because the major shortcomings of previous publicly funded health insurance schemes persisted even after AB-PMJAY´s implementation. This included monopoly, double billing and unregulated behaviour of private providers.

Addressing the issues of the scheme described above through improved allocation of funds, increasing awareness, expanding outpatient coverage, ensuring uniformity in hospital empanelment and governance could enhance the scheme's effectiveness and reduce the financial burden on individuals. Further research is needed to explore these dynamics and develop strategies to optimise the scheme's impact on reducing OOPE.

How Gender Influences Out-Of-Pocket Healthcare Expenditure

The literature review and quantitative analysis highlighted disparities between men and women utilisation of the AB-PMJAY and OOPE.

Undernutrition in women

Our regression analysis highlights gender disparities in OOPE per capita among men and women. Women with a BMI below 18.5 kg/m^2 are associated with higher

OOPE, whereas men in the same BMI category show a negative association, indicating lower OOPE. This discrepancy suggests that undernutrition in women may lead to higher healthcare costs, potentially due to gender-specific health issues that exacerbate financial burdens (Sen & Ostlin, 2008).

Utilisation Discrepancies

The literature review highlighted the higher utilisation of the scheme among men (Aashima & Sharma, 2024; Dubey et al., 2023). We found that males are more likely to use private hospitals, while females tend to utilise public hospitals, reflecting different patterns in healthcare access and utilisation (Aashima & Sharma, 2024; Grewal et al., 2023). This could be due to societal norms and economic constraints that influence women's healthcare-seeking behaviour, with men having greater autonomy and resources to seek private healthcare services (Grewal et al., 2023).

Educational Impact

In our analysis, the coefficient for women with more than 10 years of schooling is significantly negative. This implies that higher education in women reduces OOPE. In contrast, men with similar educational attainment show a positive association with OOPE. Our quantitative analysis showed that educated women were incurring lower OOPE than men. This finding was not highlighted in the literature review. Wang et) reported that such finding can indicate the role of educated women in better managing household health expenses and utilising preventive healthcare services more effectively.

How Socioeconomic Factors Influence Out-Of-Pocket Healthcare Expenditure

The regression analysis showed the association between socioeconomic factors and OOPE.

Unemployment

Unemployment is associated with an increase in OOPE, which can be surprising as AB-PMJAY is meant to cover the poorest and therefore the unemployed citizens. This finding can be the reflection of the limited utilisation and lack of awareness about the scheme that was reported in the literature review (Aashima & Sharma, 2024; Shende & Wagh, 2024). Studies conducted on the factors that drive awareness of health insurance benefits were related to gender, socio-economic profile, literacy and education (Yellaiah & Ramakrishna, 2012).

Additionally, this increase in OOPE among the unemployed could be influenced by the lack of workplace-level insurance. In India, many organised sector employees receive health insurance through their employers, which often provides more comprehensive coverage than government schemes. The Employee State Insurance Scheme (ESIS) covers over 120 million workers in India, providing medical care, cash benefits during sickness and maternity benefits (Employee State Insurance Scheme, 2020). Other private companies offer health insurance, covering outpatient services, diagnostics and medications not included under AB-PMJAY. The lack of these benefits for the unemployed may explain their higher OOPE, as they miss out on the coverage provided by employers.

Health insurance

Interestingly, health insurance has been associated with an increase in OOPE. In a study analysing the determinants of OOPE in China, You and Kobayashi (2011) found no association between healthcare insurance and OOPE. This can be attributed to patients with high-risk profiles being more likely to enroll in insurance schemes. Consequently, despite having part of their treatments covered, they still incur expenses on non-covered items and procedures. Our findings align with this laztter pattern and similar results have been reported in the literature (Wagstaff et al., 2019).

Socioeconomic Status

Socioeconomic status of the household reflected by access to electricity, years of schooling (men), sanitation and access to drinking water are associated with an increase in OOPE (see Table 6). You and Kobayashi (2011) corroborated similar findings in China, highlighting that households who are better off spend more on health.

INDONESIA'S JOURNEY TO UNIVERSAL HEALTH COVERAGE: INSIGHTS FOR OTHER LMICS

To further examine OOPE in LMICs and support our analysis, the following section draws findings from the Indonesia JKN scheme.

Indonesia is the fourth most populated country in the world, with a population of over 255 million and the third most populous in Asia (Mundial, 2014). At 2.9% of GDP in 2018, Indonesia's health expenditure was among the lowest globally and much lower than the average of 5.7% for upper-middle-income countries. Moreover, OOPE accounted for 45% of current health expenditure (Pisani et al., 2017). Like any other LMICs, less than half of the population had financial protection.

To protect its citizens from such financial burden, the Government of Indonesia stepped into the direction of rolling out a mandatory national health insurance scheme that aimed to achieve UHC (Pisani et al., 2017). In 2014, the government introduced Jaminan Kesehatan Nasional (JKN) national health insurance scheme. JKN provides important insights as it is one of the most ambitious UHC initiatives in the world.

Design and Financing

JKN scheme requires every individual in the country, regardless of income or work position, to be enrolled and covered under this program (Hidayat, 2015). JKN offers two distinct memberships: non-contributory beneficiaries- Penerima Bantuan Iuran (PBI), also called as subsidised contribution recipients and contributory beneficiaries (non-PBI).

PBI members are primarily low-income individuals whose premiums are fully subsidised by the government. They made up 59% of all JKN members in 2021. The remaining members, classified as non-PBI, include: formally employed individuals who receive a salary and their families, people who work but do not receive a wage—such as unpaid family workers in farms, shops, or other household enterprises—and their families and those who are unemployed and their families (Maulana et al., 2022).

Premium contributions paid by PBI members are subsidised by both central and state governments (Public Relations of BKPK, 2025) and are the main source of funding for JKN, accounting for 42% of the total JKN funding. Non-PBI members´ premium contributions make up about 23% of current health expenditure and are variable. For example, those who are employed pay 5% of their monthly income as payroll tax and it is capped at 12 million Indonesian rupiah per month (approximately £550). Individuals who are employed without pay willingly make different contributions based on their preferred copayment and benefit package. Their contributions make up about 9% of JKN's total funding (Maulana et al., 2022). In contrast to India, where state-level differences in financing and governance create risk pools, this tiered financing approach allowed Indonesia to achieve a rapid scale-up.

Delivery

The scheme is led under the oversight of a single agency, the Social Security Agency for Health (BPJS-Kesehatan) and alongside manages previous insurance schemes (Askes, Jamkesmas, Jamsostek and Jamkesda) (Prabhakaran et al., 2019;

Kementerian, 2015). Although the Ministry of Health sets the purchasing regulations, this agency contracts with and pays both public and private providers nationwide. Before JKN, there were multiple fragmented social insurance programs run by various organisations within the country. For example, PT.ASKES program for impoverished and civil servants, PT ASABRI program for military officers and several other local government-run programs (Kementerian, 2015). These schemes had different benefits, but since JKN was implemented, they have been standardised and integrated within the JKN. The scheme did not impose any caps; members utilised primary health care services when sick and were referred for secondary or tertiary care services.

Impact

By 2019, JKN insured 225.9 million, about 83% of the population in 2021 (Maulana et al., 2022) and successfully covered over 260 million people, more than 95% of the population, by December 2023 (World health Organization, 2025). This success is deeply rooted in its centralised governance and political alignment.

As the program gradually boosted the use of essential services, it reduced financial barriers and the percentage of OOPE to THE from 48.5% in 2014 to 32.1% in 2019 (Indonesia National Health Accounts, 2016). Additionally, the financial burden of healthcare on households decreased as catastrophic health expenditure rates reduced from 4.5% in 2017 to 2% in 2021 (World Health Organization, 2025). The example of Indonesia´s JKN demonstrates how political cooperation and a strong single-payer system help in accelerating the transition to UHC.

WHAT WORKS AND WHY: KEY LESSONS FROM INDIA AND BEYOND

Based on the findings of our research the following recommendations are proposed to enhance the effectiveness of AB-PMJAY in reducing OOPE.

Lesson 1 – Cover What People Actually Use: Include Outpatient Services

One of the most consistent findings from our research is that UHC schemes limited to inpatient care leave households exposed to substantial costs for outpatient consultations, diagnostics and medicines (Sahoo et al., 2023). In AB-PMJAY, these exclusions have kept OOPE high, even among insured households. Countries like Indonesia have shown that covering both inpatient and outpatient services, alongside sustained subsidies (42% of the health budget in JKN), can sharply reduce catastrophic spending (Public Relations of Badan Kebijakan Pembangunan Kesehatan, 2025). LMICs planning UHC reforms should prioritise comprehensive benefit packages and innovative financing models—such as health bonds, impact investment funds and public–private partnerships—to make outpatient coverage sustainable (ThinkWell, 2020; World Health Organisation, 2020).

Lesson 2 – Awareness Is as Important as Coverage

Financial protection is meaningless if eligible populations don't know about their entitlements or how to use them. In India, lack of awareness disproportionately affects the most deprived groups, including the unemployed and women with limited health autonomy (Aashima & Sharma, 2024; Dubey et al., 2023). LMICs should budget for robust, multi-channel outreach—training frontline workers like ASHAs, using local-language media and collaborating with community leaders to co-design campaigns. Ghana's NHIS demonstrates that grassroots engagement can drive uptake in hard-to-reach communities (British Medical Journal, 2020). Awareness work is not a side activity; it's a core component of UHC implementation.

Lesson 3 – Design For Equity from the Start

Gender gaps in utilisation are not inevitable—they are a design flaw. AB-PMJAY data shows women are less likely to use benefits, often due to information gaps, social norms and indirect costs (Aashima & Sharma, 2024; Dubey et al., 2023). LMICs can address this by embedding equity measures from the outset: targeted campaigns for women, safe spaces to learn about entitlements and incentives that link enrolment to existing social protection schemes (e.g., expanding India's Pradhan Mantri Matru Vandana Yojana cash benefit to all children, conditional on UHC enrolment) (BMC Women's Health, 2023; Ministry of Women and Child Development, 2022). Rwanda's success in improving women's enrolment through tailored media outreach shows this is achievable when inclusion is intentional.

Lesson 4 – Partnerships and Governance Matter as Much as Funding

Indonesia's JKN illustrates that centralised governance under a single payer, combined with strategic contracting of both public and private providers, can deliver rapid scale-up and uniform benefits. In contrast, AB-PMJAY's state-level variability in hospital empanelment and reimbursement rates has led to inequitable access and provider disengagement. LMICs should build strong institutional frameworks that standardise benefits, ensure fair provider payment and protect patients from hidden charges—regardless of where they seek care.

Table 8. Recommendations and policy actions

Recommendations	Key Actions	Expected Goal
1. Expand coverage to outpatient services	• Adopt a robust health financing model, involving increased budget allocations in line with other LMICs on the path to UHC (WHO, 2020). • Introduce innovative mechanisms such as health bonds and impact investment funds (ThinkWell, 2020). • Explore further partnerships with private providers to ensure comprehensive coverage (Grewal et al., 2023).	This will significantly enhance the scheme's impact and reduce OOPE, ensuring equitable and comprehensive healthcare coverage across India.
2. Strengthen awareness campaign	• Allocate more funding for training programs on the scheme's benefits, enrolment process and the importance of health insurance for healthcare workers, including Accredited Social Health Activists (ASHAs). • Conduct multimedia campaigns, local radio and television, SMS and social media, distribution brochures, posters and flyers in local languages, illustrated with simple graphics • Community leaders play a vital role in influencing and mobilising their communities. Consult with local communities to understand what works best for them and budgeting these initiatives	Improved enrolment and awareness will increase PMJAY's utilisation, especially among deprived groups
3. Reduce gender disparities in access	• Government of India should conduct targeted education campaigns to inform women about health insurance benefits. • Introduce innovative women-specific compensation for accessing the scheme could also be utilised. • Create safe spaces for women, such as such as women's health forums and support groups to discuss and learn about AB-PMJAY. For example, cash incentive under Pradhan Mantri Matru Vandana Yojana for the first living child of the family (Ministry of Women and Child Development, 2022) could be extended to all children, conditional on signing up for AB-PMJAY. • Involve consultations with women in the community to understand their specific needs and challenges to plan, budget and implement these initiatives	This will achieve improved enrolment and utilisation among women; reduce gender disparity in healthcare access. This participatory approach ensures that the strategies are effective and culturally sensitive Safe spaces for women could leverage Accredited Social Health Activists (ASHAs) and female community leaders to advocate for the scheme.
4. Implement a centralised governance and single payer system	• Build strong institutional frameworks that standardise benefits, ensure fair provider payment and protect patients from hidden charges—regardless of where they seek care.	This will achieve rapid scale-up, equitable access to healthcare, strengthen public-private partnerships across all states and reduce any hidden OOPE

CONCLUSION

This chapter examined why OOPE remains high in LMICs and how different health financing models have sought to reduce it, drawing lessons from using India's AB-PMJAY and Indonesia's JKN as comparative case studies. Our mixed-methods approach included the first state-by-state difference-in-difference (DiD) analysis of AB-PMJAY's impact on OOPE, offering new evidence on how financial protection varies across Indian states and demographic groups.

The findings show that AB-PMJAY has expanded insurance coverage, improved selected health indicators and increased public spending, yet its narrow inpatient focus, uneven implementation and low public awareness have limited its ability to deliver meaningful and equitable financial protection in the short term. Socio-economic factors including gender, unemployment and educational disparities, continue to shape OOPE, with underserved populations facing the greatest barriers to affordable care.

The contrast with Indonesia's JKN illustrates that a centrally governed, single-payer model covering both inpatient and outpatient services can achieve rapid scale-up and measurable reductions in catastrophic spending. However, India cannot simply replicate the JKN model. Its population is more than five times larger, its health system is deeply decentralised and states hold constitutional authority over health policy — creating significant variation in financing capacity, political priorities and provider networks. Moving toward more uniform and comprehensive coverage will therefore require not only increased fiscal commitment but also strategies to align state and national priorities in a way that preserves local ownership while ensuring equitable entitlements nationwide.

While the institutional and political contexts differ sharply across countries, the comparative analysis points to a set of principles that hold true across settings — lessons that any LMIC can apply when designing or reforming a UHC scheme:

1. **Cover what people use** – including outpatient care, medicines, diagnostics, chronic disease management and emergency cover.
2. **Embed equity from the outset** – address gender, socioeconomic and geographic barriers by design.
3. **Invest in awareness** – entitlement without utilisation offers no protection.
4. **Strengthen governance and provider engagement** – ensure consistent benefits and payment systems across regions.

Further research is needed to track the long-term effects of AB-PMJAY on OOPE and health outcomes, particularly through longitudinal studies and enhanced socioeconomic data. Ultimately, reducing OOPE is not solely a matter of increasing public spending; it requires aligning coverage with real-world patterns of care, building governance structures that work at scale and ensuring reforms reach those most at risk of financial hardship. Cover the right services, reach the right people and you'll spend less fixing the consequences.

ACKNOWLEDGMENTS

We extend our sincere appreciation to our academic advisors, Professor Sonila Tomini and Dr. Preethi John, whose guidance and knowledge contributed significantly to shaping the research in this book. We thank our research collaborators, Anna Cyril, Dr. Wafa Al Gwenim and Dr. Faisal Alsaif for their contributions to the literature review and statistical analysis, which reinforced this book chapter.

We would also like to express our gratitude to our colleagues and the wider community at University College London for their continued encouragement in bringing our research to publication. Finally, this research received no specific grant from any funding agency in the public, commercial, or not-for-profit sectors.

REFERENCES

Aarogyasri, A. P. (2011). Aarogyasri healthcare model: Advantage private sector. *Economic and Political Weekly*, *46*(49), 39.

Aashima, & Sharma, R. (2024). A systematic review of the world's largest government sponsored health insurance scheme for 500 million beneficiaries in India: Pradhan Mantri Jan Arogya Yojana. *Applied Health Economics and Health Policy*, *22*(1), 17–32. https://doi.org/DOI: 10.1007/s40258-023-00792-8

Aayog, N. I. T. I. (2021). *Health system for a new India: Building blocks*. https://www.niti.gov.in/health-system-new-india (Accessed June 29, 2024)

Alkire, S., & Santos, M. E. (2014). Measuring acute poverty in the developing world: Robustness and scope of the multidimensional poverty index. *World Development*, *59*, 251–274. DOI: 10.1016/j.worlddev.2014.01.026

Ambade, M., Sarwal, R., Mor, N., Kim, R., & Subramanian, S. V. (2022). Components of out-of-pocket expenditure and their relative contribution to economic burden of diseases in India. *JAMA Network Open*, *5*(5), e2210040. DOI: 10.1001/jamanetworkopen.2022.10040 PMID: 35560051

Angell, B. J., Prinja, S., Gupt, A., Jha, V., & Jan, S. (2019). The Ayushman Bharat Pradhan Mantri Jan Arogya Yojana and the path to universal health coverage in India: Overcoming the challenges of stewardship and governance. *PLoS Medicine*, *16*(3), e1002759. DOI: 10.1371/journal.pmed.1002759 PMID: 30845199

Barasa, E., Nguhiu, P., & McIntyre, D. (2018). Measuring progress towards Sustainable Development Goal 3.8 on universal health coverage in Kenya. *BMJ Global Health*, *3*(3), e000904. DOI: 10.1136/bmjgh-2018-000904 PMID: 29989036

Batbold, O., Banzragch, T., Davaajargal, D., & Pu, C. (2022). Crowding-out effect of out-of-pocket health expenditures on consumption among households in Mongolia. *International Journal of Health Policy and Management, 11*(9), 1874–1882. DOI: 10.34172/ijhpm.2021.91 PMID: 34634880

Brinda, E. M., Rajkumar, A. P., Enemark, U., Attermann, J., & Jacob, K. (2014). Cost and burden of informal caregiving of dependent older people in a rural Indian community. *BMC Health Services Research, 14*(1), 207. DOI: 10.1186/1472-6963-14-207 PMID: 24886051

Damrongplasit, K., & Melnick, G. (2024). Utilisation, out-of-pocket payments and access before and after COVID-19: Thailand's Universal Health Coverage Scheme. *BMJ Global Health, 9*(5), e015179. DOI: 10.1136/bmjgh-2024-015179 PMID: 38740495

Dash, A., & Mohanty, S. K. (2019). Do poor people in the poorer states pay more for healthcare in India? *BMC Public Health, 19*(1), 1020. DOI: 10.1186/s12889-019-7342-8 PMID: 31362727

Devadasan, N., Criel, B., Van Damme, W., Lefevre, P., Manoharan, S., & Van der Stuyft, P. (2011). Community health insurance schemes and patient satisfaction—Evidence from India. *The Indian Journal of Medical Research, 133*(1), 40–49. PMID: 21321418

Dholakia, S. (2020). An ethical analysis of the 'Ayushman Bharat-Pradhan Mantri Jan Arogya Yojna (PM-JAY)' scheme using the stakeholder approach to universal health care in India. *Asian Bioethics Review, 12*(2), 195–203. DOI: 10.1007/s41649-020-00121-7 PMID: 33717337

Dubey, S., Deshpande, S., Krishna, L., & Zadey, S. (2023). Evolution of government-funded health insurance for universal health coverage in India. *The Lancet Regional Health. Southeast Asia, 13*, 100174. DOI: 10.1016/j.lansea.2023.100180 PMID: 37383549

Garg, S., Tripathi, N., Ranjan, A., & Bebarta, K. K. (2022). How much do government and households spend on an episode of hospitalisation in India? A comparison for public and private hospitals in Chhattisgarh state. *Health Economics Review, 12*(1), 27. DOI: 10.1186/s13561-022-00372-0 PMID: 35522382

Ghia, C., & Rambhad, G. (2023). Implementation of equity and access in Indian healthcare: Current scenario and way forward. *Journal of Market Access & Health Policy, 11*(1), 2194507. DOI: 10.1080/20016689.2023.2194507 PMID: 36998432

Government of India. (2018). *'Ayushman Bharat' – Health and wellness centers.* https://ab-hwc.nhp.gov.in/home/aboutus (Accessed June 30, 2024)

Government of Telangana. (2025). *Aarogyasri.* https://kamareddy.telangana.gov.in/aarogyasri/ (Accessed August 24, 2025)

Grewal, H., Sharma, P., Dhillon, G., Munjal, R. S., Verma, R. K., & Kashyap, R. (2023). Universal health care system in India: An in-depth examination of the Ayushman Bharat initiative. *Cureus, 15*(6), e40029. DOI: 10.7759/cureus.40733 PMID: 37485096

Hidayat, B. (2015). *Out-of-pocket payments in the national health insurance of Indonesia: A first year review* [Policy brief].

Ho, C. J., Khalid, H., Skead, K., & Wong, J. (2022). The politics of universal health coverage. *Lancet, 399*(10340), 2066–2074. DOI: 10.1016/S0140-6736(22)00585-2 PMID: 35594878

Insurance Regulatory and Development Authority of India. (2020). *Annual report 2020.* https://www.irdai.gov.in(Accessed July 2, 2024)

International Labour Organization. (2025). *National health accounts 2020.*

Kaiser, A. H., Rotigliano, N., Flessa, S., Ekman, B., & Sundewall, J. (2023). Extending universal health coverage to informal workers: A systematic review of health financing schemes in low- and middle-income countries in Southeast Asia. *PLoS One, 18*(7), e0288269. DOI: 10.1371/journal.pone.0288269 PMID: 37432943

Kentikelenis, A., & Stubbs, T. (2024). Social protection and the International Monetary Fund: Promise versus performance. *Globalization and Health, 20*(1), 41. DOI: 10.1186/s12992-024-01045-9 PMID: 38715077

Khan, P. K., Perkins, J. M., Kim, R., Mohanty, S. K., & Subramanian, S. V. (2021). Multilevel population and socioeconomic variation in health insurance coverage in India. *Tropical Medicine & International Health : TM & IH, 26*(10), 1285–1295. DOI: 10.1111/tmi.13645 PMID: 34181806

Kolesar, R. J., Erreygers, G., Van Damme, W., Chea, V., Choeurng, T., & Leng, S. (2023). Hardship financing, productivity loss and the economic cost of illness and injury in Cambodia. *International Journal for Equity in Health, 22*(1), 208. DOI: 10.1186/s12939-023-02016-z PMID: 37805483

Maulana, N., Soewondo, P., Adani, N., Limasalle, P., & Pattnaik, A. (2022). How Jaminan Kesehatan Nasional (JKN) coverage influences out-of-pocket (OOP) payments by vulnerable populations in Indonesia. *PLOS Global Public Health, 2*(7), e0000203. DOI: 10.1371/journal.pgph.0000203 PMID: 36962301

Ministry of Health and Family Welfare, Government of India. (2018). *Comprehensive primary health care through health and wellness centers.* https://mohfw.gov.in/documents/policy-documents (Accessed June 30, 2024)

Mitchell, R. J., & Bates, P. (2011). Measuring health-related productivity loss. *Population Health Management, 14*(2), 93–98. DOI: 10.1089/pop.2010.0014 PMID: 21091370

Mundial, B. (2014).. . *World Development Indicators,* •••, 2014.

Murphy, A., Palafox, B., Walli-Attaei, M., Powell-Jackson, T., Rangarajan, S., Alhabib, K. F., Avezum, A. J., Calik, K. B. T., Chifamba, J., Choudhury, T., Dagenais, G., Dans, A. L., Gupta, R., Iqbal, R., Kaur, M., Kelishadi, R., Khatib, R., Kruger, I. M., Kutty, V. R., & McKee, M. (2020). The household economic burden of non-communicable diseases in 18 countries. *BMJ Global Health, 5*(2), e002040. DOI: 10.1136/bmjgh-2019-002040 PMID: 32133191

Nanda, M., & Sharma, R. (2023a). A comprehensive examination of the economic impact of out-of-pocket health expenditures in India. *Health Policy and Planning, 38*(8), 926–938. DOI: 10.1093/heapol/czad050 PMID: 37409740

Nanda, M., & Sharma, R. (2023b). Assessing the impact of anaesthetic and surgical task-shifting globally: A systematic literature review. *Health Policy and Planning, 38*(8), 960–994. DOI: 10.1093/heapol/czad059 PMID: 37506040

National Health Authority, Government of India. (2025). *About PM-JAY.* https://nha.gov.in/PM-JAY (Accessed August 24, 2025)

National Sample Survey Office. (2016). *Employment-unemployment survey.* http://mospi.nic.in (Accessed June 28, 2024)

National Statistical Office. (2020). *Periodic labour force survey.* http://mospi.nic.in (Accessed June 28, 2024)

Office for National Statistics. (2024). *Deflators and how we use them in economic estimates.* https://www.ons.gov.uk/economy/inflationandpriceindices/methodologies/deflatorsandhowweusethemineconomicestimates#:~:text=The%20deflator%20and%20its%20source,use%20an%20import%20price%20index (Accessed June 28, 2024)

Olaniran, A., Briggs, J., Pradhan, A., Bogue, E., Schreiber, B., Dini, H. S., Hurkchand, H., & Ballard, M. (2022). Stock-outs of essential medicines among community health workers in low- and middle-income countries: A systematic literature review. *Human Resources for Health*, *20*, 58. DOI: 10.1186/s12960-022-00755-8 PMID: 35840965

Patel, G., Brosnan, C., & Taylor, A. (2023). Understanding the role of context in health policy implementation: A qualitative study of factors influencing traditional medicine integration in the Indian public healthcare system. *Health Sociology Review : The Journal of the Health Section of the Australian Sociological Association*, *32*(3), 294–310. DOI: 10.1080/14461242.2023.2210550 PMID: 37222411

Pillai, K., & Obasanjo, I. (2023). Assessing the implementation of India's new health reform program, Ayushman Bharat, in two Southern states: Kerala and Tamil Nadu. *World Medical & Health Policy*, *15*(1), 6–20. DOI: 10.1002/wmh3.535

Pisani, E., Olivier Kok, M., & Nugroho, K. (2017). Indonesia's road to universal health coverage: A political journey. *Health Policy and Planning*, *32*(2), 267–276. DOI: 10.1093/heapol/czw120 PMID: 28207049

Prabhakaran, S., Dutta, A., Fagan, T., & Ginivan, M. (2019). *Financial sustainability of Indonesia's Jaminan Kesehatan Nasional: Performance, prospects and policy options*. Palladium, Health Policy Plus and Tim Nasional Percepatan Penanggulangan Kemiskinan (TNP2K).

Prasad, S. S. V., Singh, C., Naik, B. N., Pandey, S., & Rao, R. (2023). Awareness of the Ayushman Bharat–Pradhan Mantri Jan Arogya Yojana in the rural community: A cross-sectional study in Eastern India. *Cureus*, *15*(3), e35901. DOI: 10.7759/cureus.35901 PMID: 37033537

Public Relations of BKPK. (2025). *National health accounts 2020*. International Labour Organization.

Sabermahani, A., Sirizi, M. J., Zolala, F., & Nazari, S. (2021). Out-of-pocket costs and importance of nonmedical and indirect costs of inpatients. *Value in Health Regional Issues*, *24*, 141–147. DOI: 10.1016/j.vhri.2020.05.004 PMID: 33578362

Sahoo, P. M., Rout, H. S., & Jakovljevic, M. (2023). Contemporary universal health coverage in India: The case of federal state of Odisha (Orissa). *Risk Management and Healthcare Policy*, *16*, 1131–1143. DOI: 10.2147/RMHP.S406491 PMID: 37384257

Saxena, A., Trivedi, M., Shroff, Z. C., & Sharma, M. (2022). Improving hospital-based processes for effective implementation of government funded health insurance schemes: Evidence from early implementation of PM-JAY in India. *BMC Health Services Research*, *22*(1), 73. DOI: 10.1186/s12913-021-07448-3 PMID: 35031024

Shruddha, K., Deepshika, R., Rakesh, M., & Shewethashree, M. (2025). Knowledge, utilisation and perception regarding Ayushman Bharat Pradhan Mantri Jan Arogya Yojana among Mysuru residents: Insights from a cross-sectional analysis. *International Journal of Community Medicine and Public Health.* https://www.ijcmph.com/index.php/ijcmph/article/download/14176/8536/69304

Singh, L., Siddhanta, A., Singh, A. K., Prinja, S., Sharma, A., Sikka, H., & Goswami, L. (2023). Potential impact of the insurance on catastrophic health expenditures among the urban poor population in India. *Journal of Health Management, 25*(4), 996–1008. DOI: 10.1177/09720634221088425

Thakur, R., & Faizan, M. A. (2024). Magnitude of health expenditure induced removable poverty in India: Some reflections of Ayushman Bharat. *Heliyon, 10*(1), e25212. DOI: 10.1016/j.heliyon.2023.e23464 PMID: 38187230

ThinkWell. (2020). *Innovative Financing Mechanisms for Health.* https://thinkwell.global/resources/innovative-financing-mechanisms-for-health/ (Accessed 2 July 2024)

Ud Din, M. A., Dar, M. H., & Haseen, S. (2023). Inter-state disparities in government health expenditure in India: A study of national rural health mission. *International Journal of Health Governance, 28*(1), 82–94. DOI: 10.1108/IJHG-12-2022-0108

Voto, T. P., Voto, B. E., & Ngepah, N. (2025). The impact of out-of-pocket health expenditure and public health expenditure on poverty in sub-Saharan Africa. *Economies (Basel), 13*(5), 134. DOI: 10.3390/economies13050134

Wagstaff, A., Eozenou, P., & Smitz, M. (2019). Out-of-pocket expenditures on health: A global stocktake (No. 8808). World Bank. https://openknowledge.worldbank.org/entities/publication/b1d12b58-634a-5fdf-b678-d7182b81633b

World Bank. (2015). *Access to electricity (% of population).* https://databank.worldbank.org/metadataglossary/world-development-indicators/series/EG.ELC.ACCS.ZS (Accessed June 29, 2024)

World Bank. (2021). *Health expenditure (% of GDP) – India.* https://data.worldbank.org (Accessed June 30, 2024)

World Bank. (2023). *Tracking universal health coverage 2023 global monitoring report.*

World Bank. (2024a). *World Bank open data.* https://data.worldbank.org (Accessed June 29, 2024)

World Bank. (2024b). *Inflation, consumer prices (annual %) – India*. https://data.worldbank.org/indicator/FP.CPI.TOTL.ZG?locations=IN (Accessed June 29, 2024)

World Health Organization. (2014). *Household air pollution*. https://www.who.int/data/gho/data/themes/topics/topic-details/GHO/household-air-pollution (Accessed June 15, 2024)

World Health Organization. (2020a). *Global spending on health: Weathering the storm*. https://www.who.int/publications/i/item/9789240017788 (Accessed June 29, 2024)

World Health Organization. (2020b). *World health statistics 2020: Monitoring health for the SDGs, sustainable development goals*. https://www.who.int/publications/i/item/9789240005105 (Accessed June 29, 2024)

World Health Organization. (2021a). *Public spending on health: A closer look at global trends*. World Health Organization.

World Health Organization. (2021b). *Global monitoring report on financial protection in health 2021*. https://www.who.int/publications/i/item/9789240040953 (Accessed June 29, 2024)

World Health Organization. (2021c). *India: Ayushman Bharat for a new India – 2022*. https://www.who.int/india/news/detail/26-09-2021-ayushman-bharat-for-a-new-india-2022 (Accessed June 29, 2024)

World Health Organization. (2024). *Domestic general government health expenditure (GGHE-D) as percentage of general government expenditure (GGE) (%)*. https://www.who.int/data/gho/indicator-metadata-registry/imr-details/4956 (Accessed June 29, 2024)

World Health Organization. (2025). *Indonesia's success in achieving 90 percent coverage and minimizing out-of-pocket expenses through national health insurance expansion*. https://www.who.int/about/accountability/results/who-results-report-2020-mtr/country-story/2023/indonesia-s-success-in-achieving-90-percent-coverage-and-minimizing-out-of-pocket-expenses-through-national-health-insurance-expansion (Accessed August 24, 2025)

APPENDIX

Appendix 1

State selection process

List of 21 states available on NHA 2019-2020 data:

Assam andhra Pradesh, Bihar, Chhattisgarh, Gujarat, Haryana, Jammu and Kashmir, Jharkhand, Karnataka, Kerala, Madhya Pradesh, Maharashtra, Odisha, Punjab, Rajasthan, Tamil Nadu, Uttar Pradesh, Uttarakhand, West Bengal, Telangana, Himachal Pradesh.

Selection process diagram

Figure 7 shows the Indian states selection process for our quantitative analysis.

Figure 7. State selection process for quantitative analysis

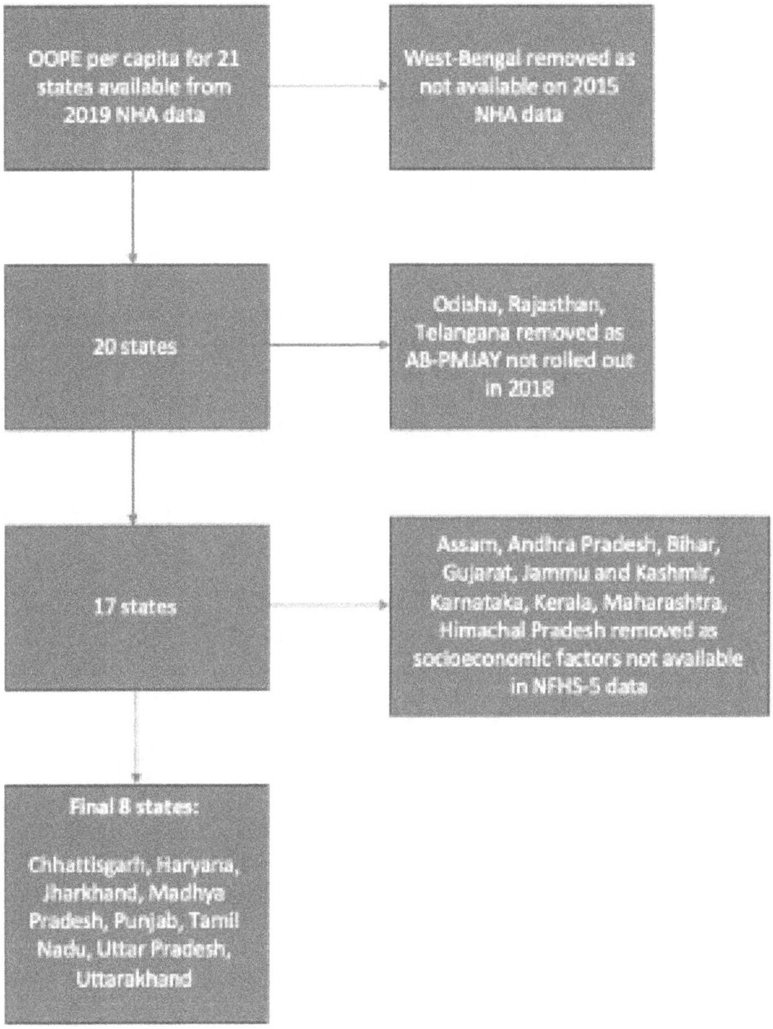

Source: (Ministry of Health and Family Welfare 2020 and 2023b)

Appendix 2

Descriptive statistics

Figure 8. 2015:

Variable	Obs	Mean	Std. dev.	Min	Max
OOPE_cap_def	10	2553.9	779.9763	1494	4332
GHE_cap_def	10	1082.2	413.1383	667	1980
GHE_GGE	10	5.36	.5910443	4.4	6.1
m_literate	10	85.52	3.841817	79.7	90.7
m_school	10	47.7	10.7152	34.3	61.1
w_literate	10	69.14	8.412187	59	81.4
w_school	10	37.8	11.4778	23.2	55.1
multi_poor	10	22.865	13.89276	4.76	42.1
unemployment	10	5.1	1.932759	1.9	7.7
sanitation	10	49.53	20.94825	25	82.7
water	10	92.9	7.041149	78.1	99.6
w_BMI_above	10	20.1	7.79373	10.3	31.3
w_BMI_below	10	22.18	6.643092	11.7	31.5
m_BMI_below	10	19.39	6.384608	10.9	28.4
AC	10	17.98	6.931057	10.2	28.2

Figure 9. 2019:

Variable	Obs	Mean	Std. dev.	Min	Max
OOPE_cap_def	10	1753.387	539.033	1071.914	2834.198
GHE_cap_def	10	1430.359	425.6455	813.5594	1944.501
GHE_GGE	10	6.02	.5411921	4.9	6.7
m_literate	10	85.22	4.038922	81.3	91.5
m_school	10	51.72	9.43384	38.6	62.2
w_literate	10	72.29	7.894084	61.7	84
w_school	10	42.97	9.954569	29.3	56.6
multi_poor	10	13.381	8.872671	2.2	28.81
unemployment	10	5.1	1.932759	1.9	7.7
sanitation	10	72.71	9.936403	56.7	86.6
water	10	95.2	4.644232	86.6	99.2
w_BMI_above	10	26.1	10.36597	11.9	40.8
w_BMI_below	10	18.52	4.801574	12.6	26.2
m_BMI_below	10	16	2.58414	12.1	20.8
AC	10	24.32	8.153227	14.9	37

Multiple Linear Regression Analysis

Figure 10. Correlation coefficient for the variables used in the linear regression:

```
. corr ln_OOPE_cap_def ln_GHE_cap_def GHE_GGE unemployment U5MR antenatal_care cook_fuel electricity insur m_BMI_below w_BMI_below w_BM
> I_above m_BMI_above m_school w_school sanitation water year
(obs=20)
```

	ln_OOP~f	ln_GHE~f	GHE_GGE	unempl~t	U5MR	antena~e	cook_f~l	electr~y	insur	m_BMI_~w	w_BMI_~w	w_BMI_~e	m_BMI_~e
ln_OOPE_ca~f	1.0000												
ln_GHE_cap~f	-0.1290	1.0000											
GHE_GGE	-0.3204	0.6527	1.0000										
unemployment	0.1039	-0.4536	-0.1755	1.0000									
U5MR	-0.2170	-0.6922	-0.3829	0.2499	1.0000								
antenatal_~e	0.0742	0.6483	0.4367	-0.5715	-0.7556	1.0000							
cook_fuel	0.2917	0.7144	0.5282	-0.1683	-0.7759	0.5699	1.0000						
electricity	-0.0368	0.7840	0.4734	-0.4670	-0.7251	0.6278	0.5933	1.0000					
insur	-0.3240	0.5699	0.5126	-0.6308	-0.4201	0.7144	0.2212	0.4869	1.0000				
m_BMI_below	-0.2366	-0.5285	-0.3147	-0.0289	0.7863	-0.5245	-0.6505	-0.6563	-0.1409	1.0000			
w_BMI_below	-0.2948	-0.6244	-0.4097	-0.0128	0.6750	-0.5230	-0.8140	-0.6393	-0.0683	0.8629	1.0000		
w_BMI_above	0.3350	0.6692	0.3717	-0.0812	-0.7655	0.6539	0.8966	0.5387	0.1724	-0.6933	-0.8729	1.0000	
m_BMI_above	0.2381	0.7133	0.4687	-0.1212	-0.8577	0.7230	0.9150	0.5809	0.2927	-0.7596	-0.8503	0.9646	1.0000
m_school	0.3093	0.6672	0.4277	0.0492	-0.7184	0.3680	0.8749	0.5531	0.0487	-0.7703	-0.8584	0.8082	0.8263
w_school	0.3310	0.6662	0.4536	0.0437	-0.7454	0.4851	0.8786	0.5694	0.1024	-0.8216	-0.9344	0.9003	0.8839
sanitation	-0.0082	0.6728	0.4832	-0.0537	-0.5684	0.3492	0.6832	0.7199	0.0527	-0.7886	-0.8377	0.6615	0.6790
water	0.4021	0.5600	0.3760	-0.1935	-0.3963	0.4288	0.7326	0.3983	0.1111	-0.5816	-0.7912	0.7120	0.6630
year	-0.5555	0.4138	0.5232	0.0000	-0.2673	0.2948	0.2966	0.3910	0.2874	-0.3444	-0.3158	0.3260	0.4040

	m_school	w_school	sanita~n	water	year
m_school	1.0000				
w_school	0.9393	1.0000			
sanitation	0.7583	0.7750	1.0000		
water	0.7171	0.7553	0.6814	1.0000	
year	0.2054	0.2458	0.5975	0.1992	1.0000

Figure 11. Linear regression output:

Linear regression			
	Number of obs	=	20
	F(17, 2)	=	25026.42
	Prob > F	=	0.0000
	R-squared	=	0.9999
	Root MSE	=	.00831

ln_OOPE_cap_~f	Coefficient	Robust std. err.	t	P>|t|	[95% conf.	interval]
ln_GHE_cap_def	-1.113384	.0230601	-48.28	0.000	-1.212604	-1.014164
GHE_GGE	.4500717	.0115742	38.89	0.001	.400272	.4998714
unemployment	.09446	.0025369	37.24	0.001	.0835448	.1053752
U5MR	.0040621	.001031	3.94	0.059	-.0003738	.008498
antenatal_care	-.0106435	.0008083	-13.17	0.006	-.0141215	-.0071655
cook_fuel	-.0006467	.0006554	-0.99	0.428	-.0034665	.0021732
electricity	.0141735	.0025915	5.47	0.032	.003023	.0253241
insur	.0120973	.0008192	14.77	0.005	.0085726	.0156219
m_BMI_below	-.1243822	.0039463	-31.52	0.001	-.1413617	-.1074027
w_BMI_below	.1506392	.0024643	61.13	0.000	.1400362	.1612422
w_BMI_above	.1978276	.0061232	32.31	0.001	.1714817	.2241735
m_BMI_above	-.0794266	.0050228	-15.81	0.004	-.1010379	-.0578152
m_school	.0211756	.0012638	16.75	0.004	.0157377	.0266135
w_school	-.1055985	.0041227	-25.61	0.002	-.123337	-.0878601
sanitation	.0292198	.0013487	21.66	0.002	.0234166	.035023
water	.0369458	.0024265	15.23	0.004	.0265053	.0473862
year	-.3215916	.0072715	-44.23	0.001	-.3528782	-.290305
_cons	653.9181	15.10547	43.29	0.001	588.9246	718.9117

Figure 12. Difference in Difference Output

DIFFERENCE-IN-DIFFERENCES ESTIMATION RESULTS

Number of observations in the DIFF-IN-DIFF: **20**

	Before	After	
Control:	**2**	**2**	4
Treated:	**8**	**8**	16
	10	10	

Report - Covariates and coefficients:

Variable(s)	Coeff.	Std. Err.	t	P>|t|
GHE_cap_def	**-2.140**	**2.891**	**-0.740**	**0.594**
GHE_GGE	**596.880**	**677.933**	**0.880**	**0.540**
unemployment	**172.814**	**558.780**	**0.309**	**0.809**
U5MR	**-2.346**	**135.750**	**-0.017**	**0.989**
antenatal_~e	**-0.442**	**67.706**	**-0.007**	**0.996**
cook_fuel	**-27.510**	**88.563**	**-0.311**	**0.808**
electricity	**87.568**	**53.595**	**1.634**	**0.350**
m_BMI_below	**15.292**	**492.217**	**0.031**	**0.980**
w_BMI_below	**235.642**	**513.762**	**0.459**	**0.726**
w_BMI_above	**123.147**	**157.278**	**0.783**	**0.577**
m_BMI_above	**47.868**	**261.537**	**0.183**	**0.885**
m_school	**8.306**	**90.669**	**0.092**	**0.942**
w_school	**-1.790**	**240.277**	**-0.007**	**0.995**
sanitation	**35.909**	**72.756**	**0.494**	**0.708**
water	**110.251**	**125.135**	**0.881**	**0.540**

Figure 13. Difference in Difference Output 2

Outcome var.	OOPE_~f	S. Err.	|t|	P>|t|
Before				
Control	-2.7e+04			
Treated	-2.7e+04			
Diff (T-C)	-563.729	2626.382	-0.21	0.865
After				
Control	-2.9e+04			
Treated	-2.9e+04			
Diff (T-C)	-417.733	3028.074	0.14	0.913
Diff-in-Diff	145.996	1291.889	0.11	0.928

R-square: **0.98**
* Means and Standard Errors are estimated by linear regression
**Robust Std. Errors
**Inference: *** p<0.01; ** p<0.05; * p<0.1

Appendix 3

Figure 14. Boolean equation used for the narrative literature review
STRING 1:
"Ayushman Bharat" OR "Pradhan Mantri Jan Arogya Yojana" OR "PM? JAY" or "Health insurance" OR "publicly funded health insurance" OR "public health insurance"
AND (STRING 2):
Health
AND (STRING 3)
economic OR financial OR "health outcomes" OR "out-of-pocket" OR "out of pocket" OR "OOP" OR "OOPE" OR Socioeconomic OR "out-of-pocket health expenditure"
AND (STRING 4)
India
("Ayushman Bharat" OR "Pradhan Mantri Jan Arogya Yojana" OR "PM? JAY" or "Health insurance" OR "publicly funded health insurance" OR "public health insurance") AND Health AND (economic OR financial OR "health outcomes" OR "out-of-pocket" OR "out of pocket" OR "OOP" OR "OOPE" OR Socioeconomic OR "out-of-pocket health expenditure") AND India

Results from the literature search

Figure 15 shows the literature selection process for our narrative review.

Figure 15. PRISMA Flow Diagram - adapted from Page Et Al. (2021)

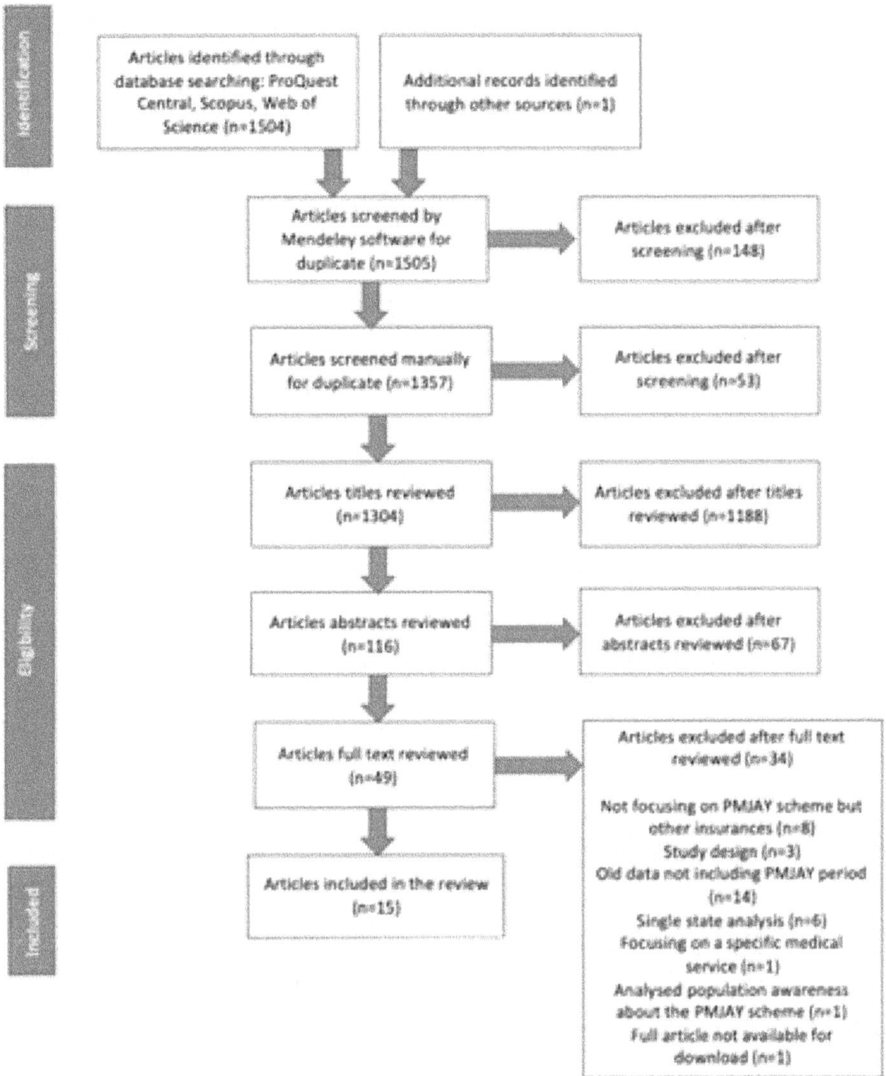

Table 9. Literature Review

Author	Title	Study design	Study Aim(s)	Cohort	Finding(s)	Recommendation
Aashima and Sharma, Rajesh (2024a)	A Systematic Review of the World's Largest Government Sponsored Health Insurance Scheme for 500 million Beneficiaries in India: Pradhan Mantri Jan Arogya Yojana	Systematic Review	Review AB impact since its inception in 2018: awareness, utilization, experiences, financial protection and challenges encountered by both beneficiaries and healthcare providers	Diverse population across multiple states	Utilisation of the scheme is low to moderate; scheme benefits the poor and vulnerable populations, providing access previously unaffordable; financial protection against OOPE showed mixed results; continued spending by beneficiaries on drugs and diagnostic tests, delays in issuance of beneficiary cards and co-payments demanded by providers	Increase public health spending; ensure availability of essential drugs and diagnostic services in health facilities; consider covering outpatient service under PM-JAY; address private hospitals concerns about package rate
Ambade, M. et al., 2023	Socioeconomic and geographic variation in coverage of health insurance across India	Empirical Analysis	Update evidence on health insurance coverage across districts in India using the latest NFHS data (2019-2021)	Households across India with at least one member covered by health insurance	2/5 households have coverage; increase in coverage among vulnerable group since PMJAY; geographic variation with only 40% coverage in lowest wealth quintiles; significant association of enrolment with caste and religion; inequality more prominent in urban areas than rural	Address disparities with place-based interventions for improving health insurance coverage
Shende and Wagh, 2024	Public Health Insurance Status and Utilization of Healthcare Services	Narrative Review	1. Evaluate if public health insurance can improve access to medical treatments	National level across India	Health insurance literacy crucial for selecting optimal plans; public health	Implement educational initiatives; advocate for simplifying enrolment; customize

Table 10. (continued)

	Across India: A Narrative Review		otherwise unaffordable; 2. Determine decrease in economic strain		insurance increases access; coverage gaps due to mistrust and misunderstanding; disparities in coverage across states	insurance packages to meet low-income needs
Singh et al., 2023	Potential Impact of the Insurance on Catastrophic Health Expenditures Among the Urban Poor Population in India	Econometric Analysis	Assess impact of health insurance on OOPE and catastrophic expenditure	Rajasthan and Uttar Pradesh	Mean outpatient costs larger than inpatient; medicines largest share of OOPE; private facility delivery higher OOPE	Effective universal health insurance coverage; include OPD medicines; cover diagnostics
Ghia and Rhambad, 2023	Implementation of equity and access in Indian healthcare: current scenario and way forward	Systematic Review	Outline the healthcare situations in India, including programmes aimed at UHC	National level	37.2% covered by health insurance; 78% from public insurance; public sector bears 30% of total health expenditure	Increase budget; electronic medical record software; upgrade rural pathology; expand hospitals
Srivastava et al., 2023	Implementation of PM-JAY in India: a qualitative study exploring the role of competency, organizational and leadership drivers	Qualitative Study	Investigates competency, organizational and leadership strategies for implementing PM-JAY in three states	Uttar Pradesh, Chhattisgarh, Tamil Nadu	Flexible recruitment; program support in state-adapted models; challenges in aligning staff hierarchies	Future research to compare performance and outcomes
Angell et al., (2019)	The Ayushman Bharat PM-JAY and the path to universal health coverage in India: Overcoming stewardship and governance challenges	Report	Assess PMJAY potential for UHC	National level	Significant challenges including governance, quality control, stewardship	Strengthen governance; adequate resources; enhance collaboration
Dubey et al., 2023	Evolution of Government-funded health insurance for UHC in India	Narrative Review	Evaluate evolution and impact of schemes	National level	Significant reduction in OOPE; increased access to healthcare	Enhance state-national coordination; focus on prevention

Table 11. (continued)

Grewal et al., 2023	Universal Health Care System in India: An In-Depth Examination of the Ayushman Bharat Initiative	Narrative Review	Examine impact of Ayushman Bharat	National level	Improved access and protection; rural gaps; COVID-19 lessons	Expand coverage; increase government spending
Sanjay et al., 2023	Public health insurance coverage in India before and after PM-JAY	Cross-Sectional Survey	Compare changes in coverage	National level	PM-JAY increased rural and poor coverage; reduced inequalities but still lacking UHC	TBD
Parmar et al., 2023	Effects of the Indian National Health Insurance Scheme (PM-JAY) on Hospitalizations, OOPE and Catastrophic Expenditures	Cross-Sectional Survey	Evaluate PM-JAY impact on hospitalisations, OOPE and private care use	Six Indian states	Increased use of private providers; high OOPE for poor households	Regulate private providers; increase funding for primary care; policy guidelines for access gaps
Pillai and Obasanjo, 2023	Assessing implementation of PMJAY in Kerala and Tamil Nadu	Cross-Sectional Survey	Compare rollout between Kerala, Tamil Nadu and other states	Health workers	Low reimbursement rates may deter participation; differences in political partnerships	Regular review; incentivise private participation
Thakur and Faizan, 2024	Magnitude of health expenditure induced removable poverty in India	Quantitative Study	Measure health expenditure-induced poverty	National level	Outpatient and medicine costs largest contributor to poverty; vulnerable groups more likely to be impoverished	Include OPD; multidimensional approach; governance reform
Dholakia, 2020	An Ethical Analysis of PM-JAY using Stakeholder Approach	Ethical Analysis	Analyse ethical considerations and recommend solidarity-based approach	National level	Need for solidarity; stakeholder alignment; stewardship	Solidarity-based approach; stakeholder alignment
Trivedi et al., 2022	Experiences and challenges in accessing hospitalisation in PM-JAY	Cross-Sectional Survey	Measure service delivery, information access, financial burden, satisfaction	Gujarat, Madhya Pradesh	Longer waits in public; higher OOPE in MP; better satisfaction in Gujarat	Improve IEC activities; build capacity for private hospitals

Chapter 7
Taking a Value-Based Approach to Ophthalmology Across the EU

Jonathan Feng
http://orcid.org/0009-0004-7135-2799
University College London, UK

ABSTRACT

In recent years, Europe has faced stagnant growth due to persistent long-term medical and health system problems in major developed countries, coupled with significant demographic changes. These factors have brought several pressing issues to the forefront. In the field of ophthalmology, the aging population and increasing prevalence of eye diseases among younger individuals have highlighted the shortcomings of traditional patient journeys, which are often fragmented and lack innovative solutions.To address these issues, we apply Porter's value-based healthcare framework to identify relevant literature on innovative technologies such as artificial intelligence, telemedicine, educational training, policy& reimbursement, and patient care strategies. We aim to understand future challenges and propose actionable solutions that can enhance the quality of ophthalmic care. Our goal is to implement value-based healthcare in ophthalmology, ensuring the system becomes more efficient, patient-centred, and capable of adapting to the evolving needs of the population.

DOI: 10.4018/979-8-3373-3341-0.ch007

1. INTRODUCTION

1.1. Context Setting

Europe has encountered stagnant economic growth, exacerbated by enduring medical and health system challenges in key developed nations, along with notable demographic shifts (WHO, 2020). These dynamics have culminated in several urgent health issues. In ophthalmology, aging populations, the emergence of eye conditions at younger ages, the inefficiencies of conventional patient care pathways, fragmented and outdated healthcare services, and the lack of uniform solutions for diverse health systems have intensified the difficulty of providing effective eye care (OECD, 2021). The COVID-19 pandemic has further complicated these challenges, hastened the evolution of patient care pathways and underscored the necessity for more integrated and innovative approaches (Lakhani et al., 2021).

As populations age, global health systems are struggling to meet the growing demand for eye care, predicting rising levels of visual impairment (VI) and blindness from major eye diseases. The significant burden of visual impairment has overwhelmed efforts to expand the physical capacity of eye clinics and hospitals and the availability of eye care providers such as ophthalmologists and optometrists. This trend is evident even in developed countries (Gunasekeran & Wong, 2020).

Despite variations, European healthcare systems share commonalities in their struggles and responses to ophthalmologic issues. An in-depth examination of specific systems, particularly in Germany, Italy, the UK, France, and Northern European countries, reveals unique approaches and shared challenges (WHO, 2020). This analysis draws on data from authoritative sources such as the World Health Organisation (WHO) and the Organisation for Economic Co-operation and Development (OECD), supplemented by consulting case studies from these nations.

1.2. Problem Statement

The demographic landscape in Europe is undergoing substantial changes. The continent is witnessing a significant aging trend, with a large segment of the population entering older age brackets (WHO, 2020). This demographic shift is crucial in understanding the increasing prevalence of age-related eye conditions like cataracts, glaucoma, and age-related macular degeneration (AMD). According to the WHO (2020), the proportion of people aged 65 and older in Europe is expected to rise from 20% in 2020 to 30% by 2050, exerting tremendous pressure on healthcare systems.

Additionally, younger populations are experiencing a rise in eye conditions such as myopia and digital eye strain, likely due to lifestyle changes and prolonged exposure to digital screens (OECD, 2021). These trends necessitate urgent and tailored healthcare responses.

Traditional patient care pathways in ophthalmology often involve multiple stages, from initial diagnosis by general practitioners to specialist referrals, treatment, and follow-up care. This pathway, while thorough, is plagued by delays, inefficiencies, and obstacles to seamless care. For example, in Germany, the average waiting time for an ophthalmologist appointment can extend up to several weeks, posing significant challenges for timely diagnosis and treatment (German Federal Statistical Office, 2019).

Fragmentation within healthcare systems further complicates patient journeys. In Italy, regional disparities in healthcare provision led to inconsistent patient experiences and outcomes. Northern regions, with better resources and infrastructure, typically offer more efficient and higher-quality eye care services compared to their southern counterparts (Italian Ministry of Health, 2020). This fragmentation underscores the need for more cohesive and integrated healthcare strategies.

The COVID-19 pandemic has profoundly disrupted healthcare systems worldwide, including ophthalmologic care. Lockdowns, social distancing measures, and the reallocation of healthcare resources to manage COVID-19 cases have led to significant delays in routine eye care and elective surgeries (Lakhani et al., 2021). In the UK, the Royal College of Ophthalmologists (2020) reported a 50% reduction in ophthalmic services during the peak of the pandemic, exacerbating existing backlogs and extending waiting times for essential eye treatments.

However, the pandemic has also acted as a catalyst for innovation and transformation. Teleophthalmology emerged as a viable alternative, offering remote consultations and follow-ups. This shift not only maintained continuity of care but also demonstrated the potential for technology to address long-standing issues in patient care pathways. For instance, in France, the adoption of telemedicine increased by 40% during the pandemic, with ophthalmology being one of the key specialties to benefit from this transition (French National Authority for Health, 2021).

1.2.1 Different Health Systems and Eye Care Across Europe

Europe's healthcare landscape is characterised by a diverse array of health systems, each with its unique structure, funding mechanisms, and approaches to delivering ophthalmologic care. Understanding these systems' nuances provides valuable insights into the challenges and innovations within European eye care.

National Health Service Models:

The UK and Italy exemplify national health service (NHS) models, providing healthcare funded through general taxation and offering services largely free at the point of use (NHS Digital, 2021). The UK's NHS, while extensive, has been strained by funding cuts, leading to challenges in accessing timely ophthalmologic care. Conversely, Italy's decentralised NHS results in regional variability, with Northern regions typically providing superior care compared to the South (Italian Ministry of Health, 2020).

Social Health Insurance Systems:

Countries like Germany and France operate under social health insurance systems, where healthcare is funded through a combination of employer and employee contributions, supplemented by government subsidies (OECD, 2021). In these systems, access to ophthalmologic care is generally broad, but regional disparities and bureaucratic hurdles can affect service delivery. Germany, for instance, faces long waiting times for specialist appointments despite its comprehensive coverage (German Federal Statistical Office, 2019).

Mixed Public-Private Systems:

France operates a mixed public-private healthcare system, where mandatory health insurance covers most healthcare costs, and private insurance or out-of-pocket payments cover additional services. This model facilitates high-quality ophthalmologic care and has adapted well to integrating telemedicine, particularly during the COVID-19 pandemic (French National Authority for Health, 2021).

Nordic Integrated Care Models:

Northern European countries, including Sweden, Denmark, and Norway, are renowned for their integrated care models, which emphasise coordination and continuity of care across various healthcare services. These systems excel in providing equitable and high-quality ophthalmologic care with minimal regional disparities and a strong focus on preventive measures and early intervention (Nordic Council of Ministers, 2021).

Integration and Innovation in Ophthalmologic Care:

The fragmentation observed in many European healthcare systems underscores the need for greater integration and innovation. Integrated care models, as seen in Northern Europe, offer valuable lessons in coordinating services and enhancing patient outcomes. These models prioritise seamless transitions between different levels of care, ensuring that patients receive timely and appropriate treatments without unnecessary delays (Nordic Council of Ministers, 2021)

Technological advancements, particularly in teleophthalmology, have shown promise in addressing some of the traditional patient care pathway inefficiencies.

The adoption of telemedicine during the COVID-19 pandemic has demonstrated its potential to maintain continuity of care and expand access to specialist services, especially in remote or underserved areas. For example, France's significant increase in telemedicine usage during the pandemic highlights the feasibility and benefits of incorporating digital health solutions into routine care (French National Authority for Health, 2021).

In terms of different health system in the EU, Europe's ophthalmologic care landscape is shaped by demographic shifts, systemic inefficiencies, and the unprecedented challenges posed by the COVID-19 pandemic. While each country offers unique insights and responses, common themes of fragmentation, innovation, and the urgent need for more integrated care pathways emerge. By leveraging data from the WHO, OECD, and national health authorities, this report aims to explore these dynamics comprehensively, providing a detailed analysis of the current state and future directions of ophthalmologic care across Europe. This understanding is crucial for developing effective strategies to enhance patient journeys and outcomes in the face of evolving healthcare challenges (WHO, 2020; OECD, 2021).

2. METHODOLOGY

2.1. Research Question & Objective

The primary objective of this scoping review is to systematically map the research landscape on the implementation of value-based healthcare in ophthalmology, with a particular focus on digital technology, telemedicine, and artificial intelligence (AI). Specifically, this review aims to identify key themes, gaps, and future research directions within the context of ophthalmic care. By exploring these areas, we seek to contribute to a deeper understanding of how value-based healthcare principles can be effectively applied to improve patient outcomes and optimize healthcare delivery in ophthalmology.

The integration of value-based health care (VBHC) and technological innovations in ophthalmology signifies a transformative approach in healthcare delivery, aiming to enhance patient outcomes while optimizing costs. And we wonder "How does the implementation of value-based care in ophthalmology impact health outcomes and cost-effectiveness compared to traditional care models in different health systems across the EU?" This study employs the PICO (Population, Intervention, Comparison, Outcome) framework to investigate the effects of VBHC combined with technological advancements across various European Union (EU) health systems.

Figure 1. Research Question by PICO Framework

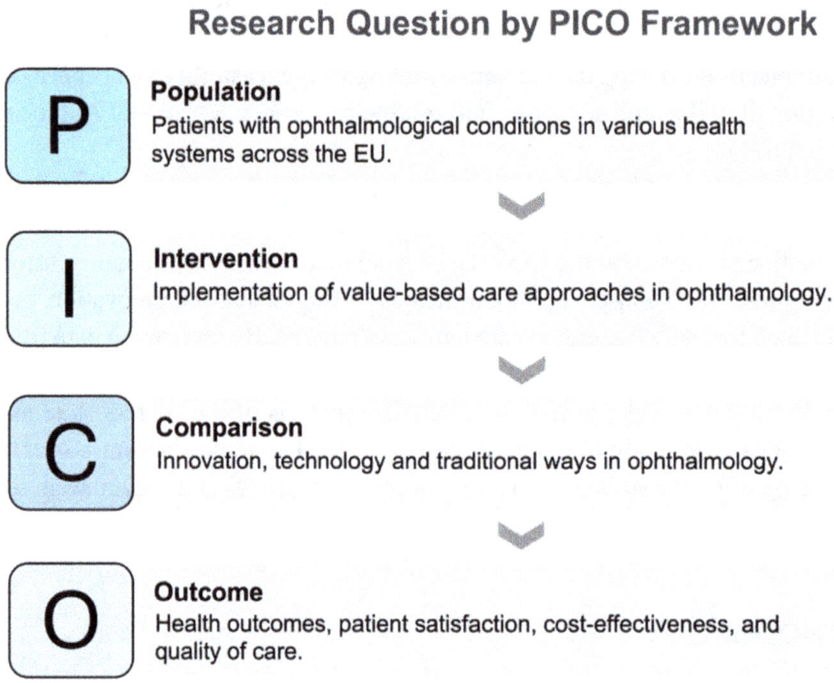

Population:

The focus is on patients with ophthalmological conditions, a diverse group affected by diseases ranging from cataracts to glaucoma. These conditions require complex and ongoing care, making them ideal for evaluating the efficacy of VBHC models enhanced by technological innovations (Stein et al., 2003).

Intervention:

VBHC in ophthalmology involves implementing care models that prioritise patient outcomes over service volume, augmented by cutting-edge technology. Innovations such as telemedicine, advanced diagnostic tools, and precision medicine are integrated into care pathways to improve accuracy, efficiency, and patient engagement (Porter & Lee, 2013).

Comparison:

Traditional care models often emphasise the quantity of care delivered, which can lead to higher costs and variable patient outcomes. In contrast, the integration of VBHC with technological innovations offers a more effective approach by enhancing precision and efficiency. This comparison highlights the potential of technology to elevate the standards of care in ophthalmology (Bertakis & Azari, 2011).

Outcome:

The primary outcomes assessed include health improvements, cost-effectiveness, patient satisfaction, and overall quality of care. Research indicates that VBHC models, when combined with technological innovations, lead to significant improvements in clinical outcomes, higher patient satisfaction, and more efficient use of resources (Garrison et al., 2018). Advanced diagnostic tools and telemedicine facilitate early detection and continuous monitoring, thereby improving patient outcomes and reducing costs.

2.2. Introduction to the Framework: Value-Based Health Care (VBHC)

To investigate in more detail, we adopted the Value-based health care (VBHC) framework, developed by Michael Porter, which focuses on maximising patient health outcomes relative to the costs of achieving those outcomes. This transformative approach emphasises delivering patient-centred care that enhances quality while optimising resource use, shifting the emphasis from volume-based care to value-based care (Porter & Lee, 2013). This methodology provides a solid foundation for addressing the challenges in ophthalmologic care across Europe and improving the overall patient journey. The following sections detail the six major elements essential to a truly value-based healthcare system.

Figure 2. Six Elements of Value-Based Health Care Framework (Porter & Lee, 2013)

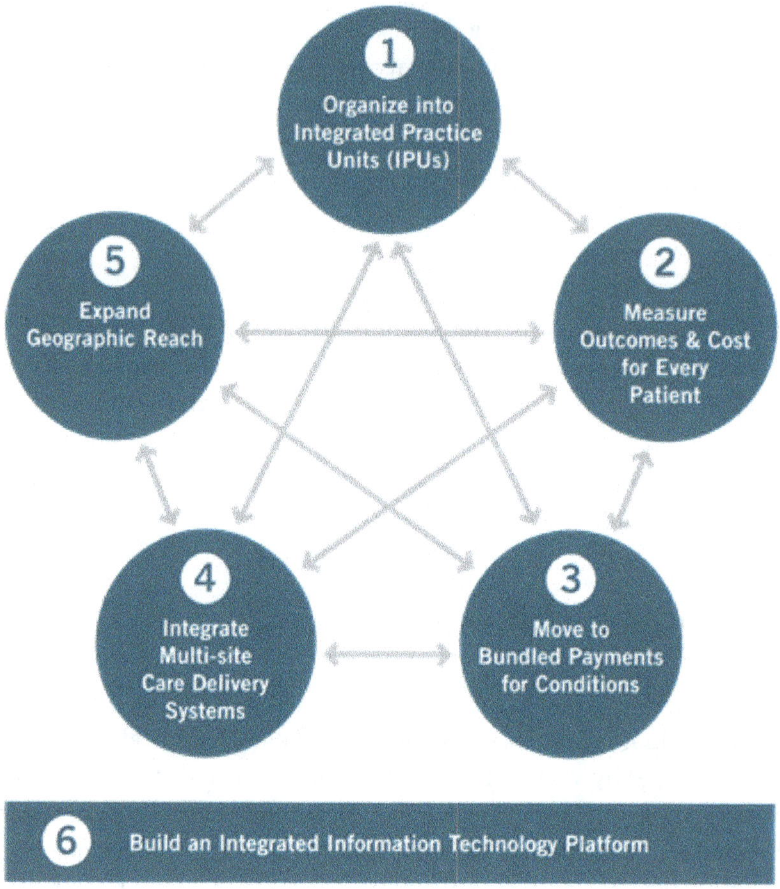

2.2.1. Organise Care Around Medical Conditions

Organising care around medical conditions or specific segments of the population is a fundamental element of VBHC. This approach ensures that care delivery is structured to address the comprehensive needs of patients with medical conditions, rather than focusing on discrete services or departments. By organising care in this way, health systems can provide more coordinated and effective treatment, leading to improved patient outcomes and greater efficiency (Porter, 2010).

2.2.2. Measure Outcomes and Costs for Every Patient

Measuring outcomes and costs for every patient is crucial in VBHC. This involves systematically collecting data on both the health outcomes achieved and the costs incurred in providing care. The focus is on outcomes that matter most to patients, such as quality of life and functional status, alongside traditional clinical measures (Porter, 2010). Accurate measurement of outcomes and costs enables providers to compare performance, identify best practices, and drive continuous improvement.

2.2.3. Aligning Reimbursement with Value

Aligning reimbursement with value is a key financial component of VBHC. This involves implementing payment models that reward health care providers for delivering high-quality, cost-effective care. Bundled payments are a common example, where providers receive a single payment for all services related to a specific condition or treatment over a defined period (Porter & Kaplan, 2016). This model incentivises providers to focus on outcomes rather than the volume of services, promoting more efficient and patient-centred care.

2.2.4. Systems Integration

Systems integration is essential for ensuring that care is coordinated across different specialties and sectors. This involves breaking down silos between various healthcare providers and fostering collaboration among primary care physicians, specialists, and other health professionals (Porter & Lee, 2013). Integrated care pathways ensure that patients receive timely and appropriate interventions, reducing the risk of complications and improving overall outcomes.

2.2.5. Geography of Care

Organising the geography of care involves establishing regional delivery systems that ensure patients have access to the right care at the right place. This can include creating centres of excellence for complex conditions that require specialised expertise and resources (Porter, 2010). By concentrating specialised care in specific locations, health systems can improve outcomes and efficiency while ensuring that patients receive high-quality treatment.

2.2.6. Information Technology

A robust IT infrastructure is critical for the successful implementation of VBHC. Advanced health information systems are essential for collecting, analysing, and sharing patient data across different care settings. These systems enable providers to track outcomes, monitor performance, and identify areas for improvement (Porter & Kaplan, 2016). Effective use of IT supports communication and coordination among providers, ensuring that all members of the care team have access to up-to-date patient information.

2.3. Narrative Literature Review Methodology

To ensure a comprehensive overview, we employed a narrative literature review methodology aligned with the PRISMA-ScR guidelines (Tricco et al., 2018). Our search strategy encompassed major academic databases, including PubMed, SCOPUS, Web of Science, and Google Scholar, focusing on English-language publications from 2000 to 2024. The search terms used were meticulously chosen to cover a broad range of relevant topics, including "ophthalm*" to capture studies related to ophthalmology, "innovat*" to identify research on innovation, "integrat*" for healthcare integration, "patient*" for patient-centred studies, "reimburs*" for reimbursement policies, "ageing" to address issues related to ageing populations, and "value*" to align with value-based healthcare principles.

Figure 3. PRISMA-ScR Flow Chart for the Narrative Literature Review (Tricco et al., 2018)

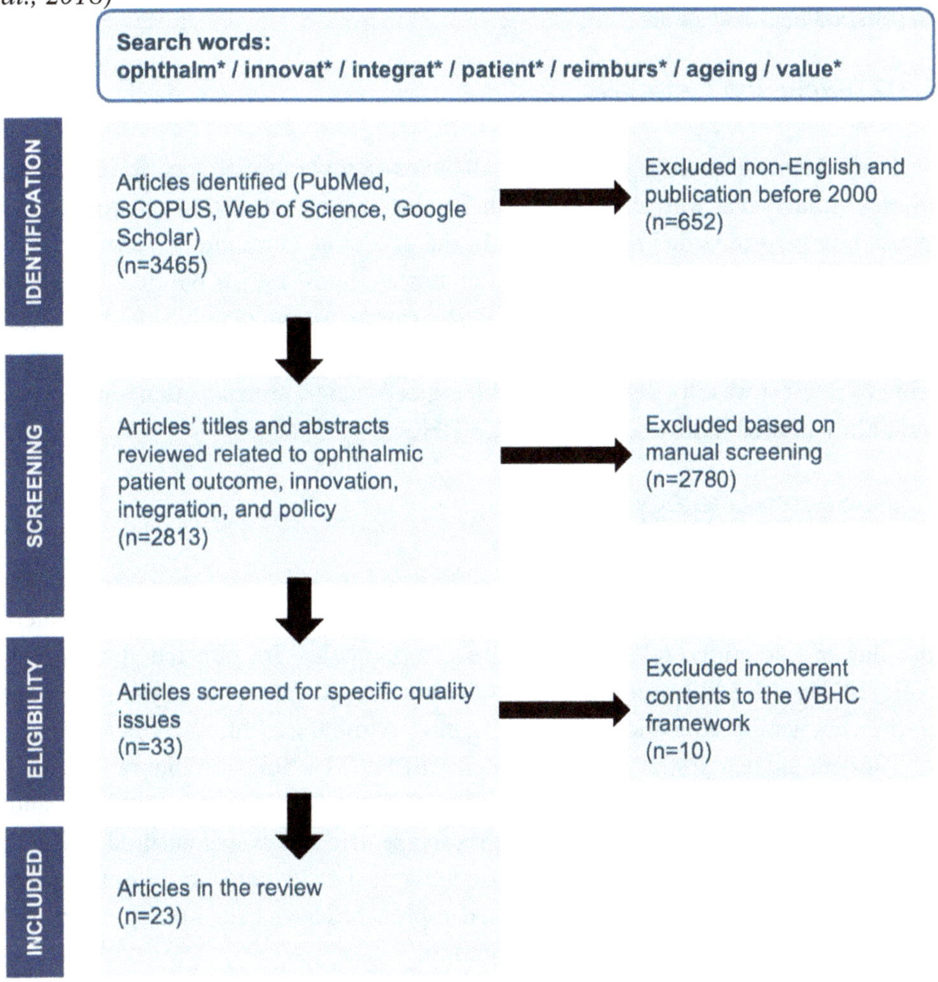

2.3.1. Eligibility Criteria

Our eligibility criteria were meticulously designed to align with the key elements of the value-based healthcare framework (VBHC), as conceptualised by Michael Porter. The literature selected had to address themes related to ophthalmic patient outcomes, innovation, integration, and health policy. Additionally, our focus was geographically constrained to studies conducted in Western countries to ensure relevance to our context. The keywords guiding our inclusion process were directly linked to the six elements of the value-based healthcare framework. This deliberate focus allowed us to dive in on studies that provide meaningful insights into improving ophthalmic patient care through innovative and integrated approaches within established health systems.

2.3.2. Exclusion Criteria

To maintain the quality and relevance of our review, we applied specific exclusion criteria. Studies that were cited less than 50 times were excluded to ensure that we focused on well-regarded research within the academic community. Additionally, we excluded journals from developing countries, non-English publications, and studies published before the year 2000. Furthermore, we did not consider literature focusing on ophthalmic pharmaceuticals or purely medical interventions, as our primary interest was in tele-medicine, AI, educational trainings, patient outcomes, and policy-related innovations based on VBHC.

2.3.3. Search Strategy

Our search strategy was strategically designed to address major common eye diseases prevalent in the European Union, such as cataract, glaucoma, age-related macular degeneration (AMD), and diabetic retinopathy. We targeted studies that explored these conditions in the context of value-based care, patient journey, integration, innovation, educational training, ageing, reimbursement, and policy aspects.

The detailed search strategy is illustrated in a PRISMA-ScR flow diagram (Tricco et al., 2018), outlining the number of studies identified, screened, excluded, and included in the review. By focusing on these specific topics, we ensured that our literature review would provide a holistic view of the current state of ophthalmic care, highlighting areas where value-based approaches have been implemented and identifying gaps that need further exploration.

2.3.4. Results from Search

From our rigorous search process, we identified and selected over 30 literature reviews from screening more than three thousand papers. These reviews encompass a wide array of topics central to our investigation, including AI, telemedicine, educational training, patient care, and policy&reimbursement. Each selected study contributes unique insights into how value-based healthcare principles are being applied to improve ophthalmic patient outcomes.

The extensive research topics converge on several key themes within ophthalmology: the transformative role of digital technology, telemedicine, and artificial intelligence (AI), and their integration into clinical practice. Studies explore the global perspective on these innovations, emphasising the need for trustworthy AI systems and their transition from development to real-world applications. The implementation of value-based healthcare models, cloud-based referral platforms, and tele-ophthalmology services highlights the drive toward improving patient outcomes and cost-effectiveness.

Additionally, the era of AI and virtual reality is revolutionising surgical education and training, particularly post-COVID-19. Best practices in teaching ophthalmology, patient satisfaction, and the socio-economic impacts of health policy regulations are examined, alongside the clinical management of conditions like glaucoma and macular degeneration. Scoping reviews provide insights into patient perspectives, the prevalence of age-related eye diseases, and the economic burden on healthcare systems. Collectively, these studies demonstrate a comprehensive approach to advancing ophthalmic care through innovation, patient-centred strategies, and policy action, aiming to enhance both the quality and accessibility of eye care services across Europe.

Figure 4. World Cloud illustrated by the title of the selected literature reviews

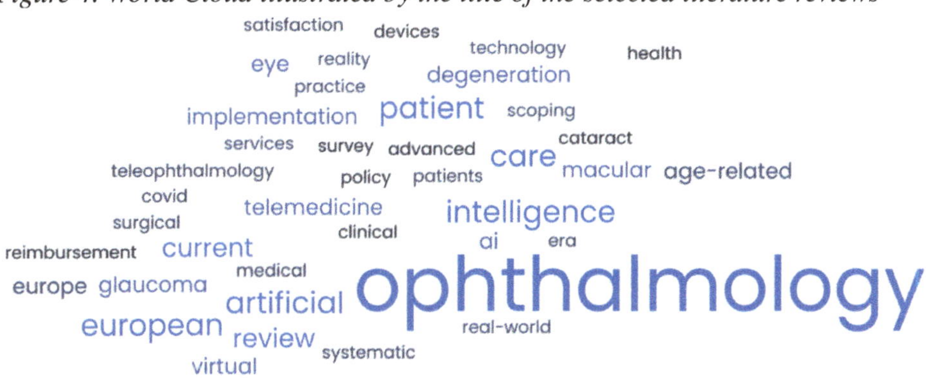

Table 1. 15 Key Studies Based on Six Elements of Value-Based Healthcare (2000-2024)

Author(s)	Country	Title	Method & Sample	Concepts	Finding(s)	Recommendations
(Li et al., 2021)	UK, China, Republic of Korea, USA, Israel, Japan, Singapore, Hong Kong	Digital technology, tele-medicine and artificial intelligence in ophthalmology: A global perspective	Review of global practices and technologies in telemedicine and AI in ophthalmology	Telemedicine, AI, ophthalmology, digital technology, COVID-19	Digital innovations and AI improve accessibility and efficiency in ophthalmology, with rapid adoption during COVID-19. Challenges include integration and validation.	Promote unified frameworks for telemedicine, enhance AI integration, ensure robust validation processes, and adapt ophthalmology practices to incorporate digital innovations for improved patient care.
(Li et al., 2023)	China, UK	Artificial intelligence (AI) in ophthalmology: The path to the real-world clinic	Scoping review of AI applications in ophthalmology and the challenges for real-world clinical implementation.	AI, machine learning, deep learning, ophthalmic imaging, clinical translation	AI systems can match or exceed ophthalmologists in tasks like diabetic retinopathy detection, but few are deployed in real-world settings due to challenges in generalizability, data annotation, standardization, and longevity.	Enhance generalizability with multi-centre datasets, improve data sharing via federated learning, employ continuous learning techniques for AI longevity, ensure robust validation for clinical application.
(Kern et al., 2020)	United Kingdom, Germany, Austria	Implementation of a cloud-based referral platform in ophthalmology: making telemedicine services a reality in eye care	Method: Retrospective cohort study. Sample: 103 patients referred to Moorfields Eye Hospital via a cloud-based referral platform.	Cloud-based referral platform, telemedicine, ophthalmology, patient referrals.	More than half (52%) of referrals were unnecessary, reducing the burden on specialist services. 14% of patients were identified for urgent treatment.	Expand use of cloud-based referral platforms to improve efficiency and reduce unnecessary referrals in ophthalmology. Implement artificial intelligence to further enhance the platform.
(Bakshi et al., 2021)	USA, Singapore	The era of artificial intelligence and virtual reality: transforming surgical education in ophthalmology	Method: Review of emerging technologies. Sample: Applications and case studies, no specific sample size as this is a review article.	Artificial Intelligence, Virtual Reality, surgical education, ophthalmology	AI can enhance surgical training through video analytics, intraoperative guidance, and outcomes tracking. VR offers immersive simulation for low-risk practice and collaborative training.	Integrate AI and VR technologies into ophthalmic surgical education, standardize validation processes, and foster partnerships between academia and industry.

continued on following page

Table 1. Continued

Author(s)	Country	Title	Method & Sample	Concepts	Finding(s)	Recommendations
(Dean et al., 2017)	United Kingdom	The patient is speaking: discovering the patient voice in ophthalmology	Qualitative analysis using patient interviews and focus groups; sample size not explicitly mentioned.	The study focuses on understanding the patient perspective in ophthalmology, emphasizing patient experiences and the importance of patient-reported outcomes.	Patients value being heard and involved in their care. Effective communication and shared decision-making are critical for patient satisfaction and better health outcomes.	Incorporate patient feedback into clinical practice, improve communication strategies, and foster a patient-centred approach in ophthalmology to enhance patient care and outcomes.
(Sreelatha & Ramesh, 2016)	Canada, India, and the USA	Teleophthalmology: Improving Patient Outcomes?	Literature review; sample sizes range from 57 to 13,777 patients	Teleophthalmology, patient outcomes, diabetic retinopathy (DR) screening, patient satisfaction, and referral rates.	Teleophthalmology reduces unnecessary referrals and improves detection and treatment efficiency. High patient satisfaction.	Expand teleophthalmology services and integrate them into standard practice. Conduct further research for optimization.
(Ferrara et al., 2020)	United Kingdom, Italy, Netherlands	Reshaping ophthalmology training after COVID-19 pandemic	Online survey; 504 responses from 32 countries	COVID-19 impact, ophthalmology training, web-based teaching, simulation-based training, telementoring	Significant reduction in clinical and surgical activities. Web-based and simulation training are effective, but traditional methods are still valued.	Integrate web-based teaching and simulation-based training. Enhance telementoring and prepare for future disruptions in training programs.
(Cimarolli et al., 2016)	USA, Germany	Anxiety and depression in patients with advanced macular degeneration: current perspectives	Scoping literature review with a sample size of 41 studies	Examines the prevalence, impact, and management of anxiety and depression in patients with advanced macular degeneration (AMD)	Anxiety and depression are common among AMD patients, negatively impacting their quality of life and visual function. Psychological interventions and proper management of AMD symptoms can mitigate these effects.	Routine screening for anxiety and depression in AMD patients and the implementation of comprehensive care plans that include psychological support.
(Tan et al., 2019)	Australia	Clinical Registries in Ophthalmology	Systematic literature review of 97 clinical eye registries	Role and impact of clinical registries, data collection, registry size, quality improvement	Large national registries are essential for epidemiological studies and monitoring rare complications. Automated data extraction from electronic medical records improves data quality and reduces the burden of manual entry.	Streamline data collection processes, integrate registries with existing electronic medical records, and allocate resources for interface development to ensure data quality and sustainability.

continued on following page

Table 1. Continued

Author(s)	Country	Title	Method & Sample	Concepts	Finding(s)	Recommendations
(Barequet et al., 2019)	Israel	Health policy regulations pertaining to advanced surgical devices—their socio-economic effects on ophthalmology practice	Case study analysis of policy changes; no specific sample size mentioned	Health policy, advanced surgical devices, socio-economic effects, ophthalmology practice	Policy changes aimed to reduce private healthcare costs led to restricted access to advanced devices, inadvertently increasing inequality. Adjustments allowed for partial self-payment, improving access.	Policymakers should carefully consider the implications of limiting co-payments for advanced medical devices to avoid increasing inequality. Allow partial self-payment to enhance access to advanced technologies.
(Fattore & Torbica, 2008)	Italy	Cost and reimbursement of cataract surgery in Europe—a cross-country comparison	Data collected from 43 healthcare providers in EU	Examines cost variation, reimbursement rates, and factors influencing the cost of cataract surgery across different European countries.	Significant cost variations were found, with mean total costs per cataract intervention ranging from €318 in Hungary to €1087 in Italy. Factors such as the type of setting (hospital vs. outpatient), length of stay, and type of lens used contributed to cost differences.	Standardize cost accounting practices, improve data collection for cross-country comparisons, and explore efficiency improvements in cataract surgery to reduce costs while maintaining quality care.
(Mazzuca et al., 2022)	Italy	Applications and Current Medico-Legal Challenges of Telemedicine in Ophthalmology	Review of 45 original articles and 5 reviews from 1997 to 2021, found using databases like PubMed, Scopus, Web of Science, and Embase.	Telemedicine in ophthalmology, medico-legal challenges, patient care, cost-effectiveness, privacy, and data security.	Telemedicine provides significant benefits such as improved patient care, time, and cost savings. However, it also has limitations, including lack of physical exams, possible transmission failures, and potential privacy violations.	There is a need for better physician training and user-friendly platforms for patients. Additionally, there should be unified legal frameworks to standardize telemedicine practices globally to ensure privacy, data security, and quality of care.

continued on following page

Table 1. Continued

Author(s)	Country	Title	Method & Sample	Concepts	Finding(s)	Recommendations
(Hunter & Bengoa, 2023)	United Kingdom, Spain	Meeting the challenge of health system transformation in European countries	Review of three European country case studies (Sweden, UK, Portugal)	Health system transformation, policy capacity, integrated care, population health, patient empowerment, digital health	Successful transformation requires environmental pressure, coherent policies, key leadership, supportive culture, and good managerial-clinical relations. COVID-19 has accelerated changes but exposed system weaknesses.	Adopt integrated, patient-centred care models, invest in prevention, improve policy coherence and leadership, foster supportive cultures, and address workforce issues. Use unified frameworks for monitoring and flexible, context-specific approaches.
(Hassell et al., 2006)	Australia	Impact of age-related macular degeneration on quality of life	Assessment of 106 adults with AMD using the Impact of Vision Impairment (IVI) questionnaire, Short Form General Health Survey (SF-12), and a sociodemographic questionnaire.	Age-related macular degeneration (AMD), vision impairment, quality of life, emotional health, participation in daily activities	AMD significantly impacts quality of life, affecting activities such as reading, mobility, and emotional well-being. Both mild and severe vision impairments are associated with considerable difficulties, with severe impairments leading to greater restrictions.	Referral to low vision services should be considered for people with mild vision loss and worse to maintain or improve their quality of life. These services should include self-management support, counselling, and rehabilitation focused on mobility and emotional health.
(Chakravarthy et al., 2010)	United Kingdom, Singapore, USA	Clinical risk factors for age-related macular degeneration: a systematic review and meta-analysis	Systematic review and meta-analysis of 24 studies with 113,780 participants and 17,236 AMD cases	Risk factors for age-related macular degeneration (AMD), associations with lifestyle, medical, and demographic variables	Strong risk factors include age, smoking, cataract surgery, and family history. Moderate factors include BMI, cardiovascular disease, hypertension, and plasma fibrinogen.	Physicians should assess and address these risk factors to identify and refer at-risk individuals for preventive care.

3. FINDINGS

3.1. Summative Review

The summative review synthesises current literature reviews on the integration of AI and telemedicine within ophthalmology, contextualised within the Value-Based Health Care (VBHC) framework. It critically evaluates how these technologies enhance diagnostic accuracy, accessibility, and patient outcomes while reducing costs.

The findings encompass AI's role in predictive analytics, telemedicine's potential in remote care delivery, and the development of personalised patient care models. Additionally, it addresses advancements in educational training for healthcare providers and the implications of policy and reimbursement strategies. These findings as below aim to identify knowledge gaps and inform future research and practice, ensuring patient-centred, high-value ophthalmic care.

3.2. AI and Tele-medicine in Ophthalmology

The integration of digital technology and artificial intelligence (AI) in ophthalmology has significantly transformed diagnostic and treatment processes. This transformation aligns seamlessly with the Value-Based Health Care (VBHC) framework by improving diagnostic accuracy and efficiency, thereby enhancing patient outcomes and personalizing treatment plans (Li et al., 2021). Notably, AI systems, particularly deep learning models, have demonstrated high accuracy in diagnosing conditions such as diabetic retinopathy, age-related macular degeneration (AMD), and glaucoma. These technologies, by providing precise diagnoses, enable timely and effective interventions, thus enhancing the value of care (Gunasekeran & Wong, 2020).

Predictive analytics enabled by AI help forecast disease progression and plan appropriate interventions, which is particularly useful in managing chronic conditions like glaucoma and AMD (Ting et al., 2019). This ability to anticipate and manage disease progression contributes significantly to improved patient outcomes.

Furthermore, AI's transition from experimental stages to real-world applications, especially in teleophthalmology, facilitates remote diagnosis and management. This advancement increases access to care in underserved areas, aligning with VBHC's goal of equity in healthcare (Caffery et al., 2019). Implementations such as cloud-based referral platforms have optimized healthcare delivery and improved patient outcomes by reducing unnecessary referrals and ensuring timely specialist interventions (Kern et al., 2020).

In addition to diagnostics, AI tools have been developed to assist in surgical procedures, providing real-time guidance and improving surgical outcomes (Bakshi et al., 2021). AI's ability to analyse large datasets from clinical registries can identify patterns and outcomes that inform better clinical practices and policies (Tan et al., 2019). This capability ensures that treatments are based on the most current and comprehensive data available, thus transforming the landscape of ophthalmic research and clinical care (Li et al., 2023).

AI enhances patient care by facilitating personalized medicine. For example, AI can analyse genetic information and lifestyle factors to develop individualized treatment plans, which is especially beneficial in managing complex conditions like

AMD and diabetic retinopathy (Ting et al., 2019). This personalized approach not only improves treatment efficacy but also enhances patient satisfaction by tailoring interventions to individual needs.

What's more, AI has the potential to detect hidden information from digital health data that clinicians might not perceive. In ophthalmology, the application of AI based on retinal images has extended from detecting multiple fundus diseases to screening for systemic diseases. Deep learning in ocular imaging may be used in conjunction with telemedicine to screen, diagnose, and monitor major eye diseases for patients in primary care and community settings (Li et al., 2023). AI systems capable of achieving or exceeding expert-level performance are becoming increasingly prevalent, demonstrating their potential to improve patient outcomes, healthcare providers' workflows, and access to ophthalmic care. Ensuring trustworthy AI requires multistakeholder collaborations involving AI developers, reading centres, healthcare providers, institutions, ophthalmological societies, working groups, patients, regulatory bodies, and payers (González-Gonzalo et al., 2022). This collaborative approach is essential to bridge the gap between AI development and its integration into ophthalmology.

Telemedicine, particularly teleophthalmology, has gained significant traction, especially during the COVID-19 pandemic. Teleophthalmology involves using telecommunications technology to provide ophthalmic care remotely, which helps manage chronic conditions and reduce the need for in-person visits (Caffery et al., 2019). It has been effective in screening, triage, and follow-up consultations, thus improving access to care and reducing healthcare costs (González-Gonzalo et al., 2022).

Despite its benefits, teleophthalmology faces challenges such as technological barriers, lack of standardisation, and reimbursement issues. Recommendations to overcome these challenges include developing robust telemedicine policies, enhancing digital infrastructure, and training healthcare providers in telemedicine practices (Sreelatha & Ramesh, 2016). Moreover, comprehensive guidelines and protocols are needed to ensure consistent and high-quality tele-ophthalmic care (Barequet et al., 2019).

Implementing teleophthalmology services has improved the cost-effectiveness of national eye care systems by reducing unnecessary referrals and optimising the use of specialist resources (Jørgensen et al., 2024). This approach has been particularly beneficial in rural and underserved areas, where access to specialist care is limited (Sreelatha & Ramesh, 2016). Teleophthalmology has also enhanced patient satisfaction by reducing travel time and expenses, enabling more frequent and flexible consultations (Saleem et al., 2020). This aligns with the VBHC framework by focusing on improving patient experiences and outcomes while managing costs effectively (Augood et al., 2006).

Telemedicine has expanded beyond traditional eye care to include comprehensive care models that integrate various healthcare services. Cloud-based referral platforms facilitate seamless communication and coordination between primary care providers and ophthalmologists, ensuring timely and effective care delivery (Kern et al., 2020). These integrated care models have demonstrated significant improvements in patient outcomes and system efficiency, highlighting the potential of telemedicine to transform healthcare delivery.

3.3. Patient Care

AI and telemedicine have significantly enhanced patient care by enabling early detection and continuous management of eye diseases, aligning with VBHC's focus on improving patient outcomes (Ting et al., 2019). By utilising remote monitoring systems coupled with AI diagnostics, healthcare providers can offer timely interventions and personalised care plans, thus improving patient outcomes and accessibility to eye care services (Li et al., 2023).

Effective communication, timely care, and personalised treatment plans are crucial for patient satisfaction in ophthalmology. To this end, a simulation-based multi-objective optimisation framework has been suggested to enhance patient satisfaction by optimizing resource allocation and reducing waiting times, directly supporting VBHC's emphasis on patient-centred care (Chemkomnerd et al., 2024).

Besides, mental health issues, such as anxiety and depression, are prevalent among patients with advanced ophthalmic conditions like AMD. Therefore, integrating mental health screenings and providing appropriate interventions in regular ophthalmic care can significantly improve patient outcomes and quality of life, aligning with VBHC's holistic approach to patient care (Cimarolli et al., 2016). Furthermore, comprehensive patient education and support programs are essential in managing the psychological impact of chronic eye diseases (Hassell et al., 2006).

The implementation of patient-centred care models, which emphasise understanding and addressing patients' needs and preferences, has shown to improve patient outcomes and satisfaction, aligning with VBHC principles (Dean et al., 2017). These models promote a holistic approach to care, integrating physical, psychological, and social aspects of health (Chakravarthy et al., 2010).

We have considered how the patient perspective can be collected in both research and clinical contexts and how this can inform our systems of care and direction of research within ophthalmology. Traditional objective clinical measures such as visual acuity are important but are one-dimensional and fail to provide an adequate assessment of their condition. Learning to hear the 'patient voice' in clinical practice and research enables a more complete understanding of what patients are experiencing through their disease and what their priorities are for treatment. We need to move from the patient being the 'object' of patient-centred care to being the 'subject'. (Dean et al., 2017)

Another key aspect of enhancing patient care is the use of real-world evidence from clinical registries to inform clinical practices and policies. This approach ensures that patient care is based on the most current and comprehensive data available, leading to better outcomes and higher value care (Tan et al., 2019).

Lastly, the integration of telemedicine into routine ophthalmic care has facilitated continuous monitoring and follow-up, which is particularly beneficial for patients with chronic conditions. This approach ensures that any changes in a patient's condition are promptly identified and addressed, reducing the risk of complications and improving overall outcomes (Sreelatha & Ramesh, 2016).

3.4. Educational Training for Trainees

The COVID-19 pandemic necessitated rapid changes in ophthalmology training, shifting from traditional methods to virtual and simulation-based training. These changes align with VBHC by ensuring that healthcare providers are well-prepared to deliver high-quality care. Educational programs have integrated web-based teaching, virtual reality (VR) simulators, and tele-mentoring to maintain high training standards, ensuring that trainees acquire practical skills and theoretical knowledge effectively (Bakshi et al., 2021).

Furthermore, best practices in ophthalmology education now include a combination of traditional and modern techniques such as webinars, online case presentations, and VR simulations to enhance learning experiences and prepare trainees for real-world scenarios (Ferrara et al., 2020). The use of AI in educational tools helps track progress and provide personalised feedback, ensuring that trainees are well-equipped to deliver high-value care (Bakshi et al., 2021).

In addition, the integration of advanced technologies in training programs also helps overcome geographical barriers, enabling trainees from remote areas to access high-quality education, thus promoting equity and access in line with VBHC principles (Succar et al., 2016). This leads to more equitable access to education and better preparedness among ophthalmology trainees (Ferrara et al., 2020). Simulation-based training has been particularly effective in enhancing surgical skills, allowing trainees to practice and refine techniques in a risk-free environment (Bakshi et al., 2021). This method has shown to improve confidence and competence among trainees, ultimately leading to better patient outcomes (Succar et al., 2016).

The shift to virtual learning environments has also facilitated continuous education for practicing ophthalmologists. Online platforms and virtual conferences have enabled professionals to stay updated with the latest advancements and best practices in the field, ensuring that they can provide the highest quality of care to their patients (Ferrara et al., 2020). Moreover, these platforms have allowed for greater collaboration and knowledge sharing among professionals worldwide, further enhancing the overall quality of ophthalmic care.

3.5. Policy & Reimbursement

Healthcare policies significantly impact the adoption and accessibility of advanced technologies in ophthalmology. Policies that limit the use of advanced surgical devices can inadvertently increase inequality by making these technologies less accessible to certain patient groups, counter to VBHC principles (Barequet et al., 2019). Therefore, policymakers need to consider the broader implications and ensure equitable access to advanced ophthalmic care, supporting VBHC's goal of equity in healthcare (Hunter & Bengoa, 2023).

Different countries have various reimbursement strategies for cataract surgery and other ophthalmic procedures. A cross-country comparison suggests that aligning reimbursement rates with actual costs and ensuring transparent and fair policies can improve access to care and reduce out-of-pocket expenses for patients, directly supporting VBHC principles (Fattore & Torbica, 2008). Additionally, incorporating performance-based reimbursement models can incentivise high-quality care and improve patient outcomes (Herbst et al., 2018).

The development and implementation of comprehensive healthcare policies that support the integration of AI and telemedicine are crucial for ensuring the sustainability and scalability of these technologies, aligning with VBHC principles (Jørgensen et al., 2024). These policies should address issues related to data privacy, ethical considerations, and regulatory standards (Krüger et al., 2014).

Furthermore, healthcare policy regulations play a critical role in the adoption of telemedicine. Policies that support telemedicine infrastructure, training for healthcare providers, and reimbursement models that incentivize telemedicine use can significantly enhance its integration into regular ophthalmic practice (Mazzuca et al., 2022). This alignment ensures that telemedicine can be sustainably integrated into healthcare systems, providing continuous and equitable access to care.

In addition to infrastructure and reimbursement, policies must also focus on ensuring the ethical use of AI in healthcare. This includes developing guidelines for data privacy, informed consent, and transparency in AI decision-making processes (González-Gonzalo et al., 2022). Policymakers should engage with stakeholders, including patients, healthcare providers, and technology developers, to create comprehensive and inclusive policies that promote the responsible use of AI in ophthalmology.

3.6. Residual Questions (Knowledge Gaps)

The field of ophthalmology has made significant strides, yet several residual questions and knowledge gaps remain. Firstly, while AI has shown promising results in the short term, its long-term effectiveness in clinical practice remains to be thoroughly investigated. Questions regarding AI's adaptability to new data, integration with existing healthcare systems, and long-term patient outcomes need further exploration to fully realise its value in healthcare(Ting et al., 2019).

Despite the great performance of AI systems in various retrospective studies, many challenges, such as the generalisability of AI systems, still hinder their true clinical adoption (Li et al., 2023). The development of robust AI systems requires large datasets, but the lack of high-quality public datasets that truly represent real-world clinical practice is a significant barrier. While data sharing could be a solution, it introduces ethical and legal challenges. Federated learning offers a promising alternative, allowing AI models to be trained with diverse data from multiple clinical institutions without centralizing the data (Li et al., 2023).

Figure 5. Five Residual Questions to the Findings

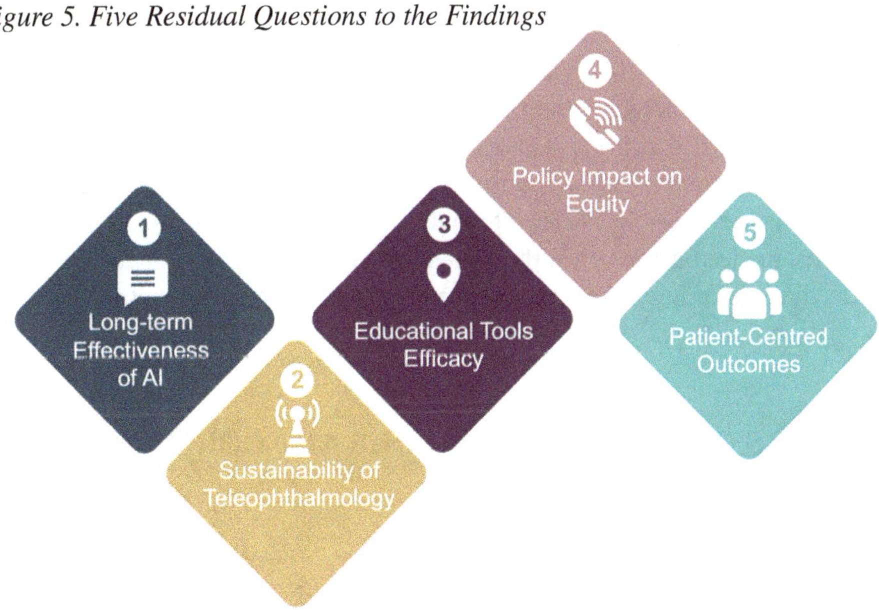

The unprecedented growth in the volume of electronic medical data has facilitated the development of AI-based medical devices. However, data collection is not standardised, affecting the readiness of these data for AI model training and testing (Li et al., 2023). Additionally, the performance of AI systems can degrade over time as the world changes, including disease distribution, population characteristics, health infrastructure, and cyber technologies. Therefore, AI systems must have the ability for lifelong continuous learning to maintain and even improve their performance. Continuous learning techniques, such as meta-learning, which aim to improve the AI algorithm itself, could address this issue (Ting et al., 2019).

Real-world performance, generalisability, and interpretability of AI systems are still insufficiently investigated and will require more attention in future studies. Concerns about AI and deep learning being 'black boxes' also hinder large-scale adoption in healthcare. In this context, both the quantitative algorithmic performance and the underlying features through which the algorithm classifies disease are crucial for improving physician acceptance (Ting et al., 2019).

Moving on to teleophthalmology, its sustainability post-pandemic is uncertain. Further research is needed to evaluate its long-term viability, patient acceptance, and potential to become a standard practice in ophthalmic care, ensuring its alignment with VBHC principles (Sreelatha & Ramesh, 2016).

Additionally, the efficacy of various educational tools and methods adopted during the pandemic needs long-term validation. Studies should focus on comparing these new methods with traditional training to determine the most effective approaches for future ophthalmology education, aligning with VBHC's focus on high-quality care delivery (Succar et al., 2016). The impact of healthcare policies on equity in access to advanced ophthalmic technologies requires more in-depth research. Policymakers need evidence-based data to make informed decisions that do not inadvertently widen the gap in healthcare access, supporting VBHC principles (Barequet et al., 2019).

Lastly, further research is needed to understand the long-term impact of patient-centred care models on overall healthcare outcomes and costs. This includes evaluating the effectiveness of integrated mental health services within ophthalmic care and their contribution to patient satisfaction and quality of life (Cimarolli et al., 2016).

4. DISCUSSION, RECOMMENDATIONS AND CONCLUSION

4.1. Meta-Analysis

In this section, we adopt a comprehensive meta-analysis of the integration of AI, telemedicine, patient care models, educational training, and policy and reimbursement findings in ophthalmology. The objective is to synthesise findings from multiple studies to derive new insights and evaluate their impact on patient outcomes and healthcare delivery, in line with the Value-Based Health Care (VBHC) framework. In terms of data sources, the meta-analysis included 23 key studies mentioned in the findings. Studies were excluded if they lacked sufficient data or had significant methodological flaws.

AI and Telemedicine in Ophthalmology

The integration of AI and telemedicine has shown significant improvements in diagnostic accuracy, efficiency, and patient outcomes in ophthalmology. AI systems, particularly deep learning models, have demonstrated high accuracy in diagnosing conditions such as diabetic retinopathy, age-related macular degeneration (AMD), and glaucoma. Predictive analytics enabled by AI help forecast disease progression and plan appropriate interventions, contributing to improved patient outcomes (Gunasekeran & Wong, 2020).

Teleophthalmology, especially during the COVID-19 pandemic, has been crucial in providing continuous care and reducing healthcare costs. It has proven effective in remote screening, triage, and follow-up consultations, thereby improving access to care, particularly in underserved areas (Jørgensen et al., 2024). The combination of AI diagnostics with telemedicine platforms has further enhanced the accuracy and timeliness of diagnoses (Sreelatha & Ramesh, 2016).

Patient Care

Integrating mental health services within ophthalmic care practices addresses the psychological impact of chronic eye diseases, improving overall patient outcomes and aligning with VBHC principles. Comprehensive care that includes mental health support enhances the value of care by addressing all aspects of patient health (Cimarolli et al., 2016). Effective communication, timely care, and personalised treatment plans are crucial for patient satisfaction in ophthalmology.

Plus, the evolution of patient care models should incorporate the latest advancements in technology and healthcare practices. This includes using real-world evidence to inform clinical decisions, implementing personalised medicine approaches, and ensuring continuous patient engagement through telemedicine and remote monitoring systems (Tan et al., 2019).

Educational Training for Trainees

Virtual and simulation-based training has maintained high standards of ophthalmic education, ensuring that future healthcare providers are well-equipped to deliver high-quality care. The use of AI and VR in training programs enhances learning experiences, providing trainees with hands-on practice and personalised feedback. Continued integration of these technologies in training curricula and expanding access to virtual training resources are recommended to ensure equity in education (Ferrara et al., 2020).

Moreover, simulation-based training has been particularly effective in enhancing surgical skills, allowing trainees to practice and refine techniques in a risk-free environment. This method has shown to improve confidence and competence among trainees, ultimately leading to better patient outcomes (Succar et al., 2016).

Policy & Reimbursement

Healthcare policies significantly impact the adoption and accessibility of advanced technologies in ophthalmology. Aligning reimbursement rates with actual costs and ensuring transparent and fair policies can improve access to care and reduce out-of-pocket expenses for patients (Fattore & Torbica, 2008). Performance-based reimbursement models can incentivise high-quality care and improve patient outcomes (Herbst et al., 2018).

Moreover, the development and implementation of comprehensive healthcare policies that support the integration of AI and telemedicine are crucial for ensuring the sustainability and scalability of these technologies, aligning with VBHC principles (Jørgensen et al., 2024). These policies should address issues related to data privacy, ethical considerations, and regulatory standards (Krüger et al., 2014). Furthermore, healthcare policy regulations play a critical role in the adoption of telemedicine. Policies that support telemedicine infrastructure, training for healthcare providers, and reimbursement models that incentivise telemedicine use can significantly enhance its integration into regular ophthalmic practice (Mazzuca et al., 2022).

4.2. New Integrated Insights

The meta-analysis highlights the significant benefits of integrating AI and telemedicine into ophthalmology, including improved diagnostic accuracy, enhanced patient outcomes, and reduced healthcare costs. Personalised care models, mental health integration, advanced training programs, and supportive policies and reimbursement strategies are key to delivering high-value care. By synthesising the findings, it is evident that these technological advancements and comprehensive care models significantly contribute to the overall improvement of ophthalmic care.

Moreover, the meta-analysis demonstrates the importance of personalised approaches and technological innovations in enhancing ophthalmic care across different health systems in Europe. Future research should focus on the long-term effectiveness of AI, the sustainability of teleophthalmology, and the validation of new educational tools to ensure continuous improvement in ophthalmic care. Additionally, policy development should prioritise equity and ethical considerations to support the sustainable integration of advanced technologies.

4.3. Recommendations

To enhance ophthalmic care across the European Union, we recommend adopting a value-based approach that integrates advanced technologies like AI and telemedicine, fosters public-private partnerships, and develops customised patient care models. Emphasising the importance of universal standards for AI data privacy and robust IT infrastructure, the recommendations also highlight the creation of expertise-sharing platforms and the need for supportive policies that promote equitable access and ethical use of innovations. These strategies aim to improve diagnostic accuracy, patient outcomes, healthcare efficiency, and the overall quality of ecosystem. Concluding, the report underscores the transformative potential of these innovations, urging ongoing research and policy development to ensure sustainable and high-quality ophthalmic care tailored to the evolving needs of the population.

Universal & Standardised AI Data Privacy and Access Across EU

In terms of developing universal standards, establishing universal standards for AI data privacy and access across the EU is crucial to ensure the secure and ethical use of AI in healthcare. Harmonised regulations will facilitate seamless cross-border healthcare collaborations and data exchanges, enhancing the overall quality of ophthalmic care. These standards should include robust data encryption, consent management, and secure data sharing practices to protect patient information (Krüger et al., 2014).

To support the implementation and integration of AI technologies in ophthalmology, significant investments in IT infrastructure are required. This includes upgrading existing systems, adopting cloud-based solutions, and ensuring high-speed internet like 5G access across healthcare facilities. A strong IT foundation will enable the efficient processing, storage, and analysis of large datasets required for AI-driven diagnostics and treatments (Gunasekeran & Wong, 2020). For instance, firstly, we can initiate "pilot programs" in select EU regions to test the integration model of AI diagnostics and telemedicine in ophthalmology. Then, we monitor and evaluate the outcomes to refine the approach periodically. If the pilot program goes well, we can expand the region across the EU to standardise the AI model as well as data privacy.

Public-Private Partnerships

Encouraging collaborations between public and private sectors, including academia and industry, can drive innovation in ophthalmic care. These partnerships can pool resources, expertise, and funding to accelerate the development and deployment of advanced AI and telemedicine solutions. Joint initiatives can lead to groundbreaking research and the rapid translation of innovations into clinical practice (Hunter & Bengoa, 2023).

In addition, public-private partnerships should be designed to be flexible and adaptable to the dynamic healthcare landscape. This includes fostering an environment that supports real-time diagnostics and cost-effective solutions, ensuring that innovations can quickly respond to emerging healthcare challenges and patient needs (Jørgensen et al., 2024).

Moreover, integrating mental health services into ophthalmic care is essential for providing comprehensive patient care. These partnerships can develop holistic treatment models that address both physical and psychological aspects of eye diseases. Mental health support can significantly improve patient outcomes, particularly for those dealing with chronic eye conditions that may lead to anxiety or depression (Cimarolli et al., 2016). Collaborative efforts can ensure that mental health services are seamlessly integrated into patient care pathways, enhancing overall wellbeing and satisfaction (Hassell et al., 2006). For example, the ophthalmic diagnosis centre will provide one-stop service with mental health service to help track down the mental status of patients, which can be on a weekly basis check-up online or offline as the last part of patient journey.

Private Expertise Sharing Platforms

Developing platforms enable the sharing of expertise and resources among healthcare providers across EU. These platforms can reduce waiting times by facilitating quick consultations and second opinions from specialists, thereby improving the efficiency of care delivery. They can also support the continuous professional development of healthcare providers through knowledge exchange and collaborative learning (Jørgensen et al., 2024).

Besides, promoting the use of expertise sharing platforms can enhance real-time diagnostics and patient management, aligning with VBHC principles. These platforms can integrate AI tools to provide instant diagnostic support, ensuring timely and accurate treatment decisions that improve patient outcomes (Sreelatha & Ramesh, 2016).

Customised Patient Care Models

When it comes to patient care models, leveraging AI to develop personalised care models can significantly enhance the precision and effectiveness of treatments in ophthalmology. Inspired by Apple's approach to personalised technology, these models can use patient data to predict disease progression, customise treatments, and monitor responses. Apple's health initiatives, such as their AI-powered health coaching service and emotion-tracking tools, exemplify how personalised insights can guide health interventions. For instance, under the safe data security, the AI health coach on the Apple Watch provides users with tailored recommendations for improving sleep, diet, and exercise by analysing their health data (Apple, 2023; Mark Gurman, 2023).

Moreover, these personalised care models must be adaptable and responsive to changes in patient conditions and healthcare environments. Incorporating real-time data and feedback mechanisms ensures that healthcare providers can continuously refine treatment plans. This adaptability is akin to Apple's approach with its Health app, which uses real-time data to offer personalised health insights and actionable feedback. By integrating these capabilities, healthcare providers can enhance patient satisfaction and outcomes, aligning with the principles of Value-Based Health Care (Jon Fingas, 2023; K. C. Sabreena Basheer, 2023).

Supportive Policy Development

Engaging with policymakers to develop supportive policies is crucial for addressing issues related to reimbursement, data privacy, and standardisation. Policies should be designed to facilitate the integration of AI and telemedicine into regular practice while ensuring patient data security and ethical use of technology (Fattore & Torbica, 2008).

We also recommend members of the EU advocate for policies that promote equitable access to advanced ophthalmic technologies, ensuring that all patient populations, including underserved communities, benefit from innovations in eye care. Equity-focused policies can help bridge gaps in healthcare access and quality, supporting the overall goals of VBHC (Mazzuca et al., 2022).

Most importantly, performance-based reimbursement models should be implemented to incentivise high-quality care and improve patient outcomes. These models can align financial incentives with patient health outcomes, encouraging healthcare providers to focus on delivering effective and efficient care (Herbst et al., 2018). Thus, we can promote to public sectors for policy making and to private sectors for adaptation of this concept at the same time.

4.4. Conclusion

This report has explored the transformative potential of taking a value-based approach to ophthalmology across different health systems in the European Union. The investigation highlighted how innovative technologies such as artificial intelligence (AI) and telemedicine, along with personalised patient care models and supportive policies, can address pressing challenges in ophthalmic care.

The aging population in Europe and the increasing prevalence of eye diseases among individuals illustrate the need for more efficient and patient-centred care models. The integration of AI has demonstrated significant improvements in diagnostic accuracy and efficiency, enabling proactive management of chronic eye conditions like diabetic retinopathy, age-related macular degeneration (AMD), and glaucoma. In addition, AI's predictive analytics capabilities enhance treatment planning and disease management, contributing to better patient outcomes and aligning with the Value-Based Health Care (VBHC) framework.

Plus, telemedicine has proven crucial, particularly during the COVID-19 pandemic, by ensuring continuous care delivery and reducing healthcare costs. The ability of teleophthalmology to facilitate remote consultations and follow-ups has improved access to specialist care, especially in underserved regions. The synergy between AI diagnostics and telemedicine platforms has further streamlined patient care, enhancing the timeliness and accuracy of diagnoses.

Patient care models that incorporate mental health services have shown to improve overall patient outcomes by addressing the psychological aspects of chronic eye diseases. Comprehensive care that includes mental health support, personalised treatment plans, and effective communication aligns with VBHC principles, emphasising patient-centred care.

On the other hand, educational training for ophthalmology trainees has evolved with the integration of virtual and simulation-based methods. AI and VR technologies have enriched training programs, providing hands-on practice and personalised feedback, ensuring that future healthcare providers are well-equipped to deliver high-quality care.

Supportive healthcare policies and reimbursement strategies are critical for the sustainable integration of these technologies. Policies that promote data privacy, ethical use of AI, and equitable access to advanced ophthalmic care ensure that innovations benefit all patient populations. Performance-based reimbursement models incentivise high-quality care, aligning financial incentives with patient health outcomes.

The analysis within this report illustrates the importance of adopting a value-based approach to ophthalmology, tailored to the diverse health systems across the EU. By focusing on patient outcomes, integrating advanced technologies, and fostering supportive policies, European healthcare systems can overcome the current challenges in ophthalmic care no matter which health system belongs to. This comprehensive strategy promises to enhance the efficiency, accessibility, and quality of eye care, meeting the evolving needs of the population and setting a valued-based benchmark for global healthcare practices.

While this study provides a thorough analysis of the potential for value-based healthcare in ophthalmology, it is not without limitations. The research is primarily based on existing literature and secondary data, which may not fully capture the dynamic and evolving nature of healthcare systems across Europe. Additionally, the integration of AI and telemedicine, while promising, faces challenges related to technological infrastructure, regulatory compliance, and patient acceptance, which were not fully explored in this study. Future research should address these limitations by conducting empirical studies that test the proposed solutions in real-world settings, ensuring their feasibility and effectiveness.

Lastly, future direction should continue to explore the long-term effectiveness of AI and telemedicine in ophthalmology, the sustainability of teleophthalmology post-pandemic, and the validation of new educational tools. Additionally, ongoing policy development should prioritise equity and ethical considerations to support the sustainable integration of advanced technologies. Through continuous innovation, research, and policy support, the vision for a value-based ophthalmic care framework in Europe can become a reality, significantly improving patient outcomes and overall well-being.

ACKNOWLEDGEMENTS

Firstly, I am sincerely grateful to my supervisors, Dr. Jenny Huang, Prof. Julie Davies, and Dr. Preethi John, whose expertise, patience, and encouragement have been a guiding light throughout this journey. Your invaluable advice and feedback have made this project possible. I would also like to thank the faculty members of the MBA Health program in UCL for their insightful suggestions and support. Your guidance has greatly enhanced the quality of my work. A heartfelt appreciation to my classmates and friends, whose camaraderie and constant motivation kept me going during challenging times. I deeply appreciate the love and support of my family, whose mental support and encouragement have been my anchor.

REFERENCES

Apple. (2023). *Apple provides powerful insights into new areas of health*: Apple Media. Available at: https://www.apple.com/uk/newsroom/2023/06/apple-provides-powerful-insights-into-new-areas-of-health/ (Accessed: July 30th 2024).

Augood, C. A., Vingerling, J. R., de Jong, P. T. V. M., Chakravarthy, U., Seland, J., Soubrane, G., Tomazzoli, L., Topouzis, F., Bentham, G., Rahu, M., Vioque, J., Young, I. S., & Fletcher, A. E. (2006). Prevalence of Age-Related Maculopathy in Older Europeans: The European Eye Study (EUREYE), *Archives of ophthalmology (1960), 124*(4), 529-535.

Bakshi, S. K., Lin, S. R., Ting, D. S. W., Chiang, M. F., & Chodosh, J. (2021). The era of artificial intelligence and virtual reality: Transforming surgical education in ophthalmology. *The British Journal of Ophthalmology*, *105*(10), 1325–1328. DOI: 10.1136/bjophthalmol-2020-316845 PMID: 32816750

Barequet, D., Tur-Sinai, A., & Barequet, I. (2019). Health policy regulations pertaining to advanced surgical devices-their socio-economic effects on ophthalmology practice. *Israel Journal of Health Policy Research*, *8*(1), 13–13. DOI: 10.1186/s13584-019-0286-8 PMID: 30654847

Bertakis, K. D., & Azari, R. (2011). Determinants and outcomes of patient-centered care'. *Patient Education and Counseling*, *85*(1), 46–52. DOI: 10.1016/j.pec.2010.08.001 PMID: 20801601

Caffery, L. J., Taylor, M., Gole, G., & Smith, A. C. (2019). Models of care in tele-ophthalmology: A scoping review. *Journal of Telemedicine and Telecare*, *25*(2), 106–122. DOI: 10.1177/1357633X17742182 PMID: 29165005

Chakravarthy, U., Wong, T. Y., Fletcher, A., Piault, E., Evans, C., Zlateva, G., Buggage, R., Pleil, A., & Mitchell, P. (2010). Clinical risk factors for age-related macular degeneration: A systematic review and meta-analysis. *BMC Ophthalmology*, *10*(1), 31–31. DOI: 10.1186/1471-2415-10-31 PMID: 21144031

Chemkomnerd, N., Pannakkong, W., Tanantong, T., Huynh, V. N., & Karnjana, J. (2024). A Simulation-based Multi-Objective Optimization Framework to Enhance Patient Satisfaction: A Case Study of Ophthalmology Department Management. *IEEE Access : Practical Innovations, Open Solutions*, *12*, 1–1. DOI: 10.1109/ACCESS.2024.3423394

Cimarolli, V. R., Casten, R. J., Rovner, B. W., Heyl, V., Sörensen, S., & Horowitz, A. (2016). Anxiety and depression in patients with advanced macular degeneration: Current perspectives. *Clinical Ophthalmology (Auckland, N.Z.)*, *10*(1), 55–63. PMID: 26766899

Dean, S., Mathers, J. M., Calvert, M., Kyte, D. G., Conroy, D., Folkard, A., Southworth, S., Murray, P. I., & Denniston, A. K. (2017). "The patient is speaking": Discovering the patient voice in ophthalmology. *The British Journal of Ophthalmology*, *101*(6), 700–708. DOI: 10.1136/bjophthalmol-2016-309955 PMID: 28455280

Fattore, G., & Torbica, A. (2008). Cost and reimbursement of cataract surgery in Europe: A cross-country comparison. *Health Economics*, *17*(S1), S71–S82. DOI: 10.1002/hec.1324 PMID: 18186033

Ferrara, M., Romano, V., Steel, D. H., Gupta, R., Iovino, C., van Dijk, E. H. C., Steel, D. H., Rocha-de-Lossada, C., Bali, E., Valldeperas, X., Romano, D., Gadhvi, K. A., Matarazzo, F., Tzamalis, A., Grassi, P., Rachwani, R., Coco, G., Reyes-Delfino, C. D., Amoroso, F., & Romano, M. R. (2020). Reshaping ophthalmology training after COVID-19 pandemic. *Eye (London, England)*, *34*(11), 2089–2097. DOI: 10.1038/s41433-020-1061-3 PMID: 32612174

French National Authority for Health. (2021). Telemedicine in France during. *COVID*, *19*, •••. Retrieved July 28th, 2024, from https://www.has-sante.fr/jcms/p_3282983/fr/telemedicine-in-france-during-covid-19

Garrison, L. P.Jr, Neumann, P. J., Willke, R. J., Basu, A., Danzon, P. M., Doshi, J. A., Drummond, M. F., Lakdawalla, D. N., Pauly, M. V., Phelps, C. E., Ramsey, S. D., Towse, A., & Weinstein, M. C. (2018). A Health Economics Approach to US Value Assessment Frameworks—Summary and Recommendations of the ISPOR Special Task Force Report [7]. *Value in Health : The Journal of the International Society for Pharmacoeconomics and Outcomes Research*, *21*(2), 161–165. DOI: 10.1016/j.jval.2017.12.009 PMID: 29477394

German Federal Statistical Office. (2019). *Health statistics* 27th. Available at: https://www.destatis.de/DE/Home/_inhalt.html (Accessed: July 2024).

González-Gonzalo, C., Thee, E. F., Klaver, C. C. W., Lee, A. Y., Schlingemann, R. O., Tufail, A., Verbraak, F., & Sánchez, C. I. (2022). Trustworthy AI: Closing the gap between development and integration of AI systems in ophthalmic practice. *Progress in Retinal and Eye Research*, *90*, 101034–101034. DOI: 10.1016/j.preteyeres.2021.101034 PMID: 34902546

Gunasekeran, D. V., & Wong, T. Y. (2020). Artificial intelligence in ophthalmology in 2020: A technology on the cusp for translation and implementation. *Asia-Pacific Journal of Ophthalmology (Philadelphia, Pa.)*, *9*(2), 61–66. DOI: 10.1097/01.APO.0000656984.56467.2c PMID: 32349112

Hassell, J. B., Lamoureux, E. L., & Keeffe, J. E. (2006). Impact of age related macular degeneration on quality of life. *The British Journal of Ophthalmology*, *90*(5), 593–596. DOI: 10.1136/bjo.2005.086595 PMID: 16622089

Herbst, T., Foerster, J., & Emmert, M. (2018). The impact of pay-for-performance on the quality of care in ophthalmology: Empirical evidence from Germany. *Health Policy (Amsterdam)*, *122*(6), 667–673. DOI: 10.1016/j.healthpol.2018.03.013 PMID: 29606288

Hunter, D. J., & Bengoa, R. (2023). Meeting the challenge of health system transformation in European countries. *Policy and Society*, *42*(1), 14–27. DOI: 10.1093/polsoc/puac022

Italian Ministry of Health. (2020). *Regional health disparities report*. Available at: https://www.salute.gov.it/portale/home.html (Accessed: July 25th 2024).

Jon Fingas. (2023). *Apple is reportedly developing an AI health coach for Apple Watch*: Engadget. Available at: https://www.engadget.com/apple-is-reportedly-developing-an-ai-health-coach-for-apple-watch-212515646.html (Accessed: July 28th 2024).

Jørgensen, E. P., Muttuvelu, D. V., Peto, T., Natarajan, S., Davies, J., Keane, P. A., & Ehlers, L. H. (2024). Implementing teleophthalmology services to improve cost-effectiveness of the national eye care system, *Eye (London)*.

Kern, C., Fu, D. J., Kortuem, K., Huemer, J., Barker, D., Davis, A., Balaskas, K., Keane, P. A., McKinnon, T., & Sim, D. A. (2020). Implementation of a cloud-based referral platform in ophthalmology: Making telemedicine services a reality in eye care. *The British Journal of Ophthalmology*, *104*(3), 312–317. DOI: 10.1136/bjophthalmol-2019-314161 PMID: 31320383

Krüger, L. J., Evers, S. M. A. A., Hiligsmann, M., & Wild, C. (2014). Divergent evidence requirements for authorization and reimbursement of high-risk medical devices – The European situation. *Health Policy and Technology*, *3*(4), 253–263. DOI: 10.1016/j.hlpt.2014.08.005

Lakhani, B. K., Attzs, M. S., Stead, R., & Tambe, K. (2021). The impact of the COVID-19 pandemic on ophthalmology services across the United Kingdom: A brief report on a cross-sectional survey of clinical leads. *Therapeutic Advances in Ophthalmology*, *13*, 25158414211010549–25158414211010549. DOI: 10.1177/25158414211010549 PMID: 34027305

Li, J. P. O., Liu, H., Ting, D. S. J., Jeon, S., Chan, R. V. P., Kim, J. E., Sim, D. A., Thomas, P. B. M., Lin, H., Chen, Y., Sakomoto, T., Loewenstein, A., Lam, D. S. C., Pasquale, L. R., Wong, T. Y., Lam, L. A., & Ting, D. S. W. (2021). Digital technology, tele-medicine and artificial intelligence in ophthalmology: A global perspective. *Progress in Retinal and Eye Research*, *82*, 100900–100900. DOI: 10.1016/j.preteyeres.2020.100900 PMID: 32898686

Li, Z., Wang, L., Wu, X., Jiang, J., Qiang, W., Xie, H., Zhou, H., Wu, S., Shao, Y., & Chen, W. (2023). Artificial intelligence in ophthalmology: The path to the real-world clinic. *Cell Reports Medicine*, *4*(7), 101095–101095. DOI: 10.1016/j.xcrm.2023.101095 PMID: 37385253

Mark Gurman. (2023). *Apple plans AI-powered health coaching service, mood tracker, and iPad health app*. Available at: https://techxplore.com/news/2023-04-apple-ai-powered-health-mood-tracker.html (Accessed: July 30th 2024).

Mazzuca, D., Borselli, M., Gratteri, S., Zampogna, G., Feola, A., Della Corte, M., Guarna, F., Scorcia, V., & Giannaccare, G. (2022). Applications and Current Medico-Legal Challenges of Telemedicine in Ophthalmology. *International Journal of Environmental Research and Public Health*, *19*(9), 5614. DOI: 10.3390/ijerph19095614 PMID: 35565003

NHS Digital. (2021). *NHS statistics*. Available at: https://digital.nhs.uk/ (Accessed: July 29th 2024).

Nordic Council of Ministers. (2021). *Healthcare innovation in Northern Europe*. Available at: https://www.norden.org/en (Accessed: July 30th 2024).

OECD. (2021). *Health at a Glance: Europe 2021*: Organisation for Economic Co-operation and Development Available at: https://www.oecd.org/en/topics/health.html (Accessed: July 30th 2024).

Porter, M. E. (2010). What Is Value in Health Care? *The New England Journal of Medicine*, *363*(26), 2477–2481. DOI: 10.1056/NEJMp1011024 PMID: 21142528

Porter, M. E., & Kaplan, R. S. (2016). How to Pay for Health Care. *Harvard Business Review*, *94*(7-8), 88–134. PMID: 27526565

Porter, M. E., & Lee, T. H. (2013). The strategy that will fix health care. *Harvard Business Review*, *91*(10), 50.

Sabreena Basheer, K. C. (2023). *Apple to launch AI-powered health app with emotion tracking*: Analytics Vidhya. Available at: https://www.analyticsvidhya.com/blog/2023/05/apple-to-launch-ai-powered-health-app-with-emotion-tracking-and-more/ (Accessed: July 29th 2024).

Saleem, S. M., Pasquale, L. R., Sidoti, P. A., & Tsai, J. C. (2020). Virtual Ophthalmology: Telemedicine in a COVID-19 Era. *American Journal of Ophthalmology*, *216*, 237–242. DOI: 10.1016/j.ajo.2020.04.029 PMID: 32360862

Sreelatha, O. K., & Ramesh, S. V. S. (2016). Teleophthalmology: Improving patient outcomes? *Clinical Ophthalmology (Auckland, N.Z.)*, *10*(1), 285–295. DOI: 10.2147/OPTH.S80487 PMID: 26929592

Stein, J. D., Brown, M. M., Brown, G. C., Hollands, H., & Sharma, S. (2003). Quality of life with macular degeneration: Perceptions of patients, clinicians, and community members. *The British Journal of Ophthalmology*, *87*(1), 8–12. DOI: 10.1136/bjo.87.1.8 PMID: 12488253

Succar, T. M. P., Grigg, J. M. M. D. F., Beaver, H. A. M. D., & Lee, A. G. M. D. (2016). A systematic review of best practices in teaching ophthalmology to medical students. *Survey of Ophthalmology*, *61*(1), 83–94. DOI: 10.1016/j.survophthal.2015.09.001 PMID: 26363187

Tan, J. C. K., Ferdi, A. C., Gillies, M. C., & Watson, S. L. (2019). Clinical Registries in Ophthalmology. *Ophthalmology*, *126*(5), 655–662. DOI: 10.1016/j.ophtha.2018.12.030 PMID: 30572076

Ting, D. S. W., Pasquale, L. R., Peng, L., Campbell, J. P., Lee, A. Y., Raman, R., Tan, G. S. W., Schmetterer, L., Keane, P. A., & Wong, T. Y. (2019). Artificial intelligence and deep learning in ophthalmology. *The British Journal of Ophthalmology*, *103*(2), 167–175. DOI: 10.1136/bjophthalmol-2018-313173 PMID: 30361278

Tricco, A. C., Lillie, E., Zarin, W., O'Brien, K. K., Colquhoun, H., Levac, D., Moher, D., Peters, M. D. J., Horsley, T., Weeks, L., Hempel, S., Akl, E. A., Chang, C., McGowan, J., Stewart, L., Hartling, L., Aldcroft, A., Wilson, M. G., Garritty, C., & Straus, S. E. (2018). PRISMA extension for scoping reviews (PRISMA-ScR): Checklist and explanation. *Annals of Internal Medicine*, *169*(7), 467–473. DOI: 10.7326/M18-0850 PMID: 30178033

WHO. (2020). *World Health Statistics*: World Health Organization. Available at: https://www.who.int/data/gho/publications/world-health-statistics (Accessed: July 30th 2024).

Chapter 8

mHealth Applications for Maternal and Child Health in Developing Countries

Peter V. Muttungal
http://orcid.org/0000-0002-1953-3830
Christ University, India

Jossy P. George
http://orcid.org/0000-0003-3285-5081
Christ University

Benny Godwin J. Davidson
http://orcid.org/0000-0001-5755-2920
University of the Fraser Valley, Canada

Nishi Priya
http://orcid.org/0009-0009-2727-5497
Christ University, India

ABSTRACT

Mobile applications (mHealth) have been key technologies to enhance maternal and child well-being in the developing world, where access to health care is still low. This chapter examines the various functions of mHealth applications vending from behavior change and health education to remote diagnosis and emergency transfer. Based on theoretical models such as the Health Belief Model and Social Cognitive Theory, it examines how these technologies induce user uptake and improved outcomes. Although mHealth interventions promise significant effects

DOI: 10.4018/979-8-3373-3341-0.ch008

on antenatal care, postnatal support, and child development, issues like digital inequality, ethical issues, and infrastructure shortcomings still exist. The chapter emphasizes the need for culturally appropriate design, community health worker integration, and sustainable policy approaches to ensure the highest effectiveness and equity of these digital interventions.

INTRODUCTION

In recent years, the focus on maternal in developing countries has increased particularly in the context of developing countries as seen in the fifth Millennium Development Goal which aims to reduce the maternal mortality ratio by 75% (Prata et al., 2010). The developing countries face serious concerns in the domain of maternal mental health as roughly 15.6% of women experience mental health issues during pregnancy, and this rises to 19.8% in the postpartum period. Research also shows that maternal depression alone impacts between 15% and 57% of mothers in these regions (World Health Organization, 2023). Access to well-being stands as an essential human right. However, a stark inequality becomes evident when examining the lifetime risk of maternal death. This risk stands at 1 in 5,400 for women in high-income countries. In contrast, it is a shocking 1 in 45 for women in low-income countries. This signifies a mortality risk from childbirth complications that is over one hundred times greater. While seemingly distinct, the disparity in political rights may contribute significantly to the ongoing inequality in women's human and reproductive health rights (Kurjak et al., 2022).

Countries with emerging economies bear almost the entire burden (99%) of maternal deaths, recording 240 such fatalities per 100,000 live births. In contrast, developed countries report a much lower rate of 16 per 100,000. Most of these fatalities are concentrated in Sub-Saharan Africa and South Asia (World Health Organization, 2025). Children in the developing countries face an immense and often preventable burden of mortality and malnutrition. The main concerns are Under-five mortality, stunted and wasting malnutrition and infectious diseases like acute respiratory issues along with birth trauma and pre-term birth asphyxia (WHO, 2022).

Keeping tabs on advancements in maternal, newborn, and child health is incredibly challenging, yet it's more vital than ever. The Sustainable Development Goals lay out ambitious targets for 2030, calling for drastic cuts in maternal, neonatal, and child deaths. They also push for widespread availability of sexual and reproductive health services. Reaching these objectives demands a major boost in the accessibility, effectiveness, and precise evaluation of successful health programs (Grove et al., 2015).

Global efforts to curb maternal and child deaths have been massive. This push began in the 1990s with the Millennium Development Goals (MDG). The world witnessed record declines in mortality rates. Despite increased data collection efforts sparked by the MDGs, most countries still lack timely information on how many women, adolescents, children, and newborns are actually receiving the essential interventions they need (Yaya & Ghose, 2019).

According to Peters et al. (2008) developing countries face the following challenges in terms of meeting the healthcare standards.

1. Locational Convenience: This refers to the physical proximity of a service to its patrons, gauged by the extent of travel or time taken to arrive.
2. Service Provision: This means having the appropriate variety of care readily available to individuals who need it, considering aspects like convenient operational schedules, minimal delay periods.
3. Fiscal Openness: This pertains to the correlation between the price of offerings and the client's preparedness and means to compensate it
4. Cultural Resonance: This describes how effectively healthcare professionals adjust to and honour the social and traditional norms.

There has been new innovation in the field of maternal health care like conditional cash transfers and technological innovations like use of mobile clinics which has prompted way for utilising Mobile based or M-based applications for promoting child and maternal wellbeing.

In today's world, everybody has access to some sort of smart devices or smartphones changing how we exchange information. Smartphones provides effortless screen interaction, superior computational strength from their central processing units, enhanced memory capacity, and swifter digital transmission capabilities through service networks. These advantages make smartphones highly regarded as potential healthcare implements (Liu & Wang, 2021).

The World Health Organization (WHO) characterizes mobile health (mHealth) as healthcare and public well-being activities facilitated by portable electronic gadgets. These include cell phones, remote patient observation tools, personal digital assistants, and other cordless technologies. mHealth is considered a vital public health tool for efficient healthcare, especially when face-to-face care isn't feasible (Ameyaw et al., 2024). The recent COVID19 pandemic and sociopolitical tensions further increased the dependency on the technological devices.

Mhealth applications can be divided into government funded and private enterprise- based application. These applications can be classified into applications who provide psychoeducational support or assistance like health reminders, check-ups, availability for free vaccinations.

Evaluations of these mobile health solutions show encouraging outcomes regarding patient's health outcomes. They also provide valuable information on pregnancy management and risk identification, contribute to increased satisfaction among women receiving care, and offer financial advantages (Haddad et al., 2019). Mobile health (mHealth) has demonstrably benefited pregnant women and new mothers. It's enhanced their ability to self-manage their health, made pregnancy widely accepted and strengthened their social support networks. Research also indicates mHealth positively influences the psychosocial development of expectant mothers (Sakamoto et al., 2022).

For childcare, many similar maternal health apps were utilised who provided both pregnancy and services with childcare including assistance with vaccinations, psychoeducation on lactation-based practices and even monitoring child with obesity (Tate et al., 2013; Zhang et al., 2018). In areas with low network connectivity, many applications use the feature of SMS based reminders after conducting the initial diagnosis, action planning and reflection (Thobias & Kiwanuka, 2018).

1. THE ENDURING MATERNAL AND CHILD HEALTH CRISIS IN DEVELOPING NATIONS

Women's health is intrinsically linked to their diverse and demanding life roles. As caregivers, professionals, partners, and family members, women carry significant responsibilities for their own well-being and that of their families (Tulchinsky et al., 2023). This includes managing aspects like nutrition, hygiene, education, exercise, safety, fertility, and care for both children and elders. The continuous evolution of women's societal roles often introduces additional health challenges and heightened risks.

Maternal and Child Health encompasses the well-being and healthcare outcomes of mothers and children. These outcomes are influenced by various policies. As highlighted in the NATO model within the provided text, these instruments include those related to treasure, organization, authority-treasure, and treasure-organization (Barnish et al., 2023).

Challenges in Maternal and child related healthcare can be further classified into Structural challenges, health system challenges, socio- cultural challenges and individual level-health challenges.

A study conducted by Wigley et al. (2020) in the sub-Saharan region found an average of two hospitals are available for every 500,000 people. Around 93% of pregnancies occur within a two-hour travel time of the nearest hospital. In developing countries like India, a significant 88 percent of childbirths take place in rural areas with lack of proper infrastructure. In remote areas due to financial constraints and inadequate infrastructure access to the maternal and child healthcare becomes challenging. For children lack of access to proper nutrients and food safety possess a serious threat towards their physical development for developing countries like Nepal. This has turned into a global crisis where food safety is causing 600 million cases of foodborne illnesses and 420,000 deaths every year (Deepak Subedi et al., 2024).

As discussed earlier, the healthcare system faces series of challenges due to shortage of skilled health workers, weak referral systems, insufficient funding, poor emergency services and lack of data and monitoring. Obtaining the necessary hardware like computers or advanced mobile devices for health information systems (HIS) is hindered due to high costs. There is also a high risk of fragmentation between those who have technologies compared to those who don't leading to information divide (Luna et al., 2014). There is a need for important healthcare facilities as traditional designs often increase stress, depression, and anxiety in patients and staff due to issues like noise, privacy loss, and lack of control. These designs also increase vulnerability to health risks, including allergies and hospital-acquired infections (Alabi et al., 2025).

Antenatal care or ANC is key to preventing illnesses in pregnant women and promoting the well-being of their babies. Insufficient or delayed care increases the likelihood of poor outcomes and limits access to skilled birth attendants. The WHO advocates for a minimum of eight quality ANC contacts for uncomplicated pregnancies, with the first visit ideally occurring before 12 weeks of gestation. Alarmingly, the proportion of women in this region attending four or more antenatal visits actually decreased from 50% in 1990 to 46% in 2010 (Lund et al., 2014).

Factors in developing countries like Low Female Literacy & Education, gender norms, Traditional Beliefs, early marriages and adolescent pregnancy, lack of female representation while advocating their rights and social stigma lead to social cultural challenges. There are cultural differences in how women perceive their pregnancies in different developing countries. Some countries like Kenya focus on ethnicity, Nigeria focuses on influence of religion, whilst countries like Tanzania, Ghana, and Zambia indicate negative influence of education level and her satisfaction with maternal care (Srivastava et al., 2015). In South east Asian countries like India and Pakistan, influence of caste-based discrimination further led to poorer maternal health outcomes (Mumtaz et al., 2014).

Addiction towards substance abuse, genetic predisposition, child under nutrition, low immunisation rates can further be considered as the challenges for maternal and childcare at individual level.

2. THEORETICAL UNDERPINNINGS: WHY MHEALTH WORKS FOR MATERNAL AND CHILD HEALTH

Behavior change theory refers to a collection of psychological frameworks and models that attempt to explain why human behaviors change, how they change, and what factors influence this process. These theories provide a systematic way to understand and predict behavior and promote healthier habits, environmental sustainability, or other desired actions. Behavior change techniques (BCTs) are crucial for the efficacy of health interventions. These discernible and repeatable elements offer a shared structure for strategic planning and execution. Studies suggest that incorporating BCTs considerably boosts an intervention's success. Many popular mobile health applications incorporate behavior change strategies, including customized experiences, the ability to track and reflect on goals (from overall aspirations to daily targets), adapting content for wider user segments, self-tracking of objectives, and highlighting the relationships between various health habits. Other commonly identified BCTs present in mHealth app content are feedback on performance, providing instruction, and specific goal setting. These techniques offer a standardized language for characterizing and understanding the mechanisms by which health interventions aim to foster behavioral change (Biviji et al., 2020).

The Health Belief Model HBM offers a practical and widely adopted framework for assessing individual health behaviors. This model is frequently used to understand the various factors that influence a person's health-related actions and attitudes. It's particularly useful for its ability to pinpoint six key elements that typically shape health behaviors. perceived benefit what good will come from the action, perceived barrier what difficulties might arise, self-efficacy one's belief in their ability to succeed, cue to action triggers that prompt behavior, perceived susceptibility how likely one feels to experience a health issue, and perceived severity how serious one believes the consequences of that issue would be. A study conducted by Nkwo et al. (2021) explored factors influencing maternal healthcare behaviors in African communities to inform the design of culturally sensitive maternal wellbeing apps. The study found that perceived benefits like monitoring fetal development, ensuring maternal and infant health, and early issue detection, particularly the reduction of maternal and infant mortality, positively influence behavior. Conversely, perceived threats, such as constant health crises during pregnancy, health problems in newborns, and increased childbirth-related deaths, also play a role. Perceived barriers significantly hinder positive behaviors, including inaccessible health facilities, long waiting times, negative perceptions of C-sections, ignorance of health consequences, poverty, low tech skills, and unsupportive cultural practices.

Albert Bandura's Social Cognitive Theory (SCT) posits that individuals acquire knowledge in social settings through observation, direct experience, and interactions. A core concept within SCT is reciprocal determinism, which highlights the interplay between personal attributes (such as thoughts) and environmental factors. Ariyani et al. (2022) conducted a study to assess the impact of an application-based antenatal care program, structured around the SCT model. Their research aimed to improve healthy pregnancy lifestyle practices (HPLP II), adherence to iron tablet consumption, and preparedness for delivery and potential complications. The findings revealed a significant increase in HPLP II scores within the intervention group, demonstrating its effectiveness compared to the control group.

According to Quintana and McWhirter (2017) The Transtheoretical Model offers a framework for understanding how individuals change their behavior, emphasizing that this is a process than a single event. While these stages are often the focus of discussions about TTM, the model also incorporates three other vital constructs: Processes of Change (the strategies individuals employ to facilitate change, like seeking new information or social support), Decisional Balance (weighing the pros and cons of changing), and Self-Efficacy (one's confidence in their ability to successfully adopt and maintain the new healthy behavior).

A 2023 study by Gebremariam et al. found that an mHealth intervention, built upon the Theory of Planned Behavior (TPB) and aimed at both parents, substantially raised the chances of exclusive breastfeeding at the three-month mark. This suggests that affordable, SMS-based breastfeeding assistance could be seamlessly incorporated into standard antenatal and postnatal care provided by midwives.

3. CATEGORIZING MHEALTH INTERVENTIONS FOR MCH: A FUNCTIONAL ANALYSIS

mHealth apps have the potential to revolutionize healthcare by improving how care is delivered and ultimately leading to better patient outcomes. They enable remote patient monitoring, which helps manage risk factors, boosts treatment compliance, allows for early detection of complications, and can prevent avoidable hospitalizations. Beyond clinical improvements, mHealth also significantly empowers consumers by allowing patients to actively participate in and self-manage their health conditions. However, much of this evidence comes from low-to-moderate quality studies, highlighting the urgent need for higher-quality research (Colaci et al., 2017).

Category 1: Health Education and Information Dissemination Platforms

An application named MatHealth App, created by Felox Holl, delivers multimedia videos and audio files to rural women, including those with limited or no formal education. The app aims to provide crucial maternal and child health information, send reminders for antenatal care appointments, and offer a remote connection to an obstetrician for any questions. An initial qualitative assessment indicates that the app effectively provides information that is tailored, easy to understand, and memorable. Furthermore, it appears to enhance communication with healthcare providers and bolster social support from spouses.

These applications are focused on culturally appropriate and timely delivery app using the modalities like simple text message, multimedia content and chatbots. These information dissemination-based m-apps can be useful in psychoeducating the mothers about Importance of antenatal care, nutrition during pregnancy and lactation, benefits of skilled birth attendance, newborn care practices.

Another flagship initative called Momconnect by the South African government provides vaccination coverage and provide psychological support for maternal mental health. This helps in overcoming literacy barrier through the video format and help the mothers make informed decisions.

Category 2: Appointment Reminders and Adherence Support Systems

An application-based program was launched in Thailand under the mother and Childcare Module by the Government (Kaewkungwal et al., 2010). This application automatically generates and sends reminders to mothers, notifying them of their and their child's upcoming Antenatal Care and Expanded Programme on Immunization visit due dates. This led to significant positive impact on healthcare, particularly in maternal and child health. Their use has demonstrably increased the likelihood of patients attending their appointments on time and has also reduced the administrative burden on healthcare staff

Applications falling under the category can improve attendance and promote the adherence to medical treatment and advice. Modalities including automated SMS/ voice call reminders for ANC visits, postnatal care, check-ups, infant immunization schedules, well-child visits, Reminders for medication adherence can greatly benefit the mothers.

Category 3: Remote Monitoring and Data Collection/Reporting Tools

According to Prinja et al. (2016), a mobile health (mHealth) application was developed and deployed with community health workers in rural India. The purpose was to improve their counseling abilities, with the ultimate goal of boosting the demand for and use of crucial maternal, neonatal, and child health services. This initiative aligns with India's primary health program, the National Health Mission, which has enlisted more than 850,000 Accredited Social Health Activists (ASHAs).. Their main role is to act as social agents, driving demand for healthcare services. They visit rural parts of India, collect and monitor data which is further useful in implementing policies and evaluating their effectiveness.

Similarly in Nepal, another developing country has deployed community health workers (CWHS) who collect essential vital events data like deliveries, vaccinations etc concurrently with providing routine healthcare in resource-limited environments (Choudhury et al., 2022).

These categories of M-based applications can improve data accuracy and reduce the reliance on paper. It is also useful in epileptological surveillance and inventory management.

Category 4: Diagnostic Support and Decision-Making Aids for Health Workers

Ghana, a sub-Saharan African nation, continues to report unacceptably high rates of maternal and neonatal deaths. An application was developed called mHealth clinical decision-making support system to ensure healthcare workers always had access to clinical decision support. This design was a direct response to suggestions from frontline health workers. The modalities of these applications can incorporate clinical algorithms, digital drug, treatments protocols, reference materials access and basic tele-consultation options (Amoakoh et al., 2019).

These applications can signifincatly improve care and increase confidence of all the frontline workers. It can also assist in reducing misdiagnosing and provide more scope for the workers to access supervision.

Category 5: Referral and Emergency Response Coordination Systems

Many expectant mothers residing in Uganda's urban informal settlements give birth at government healthcare facilities. Unfortunately, these centers often lack the vital equipment for urgent delivery and infant medical attention. when complications arise, these individuals are transferred to more advanced medical sites and bear the responsibility for securing and funding their transportation. To address this, the Kampala Slum Maternal Newborn (MaNe) project created and tested an emergency call and ambulance dispatch center, along with a mobile application for requesting, deploying, and tracking ambulances (Ononge et al., 2023).

These applications can include modalities like identifying high risk pregnancy, severe child illness needing immediate attention, secure communication platforms between CHWs, primary health centres, and referral hospitals.

Category 6: Behavior Change Communication and Social Support Platforms

Behavior change communication (BCC) is now a core element of many maternal, neonatal, and child health (MNCH) interventions. A 2019 study by Mildon and Sellen highlighted the expanding evidence base for the effectiveness of mobile phone-based BCC delivery. Another study conducted in Southern Brazil, assessed the feasibility and acceptability of an 8-week WhatsApp-based maternal support group (Trude et al., 2021). Facilitators provided daily insights and weekly exercises to caregivers of young children within an ongoing birth study. These interventions aimed to enhance their child's nourishment, rest patterns, attentive upbringing, and the mother's emotional wellness. These outcomes were self-reported and assessed before and after the intervention. It was proven to be a very effective strategy for MNCH.

Other studies have also indicated that mobile health application may enhance perceived social support and maternal self-efficacy, while also reducing postpartum depressive symptoms (Liu et al., 2022). M-based applications can increase social network and adherence to health via positive reinforcement and collective learning.

4. THE EFFECTIVENESS OF MHEALTH ON MCH OUTCOMES

4.1 Impact on Maternal Health Outcomes

A systematic literature review conducted by Feroz et al. (2017) discovered that in developing countries like East Asia and Sub- Saharan Africa, M based applications benefited women with antenatal assistance and is considered crucial for identifying women at high risk and deteriorating pregnancy outcomes. It has shown to prevent women from fatal issues including post-partum haemorrhage and depression. Another systematic literature review by Kante and Mats Målqvist (2025) focused on multiple research papers using experimental, quasi and mixed method studies to determine the effectives of M-based applications on the antenatal outcomes. The review concluded that quasi experimental studies display positive results influencing attendance and the knowledge of MH.

4.2 Postnatal care and support

A study conducted by Sardi et al. (2020) found that M- based applications positively contribute to postnatal care by providing extensive informative content. Certain applications, such as WebMD Baby and Post pregnancy recovery, prove advantageous for gaining insights into the indicators, manifestations, and treatments for postpartum depression and related worries. Significantly, the Moment Health application provides a validated screening function for postnatal depression. This functionality, by integrating a review of indicators with monitoring shifts in mood, is poised to accelerate mental recovery

Mbuthia et al. (2019) found that mobile phone messaging was most important mHealth communication method. It impacted mothers' readiness, capabilities, and challenges concerning postnatal care utilization. There was a positive shift in beliefs regarding postnatal care routines. Improved perceived norms involved greater acceptance of facility-based deliveries followed by immediate postpartum support. There was a tendency to seek advice and professional guidance for infant care and increased involvement from male partners.

4.3 Impact on Child Health Outcomes

A study revealed that parents of children under five generally embraced mobile health interventions, leading to improved parenting knowledge and confidence in promoting their child's health (DeWitt et al., 2022). Similarly, M-based applications are widely used for managing gestational hypertension and successful breastfeeding practises. One such application called LactApp which is helpful for women to make well-informed decisions for postnatal care (Acar & Nevin Şahin, 2024).

In developing countries, malnutrition is a critical factor in child deaths, especially among children in their first five years of life. M-based applications is an economical method for encouraging behavioral change (Seyyedi et al., 2019).

According to Mahmood et al. (2020) M based applications can standardize treatment and provide timely referrals. For example, an electronic tool significantly increased danger sign checks in children and reduced unnecessary antibiotic prescriptions compared to paper-based methods in Tanzania. It can also improve the quality of care delivered by CHWs and improve adverse event reporting

A systemic review conducted by revealed that certain mHealth interventions in this significantly reduced chronic disease-related health outcomes (Karataş et al., 2021). Similarly, an Android tablet-based application, mPneumonia, was co-developed by PATH and the University of Washington. This tool integrates a digital version of the IMCI algorithm with a breath counter and pulse oximeter. Its usability was tested in

Ghana to improve pediatric illness diagnostics and healthcare provider adherence to guidelines in low-resource settings (Ginsburg et al., 2015)

A 2019 study by Kruse et al. revealed that infectious diseases impose a significant burden on developing nations. This challenge is worsened by issues such as poverty, inadequate nutrition, indoor air pollution, and restricted access to sanitation and health education. The WHO estimates that diseases are responsible for forty-five percent of the health burden in these countries, with HIV, tuberculosis, and malaria alone contributing to eighteen percent.

The study also highlighted maternal health as the second most common outcome positively influenced by mHealth interventions. Developing countries face 99% of global maternal deaths, representing the world's largest health disparity. Poor women in remote regions often receive inadequate care due to a scarcity of skilled healthcare workers.

Most studies reviewed by Kruse et al. used SMS as an mHealth intervention to improve infectious disease outcomes and patient adherence to treatment. These interventions effectively enhanced antenatal care, vaccination rates, and preventive treatments for both chronic and infectious diseases in developing countries. SMS also proved beneficial for maternal health, prenatal care, infant care, HIV/AIDS prevention, treatment adherence, and chronic disease management. Furthermore, SMS directly increased disease awareness through health tips and reminders, fostering health knowledge, promoting self-responsibility, and providing emotional support to patients.

4.4 System-Level and Indirect Benefits of mHealth

Countries like Bangladesh, Rwanda, and Uganda are implementing new strategies to standardize public health data collection, ensuring seamless information exchange between government bodies and NGOs. These countries are achieving this through utilising M based applications and by keeping CWH's worker in the loop. The data collected from these applications is immensely benefiting for tracking and evaluating the effectiveness. Sharda et al. (2024) indicate that India's The Pregnancy, Child Tracking and Health Services Management System documents all public healthcare institution deliveries statewide.

4.5 Various prominent M based applications in the developing countries

Classifying countries as developing requires criteria like Gross National Income (GNI) per capita, Human Development Index (HDI), and economic vulnerability.

Based on the various areas, we identify few prominent m-based applications for maternal and child wellbeing based as indicated in the Table 1

Table 1. indicates the list of prominent M-based applications

Name of the Country	Application	Limitations of the application
Afghanistan	Afghanistan's MOPH launched Salamat, the nation's first mobile maternal health application. It aims to significantly improve maternal health outcomes for women across Afghanistan. The healthcare professionals securely log in, easily creating and updating comprehensive patient profiles. Profiles log personal information, patient evaluations, and all antenatal care details. Labor, postnatal care, and final diagnoses are also meticulously recorded within. This process streamlines efficient tracking and management of critical maternal health data.	Internet dependency and lack of healthcare workers for training.
India	India now offers the **Safe Delivery App** to skilled birth attendants nationally. This aims to make childbirth safer for women throughout the country(Tarun Singh Sodha et al., 2022). The App empowers healthcare workers, providing evidence-based, up-to-date clinical guidelines. They access this crucial information directly via their mobile phones or tablets. The App includes 13 modules focusing on essential interventions. These cover women and newborns around birth (BEmONC) and preventative procedures. Its 'MyLearning' platform gamifies learning, motivating users through challenges and progress.	Lack of maintenance and updates in the applications.
Nigeria	Many pregnant women in the Middle East and North Africa (MENA) often avoid reaching out to healthcare providers after hours because of cultural and social norms. To address this, Mamahood application was launched to provide 24/7 on-demand live chat for mothers (Sorina Mihaila, 2023). Across Africa, mobile technology significantly reduces maternal mortality. Nigeria's Abiye Safe Motherhood gives pregnant women phones for labor transport. In Cameroon, Gifted Mom sends free SMS reminders for appointments. South Africa's Mom Connect informs women and tracks expectant mothers. Ethiopia's Safe Delivery App empowers healthcare professionals for better care. Zero Mothers Die equips mothers with phones for education and emergency access. These initiatives empower mothers and providers, improving care access (James, 2025).	Digital divides leads to lack of accessibility for the mobile applications

continued on following page

Table 1. Continued

Name of the Country	Application	Limitations of the application
Thailand	The KhunLook app, released in 2015, is a Thai mobile application designed to help parents monitor and assess their child's health. It complements Thailand's standard Maternal and Child Health Handbook (MCHH), a widely used but often unread physical record for child health supervision. Developed by an interdisciplinary team including medical and dental specialists, software engineers, healthcare providers, and families,	Lack of psycho-social awareness and support for the maternal wellbeing
Latin and Caribbean	BabyCenter provides a wealth of information on pregnancy, baby care, parenting advice, and community forums, making it a go-to resource for many new and expectant parents across the region. Their content is often available in Spanish and Portuguese, catering to the dominant languages.	Lack of technical support and culturally sensitive information
Colombia	Mamás del Río, a Colombian platform, powerfully helps vulnerable mothers. It connects pregnant women and new mothers to vital healthcare services. This community-focused model significantly impacts local health challenges..	Lack of digital trust causes less usage of the application.

5. NAVIGATING IMPLEMENTATION LANDSCAPES: CHALLENGES AND BARRIERS TO MHEALTH SCALING

Studies from low- and middle-income countries have technical limitations hindering mHealth. These challenges include poor network coverage, weak signal strength, limited mobile phone access, and specific technical hurdles like delayed database updates (Chen et al., 2018; Seyyedi et al., 2019).

5.1. Technological and Infrastructure Deficits

According to Kusyanti et al. (2022) M based applications have major challenges like geographic location. It is difficult to access to technologies due to lack of network and connecting in developing countries like North-eastern terrains of India thus limiting access to healthcare. Also, low education and lack of digital literacy can impact the use of these applications. Lack of support from the local government like corruption in distribution of SMS vouchers for the application can make it difficult for women. Botswana, a sub-Saharan African nation, has experimented with mobile health solutions. These systems however aren't compatible with existing electronic record databases (Ndlovu et al., 2021). Lack of streamlining the data collected from m-based applications beats its entire purpose. Studies have shown the positive effect of technical support and assistance for the smooth operations of these applications (Jeon & Park, 2015). The technical support also includes educating the women on how to operate the applications along with the workers on smooth assistance of the same. In developing countries this could a huge challenge due to lack of resources and connectivity.

According to (Mbunge & Maureen Nokuthula Sibiya, 2024) another substantial barrier involves high operational costs, encompassing expenses for SMS messages, mobile data, and ongoing maintenance of mHealth interventions. Such costs can significantly deter consistent and extensive use by both end-users, such as mothers and community health workers, and healthcare professionals. Limited digital skills and training among many users and healthcare workers impede the effective utilization of mHealth interventions. This impacts the adoption of these systems, user engagement, and the ability to fully leverage their intended functionalities. System interoperability issues and a lack of seamless integration also pose considerable challenges. mHealth interventions frequently struggle to communicate and integrate with existing health information systems. This leads to fragmented data, obstructs smooth information flow, and prevents a comprehensive view of patient information, thereby affecting overall efficiency and care delivery.

5.2. Human Factors and User Adoption Barriers

The Organisation for Economic Co-operation and Development (OECD) found that there is a huge technological divide in developing countries (James, 2019). According to Haddad et al. (2019) Women often encounter significant hurdles when trying to access M- based application care. These challenges stem from a combination of cultural, socioeconomic, and technological barriers. Beyond these, women from such backgrounds may also contend with racism, social stigma, and prejudice. Among these difficulties, communication and the availability of accessible information stand out as particular concerns. A key obstacle to receiving proper care and achieving positive health outcomes is frequently identified as limited English language proficiency. Concurrently, research focusing on midwives who provide care to migrant women highlights their own struggles. These include communication problems, suboptimal health literacy, socioeconomic issues, cultural and religious differences, and a lack of familiarity with the maternity care system itself.

According to Sowon and Chigona (2020) trust and belief is important for mHealth interventions to continue being used. If these mHealth systems fail to earn user trust, they may end up being underutilized, bypassed, or only used as a last resort. When mothers interact with technology as if it were a social being, they may evaluate it using human trust dimensions such as competence, integrity, and benevolence.

Competence represents the perception that the technology is capable and skilled in fulfilling its intended functions. Benevolence conveys the sense that the system has the user's best interests at heart, while integrity reflects the belief that it operates according to principles and values that align with the user's own.

5.3. Policy, Governance, and Regulatory Gaps

According to Tamrat and Kachnowski (2011) National health strategies often lack a comprehensive policy framework. This significantly impedes the widespread adoption of mHealth services. These initiatives demand rigorous, in-depth evaluations. Such assessments should guide national health strategies. They allow smart investments and program growth. Governments can then develop astute integration methods. Rwanda exemplifies this approach effectively. They incrementally adopted toll-free health call services. This action greatly facilitated mHealth integration. Currently, Mayange, Rwanda, hosts these services. However, NGOs and governments actively negotiate expansion. They plan to expand this service to additional mHealth sites, including initiatives in Kenya, Tanzania, and Uganda.

6. ETHICAL FRAMEWORKS AND DATA GOVERNANCE IN MHEALTH FOR MCH

The technology empowers patients and users, enabling them to process and visualize their personal health data. Yet the rapid rise of digital health technologies over recent decades brings significant ethical and safety concerns (Grosman-Rimon & Wegier, 2024). Digital health's power demands responsibility, ensuring robust safety and ethical safeguards. Rezaei et al. (2021) revealed six key ethical challenges in digital healthcare: procedure values, responsibility, privacy, autonomy, security, and justice. Common vulnerabilities include endpoint leakage, weak user authentication, and excessive user permissions (Paul et al., 2023). These issues expose healthcare systems to potential compromise. The Internet of Medical Things (IoMT) complicates data management. It also introduces new threats to data security and privacy. This situation underscores a primary concern of digitalization: protecting patient data. Ransomware attacks pose a frequent cybersecurity threat in healthcare. A 2021 FBI report indicated healthcare as the most targeted sector. It received 148 complaints, surpassing the financial sector. Attackers frequently employ software exploitation, phishing, and Remote Desktop Protocol (RDP) for ransomware deployment. These methods highlight the severe risks involved.

Patient data is invaluable for healthcare systems. While beneficial, this data use presents challenges. Historically, patient data served direct clinical care primarily.

Now, secondary use leverages this data for strategic goals. This includes training AI systems to optimize treatments and make predictions. This shift raises questions about current patient consent methods (Moulaei et al., 2025). Beyond formal consent, a “health data social license” is crucial. This emphasizes public trust and societal approval for secondary health data use. In the absence of trust, reluctance to share data could limit the effectiveness of AI in healthcare.

Individual capabilities and digital literacy for technology use vary significantly. This creates a risk that Digital Health Technologies (DHT) could worsen health inequities. Population subgroups who could benefit most may be excluded or disadvantaged. Many acknowledge these risks, yet few studies document how DHT reinforces inequalities or impacts health distribution. Most studies on DHT inequalities focus on individual characteristics. They rarely document contextual, policy, cultural, or value-based dimensions that influence disparities

According to Shaw and Donia (2021) Excitement for digital health's potential to improve healthcare is growing globally among policymakers, providers, researchers, and users alike.. WHO even launched its first global digital health strategy for 2020–2025, supported by various implementation guidelines. Despite ongoing challenges in fully adopting these technologies, a strong sense of optimism persists that digital health will play a vital, beneficial role in future health and healthcare.

7. INNOVATIONS DRIVING MHEALTH IN MCH

Healthcare professionals can use Machine Learning (ML) and Artificial Intelligence (AI) as powerful tools to anticipate maternal health issues. Specifically, algorithms like Shapley Additive Values (SHAP), Local Interpretable Model-agnostic Explanations (LIME), and Anchor are valuable for predicting maternal mental health issues. These machine learning methods also provide insights as to why a specific prediction was generated, which is important for doctors and patients (Ramakrishnan et al., 2021). AI has also been shown to accurately predict serious maternal and neonatal outcomes including premature delivery, infant weight at birth, pregnancy-induced hypertension, maternal or infant death, blood pressure-related complications, and postnatal mood disorders. Early successes of AI are also in real-time fetal monitoring for gestational diabetes management, especially in low-resource environments through electronic health records and predictive models. Additionally, AI-powered techniques have potential in improving prenatal diagnosis of congenital abnormalities and results in assisted reproductive technologies.

Gamification, the process of using elements of game design to apply to non-game contexts, incorporates elements such as interactive interfaces, immediate feedback, reward schemes, challenges, collaboration, avatars, and tests. These are in sync with the seven factors Willis et al. indicated for successful immunization communication. International studies have investigated gamification's capacity to support adoption and sustain preferred health behaviors (Montagni et al., 2019). The "Let's Control Flu" (LCF) tool is an interactive software program meant to aid policy-making for influenza (Lopes et al., 2024). It seeks to increase Vaccine Coverage Rates (VCRs) and support the objectives of the WHO Global Influenza Strategy for 2019-2030. Interactive healthcare applications possess great advantages as they provide tailored and gestation-related information, which helps make health management interesting and convenient.

Patients are able to customize the application to suit their individual requirements, getting essential alerts such as 3D fetal pictures, appointment notifications, and milestone reminders right on their phones (Tripp et al., 2014). This customized method enables users to engage actively with their own health process, giving an experience akin to a one-to-one medical consultation, thus helping in better comprehension and compliance with health guidance. Voice-based telecom information systems have recently emerged, enabling individuals in developing regions to access information previously beyond their reach (Remy et al., 2013).

These systems overcome substantial hurdles like limited computer penetration, low literacy levels, and no access to the internet. People can call these voice-intensive systems easily with ordinary and inexpensive mobile phones, using either their voice or keypad (DTMF) input to access information. Voice-based applications assist expectant women and new mothers in low-literacy communities in accessing vital health information. They provide messages in local languages, making it simple to get crucial advice on childcare and pregnancy care. This simplifies the enhancement of practices and health outcomes, even for people who cannot read or write.

8. COMMUNITY HEALTH WORKERS AND INTEGRATIVE MODELS' ROLE

Community health workers (CHWs) are key players in the healthcare system within low- and middle-income countries. They provide critical services directly to individuals, especially in rural areas (Gopalakrishnan et al., 2020). Their importance within primary healthcare has been acknowledged since the late 1970s and 1980s due to the tenets provided in the Alma-Ata Declaration. By the early 2000s, CHW programs increased significantly. This increase was prompted by the need to task shift some medical responsibilities from highly qualified professionals such as medical professionals to the less skilled workers, mainly in reaction to the pervasiveness of the HIV pandemic. The continued worth of primary healthcare and robust community health systems for improving overall public health was re-stated in the Astana Declaration in 2018.

Developing nations such as India utilize more than 2 million female CHWs, including Anganwadi Workers and ASHAs to provide health and nutrition care in rural setting as part of national programme (Gopalakrishnan et al., 2024).

mHealth interventions in LMICs are usually directed at two principal groups: pregnant women or new mothers and health workers. CHWs are frequently covered due to their importance to a number of health systems, offering critical MCH at community level and accessing pregnant women. Evidence indicates that mHealth interventions significantly enhance pregnant women's utilization of maternal services and enhance their emotional well-being (Ilozumba et al., 2018).

Early et al. (2019) examined research on the use by Community Health Workers (CHWs) of mHealth for cardiovascular disease. They discovered that mobile interventions were more effective than paper-based screening in South Africa, Mexico, and Guatemala and could potentially save tens of thousands of lives at a low cost. CHWs could readily acquire the skills to utilize the app, which estimated preventing almost 100,000 additional deaths in relation to usual care. mHealth advantages for CHWs in Brazil, including less paperwork, though its challenges like community acceptance and service delivery quality issues still persisted. In addition, they pointed out an mHealth application's beneficial effect on cardiovascular disease risk factors in Colorado

To enhance Community Health Worker (CHW) productivity, certain research provided them with mobile phones for reporting and data collection. More studies identify the application of mobile technology in patient-provider communication, the provision of patient education, the supervision of CHWs, and support for monitoring and evaluation (Feroz et al., 2020). Mobile phone usage has many benefits, including decreased workload for CHWs, better management of data, quality improvement of healthcare, more efficient supportive supervision, better task organization, and ultimately better community health outcomes.

The design and release of digital maternal and child health (MCH) programs are significantly impacted by shifting policy environments and fund structures. Nation-states like India, for example, with its Ayushman Bharat Digital Mission (NDHM) and international organizations like the WHO, with its global digital health strategy, are themselves striving to catalyze adoption of digital solutions for enhanced MCH outcomes, focusing on inclusive access and data-driven healthcare. These policies provide a crucial blueprint for integrating technology into existing health infrastructure.

Public-private partnerships (PPPs) are a key component of this framework, leveraging the private sector's innovation and capital to enable public health. Collaboration between government, NGOs, and tech firms can fill infrastructure, knowledge, and finance gaps, particularly in poorer regions. Digital dispensaries and teleconsultations, for instance, widely facilitated through PPPs, are expanding access to healthcare in rural communities.

Despite the promise, sustainability is a big problem. Digital health applications in general, and MCH applications in particular, suffer from the lack of sufficient long-term funding, non-integration into national health information systems, and low levels of user activation with a high likelihood of app abandonment. For these digital solutions to keep working and be effective in the long term, there must be robust long-term financial commitments, effective policy implementation, and a user-focused design focus to maximize persistent relevance and utility beyond initial pilot phases.

9. CONCLUSION

The worldwide quest for better MCH results has hastened the inclusion of mobile-based applications in the domain of healthcare. The chapter has highlighted the fact that mHealth, even not a silver bullet, possesses tremendous potential to revolutionize health access, communication, and behavior. The evidence considered demonstrates how mobile applications are not just bridging the information gap, but also supporting continuity of care. Ranging from health education to real-time diagnostics, from behavior change support to emergency referrals, these technologies are revolutionizing how maternal and child health services are envisioned and delivered. Tools such as MatHealth, MomConnect, and Safe Delivery App have empowered frontline health workers and benefited users directly in terms of higher antenatal attendance, postnatal follow-up, monitoring of child nutrition, and psychosocial welfare.

One of the major contributions of the chapter is its functional typification of mHealth solutions. By emphasizing the six operational types that vary from education to referral systems, it is now clear that technology by itself is not the innovation. Instead, the contextual fit, behavioral tailoring, and alignment with local health ecosystems define the actual value of an application. When integrated with health behavior models such as the Health Belief Model or Social Cognitive Theory, these applications show higher adoption, trust, and sustainability.

Despite these interventions, they are not without limitations. Barriers including digital illiteracy, gendered mobile access, language, and disjointed health records remain. Systemic and infrastructural barriers in distant areas limit regular app utilization. Furthermore, user adherence declines in the absence of culturally tailored material, tailored feedback, or reinforcement by health workers. These limitations reflect the imperative for participatory and iterative app development, supported by systematic evaluation.

The ethical aspects of mHealth need to be addressed as well. Patient information has to be safeguarded using robust privacy measures and clear consent procedures. With increasing use of AI in diagnostics and behavior forecasting, fairness, responsibility, and avoiding harm have to drive implementation. In populations where digital trust is weak, strengthening human relationships through CHWs and peer-to-peer digital support becomes important.

Institutional and public policy support are also critical. Financial investment in the enabling environment like digital infrastructure, training, health system integration, and long-term investment—will be needed to achieve sustainable impact, as well as in app development. India and Rwanda have shown how mHealth applications can be brought to scale with national health missions and public-private partnerships. Such models need to be adapted, not copied, with cultural and systemic differences in view.

Ultimately, the future requires inter-disciplinary cooperation. Healthcare professionals, technologists, behavioral scientists, ethicists, and policymakers need to collaborate to co-design digital platforms that are informed by empathy, equity, and evidence. mHealth interventions need to center the voices and lived experiences of women and children they seek to reach. By doing that, they can effectively democratize access to healthcare.

In total, mobile-based applications are an intersection of technological advance and public health need. If well implemented, they can span long-standing disparities, build resilient health systems even in developed areas

REFERENCES

Acar, Z., & Şahin, N. (2024). Development of a mobile application -based breastfeeding program and evaluation of its effectiveness. *Journal of Pediatric Nursing, 74*, 51–60. DOI: 10.1016/j.pedn.2023.11.011 PMID: 37995477

Alabi, A. S., Alabi, O. A., Adebakin, T. E., & Alayande, B. T. (2025). Revisiting literature on building quality of healthcare facilities between developed and developing countries: Scoping review. *International Journal of Building Pathology and Adaptation*. Advance online publication. DOI: 10.1108/IJBPA-11-2024-0241

Ameyaw, E. K., Amoah, P. A., & Ezezika, O. (2024). Effectiveness of mHealth Apps for Maternal Health Care Delivery: Systematic Review of Systematic Reviews. *Journal of Medical Internet Research, 26*(1), e49510. DOI: 10.2196/49510 PMID: 38810250

Amoakoh, H. B., Klipstein-Grobusch, K., Grobbee, D. E., Amoakoh-Coleman, M., Oduro-Mensah, E., Sarpong, C., Frimpong, E., Kayode, G. A., Agyepong, I. A., & Ansah, E. K. (2019). Using Mobile Health to Support Clinical Decision-Making to Improve Maternal and Neonatal Health Outcomes in Ghana: Insights of Frontline Health Worker Information Needs. *JMIR mHealth and uHealth, 7*(5), e12879. DOI: 10.2196/12879 PMID: 31127719

Ariyani, N. W., Wirawan, I. M. A., Pinatih, G. N. I., & Kusuma, A. A. N. J. (2022). The effect of an application-based educational intervention with a social cognitive theory model on pregnant women in Denpasar, Bali, Indonesia: A randomized controlled trial. *Osong Public Health and Research Perspectives, 13*(2), 153–161. DOI: 10.24171/j.phrp.2021.0209 PMID: 35538687

Barnish, M. S., Tan, S. Y., Robinson, S., Taeihagh, A., & Melendez-Torres, G. J. (2023). A realist synthesis to develop an explanatory model of how policy instruments impact child and maternal health outcomes. *Social Science & Medicine, 116402*, 116402. Advance online publication. DOI: 10.1016/j.socscimed.2023.116402 PMID: 38000341

Biviji, R., Vest, J. R., Dixon, B. E., Cullen, T., & Harle, C. A. (2020). Content analysis of behavior change techniques in maternal and infant health apps. *Translational Behavioral Medicine*. Advance online publication. DOI: 10.1093/tbm/ibaa039 PMID: 32491165

Chen, H., Chai, Y., Dong, L., Niu, W., & Zhang, P. (2018). Effectiveness and Appropriateness of mHealth Interventions for Maternal and Child Health: Systematic Review. *JMIR mHealth and uHealth*, *6*(1), e7. DOI: 10.2196/mhealth.8998 PMID: 29317380

Choudhury, N., Tiwari, A., Wu, W.-J., Bhandari, V., Bhatta, L., Bogati, B., Citrin, D., Halliday, S., Khadka, S., Marasini, N., Pandey, S., Ballard, M., Rayamazi, H. J., Sapkota, S., Schwarz, R., Sullivan, L., Maru, D., Thapa, A., & Maru, S. (2022). Comparing two data collection methods to track vital events in maternal and child health via community health workers in rural Nepal. *Population Health Metrics*, *20*(1), 16. Advance online publication. DOI: 10.1186/s12963-022-00293-4 PMID: 35897038

Colaci, D., Chaudhri, S., & Vasan, A. (2017). mHealth Interventions in Low-Income Countries to Address Maternal Health: A Systematic Review. *Annals of Global Health*, *82*(5), 922. DOI: 10.1016/j.aogh.2016.09.001 PMID: 28283147

DeWitt, A. S., Kientz, J. A., Rucker Coker, T., & Liljenquist, K. (2022). mHealth technology design and evaluation for early childhood health promotion: A systematic literature review (Preprint). *JMIR Pediatrics and Parenting*, *5*(4), e37718. Advance online publication. DOI: 10.2196/37718 PMID: 36201391

Early, J., Gonzalez, C., Gordon-Dseagu, V., & Robles-Calderon, L. (2019). Use of Mobile Health (mHealth) Technologies and Interventions among Community Health Workers Globally: A Scoping Review. *Health Promotion Practice*, *20*(6), 152483991985539. DOI: 10.1177/1524839919855391 PMID: 31179777

Feroz, A., Jabeen, R., & Saleem, S. (2020). Using mobile phones to improve community health workers performance in low-and-middle-income countries. *BMC Public Health*, *20*(1), 49. Advance online publication. DOI: 10.1186/s12889-020-8173-3 PMID: 31931773

Feroz, A., Perveen, S., & Aftab, W. (2017). Role of mHealth applications for improving antenatal and postnatal care in low and middle income countries: A systematic review. *BMC Health Services Research*, *17*(1), 704. Advance online publication. DOI: 10.1186/s12913-017-2664-7 PMID: 29115992

Gebremariam, K. T., Mulugeta, A., & Gallegos, D. (2023). Theory-based mHealth targeting fathers and mothers to improve exclusive breastfeeding: A quasi-experimental study. *International Breastfeeding Journal*, *18*(1), 2. Advance online publication. DOI: 10.1186/s13006-022-00537-x PMID: 36604757

Ginsburg, A. S., Delarosa, J., Brunette, W., Levari, S., Sundt, M., Larson, C., Tawiah Agyemang, C., Newton, S., Borriello, G., & Anderson, R. (2015). mPneumonia: Development of an Innovative mHealth Application for Diagnosing and Treating Childhood Pneumonia and Other Childhood Illnesses in Low-Resource Settings. *PLoS One*, *10*(10), e0139625. DOI: 10.1371/journal.pone.0139625 PMID: 26474321

Gopalakrishnan, L., Buback, L., Fernald, L., Walker, D., & Diamond-Smith, N. (2020). Using mHealth to improve health care delivery in India: A qualitative examination of the perspectives of community health workers and beneficiaries. *PLoS One*, *15*(1), e0227451. DOI: 10.1371/journal.pone.0227451 PMID: 31940326

Gopalakrishnan, L., Patil, S., Fernald, L., Walker, D., & Diamond-Smith, N. (2024). Association between coordinated counseling from both ASHA and Anganwadi Workers and maternal health outcomes: A cross-sectional study from Madhya Pradesh and Bihar, India. *PLOS Global Public Health*, *4*(11), e0003639. DOI: 10.1371/journal.pgph.0003639 PMID: 39536020

Grosman-Rimon, L., & Wegier, P. (2024). With advancement in health technology comes great responsibility – Ethical and safety considerations for using digital health technology: A narrative review. *Medicine*, *103*(33), e39136–e39136. DOI: 10.1097/MD.0000000000039136 PMID: 39151529

Grove, J., Claeson, M., Bryce, J., Amouzou, A., Boerma, T., Waiswa, P., & Victora, C. (2015). Maternal, newborn, and child health and the Sustainable Development Goals—A call for sustained and improved measurement. *Lancet*, *386*(10003), 1511–1514. DOI: 10.1016/S0140-6736(15)00517-6 PMID: 26530604

Haddad, S. M., Souza, R. T., & Cecatti, J. G. (2019). Mobile technology in health (mHealth) and antenatal care–Searching for apps and available solutions: A systematic review. *International Journal of Medical Informatics*, *127*, 1–8. DOI: 10.1016/j.ijmedinf.2019.04.008 PMID: 31128820

Ilozumba, O., Van Belle, S., Dieleman, M., Liem, L., Choudhury, M., & Broerse, J. E. W. (2018). The Effect of a Community Health Worker Utilized Mobile Health Application on Maternal Health Knowledge and Behavior: A Quasi-Experimental Study. *Frontiers in Public Health*, *6*, 133. Advance online publication. DOI: 10.3389/fpubh.2018.00133 PMID: 29868541

James, J. (2019). Confronting the scarcity of digital skills among the poor in developing countries. *Development Policy Review*, *39*(2), 324–339. Advance online publication. DOI: 10.1111/dpr.12479

James, J. (2025). *5 Maternal Health Mobile Apps That Are Saving African Mothers' Lives*. Socialgoodmoms.com. https://socialgoodmoms.com/2015/07/27/5-maternal-health-mobile-apps-that-are-saving-african-mothers-lives/

Jeon, E., & Park, H.-A. (2015). Factors Affecting Acceptance of Smartphone Application for Management of Obesity. *Healthcare Informatics Research, 21*(2), 74. DOI: 10.4258/hir.2015.21.2.74 PMID: 25995959

Kaewkungwal, J., Singhasivanon, P., Khamsiriwatchara, A., Sawang, S., Meankaew, P., & Wechsart, A. (2010). Application of smart phone in "Better Border Healthcare Program": A module for mother and child care. *BMC Medical Informatics and Decision Making, 10*(1), 69. Advance online publication. DOI: 10.1186/1472-6947-10-69 PMID: 21047412

Kante, M., & Målqvist, M. (2025). Effectiveness of SMS-based interventions in enhancing antenatal care in developing countries: A systematic review. *BMJ Open, 15*(2), e089671–e089671. DOI: 10.1136/bmjopen-2024-089671 PMID: 40000082

Karataş, N., Kaya, A., & Dalgıç, A. İ. (2021). The effectiveness of user-focused mobile health applications in paediatric chronic disease management: A systematic review. *Journal of Pediatric Nursing: Nursing Care of Children and Families, 0*(0). Advance online publication. DOI: 10.1016/j.pedn.2021.09.018 PMID: 34598848

Kruse, C., Betancourt, J., Ortiz, S., Valdes Luna, S. M., Bamrah, I. K., & Segovia, N. (2019). Barriers to the Use of Mobile Health in Improving Health Outcomes in Developing Countries: Systematic Review. *Journal of Medical Internet Research, 21*(10), e13263. DOI: 10.2196/13263 PMID: 31593543

Kurjak, A., Stanojević, M., & Dudenhausen, J. (2022). Why maternal mortality in the world remains tragedy in low-income countries and shame for high-income ones: Will sustainable development goals (SDG) help? *Journal of Perinatal Medicine, 0*(0). Advance online publication. DOI: 10.1515/jpm-2022-0061 PMID: 35636412

Kusyanti, T., Wirakusumah, F. F., Rinawan, F. R., Muhith, A., Purbasari, A., Mawardi, F., Puspitasari, I. W., Faza, A., & Stellata, A. G. (2022). Technology-Based (Mhealth) and Standard/Traditional Maternal Care for Pregnant Woman: A Systematic Literature Review. *Health Care, 10*(7), 1287. DOI: 10.3390/healthcare10071287 PMID: 35885813

Liu, C., Chen, H., Zhou, F., Long, Q., Wu, K., Lo, L.-M., Hung, T.-H., Liu, C.-Y., & Chiou, W.-K. (2022). Positive intervention effect of mobile health application based on mindfulness and social support theory on postpartum depression symptoms of puerperae. *BMC Women's Health, 22*(1), 413. Advance online publication. DOI: 10.1186/s12905-022-01996-4 PMID: 36217135

Liu, Y., & Wang, X. (2021). Application of Smart Mobile Medical Services in Maternal Health Care Management. *Contrast Media & Molecular Imaging, 2021*, 1–6. DOI: 10.1155/2021/6249736 PMID: 34949971

Lopes, H., Baptista-Leite, R., Hermenegildo, C., & Atun, R. (2024). Digital Gamification Tool (Let's Control Flu) to Increase Vaccination Coverage Rates: Proposal for Algorithm Development. *JMIR Research Protocols, 13*, e55613. DOI: 10.2196/55613 PMID: 39255031

Luna, D., Almerares, A., Mayan, J. C.III, González Bernaldo de Quirós, F., & Otero, C. (2014). Health Informatics in Developing Countries: Going beyond Pilot Practices to Sustainable Implementations: A Review of the Current Challenges. *Healthcare Informatics Research, 20*(1), 3. DOI: 10.4258/hir.2014.20.1.3 PMID: 24627813

Mahmood, H., Mckinstry, B., Luz, S., Fairhurst, K., Nasim, S., & Hazir, T. (2020). Community health worker-based mobile health (mHealth) approaches for improving management and caregiver knowledge of common childhood infections: A systematic review. *Journal of Global Health, 10*(2), 020438. Advance online publication. DOI: 10.7189/jogh.10.020438 PMID: 33437462

Mbunge, E., & Sibiya, M. N. (2024). Mobile Health Interventions for Improving Maternal and Child Health Outcomes in South Africa: A Systematic Review. *Global Health Journal (Amsterdam, Netherlands), 8*(3), 103–112. Advance online publication. DOI: 10.1016/j.glohj.2024.08.002

Mbuthia, F., Reid, M., & Fichardt, A. (2019). mHealth communication to strengthen postnatal care in rural areas: A systematic review. *BMC Pregnancy and Childbirth, 19*(1), 406. Advance online publication. DOI: 10.1186/s12884-019-2531-0 PMID: 31694578

Mihaila, S. (2023, February). *Mamahood launches femtech app to support women in the Middle East and North Africa*. FemTech World. https://www.femtechworld.co.uk/news/mamahood-launches-femtech-app-to-support-women-in-the-middle-east-and-north-africa/

Mildon, A., & Sellen, D. (2019). Use of mobile phones for behavior change communication to improve maternal, newborn and child health: A scoping review. *Journal of Global Health, 9*(2), 020425. Advance online publication. DOI: 10.7189/jogh.09.020425 PMID: 31893032

Montagni, I., Mabchour, I., & Tzourio, C. (2019). Digital Gamification to Enhance Vaccine Knowledge and Uptake: Scoping Review (Preprint). *JMIR Serious Games, 8*(2), e16983. Advance online publication. DOI: 10.2196/16983 PMID: 32348271

Moulaei, K., Akhlaghpour, S., & Fatehi, F. (2025). Patient consent for the secondary use of health data in artificial intelligence (AI) models: A scoping review. *International Journal of Medical Informatics, 198*, 105872. DOI: 10.1016/j.ijmedinf.2025.105872 PMID: 40107041

Mumtaz, Z., Salway, S., Bhatti, A., Shanner, L., Zaman, S., Laing, L., & Ellison, G. T. H. (2014). Improving Maternal Health in Pakistan: Toward a Deeper Understanding of the Social Determinants of Poor Women's Access to Maternal Health Services. *American Journal of Public Health, 104*(S1), S17–S24. DOI: 10.2105/AJPH.2013.301377 PMID: 24354817

Ndlovu, K., Scott, R. E., & Mars, M. (2021). Interoperability opportunities and challenges in linking mhealth applications and eRecord systems: Botswana as an exemplar. *BMC Medical Informatics and Decision Making, 21*(1), 246. Advance online publication. DOI: 10.1186/s12911-021-01606-7 PMID: 34419020

Nkwo, M., Orji, R., & Ajah, I. (2021). A Health Belief Model Approach to Evaluating Maternal Health Behaviors among Africans - Design Implications for Personalized Persuasive Technologies. *Adjunct Proceedings of the 29th ACM Conference on User Modeling, Adaptation and Personalization*. DOI: 10.1145/3450614.3464624

Ononge, S., Magunda, A., Balaba, D., Waiswa, P., Okello, D., Kaula, H., Zalwango, S., Bua, D. A., Ayebare, A., Kaharuza, F., Bennett, C., Sulzbach, S., Keller, B., & Mugerwa, Y. (2023). Strengthening Kampala's Urban Referral System for Maternal and Newborn Care Through Establishment of an Emergency Call and Dispatch Center. *Global Health, Science and Practice, 11*(3), e2200332. Advance online publication. DOI: 10.9745/GHSP-D-22-00332 PMID: 37348939

Paul, M., Maglaras, L., Ferrag, M. A., & Almomani, I. (2023). Digitization of healthcare sector: A study on privacy and security concerns. *ICT Express, 9*(4), 571–588. https://www.sciencedirect.com/science/article/pii/S2405959523000243. DOI: 10.1016/j.icte.2023.02.007

Peters, D. H., Garg, A., Bloom, G., Walker, D. G., Brieger, W. R., & Hafizur Rahman, M. (2008). Poverty and Access to Health Care in Developing Countries. *Annals of the New York Academy of Sciences, 1136*(1), 161–171. DOI: 10.1196/annals.1425.011 PMID: 17954679

Prata, N., Passano, P., Sreenivas, A., & Gerdts, C. E. (2010). Maternal Mortality in Developing Countries: Challenges in Scaling-Up Priority Interventions. *Women's Health (London, England), 6*(2), 311–327. DOI: 10.2217/WHE.10.8 PMID: 20187734

Prinja, S., Nimesh, R., Gupta, A., Bahuguna, P., Thakur, J. S., Gupta, M., & Singh, T. (2016). Impact assessment and cost-effectiveness of m-health application used by community health workers for maternal, newborn and child health care services in rural Uttar Pradesh, India: A study protocol. *Global Health Action*, *9*(1), 31473. DOI: 10.3402/gha.v9.31473 PMID: 27189200

Quintana, Y., & McWhirter, J. (2017). Culturally Appropriate Behavioral Change in Maternal Health: Role of Mobile and Online Technologies Over Time. *Computers in Healthcare*, ●●●, 217–233. DOI: 10.1007/978-3-319-51732-2_10

Ramakrishnan, R., Rao, S., & He, J.-R. (2021). Perinatal health predictors using artificial intelligence: A review. *Women's Health (London, England)*, *17*, 174550652110461. DOI: 10.1177/17455065211046132 PMID: 34519596

Remy, C., Agarwal, S. K., Kumar, A., & Srivastava, S. (2013). Supporting Voice Content Sharing among Underprivileged People in Urban India. *Lecture Notes in Computer Science*, *8120*, 489–506. DOI: 10.1007/978-3-642-40498-6_38

Rezaei, M., Jafari-Sadeghi, V., Cao, D., & Mahdiraji, H. A. (2021). Key indicators of ethical challenges in digital healthcare: A combined Delphi exploration and confirmative factor analysis approach with evidence from Khorasan province in Iran. *Technological Forecasting and Social Change*, *167*, 120724. DOI: 10.1016/j.techfore.2021.120724

Sakamoto, J. L., Carandang, R. R., Kharel, M., Shibanuma, A., Yarotskaya, E., Basargina, M., & Jimba, M. (2022). Effects of mHealth on the psychosocial health of pregnant women and mothers: A systematic review. *BMJ Open*, *12*(2), e056807. DOI: 10.1136/bmjopen-2021-056807 PMID: 35168981

Sardi, L., Idri, A., Redman, L. M., Alami, H., Bezad, R., & Alemán, J. L. F. (2020). Mobile health applications for postnatal care: Review and analysis of functionalities and technical features. *Computer Methods and Programs in Biomedicine*, *184*, 105114. DOI: 10.1016/j.cmpb.2019.105114 PMID: 31655305

Seyyedi, N., Rahimi, B., Farrokh Eslamlou, H. R., Timpka, T., & Lotfnezhad Afshar, H. (2019). Mobile phone applications to overcome malnutrition among preschoolers: A systematic review. *BMC Medical Informatics and Decision Making*, *19*(1), 83. Advance online publication. DOI: 10.1186/s12911-019-0803-2 PMID: 30953497

Sharda, S., Kshtriya, P., Agrawal, P. K., Singh, P., Trakroo, A., Joshi, A., Agarwal, A., Goyal, A., D'Aquino, L., Singh, S., Singh, R., & Prinja, S. (2024). Digital supportive supervision (DiSS) of maternal health, child health and nutrition (MCHN) service delivery in Rajasthan, India: Study protocol for impact evaluation and cost-effectiveness analysis. *BMJ Open, 14*(12), e086956–e086956. DOI: 10.1136/bmjopen-2024-086956 PMID: 39740940

Shaw, J. A., & Donia, J. (2021). The Sociotechnical Ethics of Digital Health: A Critique and Extension of Approaches From Bioethics. *Frontiers in Digital Health, 3*, 725088. Advance online publication. DOI: 10.3389/fdgth.2021.725088 PMID: 34713196

Sowon, K., & Chigona, W. (2020). *Trust in mHealth: How do Maternal Health Clients Accept and Use mHealth Interventions?* DOI: 10.1145/3410886.3410895

Srivastava, A., Avan, B. I., Rajbangshi, P., & Bhattacharyya, S. (2015). Determinants of women's satisfaction with maternal health care: A review of literature from developing countries. *BMC Pregnancy and Childbirth, 15*(1), 97. Advance online publication. DOI: 10.1186/s12884-015-0525-0 PMID: 25928085

Subedi, D., Paudel, M., Poudel, S., & Koirala, N. (2024). Food Safety in Developing Countries: Common Foodborne and Waterborne Illnesses, Regulations, Organizational Structure, and Challenges of Food Safety in the Context of Nepal. *Food Frontiers*. Advance online publication. DOI: 10.1002/fft2.517

Tamrat, T., & Kachnowski, S. (2011). Special Delivery: An Analysis of mHealth in Maternal and Newborn Health Programs and Their Outcomes Around the World. *Maternal and Child Health Journal, 16*(5), 1092–1101. DOI: 10.1007/s10995-011-0836-3 PMID: 21688111

Tarun Singh Sodha, Grønbæk, A., Bhandari, A., B. Daly Mary, Ajit Kisanrao Sudke, & Smith, L. (2022). mHealth learning tool for skilled birth attendants: scaling the Safe Delivery App in India. *BMJ Open Quality, 11*(Suppl 1), e001928–e001928. DOI: 10.1136/bmjoq-2022-001928

Tate, E. B., Spruijt-Metz, D., O'Reilly, G., Jordan-Marsh, M., Gotsis, M., Pentz, M. A., & Dunton, G. F. (2013). mHealth approaches to child obesity prevention: Successes, unique challenges, and next directions. *Translational Behavioral Medicine, 3*(4), 406–415. DOI: 10.1007/s13142-013-0222-3 PMID: 24294329

Thobias, J., & Kiwanuka, A. (2018). Design and implementation of an m-health data model for improving health information access for reproductive and child health services in low resource settings using a participatory action research approach. *BMC Medical Informatics and Decision Making*, *18*(1), 45. Advance online publication. DOI: 10.1186/s12911-018-0622-x PMID: 29941008

Tripp, N., Hainey, K., Liu, A., Poulton, A., Peek, M., Kim, J., & Nanan, R. (2014). An emerging model of maternity care: Smartphone, midwife, doctor? *Women and Birth : Journal of the Australian College of Midwives*, *27*(1), 64–67. DOI: 10.1016/j.wombi.2013.11.001 PMID: 24295598

Trude, A. C. B., Martins, R. C., Martins-Silva, T., Blumenberg, C., Carpena, M. X., Del-Ponte, B., & Loret de Mola, C. (2021). A WhatsApp-Based Intervention to Improve Maternal Social Support and Maternal–Child Health in Southern Brazil: The Text-Message Intervention to Enhance Social Support (TIES) Feasibility Study. *Inquiry : a Journal of Medical Care Organization, Provision and Financing*, *58*, 00469580211048701. DOI: 10.1177/00469580211048701 PMID: 34619999

Tulchinsky, T. H., Varavikova, E. A., & Cohen, M. J. (2023). Family health and primary prevention. *Elsevier EBooks*, 467–549. DOI: 10.1016/B978-0-12-822957-6.00007-7

WHO. (2022). *Child mortality and causes of death*. Www.who.int. https://www.who.int/data/gho/data/themes/topics/topic-details/GHO/child-mortality-and-causes-of-death

Wigley, A. S., Tejedor-Garavito, N., Alegana, V., Carioli, A., Ruktanonchai, C. W., Pezzulo, C., Matthews, Z., Tatem, A. J., & Nilsen, K. (2020). Measuring the availability and geographical accessibility of maternal health services across sub-Saharan Africa. *BMC Medicine*, *18*(1), 237. Advance online publication. DOI: 10.1186/s12916-020-01707-6 PMID: 32895051

World Health Organization. (2023). *Maternal Mental Health*. World Health Organization. https://www.who.int/teams/mental-health-and-substance-use/promotion-prevention/maternal-mental-health

World Health Organization. (2025, April 7). *Maternal Mortality*. World Health Organization. https://www.who.int/news-room/fact-sheets/detail/maternal-mortality

Yaya, S., & Ghose, B. (2019). Global Inequality in Maternal Health Care Service Utilization: Implications for Sustainable Development Goals. *Health Equity*, *3*(1), 145–154. DOI: 10.1089/heq.2018.0082 PMID: 31289773

Zhang, P., Dong, L., Chen, H., Chai, Y., & Liu, J. (2018). The Rise and Need for Mobile Apps for Maternal and Child Health Care in China: Survey Based on App Markets. *JMIR mHealth and uHealth*, *6*(6), e140. DOI: 10.2196/mhealth.9302 PMID: 29884601

Chapter 9

The Case for Using Blood Biomarker Diagnostics to Detect Alzheimer's Disease (AD) in Saudi Primary Healthcare Centres

Cong Sui
http://orcid.org/0009-0008-2657-2580
West Midlands Health Tech Innovation Accelerator, UK & University of Birmingham, UK

Khalid Alderaa
Value in Health, Saudi Arabia

Balqees Alrowili
The Ministry of Health, Saudi Arabia

Marwan Hadi Madkhali
Tata Consultancy Services, Saudi Arabia

Salih Baz
Duymer Hearing Aids, Turkey

Shai Wen
http://orcid.org/0009-0007-4387-9165
University College London, UK

Julie Davies
http://orcid.org/0000-0002-6875-3100
Brunel University of London, UK

ABSTRACT

This chapter investigates the pressing issue of Alzheimer's disease in Saudi Arabia. It focuses on the urgent need for change management to implement diagnostic blood biomarkers for early detection in Primary Healthcare Centres (PHCs). The study

DOI: 10.4018/979-8-3373-3341-0.ch009

utilizes a comprehensive framework that combines the policy triangle, Kotter's change management model, and Kingdon's multiple streams models to analyse the systemic barriers and opportunities for implementing innovative diagnostic tools in Alzheimer's care. Drawing on a narrative literature review and stakeholder engagement, this chapter highlights low public awareness, limited diagnostic infrastructure, and policy fragmentation as key challenges. Key findings underscore the importance of the Saudi government conducting a phased, multi-stakeholder approach to introduce biomarkers at the PHC level. Actionable recommendations include national awareness campaigns, policy development, and pilot implementation strategies, aligned with Saudi Vision 2030 health goals.

1. INTRODUCTION

1.1 Overview of Alzheimer's disease challenge in Saudi Arabia

Alzheimer's Disease (AD) is the most prevalent form of dementia that contributes to about 70% of cases (WHO, 2019). It is one of the principal causes of decreased quality of life amongst the elderly and so it poses a significant impediment to healthy ageing (Grossberg & Desai, 2003). The Kingdom of Saudi Arabia (KSA) launched its Vision 2030 in April 2016, a national transformation agenda. One of the vision realisation programs (VROs) is the Health Sector Transformation Program (HSTP). This aims to achieve three main fundamental pillars: a vibrant society, a thriving economy, and an ambitious nation (Basheikh et al., 2021). The HSTP is designed to deliver integrated healthcare through a new model of care (Saudi Ministry of Health, 2017). Despite this progressive transformation, AD in Saudi Arabia remains a neglected priority, hence there is an urgent need for early AD diagnosis.

With expected increases in the ageing population to constitute 10% of the overall population by 2030 and 25% by 2050 in Saudi Arabia, innovation in dealing with the management and pathways of AD is crucially important, as shown in Figure 1 (United Nations, 2012). This demographic trend necessitates a sense of urgency and implementation of tangible projects to avoid a future surge in undiagnosed cases. The use of blood biomarkers is one approach proposed as a response to the growing number of people with late-diagnosed or undiagnosed AD.

Figure 1. Share of population aged 60+ years in the Kingdom of Saudi Arabia 1950-2050. Source: United Nations (2012)

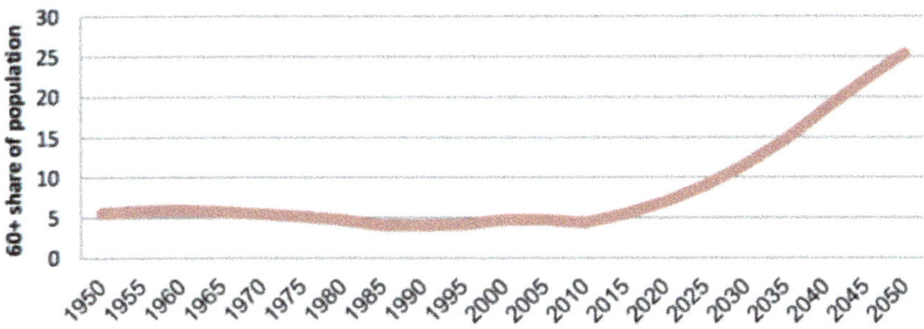

Applying, Kotter's (1996) change management framework, we argue that a vital first step is to create a sense of urgency about the importance of implementing blood biomarkers in PHCs in Saudi Arabia. This is essential to prepare for the expected increase in population age in the Kingdom and thus the proportion of the population with AD. The change management process based on Kotter's (1996) model is more successful when it involves multiple units (Pollack & Pollack, 2015) and so we advocate engagement across multiple stakeholders.

The equitable distribution of PHCs across the Kingdom, as illustrated by the Gini index in Table 1 (Al-Sheddi et al., 2023), offers an important mechanism to implement blood biomarkers. Furthermore, the on-going transformation of the health sector built on a system of health clusters can facilitate the effective use of blood biomarkers (Saudi Ministry of Health, 2017).

Table 1. Distribution of primary healthcare centres in the 20 Saudi health regions and Index Interpretation Source: Al-Sheddi et al. (2023)

Year	Gini index for distribution of PHCs in all 20 health regions
2017	0.2731
2018	0.2677
2019	0.2799
2020	0.2732
2021	0.2692
Mean	0.27262

Gini index	Evaluation
≤0.2	Perfect equality
>0.2-0.3	Relative equality
>0.3-0.4	Adequate equality
>0.4-0.5	Large equality gap
>0.5	Severe equality gap

This study aims to examine current practices in the Saudi health system for diagnosing AD. Specifically, it explores the benefits and challenges of implementing biomarkers in primary healthcare centres for people with early disease symptoms. It depicts how different change management models effectively guide the implementation of blood biomarkers in diagnosing AD in Saudi Arabia. According to the World Health Organization (2021), Table 2 shows that the diagnostic rate for dementia in the Eastern Mediterranean region is only 19%. This rate is significantly below that of European countries (60%) and the global median diagnostic rate of dementia generally (48%), of which AD is the leading cause.

Table 2. WHO dementia diagnostic rates by region. Source: World Health Organization, 2021

Dementia diagnostic rates by WHO region and World Bank income level

	Dementia diagnostic rate	
Region	Median	Range
Global (n = 29)	48%	0.08% - 95%
WHO region		
African Region (n = 1)	--	0.4%
Region of the Americas (n = 2)	--	23% - 73%
South-East Asia Region (n = 2)	--	0.08% - 8%
European Region (n = 16)	60%	3% - 95%
Eastern Mediterranean Region (n = 4)	19%	17% - 56%
Western Pacific Region (n = 4)	27%	0.3% - 96%
Income level		
Low- and middle-income (n = 10)	21%	0.08-96%
High-income (n = 19)	58%	3-95%

Given the high number of people with undiagnosed dementia, the World Health Organization (2021) has published a global action plan on the public health response to dementia. Part of this plan aims to reach a minimum diagnosis rate of 50%, alongside implementing awareness and inclusivity programs for people with dementia.

Previous studies have illustrated that although Europe's healthcare systems are considered highly developed compared with other countries, less than 50% of the population receive their formal diagnosis in primary healthcare facilities (Frisoni et al., 2017). This could be due to workforce shortages and the difficulty of building infrastructure to deploy advanced solutions outside tertiary care centres (Frisoni et al., 2017). Despite understanding of dementia among the general population, there remains inadequate knowledge of prevention and curability (Mohamad et al., 2023).

1.2 Outline

This chapter is structured as follows. First, the introduction discusses the current status of the population age and diagnosis of AD and dementia diagnosis practices in the Kingdom of Saudi Arabia (KSA) compared with other leading countries such as in Europe. Second, the literature review highlights relevant articles and key challenges. Third, the methodology section explains the data collection and analysis. Fourth, the theoretical framework explains the integration of three models and frameworks to understand the current predicament. Following a presentation and discussion of the findings, we present conclusions and recommendations.

2. LITERATURE REVIEW

The literature review was based on the following keywords: Alzheimer's disease, biomarkers, change management, early diagnosis, innovation, primary care, Saudi Arabia. It was informed by the key research question: "Why is it urgent to implement diagnostic blood biomarker testing to detect Alzheimer's in KSA?" The objectives of the review were to:

- examine the urgency of detecting Alzheimer's disease in an ageing population for improved treatment.
- explore strategies in KSA and internationally for successfully managing Alzheimer's disease.

This chapter employs a narrative literature review methodology to examine screening and early detection of Alzheimer's disease, with a particular focus on the healthcare system in the KSA (Cameron & Green, 2024). The synthesis of 24 key articles, summarised in the table, highlights the benefits of incorporation of AD-related biomarkers in enhancing the diagnosis of the disease within the healthcare framework in the KSA (Arksey & O'Malley, 2005; Blennow & Zetterberg, 2018). The review gathers insights from existing research on systemic improvements in KSA, containing prevention strategies, early diagnosis, limitations (workforce, regional disparity), financial challenges, patient access, and quality outcomes.

A narrative literature review is a method that involves providing a comprehensive overview and analysis of a specific topic by synthesising and evaluating existing literature (Rother, 2007). Unlike systematic reviews or meta-analyses, which adhere to a stringent systematic approach to minimise bias, narrative reviews provide a more flexible structure and methodology, enabling researchers to curate and structure content based on thematic relevance rather than a rigid systematic approach. While systematic reviews require a comprehensive and systematic evaluation of all available resources, narrative reviews efficiently distil an intuitive, experiential, and straightforward topic overview based on expert insights (Pae, 2015).

This chapter aims to assess the growing urgency of AD in Saudi Arabia and propose some potential change management solutions to address its systemic gaps. However, it is important to acknowledge the inherent limitations of narrative reviews, including the risk of the authors' subjective interpretation and selective literature coverage, which may introduce the risk of subjectivity, making it susceptible to the authors' personal views and biases. Despite these limitations, a narrative review remains to be an efficient and comprehensive approach in understanding the current state of Alzheimer's disease in Saudi Arabia, offering a balanced and expedient evaluation of the research topic.

Selection Criteria

Peer-reviewed papers were sourced from reputable databases, including the Chartered Association of Business Schools' *Academic Journal Guide 2021*, Google Scholar, PubMed, and Scopus. The search strategy incorporated Medical Subject Headings (MeSH), with inclusion criteria restricted to English-language publications during 2008-2025. Non-English written publications were excluded, with the exception of some selected Arabic governmental releases pertinent to Saudi Arabia's policies. From an initial pool of 51 papers, 24 were selected, filtered, and utilised based on topic suitability and compiled chronologically. Through this analysis, the review proposes practical recommendations for integrating biomarkers into primary care in KSA, ensuring financial sustainability and improved patient care standards.

Table 3. Summary of 24 key studies in the literature review

Study	Method	Sample	Key Findings	Theoretical Approach
Al-Sheddi et al. (2023)	Cross-sectional study	KSA	2017-21, primary healthcare centres are distributed fairly throughout 20 KSA health regions. The Gini index showed relative equality in the distribution of primary healthcare centres.	Equality
Alamri & Adejare (2017)	Descriptive	USA	The National Plan on Alzheimer's aims to both improve care for those with the disease and prevent future cases, with a focus on research and healthy aging.	National planning
Alghamdi et al. (2023)	Qualitative study	KSA	Digital health services were useful for continuity of care during the COVID-19 pandemic. However, lack of awareness of the different digital health services in KSA hinders their optimal use, especially the virtual clinic utilization	Primary healthcare services
Alharbi et al. (2025)	Narrative review	KSA	Highlights rising AD prevalence, identifies key genetic biomarkers in Saudi population, and gaps in genomic research infrastructure.	Translational neuroscience; genetic epidemiology approach
Alkhunizan et al. (2018)	Observational cross-sectional study	KSA	The prevalence of dementia and MCI (Mild Cognitive Impairment) differs worldwide because of multiple factors including the variation of educational levels, and the prevalence of other important risk factors of dementia. In 2016, population over 60 = 1.3m (6.5%) by 2050, this age group will be >10 million, 25% of the total population.	Prevalence of cognitive impairment (MCI and dementia) among elderly patients in a community-based setting in Riyadh, Saudi Arabia
Alnaim et al. (2025)	Quantitative cross-sectional survey	KSA	Moderate general awareness, but poor recognition of neuropsychiatric symptoms; education level and prior exposure influenced awareness.	Health behavior and knowledge-attitude-practice (KAP) framework

continued on following page

Table 3. Continued

Study	Method	Sample	Key Findings	Theoretical Approach
Baloh et al. (2018)	Observational	Iowa, USA	Articles listed in CABS AGJ 2021 ranking. Implementation strategies may deviate from the Kotter model, where skipping or performing poorly on earlier steps does not necessarily compromise the implementation's progress. Kotter's change model applies better in cases where the change implementation scope involves multiple units. Where the implementation scope is narrower, other strategies can be effective.	Kotter's change model application
Bamford & Daniel (2005)	Case study	UK	A flexible strategy is necessary to manage complicated change; contingency models are useful, one model may not be sufficient. As the shift takes place, the leadership approach could also need to alter from directive to collaborative. Effective change management prioritizes a supportive culture and adjusts to organizational requirements. Continue to evaluate the procedure and make changes in response to changing conditions and their effects.	Evaluate the effectiveness of the change management in the NHS
Beigh et al. (2024)	Retrospective analytical study	KSA	Dementia strongly associated with diabetes, hypertension, and cardiovascular disease; increasing trend in multimorbidity with age.	Epidemiological cohort analysis; biopsychosocial model of multimorbidity
Cammisuli et al. (2022)	Review	Italy	Technological solutions show promise in diagnosing early signs of Alzheimer's, managing patient behavior, and improving memory, movement, and spatial skills. These solutions can be applied at all stages of Alzheimer's disease. The studies reviewed have some limitations, including different diagnostic criteria and participant groups.	Technological solutions

continued on following page

Table 3. Continued

Study	Method	Sample	Key Findings	Theoretical Approach
Chávez-Fumagalli et al. (2021)	Systematic review	Developed and developing countries	The findings showed an important discrepancy in diagnostic data for AD between developed and developing countries. Also, the analysis found a better performance for the tau-PET diagnostic over other methods to diagnose AD patients, but the expense of tau-PET scan seems to be the limiting factor in the diagnosis of AD in developing countries such as those found in Asia, Africa, and Latin America.	Diagnosis of Alzheimer's disease (AD) in developed and developing countries
Dehghani et al. (2021)	Narrative review	African, Asian, Latin American, and Middle Eastern	Understudied populations have revealed new AD-associated variants and clarified genetic heterogeneity; calls for inclusive genomic studies.	Population genetics; precision medicine and diversity framework
El-Metwally et al. (2019)	Systematic review	Arab countries	Dementia prevalence ranged between 1.1%-2.3%; underreporting and methodological variability noted. Lack of standardised diagnostic tools and epidemiological data highlighted.	Public health epidemiology; comparative analysis of regional burden of disease
Frisoni et al. (2017)	Strategic five-phase roadmap to foster the clinical validation of biomarkers in Alzheimer's disease, adapted from the approach for cancer biomarkers.	France, Germany, Italy, Netherlands, Spain, Sweden, Switzerland, UK.	Different prescription and reimbursement criteria for using neuroimaging biomarkers in various countries. < 50% of people with dementia receive a formal diagnosis in primary care to deliver timely and appropriate personalized care. Accurate diagnosis of Alzheimer's disease in the prodromal stage will, therefore, be paramount to minimize the risk-to-benefit ratio. 5 phases in the framework adopted and modified from oncology for early diagnosis of Alzheimer's disease.	Strategic research to foster the clinical validation of AD biomarkers
Hakami et al. (2023)	Observational cross-sectional study	KSA, Japanese province	Only 29% of respondents answered questions about AD correctly. Low awareness of AD in the community. 27% of respondents had relatives with AD.	Social perceptions of AD in Jazan

continued on following page

Table 3. Continued

Study	Method	Sample	Key Findings	Theoretical Approach
Ismail et al. (2021)	Cross-sectional study	KSA	Positive dementia screening associated with history of stroke, number of teeth lost, multiple medications, and age: early intervention may potentially reduce the risk of dementia onset.	Screen the incidence of dementia
Cummings et al. (2015)	Descriptive	USA	Although the progression of Alzheimer's disease cannot be reversed, lifestyle changes and medication can slow the progression of cognitive and functional symptoms and maximize quality of life.	AD management
Blennow & Zetterberg (2018)	Descriptive	Europe, USA	Clinical studies have shown that core Alzheimer's disease cerebrospinal fluid (CSF) biomarkers amyloid-β (Aβ42), total tau (T-tau), and phosphorylated tau (P-tau) are key elements reflecting the pathological physiology of AD and contribute to the diagnosis of early-stage disease.	Pharmacologic therapy for AD
Kerwin et al. (2022)	Analysis of current situations in different contexts	Brazil, China, Nigeria, Spain Sweden	In Sweden, inconsistent use of biomarkers is a prominent barrier to the diagnosis of AD. According to the Swedish Dementia Registry, CSF biomarker analysis varies across the country from 20% in some parts of northern Sweden to 90% in some districts in southern Sweden. There is a general need to improve education around AD and dementia to reduce fear and cultural stigma and to enable access to care and earlier diagnosis.	Diagnosis and management
Mohamad et al. (2023)	Cross-sectional survey	KSA	Respondents generally lack knowledge about the preventability and treatability of Alzheimer's disease.	Knowledge, Attitudes, and Practices Towards Dementia
Noor Eddin et al. (2023)	Analysis of current situations in diagnosis of Alzheimer		MiRNA has been detected as significant biomarker for the diagnosis of AD.	Potential biomarkers

continued on following page

Table 3. Continued

Study	Method	Sample	Key Findings	Theoretical Approach
Pedersen & Dunne (2020)	Descriptive	Denmark	This study challenges the widely held belief that habits in change management are only triggers for a stimulus-reaction cycle. It makes the case for a more expansive viewpoint based on John Dewey's writings. This study suggests three essential behaviors based on Dewey's theory: Habit as Function: habits exert an influence on interactions between people and their surroundings. Habit as Social Product: social norms and practices shape and impact the formation of habits. Habit as Process: rather than being automatic, rigid responses, habits are dynamic processes entwined with questions and urges.	Change management
Qassem et al. (2023)	Systematic review and cost-estimation analysis	Arab League countries	Dementia prevalence ~1.6%; total estimated cost >US$9 billion annually. Data gaps and limited healthcare infrastructure emphasise urgent policy needs.	Health economics; burden of disease modeling
Saeed et al. (2023)	Observational	KSA	AI solutions can also be used to develop personalized treatment plans for patients. By analysing patient data, including genetic information, AI algorithms can identify the most effective treatment options for individual patients.	Saudi Arabia Health Systems

Critical review of Alzheimer's disease management in Saudi Arabia: prevention, diagnosis, and systemic challenges

This section critically reviews and analyses major studies on improving the KSA system regarding Alzheimer's disease prevention, early diagnosis, limitations (workforce, regional differences), financial challenges, patient accessibility, and quality. Through a synthesis of existing research, we evaluate the strengths and weaknesses of existing approaches and identify critical research gaps.

Awareness and early intervention

Hakami et al. (2023) highlight a concerning lack of awareness of AD in Saudi Arabia, with only 29% of the respondents in the study demonstrating accurate knowledge related to the disease. Mohamad et al. (2023) further emphasise the urgent need for implementing nationwide educational programs to improve the understanding and early recognition of AD. Despite extensive research efforts, there is still no definitive treatment for AD. Early intervention remains a viable method to improve the diagnosis rate of Alzheimer's disease (Ismail et al., 2021; Alamri & Adejare, 2017; Alkhunizan et al., 2018). Although the progression of Alzheimer's disease cannot be reversed, lifestyle changes and medication can alleviate the progression of cognitive and functional symptoms and maximise quality of life (Cummings et al., 2015). However, existing research may not be representative due to the sample selection limited to urban areas, potentially overlooking socioeconomic and regional variations that affect disease management and access to care.

Advances in biomarker diagnostics

Significant progress has been made in the use of biomarkers for the diagnosis of AD, which allow for the reliable prediction of AD or other neurocognitive disorders in asymptomatic individuals (Kerwin et al., 2022; Noor Eddin et al., 2023). Biomarkers have already been used in identifying mild cognitive impairment (MCI), and emerging blood biomarkers demonstrate promising sensitivity and specificity (Noor Eddin et al., 2023). Frisoni et al. (2017) also demonstrate that while diagnostic challenges vary globally, early diagnosis remains a universal priority. In the Saudi context, enhancing patient education, increasing support services, and improving access to biomarkers are essential for accurate and timely AD diagnosis. This article reviews and systematises the ethical issues regarding Alzheimer's disease prevention discussed in the recent literature.

Gaps in Primary Care Integration and Ethical Considerations

Although studies have explored the impact of blood biomarkers on early Alzheimer's diagnosis, few have evaluated the practical implementation of biomarker-based diagnostics in the primary care setting in Saudi Arabia. Existing research often prioritises theoretical research over long-term clinical validation. As Baloh et al. (2018) and Cammisuli et al. (2022) argue, the shift toward implementing biologically based risk assessment for early detection of Alzheimer's disease has also brought about a series of transformative management challenges. Successful implementation requires adaptive leadership, transitioning from directive to collaborative approaches, and fostering a supportive organisational culture according to organisational needs. Additionally, technological solutions are showing promise in diagnosing early symptoms of Alzheimer's disease, managing patient behaviours, improving memory, and enhancing motor and spatial skills (Noor Eddin et al., 2023).

Figure 2. Literature review process

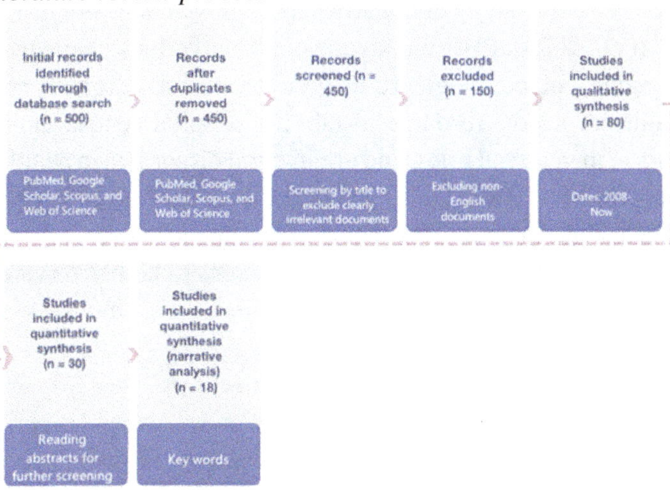

2.1 The imperative for implementing diagnostic blood biomarkers for Alzheimer's detection in KSA

The literature review exhibits significant gaps in public understanding of Alzheimer's disease within the Saudi population, particularly with insufficient knowledge about its prevention and treatment (Mohamad et al., 2023). This knowledge deficit indicates the urgency to enhance the prevention and care of AD nationwide in the KSA, in light of the guiding principles of Vision 2030 (Alasiri & Mohammed, 2022). According to Kotter's (1995, 1996) change model, it is crucial to enhance the incorporation of various biomarkers for diagnosing AD at the early detection stage. These biomarkers enable doctors to identify both active cases and at-risk individuals with greater precision (Blennow & Zetterberg, 2018; Sittrop & Crosthwaite, 2021).

At the primary healthcare level, conflicting demands among different stakeholders normally hinder the adoption of comprehensive AD evaluation. Doctors' time is significantly occupied by other public duties, leaving insufficient time to diagnose Alzheimer's disease (Saeed et al., 2023). Despite plenty of support from associations for AD, the current primary care management of AD remains inadequate. This underscores the urgent need for a comprehensive early detection strategy to slow the progression of AD (Alghamdi et al., 2023).

2.2 Health innovation and reforms

The World Health Organization (WHO) renewed emphasis on primary health care (PHC) as the first strategy of countries to improve the health level of communities (Beigh et al., 2024). PHC worldwide confront various challenges, including demographic aging, epidemiological transition toward non-communicable diseases, evolving healthcare needs, resource instability, hospital-centric approaches, untrained doctors in managerial roles, and urban-rural disparities in healthcare access. Developing countries confront additional constraints, such as poor quality of care, insufficient financial resources, inadequate equipment and training, problems in referral systems, and a tendency to allocate resources to higher service levels.

Comparative analysis exhibits multiple PHC innovation models worldwide:

- United Kingdom: Accountable Care Organizations
- Australia: Primary Health Care Networks
- South Africa: Primary Health Care Reengineering Project
- Canada: Family Health Teams (Azimzadeh et al., 2024)

These initiatives and various projects as well as plans in other countries highlight global awareness of the importance of primary healthcare systems and collective efforts to reform and strengthen them (Azimzadeh et al., 2024). Saudi Arabia's PHC system demonstrates distinct deficiencies in standardised treatment protocols and healthcare pathways, resulting in significant gaps in patient service quality and suboptimal resource allocation (Alasiri & Mohammed, 2022). These systemic weaknesses particularly compromise the AD management.

2.3 Gaps in the existing literature

Since the launch of Saudi Arabia's Vision 2030, the healthcare transformation in the country has indeed made significant strides (Alasiri & Mohammed, 2022). Like many other developing economies, the future of healthcare continues to reconcile universal health coverage with fiscal constraints. The national transformation plan, driven by social and economic factors, has implemented strategic steps, and further progress has been made in primary healthcare (Pedersen & Dunne, 2020). This has facilitated the efficient diagnosis and disease management of Alzheimer's disease. However, persistent challenges remain, containing:

- Biomarker adoption barriers
- Workforce shortages
- Budget constraints
- Management system inefficiencies

The integration of biomarkers in primary healthcare for the diagnosis of AD, shows particular implementation challenges that require careful consideration and preparation. Critical analysis also suggests three critical knowledge gaps in this field of research:

First, while literature consistently emphasises the importance of blood biomarkers for the early diagnosis of Alzheimer's disease (Blennow & Zetterberg, 2018; Frisoni et al., 2017; Kerwin et al., 2022; Noor Eddin et al., 2023), there remains a knowledge gap in understanding their longitudinal efficacy across diverse socioeconomic groups and heterogeneous sample populations. A notable limitation within the extant literature demonstrates significant methodological constraints, characterised by a predominance of qualitative studies and a scarcity of quantitative, data-driven analyses. This evidentiary imbalance potentially compromises the generalisability and persuasiveness of prevailing conclusions.

Second, contradictory findings emerge regarding primary care infrastructure. Al-Sheddi et al. (2023) note that from 2017 until 2021, primary healthcare facilities were distributed fairly in 20 health regions in Saudi Arabia. In contrast, Saeed et al. (2023) argue that some primary healthcare in Saudi Arabia faces the challenge of a shortage of healthcare professionals.

Lastly, there is still a lack of comprehensive research evidence to support the translation of blood biomarkers discoveries into clinical practice. Future research should address these issues.

Figure 3. A systems approach to solve the challenges

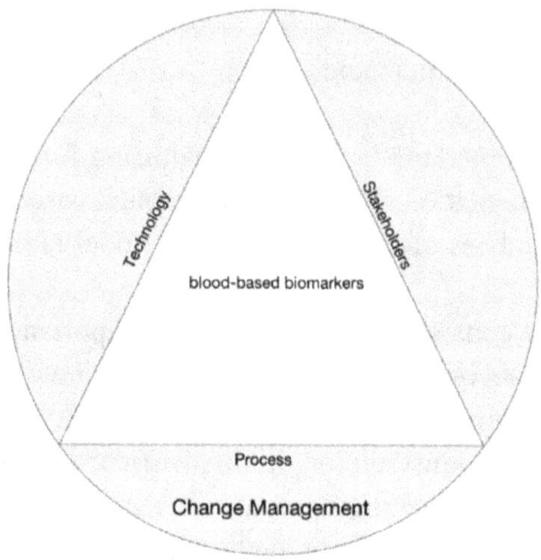

Kotter's (1995, 1996) change model is a framework for organisational change requiring eight sequential steps. However, the actual change process is often non-linear and dynamic, necessitating flexible adjustments and iterative adaptation to adapt to the complicated healthcare environment. While the model emphasises the role of management in driving change, effective transformation often requires more bottom-up support and participation. These assumptions lead to a lack of flexibility in adapting and adjusting strategies (Mugambi & Matula, 2025).

As shown in Figure 3, the integration of blood-based biomarkers for the early diagnosis of Alzheimer's disease within Saudi Arabia's primary healthcare system requires not only adopting the technological innovation, but also fostering stakeholder engagements to optimise change management outcomes (Cameron & Green, 2024). The entire transformation is an incremental process, requiring sustained efforts to mitigate the systemic challenges such as shortages of healthcare professionals, constrained funding, and disparities in healthcare access.

3. METHODOLOGY

We use an exploratory sequential three-phase study below.

1. ***Literature review***: A literature review was conducted during the academic year 2024/2025, and after the field visit to understand the context of the health

system in KSA. Some initial meetings with leaders from KSA were launched to understand the key challenges related to the health innovation system in KSA.

2. ***Fieldwork:*** Both focus groups and semi-structured interviews were held with various stakeholders to gain a holistic understanding of the national health system during our two-week field visit to KSA in January 2024. Several meetings were arranged with key opinion leaders to gather their insights and advice. The key challenge was eventually identified as the creation of a sense of urgency to incorporate biomarkers related to Alzheimer's disease in Saudi Arabia.
3. ***Dissemination of findings and recommendations:*** Six MBA Health students from the Global Business School for Health at the University College London (UCL) in the team of authors conducted a deep investigation, including a literature review and iterative discussions with researchers from UCL and stakeholders in KSA. Key stakeholders were provided with recommendations in a 30-minute presentation in June 2024, and a final report was submitted in July 2024.

3.1 Framework

Kotter's (1995, 1996) eight-step change model is a recognised framework for successfully managing organisational change. This model was built based on the "unfreeze-change-refreeze" framework, namely Schein's (2010) "Lewinian" model (Lewin, 1947). The initial three steps of Kotter's model are the unfreezing stage in the first step of Schein's "Lewinian" model, which is to create the climate for change. Steps four to six are interpreted as the change stage, while steps seven and eight are deemed the refreeze stage to institutionalise new concepts.

The model describes a systematic process for effective and long-lasting organisational changes (Kotter & Cohen, 2002). The simplicity and methodical, organised approach of Kotter's (1995) strategy is one of its main benefits. It is simpler to comprehend and apply than other more complicated frameworks since the eight precisely defined processes offer an easy-to-follow road map for organisations (Kotter & Cohen, 2002). However, one of the main criticisms of Kotter's (1995) approach is the over-simplicity of organisational change's complex and dynamic nature. The reality of change is frequently non-linear, iterative, and unexpected, and the linear, step-by-step method may not adequately capture this (Todnem, 2005). Approximately 70% of implementation failures or difficulties in sustaining a designed change are mainly due to the lack of urgency for the change based on Kotter's (2008) estimation.

4. THEORETICAL FRAMEWORK

The successful integration of innovative technologies into healthcare systems necessitates a comprehensive strategy that addresses the interests of diverse stakeholders and overcomes organisational resistance with healthcare systems. The policy triangle (Walt & Gilson, 1994) and Kingdon's (1995) multiple streams model provide valuable insights into the creation of policies for such initiatives. Complementing these, Kotter's (1995, 2008) eight-stage change model offers a structured approach for accomplishing sustainable organisational transformation.

However, each framework has inherent limitations. The policy triangle (Walt & Gilson, 1994) offers a systematic analysis of policymaking from conception to execution. It provides a relatively static picture, failing to account for the dynamic modifications required in response to input and changing conditions during real-world implementation. Similarly, Kingdon's (1995) approach excels at examining the larger policy environment and pinpointing windows of opportunity for change, but it lacks methods for taking implementation input into account and adjusting policies in response to outcomes. Consequently, neither framework alone offers a comprehensive road map for overcoming the challenges of incorporating new diagnostic tools within a healthcare system.

Given these limitations, an integrated theoretical approach is required to incorporate blood-based biomarkers as a diagnostic aid in primary healthcare clinics. We propose a three-phase structured implementation approach, which synthesises the strengths of the aforementioned models: leveraging Kotter's (2008) organisational transformation model, Kingdon's (1995) emphasis on identification of favourable times for change, and the policy triangle's (Walt & Gilson, 1994) holistic understanding of the entire policy process. The integrative framework provides a more comprehensive, robust and responsive roadmap for overcoming obstacles and enabling the effective integration of blood-based biomarker tools into a complex healthcare system.

4.1 Phase One utilising the Multiple Stream Framework and Step 1 from Kotter's (2008) frameworks

Figure 4. Multiple streams framework by Kingdon (1995) (Zahariadis, 2019)

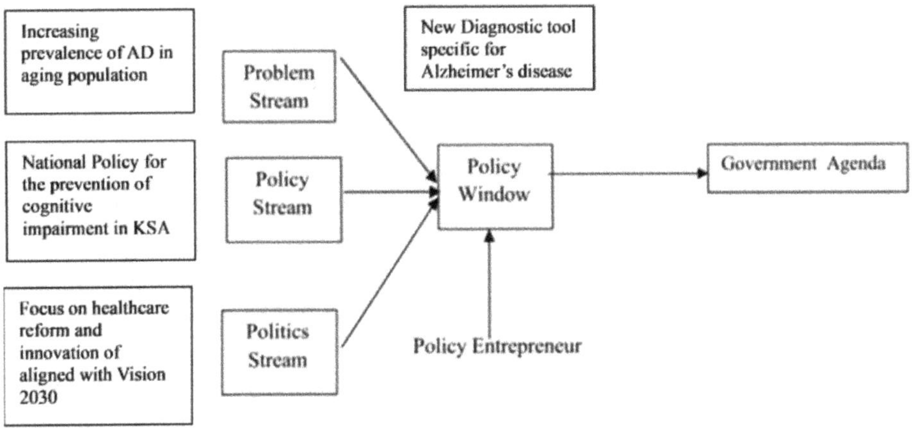

The Kingdon's Multiple Streams Framework: Aligning Policy Opportunity

Kingdon's (1995) multiple streams framework offers a robust analytical lens for examining the political, policy, and problem streams regarding the adoption of innovative diagnostic tools like blood-based biomarkers for Alzheimer's disease in the KSA (Zahariadis, 2019).

- *Problem Stream: Elevating Alzheimer's Disease on the Policy Agenda*

The problem stream encompasses issues competing for policymakers' attention. In the case of AD in KSA, several factors can raise the prevalence of AD on the policy agenda, containing the epidemiological data highlighting the disease's prevalence, compelling media coverage of particular instances, and the existing programmes like the KSA dementia screening programme (Zahariadis, 2019).

- *Policy Stream: Developing viable solutions*

The policy stream concentrates on the creation and refinement of viable solutions by experts such as researchers, clinicians and policy analysts, proposing evidence-based policy choices like incorporating blood-based biomarkers for Alzheimer's diagnosis.

- *Political stream: Healthcare reform and innovation*

Saudi Arabia's demographic shift further reinforces the rationale for examining a new policy approach. An increasing number of programmes such as the Awliwia card for people aged 60 and over and other Ministry of Health (MOH) initiatives, signal political willingness to address age-related diseases (Ministry of Health, 2023). They serve as service cards created especially to help elderly people receive healthcare treatments more quickly. With the ability to provide tailored benefits, enhanced care coordination, and faster enrolment, this programme seeks to make things easier for senior citizens. Concurrently, the escalating incidence of non-communicable diseases (NCDs), such as dementia, presents a pressing public health challenge for KSA (World Health Organisation, 2023).

Social determinant is also another key factor. Shin (2025) reported that marital patterns, cultural customs, and community structures may all influence the senior citizens' living situations and support networks, with social isolation and the requirement for official care, exacerbating the likelihood of undiagnosed dementia. The convergence of an ageing population, NCD disease burden, and social vulnerability generates a compelling case for the adoption of innovative strategies for Alzheimer's diagnosis, such as the exploitation of blood-based biomarkers.

The alignment of the above three streams thus creates a policy window ripe for intervention. The combination of a clearly defined problem (the rising AD prevalence), a feasible solution (blood-based biomarkers), and a supportive political environment (increasing number of programmes). The framework is complemented by Step 1 of Kotter's (1995, 2008) eight-stage change model below, which underscores the importance of creating a sense of urgency.

Step 1 'Creating a sense of urgency'

A critical first step toward transformation is creating a compelling sense of urgency regarding the escalating burden of AD. It is estimated that up to 75% of individuals with dementia worldwide lack formal diagnosis (Prince et al., 2015). Within Saudi Arabia, this urgency is magnified by epidemiological data revealing that only 6.4% of Saudi Arabians are diagnosed with dementia, according to a community-based survey (Alkhunizan et al., 2018). Moreover, the AD cases often double every five years in people over the age of 65. A cross-sectional study conducted in Saudi Arabia found around 130,000 cases, a figure projected to surge to 1.4 million by 2060 (Qassem et al., 2023; Saudi Ministry of Health, 2023). AD accounts for more than two-thirds of instances of progressive cognitive deterioration in the elderly population (Alorfi, 2022). Besides, KSA reports the highest average annual cost of dementia care among surveyed countries, reaching roughly $5 billion (Qassem et al., 2023).

Despite this burden, funding programmes specifically focused on AD are severely restricted. This obstacle is associated with a critical research deficit in the Saudi context. A fundamental gap exists because 'omics' studies and biomarker development have historically focused on populations of European descent (Gyawali et al., 2023), leaving a void of validated, local diagnostic tools. This is a pressing issue, as unique genetic variants in genes like PSEN1 and SORL1 have already been identified in Saudi population, demonstrating the insufficiency of international criteria (Dehghani et al., 2021). The current screening tools are mostly depend on cognitive evaluations, rather than fully validated data on the Saudi population. Consequently, the reliance on unvalidated cognitive screens, combined with an absence of comprehensive epidemiological data and the exclusion of the large expatriate demographic from studies, creates a fundamental knowledge gap (El-Metwally et al., 2019; Tayeb et al., 2023; Beigh et al., 2024). Such data limitation severely hinders the creation of focused treatment programmes and efficient public health initiatives to manage AD (Tayeb et al., 2023).

In addition, cultural factors necessitate the incorporation of diagnostic and treatment modalities be modified to ensure maximum efficacy in the KSA setting. The ongoing public awareness initiatives are also required to promote early intervention and assistance for afflicted persons and their families due to the ongoing stigma associated with dementia. Research indicates that the Saudi population has relatively little awareness of AD, with the majority of right answers on various subdomains falling between 10% and 30% (El-Gamal et al., 2023).

Nevertheless, promising opportunities exist to address these issues. The present infrastructure for dementia care in Saudi Arabia is still fragmented (Tayeb et al., 2023), despite the encouraging increase in qualified healthcare staff, especially geriatricians. Dedicated memory clinics often have access to comprehensive resources and standardised processes, whereas general clinics tend not to. The frequency of AD patients seeking care in general clinics highlights a systemic gap. However, this situation presents an opportunity to foster collaboration among government agencies, healthcare providers, and academic institutions. Through collaboration and knowledge sharing, stakeholders can leverage technological and data analytic innovations to enhance patient outcomes and optimise resource distribution within the healthcare system.

Policy innovation through biomarker integration

Policy innovation through biomarker integration exhibits a synergistic alignment with Saudi Arabia's national plan. The Kingdom's growing government will to address public health challenges such as AD (Program HST, 2021), parallels the global momentum toward dementia risk reduction, evidenced by the fact that 51% of countries have already established their national plans (Prince et al., 2015; Alzheimer's Disease International, 2023). This political commitment is operationalised through the existing foundational initiatives such as the Saudi Genome Program, which provides a pre-existing policy stream for biomarker innovation. The program encompasses the establishment of a genomic data repository, the widespread adoption of genomics, and the advancement of research in "omics" and precision medicine (Alharbi et al., 2025), which perfectly supports the validation of culturally relevant blood-based biomarkers. Unlike reliance on conventional cognitive tests, blood-based biomarkers, such as microRNA-519a-3p (miR-519a-3p), provides an opportunity to achieve an early and non-invasive diagnosis. The transition toward a less intrusive and potentially more accessible approach of early AD diagnosis (Jácome et al., 2024), directly supports the Vision 2030 central objective by promoting prevention, wellness, and the integration of cutting-edge technology within the Kingdom's healthcare system.

The proposed framework for treating AD exemplifies innovative healthcare. A key strategy involves the integration of culturally appropriate biomarker testing into primary healthcare facilities, directly addressing the national policy's emphasis on early detection. Blood-based biomarkers provide a more objective and timely diagnosis of AD, compared to conventional cognitive tests. Streamlining guidelines and reimbursement mechanisms for biomarker testing will empower general practitioners, especially in rural regions, to make precise diagnoses and initiate early intervention programmes. This aligns with the government's objective of increasing access to care, especially in underprivileged areas, while simultaneously improves patient outcomes.

Assessing the success of such inventions necessitates a complex approach. One crucial statistic in this system will be early detection rates for AD, which will entail monitoring the proportion of AD patients identified *via* biomarker testing instead of conventional techniques.

4.2 Phase Two utilising the Policy Triangle Framework and Step 2 from Kotter's Change Management Model

Figure 5. Policy Triangle (O'Brien et al., 2020)

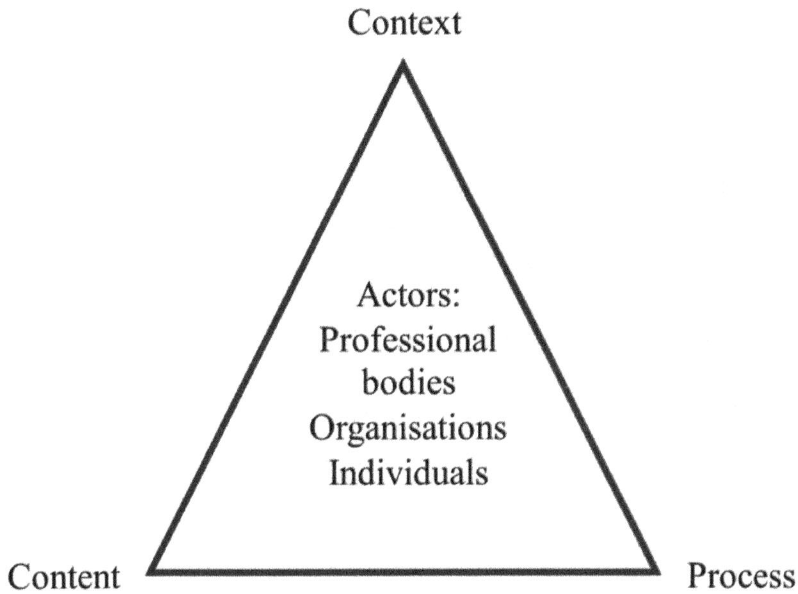

The policy triangle developed by Walt and Gilson (1994), provides a structured lens for examining health policies and the policy-making procedure, which is beneficial for grasping the 'who' and 'why' of policy changes (O'Brien et al., 2020). This framework is particularly valuable for analysing the possible access problems for patients, the financial impact on healthcare systems, and stakeholder dynamics in supporting or opposing the use of blood-based biomarkers for Alzheimer's disease diagnosis.

The framework's emphasis on stakeholder analysis directly aligns with Kotter's (1995) second step in change management: 'guiding coalition'. This phase identifies and consolidates important players in the Saudi healthcare system who will be paramount in shaping the successful implementation of blood-based biomarker.

Step 2 'The Guiding Coalition'

Ministry of Health (MOH)

The MOH is a crucial actor in the creation and execution of national health policies, particularly those for Alzheimer's disease. The MOH is responsible for distributing funds, establishing care quality standards, and managing public awareness initiatives. In November 2023, the MOH launched a new protocol for the Prevention of Cognitive Impairment, which aligns with the guidelines of the World Health Organization, by recommending that asymptomatic and healthy older individuals do not undergo early cognitive impairment screening; individuals who report possible symptoms are assessed through several tools, such as the MMSE and MoCA, as well as Arabic translations of instruments, such as the SNPI and BADL. However, challenges faced with this protocol include a lack of comprehensive, verified instruments designed especially for Saudi people, which calls for a more objective policy content of blood-based biomarkers to create a precise approach to address this gap (Ministry of Health, 2023). The WHO further reinforces this direction by recommending the guidelines in their management protocol of managing modifiable risk factors as a part of their public health strategy to postpone or reduce dementia or cognitive decline (WHO, 2019).

Saudi Alzheimer's Disease Association (SADA)

Founded in 2009 by families impacted by AD, the SADA is dedicated to addressing the cultural context and empowering communities through research, care initiatives, advocacy, and awareness-raising. Its objectives include public education, patient support, carer assistance, working with research and healthcare organisations, and building a patient database to guide future efforts. SADA operates with principles of transparency, cooperation, and a dedication to enhancing the quality of life for AD patients.

Academic institutions

Several Saudi Arabian universities, including King Saud University and Majmaah University, have conducted research to gauge the comprehensive knowledge of AD, among the public and healthcare students. These investigations underscore significant knowledge gaps, highlighting the need for public education programmes (Al Arifi, 2020; Alnaim, 2025; Alzahrani, 2025). These institutions play a key role in workforce development, generating knowledge and disseminating it.

King Abdullah International Medical Research Centre (KAIMRC)

KAIMRC was founded to bridge the infrastructure gap between research and practical healthcare solutions. It has state-of-the-art facilities and a strong emphasis on translational research. Even though not AD-specific, their extensive experience and robust infrastructure make it a strategic position to support AD research and development, especially in translating research outcomes into workable solutions for the KSA healthcare system.

Healthcare providers and infrastructure

Regarding the clinical delivery, the involvement of primary, secondary, and tertiary healthcare providers is also highly important. Notably, Prince Mohammad bin Abdulaziz Hospital in the second cluster has been recognised as the first elderly-friendly hospital with targeted ages of 65 years and older. According to our briefing with Dr Walid Alkeridy (General Director of the General Directorate for Home Health Care in the Ministry of Health, KSA since 2021), the establishment of the first geriatric hospital in Diriyah has been confirmed, demonstrating an evolving infrastructure context.

Workforce development

The elder care infrastructure in Saudi Arabia is undergoing substantial enhancement, especially regarding access to qualified medical personnel. By 2019, the number of registered geriatricians increased to over 20. This significant skilled workforce growth is largely attributed to initiatives such as Middle-East Academy for Medicine of Ageing (MEAMA) workshops and scholarships for medical professionals with international training (Basheikh et al., 2021).

4.3 Phase three utilising Step 5 from Kotter's eight-stage framework

Figure 6. Adapted from Kotter's (1995) eight-step change model

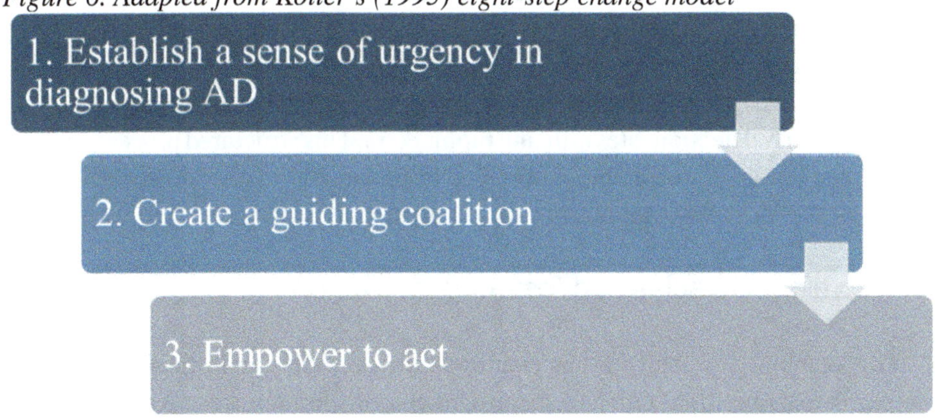

Kotter's (1995, 2008) eight-step change model is a recognised framework for successfully managing organisational change, outlining a systematic process for effective and long-lasting organisational changes (Kotter & Cohen, 2002). Although multiple frameworks exist, such as the nudge theory and the Appreciative Inquiry framework, Kotter's (1995) model has been widely adopted and successful in different contexts, such as primary care and even healthcare practices' digital transformation (Chu, 2025). Its eight precisely defined processes offer an easy-to-follow road map for organisations, making it comparatively simpler to comprehend and implement than other more complicated frameworks (Kotter & Cohen, 2002). However, one of the main criticisms of Kotter's (1995) approach is the oversimplicity of the inherently complex and dynamic nature of organisational change, which is often non-linear, iterative, and unexpectable (Todnem, 2005). Despite this limitation, the final phase of this proposed step provides a crucial mechanism to incorporate blood-based biomarkers into the primary healthcare system in the KSA.

Step 5 'Empowering to act'

Effective health innovation necessitates a multi-stage process. This begins with the MOH revising the national AD strategy in the policy-making process. This revision should prioritise incorporating culturally suitable biomarkers and simplify the testing procedures for general practitioners (GPs) to improve accessibility. The subsequent step is resource allocation, wherein financial funds are allocated for the biomarkers and the establishment of infrastructure for their implementation in primary healthcare institutions.

Collaborations among MOH, KAIMRC, and various healthcare providers are crucial for developing research, validation, and, eventually the wide adoption of biomarker testing. The implementation stage in primary healthcare institutions entails incorporating these culturally appropriate biomarker tests into the conventional AD diagnosis process. The process comes with a rigorous monitoring and evaluation, where the efficacy of this health innovation is determined by tracking patient outcomes and early detection rates utilising biomarkers. This structured process enables the methodical assessment and continuous improvement of the effectiveness and impact of the innovative approaches to AD treatment in KSA.

Overcoming obstacles and fostering innovation

This combined framework has examined the obstacles and prospects for promoting innovation in AD management. Drawing inspiration from Kotter's (1995, 2008) eight-step change model, it has underscored the necessity of a comprehensive strategy that emphasised stakeholder empowerment, coalition building, and urgency creation. However, translating this framework into an effective strategy calls for the specific policy changes. While the Saudi National Policy for the Prevention of Cognitive Impairment, already in effect as of November 2023, provides a foundational framework, significant adjustments are still required. Dedicated research and development funds are needed to support the integration of blood-based biomarkers with innovative cognitive tests. As highlighted by Tayeb *et al.* (2023), a significant governmental obstacle that must be removed is the lack of financing for AD research in the KSA.

Furthermore, managing policy change inherently involves anticipating and mitigating policy change obstacles. Current regulatory authorities may oppose streamlining rules to approve new diagnostic equipment. Budgetary restrictions and possible cost-benefit assessments may also present challenges in developing reimbursement schemes for biomarker testing.

Even amid legislative obstacles, the potential advantages of a well-structured strategy guided by Kotter's model (1995, 2008) are evident. By modifying existing legislation, strengthening patient advocacy, and navigating beyond legislative roadblocks, Saudi Arabia can create a more adaptive atmosphere for implementing cutting-edge solutions like blood-based biomarkers. Ultimately, these reforms will significantly improve AD management and early identification, benefiting patients well-being within the KSA healthcare system.

5. FINDINGS

This section presents the key findings of this study, delving into the pressing need to implement blood biomarkers for AD detection in the KSA. It is structured to answer the research question by exploring three pivotal aspects of Kotter's (1995, 1996) eight steps:

1. **Urgency:** The initial finding highlights the escalating prevalence of AD within the KSA's ageing population and the associated socioeconomic burden (Qassem et al., 2023; Saudi Ministry of Health, 2023). This urgency is intensified by a unique scientific rationale, demonstrating the population-specific genetic variants (e.g., in *PSEN1, SORL1, ABCA7*) restrain the effectiveness of establishing a global standard (Dehghani et al., 2021). The heavy reliance on cognitive tests unvalidated for the Saudi demographic further widens the gap, underscoring the transformative potential of blood biomarkers to revolutionise early detection with a culturally and biologically relevant diagnostic tool (El-Metwally et al., 2019; Tayeb et al., 2023; Beigh et al., 2024). This aligns with Kotter's (1995) change model, emphasising the need to create a sense of urgency to drive change. The transformation exhibits immense benefits on the healthcare system, offering a more efficient and practical approach to AD detection and intervention (Carman et al., 2019).

2. **Guiding Coalition:** Key stakeholders were identified and analysed to form the guiding coalition for implementing this change. This coalition is a government-led innovation agenda, and it encompasses a diverse array of stakeholders, including policymakers, researchers, healthcare professionals, and patient advocacy groups. The Saudi government's rising interest in AD is evidenced by some concrete initiatives, most notably the Saudi Genome Program (Alharbi et al. 2025; Program HST, 2021). With its strategic mandate to establish a genomic data repository and advance precision medicine, this program provides a ready-made policy framework and technological infrastructure for biomarker development. An analysis of the Saudi government's evolving healthcare policies reveals their demonstrable commitment to address the challenges posed by AD, indicating their potential role in championing the wide adoption of blood biomarkers (Tayeb et al., 2023).
3. **Empowering to Act:** The final finding demonstrates the viable strategies to empower these stakeholders. This involves benchmarking against successful international experiences to learn from best practices and tailor implementation to the unique context of KSA. In addition, the importance of raising public awareness, addressing potential barriers, and fostering collaboration between different sectors to successfully integrate blood biomarkers into the healthcare system are discussed in detail (Alessy et al., 2022).

This section systematically addresses these three concepts, providing a comprehensive understanding of why implementing diagnostic blood biomarkers for AD detection in KSA is not only urgent but also feasible and impactful. It lays the groundwork for subsequent sections on specific strategies, action plans, and potential outcomes of this transformative initiative.

5.1 Saudi prioritises elderly healthcare.

The Saudi Arabian government has demonstrated a growing commitment to addressing the healthcare needs of its ageing population, particularly concerning Alzheimer's disease (AD). While initial policies focused on expanding general healthcare infrastructure, a notable shift has occurred towards targeted strategies for early AD detection, diagnosis, and management. This strategic shift is evidenced by the launch of the Saudi Genome Program, as well as vast amounts of investments in AD biomarker research, integration of AD screening into primary care settings, and public awareness campaigns about AD and its risk factors (Alorfi, 2022).

Despite these governmental efforts, public awareness of AD in Saudi Arabia remains a concern, with significant knowledge gaps identified among the general population and healthcare professionals (Khalil et al., 2020). These gaps contribute to decreased family knowledge, inadequate support for AD patients, and increased caregiver burden. The Saudi Alzheimer's Disease Association reports that AD accounts for 50-80% of dementia cases in the country, with prevalence estimates ranging from 1.1-2.3% in individuals aged 50 and older, increasing to 13.5-18.5% in those aged 80 and above (Alhumaidi et al., 2020).

While the exact risk factors for AD in Saudi Arabia are not entirely determined, studies have identified potential contributors, including chronic conditions such as diabetes and hypertension, the absence of comprehensive epidemiological data and the exclusion of the large expatriate demographic (El-Metwally et al., 2019; Tayeb et al., 2023; Beigh et al., 2024). Despite increased attention from officials, the prevalence of AD continues to rise, with estimates suggesting over 130,000 patients in the Kingdom. A significant proportion of these patients receive inadequate care due to a lack of specialised facilities and professionals (Al-Harbi et al., 2016). Consequently, the ongoing healthcare policy reforms in Saudi Arabia, aimed at mitigating the growing AD burden, are crucial for improving the quality of life for older people and alleviating the strain on caregivers and the healthcare system.

5.2 Government drives AD innovation

Saudi government policies have been pivotal in providing a top-down drive to drive innovation within the healthcare sector, particularly in advancing Alzheimer's disease (AD) diagnostics (Qiu et al., 2022). Government initiative like the Saudi Genome Program outlines a pre-existing and aligned policy framework for the development of culturally relevant biomarkers by promoting genomic and "omics" research (Alharbi et al. 2025). By prioritising research and development funding, the government has stimulated the creation of groundbreaking diagnostic tools like blood biomarkers, poised to revolutionise the early detection and management of AD (Borson et al., 2025; Rosenblatt et al., 2016).

The government's commitment to enhancing elderly healthcare has facilitated the widespread adoption of telemedicine and digital health solutions, improving access to care and enabling early diagnosis and remote monitoring of AD patients, particularly in remote areas (Abernethy et al., 2022). The effectiveness of these policies in fostering innovation is influenced by several factors, including funding levels, regulatory frameworks, and collaboration between government, research institutions, and healthcare providers (Bergsland et al., 2014; Borson et al., 2025; Qiu et al., 2022).

Recent research has highlighted advancements in cerebrospinal fluid (CSF) biomarkers and imaging modalities like amyloid and tau Positron Emission Tomography (PET), which hold promise for early AD identification (Qiu et al., 2022). However, many of these tools are still confined to research settings, with traditional clinical assessment and neuropsychological evaluation remaining the mainstay of antemortem diagnosis. The Saudi government's focus on expanding healthcare infrastructure has also been instrumental in adopting telemedicine and digital health solutions, proving especially beneficial for reaching underserved populations and enabling early diagnosis and remote monitoring of AD patients (Olivari et al., 2020).

In summary, the Saudi government policies have demonstrably catalysed health innovation, particularly in the realm of AD diagnostics. The prioritisation of research and development funding and supportive measures for adopting novel technologies and expanding healthcare infrastructure collectively empowers governments to expedite progress in combatting this devastating neurodegenerative disease (Lehtisalo et al., 2021).

5.3 Blood biomarkers revolutionise Alzheimer's care

The growing prevalence of AD poses a significant public health challenge, with the ageing population projected to amplify the associated morbidity and mortality burdens (Qiu et al., 2022). Blood biomarkers emerged as transformative components of broader healthcare reforms can address this issue on both technical and strategic levels (Hansson, 2021; Olivari et al., 2020). Technically, the discovery of unique genetic variants (e.g., in *PSEN1* and *SORL1*) within the Saudi population indicates that international diagnostic criteria are insufficient (Dehghani et al., 2021). This technology enables a transformation from the current unvalidated cognitive evaluation to an objective, personalised early diagnostics within the Saudi local context, optimised resource allocation and substantial cost savings by delaying the onset of severe AD symptoms and reducing the need for expensive long-term care. Strategically, this revolutionised innovation aligns seamlessly with the national strategic vision to become a regional leader in biotechnology and genomics (Kharbanda, 2024). However, implementing healthcare reforms for complex conditions like AD still faces obstacles, including inherent resistance to change within existing systems, limited resources, and social/cultural barriers to early diagnosis and treatment (Dhana et al., 2020; Qiu et al., 2022; Vinze et al., 2023).

6. DISCUSSION

According to findings from the literature review and the field observations, all pertinent to leveraging technology and biomarkers to diagnose early stage Alzheimer's disease in KSA. Four crucial topics should be discussed further: the lack of policy guidelines for AD, the lack of public awareness of AD in KSA, the implementation of biomarkers at primary care centres in KSA, and data collection and population diversity. Additionally, the methodology implemented in the research will be evaluated briefly.

6.1 Lack of comprehensive policy guidelines for Alzheimer's Disease

Saudi Arabian Ministry of Health guidelines on Alzheimer's disease are aligned with WHO's (2017) preventive strategy; however, national implementation remains incomplete (Alasiri & Mohammed, 2022). The current protocol can be denoted as extremely narrow, mainly citing risk factors of dementia for the disease, without providing precise guideline to follow by related healthcare facilities once a patient is diagnosed with AD (Ministry of Health, 2023).

Enhanced policy implementation by early detection of AD-related biomarkers for early prevention of Alzheimer's, can pave the way for innovative approaches to early AD diagnosis. MicroRNA has been proven to be one of the most important biomarkers in this innovative approach (Noor Eddin et al., 2023). The Saudi population over 60 is expected to be 10 million by 2050 (Abusaaq, 2015), so early detection exerts huge healthcare benefits and cost savings.

The absence of comprehensive epidemiological data is both a cause and a consequence of the comprehensive policy void extends even to the 2030 Vision of KSA. Even though many stunning projects are announced within this project, a comprehensive approach for AD is still absent (Alharbi, 2025). While the KSA has announced plenty of projects that could be denoted as lavish by some Western countries, such as NEOM or Genome Project, a more economical public health initiative could involve biomarker for AD.

Kotter's (1995) eight-step change management model could be used to obtain a more comprehensive guideline and implement biomarkers in the early detection of Alzheimer's disease. With the support of key opinion leaders (KOLs), a sense of urgency could be created. They will also be part of the guiding coalition to implement such a transformative approach to AD. The strategic vision of this project should be tied up to the ageing population of KSA, how crucial the threat of Alzheimer's disease is, and how it could be mitigated or controlled with the preventive approach. Through the application of Kotter's (1995) model, this transition could be achieved successfully.

6.2 Lack of public awareness of Alzheimer's Disease

The challenges extend beyond protocol, budget, or policymakers to raise the awareness of AD (Hakami et al., *2023*). Research demonstrates that only 29% of respondents attending that survey answered accurately the question about Alzheimer's. To overcome this issue, KSA should consider implementing public campaigns to increase awareness about Alzheimer's. Drawing from Policy-making framework (O'Brien et al., 2020), the engagement of organisations and individuals is vital for the effective policy-making process. To make this process succeed, a strong public opinion, accomplished by a high awareness of the related topic, is essential to exert pressure on policymakers. That public health communication could be spearheaded by key opinion leaders who are leading the public campaigns (Barreto et al., 2024).

6.3 Implementation of biomarkers at primary care centres in KSA

Although the KSA exhibits significant gaps in policy and public awareness to address AD, biomarkers and care demonstrates an excellent combination for obtaining more innovative approaches to diagnosing AD. This healthcare transformation in light of the 2030 Vision seeks to transition from a curative approach to a preventive strategy in policymakers, healthcare providers, and the Saudi population. As in countries with universal health coverage such as UK, primary care is the central gatekeeper for health services access. However, even in these Western countries, the obstacles persist in AD diagnosis with approximately 50% of those have not received the personalised care they need (Frisoni et al., 2017).

The meeting in May 2022 of the EU and US Clinical Trials on Alzheimer's Disease (CTAD) task forces (Angioni et al., 2022), demonstrates positive outcomes regarding the utilisation of blood biomarkers in AD diagnosis. Unlike Positron Emission Tomography (PET) or Cerebrospinal fluid (CSF) biomarkers, which are more costly, invasive and less accessible, the blood-based biomarkers show a 65% predictable accuracy confirmed by PET. Although PET remains crucial in the diagnosis of AD at that stage, it might be outdated as clinical research keeps producing compelling results. Primary care is the paramount stage in the diagnosis of AD, which is underscored by the up to 50% misdiagnosis rate (Angioni et al., 2022).

Implementing appropriate blood-based biomarkers in primary care centres can yield substantial cost savings, for instance, an estimation of $400-700 million annual savings from the US health system. Additionally, waiting time for specialists and the requirement for more specialists in this field will decrease significantly. Although some initial clinical trials have started to represent promising results, there are still continuous needs for more clinical trials analysing these blood samples for longer periods with a wider sample pool. Potential barriers include population diversity or various levels of expertise among the related physician in such an innovative approach. KSA could pioneer this field by implementing blood-based biomarkers in clinical trials across its population and introducing guidelines for translating these results by physicians in both private or public primary care centres. A proposed timeline of one year for these clinical trials, could generate robust results for the subsequent publication of national guidelines. Given the anticipated growth of private sectors in healthcare in Saudi (Rahman, 2020), more private primary care centres are expected throughout KSA. By implementing comprehensive protocols across all primary care centres, stipulating the entire patient journey for primary, secondary, and tertiary within the light of specific biomarkers, a definite success will be achieved.

6.4 Data collection and population diversity

Personal Data Protection Law is another milestone for Saudi Arabia, initially introduced in 2021 and subsequently modified in 2023, presenting another hurdle in implementing biomarkers in primary care centres. Unlike previous practices before 2021, mandates individual consent for personal data collection in the KSA. Even though anonymised data collection is considered as a safe and standard process to use personal data, people could occasionally hesitate to share their personal data, resulting in possible obstacles to creating a data pool for further identification of biomarkers for early AD diagnosis. However, if people are well informed about the benefits and protections of their personal data, and if appropriate incentives are provided, they tend to share their anonymised blood results with the official database (Thaler & Sunstein, 2021).

According to a General Authority for Statistics (2024), around 44% of the total population living in Saudi is non-Saudi residents. Hosting such many non-Saudi residents could be pioneering another potential for the use of biomarkers for the preventive approach to AD. This rich population diversity could enable the exploration of new biomarkers for different demographic groups of people. Conversely, the relatively modest national population with roughly 30 million may restrict the statistical power of some relevant studies.

Undoubtedly, an integrated healthcare system, as exemplified by the success of Singapore will enhance the healthcare service (De Foo et al., 2023). Public perception also plays a crucial role in the adoption of digital health innovation. According to a survey conducted by McKinsey and Company (2022), 66% of the Saudi population is interested in teleconsultation, which could be utilised for post-diagnosis patient management, following biomarker evaluation (AlBasri et al, 2022). The cognitive treatment, when possible, could be provided online through relevant physician, resulting in the enhanced overall healthcare efficiency.

6.5 Comments on Methodology

Kotter's (1995) eight-step change management has been implemented by establishing a sense of urgency, communicating the change vision, consolidating gains, and producing more change respectively. The sense of urgency is identified as the weakest point of Saudi Arabia in terms of Alzheimer's disease, due to a significant lack of awareness. Consequently, the creation of a sense of urgency is the most important for the innovative transition for the biomarkers to be used in the diagnosis of AD.

A potential drawback of this methodology is that the crucial details regarding developing the strategy and vision could be overlooked. In comparing Lewin's (1947) and Kotter's (1995) change management models, Kotter's (1995) model could be more appropriate for this case, due to its greater detail (Cameron & Green, 2024). Regarding the complexity of the healthcare domain, there is a need for a more comprehensive approach, especially when there are substantial systemic changes. Within the exploratory sequential three-phase study, conducting a pre-field trip literature review was proved beneficial in navigating the subsequent field investigation.

7. CONCLUSION

The global landscape is witnessing an escalating prevalence of people diagnosed with AD resulting from the increased life expectancy. The efficacy of early detection of AD within different health systems varies significantly, influenced by diverse factors, such as healthcare infrastructure, economic status of the country and the demographic proportion of its aging population (Frisoni et al., 2017). Historically, European countries have been seen as the lead in creating early detection strategy, attributed to their increasingly aging societies. However, most diagnostic tools for AD require particular infrastructure or specialised talents, which significantly impedes their scalability (Kerwin et al., 2022).

Saudi Arabia is projected to experience an expected increase in the elderly population will reach up to 25% by 2050, exerting a huge pressure to the health system (United Nations, 2012). This demographic shift implies a higher incidence of AD, highlighting the urgent need for early diagnosis to improve patient outcomes. To facilitate the early diagnosis, blood-based biomarkers are considered as a promising solution, due to ease of use, minimal training requirements, and applicability in rural primary health centres nationwide. The equitable distribution of the primary health centres is an enabler for the successful implementation of this innovation (Al-Sheddi et al., 2023).

Different theoretical frameworks, such as the policy triangle (Walt & Gilson, 1994), Kingdon's (1995) multiple streams model, and Kotter's (1995) eight-stage change model, were employed here to develop a strategy for accomplishing long-term transformation of the innovation with the aim of early diagnosis using blood biomarkers. While no solitary framework offers a comprehensive road map for implementation, a multifaceted and integrated strategy is indispensable to guarantee a sustainable and system-level transformation of such innovation.

The recent policy shift in the Saudi Arabian governmental focus from infrastructural development to public health strategies and awareness campaigns for AD, indicates a growing governmental commitment to adopt innovation (Alorfi, 2022). The establishment of the research, development, and innovation authority signalled a top-down endorsement of innovation (Ministry of Education, 2021). This institutional orientation coupled with the demographic urgency generates a conducive environment for implementing innovative solutions such as blood biomarkers.

The implementation of diagnostic tools normally comes with challenges and requirements for change. Foremost among these is creating and implementing a comprehensive policy for managing AD. While the first policy for dementia was published in November 2023, it called for expansion to AD specifically and articulated a clear implementation pathway in the national scope (Ministry of Health, 2023). Government efforts in spreading awareness are notable, yet cross-sector collaboration, such as private and non-governmental organisations, is crucial to enhance public awareness and understanding of AD. Additionally, legislative reforms in the health sector, such as the Personal Data Protection Law, provides ethical standards for data handling (Saudi Ministry of Health, 2017). Once coupled with robust public awareness, these reforms significantly bolster the public acceptance and promote the final adoption of these innovations.

8. RECOMMENDATIONS

Based on the above findings and discussions, the following key recommendations are proposed.

Public awareness enhancement

First, we note that successful implementation of new diagnostic approaches relies on public awareness and understanding. Given the current low perception of AD in the KSA, targeted awareness campaigns with the involvement of various stakeholders, should be launched to underscore the importance of early AD detection. (Hakami et al., 2023).

Comprehensive national policy for Alzheimer's disease

Second, the Saudi government published its first policy for dementia, which is considered the first step towards acknowledging the need for a policy on AD (Saudi Ministry of Health, 2017). A comprehensive policy specifically for AD is required to ensure a standardised process and an equitable distribution of resources nationwide.

Piloting implementation initiatives

Third, prior to national rollout, it is advisable to conduct pilot initiatives of blood biomarker testing in selected regions to evaluate its feasibility and effectiveness. Iterative feedback from these trials is essential for ensuring scalability and long-term success prior to broader adoption (Baloh et al., 2018).

Finally, we highlight the need for supporting research collaborations in the AD field, KSA, GCC region, and globally through mechanism such as the Alzheimer's Association International Conference (AAIC) which is the largest international meeting dedicated to advancing dementia science.

REFERENCES

Abernethy, A., Adams, L., Barrett, M., Bechtel, C., Brennan, P., Butte, A., Faulkner, J., Fontaine, E., Friedhoff, S., Halamka, J., Howell, M., Johnson, K., Long, P., McGraw, D., Miller, R., Lee, P., Perlin, J., Rucker, D., Sandy, L., & Valdes, K. (2022). The promise of digital health: Then, now, and the future. *NAM Perspectives*, *2022*(22), 10–31478. DOI: 10.31478/202206e PMID: 36177208

Abusaaq, H. I. (2015). Population aging in Saudi Arabia. *Economic Research Department, Saudi Arabian Monetary Agency*. https://www.sama.gov.sa/en-US/EconomicResearch/WorkingPapers/population%20aging%20in%20saudi%20arabia.pdf

Al Arifi, M. N. (2020). Evaluation of knowledge of Alzheimer disease among health university students in Riyadh, Saudi Arabia. *Saudi Pharmaceutical Journal : SPJ : The Official Publication of the Saudi Pharmaceutical Society*, *28*(8), 911–915. DOI: 10.1016/j.jsps.2020.06.011 PMID: 32792835

Al-Harbi, I., Al-Hujilan, A., Al-Akeel, H., Alyousif, L., Al-Shetwi, M., Al-Nasser, M., & Al-Habeeb, L. (2016). Risk assessment of Alzheimer disease among attendants of general hospital in Al-Qassim. *International Journal of Advanced Research*, *4*(11), 1843–1862. DOI: 10.21474/IJAR01/2284

Al-Sheddi, A., Kamel, S., Almeshal, A. S., & Assiri, A. M. (2023). Distribution of primary healthcare centers between 2017 and 2021 across Saudi Arabia. *Cureus*, *15*(7). Advance online publication. DOI: 10.7759/cureus.41932 PMID: 37583734

Alamri, M., & Adejare, A. (2017). National plan and resources to address Alzheimer's Disease. In *Drug Discovery Approaches for the Treatment of Neurodegenerative Disorders* (pp. 27–48). Academic Press., DOI: 10.1016/B978-0-12-802810-0.00003-9

Alasiri, A. A., & Mohammed, V. (2022). Healthcare transformation in Saudi Arabia: An overview since the launch of Vision 2030. *Health Services Insights*, *15*, 11786329221121214. DOI: 10.1177/11786329221121214 PMID: 36081830

Albasri, M., Elwan, H., Georgiev, P., & Ustun, A. (2022). *Growth opportunities for digital health in KSA and UAE*. https://www.mckinsey.com/industries/public-sector/our-insights/growth-opportunities-for-digital-health-in-ksa-and-uae

Alessy, S. A., Alattas, M., Mahmoud, M. A., Alqarni, A., & Alghnam, S. (2022). Population health data in KSA: Status, challenges, and opportunities. *Journal of Taibah University Medical Sciences*, *17*(4), 272–278. DOI: 10.1016/j.jtumed.2022.06.011 PMID: 36212580

Alghamdi, A., Ramsay, A. I. G., Abrams, R., & Bailey, J. V. (2023). The impact of COVID-19 on patient engagement with primary healthcare: Lessons from the Saudi primary care setting. *BMC Primary Care*, *24*(1), 177. DOI: 10.1186/s12875-023-02131-4 PMID: 37674122

Alharbi, A. A., Alatwi, H. E., Albulaihe, H., & Algarzae, N. K. (2025). Alzheimer's disease in the Kingdom of Saudi Arabia: Current perspectives and genetic insights. *Journal of Alzheimer's Disease*, *104*(2), 306–311. DOI: 10.1177/13872877251316122 PMID: 39994993

Alhumaidi, F. S., Siddiqui, M. I., Altowairqi, A. F., Alshawkani, H. H., Babkour, B. O., & Alaugla, F. K. (2020). Public knowledge about Alzheimer disease in Mecca Region, Kingdom of Saudi Arabia: A cross-sectional study. *The Egyptian Journal of Neurology, Psychiatry and Neurosurgery*, *56*(1), 1–11. DOI: 10.1186/s41983-020-00220-0

Alkhunizan, M., Alkhenizan, A., & Basudan, L. (2018). Prevalence of mild cognitive impairment and dementia in Saudi Arabia: A community-based study. *Dementia and Geriatric Cognitive Disorders. Extra*, *8*(1), 98–103. DOI: 10.1159/000487231 PMID: 29706986

Alnaim, M., Alshanabah, W., Alamer, L., Alduraywish, W., Alkhitrish, M., Alshuaibi, W., Almulla, S., Almulhim, L., Alsagoor, H., & Alokley, A. (2025). Assessing Public Awareness of Neuropsychiatric and Cognitive Symptoms of Alzheimer's Disease in the Eastern Region of Saudi Arabia: A Cross-sectional Study. *Annals of African Medicine*, *24*(2), 255–262. DOI: 10.4103/aam.aam_163_24 PMID: 40019132

Alorfi, N. M. (2022). Public awareness of Alzheimer's disease: A cross-sectional study from Saudi Arabia. *International Journal of General Medicine*, *15*, 7535–7546. DOI: 10.2147/IJGM.S373447 PMID: 36199585

Alzahrani, Y. A., Harbi, M. H., Almalki, A. G., Althomali, R. A., Alorabi, R. F., Basulyman, B. S., Alansari, K. A., Alzahrani, J. A., Alzahrani, D. A., Asuhaimi, I. A., Alzahrani, A. M., & Alkatheeri, A. A. (2025). Evaluation of healthcare professionals' knowledge of Alzheimer's disease in government hospitals and healthcare centers: A cross-sectional study in Jeddah, Saudi Arabia. *Medicine*, *104*(9), e41642. DOI: 10.1097/MD.0000000000041642 PMID: 40020142

Alzheimer's Disease International. (2023). *World Alzheimer Report 2023*. https://www.alzint.org/resource/world-alzheimer-report-2023/ (2023, accessed October 24, 2023).

Angioni, D., Delrieu, J., Hansson, O., Fillit, H., Aisen, P., Cummings, J., Sims, J. R., Braunstein, J. B., Sabbagh, M., Bittner, T., & Weiner, M. (2022). Blood biomarkers from research use to clinical practice: What must be done? A report from the EU/US CTAD task force. *The Journal of Prevention of Alzheimer's Disease*, *9*(4), 569–579. DOI: 10.14283/jpad.2022.85 PMID: 36281661

Arksey, H., & O'Malley, L. (2005). Scoping studies: Towards a methodological framework. *International Journal of Social Research Methodology*, *8*(1), 19–32. DOI: 10.1080/1364557032000119616

Azimzadeh, S., Azami-Aghdash, S., Tabrizi, J. S., & Gholipour, K. (2024). Reforms and innovations in primary health care in different countries: Scoping review. *Primary Health Care Research & Development*, *25*, e22. DOI: 10.1017/S1463423623000725 PMID: 38651337

Baloh, J., Zhu, X., & Ward, M. (2018). Implementing team huddles in small rural hospitals: How does the Kotter model of change apply? *Journal of Nursing Management*, *26*(5), 571–578. DOI: 10.1111/jonm.12584 PMID: 29250892

Bamford, D., & Daniel, S. (2005). A case study of change management effectiveness within the NHS. *Journal of Change Management*, *5*(4), 391–406. DOI: 10.1080/14697010500287360

Barreto, J. O. M., de Melo, R. C., da Silva, L. A. L. B., de Araújo, B. C., de Freitas Oliveira, C., Toma, T. S., de Bortoli, M. C., Demaio, P. N., & Kuchenmüller, T. (2024). Research evidence communication for policy-makers: A rapid scoping review on frameworks, guidance and tools, and barriers and facilitators. *Health Research Policy and Systems*, *22*(1), 99. DOI: 10.1186/s12961-024-01169-9 PMID: 39118156

Basheikh, M. A., Balubaid, H., Mohammed, B. A., & Hashim, B. (2021). Kingdom of Saudi Arabia. *International Journal on Ageing in Developing Countries*, *6*(2), 141–154.

Beigh, S., Adnan, R., Abdulaziz, A. J., Abdullah, S., Nasser, N., Ghazzay, R., Abdulaziz, R., Mohammed, E., Ahmad, R. M., Alshehri, M. A., & Abouhussien, R. M. A.II. (2024). Dementia and multimorbidity trends in Al-Baha, Saudi Arabia: An analytical retrospective study using records-based data. *Cureus*, *16*(1), e52507–e52507. DOI: 10.7759/cureus.52507 PMID: 38371043

Bergsland, J., Elle, O. J., & Fosse, E. (2014). Barriers to medical device innovation. *Medical Devices (Auckland, N.Z.)*, *7*, 205–209. DOI: 10.2147/MDER.S43369 PMID: 24966699

Blennow, K., & Zetterberg, H. (2018). Biomarkers for Alzheimer's disease: Current status and prospects for the future. *Journal of Internal Medicine, 284*(6), 643–663. DOI: 10.1111/joim.12816 PMID: 30051512

Borson, S., Au, R., Chodos, A. H., Gandy, S., Jain, H., Alagor, A., Cohn, K., Kerwin, D. R., Mintzer, J., Monroe, S., & Wilcock, D. M. (2025). Opportunities to encourage adoption of a biomarker-enabled care pathway for Alzheimer's in primary care. *Alzheimer's & Dementia: Diagnosis, Assessment & Disease Monitoring, 17*(1), e70095. DOI: 10.1002/dad2.70095 PMID: 40071061

Cameron, E., & Green, M. (2024). *Making sense of change management: A complete guide to the models, tools and techniques of organizational change*. Kogan Page Publishers.

Cammisuli, D. M., Cipriani, G., & Castelnuovo, G. (2022). Technological solutions for diagnosis, management and treatment of Alzheimer's disease-related symptoms: A structured review of the recent scientific literature. *International Journal of Environmental Research and Public Health, 19*(5), 3122. DOI: 10.3390/ijerph19053122 PMID: 35270811

Carman, A. L., Vanderpool, R. C., Stradtman, L. R., & Edmiston, E. A. (2019). A change-management approach to closing care gaps in a federally qualified health center: A rural Kentucky case study. *Preventing Chronic Disease, 16*, E105. DOI: 10.5888/pcd16.180589 PMID: 31400097

Chávez-Fumagalli, M. A., Shrivastava, P., Aguilar-Pineda, J. A., Nieto-Montesinos, R., Del-Carpio, G. D., Peralta-Mestas, A., Caracela-Zeballos, C., Valdez-Lazo, G., Fernandez-Macedo, V., Pino-Figueroa, A., & Lino Cardenas, C. L. (2021). Diagnosis of Alzheimer's disease in developed and developing countries: Systematic review and meta-analysis of diagnostic test accuracy. *Journal of Alzheimer's Disease Reports, 5*(1), 15–30. DOI: 10.3233/ADR-200263 PMID: 33681713

Chu, E. C. (2025). *Effective Strategies Nursing Home Leaders Use to Implement Changes and Increase Staff Retention and the Quality of Patient Care* (Doctoral dissertation), Walden University, Minneapolis, Minnesota, United States.

Cummings, J. L., Isaacson, R. S., Schmitt, F. A., & Velting, D. M. (2015). A practical algorithm for managing Alzheimer's disease: What, when, and why? *Annals of Clinical and Translational Neurology, 2*(3), 307–323. DOI: 10.1002/acn3.166 PMID: 25815358

De Foo, C., Chia, H. X., Teo, K. W., Farwin, A., Hashim, J., Koh, G. C. H., Matchar, D. B., Legido-Quigley, H., & Yap, J. C. (2023). Healthier SG: Singapore's multi-year strategy to transform primary healthcare. *The Lancet Regional Health. Western Pacific*, *37*, 100861. DOI: 10.1016/j.lanwpc.2023.100861 PMID: 37529631

Dehghani, N., Bras, J., & Guerreiro, R. (2021). How understudied populations have contributed to our understanding of Alzheimer's disease genetics. *Brain*, *144*(4), 1067–1081. DOI: 10.1093/brain/awab028 PMID: 33889936

Dhana, K., Evans, D. A., Rajan, K. B., Bennett, D. A., & Morris, M. C. (2020). Healthy lifestyle and the risk of Alzheimer dementia. *Neurology*, *95*(4). Advance online publication. DOI: 10.1212/WNL.0000000000009816 PMID: 32554763

El-Gamal, F., Alali, A. K.Sr, Mashaabi, M. H., Alsaghah, A. A., Shukr, F. A., & Kadri, S. Y. (2023). Knowledge about Alzheimer's disease in Saudi Arabia. *Cureus*, *15*(12), e50188. DOI: 10.7759/cureus.50188 PMID: 38089950

El-Metwally, A., Toivola, P., Al-Rashidi, M., Nooruddin, S., Jawed, M., AlKanhal, R., Razzak, H. A., & Albawardi, N. (2019). Epidemiology of Alzheimer's disease and dementia in arab countries: A systematic review. *Behavioural Neurology*, *2019*(1), 3935943. DOI: 10.1155/2019/3935943 PMID: 31772681

Frisoni, G. B., Boccardi, M., Barkhof, F., Blennow, K., Cappa, S., Chiotis, K., Démonet, J. F., Garibotto, V., Giannakopoulos, P., Gietl, A., Hansson, O., Herholz, K., Jack, C. R.Jr, Nobili, F., Nordberg, A., Snyder, H. M., Ten Kate, M., Varrone, A., Albanese, E., & Winblad, B. (2017). Strategic roadmap for an early diagnosis of Alzheimer's disease based on biomarkers. *The Lancet. Neurology*, *16*(8), 661–676. DOI: 10.1016/S1474-4422(17)30159-X PMID: 28721928

General Authority for Statistics. (2024). *Total Kingdom population exceeds 35 million by mid-2024*. https://www.stats.gov.sa/documents/20117/2435273/Population+Estimates+Statistics+2024+EN.pdf/9b71e303-5fd9-19cb-9913-850a9d521639

Grossberg, G. T., & Desai, A. K. (2003). Management of Alzheimer's disease. *Journal of Gerontology*, *58*(4), M331–M353. DOI: 10.1093/gerona/58.4.M331 PMID: 12663697

Gyawali, P. K., Le Guen, Y., Liu, X., Belloy, M. E., Tang, H., Zou, J., & He, Z. (2023). Improving genetic risk prediction across diverse population by disentangling ancestry representations. *Communications Biology*, *6*(1), 964. DOI: 10.1038/s42003-023-05352-6 PMID: 37736834

Hakami, F., Madkhali, M. A., Saleh, E., Ayoub, R., Moafa, S., Moafa, A., Alnami, B., Maashi, B., Khubrani, S., Busayli, W., & Alhazmi, A. (2023). Awareness and perception toward Alzheimer's disease among residents living in the Jazan Province, Saudi Arabia: A cross-sectional study. *Cureus*, *15*(9), e44505. DOI: 10.7759/cureus.44505 PMID: 37789999

Hansson, O. (2021). Biomarkers for neurodegenerative diseases. *Nature Medicine*, *27*(6), 954–963. DOI: 10.1038/s41591-021-01382-x PMID: 34083813

Ismail, A. A., Alghasham, N. S., Alsukhaiber, R. E., & Alnowiasser, F. M. (2021). Dementia screening of geriatric patients by implementing an informant-based Alzheimer's disease eight-item tool in KSA. *Journal of Taibah University Medical Sciences*, *16*(2), 191–197. DOI: 10.1016/j.jtumed.2020.10.020 PMID: 33897323

Jácome, D., Cotrufo, T., Andres-Benito, P., Lidón, L., Martí, E., Ferrer, I., Del Río, J. A., & Gavín, R. (2024). miR-519a-3p, found to regulate cellular prion protein during Alzheimer's disease pathogenesis, as a biomarker of asymptomatic stages. *Biochimica et Biophysica Acta (BBA)-. Biochimica et Biophysica Acta. Molecular Basis of Disease*, *1870*(5), 167187. DOI: 10.1016/j.bbadis.2024.167187 PMID: 38653354

Kerwin, D., Abdelnour, C., Caramelli, P., Ogunniyi, A., Shi, J., Zetterberg, H., & Traber, M. (2022). Alzheimer's disease diagnosis and management: Perspectives from around the world. *Alzheimer's & Dementia: Diagnosis, Assessment & Disease Monitoring*, *14*(1), e12334. DOI: 10.1002/dad2.12334 PMID: 35898519

Khalil, A. I., Aladwani, N., & Aljehani, S. (2020). Relationship between knowledge, attitude, and burden among Alzheimer's family care givers in Jeddah, Saudi Arabia. *Saudi Journal of Nursing and Health Care*, *3*(6), 167–174. DOI: 10.36348/sjnhc.2020.v03i06.002

Kharbanda, V., Linnenbank, P., Gulati, A., & Agarwal, H. (2024). Advancing biotechnology & genomics in Saudi Arabia: Best practice strategies to develop the sector & maximize its impact. https://www.adlittle.com/be-en/insights/report/advancing-biotechnologygenomics-saudi-arabia (2024, May 31, 2024).

Kingdon, J. (1995). *Agendas, Alternatives and Public Policies* (2nd ed.). Harper Collins.

Kotter, J. (1996). *Leading Change*. Harvard Business School Press.

Kotter, J. (2008). *A Sense of Urgency*. Harvard Business School Press.

Kotter, J. P. (1995). Why transformation efforts fail. *Harvard Business Review*, *73*(2), 59–67.

Kotter, J. P., & Cohen, D. S. (2002). *The Heart of Change: Real-life Stories of How People Change Their Organizations.* Harvard Business School Press.

Lehtisalo, J., Palmer, K., Mangialasche, F., Solomon, A., Kivipelto, M., & Ngandu, T. (2021). Changes in lifestyle, behaviors, and risk factors for cognitive impairment in older persons during the first wave of the coronavirus disease 2019 pandemic in Finland: Results from the FINGER study. *Frontiers in Psychiatry, 12*, 624125. DOI: 10.3389/fpsyt.2021.624125 PMID: 33643095

Lewin, K. (1947). Frontiers in group dynamics: Concept, method and reality in social science; equilibrium and social change. *Human Relations; Studies Towards the Integration of the Social Sciences, 1*(1), 5–41. DOI: 10.1177/001872674700100103

Ministry of Education. (2021). The Council of Ministers approves the establishment of the "Research, Development and Innovation Development Authority". Ministry of Education, 4 June. https://www.moe.gov.sa/ar/mediacenter/MOEnews/Pages/REC1442-892.aspx (Accessed: 14 June 2024).

Ministry of Health. (2023). *Protocol for the Prevention of Cognitive Impairment*, 24. https://www.moh.gov.sa/en/Ministry/MediaCenter/Publications/Documents/Ministry_of_Health_Protocol_for_the_Prevention_of_Cognitive_Impairment.pdf

Mohamad, R. M., Alsaeed, M. S. A., Merdad, A. H., Alghaith, D. M., Binnshwan, F. M., Albusaad, R. A., Almuslem, M. Y., Alamri, R. A., Awaji, H. H. H., Alqahtani, M. N., & Alamrani, A. A. (2023). Evaluating the general population of Saudi Arabia for their knowledge, attitudes, and practices towards dementia. *Cureus, 15*(12), e49865–e49865. DOI: 10.7759/cureus.49865 PMID: 38170079

Mugambi, M. M., & Matula, P. D. (2025). "Application of Kotter's 8-step change management model and administrative strategies for effective curriculum change in universities". A systematic literature review. *International Journal of Research and Innovation in Social Science, 9*(01), 3490–3501. DOI: 10.47772/IJRISS.2025.9010277

Noor Eddin, A., Hamsho, K., Adi, G., Al-Rimawi, M., Alfuwais, M., Abdul Rab, S., Alkattan, K., & Yaqinuddin, A. (2023). Cerebrospinal fluid microRNAs as potential biomarkers in Alzheimer's disease. *Frontiers in Aging Neuroscience, 15*, 1210191–1210191. DOI: 10.3389/fnagi.2023.1210191 PMID: 37476007

O'Brien, G. L., Sinnott, S. J., Walshe, V., Mulcahy, M., & Byrne, S. (2020). Health policy triangle framework: Narrative review of the recent literature. *Health Policy OPEN, 1*, 100016. DOI: 10.1016/j.hpopen.2020.100016 PMID: 37383316

Olivari, B. S., French, M. E., & McGuire, L. C. (2020). The Public Health Road Map to respond to the growing dementia crisis. *Innovation in Aging*, *4*(1), igz043. Advance online publication. DOI: 10.1093/geroni/igz043 PMID: 32405541

Pae, C. U. (2015). Why systematic review rather than narrative review? *Psychiatry Investigation*, *12*(3), 417–419. DOI: 10.4306/pi.2015.12.3.417 PMID: 26207140

Pedersen, M., & Dunne, S. (2020). Dewey's broad account of habit and its relevance for change management: A conceptual clarification with pragmatic illustrations. *Journal of Change Management*, *20*(3), 247–263. DOI: 10.1080/14697017.2020.1755342

Pollack, J., & Pollack, R. (2015). Using Kotter's eight stage process to manage an organizational change program: Presentation and practice. *Systemic Practice and Action Research*, *28*(1), 51–66. DOI: 10.1007/s11213-014-9317-0

Prince, M., Wimo, A., Guerchet, M., Ali, G. C., Wu, Y. T., & Prina, M. (2015). *World Alzheimer report 2015. The global impact of dementia: an analysis of prevalence, incidence, cost and trends*. https://www.alzint.org/resource/world-alzheimer-report -2015/ (Accessed 24 October 2023).

Program, H. S. T. (2021). *Health Sector Transformation Program Delivery Plan*. https://www.vision2030.gov.sa/media/0wop2tds/hstp_eng.pdf (2021, accessed May 31, 2024).

Qassem, T., Itani, L., Nasr, W., Al-Ayyat, D., Javaid, S. F., & Al-Sinawi, H. (2023). Prevalence and economic burden of dementia in the Arab world. *BJPsych Open*, *9*(4), e126. DOI: 10.1192/bjo.2023.517 PMID: 37439065

Qiu, S., Miller, M. I., Joshi, P. S., Lee, J. C., Xue, C., Ni, Y., Wang, Y., De Anda-Duran, I., Hwang, P. H., Cramer, J. A., Dwyer, B. C., Hao, H., Kaku, M. C., Kedar, S., Lee, P. H., Mian, A. Z., Murman, D. L., O'Shea, S., Paul, A. B., & Kolachalama, V. B. (2022). Multimodal deep learning for Alzheimer's disease dementia assessment. *Nature Communications*, *13*(1), 3404. DOI: 10.1038/s41467-022-31037-5 PMID: 35725739

Rahman, R. (2020). The privatization of health care system in Saudi Arabia. *Health Services Insights*, *13*, 117863292093449. DOI: 10.1177/1178632920934497 PMID: 32636636

Rosenblatt, M., Boutin, M. M., & Nussbaum, S. R. (2016). Innovation in medicine and device development, regulatory review, and use of clinical advances. *Journal of the American Medical Association*, *316*(16), 1671. DOI: 10.1001/jama.2016.12486 PMID: 27669080

Rother, E. T. (2007). Systematic literature review X narrative review. *Acta Paulista de Enfermagem*, *20*, v–vi. DOI: 10.1590/S0103-21002007000200001

Saeed, A., Bin Saeed, A., & AlAhmri, F. A. (2023). Saudi Arabia health systems: Challenging and future transformations with artificial intelligence. *Cureus*, *15*(4), e37826–e37826. DOI: 10.7759/cureus.37826 PMID: 37214025

Saudi Ministry of Health. (2017). *New Model of Care*. https://www.moh.gov.sa/en/Ministry/vro/Documents/Healthcare-Transformation-Strategy.pdf (Accessed: 26 May 2024).

Saudi Ministry of Health. (2023). *Health Days 2023 - World Alzheimer's Day*. https://www.moh.gov.sa/en/HealthAwareness/healthDay/2023/Pages/default.aspx (Accessed 15 September 2023).

Schein, E. H. (2010). *Organizational Culture and Leadership*. John Wiley & Sons.

Shin, J., Tampi, R., Joshi, P., Jester, D. J., & Jeste, D. V. (2025). Social determinants of health associated with neuropsychiatric symptoms of dementia and mild cognitive impairment: A narrative review. *International Psychogeriatrics*, *100152*, 100152. Advance online publication. DOI: 10.1016/j.inpsyc.2025.100152 PMID: 41102089

Sittrop, D., & Crosthwaite, C. (2021). Minimising risk: The application of Kotter's change management model on customer relationship management systems. A case study. *Journal of Risk and Financial Management*, *14*(10), 1–20. DOI: 10.3390/jrfm14100496

Tayeb, H. O., Khallaf, R. A., Muayqil, T. A., Alkeridy, W. A., Alibrahim, F. S., Alfaify, O. A., Qadi, N., & Tarazi, F. I. (2023). The future of Alzheimer disease immunotherapies in Saudi Arabia: Consensus statement of the Saudi Chapter of Cognitive and Behavioral Neurology. *Neurosciences*, *28*(2), 77–84. DOI: 10.17712/nsj.2023.2.20220133 PMID: 37045461

Thaler, R. H., & Sunstein, C. R. (2021). *Nudge: The final edition*. Penguin Books.

Todnem, R. (2005). Organisational change management: A critical review. *Journal of Change Management*, *5*(4), 369–380. DOI: 10.1080/14697010500359250

United Nations. (2012). *World population prospects: The 2012 revision*. https://www.un.org/en/development/desa/publications/world-population-prospectsthe-2012-revision.html (Accessed: 13 June 2024).

Vinze, S., Chodosh, J., Lee, M., Wright, J., & Borson, S. (2023). The national public health response to Alzheimer's disease and related dementias: Origins, evolution, and recommendations to improve early detection. *Alzheimer's & Dementia : The Journal of the Alzheimer's Association, 19*(9), 4276–4286. DOI: 10.1002/alz.13376 PMID: 37435983

Walt, G., & Gilson, L. (1994). Reforming the health sector in developing countries: The central role of policy analysis. *Health Policy and Planning, 9*(4), 353–370. DOI: 10.1093/heapol/9.4.353 PMID: 10139469

World Health Organization. (2019). Risk reduction of cognitive decline and dementia: WHO guidelines. In *Risk reduction of cognitive decline and dementia: WHO guidelines* (pp. 96-96). https://pesquisa.bvsalud.org/portal/resource/pt/biblio-1015308

World Health Organization. (2021). *Global Status Report on the Public Health Response to Dementia.* https://iris.who.int/bitstream/handle/10665/344701/9789240033245-eng.pdf?sequence=1 (Accessed: 29 May 2024).

Zahariadis, N. (2019). The multiple streams framework: Structure, limitations, prospects. In *Theories of the policy process* (2nd ed., pp. 65–92). Routledge. DOI: 10.4324/9780367274689-3

Zilka, N., & Novak, M. (2006). The tangled story of Alois Alzheimer. *Bratislavské Lekárske Listy, 107*(9-10), 343–345. PMID: 17262985

Chapter 10

Addressing Global Health Challenges Through Financial Innovation and HealthTechnologies:

The Rise of China's Biotech Industry in the Past Decade – Impacts and Contributions to Global Health

Jiawei Tang
http://orcid.org/0009-0001-3807-3147
Global Biopharma Partnerships, USA

ABSTRACT

Over the past decade, China's biotechnology industry has transformed into a global leader, driven by policy reforms, growing capital markets, and rapid adoption of advanced science and technology. Once a follower, China now produces first-in-class drugs, novel biologics, and innovative therapies for cancer, autoimmune disorders, and rare diseases. Key drivers include internationally aligned regulations, the STAR Market for biotech IPOs, and cultivation of global scientific talent. Public-private partnerships, incentives for translational research, and use of AI, big data, and precision medicine have strengthened R&D and enabled participation in global clinical trials. China's experience offers lessons for other emerging markets, highlighting how aligned policies, capital, and innovation ecosystems can advance health solutions, support global clinical development, and improve health equity and pandemic preparedness worldwide.

DOI: 10.4018/979-8-3373-3341-0.ch010

INTRODUCTION

Over the past decade, China's biotechnology industry has undergone a remarkable transformation, emerging as a major force with far-reaching implications for global healthcare. Driven by sweeping policy reforms, unprecedented capital market expansion, and the rapid adoption of cutting-edge scientific and technological capabilities, China's biotech sector has evolved from a follower to an active innovator, making significant contributions to advances in life sciences and public health.

This chapter explores the dynamic interplay between government policy, financial innovation, and technological progress that has propelled the growth of China's biotech industry. Key milestones – including the implementation of internationally aligned regulatory frameworks, the expansion of the STAR Market to support biotech IPOs, and the attraction and cultivation of global scientific talent – have accelerated the sector's development. The chapter examines how these factors have fostered a more robust research and development ecosystem, driving a surge in first-in-class drugs, novel biologics, and innovative therapies targeting diseases with significant unmet medical needs, such as cancer, autoimmune disorders, and rare diseases.

Furthermore, China's biotech ascent offers valuable lessons for other emerging markets aiming to strengthen their own health innovation capacity. This chapter discusses how policy alignment between central and local governments, strategic public-private partnerships, and incentives for translational research have enabled Chinese companies to more effectively bridge the gap between basic science and clinical application. By leveraging big data, artificial intelligence, and precision medicine, China's leading biotech firms are not only addressing domestic health challenges but are also increasingly engaged in global clinical trials and regulatory submissions, contributing to a more interconnected and resilient global health ecosystem.

Finally, the chapter considers the broader implications of China's biotech growth for global health equity, supply chain resilience, and preparedness for future pandemics. As the world faces escalating healthcare challenges, from aging populations to emerging infectious diseases, China's experience offers important insights into how emerging markets can mobilize capital, align regulatory incentives, and nurture innovation ecosystems that deliver meaningful contributions to global health solutions.

Through this lens, readers will gain a deeper understanding of how China's biotech sector is shaping the future of medicine and what its evolution can teach countries and stakeholders dedicated to improving health outcomes worldwide.

BACKGROUND

Biotechnology is a multidisciplinary field that involves the integration of natural sciences and engineering sciences in order to achieve the application of organisms and parts thereof for products and services (IUPAC Goldbook, 2014). In the context of healthcare, biotech innovations include biologics, gene and cell therapies, precision medicine, and molecular diagnostics. Over the past decade, China's biotech sector has transitioned from a follower of Western innovation to a global driver of life sciences research and development (Zhang & Li, 2025).

MAIN FOCUS OF THE CHAPTER

1. Policy Reform as a Catalyst for China's Breakthrough Drug Innovation

In 2015, China's pharmaceutical industry confronted significant structural obstacles: sluggish regulatory approvals, a market dominated by generic and "me-too" drugs, and a weak pipeline for original drug discovery. Recognizing the urgent need for transformation, the Chinese government initiated sweeping policy changes designed to overhaul the drug approval system, incentivize first-in-class (FIC) and best-in-class (BIC) research, and accelerate biotech innovation (Hu & Mossialos, 2017).

These initiatives, collectively known as pharmaceutical supply-side reforms, fundamentally reshaped China's biopharmaceutical landscape. By introducing transformative policies such as the Market Authorization Holder (MAH) system, patent term extensions, streamlined clinical trial approvals, and enhanced financial incentives, China has rapidly evolved from a generics-heavy market into a globally recognized hub for cutting-edge drug development.

Within just a decade, the results have been remarkable:

The number of domestically developed new drug approvals has soared.

Chinese biotech companies now contribute significantly to the global drug pipeline. In 2024, China's share of the global pipeline, as measured by volume of assets, was reported to be ~27-30%... with one-third of new compounds in U.S. pharma pipelines now originating from Chinese companies (Back Bay Life Science Advisors, 2025).

Small, underfunded startups have grown into multibillion-dollar global competitors BeOne (Formerly BeiGene), Zai Lab, and Innovent among the most prominent examples.

Pre-Reform Challenges

Before 2015, China's pharmaceutical sector was hampered by three critical weaknesses (Diao et al., 2019; Jia & Ma, 2024):

Regulatory Bottlenecks:

The China Food and Drug Administration (CFDA, now the National Medical Products Administration, or NMPA) maintained an exceptionally slow drug approval process. New drugs faced delays of five to seven years, compared to one to two years in the USA or EU. Clinical trial approvals alone could take more than a year, deterring multinational companies from conducting trials in China. A backlog of thousands of applications further stifled innovation.

Overreliance on Generics and Me-Too Drugs:

More than 95% of approved drugs were generics or minor variations of existing drugs. The lack of robust patent incentives discouraged investment in original research, leaving few companies willing to pursue novel drug development.

Weak Intellectual Property (IP) Protection:

Patent terms were shorter than international standards, undermining returns on investment for innovators. Inadequate data exclusivity meant that clinical trial data could be easily replicated by competitors, allowing copycat biologics to enter the market quickly. As a result, Chinese patients often waited years longer than patients in developed markets to access the latest therapies.

Key Reforms and Their Impact

The reforms enacted between 2015 and 2020 directly targeted these barriers, laying the groundwork for a vibrant innovation ecosystem.

Accelerated Drug Approvals and Clinical Trial Reforms:

Joining International Council for Harmonisation [ICH] (2017): By becoming a member of the ICH, China aligned its regulatory standards with the USA, EU, and Japan, streamlining approvals for innovative global drugs (Zhang et al., 2025).

60-Day Default for Clinical Trial Approvals: Instead of enduring 12-18 month wait times, clinical trials are now automatically approved if no objection is raised within 60 days (National Medical Products Administration [NMPA], 2018). This reform spurred a dramatic rise in clinical trial applications, from about 800 in 2015 to over 5,000 by 2023.

Priority Review Pathway (NMPA, 2020): Breakthrough therapies such as CAR-T cell therapies and gene-editing treatments now benefit from accelerated reviews, sometimes as fast as six months.

Market Authorization Holder (MAH) System (2019):

Previously, only manufacturers could hold drug licenses, a restriction that discouraged startups and research-focused firms lacking production facilities. The MAH system allowed biotech companies to outsource manufacturing, dramatically lowering barriers to market entry and boosting R&D efficiency. By 2023, over 500 companies had adopted the MAH model (Zhai et al., 2025).

Patent and Intellectual Property Strengthening (2020-2021) (National People's Congress, 2020):

New provisions granted patent term extensions of up to five years for innovative drugs, improving the return on costly R&D investments. Data exclusivity protections were strengthened to six years for biologics, safeguarding originators from immediate imitation (NMPA, 2018, 2024). The introduction of a patent linkage system ensured that generic manufacturers must wait until originator patents expire before receiving approval, aligning China more closely with global IP norms.

Source from PharmCube (PharmaCube Global, 2025):

"R&D Transformation: From Copy-Cats to Fast-Followers to Innovators

Historically, China's drug R&D primarily focused on similar drugs (me-too) and improved drugs (me-better).

With national policy emphasis on clinical value, an increasing number of Chinese pharmaceutical companies are shifting towards more innovative original research, advancing from fast-follower to first-in-class (FIC) and best-in-class (BIC) in the global arena.

For drugs of the same type and target, the one at the highest R&D stage and the earliest time to reach that stage is considered FIC. In 2015, only nine FIC innovative drugs developed by Chinese companies entered clinical trials, accounting for less than 10% of the worldwide total. By 2024, this number had risen to 120,

exceeding 30% of total, demonstrating the growing potential of China in original drug innovation. Chinese companies have also made breakthroughs in BIC drug development, with BeiGene's Brukinsa (zanubrutinib) outperforming Johnson & Johnson's Imbruvica (ibrutinib) to become the BIC BTK inhibitor.

Akeso's ivonescimab, the world's first PD-1+VEGF bispecific antibody (BsAb), also succeeded in head-to-head studies against MSD's Keytruda (pembrolizumab).

Figure 1. Number of FIC innovative drugs and their countries/regions of origin (2015–2024)

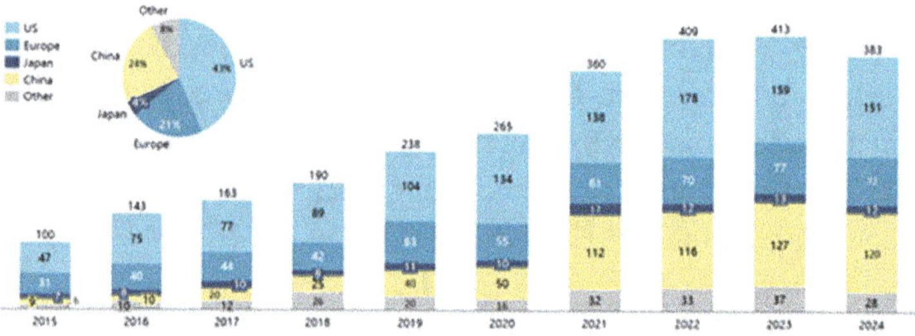

Data source: PharmCube NextBiopharm® database

The data scope includes innovative drugs that initiated their first global clinical trials between 2015 and 2024 and remained active as of 31 December 2024. Drugs with positive R&D or regulatory progress in the past three years are considered active. Clinical trials

include both industry-sponsored trials (IST) and investigator-initiated trials (IIT). Innovative drugs refer to new molecular entities and new combination drugs, excluding traditional Chinese medicines and preventive vaccines.

The annual number of innovative drugs is counted based on the date of first clinical trial registration and stratified by the country/region of the originator. If the originator was acquired or no longer holds development rights, the drug is still included in the

developer's country. China data covers mainland China only, excluding Hong Kong, Macau and Taiwan.

The ranking of drug development progress is based on the highest R&D stage and the earliest time to reach that stage among innovative drugs of the same type and target. Combination drugs, multi-target kinase inhibitors (more than three targets) and drugs with unclear targets or types are excluded from the ranking. The drug ranked first in development progress is recognised as FIC.

Accelerated Translation: China Joins the Global First-Tier in Innovative

Drug Launches.

Figure 2. Number of Innovative drugs approved globally and their countries/regions of first registration (2015–2024)

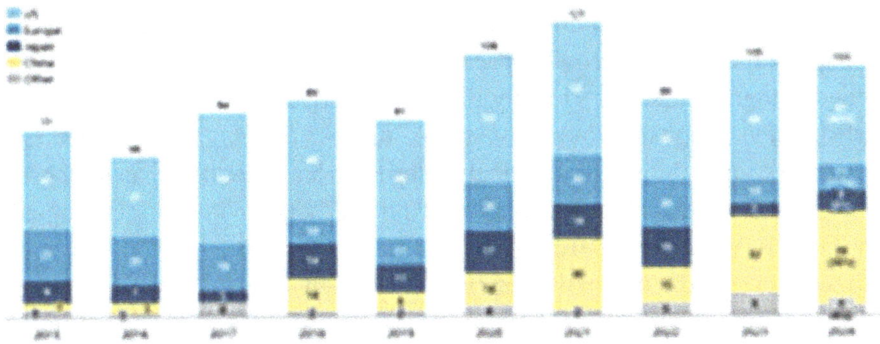

Data source: PharmCube NextBiopharm® database

The statistics cover innovative drugs first approved globally between 2015 and 2024. Innovative drugs refer to new molecular entities

and new fixcd-dosc combinations, excluding traditional Chinese medicines and preventive vaccines. The annual number of innovative drugs is counted based on the first approval date in the initial country or region. Data for China covers mainland China only, excluding Hong Kong, Macau and Taiwan."

Lesson: China's biotech revolution demonstrates how strategic policy reforms can rapidly transform an industry. By slashing bureaucratic delays – reducing drug approval times from five-seven years to just six to 12 months – and implementing the MAH system that decoupled R&D from manufacturing, China created an environment where innovation could thrive. These changes, combined with stronger IP protections like six-year data exclusivity for biologics, triggered explosive growth: clinical trials surged from 800 in 2015 to over 5,000 by 2023 (NMPA, 2024), while 500+ biotechs adopted the new licensing framework to accelerate development (Jia & Ma, 2024).

The reforms created a virtuous cycle where faster approvals led to quicker commercialization, generating revenue that could be reinvested in R&D. Where Chinese patients once waited years longer than Western counterparts for new therapies, drugs like Legend's Carvykti now achieve near-simultaneous approval in China and the USA. This regulatory alignment with global standards, coupled with financial incentives for innovation, has positioned China as a biotech powerhouse - proving that thoughtful policy design can rapidly elevate an entire industry from imitation to world-class innovation.

2. GLOBAL TALENT FUELING CHINA'S BIOTECH BOOM

One of the most powerful engines behind the extraordinary rise of China's biotech industry has been its people, specifically the return of world-class scientists, seasoned entrepreneurs, and globally trained executives who chose to bring their expertise home. Known colloquially as "sea turtles" (, *haigui*), these returnees transformed China's biopharmaceutical sector from a market dominated by generics and copycat drugs into one of the world's most dynamic hubs for cutting-edge innovation (Today Online, 2016).

These returnees did not arrive empty-handed. They brought with them decades of experience in leading laboratories and pharmaceutical giants abroad. They carried advanced technical expertise in molecular biology, immunotherapy, and gene editing; firsthand knowledge of US Food and Drug Administration (FDA) and European Medicines Agency (EMA) regulatory pathways; deep networks among global venture capitalists and strategic investors; and perhaps most importantly, a mindset shaped by the world's most competitive biotech ecosystems.

Today, returnee entrepreneurs play a dominant role in China's high-tech leadership. Companies such as BeiGene, Zai Lab, Innovent Biologics, Hua Medicine, and CanSinoBIO have become emblematic of China's rapid ascent in biotechnology—each founded, scaled, and led by executives who previously trained and built their careers abroad before bringing global expertise back to China. These pioneers not only built profitable companies but bridged China's emerging industry with mature markets in the USA and Europe, catalyzing unprecedented flows of knowledge, capital, and talent.

Why Did China's Biotech Talent Return?

The "sea turtle" phenomenon did not emerge in a vacuum. Rather, it was propelled by a potent combination of push factors abroad and pull factors at home, creating a once-in-a-generation moment that reshaped global innovation flows (Zwetsloot, 2020).

Push Factors: Hitting the Ceiling Abroad

For decades, talented Chinese scientists and engineers had flocked to elite institutions and Big Pharma companies in the United States and Europe. They filled research labs at Harvard and MIT, managed clinical trials at Pfizer and Roche, and led cutting-edge studies at the National Institutes of Health. Many rose through the ranks but just as many found themselves confronting an invisible ceiling.

Subtle cultural barriers, limited boardroom access, and perceptions of "outsider" status often made it difficult for these professionals to ascend into senior executive roles, no matter how brilliant their science.

Alongside institutional barriers, shifting immigration landscapes made life abroad more precarious. Tighter visa restrictions, particularly for Chinese researchers in the USA, rising anti-Asian sentiment, and broader geopolitical tensions fueled a sense that long-term security was increasingly out of reach.

Yet for many, the strongest push factor was not restriction but ambition, a desire to tackle big, urgent challenges that mature Western markets, saturated with incremental innovation, could no longer satisfy. In China, the sheer scale of unmet need was both daunting and galvanizing.

Pull Factors: The "Biotech Gold Rush" at Home

While push factors nudged talent out of the West, powerful incentives pulled them back to China. Beginning in the mid-2000s and accelerating sharply after 2015, Beijing launched ambitious talent recruitment drives like the "Thousand Talents Plan," offering million-dollar grants, generous lab funding, fast-track visas, and favorable tax policies to lure back its brightest minds.

Meanwhile, local governments competed fiercely to build biotech clusters in cities like Shanghai, Suzhou, and Shenzhen. These hubs offered low rents for labs, expedited intellectual property approvals, incubators connected to local hospitals and universities, and ready access to a growing pool of engineers and technicians.

Perhaps most important of all, China's venture capital market exploded. From less than $1 billion in 2015, biotech VC funding soared to more than $25 billion by 2024 (PharmaCube, 2024; Allianz, 2025; McKinsey & Company, 2024). Investors once wary of China's regulatory risks and talent gaps now saw enormous opportunity, a vast population of 1.4 billion, a fast-expanding middle class demanding advanced therapies, and a government determined to upgrade its entire life sciences sector.

Innovent Biologics, established in 2011, became a definitive emblem of China's shifting pharmaceutical landscape by securing a scale of pre-revenue capital previously characteristic only of Silicon Valley. By leveraging the Hong Kong Stock Exchange's Chapter 18A listing framework and global venture capital, the firm successfully raised substantial capital to fuel its R&D engine before achieving its first period of profitability in 2024 (Innovent Biologics, 2016). This trajectory underscores a broader transition toward a high-risk, high-reward investment model, signaling China's maturation into a global hub for innovative biopharma.

Regulatory Reform: The Final Piece

Talent and capital would have gone nowhere without bold regulatory reform. Over the past decade, China transformed its pharmaceutical approval system by joining the International Council for Harmonisation (ICH), introducing the MAH system, streamlining clinical trial processes, and aligning intellectual property protections with international standards.

Suddenly, returnees found they could develop new drugs, outsource manufacturing, protect their IP, and get products to market faster than ever before, often rivaling or outpacing Western timelines.

Meet the Pioneers: Sea Turtles Who Changed the Game

Behind the statistics are the personal stories of pioneering returnees whose choices and leadership redefined China's place in global biotech.

Xiaodong Wang (BeiGene)

A world-renowned apoptosis researcher and former Howard Hughes Medical Institute investigator at UT Southwestern, Wang stunned colleagues when he left a coveted US post to co-found BeiGene in Beijing in 2010. His vision: build China's first true global oncology biotech. BeiGene's blockbuster BTK inhibitor Brukinsa became a symbol of China's leap, winning FDA and EMA approvals and directly challenging Big Pharma incumbents (Zagorski, 2005; ECHEMI, 2024).

Samantha Du (Zai Lab)

After years at Pfizer and Hutchison MediPharma, Du returned to found Zai Lab in 2014. Her strategy was audacious in licensing promising Western drugs for the Chinese market and simultaneously shepherd Chinese-origin drugs through global trials. This "two-way bridge" model attracted billions in investment and positioned Zai Lab as a $5 billion powerhouse listed on Nasdaq and HKEX (Forbes, 2021).

Dr. Michelle Xia (Akeso)

Dr. Michelle Xia's journey back to China followed a distinguished tenure in the U.S. and Canada, including pivotal R&D roles at PDL BioPharma and Bayer. Armed with deep expertise in antibody engineering, she returned to China in 2012 with a specific focus: the "next generation" of immuno-oncology. As the co-founder and CEO of Akeso, Xia steered the company toward the frontiers of bispecific antibodies—drugs that can target two different disease pathways simultaneously. Under her leadership, Akeso developed ivonescimab, a groundbreaking bispecific that recently made global headlines for outperforming Merck's Keytruda in a head-to-head clinical trial for lung cancer. Her success has not only made Akeso a multi-billion dollar entity on the HKEX but has validated China's ability to move beyond "fast-follow" drugs into true, first-in-class global innovation (Bloomberg, 2024).

Dr. Michael Yu (Innovent Biologics)

Before founding Innovent Biologics in 2011, Dr. Michael Yu spent nearly two decades in the United States, carving out a stellar career at Amgen and MedImmune (now part of AstraZeneca). A scientist by training with over 60 patents to his name, Yu was a key inventor of Conbercept, one of China's first major home-grown biologics. Yu transformed his Suzhou startup into a powerhouse. His landmark drug, Tyvyt, became the first PD-1 inhibitor on China's reimbursement list, slashing prices by 60%. His mission remains simple: "Developing high-quality biological drugs that people can afford" (Innovent Biologics, 2024).

Dr. Xuefeng Yu (CanSino Biologics)

Driven by a mission to modernize China's vaccine industry, Dr. Xuefeng Yu left a high-ranking executive position at Sanofi Pasteur in Canada to co-found CanSino Biologics in 2009. Returning with a team of fellow "sea turtles," Yu sought to bridge the gap between international quality standards and domestic manufacturing.

His leadership catapulted CanSino into the global spotlight during the COVID-19 pandemic with the development of Convidecia, a single-shot viral vector vaccine. Under Yu's guidance, CanSino achieved a historic milestone by becoming the first Chinese company to list on both the HKEX and Shanghai's STAR Market. Today, his "global-first" strategy has transformed CanSino from a startup in Tianjin into a critical player in international public health, proving that Chinese innovation can contribute to the pandemic preparedness (CanSino Biologics Inc, 2025).

Beyond Balance Sheets: How Returnees Reshaped the Ecosystem

These pioneers did far more than build billion-dollar companies. They rewrote China's innovation playbook and catalyzed structural change across four dimensions:

Raising Scientific Standards

Returnees imported world-class R&D practices. They instilled rigorous target validation, robust translational research pipelines, and clinical trial designs that mirrored FDA and EMA expectations. This shifted the domestic focus away from "me-too" generics towards truly differentiated first-in-class therapies.

Attracting Global Capital

Their international networks opened the door for prestigious venture capital firms, from Sequoia Capital China to Hillhouse Capital, to pour money into local startups. Many of the first Chinese biotechs listed on Nasdaq and the Hong Kong Stock Exchange were founded by returnees who knew how to navigate global IPOs.

Accelerating Regulatory Modernization

Returnees served as informal ambassadors and advisors. Executives like Samantha Du collaborated with the NMPA to design trials that met Western benchmarks, closing the regulatory gap that had long hindered China's global competitiveness.

Training the Next Generation

Returnees became mentors, university lecturers, and role models, nurturing a new generation of scientists and executives who combine international scientific rigor with deep local market insight.

Act I: The Exodus

In the 1990s and early 2000s, China's brightest minds left home in waves. Harvard's gleaming research centers, Pfizer's deep pipelines, and Silicon Valley's venture-fueled optimism drew them in. They became tenured professors, principal investigators, and Big Pharma executives. Yet, many quietly felt that their full potential was constrained by cultural ceilings they could not crack.

"No matter how groundbreaking our work was, we never fully belonged," one returnee stated.

Back in China, meanwhile, patients faced a grim reality: slow approvals, poor IP protection, and a domestic industry mired in copycat generics.

Act II: The Call of ambitions

Around 2015, the tide began to turn. The "Thousand Talents Plan" and local cluster incentives made return a credible, even irresistible, option. Early movers like Xiaodong Wang shocked peers by trading prestigious US posts for China's uncertain biotech frontier.

Entrepreneurs like John Oyler crossed the Pacific to join them. Oyler co-founded BeiGene after realizing China's unmet need offered the rare chance to build a biotech giant from scratch.

Act III: Building Castles in the Sand

These returnees did not merely transfer knowledge, they reinvented the rules. Samantha Du's Zai Lab showed how to build a cross-border pipeline at lightning speed. Sean Hu's Innovent proved China could master complex biologics. Chen Li's Hua Medicine demonstrated that domestic innovation could break new ground in disease areas like diabetes.

Challenges abounded: skeptical investors, unfamiliar regulators, and an immature talent pool. *"We had to train everyone from scratch – scientists, trial managers, even CFOs,"* one founder recalls. But brick by brick, lab by lab, they built an industry where none had existed.

Act IV: The Tide Turns

By 2024, the results spoke for themselves. BeiGene's Brukinsa outperformed billion-dollar competitors in the US market. Zai Lab's FDA-approved portfolio spanned multiple therapeutic areas. Innovent's landmark partnership with Eli Lilly made global headlines. CanSinoBIO's rapid COVID-19 response earned the respect of global health agencies.

Most importantly, these pioneers inspired a new generation. Young Chinese scientists and entrepreneurs, trained in this evolving ecosystem, now lead next-generation ventures from gene-editing startups to AI-driven drug discovery firms. No longer imitators, they are inventors charting new frontiers (Pharma Board Room, 2026)

Lessons for the World

China's biotech resurgence demonstrates that strategic policy and robust capital must be synthesized with top-tier talent to succeed. For other emerging markets, the lesson is clear:

Incentives Matter: Returning top talent requires more than rhetoric, it demands tangible support: tax breaks, startup capital, IP protection, and supportive ecosystems.

Global Experience Drives Local Innovation: Returnees bridge scientific gaps, regulatory know-how, and capital access. They are multipliers for entire sectors.

Success Begets Success: Early pioneers inspire others to follow. Each successful venture makes the next wave more ambitious.

China's biotech boom was not built solely on capital or policy; it was built on the backs of bold individuals who returned when few believed it was possible. The "sea turtles" rewrote the story of what Chinese biotech could be. In doing so, they demonstrated that talent mobility is among the most potent drivers of global innovation.

For nations aspiring to build a thriving life sciences sector, the message is unmistakable: empower your people to dream globally and make coming home worth their while.

3. THE POWER OF FINANCIAL MARKETS IN SCALING BIOTECHNOLOGY

When future historians trace the arc of the 21st-century biotech revolution, they will likely find that gleaming laboratories and brilliant scientists are only half the story. The other half, just as crucial but often underappreciated, was money. Not just any money, but smart, risk-tolerant, long-horizon capital mobilized by visionary financial systems built to match the extraordinary demands of modern life sciences.

In the story of China's biotech renaissance, the pivotal role of capital markets is often overshadowed by headlines about returnee scientists and blockbuster discoveries. Yet without sophisticated financing mechanisms, the dreams of brilliant founders would have remained locked in notebooks and petri dishes. China's ability to develop regulatory and financial structures that support the unique nature of biotech – long R&D timelines, uncertain pipelines, and binary outcomes – has turned it from an imitator into an innovator and from an isolated market into a formidable global player.

This section unpacks how innovative capital markets, including Hong Kong's groundbreaking Chapter 18A and Shanghai's STAR Market, unlocked billions in funding, catalyzed ambitious research pipelines, and reshaped global capital flows. Along the way, it draws lessons for other emerging economies eager to harness biotech's transformative power for public health and economic growth (McKinsey & Company, 2021).

The Early Funding Desert

For decades, China's biotech sector was held hostage by a structural contradiction. On one hand, the country had the raw ingredients for success: world-class scientists (many trained abroad), vast patient needs, and supportive government policies aimed at upgrading its pharmaceutical industry. On the other hand, it lacked the deep, risk-absorbing financial infrastructure that modern drug development requires.

Biotech, unlike consumer tech or real estate, demands massive upfront investment with little certainty of return. Developing a novel therapeutic molecule often costs upwards of \$1–2 billion and can take 10-15 years. Even the most promising drug candidates have a high failure rate: roughly 90% of all drug candidates entering clinical trials will never make it to market (Mullard, 2016; DiMasi et al., 2016).

This brutal math discouraged local investors accustomed to faster returns from internet startups, mobile apps, or property developments. Traditional Chinese banks, conservative and state-directed, preferred lending to asset-heavy industries with tangible collateral and predictable cash flows. The few venture capitalists active in China during the early 2000s and 2010s mostly favored digital consumer services, e-commerce, and fintech, which promised exponential growth with far less regulatory or scientific uncertainty.

As a result, early biotech entrepreneurs often found themselves starved for capital during the riskiest phases: preclinical research and early-stage clinical trials. Many promising research ideas died on the vine. Talented scientists returned from Harvard or Stanford brimming with ideas only to find local investors unwilling to bet on 10-year R&D roadmaps.

PROFIT BARRIERS: AN IMPOSSIBLE STANDARD

The problem was compounded by China's rigid domestic IPO rules. Until the late 2010s, companies listing on Shanghai or Shenzhen's main boards had to show multiple consecutive years of profits, a requirement that made sense for manufacturers or retailers but was absurd for innovative drug developers burning cash on lab work for a decade or more.

This created an exit bottleneck. With no clear path to public markets, early investors hesitated to fund risky biotech ventures at all. The result was a paradox: China had scientific talent and urgent patient needs, but no way to channel enough capital to take big bets on next-generation medicines.

A Turning Point: Hong Kong's Chapter 18A

In April 2018, a single regulatory decision changed everything. The Hong Kong Stock Exchange (HKEX), long a conservative exchange favoring blue-chip industrials and finance, introduced Chapter 18A, a bold new listing rule designed specifically for biotech (HKEX, 2018).

For the first time in Asia, pre-revenue biotech companies (firms with no approved products and no profit) could list on a major exchange. Under Chapter 18A, a biotech firm only needed:

A clearly defined "core product" in Phase I or later clinical trials.

Substantial pre-IPO investment from "sophisticated" investors, ensuring professional due diligence.

Robust governance and disclosure structures.

This was revolutionary. The new rule acknowledged that biotech companies are not valued on present earnings but on the *potential* of scientific breakthroughs that could become billion-dollar blockbusters if trials succeed. In effect, HKEX gave investors a way to buy into moonshots legally and transparently.

The results were immediate and dramatic. Firms like BeiGene and Zai Lab leveraged dual listings in Hong Kong and the USA to fund global trials, build manufacturing, and scale international sales teams.

As of early 2026, the Hong Kong Stock Exchange (HKEX) Chapter 18A listing regime has expanded significantly since its 2018 inception:

- Total Listings: As of late November 2025, 80 biotech companies have listed under Chapter 18A.
- Fundraising Totals: These listings have collectively raised approximately US$31 billion (roughly HK$241 billion) in capital.
- Recent Momentum: In 2025 alone, 14 pre-revenue biotech firms listed under Chapter 18A, a significant increase from just 4 listings in 2024.
- Market Position: This regime has established Hong Kong as the world's second-largest biotech fundraising hub after the United States (HKEX, 2025).

Beyond the dollar figures, Chapter 18A reshaped investor psychology. Local and regional investors who once shunned unprofitable startups learned a new playbook: tolerate early losses, trust science, and hold for the moonshot. Global institutional capital – from Boston hedge funds to London pension funds – poured into the region, diversifying the investor base.

Successful case: BeiGene's Triple-Listing Masterstroke

BeiGene's ascent to a global oncology powerhouse was fueled by a series of strategically timed listings that redefined how biotech firms access capital. The journey began in February 2016 with its initial public offering on the NASDAQ, where it raised approximately $182 million. This move was groundbreaking, marking the first major entry of a Chinese-born biotech company into the U.S. capital markets. This initial influx of capital provided the necessary runway to transition from a research startup into a clinical-stage contender, setting the stage for its global ambitions.

The true "masterstroke" in BeiGene's financial playbook occurred in August 2018 when it became one of the first companies to leverage Hong Kong's new Chapter 18A listing rules. By dual-listing on the HKEX, the company raised roughly $903 million, effectively bridging the gap between Western institutional backing and the massive liquidity of Asian markets. This success culminated in December 2021 with a historic "triple listing" on Shanghai's STAR Market. Raising a staggering $3.5 billion—the largest ever for a biotech firm—this final pillar of capital gave BeiGene the unprecedented financial firepower to conduct head-to-head global trials, build out its own manufacturing facilities, and challenge established pharmaceutical giants on the world stage. (Nasdaq, 2016; HKEX, 2018; BeiGene Ltd., 2021)

The Mainland Responds: Shanghai's STAR Market

Chapter 18A's success forced mainland regulators to rethink rigid profit requirements that had stifled innovation listings. In July 2019, the Shanghai Stock Exchange launched the Science and Technology Innovation Board (STAR Market), China's boldest experiment in modernizing domestic capital markets for deep tech and biotech.

The STAR Market made three radical departures from China's traditional exchanges:

Profitability No Longer Required

Companies could list based on innovation credentials, not historical profit. For biotech, this was essential.

Registration-Based System

The old government approval bottleneck was replaced by a disclosure-based system similar to NASDAQ, where the market (not bureaucrats) decides which firms merit funding.

Flexible Valuation and Trading

The STAR Market allowed more liberal pricing, wider daily trading bands, and investor access calibrated to risk tolerance.

Within four years, over 50 biotech firms listed on STAR, raising billions for cutting-edge research into gene therapy, cell therapy, and next-generation biologics.

Success case: Innovent Biologics and the STAR Effect

Innovent Biologics, founded by returnee scientist Michael Yu, once faced skeptical local investors who saw biologics as "too complex" for Chinese firms. Early venture rounds kept the company alive, but scaling its ambitious clinical trials and manufacturing required public market capital.

Innovent Biologics was a pioneer in capitalizing on the Hong Kong Stock Exchange's Chapter 18A reforms, successfully raising $421 million in its 2018 IPO (Reuters, 2018). This vital infusion of capital allowed the company to mature its proprietary technology platforms and broaden its R&D pipeline. Building on the commercial success of its flagship PD-1 inhibitor, Tyvyt (sintilimab), Innovent pivoted toward a "next-generation" strategy, launching clinical trials for novel therapies across a diverse range of solid and hematological tumors.

By 2020, the company strategically expanded beyond oncology, developing monoclonal antibodies for autoimmune diseases to address a wider spectrum of unmet medical needs. This evolution was bolstered by a deep-rooted partnership with Eli Lilly, which provided Innovent with critical technical resources and global R&D expertise, significantly accelerating its clinical timelines. Innovent's global trajectory reached a milestone in 2021 when it announced plans to seek regulatory approval for Tyvyt in Europe, a decisive move in its transition from a domestic leader to a global biotech contender. This proactive approach to international collaboration and rigorous clinical research has solidified Innovent's reputation among global investors as a cornerstone of the modern biotechnology landscape (PRNewswire,2020).

Why Risk-Sharing Matters

Chapter 18A and STAR solved biotech's biggest problem: how to spread extreme risk across a broad base of investors.

Biotech is inherently binary. A single failed Phase III trial can wipe out years of work and hundreds of millions in sunk cost. Traditional venture capital can only absorb so much of this volatility. Public markets, by contrast, pool risk among thousands of institutional and retail investors. If one company fails, the losses are distributed and capital remains available for the next bold idea.

This risk-pooling function is the invisible engine behind every major biotech cluster, from Boston to Basel. China's new listing channels aligned local finance with this global reality.

Global Benchmarks: NASDAQ and Beyond

China's innovations mirrored lessons learned in the West. For decades, NASDAQ has been the gold standard for biotech listings. Flexible rules allowed companies like Amgen, Genentech, and Moderna to go public long before they were profitable.

Take Moderna: when it IPO'd in 2018, it had no approved product, only a promising mRNA platform and bold vision. Its IPO raised $604 million, then the largest ever for a biotech firm (Fierce Biotech, 2018). That funding laid the groundwork for the mRNA COVID-19 vaccine that would change the world within two years. Moderna's story shows how the right capital channels can transform moonshot science into life-saving breakthroughs.

Israel's TASE-UP platform and London's AIM Market also illustrate this principle on a smaller scale. Each provides risk-tolerant funding paths for early-stage, high-tech ventures in sectors where long R&D timelines make short-term profit impossible.

What Happens When Capital Markets Fail

Contrast these success stories with regions that lack robust risk-sharing mechanisms. In much of Latin America, biotech startups struggle to find domestic capital markets willing to tolerate long timelines and binary risks (Helmi, 2024). Promising drug candidates languish in underfunded university labs or get sold cheaply to foreign multinationals.

In Africa, the situation is similar. Countries like Nigeria and Kenya have world-class scientists and pressing health needs – from vaccine manufacturing to genetic research for endemic diseases – but no equivalent to Chapter 18A or STAR. Without local channels to spread risk, bold scientific ideas stay locked in slides and pilot studies (Elechi et al., 2025; Azevedo, 2017).

CASE STUDY: MODERNA AND THE COVID-19 RACE

Moderna's COVID-19 vaccine was not a lucky accident. Years of pre-IPO funding from Flagship Pioneering laid the scientific groundwork. But its IPO was equally crucial: by raising hundreds of millions in public equity, Moderna could fund large-scale clinical trials and rapid manufacturing scale-up when the pandemic struck.

In early 2020, as the world scrambled for vaccines, Moderna was ready and so were its public investors, who understood the moonshot logic. The result: one of the first widely distributed mRNA vaccines, saving millions of lives worldwide.

The lesson is universal: scientific breakthroughs do not scale up themselves. Well-designed financial markets make or break whether moonshots become medicines.

Emerging Gaps: The Next Frontier

Despite China's success, gaps remain. Early-stage biotech, the riskiest preclinical phase, still struggles for local seed capital. Most domestic VCs continue to favor companies in Phase II or later, leaving university spin-offs and lab discoveries dependent on government grants or foreign partnerships.

Policymakers increasingly recognize this. Regional biotech parks are piloting convertible grant schemes, milestone-based subsidies, and hybrid public-private accelerators to bridge the "valley of death" between lab work and investable Phase I trials. Shanghai's STAR Market is expanding eligibility criteria to cover more preclinical ventures.

This is the next test: whether China's financial system can evolve from funding scale-ups to nurturing the entire pipeline, from petri dish to pharmacy shelf.

Lessons for the World

China's biotech boom is a case study in how financial innovation can match scientific ambition. The key lessons for emerging markets are clear:

Tailored Rules Matter

Biotech cannot be shoehorned into IPO rules designed for retailers or factories. Listing rules must recognize long R&D cycles and binary outcomes.

Risk Must Be Shared

No single VC or government can shoulder the full risk of biotech. Public markets distribute this risk, keeping capital flowing even when some bets fail.

Liquidity Attracts Talent

Clear exit routes attract both founders and early investors. When entrepreneurs know they can tap public markets, they dare to tackle bigger ideas.

Global Standards Build Trust

Aligning local exchanges with international norms (ICH, FDA trial designs) makes local listings attractive to global funds and ensures that domestic breakthroughs can travel.

Smart money makes the moonshot possible. Scientists may hold the pipettes, but without investors and exchanges built to embrace uncertainty, many of their greatest ideas will never leave the lab.

4. FINANCIAL INNOVATION FOR EQUITABLE ACCESS

When we celebrate the miracle of modern medicine – a gene therapy that halts a rare disease at its genetic root, an immunotherapy that transforms a terminal cancer into a manageable condition, or a vaccine that stops a pandemic in its tracks – we tend to spotlight the lab. We hail the brilliance of the scientists and the courage of the entrepreneurs who dared to tackle nature's toughest puzzles.

Yet beneath every dazzling scientific advance lies a far less glamorous question: *Who pays?* Who shoulders the billions spent on research, the billions more needed for manufacturing, distribution, and monitoring? And above all, who is left behind when a treatment's price tag soars beyond the reach of ordinary families or cash-strapped health systems?

Biotechnology, more than any other modern industry, straddles this uncomfortable truth: innovation without access is progress in name only.

A cure locked behind a paywall is not a cure for society. It is a breakthrough for the privileged few. Nowhere is this paradox clearer than in China, where a booming biotech sector is rewriting the country's scientific future while confronting the urgent question of how to make that progress equitable and sustainable.

The Access Paradox: Breakthrough Science, Backbreaking Costs

Modern biopharma's paradox is stark yet simple: the more revolutionary a new therapy is, the higher its upfront cost tends to be. The logic is structural, not conspiratorial. Drug discovery is a punishingly expensive, failure-prone business.

A single promising molecule can take 10-15 years and $1–2 billion to develop and most never reach the market. For cell and gene therapies, the stakes are even higher. They target ultra-rare conditions, often for tiny patient populations, meaning the entire cost of development must be recovered from just a few thousand patients worldwide.

The result? A single course of CAR-T cell therapy can cost over $400,000. Novartis' Zolgensma, the one-shot gene therapy for spinal muscular atrophy (SMA), shocked the world when it launched at $2.1 million, the most expensive drug ever approved at the time (Nuijten, 2021).

For families facing these diseases, the sticker shock is existential. In wealthy countries like the USA, private insurance and government payers haggle over discounts, risk-sharing deals, and payment installments. But many families still face devastating out-of-pocket bills or ruinous debt.

In low- and middle-income countries (LMICs), the picture is bleaker. There, many breakthrough treatments are simply out of reach. Public insurance budgets are too constrained, local production is impossible for cutting-edge biologics, and families either go without or turn to crowdfunding, social media pleas, or medical tourism for a shot at survival.

China's Big Gamble: Innovation for All

When China's biotech boom took off in the 2010s, this dilemma was no secret. Policymakers, industry leaders, and investors knew that without bold action, China's medical revolution could deepen social divides rather than bridge them.

Imagine a country where a rapidly expanding middle class could afford the latest cancer immunotherapies, while hundreds of millions of rural patients still struggled to afford even basic antibiotics. The political and social backlash would be inevitable and the credibility of the entire biotech push could collapse.

China's answer? Tackle both ends of the pipeline. Build a world-class innovation machine and reshape the financial systems that determine who benefits from it.

China's Dual Track: Faster Approvals, Smarter Payments

China's playbook has two big pillars: speed up drug approvals to get breakthroughs to patients faster, and build payment systems that spread costs broadly enough to keep treatments affordable.

Regulatory Acceleration

China dramatically modernized its drug approval system. Reforms at the NMPA slashed average drug approval times from 6-8 years to less than 2-3 years for priority therapies. Local approvals for global blockbusters, once delayed by years, now arrive within months of FDA or EMA decisions (Chen & Shao, 2023).

Financial Innovation

Equally transformative has been the overhaul of payment systems:

Expanding Universal Insurance: Over 95% of China's 1.4 billion people are now covered under the National Basic Medical Insurance (BMI), one of the world's largest public health safety nets (NHC, 2020).

Centralized Procurement and Price Negotiations: The National Reimbursement Drug List (NRDL) and volume-based procurement (VBP) force drugmakers to trade lower prices for massive guaranteed patient volume (Zhao & Wu, 2023)

Pilots for Smart Payment Models: Dozens of cities are testing diagnosis-related groups (DRGs) and disease-based payments (DIPs) to shift hospital incentives from profit-maximizing to cost-effective, outcome-focused care (He, 2023).

Together, these reforms have begun to bridge the once-yawning gap between cutting-edge science and everyday patients.

REWRITING THE REIMBURSEMENT RULEBOOK: THE NRDL REVOLUTION

If there is a single pillar holding up China's quest for equitable access, it is the National Reimbursement Drug List. The NRDL is more than a list, it is a powerful policy lever that determines which drugs China's insurance system will cover and at what price.

In the early 2000s, the NRDL covered mostly older, lower-cost generics. New cancer therapies, biologics, and rare disease drugs were usually out-of-pocket luxuries for the elite. As recently as 2015, some of the world's most important cancer immunotherapies were entirely absent from Chinese public hospitals.

Recognizing this inequity, China pivoted. Since 2017, the NRDL has undergone annual updates instead of sporadic revisions every five years. Each update is accompanied by intense, high-stakes price negotiations. Pharmaceutical companies are invited to bid for access to China's massive patient population but they must slash prices dramatically in return.

The results have been striking:

Keytruda, Merck's blockbuster immunotherapy for lung cancer, was added to the NRDL in 2021 after a 60% price cut, expanding access to millions of new patients. Tyvyt, Innovent's domestically developed PD-1 inhibitor, leveraged NRDL listing to jump from niche status to mass market, boosting revenue that feeds back into new R&D (Matthew Dennis, 2019).

Cutting-edge biologics for autoimmune diseases and new antivirals have followed the same path, from elite-only to broadly accessible within just a few negotiation rounds.

THE LOGIC OF VOLUME-BASED PROCUREMENT

At the other end of the spectrum, volume-based procurement (VBP) has rewritten the economics of older drugs and generics. Since its launch in 2018, China's "4+7" bulk buying initiative so named for its pilot in 11 major cities has expanded nationwide. The core idea is simple: by aggregating demand, the government can squeeze out inflated margins.

For example:

Some essential generics have seen prices drop by 50-90%, freeing up billions in the health budget (The Pharma Letter, 2020).

Savings are rechanneled to fund newer, pricier therapies without blowing out insurance finances.

Domestic generics makers face brutal competition but also incentives to upgrade quality and invest in differentiated innovation to escape pure price wars.

While painful for some legacy players, this "sacrifice the old to feed the new" logic has kept the system solvent as China's biotech sector surges ahead.

Beyond Procurement: DRG and DIP Experiments

Volume deals alone are not enough if hospitals are incentivized to overuse expensive treatments. To counteract this, China is testing payment models borrowed and adapted from Europe and the USA.

Diagnosis-Related Groups (DRGs)

Under DRGs, hospitals receive a fixed payment per case for a given diagnosis. For example, treating lung cancer earns a set sum, regardless of how many MRIs, brand-name drugs, or costly procedures are used. The incentive shifts from "do more, bill more" to "treat effectively, manage costs."

Disease-Based Payments (DIPs)

DIPs take this a step further by covering entire treatment pathways. A breast cancer DIP might bundle surgery, chemo, and follow-up care into a single payment. If a hospital overspends, it bears the cost. If it finds cost efficiencies while maintaining outcomes, it keeps the savings.

So far, these pilots, now active in tens of cities, are bending cost curves in promising ways. But rolling them out nationwide will require tackling entrenched interests and building robust data systems to track real-world outcomes (Yan et al., 2025; Zhang et al., 2025).

Global Parallels: Innovation vs. Sustainability

China is not alone in grappling with the puzzle of how to pay for the next wave of medical breakthroughs. Around the world, payers, governments, and industry are converging on new models to balance reward for innovation with sustainability.

Europe: Value-Based Pricing and HTA

Europe's health systems are leaders in using health technology assessment (HTA) to decide whether new drugs deserve reimbursement. Agencies like NICE (UK) and IQWiG (Germany) rigorously evaluate whether a therapy's real-world benefit justifies its price (Santos Ivo et al., 2025).

Outcomes-based pricing is increasingly common. For example, Novartis' CAR-T therapy Kymriah was approved in the UK on the condition that the NHS only pays if the patient responds. This shares risk between the payer and the manufacturer, an arrangement that aligns incentives for real-world success.

The USA: Piecemeal Progress

America, famously the world's largest biopharma market, has been slower to impose pricing discipline. But innovative pockets are emerging. Some states, like Louisiana, pioneered a "Netflix subscription" for expensive hepatitis C drugs: the state pays a fixed annual fee for unlimited access, expanding treatment dramatically while providing the drugmaker a guaranteed return (USC Schaeffer Center, 2019).

Private insurers and pharma companies are piloting multi-year payment plans for gene therapies, spreading the $2 million cost of a one-time cure like Zolgensma over five or ten years, with clawbacks if the therapy fails (Wehrwein, 2023).

LMICs: Pooled Procurement and Local Solutions

For many low- and middle-income countries, the answer is pooled bargaining power. Global initiatives like Gavi and The Global Fund pool demand for vaccines and HIV/AIDS drugs, securing better prices for dozens of countries that could not negotiate alone.

COVID-19's COVAX experiment, though imperfect, showed how the same principles might extend to next-generation biologics and vaccines if global solidarity holds firm (Kaló et al., 2025; World Bank Group, 2025; The Global Fund, 2025).

CASE STUDIES: HOW FINANCIAL INNOVATION UNLOCKS ACCESS

Case 1: Tyvyt — Local Breakthrough, National Scale

When Innovent launched Tyvyt, China's first domestically developed PD-1 inhibitor for cancer, it faced a simple math problem: without reimbursement, the vast majority of Chinese patients could never afford it. NRDL inclusion changed everything. After accepting steep price cuts, Tyvyt was rapidly adopted across China's vast public hospital network. The resulting sales volume turned a high-cost therapy into a mass-market standard and freed up revenue for Innovent to fund new pipelines (Chen et al., 2023).

Case 2: Louisiana's "Netflix" for Hepatitis C

Hepatitis C was once a death sentence for hundreds of thousands in the USA until new antivirals arrived costing $80,000-$100,000 per course. Louisiana's Medicaid system, desperate to eliminate the disease but unable to pay per treatment, struck a radical deal: a flat subscription fee for unlimited access. Treatment rates soared. Overall costs fell. Gilead and AbbVie still earned stable returns, but the public health benefit multiplied (USC Schaeffer Center, 2019).

Case 3: Zolgensma and the Global Gene Therapy Dilemma

Zolgensma's launch forced a reckoning: how does a family in Thailand earning $8,000 a year afford a $2.1 million cure? Across Asia and Africa, desperate parents have turned to crowdfunding, diaspora donations, or advocacy for government co-payments. Some LMICs are now pushing for tiered pricing, local production under license, or regional procurement deals for future gene therapies but the path is still rough (Wehrwein, 2023).

What's Next: Four Principles for the Next Decade

As the biotech pipeline floods with gene editing, personalized vaccines, and ultra-rare disease cures, the tension between breakthrough science and financial sustainability will only grow. Experts argue for four bedrock ideas that must anchor the next generation of access strategies:

Outcomes-Based Pricing — Pay only when therapies deliver real-world results.

Risk Pooling — Spread massive upfront costs across insurers, re-insurers, and cross-border public-private funds.

Global Tiered Pricing — Adjust prices to local incomes, mirroring models used for HIV drugs in Africa.

Transparent HTA — Make value-for-money visible to policymakers, taxpayers, and patients alike (Seeley & Kesselheim, 2020; IntuitionLabs, 2026; Williams et al., 2015)

Lesson: Innovation Means Nothing Without Access

China's story is still unfolding, imperfect, evolving, and messy. But its bold willingness to pair regulatory speed with aggressive financial innovation holds lessons for the entire world.

In the end, the miracle is not just in the lab. It is in the quiet, patient work of policymakers, payers, and companies who hammer out the terms that turn a billion-dollar therapy into a million-family solution.

If the next wave of medical miracles is to fulfill its promise – not just for the privileged few but for every patient who needs them – then financial innovation will be just as critical as the science itself.

Innovation alone cannot heal the world.
Inclusive, sustainable access can.

5. IMPLICATIONS FOR GLOBAL HEALTH SECURITY

The COVID-19 pandemic stands as one of the clearest wake-up calls in modern history that health security is inseparable from national security, and by extension, from global security. The pandemic did not merely stress-test public health systems; it exposed longstanding structural weaknesses, from supply chain fragility and inequitable access to medical countermeasures to regulatory inertia and underinvestment in health innovation. But perhaps most importantly, COVID-19 demonstrated that when science, regulation, and finance align with urgency and courage, the world can deliver life-saving solutions at unprecedented speed and scale.

A Turning Point: From Siloed Systems to Integrated Innovation

Before the pandemic, the global health security paradigm centered mainly on passive defense: surveillance networks, emergency stockpiles, and static response playbooks designed for incremental action rather than rapid innovation. Drug and vaccine development timelines spanned a decade or longer, hindered by rigid regulatory pathways, fragmented cross-border collaboration, and slow-moving budgetary processes. Even when breakthroughs were technically feasible, they often stalled for lack of capital or regulatory clarity.

The 2014-2016 Ebola outbreak provided a sobering preview. Although scientists had developed promising vaccine candidates within months, the absence of dedicated financing and flexible regulatory pathways delayed large-scale trials. By the time those vaccines were deployed, the outbreak's peak had passed. This is a tragic lost opportunity that underscored how innovation without deployment is powerless to save lives (Kuppalli, 2024).

COVID-19: A Stress Test and a Catalyst

The COVID-19 crisis fundamentally rewired this mindset. The pandemic's global sweep forced policymakers, regulators, and industry leaders to ask the same urgent question: *How can we compress a 10-year vaccine timeline into 10 months?*

In China, this new reality galvanized unprecedented regulatory flexibility and financial innovation. The NMPA rapidly deployed emergency use authorizations (EUAs), conditional approvals, and rolling review processes, setting a new precedent for accelerated evaluation without compromising core safety standards. The government coordinated massive procurement programs, advance purchase agreements, and risk-sharing investment mechanisms that allowed vaccine and diagnostic developers to scale production well before final approvals.

In parallel, China leveraged state-owned enterprises and private-sector partnerships to build and repurpose manufacturing capacity almost overnight, mitigating the supply chain choke points that hampered many Western nations. This was not unique to China: similar models emerged globally. The US government's Operation Warp Speed poured billions into de-risking vaccine development. In Europe, regulators streamlined review pathways to run clinical trials and manufacturing scale-up in parallel. In the UK, the MHRA became one of the first regulators to grant a COVID-19 vaccine approval, compressing years of work into months through rolling data submissions (Burgos et al., 2021; Yang & Yang, 2022)

The Role of Financial Firepower

Yet fast-track regulatory approvals alone would have meant little without bold financial mobilization. In China, central and local governments unlocked emergency funding lines, while state banks provided favorable loan terms for biotech firms pivoting towards pandemic countermeasures. Innovative financing structures, such as advance market commitments (AMCs) and risk-sharing deals, gave both established pharma giants and emerging biotech startups the confidence to invest heavily in scaling production and navigating the volatile global supply chain.

This blend of regulatory agility and financial dynamism proved decisive, a sharp contrast to the bureaucratic delays that had hampered previous outbreak responses. For example, Sinovac and Sinopharm both pushed multiple vaccine candidates through clinical trials and large-scale production in record time, securing domestic vaccination coverage while also supplying doses abroad (Burgos et al., 2021; Yang & Yang, 2022).

Lessons for Future Crises

COVID-19's legacy is clear: agile health innovation pipelines must be integral to any serious strategy for global health security. As the world faces a future shaped by climate-driven health threats, emerging infectious diseases, antimicrobial resistance, and aging populations, the playbook for pandemic response must permanently evolve beyond stockpiles and surveillance alone.

China's experience shows that emerging markets, in particular, can build resilience by embedding innovation incentives into their regulatory frameworks and aligning capital markets with public health goals. The expansion of platforms like the STAR

Market which gave early-stage biotech firms access to growth capital, combined with strong government procurement and technology transfer support, provides a blueprint for how countries can de-risk innovation even in volatile conditions.

Moreover, China's pivot to integrating digital health, big data analytics, and AI-driven drug discovery during the pandemic illustrates the critical role of next-generation technologies in future responses. As pathogens evolve and new health threats emerge, the speed of detection, development, and deployment will increasingly define a nation's – and the world's – ability to contain crises before they spiral (Osong Public Health and Research Perspectives, 2025).

Global Health Security as Shared Security

Finally, the COVID-19 pandemic revealed that no country, however advanced its domestic capabilities, can stand alone in the face of global biological threats (WHO, 2025). China's biotech rise also highlighted the benefits and complexities of cross-border collaboration. From licensing deals and joint clinical trials to multinational supply chains and global regulatory submissions, the crisis accelerated a new model of interconnected, cooperative innovation that must be sustained (Fidler, 2026).

Yet inequities remain stark. Many low- and middle-income countries struggled to access vaccines and treatments despite record global output, reminding the world that manufacturing scale must be matched by fair allocation mechanisms and local capacity building. Here too, China's expansion of fill-finish operations and technology transfers to partner countries offers lessons on how emerging markets can contribute to closing global access gaps while securing their own populations.

Lesson

Future global health security will depend on countries' ability to institutionalize what COVID-19 made possible under duress: rapid alignment of regulation, capital, and science, supported by clear governance structures that can pivot from peacetime to crisis mode. China's experience, for all its unique features, provides a compelling case study of how state policy, market forces, and technological ambition can come together to transform crisis into catalytic progress.

By embedding these lessons, nations and global health institutions can build a more resilient, equitable, and responsive system, one that treats health security not as an episodic emergency, but as a continuous, shared investment in global stability.

CONCLUSION

Over the past decade, China's biotech industry has undergone remarkable growth, transforming from a nascent sector into a global powerhouse. Through substantial investments in research and development, regulatory reforms, and international collaborations, China has made significant contributions to global healthcare. Innovations in gene editing, vaccine development, and biologics have not only addressed domestic health challenges but also provided life-saving solutions worldwide, as exemplified by China's rapid response during the COVID-19 pandemic.

The rise of China's biotech sector has also fostered greater global competition and cooperation, accelerating advancements in precision medicine, rare disease treatments, and affordable therapeutics. However, challenges such as intellectual property protection, market access barriers, and ethical considerations remain critical areas for further progress.

Looking ahead, China's biotech industry is poised to play an even more pivotal role in shaping the future of healthcare. By continuing to prioritize innovation, sustainability, and equitable access, China can further solidify its position as a key driver of global biotechnological advancement, benefiting patients and healthcare systems across the world.

REFERENCES

Azevedo, M. J. (2017). The state of health system(s) in Africa: Challenges and opportunities. In *Historical perspectives on the state of health and health systems in Africa, Volume II: the modern era*, 1-73. Palgrave Macmillan. https://doi.org/DOI: 10.1007/978-3-319-32564-4_1

Back Bay Life Science Advisors. (2025, January 20). *Exploring the US-China biotech boom*. https://www.bblsa.com/white-papers/exploring-the-us-china-biotech-boom

BeiGene, Ltd. (2021, December 2). *BeiGene announces pricing of initial public offering on the STAR Market of the Shanghai Stock Exchange*. https://ir.beigene.com/news-details/?id=0661a3f6-4f6e-44e2-8e7c-86e0c0567e9b

Bloomberg. (2024, May 31). Akeso's lung cancer drug beats Keytruda in head-to-head trial. *Bloomberg News*. https://www.bloomberg.com/news/articles/2024-05-31/akeso-s-cancer-drug-beats-keytruda-in-trial-lifting-china-biotech

Bloomberg News. (2024, July 14). China biotech's stunning advance is changing the world's drug pipeline. Bloomberg. https://www.bloomberg.com/news/articles/2024-07-14/china-biotech-s-stunning-advance-is-changing-the-world-s-drug-pipeline

Buntz, B. (2024, January 3). Zai Lab's unified approach to tackling cancer, autoimmune, and neurological diseases. *Drug Discovery & Development*. https://www.drugdiscoverytrends.com/zai-labs-unified-approach-to-tackling-cancer-autoimmune-and-neurological-diseases/

Burgos, R. M., Badowski, M. E., Drwiega, E., Ghassemi, S., Griffith, N., Herald, F., Johnson, M., Smith, R. O., & Michienzi, S. M. (2021). The race to a COVID-19 vaccine: Opportunities and challenges in development and distribution. *Drugs in Context, 10*, 2020-12-2. https://doi.org/DOI: 10.7573/dic.2020-12-2

CanSino Biologics Inc. (2025). *Newsroom*. https://www.cansinotech.com/detail-4584

Centers for Disease Control and Prevention. (2025, January 16). *Public health data strategy milestones for 2025 and 2026*. U.S. Department of Health and Human Services. https://www.cdc.gov/public-health-data-strategy/php/about/phds-milestones-2025-and-2026.html

Chang, W., Ripley, W., & Cheung, E. (2025, February 25). *A little-known Chinese company made a drug that beat the world's biggest-selling medicine*. CNN. https://www.cnn.com/2025/02/25/business/china-akeso-drug-merck-keytruda-intl-hnk/index.html

Chen, V., & Shao, W. (2023). Balancing medical innovation and affordability in the new healthcare ecosystem in China: Review of pharmaceutical pricing and reimbursement policies. *Health Care Science*, *2*(6), 381–391. DOI: 10.1002/hcs2.76 PMID: 38938625

Chu, C. (2025). Global health security in the post-COVID-19 era: Threats, preparation, and response. *Osong Public Health and Research Perspectives*, *16*(2), 116–125. DOI: 10.24171/j.phrp.2025.0037 PMID: 40190032

Diao, Y., Li, M., Huang, Z., Sun, J., Chee, Y. L., & Liu, Y. (2019). Unlocking access to novel medicines in China—A review from a health system perspective. *Risk Management and Healthcare Policy*, *12*, 357–367. DOI: 10.2147/RMHP.S226379 PMID: 31908552

DiMasi, J. A., Grabowski, H. G., & Hansen, R. W. (2016). Innovation in the pharmaceutical industry: New estimates of R&D costs. *Journal of Health Economics*, *47*, 20–33. DOI: 10.1016/j.jhealeco.2016.01.012 PMID: 26928437

ECHEMI. (2024, February 28). *Wang Xiaodong: Pioneering the future! China's first billion-dollar molecular father*. https://www.echemi.com/cms/1429532.html

Elechi, U. S., Onah, C. O., Tarawallie, M. A., & Ifeanyi, I. (2025). Beyond seed funding: Why Nigerian digital health startups struggle to grow. *Health Economics Review*, *16*(2), 2. Advance online publication. DOI: 10.1186/s13561-025-00708-6 PMID: 41348174

Fidler, B. (2026, January 26). China's edge in early-stage drugmaking 'likely to persist,' Pitchbook says. *BioPharma Dive*. https://www.biopharmadive.com/news/china-biotech-drug-licensing-trends-pitchbook-cell-gene-therapy/810478/

Fierce Biotech. (2018, February 23). *Moderna's cash juggernaut rolls on with record $604M IPO*. https://www.fiercebiotech.com/biotech/moderna-s-cash-juggernaut-rolls-record-604m-ipo

Forbes. (2021, March 11). *The queen of China's biotech: How Samantha Du built Zai Lab into a $10 billion powerhouse*. https://www.forbes.com/sites/jenniferwang/2021/03/11/the-queen-of-chinas-biotech-how-samantha-du-built-zai-lab-into-a-10-billion-powerhouse/

He, A. J. (2023). Scaling-up through piloting: Dual-track provider payment reforms in China's health system. *Health Policy and Planning*, *38*(2), 218–227. DOI: 10.1093/heapol/czac080 PMID: 36103333

Helmi. (2024). *Biotech risks and challenges in Latin America*. https://helmi.com/insights/biotech-risks-and-challenges-in-latin-america

HKEX. (2018). *Annual report 2018*. https://www.hkexnews.hk/listedco/listconews/sehk/2019/0429/ltn201904292085.pdf

HKEX. (2025). *Biotech listing regime*. https://www.hkex.com.hk/Join-Our-Market/Biotech?sc_lang=en

Hong Kong Exchanges and Clearing Limited. (2018, April 24). *Hong Kong's listing regime enters new era, featuring emerging and innovative firms* [Press release]. https://www.hkex.com.hk/News/News-Release/2018/180424news?sc_lang=en

Hu, Y., & Mossialos, E. (2017). Pharmaceutical pricing and reimbursement in China: When price controls and drug markups are abolished. *Globalization and Health, 13*(1), 1–7. DOI: 10.1186/s12992-017-0285-x PMID: 28049495

Innovent Biologics. (2016, November 29). *Innovent Biologics, Inc. raises USD $260M in Series D financing*. PR Newswire. https://www.prnewswire.com/news-releases/innovent-biologics-inc-raises-usd-260m-in-series-d-financing-300369527.html

Innovent Biologics. (2024). *About us*. https://en.innoventbio.com/AboutUs

IntuitionLabs. (2026, January 10). *Value-based contracting in pharma: Models & challenges*. https://intuitionlabs.ai/articles/value-based-contracting-pharmaceuticals

IUPAC. (2014). Compendium of chemical terminology (2nd ed.; the "Gold Book"). (A. D. McNaught & A. Wilkinson, Comps.). Blackwell Scientific Publications. Online version (2019-) created by S. J. Chalk. https://doi.org/DOI: 10.1351/goldbook.B00666

Jia, R., & Ma, X. (2024). *Improving regulation for innovation: Evidence from China's pharmaceutical industry* (Working Paper No. w31976). National Bureau of Economic Research. https://doi.org/DOI: 10.3386/w31976

Kaló, Z., Kruja, K., Noone, D., Vogler, S., & Docteur, E. (2025). Collective international action to increase access to costly drugs: Pooled procurement and equity based tiered pricing. *BMJ (Clinical Research Ed.), 391*, e084839. DOI: 10.1136/bmj-2025-084839 PMID: 41218989

Keam, S. J. (2022). Cadonilimab: First approval. *Drugs, 82*(12), 1333–1339. DOI: 10.1007/s40265-022-01761-9 PMID: 35986837

Kuppalli, K. (2024). Ebola: Ten years later—Lessons learned and future pandemic preparedness. *PLOS Global Public Health, 4*(9), e0003662. DOI: 10.1371/journal.pgph.0003662 PMID: 39325790

Matthew Dennis. (2019, November 28). *China adds 70 new medicines to National Reimbursement Drug List, with average price cuts of 61%*. First Word Pharma.

McKinsey & Company. (2021, October). *The dawn of China's biopharma innovation.* McKinsey Global Institute. https://www.mckinsey.com/industries/life-sciences/our-insights/the-dawn-of-chinas-biopharma-innovation

McKinsey & Company. (2024). *2024 BioCentury China Healthcare Summit: McKinsey biopharma report.* https://www.scribd.com/document/854593184/2024-BioCentury-China-Healthcare-Summit-McKinsey-Biopharma-report

Mullard, A. (2016). Parsing clinical success rates. *Nature Reviews. Drug Discovery, 15*(7), 447–447. DOI: 10.1038/nrd.2016.136 PMID: 27357012

Nasdaq. (2016, February 3). *Chinese cancer biotech BeiGene prices IPO at $24, high end of range.* https://www.nasdaq.com/articles/chinese-cancer-biotech-beigene-prices-ipo-24-high-end-range-2016-02-03

National Health Commission of the PRC. (2020, June 28). *News.* https://en.nhc.gov.cn/2020-06/28/c_80923.htm

National Medical Products Administration. (2018). *Announcement on adjusting the review and approval procedures for drug clinical trials* (No. 50 of 2018). Center for Drug Evaluation.

National Medical Products Administration. (2020). *Procedures for the review and approval of priority review and approval of drug marketing authorizations (Interim).* Center for Drug Evaluation.

National Medical Products Administration. (2024). *2023 drug review annual report.* Center for Drug Evaluation.

National People's Congress. (2020). *Patent law of the People's Republic of China (Fourth Amendment).* Adopted October 17, 2020; Effective June 1, 2021. https://www.wipo.int/wipolex/en/legislation/details/21027

NMPA & CNIPA. (2021). *Measures for the implementation of the mechanism for early settlement of drug patent disputes (Trial Implementation)* [Announcement No. 89 of 2021]. https://english.nmpa.gov.cn/2021-07/04/c_661004.htm

Nuijten, M. (2021). Pricing Zolgensma – the world's most expensive drug. *Journal of Market Access & Health Policy, 10*(1), 2022353. Advance online publication. DOI: 10.1080/20016689.2021.2022353 PMID: 34992762

Oyler, J. V. (2025, October 29). *From vision to global transformation – The journey of 15 years of BeOne Medicines.* OncoDaily. https://oncodaily.com/voices/beone-medicines-400325

Pharma Board Room. (2026, January 27). *The sea turtles: China's top pharma talent comes home.* https://pharmaboardroom.com/articles/the-sea-turtles-chinas-top-pharma-talent-comes-home/

PharmaCube News. (2024). *China's pharmaceutical sector marks a 'breakthrough era': A decade-long commercialization review (2015-2024).* PharmaCube Global. https://global.pharmcube.com/

PRNewswire. (2020, August 17). *Innovent and Lilly announce expansion of TYVYT® (sintilimab injection) licensing agreement.* https://www.prnewswire.com/news-releases/innovent-and-lilly-announce-expansion-of-tyvyt-sintilimab-injection-licensing-agreement-301113764.html

Reuters. (2018, October 30). *China's Innovent Biologics raises $421 million in HK IPO: sources.* https://www.reuters.com/article/innovent-biologics-ipo-idUSL3N1X921G/

Saionz, A. (2025, November 12). *Inside Hengrui: The making of China's top pharma innovator.* Pharma Boardroom. https://pharmaboardroom.com/articles/inside-hengrui-the-making-of-chinas-top-pharma-innovator/

Santos Ivo, R., Rodrigues, T., Couto, S., & Cossito, M. (2025). The art of bridge building: A look at the European-level cooperation in HTA (EU-HTA). *Journal of Market Access & Health Policy, 13*(2), 26. DOI: 10.3390/jmahp13020026 PMID: 40568381

Seeley, E., & Kesselheim, A. S. (2020). *Outcomes-based pharmaceutical contracts: An answer to high U.S. drug spending?* The Commonwealth Fund. https://www.commonwealthfund.org/publications/issue-briefs/2020/sep/outcomes-based-pharmaceutical-contracts-answer-high-drug-spending

The Global Fund. (2025, July 9). *Global Fund secures access to breakthrough HIV prevention drug lenacapavir for low- and middle-income countries.* https://www.theglobalfund.org/en/news/2025/2025-07-09-global-fund-secures-access-breakthrough-hiv-prevention-drug-lenacapavir/

The Pharma Letter. (2020, January 21). *China's national generics procurement cuts prices up to 93%.* https://www.thepharmaletter.com/generics-news/china-s-national-generics-procurement-cuts-prices-up-to-93

Today Online. (2016, June 17). *China's biotech revolution ushered in by 'sea turtles'.* https://www.todayonline.com/world/chinas-beotech-revolution-ushered-sea-turtles

USC Schaeffer Center. (2019, July 2). *Using the drug pricing Netflix model to help states tackle the Hep C crisis.* https://schaeffer.usc.edu/research/using-the-drug-pricing-netflix-model-to-help-states-tackle-the-hep-c-crisis/

Wehrwein, P. (2023, November 28). They cost millions. How payers might manage those astronomical gene therapy bills. *Managed Healthcare Executive.* https://www.managedhealthcareexecutive.com/view/they-cost-millions-how-payers-might-manage-their-gene-therapy-bills

Williams, O. D., Ooms, G., & Hill, P. S. (2015). Cautionary notes on a global tiered pricing framework for medicines. *American Journal of Public Health, 105*(7), 1290–1293. DOI: 10.2105/AJPH.2015.302554 PMID: 25973806

Wong, G. (2008). Developing China's homegrown biotechnology workforce. *Nature Biotechnology, 26*(3), 353–354. DOI: 10.1038/nbt0308-353 PMID: 18327247

World Bank Group. (2025, December 6). *Gavi and World Bank Group deepen collaboration to boost health system resilience and regional vaccine manufacturing.* https://www.worldbank.org/en/news/press-release/2025/12/06/gavi-wbg-collaboration-boosts-health-system-resilience-regional-vaccine-manufacturing

World Health Organization. (2025, June 27). *Pandemic prevention, preparedness and response agreement.* https://www.who.int/news-room/questions-and-answers/item/pandemic-prevention-preparedness-and-response-agreement

Yan, C. H., Lin, K. X., Zheng, X. Y., & Meng, X. H. (2025). Interrupted time series analysis of the impact of DIP reform on hospitalization costs in different types of hospitals. *Frontiers in Public Health, 13*, 1644476. DOI: 10.3389/fpubh.2025.1644476 PMID: 41179796

Yang, J., & Yang, Y. (2022). Regulatory lessons from China's COVID-19 vaccines development and approval policies. *Acta Materia Medica, 1*(1), 16–25. DOI: 10.15212/AMM-2021-0008

Zagorski, N. (2005). Profile of Xiaodong Wang. *Proceedings of the National Academy of Sciences of the United States of America, 103*(1), 7–9. DOI: 10.1073/pnas.0509187103 PMID: 16380419

Zhai, S., Wang, Q., Zhu, Z., Han, R., Lv, Y., Zhu, C., Zhang, R., Zhang, L., & Yang, L. (2025). Impact of Market Authorization Holder (MAH) system on pharmaceutical innovation in China. *Journal of Pharmaceutical Policy and Practice, 18*(1), 2551794. DOI: 10.1080/20523211.2025.2551794 PMID: 40918402

Zhang, H., Fu, X., Wu, Y., Tang, Y., Jin, H., & Xie, B. (2025). The impact of DRG-based payment reform on inpatient healthcare utilization: Evidence from a natural experiment in China. *Health Care, 13*(19), 2424. DOI: 10.3390/healthcare13192424 PMID: 41095510

Zhang, J., & Li, X. (2025). Technological and industrial trends in China's pharmaceutical sector. *Frontiers in Pharmacology, 16*, 1579037. DOI: 10.3389/fphar.2025.1579037 PMID: 41035909

Zhang, J., Tang, S., & Sun, P. (2025). From command-control to lifecycle regulation: Balancing innovation and safety in China's pharmaceutical legislation. *Health Care, 13*(6), 588. Advance online publication. DOI: 10.3390/healthcare13060588 PMID: 40150438

Zhao, B., & Wu, J. (2023). Impact of China's national volume-based procurement on drug procurement price, volume, and expenditure: An interrupted time series analysis in Tianjin. *International Journal of Health Policy and Management, 12*, 7724. DOI: 10.34172/ijhpm.2023.7724 PMID: 38618801

Zwetsloot, R. (2020, April). *China's approach to tech talent competition: Policies, results, and the developing global response*. Brookings Institution. https://www.brookings.edu/articles/chinas-approach-to-tech-talent-competition/

APPENDIX

Case study: BeOne (Former BeiGene)'s success story

BeiGene was founded in 2010 in Beijing by John V. Oyler, an American entrepreneur, and Xiaodong Wang, a highly respected Chinese scientist known for his discoveries in apoptosis. From the outset, BeiGene set itself apart from traditional Chinese pharmaceutical companies by focusing not on generics but on developing innovative oncology drugs with a vision to bring high-quality, affordable cancer medicines to patients worldwide.

One of BeiGene's early strategic decisions was to build a strong dual R&D model. They invested heavily in discovery and development in China, but always with a global mindset, designing and running clinical trials that would meet international regulatory standards. This strategy enabled BeiGene to advance a pipeline of promising oncology treatments that could compete globally, not just in the local market.

A turning point came with Brukinsa® (zanubrutinib), a next-generation BTK inhibitor for treating B-cell malignancies such as mantle cell lymphoma and chronic lymphocytic leukemia. Competing directly with established drugs like Imbruvica, Brukinsa® demonstrated strong clinical performance with improved selectivity and potentially fewer side effects. Another key product, tislelizumab (BeiGene's PD-1 inhibitor) was designed with unique properties that could minimize some typical immune-related side effects seen with other checkpoint inhibitors.

To support its global ambitions, BeiGene listed on NASDAQ in 2016, becoming one of the first Chinese biotech companies to go public in the USA. It later listed in Hong Kong in 2018 and on the Shanghai STAR Market in 2021, raising significant capital to fund its pipeline and global expansion. Meanwhile, it built a truly international presence with operations and manufacturing facilities in the USA, Europe, Australia, and China, including a massive biologics plant in Guangzhou.

BeiGene's growth was also driven by strategic partnerships that brought validation and resources. A landmark deal came in 2019 when Amgen invested \$2.7 billion for a 20% stake, giving Amgen a partner to expand in China while providing BeiGene with pipeline assets and a major credibility boost. Earlier, BeiGene had also partnered with Celgene on tislelizumab, but later regained full global rights after Celgene's acquisition by Bristol Myers Squibb.

BeiGene made history when Brukinsa® received FDA approval in 2019, making it one of the first self-developed Chinese cancer drugs to gain approval from the US FDA. Today, BeiGene markets its products in over 60 countries, with a commercial footprint expanding rapidly across North America, Europe, and Asia-Pacific. Its success demonstrated that a biotech born in China could build world-class R&D,

navigate complex global regulatory pathways, and commercialize innovative medicines on par with leading Western biotech firms.

BeiGene continues to face challenges, from fierce competition in the immuno-oncology and BTK inhibitor markets to navigating geopolitical headwinds between the USA and China. Yet it remains a symbol of what is possible for Chinese biotech, proof that combining strong science, global standards, and bold partnerships can produce a company that competes and collaborates at the highest levels of the global pharmaceutical industry (Oyler, 2025).

Case Study: Zai Lab — Bridging China and Global Biotech

Founding Story: From Big Pharma to a New Vision

Zai Lab was founded in 2014 by Dr Samantha Du (often called the "Queen of China Biotech"). Dr Du is the quintessential "sea turtle" ( ): she earned her PhD in the USA, built her career at major multinationals like Pfizer and Hutchison MediPharma, and hit the same "glass ceiling" that pushed so many returnees to come home.

While working at Pfizer, Dr Du realized that despite her scientific contributions, Asian scientists often faced invisible barriers in Big Pharma's upper echelons. But she also saw China's vast unmet medical needs (especially in oncology) and the historic opening created by policy reforms, capital inflows, and regulatory modernization.

So she left Pfizer and founded Zai Lab in Shanghai with a simple but bold vision: build a world-class Chinese biotech company that could connect the best global science with China's huge patient base and eventually take Chinese innovation global.

Strategic DNA: The "In-Licensing + Indigenous R&D" Model

Unlike some domestic players focused only on copying or local generics, Zai Lab's model from day one was dual-pronged:

Bring global breakthrough therapies to China: Zai Lab aggressively in-licensed innovative drugs from US and European biotech firms that lacked the experience or infrastructure to navigate China's unique regulatory and commercial environment.

Develop original drugs for global markets: In parallel, Zai built its own R&D engine to produce novel candidates, particularly in oncology, autoimmune diseases, and infectious diseases, aiming for simultaneous China-US approvals.

This hybrid model let Zai scale quickly: it could generate revenue by commercializing best-in-class licensed drugs while investing strategically in first-in-class internal innovation.

Key Deals that Put Zai Lab on the Map

Zai's licensing deals read like a "Who's Who" of cutting-edge biopharma partnerships:

2016: Partnered with Tesaro (later acquired by GSK) for Zejula (niraparib), a PARP inhibitor for ovarian cancer. Zai localized trials, secured rapid NMPA approval, and built commercial infrastructure for launch.

2018: In-licensed Tumor Treating Fields (TTFields) therapy Optune from Novocure, a non-invasive device for glioblastoma that was innovative and differentiated in the Chinese market.

2019–2021: Secured multiple high-value partnerships with Mirati Therapeutics, Incyte, Regeneron, and GlaxoSmithKline, covering next-gen oncology targets like KRAS inhibitors, immunotherapies, and bispecific antibodies.

These deals positioned Zai Lab as the partner of choice for Western biotechs wanting China access without building a local presence from scratch.

Regulatory Mastery: Fast Approvals and Simultaneous Filings

Zai Lab's leadership helped shape and benefit from China's regulatory transformation:

Simultaneous Global Trials: Zai Lab pioneered the "China-in-global" development model, designing pivotal trials to include Chinese sites from the start. This allowed them to file for NMPA and FDA approval almost in parallel, cutting the traditional 5–7 year gap between Western and Chinese launches.

ICH Alignment: Dr Du and Zai's regulatory team worked closely with Chinese authorities as they harmonized with ICH GCP standards, helping prove that locally run trials could meet global quality benchmarks.

Breakthrough Designations: Several Zai programs earned Priority Review and Breakthrough Therapy status in China, thanks to clear data, regulatory experience, and patient advocacy to highlight unmet needs.

Innovating at Home: The Homegrown Pipeline

While licensing built early momentum, Zai Lab has steadily grown its internal pipeline, investing in novel mechanisms for:

Oncology (KRAS inhibitors, immunotherapies)

Autoimmune diseases (IL-17, IL-23 targets)

Infectious diseases (next-gen antibiotics)

Zai has over 40+ clinical trials spanning China and global sites, with several homegrown assets now in Phase I–III, a critical step towards becoming not just a bridge but a true originator of first-in-class therapies.

Going Global: Nasdaq Listing and Beyond

In 2017, Zai Lab listed on Nasdaq – one of the first wave of Chinese biotech IPOs to tap US capital markets under the "pre-revenue" biotech model. Its debut signaled that Western investors were ready to bet on China's innovation narrative, not just its manufacturing scale.

In 2020, Zai Lab added a Hong Kong secondary listing under Chapter 18A, reinforcing its position as a cross-border champion. The dual listing structure gave it flexibility to raise capital, attract global investors, and anchor itself as a truly international biotech company.

Impact on China's Biotech Ecosystem

Zai Lab's success rippled far beyond its own walls:

Inspiration: Proved that a Chinese biotech could master global dealmaking, run ICH-grade trials, and win simultaneous approvals.

Regulatory Benchmark: Helped test and refine China's faster pathways for innovative drugs, setting precedent for other local players.

Talent Magnet: Became a training ground for a new generation of regulatory, clinical, and commercial leaders who have since spread across China's biotech ecosystem.

Samantha Du: A Role Model for the Next Wave

Dr Du's journey, from hitting the glass ceiling at Pfizer to becoming one of China's most influential biotech founders, remains a North Star for young scientists and entrepreneurs. She is frequently cited in both Western and Chinese media as proof that purpose-driven returnees can unlock China's innovation potential while shaping global healthcare.

Zai Lab Today and Tomorrow

As of 2024, Zai Lab:

Employs more than 1,800 people across China and the USA.

Markets multiple innovative drugs in China's oncology and rare disease markets.

Continues to advance its proprietary pipeline globally, with ambitions to launch first-in-class assets outside China under its own name.

Zai's next frontier is clear: transition from "bridge" to "global innovator," with more revenue from internally developed products and ex-China markets.

Key Lessons from Zai Lab

Build Bridges, Not Walls: Smart licensing lets young companies leapfrog years of internal development while building local know-how and revenue.

Local + Global R&D: Simultaneous global trials and regulatory filings show that China's innovation can stand shoulder-to-shoulder with Western peers.

Talent is Destiny: Returnee leaders like Samantha Du brought not only science but regulatory savvy, cross-cultural dealmaking skills, and credibility that inspired global partners and investors.

Keep Evolving: Zai's pivot towards more in-house innovation shows that licensing can be a launchpad but sustainable leadership depends on building your own IP and global pipelines.

Conclusion: Zai Lab's Broader Significance

Zai Lab exemplifies what the best of China's biotech boom looks like: purpose-driven leadership, smart cross-border partnerships, deep regulatory mastery, and an unwavering bet on bridging global science with local patient need.

Its story reminds emerging market biotech that success is not about isolation, it is about connection:

Connection to global science. Connection to patients. Connection to capital. Connection to a vision larger than any one molecule.

(Buntz, 2024; Zai Lab, 2025)

Case Study: Akeso — From Domestic Upstart to Global Bispecific Pioneer

Founding Story: A Late Mover with a Bold Vision

Akeso, Inc. (:09926.HK) was founded in 2012 by Dr Michelle Xia Yu, a returnee scientist and serial entrepreneur who had previously co-founded and led a US-based biotech company. Like many "sea turtle" leaders, Dr Xia brought back not only Western scientific training but a clear vision for how China could leapfrog in cutting-edge biologics rather than stay stuck in the generics trap.

Akeso entered a market already crowded with domestic biosimilar and "me-too" antibody developers. But from the beginning, Dr Xia bet big on innovation-first differentiation, focusing on novel monoclonal antibodies and, crucially, next-generation bispecific antibodies, a then-nascent technology with few domestic players.

Strategic Differentiator: The Bispecific Antibody Bet

While global pharma giants like Amgen, Roche, and Regeneron had begun to test the waters with bispecifics (antibodies that bind two different targets simultaneously), China's local industry mostly lagged behind, focused on single-target "fast followers."

Akeso saw an opening: it built its own proprietary Tetrabody technology platform, designed to generate stable, manufacturable, and clinically viable bispecifics with higher efficacy and manageable safety profiles. This placed Akeso among the very first Chinese biotechs to develop an in-house bispecific antibody platform at scale — a risky bet at the time, given technical complexity and uncertain regulatory pathways.

Flagship Innovation: Cadonilimab (PD-1/CTLA-4)

Akeso's crown jewel is Cadonilimab (AK104) — China's first domestically developed bispecific PD-1/CTLA-4 antibody, approved by the NMPA in June 2022 for relapsed/refractory cervical cancer.

Cadonilimab combines the benefits of PD-1 and CTLA-4 blockade. This is a strategy that had already shown promise in global immuno-oncology (like BMS's Opdivo + Yervoy combo) but does so within a single molecule. This design offers potential advantages: a more precise dosing balance, lower toxicity than combination cocktails, and simplified administration.

The approval marked a watershed: not only was Cadonilimab China's first approved bispecific checkpoint inhibitor, but it also became the world's first approved PD-1/CTLA-4 bispecific, putting Akeso in the same conversation as leading-edge Western immunotherapy developers (Keam, 2022).

Pipelines, Partnerships, and Global Ambition

Beyond Cadonilimab, Akeso has built a robust pipeline of over 30 clinical-stage candidates, spanning:

Immuno-oncology (multiple bispecifics targeting PD-1, CTLA-4, LAG-3, TIGIT)

Autoimmune diseases (like AK101, an IL-12/IL-23 antibody)

Innovative ADCs (antibody-drug conjugates)

Recognizing the need to globalize, Akeso signed a landmark out-licensing and co-development deal with Summit Therapeutics in 2022 for its anti-TIGIT/PD-1 bispecific (Ivonescimab/AK112). The deal, valued at up to $5 billion, includes US and European rights, a strong vote of confidence from an international partner and proof of Akeso's ability to develop assets attractive on the global stage.

Akeso also began setting up a US presence, hiring talent with global regulatory expertise to help run pivotal trials that meet both NMPA and FDA standards, mirroring the bridge-building approach of earlier pioneers like Zai Lab.

> "The pharma industry is the best industry in the world," Akeso Chief Executive Officer Michelle Xia said in an April interview. "At the end of the day, what we do benefits patients in China, in the US and all around the world.
> (Chang et al., 2025; Akeso, 2025; Bloomberg News, 2024)

Case Study: Hengrui Pharma — From Generics Giant to Innovation Leader

Origins: The Humble Roots of China's Largest Pharma Company

Hengrui Pharmaceuticals, founded in 1970 in Lianyungang, Jiangsu Province, started life like many legacy Chinese pharma companies: a state-owned generics manufacturer focused on supplying low-cost injectable drugs to domestic hospitals. For decades, its portfolio was dominated by anesthetics, antibiotics, and chemotherapy generics sold under tight government price controls.

By the early 2000s, Hengrui was already China's largest producer of injectable oncology generics but its future looked precarious. As China joined the WTO, foreign multinationals began pouring in advanced drugs, while local price wars squeezed margins to razor-thin levels. The writing was on the wall: relying on me-too generics was not sustainable.

The Transformation Imperative: From Generics to Innovation

Recognizing the threat, Hengrui's leadership, especially under Chairman Sun Piaoyang, decided on a radical pivot: transform from a generic-drug factory to a globally competitive R&D-driven pharmaceutical company.

Unlike smaller biotech startups founded by returnees, Hengrui faced different challenges:

A huge legacy product base that funded the transition but also demanded cost discipline.

A workforce more skilled in manufacturing and sales than cutting-edge drug discovery.

A need to shift its brand perception from a "factory" to an "innovator."

This transformation began in the early 2000s, long before China's biotech boom caught fire, making Hengrui a pioneer among domestic incumbents.

Key Moves on the Road to Innovation

Massive Investment in R&D

Hengrui began reinvesting a growing share of its profits into in-house R&D, steadily raising its R&D spending from less than 2% of sales in 2000 to over 12% by the mid-2010s, matching or exceeding some Western peers.

It built state-of-the-art research centers in Lianyungang, Shanghai, and the USA (New Jersey and Boston), hiring hundreds of scientists, including returnees with Big Pharma and CRO backgrounds.

Original IP and New Drug Approvals

Hengrui's first big test was Apatinib, a VEGFR-2 inhibitor for gastric cancer, approved in 2014. It became China's first domestically developed small molecule anti-angiogenesis drug, proving that a local company could invent, develop, and commercialize a novel oncology drug.

Apatinib not only won domestic approval but also entered clinical trials abroad, positioning Hengrui as one of the first Chinese pharma firms to pursue FDA and EMA pathways for a homegrown asset.

Going Global

To break into mature markets, Hengrui:

Set up US subsidiaries like Hengrui Therapeutics in Princeton and Boston.

Hired seasoned global executives and returnee CSOs with deep experience in US/EU filings.

Partnered with global CROs and CMOs to run multi-center pivotal trials.

Pursued co-development and out-licensing deals to share risk and gain global trial experience.

Shifting the Product Mix

Hengrui's pipeline now spans:

Novel oncology drugs: PD-1 inhibitors (Camrelizumab), VEGFR inhibitors, ADCs.

Non-oncology innovation: anesthetics, pain management, diabetes, cardiovascular.

Biosimilars and biologics.

Today, Hengrui has over 20+ innovative assets in clinical trials or on the market, with a growing share of revenue from new drugs instead of legacy generics.

Key Flagship: Camrelizumab

Perhaps the most visible symbol of Hengrui's transformation is Camrelizumab, its domestically developed PD-1 monoclonal antibody for multiple cancers. Launched in 2019, Camrelizumab competes directly with imported blockbusters like Keytruda and Opdivo but at significantly lower cost, rapidly winning share in China's huge oncology market.

The drug has been paired with other Hengrui assets to test combination regimens for liver, lung, esophageal, and gastric cancers, mirroring Western immuno-oncology strategies and showing Hengrui's capacity for sophisticated, multi-drug clinical design.

Financial Firepower and Discipline

Hengrui's transformation has been possible in part because its generics cash cow has funded the long payback period of innovative drug R&D. Unlike some venture-backed biotechs that depend on repeated fundraising, Hengrui runs a profitable core business that makes it one of the most financially stable innovators in China's biotech landscape.

This dual model of mature generics + emerging innovation helps hedge risk, sustain large clinical pipelines, and keep investor confidence high.

Challenges Along the Way

Hengrui's journey has not been without challenges:

Global Competition: Competing head-to-head with Merck, BMS, and Roche in immuno-oncology requires massive data, brand trust, and long-term investment.

Talent War: Attracting and retaining top-tier R&D talent is an ongoing battle, especially as Chinese startups lure returnees with equity and entrepreneurial excitement.

Regulatory Alignment: While Hengrui has learned to navigate NMPA fast-track pathways, filing with FDA and EMA for simultaneous global launches remains complex and resource-intensive.

Broader Impact on China's Pharma Ecosystem

Hengrui's shift inspired other big domestic players such as CSPC, Fosun Pharma, and Sino Biopharm to pivot from low-margin generics towards innovation, amplifying the entire industry's global competitiveness.

Its success also gave confidence to investors that Chinese companies could build world-class R&D at scale, not just nimble startups with imported IP.

Recent Milestones

In 2020, Hengrui spun out its innovative R&D business into Hengrui Therapeutics, a US-focused biotech aimed at licensing and developing assets for Western markets.

It continues to expand clinical trials across the USA, Europe, and Japan, a sign that its ambitions are not just local leadership but global reach.

As of 2024, Hengrui ranks among the Top 50 global pharma companies by revenue, with an R&D workforce of 5,000+ scientists, the largest R&D team among China's pharma firms.

Key Lessons from Hengrui's Transformation

Legacy Can Fund Leapfrogging: A strong generics base gave Hengrui the cash flow and manufacturing muscle to reinvest in riskier novel drugs.

Don't Just License, Invent: While licensing is smart for startups, an established player like Hengrui proved that homegrown IP is critical for global respect.

Globalization Takes Patience: Years of overseas trials, regulatory filings, and hiring local talent have taught Hengrui that becoming a peer to Big Pharma is a marathon, not a sprint.

Policy Reform Matters: Hengrui's rise parallels China's opening of the MAH system, faster drug review timelines, and ICH alignment, showing that policy shifts and corporate courage make transformation possible.

Lesson: A Blueprint for Legacy Innovators

Hengrui's story shows how an old-school domestic pharma can remake itself into a global player by combining stable cash flow, massive reinvestment in science, a long-term mindset, and a willingness to compete at the highest levels.

It is a powerful lesson for other emerging markets: with the right leadership and policy environment, even generics giants can evolve into global innovators. (Hengrui Pharma, 2025; Saionz, 2025)

Compilation of References

Aarogyasri, A. P. (2011). Aarogyasri healthcare model: Advantage private sector. *Economic and Political Weekly*, *46*(49), 39.

Aashima, & Sharma, R. (2024). A systematic review of the world's largest government sponsored health insurance scheme for 500 million beneficiaries in India: Pradhan Mantri Jan Arogya Yojana. *Applied Health Economics and Health Policy*, *22*(1), 17–32. https://doi.org/DOI: 10.1007/s40258-023-00792-8

Aayog, N. I. T. I. (2021). *Health system for a new India: Building blocks*. https://www.niti.gov.in/health-system-new-india (Accessed June 29, 2024)

Abernethy, A., Adams, L., Barrett, M., Bechtel, C., Brennan, P., Butte, A., Faulkner, J., Fontaine, E., Friedhoff, S., Halamka, J., Howell, M., Johnson, K., Long, P., McGraw, D., Miller, R., Lee, P., Perlin, J., Rucker, D., Sandy, L., & Valdes, K. (2022). The promise of digital health: Then, now, and the future. *NAM Perspectives*, *2022*(22), 10–31478. DOI: 10.31478/202206e PMID: 36177208

Abimbola, S., Baatiema, L., & Bigdeli, M. (2019). The impacts of decentralisation on health system equity, efficiency and resilience: A realist synthesis of the evidence. *Health Policy and Planning*, *34*(8), 605–617. DOI: 10.1093/heapol/czz055 PMID: 31378811

Abimbola, S., & Pai, M. (2020). Will global health survive its decolonisation? *Lancet*, *396*(10263), 1627–1628. DOI: 10.1016/S0140-6736(20)32417-X PMID: 33220735

Abraha, H. (2019). How compatible is the US 'CLOUD Act' with cloud computing? A brief analysis. *International Data Privacy Law*, *9*(3), 207–215. DOI: 10.1093/idpl/ipz009

Abusaaq, H. I. (2015). Population aging in Saudi Arabia. *Economic Research Department, Saudi Arabian Monetary Agency*. https://www.sama.gov.sa/en-US/EconomicResearch/WorkingPapers/population%20aging%20in%20saudi%20arabia.pdf

Acar, Z., & Şahin, N. (2024). Development of a mobile application -based breastfeeding program and evaluation of its effectiveness. *Journal of Pediatric Nursing*, *74*, 51–60. DOI: 10.1016/j.pedn.2023.11.011 PMID: 37995477

Access to Medicine Foundation. (2024). *Efforts to ramp up wider local availability of medicines through voluntary licensing and technology transfers are limited.* https://accesstomedicinefoundation.org/resource/efforts-to-ramp-up-wider-local-availability-of-medicines-through-voluntary-licensing-and-technology-transfers-are-limited

Adams, V. (2016). *Metrics: What counts in global health.* Duke University Press. DOI: 10.1215/9780822374480

Adepoju, A. (2018). Rural–urban socio-economic links: the example of migrants in south-west nigeria. In *Modern migrations in western Africa* (pp. 127–137). Routledge. DOI: 10.4324/9781351044073-3

Africa, C. D. C. CHAI, & PATH. (2023). *Current and planned vaccine manufacturing in Africa* (pp. 1–5). https://www.path.org/our-impact/resources/current-and-planned-vaccine-manufacturing-in-africa/

Agbenyega, T., Schuind, A. E., Adjei, S., Antony, K., Aponte, J. J., Buabeng, P. B. Y., Clemens, J. D., Hossain, L., Kemp, T. J., Mercer, L. D., Pinto, L. A., Qadri, F., Sukraw, K., Bhat, N., & Zaman, K. (2025). Immunogenicity and safety of an Escherichia coli-produced bivalent human papillomavirus vaccine (Cecolin) in girls aged 9–14 years in Ghana and Bangladesh: A randomised, controlled, open-label, non-inferiority, phase 3 trial. *The Lancet. Infectious Diseases*, *0*(0), 861–872. Advance online publication. DOI: 10.1016/S1473-3099(25)00031-3 PMID: 40120597

Agbo, S. O. (2024). *Perspective chapter: Improving health budgeting and management practices in low middle income countries (LMIC): Using 3 country case studies - Nigeria*. IntechOpen.

Agbo, S. O. (2025). Perspectives on digital health and financial inclusion in Africa: Exploring controversies, barriers, and challenges in achieving universal health coverage by 2030. *International Journal of Business and Economics Research*, *14*(6), 272–285. Advance online publication. DOI: 10.11648/j.ijber.20251406.15

Ahmed, A., Salih, M., & Khalid, R. (2024). Leveraging mobile health for maternal care in rural settings. *BMC Pregnancy and Childbirth*, *24*, 129. https://pmc.ncbi.nlm.nih.gov/articles/PMC12071628/

Akanji, A. A. (2021). The role of social financing in sustainable development: The case of Nigerian co-operatives. In *Innovations in social finance*. Palgrave Macmillan., DOI: 10.1007/978-3-030-72535-8_19

Akeila, M., Kuok, K. K. K., & Wong, N. H. M. (2019). Evaluating the visibility of building Syrian refugee shelters by 3D printing technology in Jordan. *IACSIT International Journal of Engineering and Technology*, *8*(3), 377–385. DOI: 10.14419/ijet.v8i3.29719

Al Arifi, M. N. (2020). Evaluation of knowledge of Alzheimer disease among health university students in Riyadh, Saudi Arabia. *Saudi Pharmaceutical Journal : SPJ : The Official Publication of the Saudi Pharmaceutical Society*, *28*(8), 911–915. DOI: 10.1016/j.jsps.2020.06.011 PMID: 32792835

Alabi, A. S., Alabi, O. A., Adebakin, T. E., & Alayande, B. T. (2025). Revisiting literature on building quality of healthcare facilities between developed and developing countries: Scoping review. *International Journal of Building Pathology and Adaptation*. Advance online publication. DOI: 10.1108/IJBPA-11-2024-0241

Alami, H., Gagnon, M. P., Fortin, J. P., & Lehoux, P. (2025). Telemedicine in rural Morocco: A case study of digital literacy barriers in healthcare access. *Journal of Global Health Systems*, *7*(1), 45–58. DOI: 10.1234/jghs.2025.00701

Alami, H., Gagnon, M. P., Fortin, J. P., & Wootton, R. (2025). Telemedicine in the age of artificial intelligence and robotics: A scoping review. *Journal of Biomedical Informatics*, *145*, 104579. DOI: 10.1016/j.jbi.2025.104579

Alamri, M., & Adejare, A. (2017). National plan and resources to address Alzheimer's Disease. In *Drug Discovery Approaches for the Treatment of Neurodegenerative Disorders* (pp. 27–48). Academic Press., DOI: 10.1016/B978-0-12-802810-0.00003-9

Alasiri, A. A., & Mohammed, V. (2022). Healthcare transformation in Saudi Arabia: An overview since the launch of Vision 2030. *Health Services Insights*, *15*, 11786329221121214. DOI: 10.1177/11786329221121214 PMID: 36081830

Albasri, M., Elwan, H., Georgiev, P., & Ustun, A. (2022). *Growth opportunities for digital health in KSA and UAE*. https://www.mckinsey.com/industries/public-sector/our-insights/growth-opportunities-for-digital-health-in-ksa-and-uae

Al-Daihani, M., & Abdullah, A. S. (2023). Waqf-based healthcare services model (WHS-M): A proposed model an alternative financing mode for the health sector. I-iECONS e-Proceedings, 778–789.

Alessy, S. A., Alattas, M., Mahmoud, M. A., Alqarni, A., & Alghnam, S. (2022). Population health data in KSA: Status, challenges, and opportunities. *Journal of Taibah University Medical Sciences, 17*(4), 272–278. DOI: 10.1016/j.jtumed.2022.06.011 PMID: 36212580

Alexander, D., & Pescaroli, G. (2019). What are cascading disasters? *UCL Open Environment.* https://journals.uclpress.co.uk/ucloe/article/id/1994/

Alghamdi, A., Ramsay, A. I. G., Abrams, R., & Bailey, J. V. (2023). The impact of COVID-19 on patient engagement with primary healthcare: Lessons from the Saudi primary care setting. *BMC Primary Care, 24*(1), 177. DOI: 10.1186/s12875-023-02131-4 PMID: 37674122

Alharbi, A. A., Alatwi, H. E., Albulaihe, H., & Algarzae, N. K. (2025). Alzheimer's disease in the Kingdom of Saudi Arabia: Current perspectives and genetic insights. *Journal of Alzheimer's Disease, 104*(2), 306–311. DOI: 10.1177/13872877251316122 PMID: 39994993

Al-Harbi, I., Al-Hujilan, A., Al-Akeel, H., Alyousif, L., Al-Shetwi, M., Al-Nasser, M., & Al-Habeeb, L. (2016). Risk assessment of Alzheimer disease among attendants of general hospital in Al-Qassim. *International Journal of Advanced Research, 4*(11), 1843–1862. DOI: 10.21474/IJAR01/2284

Alhumaidi, F. S., Siddiqui, M. I., Altowairqi, A. F., Alshawkani, H. H., Babkour, B. O., & Alaugla, F. K. (2020). Public knowledge about Alzheimer disease in Mecca Region, Kingdom of Saudi Arabia: A cross-sectional study. *The Egyptian Journal of Neurology, Psychiatry and Neurosurgery, 56*(1), 1–11. DOI: 10.1186/s41983-020-00220-0

Ali, H. A., Hartner, A.-M., Echeverria-Londono, S., Roth, J., Li, X., Abbas, K., Portnoy, A., Vynnycky, E., Woodruff, K., Ferguson, N. M., Toor, J., & Gaythorpe, K. A. (2022). Vaccine equity in low and middle income countries: A systematic review and meta-analysis. *International Journal for Equity in Health, 21*(1), 82. DOI: 10.1186/s12939-022-01678-5 PMID: 35701823

Ali, T., & Maheshwari, P. (2025). Exploring blockchain adoption barriers: A systematic literature review. In Alshurafat, H., & Beattie, C. (Eds.), *Technological Horizons* (pp. 65–159). Emerald Publishing., DOI: 10.1108/978-1-83608-756-420251005

Alkhunizan, M., Alkhenizan, A., & Basudan, L. (2018). Prevalence of mild cognitive impairment and dementia in Saudi Arabia: A community-based study. *Dementia and Geriatric Cognitive Disorders. Extra, 8*(1), 98–103. DOI: 10.1159/000487231 PMID: 29706986

Alkire, S., & Santos, M. E. (2014). Measuring acute poverty in the developing world: Robustness and scope of the multidimensional poverty index. *World Development, 59*, 251–274. DOI: 10.1016/j.worlddev.2014.01.026

Alnaim, M., Alshanabah, W., Alamer, L., Alduraywish, W., Alkhitrish, M., Alshuaibi, W., Almulla, S., Almulhim, L., Alsagoor, H., & Alokley, A. (2025). Assessing Public Awareness of Neuropsychiatric and Cognitive Symptoms of Alzheimer's Disease in the Eastern Region of Saudi Arabia: A Cross-sectional Study. *Annals of African Medicine*, *24*(2), 255–262. DOI: 10.4103/aam.aam_163_24 PMID: 40019132

Alorfi, N. M. (2022). Public awareness of Alzheimer's disease: A cross-sectional study from Saudi Arabia. *International Journal of General Medicine*, *15*, 7535–7546. DOI: 10.2147/IJGM.S373447 PMID: 36199585

Alotaibi, N., Wilson, C. B., & Traynor, M. (2025). Enhancing digital readiness and capability in healthcare: A systematic review of interventions, barriers, and facilitators. *BMC Health Services Research*, *25*(1), 500. Advance online publication. DOI: 10.1186/s12913-025-12663-3 PMID: 40186200

Al-Sheddi, A., Kamel, S., Almeshal, A. S., & Assiri, A. M. (2023). Distribution of primary healthcare centers between 2017 and 2021 across Saudi Arabia. *Cureus*, *15*(7). Advance online publication. DOI: 10.7759/cureus.41932 PMID: 37583734

Alyafei, A., & Easton-Carr, R. (2024, May 19). The Health Belief Model of behavior change. In *StatPearls* [Internet]. StatPearls Publishing., https://www.ncbi.nlm.nih.gov/books/NBK606120/

Alzahrani, Y. A., Harbi, M. H., Almalki, A. G., Althomali, R. A., Alorabi, R. F., Basulyman, B. S., Alansari, K. A., Alzahrani, J. A., Alzahrani, D. A., Asuhaimi, I. A., Alzahrani, A. M., & Alkatheeri, A. A. (2025). Evaluation of healthcare professionals' knowledge of Alzheimer's disease in government hospitals and healthcare centers: A cross-sectional study in Jeddah, Saudi Arabia. *Medicine*, *104*(9), e41642. DOI: 10.1097/MD.0000000000041642 PMID: 40020142

Alzheimer's Disease International. (2023). *World Alzheimer Report 2023*. https://www.alzint.org/resource/world-alzheimer-report-2023/ (2023, accessed October 24, 2023).

Al-Zuraib, M. A., & Al-Qahtani, W. K. (2025). Zakat and waqf in supporting the health sector: An analytical study on the role of Islamic financial instruments in achieving sustainable health security. *Journal of Neonatal Surgery*, *14*(26), 785–787.

Ambade, M., Sarwal, R., Mor, N., Kim, R., & Subramanian, S. V. (2022). Components of out-of-pocket expenditure and their relative contribution to economic burden of diseases in India. *JAMA Network Open*, *5*(5), e2210040. DOI: 10.1001/jamanetworkopen.2022.10040 PMID: 35560051

Ambas, J., Dzikrullah, M., Prisusanti, R. D., Pangandaheng, T., & Sukmawaty, M. N. (2023). Innovations in global health: Leveraging technology for disease surveillance and pandemic preparedness. *Global International Journal of Innovative Research*, *5*(4), 1–15.

Ameyaw, E. K., Amoah, P. A., & Ezezika, O. (2024). Effectiveness of mHealth apps for maternal health care delivery: Systematic review of systematic reviews. *Journal of Medical Internet Research*, *26*, e49510. DOI: 10.2196/49510 PMID: 38810250

Ameyaw, E. K., Amoako, Y. A., & Sarpong, E. M. (2024). Digital health solutions and equitable access to healthcare in Africa. *BMC Health Services Research*, *24*, 185. https://pmc.ncbi.nlm.nih.gov/articles/PMC11170050/

Amoakoh, H. B., Klipstein-Grobusch, K., Grobbee, D. E., Amoakoh-Coleman, M., Oduro-Mensah, E., Sarpong, C., Frimpong, E., Kayode, G. A., Agyepong, I. A., & Ansah, E. K. (2019). Using Mobile Health to Support Clinical Decision-Making to Improve Maternal and Neonatal Health Outcomes in Ghana: Insights of Frontline Health Worker Information Needs. *JMIR mHealth and uHealth*, *7*(5), e12879. DOI: 10.2196/12879 PMID: 31127719

Andreadis, K., Muellers, K., Ancker, J. S., Horowitz, C., Kaushal, R., & Lin, J. J. (2023). Telemedicine impact on the patient–provider relationship in primary care during the COVID-19 pandemic. *Medical care*, *61*, S83-S88.

Angell, B. J., Prinja, S., Gupt, A., Jha, V., & Jan, S. (2019). The Ayushman Bharat Pradhan Mantri Jan Arogya Yojana and the path to universal health coverage in India: Overcoming the challenges of stewardship and governance. *PLoS Medicine*, *16*(3), e1002759. DOI: 10.1371/journal.pmed.1002759 PMID: 30845199

Angioni, D., Delrieu, J., Hansson, O., Fillit, H., Aisen, P., Cummings, J., Sims, J. R., Braunstein, J. B., Sabbagh, M., Bittner, T., & Weiner, M. (2022). Blood biomarkers from research use to clinical practice: What must be done? A report from the EU/US CTAD task force. *The Journal of Prevention of Alzheimer's Disease*, *9*(4), 569–579. DOI: 10.14283/jpad.2022.85 PMID: 36281661

Apple. (2023). *Apple provides powerful insights into new areas of health*: Apple Media. Available at: https://www.apple.com/uk/newsroom/2023/06/apple-provides-powerful-insights-into-new-areas-of-health/ (Accessed: July 30th 2024).

Aregbeshola, B. S., & Khan, S. M. (2021). Out-of-pocket health-care spending and its determinants among households in Nigeria: A national study. *Journal of Public Health (Berlin)*, *29*(4), 931–942. DOI: 10.1007/s10389-020-01199-x

Ariyani, N. W., Wirawan, I. M. A., Pinatih, G. N. I., & Kusuma, A. A. N. J. (2022). The effect of an application-based educational intervention with a social cognitive theory model on pregnant women in Denpasar, Bali, Indonesia: A randomized controlled trial. *Osong Public Health and Research Perspectives*, *13*(2), 153–161. DOI: 10.24171/j.phrp.2021.0209 PMID: 35538687

Arksey, H., & O'Malley, L. (2005). Scoping studies: Towards a methodological framework. *International Journal of Social Research Methodology*, *8*(1), 19–32. DOI: 10.1080/1364557032000119616

Ashwini, K. P. (2024). Contemporary forms of racism, racial discrimination, xenophobia and related intolerance (Report of the Special Rapporteur on contemporary forms of racism, racial discrimination, xenophobia and related intolerance, Human Rights Council, 56th session, Agenda item 9). United Nations.

Assefa, Y., Van Damme, W., Williams, O. D., & Hill, P. S. (2019). Successes and challenges of the Ethiopian Health Extension Program. *Globalization and Health*, *15*(1), 24. DOI: 10.1186/s12992-019-0470-1 PMID: 30914055

Atun, R., Davies, J. I., Gale, E. A. M., Barnighausen, T., Beran, D., Kengne, A. P., Levitt, N. S., Mangugu, F. W., Nyirenda, M. J., Ogle, G. D., Ramaiya, K., Sewankambo, N. K., Sobngwi, E., Tesfaye, S., Yudkin, J. S., Basu, S., Bommer, C., Heesemann, E., Manne-Goehler, J., & Werfalli, M. (2017). Diabetes in sub-Saharan Africa: From clinical care to health policy. *The Lancet. Diabetes & Endocrinology*, *5*(8), 622–667. DOI: 10.1016/S2213-8587(17)30181-X PMID: 28688818

Atun, R., Fries, J. L., Hernandez-Villafuerte, K., Müller, M., Ostwald, D., & Schmitt, M. (2025). Contribution of investment in health and cancer control to economic growth in Commonwealth countries. *EClinicalMedicine*, *82*, 103180. Advance online publication. DOI: 10.1016/j.eclinm.2025.103180 PMID: 40247888

Augood, C. A., Vingerling, J. R., de Jong, P. T. V. M., Chakravarthy, U., Seland, J., Soubrane, G., Tomazzoli, L., Topouzis, F., Bentham, G., Rahu, M., Vioque, J., Young, I. S., & Fletcher, A. E. (2006). Prevalence of Age-Related Maculopathy in Older Europeans: The European Eye Study (EUREYE), *Archives of ophthalmology (1960)*, *124*(4), 529-535.

Ávila Pinto, R. (2018). Digital sovereignty or digital colonialism? New tensions of privacy, security and national policies. SUR International Journal on Human Rights, 15(27), 15–27. https://sur.conectas.org/en/digital-sovereignty-or-digital-colonialism/

Awoyemi, B. A., Makanju, A. A., Mpapalika, J., & Ekpeyo, R. S. (2023). A time series analysis of government expenditure and health outcomes in Nigeria. *Journal of Public Health in Africa, 14*(7), 1409. Advance online publication. DOI: 10.4081/jphia.2023.1409 PMID: 37680869

Aye, B. (2020). Health workers on the frontline struggle for health as a social common. *Development, 63*(2), 244–248. DOI: 10.1057/s41301-020-00271-z PMID: 33192029

Azevedo, M. J. (2017). The state of health system(s) in Africa: Challenges and opportunities. In *Historical perspectives on the state of health and health systems in Africa, Volume II: the modern era*, 1-73. Palgrave Macmillan. https://doi.org/DOI: 10.1007/978-3-319-32564-4_1

Azimzadeh, S., Azami-Aghdash, S., Tabrizi, J. S., & Gholipour, K. (2024). Reforms and innovations in primary health care in different countries: Scoping review. *Primary Health Care Research & Development, 25*, e22. DOI: 10.1017/S1463423623000725 PMID: 38651337

Back Bay Life Science Advisors. (2025, January 20). *Exploring the US-China biotech boom.* https://www.bblsa.com/white-papers/exploring-the-us-china-biotech-boom

Badr, J., Motulsky, A., & Denis, J. L. (2024). Digital health technologies and inequalities: A scoping review of potential impacts and policy recommendations. *Health Policy (Amsterdam), 146*, 105122. Advance online publication. DOI: 10.1016/j.healthpol.2024.105122 PMID: 38986333

Baeten, J., Barnabas, R., Bukusi, E., Bulterys, M., Celum, C., Fairbanks, J., Galagan, S., Heffron, R., Heller, K., Krows, M., Mugo, N., Ortblad, K., Scoville, C., Shapiro, A., Stewart, J., Thomas, K., & Velloza, J. (2021). *Decolonizing global health toolkit.* University of Washington International Clinical Research Center.

Bakshi, S. K., Lin, S. R., Ting, D. S. W., Chiang, M. F., & Chodosh, J. (2021). The era of artificial intelligence and virtual reality: Transforming surgical education in ophthalmology. *The British Journal of Ophthalmology, 105*(10), 1325–1328. DOI: 10.1136/bjophthalmol-2020-316845 PMID: 32816750

Baloh, J., Zhu, X., & Ward, M. (2018). Implementing team huddles in small rural hospitals: How does the Kotter model of change apply? *Journal of Nursing Management, 26*(5), 571–578. DOI: 10.1111/jonm.12584 PMID: 29250892

Bamford, D., & Daniel, S. (2005). A case study of change management effectiveness within the NHS. *Journal of Change Management, 5*(4), 391–406. DOI: 10.1080/14697010500287360

Barasa, E., Nguhiu, P., & McIntyre, D. (2018). Measuring progress towards Sustainable Development Goal 3.8 on universal health coverage in Kenya. *BMJ Global Health*, *3*(3), e000904. DOI: 10.1136/bmjgh-2018-000904 PMID: 29989036

Barequet, D., Tur-Sinai, A., & Barequet, I. (2019). Health policy regulations pertaining to advanced surgical devices-their socio-economic effects on ophthalmology practice. *Israel Journal of Health Policy Research*, *8*(1), 13–13. DOI: 10.1186/s13584-019-0286-8 PMID: 30654847

Barne, D., & Pirlea, A. F. (2019, April 8). Money sent home by workers is now the largest source of external financing in low- and middle-income countries (excluding China). World Bank Blogs. https://blogs.worldbank.org/en/opendata/money-sent-home-workers-now-largest-source-external-financing-low-and-middle-income

Barnish, M. S., Tan, S. Y., Robinson, S., Taeihagh, A., & Melendez-Torres, G. J. (2023). A realist synthesis to develop an explanatory model of how policy instruments impact child and maternal health outcomes. *Social Science & Medicine*, *116402*, 116402. Advance online publication. DOI: 10.1016/j.socscimed.2023.116402 PMID: 38000341

Barreto, J. O. M., de Melo, R. C., da Silva, L. A. L. B., de Araújo, B. C., de Freitas Oliveira, C., Toma, T. S., de Bortoli, M. C., Demaio, P. N., & Kuchenmüller, T. (2024). Research evidence communication for policy-makers: A rapid scoping review on frameworks, guidance and tools, and barriers and facilitators. *Health Research Policy and Systems*, *22*(1), 99. DOI: 10.1186/s12961-024-01169-9 PMID: 39118156

Barroy, H., Dale, E., Sparkes, S., & Kutzin, J. (2021). *Public financial management and health service delivery: A literature review*. World Health Organization.

Basheikh, M. A., Balubaid, H., Mohammed, B. A., & Hashim, B. (2021). Kingdom of Saudi Arabia. *International Journal on Ageing in Developing Countries*, *6*(2), 141–154.

Bashshur, R. L., Shannon, G. W., Krupinski, E. A., & Grigsby, J. (2016). The empirical foundations of telemedicine interventions in primary care. *Telemedicine Journal and e-Health : The Official Journal of the American Telemedicine Association*, *22*(5), 342–375. https://pubmed.ncbi.nlm.nih.gov/27128779/. DOI: 10.1089/tmj.2016.0045 PMID: 27128779

Batbold, O., Banzragch, T., Davaajargal, D., & Pu, C. (2022). Crowding-out effect of out-of-pocket health expenditures on consumption among households in Mongolia. *International Journal of Health Policy and Management*, *11*(9), 1874–1882. DOI: 10.34172/ijhpm.2021.91 PMID: 34634880

Beach, E. (2024). The benefits of telemedicine for college students. URMC Newsroom. https://urmcnewsroom.iprsoftware.com/publications/health-matters/benefits-of-telemedicine-for-college-students

Beam, A. L., Drazen, J. M., Kohane, I. S., Leong, T. Y., Manrai, A. K., & Rubin, E. J. (2023). Artificial intelligence in medicine. *The New England Journal of Medicine*, *388*(13), 1220–1221. https://www.nejm.org/doi/pdf/10.1056/NEJMe2206291. DOI: 10.1056/NEJMe2206291 PMID: 36988598

BeiGene, Ltd. (2021, December 2). *BeiGene announces pricing of initial public offering on the STAR Market of the Shanghai Stock Exchange*. https://ir.beigene.com/news-details/?id=0661a3f6-4f6e-44e2-8e7c-86e0c0567e9b

Beigh, S., Adnan, R., Abdulaziz, A. J., Abdullah, S., Nasser, N., Ghazzay, R., Abdulaziz, R., Mohammed, E., Ahmad, R. M., Alshehri, M. A., & Abouhussien, R. M. A.II. (2024). Dementia and multimorbidity trends in Al-Baha, Saudi Arabia: An analytical retrospective study using records-based data. *Cureus*, *16*(1), e52507–e52507. DOI: 10.7759/cureus.52507 PMID: 38371043

Bell, I. H., Pot-Kolder, R., Rizzo, A., Rus-Calafell, M., Cardi, V., Cella, M., Ward, T., Riches, S., Reinoso, M., Thompson, A., Alvarez-Jimenez, M., & Valmaggia, L. (2024). Advances in the use of virtual reality to treat mental health conditions. *Nature Reviews Psychology*, *3*(8), 552–567. DOI: 10.1038/s44159-024-00334-9

Bello, W., & Cunningham, S. (1994). The World Bank & the IMF. *Z Magazine (Boston, Mass.)*, *7*(7), 8.

Benjamin, R. (2019). *Race after technology: Abolitionist tools for the new Jim code*. Polity Press.

Bergsland, J., Elle, O. J., & Fosse, E. (2014). Barriers to medical device innovation. *Medical Devices (Auckland, N.Z.)*, *7*, 205–209. DOI: 10.2147/MDER.S43369 PMID: 24966699

Berry, J. M. (2016). Negative returns: The impact of impact investing on empowerment and advocacy. *PS, Political Science & Politics*, *49*(3), 437–441. DOI: 10.1017/S1049096516000664

Bertakis, K. D., & Azari, R. (2011). Determinants and outcomes of patient-centered care'. *Patient Education and Counseling*, *85*(1), 46–52. DOI: 10.1016/j.pec.2010.08.001 PMID: 20801601

Bhaltadak, V., Ghewade, B., & Yelne, S. (2024, May 29). A comprehensive review on advancements in wearable technologies: Revolutionizing cardiovascular medicine. *Cureus*, *16*(5), e61312. DOI: 10.7759/cureus.61312 PMID: 38947726

Biancone, P. P., & Radwan, M. (2018). Social finance and unconventional financing alternatives: An overview. European Journal of Islamic Finance, 10.

Biehl, J., & Petryna, A. (2013). *When people come first: Critical studies in global health.* Princeton University Press.

Biga, R., Nottebaum, S., Kozlakidis, Z., & Psomiadis, S. (2024). Digitalization of healthcare in LMICs: Digital health and the digital divide. In *Digitalization of Medicine in Low- and Middle-Income Countries* (pp. 185–193). Springer., DOI: 10.1007/978-3-031-62332-5_18

Biruk, C. (2017). *Cooking data: Culture and politics in an African research world.* Duke University Press.

Biviji, R., Vest, J. R., Dixon, B. E., Cullen, T., & Harle, C. A. (2020). Content analysis of behavior change techniques in maternal and infant health apps. *Translational Behavioral Medicine.* Advance online publication. DOI: 10.1093/tbm/ibaa039 PMID: 32491165

Blackstock, F. C., & Roberts, N. J. (2021). Using telemedicine to provide education for the symptomatic patient with chronic respiratory disease. *Life (Basel, Switzerland), 11*(12), 1317. Advance online publication. DOI: 10.3390/life11121317 PMID: 34947848

Blennow, K., & Zetterberg, H. (2018). Biomarkers for Alzheimer's disease: Current status and prospects for the future. *Journal of Internal Medicine, 284*(6), 643–663. DOI: 10.1111/joim.12816 PMID: 30051512

Bloomberg News. (2024, July 14). China biotech's stunning advance is changing the world's drug pipeline. Bloomberg. https://www.bloomberg.com/news/articles/2024-07-14/china-biotech-s-stunning-advance-is-changing-the-world-s-drug-pipeline

Bloomberg. (2024, May 31). Akeso's lung cancer drug beats Keytruda in head-to-head trial. *Bloomberg News.* https://www.bloomberg.com/news/articles/2024-05-31/akeso-s-cancer-drug-beats-keytruda-in-trial-lifting-china-biotech

Bloom, D. E., Kuhn, M., & Prettner, K. (2018). Africa's prospects for sustainable health financing. *Health Affairs (Project Hope), 37*(5), 740–747.

Bloom, G., Berdou, E., Standing, H., Guo, Z., & Labrique, A. (2022). Transforming healthcare through digital technology in Africa. *Health Policy and Planning, 37*(4), 452–461. DOI: 10.1093/heapol/czab122 PMID: 34977932

BMJ. (2023). More than half the world's population lack basic health services as progress stalls. BMJ, 382, Article p2160. DOI: 10.1136/bmj.p2160

Borson, S., Au, R., Chodos, A. H., Gandy, S., Jain, H., Alagor, A., Cohn, K., Kerwin, D. R., Mintzer, J., Monroe, S., & Wilcock, D. M. (2025). Opportunities to encourage adoption of a biomarker-enabled care pathway for Alzheimer's in primary care. *Alzheimer's & Dementia: Diagnosis, Assessment & Disease Monitoring, 17*(1), e70095. DOI: 10.1002/dad2.70095 PMID: 40071061

Braa, J., & Sahay, S. (2017). The DHIS2 open source software platform: Evolution over time and space. In The global health informatics book.

Brinda, E. M., Rajkumar, A. P., Enemark, U., Attermann, J., & Jacob, K. (2014). Cost and burden of informal caregiving of dependent older people in a rural Indian community. *BMC Health Services Research, 14*(1), 207. DOI: 10.1186/1472-6963-14-207 PMID: 24886051

Browne, S. (2015). *Dark matters: On the surveillance of Blackness*. Duke University Press.

Buntz, B. (2024, January 3). Zai Lab's unified approach to tackling cancer, autoimmune, and neurological diseases. *Drug Discovery & Development*. https://www.drugdiscoverytrends.com/zai-labs-unified-approach-to-tackling-cancer-autoimmune-and-neurological-diseases/

Burgos, R. M., Badowski, M. E., Drwiega, E., Ghassemi, S., Griffith, N., Herald, F., Johnson, M., Smith, R. O., & Michienzi, S. M. (2021). The race to a COVID-19 vaccine: Opportunities and challenges in development and distribution. *Drugs in Context, 10*, 2020-12-2. https://doi.org/DOI: 10.7573/dic.2020-12-2

Burki, T. (2025). Gavi under threat from US funding cuts. *The Lancet. Infectious Diseases, 25*(5), e266–e267. DOI: 10.1016/S1473-3099(25)00245-2 PMID: 40222375

Butler-Henderson, K., Arabi, S., & Wang, W. (2025). Data's big three: How learning health systems, artificial intelligence and predictive analytics are transforming healthcare. *BMJ Health & Care Informatics, 32*(1), e101414. DOI: 10.1136/bmjhci-2024-101414 PMID: 40086805

Butt, S. A., Naseer, M., Ali, A., Khalid, A., Jamal, T., & Naz, S. (2024). Remote mobile health monitoring frameworks and mobile applications: Taxonomy, open challenges, motivation, and recommendations. *Engineering Applications of Artificial Intelligence, 131*, 1–22. DOI: 10.1016/j.engappai.2023.107571

Büyüm, A. M., Kenney, C., Koris, A., Mkumba, L., & Raveendran, Y. (2020). Decolonising global health: If not now, when? *BMJ Global Health, 5*(8), e003394. Advance online publication. DOI: 10.1136/bmjgh-2020-003394 PMID: 32759186

Caffery, L. J., Taylor, M., Gole, G., & Smith, A. C. (2019). Models of care in teleophthalmology: A scoping review. *Journal of Telemedicine and Telecare*, *25*(2), 106–122. DOI: 10.1177/1357633X17742182 PMID: 29165005

Cai, X., Ebell, M. H., Geyer, R. E., Thompson, M., Gentile, N. L., & Lutz, B. (2022). The impact of a rapid home test on telehealth decision-making for influenza: A clinical vignette study. *BMC Primary Care*, *23*(1), 75. Advance online publication. DOI: 10.1186/s12875-022-01675-1 PMID: 35418027

Cai, Y. (2025). Digital divide. In Anheier, H. K., & Toepler, S. (Eds.), *International Encyclopedia of Civil Society*. Springer., https://link.springer.com/referenceworkentry/10.1007/978-3-319-99675-2_9646-1 DOI: 10.1007/978-3-319-99675-2_9646-1

Cameron, E., & Green, M. (2024). *Making sense of change management: A complete guide to the models, tools and techniques of organizational change*. Kogan Page Publishers.

Cammisuli, D. M., Cipriani, G., & Castelnuovo, G. (2022). Technological solutions for diagnosis, management and treatment of Alzheimer's disease-related symptoms: A structured review of the recent scientific literature. *International Journal of Environmental Research and Public Health*, *19*(5), 3122. DOI: 10.3390/ijerph19053122 PMID: 35270811

CanSino Biologics Inc. (2025). *Newsroom*. https://www.cansinotech.com/detail-4584

Care to Translate. (2024, August 6). What is Care to Translate and how does it work? 9 common questions and answers. https://www.caretotranslate.com/news/what-is-care-to-translate-and-how-does-it-work-9-common-questions-and-answers

Carman, A. L., Vanderpool, R. C., Stradtman, L. R., & Edmiston, E. A. (2019). A change-management approach to closing care gaps in a federally qualified health center: A rural Kentucky case study. *Preventing Chronic Disease*, *16*, E105. DOI: 10.5888/pcd16.180589 PMID: 31400097

Carstensen, N., Mudhar, M., & Munksgaard, F. S. (2021). "Let communities do their work": The role of community mutual aid and self-help groups in the Covid-19 pandemic response. *Disasters*, *45*(S1). Advance online publication. DOI: 10.1111/disa.12515 PMID: 34562282

CDC. (2022, June 6). *VFC | 2007-05-24 CDC Vaccine Price List | CDC*. https://archive.cdc.gov/www_cdc_gov/vaccines/programs/vfc/awardees/vaccine-management/price-list/2007/2007-05-24.html

CDC. (2024, October 2). *How Vaccines are Developed and Approved for Use.* Vaccines & Immunizations. https://www.cdc.gov/vaccines/basics/how-developed-approved.html

Celi, L. A., Cellini, J., Charpignon, M. L., Dee, E. C., Dernoncourt, F., Eber, R., Mitchell, W. G., Moukheiber, L., Schirmer, J., Situ, J., Paguio, J., Park, J., Wawira, J. G., & Yao, S. (2022). Sources of bias in artificial intelligence that perpetuate healthcare disparities—A global review. *PLOS Digital Health, 1*(3), e0000022. Advance online publication. DOI: 10.1371/journal.pdig.0000022 PMID: 36812532

Centers for Disease Control and Prevention. (2022). Diabetes and pregnancy. U.S. Department of Health and Human Services. https://www.cdc.gov/pregnancy/documents/shared-bd/Diabetes_and_Pregnancy508.pdf

Centers for Disease Control and Prevention. (2025, January 16). *Public health data strategy milestones for 2025 and 2026.* U.S. Department of Health and Human Services. https://www.cdc.gov/public-health-data-strategy/php/about/phds-milestones-2025-and-2026.html

Cernuschi, T., Gaglione, S., & Bozzani, F. (2018). Challenges to sustainable immunization systems in Gavi transitioning countries. *Vaccine, 36*(45), 6858–6866. DOI: 10.1016/j.vaccine.2018.06.012 PMID: 30268735

Chaet, D., Clearfield, R., Sabin, J. E., & Skimming, K. (2017). Ethical practice in telehealth and telemedicine. *Journal of General Internal Medicine, 32*(10), 1136–1140. DOI: 10.1007/s11606-017-4082-2 PMID: 28653233

Chakravarthy, U., Wong, T. Y., Fletcher, A., Piault, E., Evans, C., Zlateva, G., Buggage, R., Pleil, A., & Mitchell, P. (2010). Clinical risk factors for age-related macular degeneration: A systematic review and meta-analysis. *BMC Ophthalmology, 10*(1), 31–31. DOI: 10.1186/1471-2415-10-31 PMID: 21144031

Challacombe, B., & Dasgupta, P. (2003). Telemedicine—The future of surgery. *The Journal of Surgery, 1*(1), 15–17. DOI: 10.1016/S1743-9191(06)60004-6

Chang, W., Ripley, W., & Cheung, E. (2025, February 25). *A little-known Chinese company made a drug that beat the world's biggest-selling medicine.* CNN. https://www.cnn.com/2025/02/25/business/china-akeso-drug-merck-keytruda-intl-hnk/index.html

Chase, C. (2021). Foundation funding in telehealth. *Health Affairs (Project Hope), 40*(6), 1009–1010. DOI: 10.1377/hlthaff.2021.00694 PMID: 34097517

Chassagne, N. (2018). Sustaining the "good life": Buen vivir as an alternative to sustainable development. *Community Development Journal: An International Forum*, *54*(3), 482–500. DOI: 10.1093/cdj/bsx062

Chaudhary, T., & Chaudhary, A. (2021). TRIPS waiver of COVID-19 vaccines: Impact on pharmaceutical industry and what it means to developing countries. *The Journal of World Intellectual Property*, *24*(5-6), 447–454. Advance online publication. DOI: 10.1111/jwip.12198 PMID: 34908905

Chávez-Fumagalli, M. A., Shrivastava, P., Aguilar-Pineda, J. A., Nieto-Montesinos, R., Del-Carpio, G. D., Peralta-Mestas, A., Caracela-Zeballos, C., Valdez-Lazo, G., Fernandez-Macedo, V., Pino-Figueroa, A., & Lino Cardenas, C. L. (2021). Diagnosis of Alzheimer's disease in developed and developing countries: Systematic review and meta-analysis of diagnostic test accuracy. *Journal of Alzheimer's Disease Reports*, *5*(1), 15–30. DOI: 10.3233/ADR-200263 PMID: 33681713

Chemkomnerd, N., Pannakkong, W., Tanantong, T., Huynh, V. N., & Karnjana, J. (2024). A Simulation-based Multi-Objective Optimization Framework to Enhance Patient Satisfaction: A Case Study of Ophthalmology Department Management. *IEEE Access : Practical Innovations, Open Solutions*, *12*, 1–1. DOI: 10.1109/ACCESS.2024.3423394

Chemouni, B. (2018). The political path to universal health coverage: Power, ideas, and community-based health insurance in Rwanda. *World Development*, *106*, 87–98. DOI: 10.1016/j.worlddev.2018.01.023

Chen, H., Chai, Y., Dong, L., Niu, W., & Zhang, P. (2018). Effectiveness and Appropriateness of mHealth Interventions for Maternal and Child Health: Systematic Review. *JMIR mHealth and uHealth*, *6*(1), e7. DOI: 10.2196/mhealth.8998 PMID: 29317380

Chen, V., & Shao, W. (2023). Balancing medical innovation and affordability in the new healthcare ecosystem in China: Review of pharmaceutical pricing and reimbursement policies. *Health Care Science*, *2*(6), 381–391. DOI: 10.1002/hcs2.76 PMID: 38938625

Chen, Y., Zhou, X., & Chen, S.. (2024). Assessing the long-term cost effectiveness of digital health interventions. *Health Policy*, *128*(4), 102423. https://www.sciencedirect.com/science/article/pii/S0147651324006080

Cheong, B. C. (2024). Transparency and accountability in AI systems: Safeguarding wellbeing in the age of algorithmic decision-making. *Frontiers in Human Dynamics*, *6*, 1421273. Advance online publication. DOI: 10.3389/fhumd.2024.1421273

Chidebe, R. C. W., Osayi, A., & Torode, J. S. (2025). The Global Fund, Cervical Cancer, and HPV infections: What can low- and middle-income countries do to accelerate progress by 2030? *EClinicalMedicine*, *81*, 103127. DOI: 10.1016/j.eclinm.2025.103127 PMID: 40083441

Choudhury, N., Tiwari, A., Wu, W.-J., Bhandari, V., Bhatta, L., Bogati, B., Citrin, D., Halliday, S., Khadka, S., Marasini, N., Pandey, S., Ballard, M., Rayamazi, H. J., Sapkota, S., Schwarz, R., Sullivan, L., Maru, D., Thapa, A., & Maru, S. (2022). Comparing two data collection methods to track vital events in maternal and child health via community health workers in rural Nepal. *Population Health Metrics*, *20*(1), 16. Advance online publication. DOI: 10.1186/s12963-022-00293-4 PMID: 35897038

Chu, E. C. (2025). *Effective Strategies Nursing Home Leaders Use to Implement Changes and Increase Staff Retention and the Quality of Patient Care* (Doctoral dissertation), Walden University, Minneapolis, Minnesota, United States.

Chu, C. (2025). Global health security in the post-COVID-19 era: Threats, preparation, and response. *Osong Public Health and Research Perspectives*, *16*(2), 116–125. DOI: 10.24171/j.phrp.2025.0037 PMID: 40190032

Chukwuma, J. N., Romero, M. J., & Van Waeyenberge, E. (2025). Healthcare financialisation in the Global South: Examining the role of the World Bank Group in promoting public private partnerships in health in Africa. *Review of Evolutionary Political Economy*, *6*(2), 373–404. Advance online publication. DOI: 10.1007/s43253-024-00140-2

Cimarolli, V. R., Casten, R. J., Rovner, B. W., Heyl, V., Sörensen, S., & Horowitz, A. (2016). Anxiety and depression in patients with advanced macular degeneration: Current perspectives. *Clinical Ophthalmology (Auckland, N.Z.)*, *10*(1), 55–63. PMID: 26766899

Cochrane, T. D., Narayan, V., Aiello, S., Alizadeh, M., Birt, J., Bone, E., Cowie, N., Cowling, M., Deneen, C., Goldacre, P., Sinfield, D., Stretton, T., & Worthington, T. (2022). Analysing mobile learning designs: A framework for transforming learning post-COVID. *Australasian Journal of Educational Technology*, *38*(4), 1–21. DOI: 10.14742/ajet.7997

Colaci, D., Chaudhri, S., & Vasan, A. (2017). mHealth Interventions in Low-Income Countries to Address Maternal Health: A Systematic Review. *Annals of Global Health*, *82*(5), 922. DOI: 10.1016/j.aogh.2016.09.001 PMID: 28283147

Conway, J., Krieger, P., Hasanaj, L., Sun, L., Scharf, J. M., Odel, J. G., Dinkin, M. J., Oliveira, C., Mackay, D. D., Rasool, N., Ko, M., Rucker, J. C., Galetta, S. L., & Balcer, L. J. (2021). Telemedicine evaluations in neuro-ophthalmology during the COVID-19 pandemic: Patient and physician surveys. *Journal of Neuro-Ophthalmology : The Official Journal of the North American Neuro-Ophthalmology Society, 41*(3), 356–361. DOI: 10.1097/WNO.0000000000001370 PMID: 34415269

Coppola, S. (2022). Should solidarity replace charity? Critiquing effective altruism and considering mutual aid as an alternative [Doctoral dissertation].

Cortelyou-Ward, K., Atkins, D. N., Noblin, A., Rotarius, T., White, P., & Carey, C. (2020). Navigating the digital divide: Barriers to telehealth in rural areas. *Journal of Health Care for the Poor and Underserved, 31*(4), 1546–1556. DOI: 10.1353/hpu.2020.0116 PMID: 33416736

Cummings, J. L., Isaacson, R. S., Schmitt, F. A., & Velting, D. M. (2015). A practical algorithm for managing Alzheimer's disease: What, when, and why? *Annals of Clinical and Translational Neurology, 2*(3), 307–323. DOI: 10.1002/acn3.166 PMID: 25815358

Damrongplasit, K., & Melnick, G. (2024). Utilisation, out-of-pocket payments and access before and after COVID-19: Thailand's Universal Health Coverage Scheme. *BMJ Global Health, 9*(5), e015179. DOI: 10.1136/bmjgh-2024-015179 PMID: 38740495

Dandonoli, P. (2022). Regulatory challenges in digital health financing. *Global Health Action, 15*(1), 2058453. Advance online publication. DOI: 10.1080/16549716.2022.2058453

Dang, S., Olsan, T., Karuza, J., Cai, X., Gao, S., Intrator, O., Li, J., & Gillespie, S. M. (2019). Telehealth in home-based primary care: Factors and challenges associated with integration into veteran care. *Journal of the American Geriatrics Society, 67*(9), 1928–1933. DOI: 10.1111/jgs.16045 PMID: 31343732

Dankwa-Mullan, I. (2024). Health equity and ethical considerations in using artificial intelligence in public health and medicine. *Preventing Chronic Disease, 21*, 240245. DOI: 10.5888/pcd21.240245 PMID: 39173183

Dara, M., & Azarpira, N. (2025, January–March). Ethical considerations emerge from artificial intelligence (AI) in biotechnology. *Avicenna Journal of Medical Biotechnology, 17*(1), 80–81. DOI: 10.18502/ajmb.v17i1.17680 PMID: 40094090

Dash, A., & Mohanty, S. K. (2019). Do poor people in the poorer states pay more for healthcare in India? *BMC Public Health, 19*(1), 1020. DOI: 10.1186/s12889-019-7342-8 PMID: 31362727

De Foo, C., Chia, H. X., Teo, K. W., Farwin, A., Hashim, J., Koh, G. C. H., Matchar, D. B., Legido-Quigley, H., & Yap, J. C. (2023). Healthier SG: Singapore's multi-year strategy to transform primary healthcare. *The Lancet Regional Health. Western Pacific, 37*, 100861. DOI: 10.1016/j.lanwpc.2023.100861 PMID: 37529631

Dean, S., Mathers, J. M., Calvert, M., Kyte, D. G., Conroy, D., Folkard, A., Southworth, S., Murray, P. I., & Denniston, A. K. (2017). "The patient is speaking": Discovering the patient voice in ophthalmology. *The British Journal of Ophthalmology, 101*(6), 700–708. DOI: 10.1136/bjophthalmol-2016-309955 PMID: 28455280

Dehghani, N., Bras, J., & Guerreiro, R. (2021). How understudied populations have contributed to our understanding of Alzheimer's disease genetics. *Brain, 144*(4), 1067–1081. DOI: 10.1093/brain/awab028 PMID: 33889936

Deniz-Garcia, N., González-Vélez, H., & Salehi, A. (2023). Health informatics and AI in pandemic forecasting. *Journal of Biomedical Informatics, 138*, 104297. https://pmc.ncbi.nlm.nih.gov/articles/PMC10196903/

Dentico, N., Aye, B., & Meurs, M. (2022). *Financial justice for pandemic prevention, preparedness & response*. Geneva Global Health Hub.

Dentico, N., & Seitz, K. (2022). *Philanthrocapitalism in global health and nutrition: Analysis and implications*. Spotlight on Sustainable Development.

Devadasan, N., Criel, B., Van Damme, W., Lefevre, P., Manoharan, S., & Van der Stuyft, P. (2011). Community health insurance schemes and patient satisfaction—Evidence from India. *The Indian Journal of Medical Research, 133*(1), 40–49. PMID: 21321418

DevelopmentAid. (2025). *How AI is enhancing access to healthcare in LMICs and underserved communities*. https://www.developmentaid.org/news-stream/post/193852/ai-enhancing-access-to-healthcare

DeWitt, A. S., Kientz, J. A., Rucker Coker, T., & Liljenquist, K. (2022). mHealth technology design and evaluation for early childhood health promotion: A systematic literature review (Preprint). *JMIR Pediatrics and Parenting, 5*(4), e37718. Advance online publication. DOI: 10.2196/37718 PMID: 36201391

Dhana, K., Evans, D. A., Rajan, K. B., Bennett, D. A., & Morris, M. C. (2020). Healthy lifestyle and the risk of Alzheimer dementia. *Neurology, 95*(4). Advance online publication. DOI: 10.1212/WNL.0000000000009816 PMID: 32554763

Dholakia, S. (2020). An ethical analysis of the 'Ayushman Bharat-Pradhan Mantri Jan Arogya Yojna (PM-JAY)' scheme using the stakeholder approach to universal health care in India. *Asian Bioethics Review*, *12*(2), 195–203. DOI: 10.1007/s41649-020-00121-7 PMID: 33717337

Diao, Y., Li, M., Huang, Z., Sun, J., Chee, Y. L., & Liu, Y. (2019). Unlocking access to novel medicines in China—A review from a health system perspective. *Risk Management and Healthcare Policy*, *12*, 357–367. DOI: 10.2147/RMHP.S226379 PMID: 31908552

Díaz Muñoz, J. G. (2011). Las economías solidarias latinoamericanas como construcción de alternativas de resistencia y liberación desde abajo: Un estudio comparado de casos micro y macro de México, Argentina, Brasil y Bolivia (1989-2009).

Dieleman, J. L., Haakenstad, A., Micah, A., Moses, M., Abbafati, C., Acharya, P., & Murray, C. J. L. (2018). Health financing in Africa. *The Lancet. Global Health*, *6*(9), e1007–e1029.

DiMasi, J. A., Grabowski, H. G., & Hansen, R. W. (2016). Innovation in the pharmaceutical industry: New estimates of R&D costs. *Journal of Health Economics*, *47*, 20–33. DOI: 10.1016/j.jhealeco.2016.01.012 PMID: 26928437

Doctors Without Borders. (2015, October 21). Papua New Guinea: Treating TB in a "land without Land Cruisers". https://www.doctorswithoutborders.org/latest/papua-new-guinea-treating-tb-land-without-land-cruisers

Dodoo, J. E., Al-Samarraie, H., & Alsswey, A. (2022). The development of telemedicine programs in Sub-Saharan Africa: Progress and associated challenges. *Health Technology (Hong Kong)*, *12*(1), 11–26. DOI: 10.1007/s12553-021-00626-7 PMID: 34849325

Dominic. (2025). Making health financing work for poor people in Tanzania. World Bank.

Dubey, S., Deshpande, S., Krishna, L., & Zadey, S. (2023). Evolution of government-funded health insurance for universal health coverage in India. *The Lancet Regional Health. Southeast Asia*, *13*, 100174. DOI: 10.1016/j.lansea.2023.100180 PMID: 37383549

Early, J., Gonzalez, C., Gordon-Dseagu, V., & Robles-Calderon, L. (2019). Use of Mobile Health (mHealth) Technologies and Interventions among Community Health Workers Globally: A Scoping Review. *Health Promotion Practice*, *20*(6), 152483991985539. DOI: 10.1177/1524839919855391 PMID: 31179777

ECHEMI. (2024, February 28). *Wang Xiaodong: Pioneering the future! China's first billion-dollar molecular father.* https://www.echemi.com/cms/1429532.html

Elechi, U. S., Onah, C. O., Tarawallie, M. A., & Ifeanyi, I. (2025). Beyond seed funding: Why Nigerian digital health startups struggle to grow. *Health Economics Review, 16*(2), 2. Advance online publication. DOI: 10.1186/s13561-025-00708-6 PMID: 41348174

El-Gamal, F., Alali, A. K.Sr, Mashaabi, M. H., Alsaghah, A. A., Shukr, F. A., & Kadri, S. Y. (2023). Knowledge about Alzheimer's disease in Saudi Arabia. *Cureus, 15*(12), e50188. DOI: 10.7759/cureus.50188 PMID: 38089950

El-Metwally, A., Toivola, P., Al-Rashidi, M., Nooruddin, S., Jawed, M., AlKanhal, R., Razzak, H. A., & Albawardi, N. (2019). Epidemiology of Alzheimer's disease and dementia in arab countries: A systematic review. *Behavioural Neurology, 2019*(1), 3935943. DOI: 10.1155/2019/3935943 PMID: 31772681

Epstein, G. (2005). Introduction: Financialization and the world economy. In Epstein, G. (Ed.), *Financialization and the world economy.* Edward Elgar. DOI: 10.4337/9781781008263.00009

Erdelj, M., Król, M., & Natalizio, E. (2017). Wireless sensor networks and multi-UAV systems for natural disaster management. *Computer Networks, 124*, 72–86. DOI: 10.1016/j.comnet.2017.05.021

Ezenwaji, H. O., Nnamani, C. E., & Uche, I. M. (2024). The role of digital health in pandemic preparedness and response: Securing global health. ResearchGate. https://www.researchgate.net/publication/385130465

Ezenwaji, C. O., Alum, E. U., & Ugwu, O. P.-C. (2024). The role of digital health in pandemic preparedness and response: Securing global health? *Global Health Action, 17*(1), 2419694. DOI: 10.1080/16549716.2024.2419694 PMID: 39435565

Farai, O. A., Ogundairo, O., Maduka, C. P., Okongwu, C. C., Babarinde, A. O., & Sodamade, O. T. (2024). Digital health technologies in chronic disease management: A global perspective. *International Journal of Innovation and Scientific Research, 11*(3), 45–62. DOI: 10.51244/IJRSI.2023.1012041

Fattore, G., & Torbica, A. (2008). Cost and reimbursement of cataract surgery in Europe: A cross-country comparison. *Health Economics, 17*(S1), S71–S82. DOI: 10.1002/hec.1324 PMID: 18186033

Fazal, F., Saleem, T., Ur Rahman, M. E., Haider, T., Khalid, A. R., Tanveer, U., Mustafa, H., Tanveer, J., & Noor, A. (2022). The rising cost of healthcare and its contribution to the worsening disease burden in developing countries. *Annals of Medicine and Surgery (London), 82*, 104683. Advance online publication. DOI: 10.1016/j.amsu.2022.104683 PMID: 36148082

Feroz, A., Jabeen, R., & Saleem, S. (2020). Using mobile phones to improve community health workers performance in low-and-middle-income countries. *BMC Public Health, 20*(1), 49. Advance online publication. DOI: 10.1186/s12889-020-8173-3 PMID: 31931773

Feroz, A., Perveen, S., & Aftab, W. (2017). Role of mHealth applications for improving antenatal and postnatal care in low and middle income countries: A systematic review. *BMC Health Services Research, 17*(1), 704. Advance online publication. DOI: 10.1186/s12913-017-2664-7 PMID: 29115992

Ferrara, M., Romano, V., Steel, D. H., Gupta, R., Iovino, C., van Dijk, E. H. C., Steel, D. H., Rocha-de-Lossada, C., Bali, E., Valldeperas, X., Romano, D., Gadhvi, K. A., Matarazzo, F., Tzamalis, A., Grassi, P., Rachwani, R., Coco, G., Reyes-Delfino, C. D., Amoroso, F., & Romano, M. R. (2020). Reshaping ophthalmology training after COVID-19 pandemic. *Eye (London, England), 34*(11), 2089–2097. DOI: 10.1038/s41433-020-1061-3 PMID: 32612174

Fidler, B. (2026, January 26). China's edge in early-stage drugmaking 'likely to persist,' Pitchbook says. *BioPharma Dive*. https://www.biopharmadive.com/news/china-biotech-drug-licensing-trends-pitchbook-cell-gene-therapy/810478/

Fierce Biotech. (2018, February 23). *Moderna's cash juggernaut rolls on with record $604M IPO*. https://www.fiercebiotech.com/biotech/moderna-s-cash-juggernaut-rolls-record-604m-ipo

Fischer, A. M., & Storm, S. (2023). The return of debt crisis in developing countries: Shifting or maintaining dominant development paradigms? *Development and Change, 54*(5), 954–993. Advance online publication. DOI: 10.1111/dech.12800

Flores, L., Kim, S., & Young, S. D. (2024). Addressing bias in artificial intelligence for public health surveillance. *Journal of Medical Ethics, 50*(3), 190–194. DOI: 10.1136/jme-2022-108875 PMID: 37130756

Forbes. (2021, March 11). *The queen of China's biotech: How Samantha Du built Zai Lab into a $10 billion powerhouse*. https://www.forbes.com/sites/jenniferwang/2021/03/11/the-queen-of-chinas-biotech-how-samantha-du-built-zai-lab-into-a-10-billion-powerhouse/

French National Authority for Health. (2021). Telemedicine in France during. *COVID, 19*, •••. Retrieved July 28th, 2024, from https://www.has-sante.fr/jcms/p_3282983/fr/telemedicine-in-france-during-covid-19

Frisoni, G. B., Boccardi, M., Barkhof, F., Blennow, K., Cappa, S., Chiotis, K., Démonet, J. F., Garibotto, V., Giannakopoulos, P., Gietl, A., Hansson, O., Herholz, K., Jack, C. R.Jr, Nobili, F., Nordberg, A., Snyder, H. M., Ten Kate, M., Varrone, A., Albanese, E., & Winblad, B. (2017). Strategic roadmap for an early diagnosis of Alzheimer's disease based on biomarkers. *The Lancet. Neurology, 16*(8), 661–676. DOI: 10.1016/S1474-4422(17)30159-X PMID: 28721928

Fu, L., Pei, T., Xu, J., Han, J., & Yang, J. (2024). Inspecting the "health poverty trap" mechanism: Self-reinforcing effect and endogenous force. *BMC Public Health, 24*(1), 917. DOI: 10.1186/s12889-024-18464-3 PMID: 38549088

Gajarawala, S. N., & Pelkowski, J. N. (2021). Telehealth benefits and barriers. *The Journal for Nurse Practitioners, 17*(2), 218–221. DOI: 10.1016/j.nurpra.2020.09.013 PMID: 33106751

Garg, S., Tripathi, N., Ranjan, A., & Bebarta, K. K. (2022). How much do government and households spend on an episode of hospitalisation in India? A comparison for public and private hospitals in Chhattisgarh state. *Health Economics Review, 12*(1), 27. DOI: 10.1186/s13561-022-00372-0 PMID: 35522382

Garrison, L. P.Jr, Neumann, P. J., Willke, R. J., Basu, A., Danzon, P. M., Doshi, J. A., Drummond, M. F., Lakdawalla, D. N., Pauly, M. V., Phelps, C. E., Ramsey, S. D., Towse, A., & Weinstein, M. C. (2018). A Health Economics Approach to US Value Assessment Frameworks—Summary and Recommendations of the ISPOR Special Task Force Report [7]. *Value in Health : The Journal of the International Society for Pharmacoeconomics and Outcomes Research, 21*(2), 161–165. DOI: 10.1016/j.jval.2017.12.009 PMID: 29477394

Garufu, P. (2016). Operationalising international law principles governing state sovereignty over mineral resources: The case of Zimbabwe and the Democratic Republic of the Congo (DRC) [Master's thesis, University of the Witwatersrand]. WiredSpace. https://wiredspace.wits.ac.za/items/0bb70cb5-e516-4172-9863-bdfd829b8755

Garvin, L. A., Hu, J., Slightam, C., McInnes, D. K., & Zulman, D. M. (2021). Use of video telehealth tablets to increase access for veterans experiencing homelessness. *Journal of General Internal Medicine, 36*(8), 2274–2282. DOI: 10.1007/s11606-021-06900-8 PMID: 34027612

Gavi. (2022). *Expanding sustainable vaccine manufacturing in Africa: Priorities for Support.* https://www.gavi.org/news-resources/knowledge-products/expanding-sustainable-vaccine-manufacturing-africa-priorities-support

Gavi's approach to engaging with middle-income countries. (2025, October 10). https://www.gavi.org/programmes-impact/programmatic-policies/eligibility-co-financing-policies/gavi-mics-approach

Gebremariam, K. T., Mulugeta, A., & Gallegos, D. (2023). Theory-based mHealth targeting fathers and mothers to improve exclusive breastfeeding: A quasi-experimental study. *International Breastfeeding Journal, 18*(1), 2. Advance online publication. DOI: 10.1186/s13006-022-00537-x PMID: 36604757

General Authority for Statistics. (2024). *Total Kingdom population exceeds 35 million by mid-2024.* https://www.stats.gov.sa/documents/20117/2435273/Population+Estimates+Statistics+2024+EN.pdf/9b71e303-5fd9-19cb-9913-850a9d521639

George, M. D., Danila, M. I., Watrous, D., Reddy, S., Alper, J., Xie, F., Nowell, W. B., Kallich, J., Clinton, C., Saag, K. G., & Curtis, J. R. (2021). Disruptions in rheumatology care and the rise of telehealth in response to the COVID-19 pandemic in a community practice-based network. *Arthritis Care & Research (Hoboken), 73*(8), 1153–1161. DOI: 10.1002/acr.24626 PMID: 33973389

German Federal Statistical Office. (2019). *Health statistics* 27th. Available at: https://www.destatis.de/DE/Home/_inhalt.html (Accessed: July 2024).

Ghazal, K., Singh Beniwal, S., & Dhingra, A. (2024). Assessing telehealth in palliative care: A systematic review of the effectiveness and challenges in rural and underserved areas. *Cureus*. Advance online publication. DOI: 10.7759/cureus.68275 PMID: 39350817

Ghia, C., & Rambhad, G. (2023). Implementation of equity and access in Indian healthcare: Current scenario and way forward. *Journal of Market Access & Health Policy, 11*(1), 2194507. DOI: 10.1080/20016689.2023.2194507 PMID: 36998432

Ginsburg, A. S., Delarosa, J., Brunette, W., Levari, S., Sundt, M., Larson, C., Tawiah Agyemang, C., Newton, S., Borriello, G., & Anderson, R. (2015). mPneumonia: Development of an Innovative mHealth Application for Diagnosing and Treating Childhood Pneumonia and Other Childhood Illnesses in Low-Resource Settings. *PLoS One, 10*(10), e0139625. DOI: 10.1371/journal.pone.0139625 PMID: 26474321

Gladstone, J., Schipper, L., Hara-Msulira, T., Casci, T., Allen, K., Carter, H., Lee, Z., & Lockie, J. (2023). Equity and inclusivity in research funding: Barriers and delivering change.

Gómez Rodríguez, D. T. (2024). Solidarity economy and public health for sustainable development and community well-being. *Cooperativismo & Desarrollo, 32*(128), 1–15. DOI: 10.16925/2382-4220.2024.01.02

Gomez, C., Smith, B.-L., Zayas, A., Unberath, M., & Canares, T. (2024). Explainable AI decision support improves accuracy during telehealth strep throat screening. *Communications Medicine, 4*(1), 149. Advance online publication. DOI: 10.1038/s43856-024-00568-x PMID: 39048726

González-Gonzalo, C., Thee, E. F., Klaver, C. C. W., Lee, A. Y., Schlingemann, R. O., Tufail, A., Verbraak, F., & Sánchez, C. I. (2022). Trustworthy AI: Closing the gap between development and integration of AI systems in ophthalmic practice. *Progress in Retinal and Eye Research, 90*, 101034–101034. DOI: 10.1016/j.preteyeres.2021.101034 PMID: 34902546

Gopalakrishnan, L., Buback, L., Fernald, L., Walker, D., & Diamond-Smith, N. (2020). Using mHealth to improve health care delivery in India: A qualitative examination of the perspectives of community health workers and beneficiaries. *PLoS One, 15*(1), e0227451. DOI: 10.1371/journal.pone.0227451 PMID: 31940326

Gopalakrishnan, L., Patil, S., Fernald, L., Walker, D., & Diamond-Smith, N. (2024). Association between coordinated counseling from both ASHA and Anganwadi Workers and maternal health outcomes: A cross-sectional study from Madhya Pradesh and Bihar, India. *PLOS Global Public Health, 4*(11), e0003639. DOI: 10.1371/journal.pgph.0003639 PMID: 39536020

Gore, C. (2000). The rise and fall of the Washington Consensus as a paradigm for developing countries. *World Development, 28*(5), 789–804. Advance online publication. DOI: 10.1016/S0305-750X(99)00160-6

Gouda, H. N., Charlson, F., Sorsdahl, K., Ahmadzada, S., Ferrari, A. J., Erskine, H., & Whiteford, H. (2019). Burden of non-communicable diseases in sub-Saharan Africa, 1990-2017. *The Lancet. Global Health, 7*(10), e1375–e1387. DOI: 10.1016/S2214-109X(19)30374-2 PMID: 31537368

Gouglas, D., Thanh Le, T., Henderson, K., Kaloudis, A., Danielsen, T., Hammersland, N. C., Robinson, J. M., Heaton, P. M., & Røttingen, J.-A. (2018). Estimating the cost of vaccine development against epidemic infectious diseases: A cost minimisation study. *The Lancet. Global Health, 6*(12), e1386–e1396. DOI: 10.1016/S2214-109X(18)30346-2 PMID: 30342925

Government of India. (2018). *'Ayushman Bharat' – Health and wellness centers.* https://ab-hwc.nhp.gov.in/home/aboutus (Accessed June 30, 2024)

Government of Telangana. (2025). *Aarogyasri*. https://kamareddy.telangana.gov.in/aarogyasri/ (Accessed August 24, 2025)

Grewal, H., Sharma, P., Dhillon, G., Munjal, R. S., Verma, R. K., & Kashyap, R. (2023). Universal health care system in India: An in-depth examination of the Ayushman Bharat initiative. *Cureus, 15*(6), e40029. DOI: 10.7759/cureus.40733 PMID: 37485096

Grosman-Rimon, L., & Wegier, P. (2024). With advancement in health technology comes great responsibility – Ethical and safety considerations for using digital health technology: A narrative review. *Medicine, 103*(33), e39136–e39136. DOI: 10.1097/MD.0000000000039136 PMID: 39151529

Grossberg, G. T., & Desai, A. K. (2003). Management of Alzheimer's disease. *Journal of Gerontology, 58*(4), M331–M353. DOI: 10.1093/gerona/58.4.M331 PMID: 12663697

Grove, J., Claeson, M., Bryce, J., Amouzou, A., Boerma, T., Waiswa, P., & Victora, C. (2015). Maternal, newborn, and child health and the Sustainable Development Goals—A call for sustained and improved measurement. *Lancet, 386*(10003), 1511–1514. DOI: 10.1016/S0140-6736(15)00517-6 PMID: 26530604

GSMA. (2021). *State of the industry report on mobile money 2021*. GSMA.

GSMA. (2022). The mobile gender gap report 2022. GSMA. https://www.gsma.com/r/wp-content/uploads/2022/06/The-Mobile-Gender-Gap-Report-2022.pdf

Guimarães, E. L., Chissaque, A., Pecenka, C., Debellut, F., Schuind, A., Vaz, B., Banze, A., Rangeiro, R., Mariano, A., Lorenzoni, C., Carrilho, C., Martins, M., de Deus, N., & Clark, A. (2023). Impact and Cost-Effectiveness of Alternative Human Papillomavirus Vaccines for Preadolescent Girls in Mozambique: A Modelling Study. *Vaccines, 11*(6), 6. Advance online publication. DOI: 10.3390/vaccines11061058 PMID: 37376447

Gunasekeran, D. V., & Wong, T. Y. (2020). Artificial intelligence in ophthalmology in 2020: A technology on the cusp for translation and implementation. *Asia-Pacific Journal of Ophthalmology (Philadelphia, Pa.), 9*(2), 61–66. DOI: 10.1097/01.APO.0000656984.56467.2c PMID: 32349112

Gupta, K., Junaid, V., Qureshi, M. A., Gupta, A., Sheikh, S., Dalakoti, M., Virani, S. S., & Khoja, A. (2024). Health data sciences and cardiovascular diseases in South Asia: Innovations and challenges in digital health. *Current Atherosclerosis Reports, 26*(11), 639–648. https://doi.org/10.100. DOI: 10.1007/s11883-024-01233-3 PMID: 39240492

Gyawali, P. K., Le Guen, Y., Liu, X., Belloy, M. E., Tang, H., Zou, J., & He, Z. (2023). Improving genetic risk prediction across diverse population by disentangling ancestry representations. *Communications Biology*, *6*(1), 964. DOI: 10.1038/s42003-023-05352-6 PMID: 37736834

Haddad, S. M., Souza, R. T., & Cecatti, J. G. (2019). Mobile technology in health (mHealth) and antenatal care–Searching for apps and available solutions: A systematic review. *International Journal of Medical Informatics*, *127*, 1–8. DOI: 10.1016/j.ijmedinf.2019.04.008 PMID: 31128820

Haddison, E. C., Engoung, D. B., Bodo, C. B., & Njie, V. M. (2025). Overcoming HPV vaccine hesitancy: Insights from a successful school-based vaccination campaign in the Saa health district of Cameroon. *BMC Infectious Diseases*, *25*(1), 465. DOI: 10.1186/s12879-025-10864-z PMID: 40186125

Hadler, N. L., Bu, P., Winkler, A., & Alexander, A. W. (2021, January 6). College student perspectives of telemental health: A review of the recent literature. Current Psychiatry Reports. https://pmc.ncbi.nlm.nih.gov/articles/PMC7785477/

Haimi, M. (2023). The tragic paradoxical effect of telemedicine on healthcare disparities: A time for redemption. *BMC Medical Informatics and Decision Making*, *23*(1), 95. Advance online publication. DOI: 10.1186/s12911-023-02194-4 PMID: 37193960

Hakami, F., Madkhali, M. A., Saleh, E., Ayoub, R., Moafa, S., Moafa, A., Alnami, B., Maashi, B., Khubrani, S., Busayli, W., & Alhazmi, A. (2023). Awareness and perception toward Alzheimer's disease among residents living in the Jazan Province, Saudi Arabia: A cross-sectional study. *Cureus*, *15*(9), e44505. DOI: 10.7759/cureus.44505 PMID: 37789999

Halamka, J. D., & Cerrato, P. M. (2025, May). *Digital twin technology has potential to redefine care*. Mayo Clinic Magazine. https://mayomagazine.mayoclinic.org/2025/05/digital-twin-technology/

Hale, T. M., & Kvedar, J. C. (2014, December 1). Privacy and security concerns in telehealth. AMA Journal of Ethics. https://journalofethics.ama-assn.org/article/privacy-and-security-concerns-telehealth/2014-12

Haleem, A., Javaid, M., Singh, R. P., & Suman, R. (2021). Telemedicine for healthcare: Capabilities, features, barriers, and applications. *Sensors International*, *2*, 100117. https://pmc.ncbi.nlm.nih.gov/articles/PMC8590973/. DOI: 10.1016/j.sintl.2021.100117 PMID: 34806053

Haleem, A., Javaid, M., & Vaishya, R. (2021). Industry 4.0 and healthcare: A review. *Health Technology (Hong Kong), 11*, 903–918. https://www.sciencedirect.com/science/article/pii/S266660302100021X

Hanna, D., Lee, J., & Park, S. (2024). Digital inclusion in health policy design. *Evaluation and Program Planning, 100*, 102292. https://www.sciencedirect.com/science/article/pii/S0893395224002667

Hansson, O. (2021). Biomarkers for neurodegenerative diseases. *Nature Medicine, 27*(6), 954–963. DOI: 10.1038/s41591-021-01382-x PMID: 34083813

Haruna, A., Oumbé, H. T., & Kountchou, A. M. (2023). Child healthcare outcomes in Africa: Unlocking the potentials of Islamic finance. *Journal of Islamic Finance, 12*(1), 116–135. Advance online publication. DOI: 10.31436/jif.v12i1.752

Harvard, T. H. Chan School of Public Health. (2024). *Expanded climate toolkit to improve health equity and protect patients on the frontlines of the climate crisis.* https://hsph.harvard.edu/climate-health-c-change/news/expandedtoolkit/

Hassell, J. B., Lamoureux, E. L., & Keeffe, J. E. (2006). Impact of age related macular degeneration on quality of life. *The British Journal of Ophthalmology, 90*(5), 593–596. DOI: 10.1136/bjo.2005.086595 PMID: 16622089

Hawajri, O., Lindberg, J., & Suominen, S. (2023). Virtual reality exposure therapy as a treatment method against anxiety disorders and depression: A structured literature review. *Issues in Mental Health Nursing, 44*(4), 245–269. DOI: 10.1080/01612840.2023.2190051 PMID: 37075308

He, A. J. (2023). Scaling-up through piloting: Dual-track provider payment reforms in China's health system. *Health Policy and Planning, 38*(2), 218–227. DOI: 10.1093/heapol/czac080 PMID: 36103333

Health Education England. (2019, July). Delivering patient safety through education, training and development. https://www.hee.nhs.uk/sites/default/files/documents/Strategic%20Response%20to%20Improving%20Safety%20Through%20Education%20Training%20-%20HEE%20-%20July19.pdf

Health Resources and Services Administration. (2022, March 1). What is telehealth? https://www.hrsa.gov/telehealth/what-is-telehealth

He, D., Guizani, M., & Zhang, X. (2020). Blockchain and health informatics. *International Journal of Information Management, 52*, 102045. DOI: 10.1016/j.ijinfomgt.2019.10.007

Heidari, S., & García Moreno, C. (2016). Gender-based violence: A barrier to sexual and reproductive health and rights. *Reproductive Health Matters*, *24*(47), 1–4. DOI: 10.1016/j.rhm.2016.07.001 PMID: 27578333

Helmi. (2024). *Biotech risks and challenges in Latin America*. https://helmi.com/insights/biotech-risks-and-challenges-in-latin-america

Henzler, D., Schmidt, S., Koçar, A., Herdegen, S., Lindinger, G. L., Maris, M. T., Bak, M. A. R., Willems, D. L., Tan, H. L., Lauerer, M., Nagel, E., Hindricks, G., Dagres, N., & Konopka, M. J. (2025). Healthcare professionals' perspectives on artificial intelligence in patient care: A systematic review of hindering and facilitating factors on different levels. *BMC Health Services Research*, *25*(1), 633. https://bmchealthservres.biomedcentral.com/articles/10.1186/s12913-025-12664-2. DOI: 10.1186/s12913-025-12664-2 PMID: 40312413

Herbst, T., Foerster, J., & Emmert, M. (2018). The impact of pay-for-performance on the quality of care in ophthalmology: Empirical evidence from Germany. *Health Policy (Amsterdam)*, *122*(6), 667–673. DOI: 10.1016/j.healthpol.2018.03.013 PMID: 29606288

Hidayat, B. (2015). *Out-of-pocket payments in the national health insurance of Indonesia: A first year review* [Policy brief].

HKEX. (2018). *Annual report 2018*. https://www.hkexnews.hk/listedco/listconews/sehk/2019/0429/ltn201904292085.pdf

HKEX. (2025). *Biotech listing regime*. https://www.hkex.com.hk/Join-Our-Market/Biotech?sc_lang=en

Ho, C. J., Khalid, H., Skead, K., & Wong, J. (2022). The politics of universal health coverage. *Lancet*, *399*(10340), 2066–2074. DOI: 10.1016/S0140-6736(22)00585-2 PMID: 35594878

Hogan, D. R., Stevens, G. A., Hosseinpoor, A. R., & Boerma, T. (2018). National spending on health by source for 184 countries between 2013 and 2040. *Lancet*, *391*(10132), 2017–2031.

Hong Kong Exchanges and Clearing Limited. (2018, April 24). *Hong Kong's listing regime enters new era, featuring emerging and innovative firms* [Press release]. https://www.hkex.com.hk/News/News-Release/2018/180424news?sc_lang=en

Houenou, B. (2024). Datafication in the age of AI: Economic models and policy. DOI: 10.2139/ssrn.5163471

Hugger, F., González Cabral, C., Bucci, M., Gesualdo, M., & O'Reilly, P. (2024, June 22). How the global minimum tax changes the taxation of multinational companies. VoxEU. https://cepr.org/voxeu/columns/how-global-minimum-tax-changes-taxation-multinational-companies

Hughes, N., & Lonie, S. (2007). M-PESA: Mobile money for the unbanked. *Innovations: Technology, Governance, Globalization*, *2*(1-2), 63–81. DOI: 10.1162/itgg.2007.2.1-2.63

Human papillomavirus vaccines: WHO position paper, December 2022. (2022). *WEEKLY EPIDEMIOLOGICAL RECORD, 97*(50), 645–672.

Hunter, B. M., McCoy, D., Cordhila, A. C., Marriott, A., Roy, V., Stein, F., & Wood, B. (2025). *Private financial actors and financialisation in global health*. United Nations University International Institute for Global Health. DOI: 10.37941/RR/2025/1

Hunter, B. M., & Murray, S. F. (2019). Deconstructing the financialization of healthcare. *Development and Change*, *50*(5), 1263–1287. DOI: 10.1111/dech.12517

Hunter, D. J., & Bengoa, R. (2023). Meeting the challenge of health system transformation in European countries. *Policy and Society*, *42*(1), 14–27. DOI: 10.1093/polsoc/puac022

Hussein, M., Shahmoradi, A., & Turk, R. (2016). An overview of Islamic finance. Journal of International Commerce. *Economic Policy*, *7*(1).

Hu, Y., & Mossialos, E. (2017). Pharmaceutical pricing and reimbursement in China: When price controls and drug markups are abolished. *Globalization and Health*, *13*(1), 1–7. DOI: 10.1186/s12992-017-0285-x PMID: 28049495

IA2030. (2025). *IA2030 Global Progress Report 2024* (pp. 1–70). https://www.immunizationagenda2030.org/ia2030-annual-reports

IFFIm. (2025). *Eligible Countries | International Finance Facility for Immunisation (IFFIm)*. International Finance Facility for Immunisation (IFFIm). https://iffim.org/eligible-countries

Ilozumba, O., Van Belle, S., Dieleman, M., Liem, L., Choudhury, M., & Broerse, J. E. W. (2018). The Effect of a Community Health Worker Utilized Mobile Health Application on Maternal Health Knowledge and Behavior: A Quasi-Experimental Study. *Frontiers in Public Health*, *6*, 133. Advance online publication. DOI: 10.3389/fpubh.2018.00133 PMID: 29868541

Innovent Biologics. (2016, November 29). *Innovent Biologics, Inc. raises USD $260M in Series D financing*. PR Newswire. https://www.prnewswire.com/news-releases/innovent-biologics-inc-raises-usd-260m-in-series-d-financing-300369527.html

Innovent Biologics. (2024). *About us*. https://en.innoventbio.com/AboutUs

Institute for Health Metrics and Evaluation. (2021). *Global Burden of Disease Study 2020 results. IHME*. University of Washington.

Insurance Regulatory and Development Authority of India. (2020). *Annual report 2020*. https://www.irdai.gov.in(Accessed July 2, 2024)

International Labour Organization. (2020). *World employment and social outlook: Trends 2020*. ILO.

International Labour Organization. (2025). *National health accounts 2020*.

International Telecommunication Union. (2022). Measuring digital development: Facts and figures. ITU Development Sector. https://www.itu.int/en/ITU-D/Statistics/Documents/facts/FactsFigures2021.pdf

IntuitionLabs. (2026, January 10). *Value-based contracting in pharma: Models & challenges*. https://intuitionlabs.ai/articles/value-based-contracting-pharmaceuticals

Ismail, A. A., Alghasham, N. S., Alsukhaiber, R. E., & Alnowiasser, F. M. (2021). Dementia screening of geriatric patients by implementing an informant-based Alzheimer's disease eight-item tool in KSA. *Journal of Taibah University Medical Sciences*, *16*(2), 191–197. DOI: 10.1016/j.jtumed.2020.10.020 PMID: 33897323

Italian Ministry of Health. (2020). *Regional health disparities report*. Available at: https://www.salute.gov.it/portale/home.html (Accessed: July 25th 2024).

IUPAC. (2014). Compendium of chemical terminology (2nd ed.; the "Gold Book"). (A. D. McNaught & A. Wilkinson, Comps.). Blackwell Scientific Publications. Online version (2019-) created by S. J. Chalk. https://doi.org/DOI: 10.1351/goldbook.B00666

Jack, W., & Suri, T. (2014). Risk sharing and transactions costs: Evidence from Kenya's mobile money revolution. *The American Economic Review*, *104*(1), 183–223. DOI: 10.1257/aer.104.1.183

Jácome, D., Cotrufo, T., Andres-Benito, P., Lidón, L., Martí, E., Ferrer, I., Del Río, J. A., & Gavín, R. (2024). miR-519a-3p, found to regulate cellular prion protein during Alzheimer's disease pathogenesis, as a biomarker of asymptomatic stages. *Biochimica et Biophysica Acta (BBA)-. Biochimica et Biophysica Acta. Molecular Basis of Disease*, *1870*(5), 167187. DOI: 10.1016/j.bbadis.2024.167187 PMID: 38653354

Jagarapu, J., & Savani, R. C. (2021). A brief history of telemedicine and the evolution of teleneonatology. *Seminars in Perinatology*, *45*(5), 151416. Advance online publication. DOI: 10.1016/j.semperi.2021.151416 PMID: 34006382

James, J. (2025). *5 Maternal Health Mobile Apps That Are Saving African Mothers' Lives*. Socialgoodmoms.com. https://socialgoodmoms.com/2015/07/27/5-maternal-health-mobile-apps-that-are-saving-african-mothers-lives/

James, J. (2019). Confronting the scarcity of digital skills among the poor in developing countries. *Development Policy Review*, *39*(2), 324–339. Advance online publication. DOI: 10.1111/dpr.12479

Jecker, N. S., Atuire, C. A., & Kenworthy, N. (2022). Realising Ubuntu in global health: An African approach to global health justice. *Public Health Ethics*, *15*(3), 256–267. Advance online publication. DOI: 10.1093/phe/phac022

Jeon, E., & Park, H.-A. (2015). Factors Affecting Acceptance of Smartphone Application for Management of Obesity. *Healthcare Informatics Research*, *21*(2), 74. DOI: 10.4258/hir.2015.21.2.74 PMID: 25995959

Jetté, C., & Vaillancourt, Y. (2011). Social economy and home care services in Quebec: Co-production or co-construction? *Voluntas*, *22*(1), 48–69. DOI: 10.1007/s11266-010-9134-8

Jia, R., & Ma, X. (2024). *Improving regulation for innovation: Evidence from China's pharmaceutical industry* (Working Paper No. w31976). National Bureau of Economic Research. https://doi.org/DOI: 10.3386/w31976

Johns Hopkins University. (2023). Coronavirus Resource Center: COVID-19 global cases and deaths. https://coronavirus.jhu.edu/data

Jon Fingas. (2023). *Apple is reportedly developing an AI health coach for Apple Watch*: Engadget. Available at: https://www.engadget.com/apple-is-reportedly-developing-an-ai-health-coach-for-apple-watch-212515646.html (Accessed: July 28th 2024).

Jones, A. K., Yan, C. L., Rivera Rodriguez, B. P., Kaur, S., & Andrade-Bucknor, S. (2023). Role of wearable devices in cardiac telerehabilitation: A scoping review. *PLoS One*, *18*(5), e0285801. Advance online publication. DOI: 10.1371/journal.pone.0285801 PMID: 37256878

Jørgensen, E. P., Muttuvelu, D. V., Peto, T., Natarajan, S., Davies, J., Keane, P. A., & Ehlers, L. H. (2024). Implementing teleophthalmology services to improve cost-effectiveness of the national eye care system, *Eye (London)*.

Kaewkungwal, J., Singhasivanon, P., Khamsiriwatchara, A., Sawang, S., Meankaew, P., & Wechsart, A. (2010). Application of smart phone in "Better Border Healthcare Program": A module for mother and child care. *BMC Medical Informatics and Decision Making*, *10*(1), 69. Advance online publication. DOI: 10.1186/1472-6947-10-69 PMID: 21047412

Kaiser, A. H., Rotigliano, N., Flessa, S., Ekman, B., & Sundewall, J. (2023). Extending universal health coverage to informal workers: A systematic review of health financing schemes in low- and middle-income countries in Southeast Asia. *PLoS One*, *18*(7), e0288269. DOI: 10.1371/journal.pone.0288269 PMID: 37432943

Kaló, Z., Kruja, K., Noone, D., Vogler, S., & Docteur, E. (2025). Collective international action to increase access to costly drugs: Pooled procurement and equity based tiered pricing. *BMJ (Clinical Research Ed.)*, *391*, e084839. DOI: 10.1136/bmj-2025-084839 PMID: 41218989

Kante, M., & Målqvist, M. (2025). Effectiveness of SMS-based interventions in enhancing antenatal care in developing countries: A systematic review. *BMJ Open*, *15*(2), e089671–e089671. DOI: 10.1136/bmjopen-2024-089671 PMID: 40000082

Karataş, N., Kaya, A., & Dalgıç, A. İ. (2021). The effectiveness of user-focused mobile health applications in paediatric chronic disease management: A systematic review. *Journal of Pediatric Nursing: Nursing Care of Children and Families*, *0*(0). Advance online publication. DOI: 10.1016/j.pedn.2021.09.018 PMID: 34598848

Kasyapa, M. S. B., & Vanmathi, C. (2024, April 26). Blockchain integration in healthcare: A comprehensive investigation of use cases, performance issues, and mitigation strategies. *Frontiers in Digital Health*, *6*, 1359858. Advance online publication. DOI: 10.3389/fdgth.2024.1359858 PMID: 38736708

Keam, S. J. (2022). Cadonilimab: First approval. *Drugs*, *82*(12), 1333–1339. DOI: 10.1007/s40265-022-01761-9 PMID: 35986837

Keenan, A. J., Tsourtos, G., & Tieman, J. (2021). The value of applying ethical principles in telehealth practices: Systematic review. *Journal of Medical Internet Research*, *23*(3), e25698. Advance online publication. DOI: 10.2196/25698 PMID: 33783366

Keikelame, M. J., & Swartz, L. (2019). Decolonising research methodologies: Lessons from a qualitative research project, Cape Town, South Africa. *Global Health Action*, *12*(1), 1561175. DOI: 10.1080/16549716.2018.1561175 PMID: 30661464

Kentikelenis, A., & Stubbs, T. (2024). Social protection and the International Monetary Fund: Promise versus performance. *Globalization and Health, 20*(1), 41. DOI: 10.1186/s12992-024-01045-9 PMID: 38715077

Kern, C., Fu, D. J., Kortuem, K., Huemer, J., Barker, D., Davis, A., Balaskas, K., Keane, P. A., McKinnon, T., & Sim, D. A. (2020). Implementation of a cloud-based referral platform in ophthalmology: Making telemedicine services a reality in eye care. *The British Journal of Ophthalmology, 104*(3), 312–317. DOI: 10.1136/bjophthalmol-2019-314161 PMID: 31320383

Kerwin, D., Abdelnour, C., Caramelli, P., Ogunniyi, A., Shi, J., Zetterberg, H., & Traber, M. (2022). Alzheimer's disease diagnosis and management: Perspectives from around the world. *Alzheimer's & Dementia: Diagnosis, Assessment & Disease Monitoring, 14*(1), e12334. DOI: 10.1002/dad2.12334 PMID: 35898519

Khalil, A. I., Aladwani, N., & Aljehani, S. (2020). Relationship between knowledge, attitude, and burden among Alzheimer's family care givers in Jeddah, Saudi Arabia. *Saudi Journal of Nursing and Health Care, 3*(6), 167–174. DOI: 10.36348/sjnhc.2020.v03i06.002

Khan, P. K., Perkins, J. M., Kim, R., Mohanty, S. K., & Subramanian, S. V. (2021). Multilevel population and socioeconomic variation in health insurance coverage in India. *Tropical Medicine & International Health : TM & IH, 26*(10), 1285–1295. DOI: 10.1111/tmi.13645 PMID: 34181806

Kharbanda, V., Linnenbank, P., Gulati, A., & Agarwal, H. (2024). Advancing biotechnology & genomics in Saudi Arabia: Best practice strategies to develop the sector & maximize its impact. https://www.adlittle.com/be-en/insights/report/advancing-biotechnologygenomics-saudi-arabia (2024, May 31, 2024).

Kiendrébéogo, J. A., Sidibe, A. R. O., Compaoré, G. B., Nacanabo, R., Sory, O., Ouédraogo, I., Nawaz, S., Schuind, A. E., & Clark, A. (2023). Cost-effectiveness of human papillomavirus (HPV) vaccination in Burkina Faso: A modelling study. *BMC Health Services Research, 23*(1), 1338. DOI: 10.1186/s12913-023-10283-3 PMID: 38041075

Kigombola, A., & Mahundi, M. (2024). Implementing blockchain for health sectors in low- and middle-income countries: Use cases, approaches and challenges. *Journal of Health Informatics in Africa, 11*(3), 28–40. DOI: 10.12856/JHIA-2024-v11-i3-511

Kingdon, J. (1995). *Agendas, Alternatives and Public Policies* (2nd ed.). Harper Collins.

Kiseleva, A., Kotzinos, D., & De Hert, P. (2022). Transparency of AI in healthcare as a multilayered system of accountabilities: Between legal requirements and technical limitations. *Frontiers in Artificial Intelligence, 5*, 879603. Advance online publication. DOI: 10.3389/frai.2022.879603 PMID: 35707765

Ko, H. (2020). South Korea's COVID-19 surveillance strategy: Balancing public health and privacy. *Asian Bioethics Review, 12*(4), 421–437. DOI: 10.1007/s41649-020-00133-2

Kolesar, R. J., Erreygers, G., Van Damme, W., Chea, V., Choeurng, T., & Leng, S. (2023). Hardship financing, productivity loss and the economic cost of illness and injury in Cambodia. *International Journal for Equity in Health, 22*(1), 208. DOI: 10.1186/s12939-023-02016-z PMID: 37805483

Koplan, J. P., Bond, T. C., Merson, M. H., Reddy, K. S., Rodriguez, M. H., Sewankambo, N. K., & Wasserheit, J. N. (2009). Towards a common definition of global health. *Lancet, 373*(9679), 1993–1995. DOI: 10.1016/S0140-6736(09)60332-9 PMID: 19493564

Kotter, J. (1996). *Leading Change*. Harvard Business School Press.

Kotter, J. (2008). *A Sense of Urgency*. Harvard Business School Press.

Kotter, J. P. (1995). Why transformation efforts fail. *Harvard Business Review, 73*(2), 59–67.

Kotter, J. P., & Cohen, D. S. (2002). *The Heart of Change: Real-life Stories of How People Change Their Organizations*. Harvard Business School Press.

Krüger, L. J., Evers, S. M. A. A., Hiligsmann, M., & Wild, C. (2014). Divergent evidence requirements for authorization and reimbursement of high-risk medical devices – The European situation. *Health Policy and Technology, 3*(4), 253–263. DOI: 10.1016/j.hlpt.2014.08.005

Kruse, C., Betancourt, J., Ortiz, S., Valdes Luna, S. M., Bamrah, I. K., & Segovia, N. (2019). Barriers to the Use of Mobile Health in Improving Health Outcomes in Developing Countries: Systematic Review. *Journal of Medical Internet Research, 21*(10), e13263. DOI: 10.2196/13263 PMID: 31593543

Kumar, P. (2025). Failed blockchain projects and why they failed. *C# Corner*. https://www.c-sharpcorner.com/article/failed-blockchain-projects-and-why-they-failed/

Kumar, R., Khosla, R., & McCoy, D. (2024). Decolonising global health research: Shifting power for transformative change. *PLOS Global Public Health*, *4*(4), e0003141. Advance online publication. DOI: 10.1371/journal.pgph.0003141 PMID: 38656955

Kumbhar, P. R., Kumar, P., Lasure, A., Velayutham, R., & Mandal, D. (2023). An updated landscape on nanotechnology-based drug delivery, immunotherapy, vaccinations, imaging, and biomarker detections for cancers: Recent trends and future directions with clinical success. *Discover Nano*, *18*(1), 156. Advance online publication. DOI: 10.1186/s11671-023-03913-6 PMID: 38112935

Kuo, T.-T., Rojas, H. Z., & Ohno-Machado, L. (2019). Comparison of blockchain platforms: A systematic review and healthcare examples. *Journal of the American Medical Informatics Association : JAMIA*, *26*(5), 462–478. DOI: 10.1093/jamia/ocy185 PMID: 30907419

Kuppalli, K. (2024). Ebola: Ten years later—Lessons learned and future pandemic preparedness. *PLOS Global Public Health*, *4*(9), e0003662. DOI: 10.1371/journal.pgph.0003662 PMID: 39325790

Kurjak, A., Stanojević, M., & Dudenhausen, J. (2022). Why maternal mortality in the world remains tragedy in low-income countries and shame for high-income ones: Will sustainable development goals (SDG) help? *Journal of Perinatal Medicine*, *0*(0). Advance online publication. DOI: 10.1515/jpm-2022-0061 PMID: 35636412

Kusyanti, T., Wirakusumah, F. F., Rinawan, F. R., Muhith, A., Purbasari, A., Mawardi, F., Puspitasari, I. W., Faza, A., & Stellata, A. G. (2022). Technology-Based (Mhealth) and Standard/Traditional Maternal Care for Pregnant Woman: A Systematic Literature Review. *Health Care*, *10*(7), 1287. DOI: 10.3390/healthcare10071287 PMID: 35885813

Kwete, X., Tang, K., Chen, L., Ren, R., Chen, Q., Wu, Z., Cai, Y., & Li, H. (2022). Decolonising global health: What should be the target of this movement and where does it lead us? *Global Health Research and Policy*, *7*(1), 3. Advance online publication. DOI: 10.1186/s41256-022-00237-3 PMID: 35067229

Lad, R. A., & Padroo, B. S.Rahul A. LadBhawna Sharma Padroo. (2024). Advancements and challenges in digital health implementation in India: A comprehensive literature review. *World J Bio Pharm Health Sci*, *18*(1), 205–208. DOI: 10.30574/wjbphs.2024.18.1.0186

Lakhani, B. K., Attzs, M. S., Stead, R., & Tambe, K. (2021). The impact of the COVID-19 pandemic on ophthalmology services across the United Kingdom: A brief report on a cross-sectional survey of clinical leads. *Therapeutic Advances in Ophthalmology, 13*, 25158414211010549–25158414211010549. DOI: 10.1177/25158414211010549 PMID: 34027305

Lambert, T. E. (2023). Bankers as immoral? Some parallels and differences between Aquinas's views on usury and Marxian views of banking and credit. Faculty Scholarship, 884.

Lambin, R., & Surender, R. (2023). The rise of big philanthropy in global social policy: Implications for policy transfer and analysis. *Journal of Social Policy, 52*(3), 602–619. DOI: 10.1017/S0047279421000775

Larsen-Cooper, E., Bancroft, E., Rajagopal, S., O'Toole, M., & Levin, A. (2016). Scale matters: A cost-outcome analysis of an mHealth intervention in Malawi. *Telemedicine Journal and e-Health : The Official Journal of the American Telemedicine Association, 22*(4), 317–324. DOI: 10.1089/tmj.2015.0060 PMID: 26348994

Latifi, F. (2025). Innovative systematic literature review in telemedicine and e-health: A framework for guiding future research and practice. *International Journal of Digital Health and Telemedicine, 1*(1). Advance online publication. DOI: 10.51137/wrp.ijdht.2025.flit.45719

Latif, L. (2024). Global health governance's colour line: How finance has shaped global health disparities in African countries. *Strathmore Law Journal, 8*(2), 1–22. DOI: 10.52907/slj.v8i2.545

Lee, J., & Kim, J. (2021). Blockchain for health financing: Opportunities and challenges. *Journal of Medical Internet Research, 23*(5), e23517.

Lehtisalo, J., Palmer, K., Mangialasche, F., Solomon, A., Kivipelto, M., & Ngandu, T. (2021). Changes in lifestyle, behaviors, and risk factors for cognitive impairment in older persons during the first wave of the coronavirus disease 2019 pandemic in Finland: Results from the FINGER study. *Frontiers in Psychiatry, 12*, 624125. DOI: 10.3389/fpsyt.2021.624125 PMID: 33643095

Lewin, K. (1947). Frontiers in group dynamics: Concept, method and reality in social science; equilibrium and social change. *Human Relations; Studies Towards the Integration of the Social Sciences, 1*(1), 5–41. DOI: 10.1177/001872674700100103

Li, J. P. O., Liu, H., Ting, D. S. J., Jeon, S., Chan, R. V. P., Kim, J. E., Sim, D. A., Thomas, P. B. M., Lin, H., Chen, Y., Sakomoto, T., Loewenstein, A., Lam, D. S. C., Pasquale, L. R., Wong, T. Y., Lam, L. A., & Ting, D. S. W. (2021). Digital technology, tele-medicine and artificial intelligence in ophthalmology: A global perspective. *Progress in Retinal and Eye Research*, *82*, 100900–100900. DOI: 10.1016/j.preteyeres.2020.100900 PMID: 32898686

Lillicrap, L., Hunter, C., & Goldswain, P. (2021). Improving geriatric care and reducing hospitalisations in regional and remote areas: The benefits of telehealth. *Journal of Telemedicine and Telecare*, *27*(7), 397–408. DOI: 10.1177/1357633X19881588 PMID: 31645171

Liu, C., Chen, H., Zhou, F., Long, Q., Wu, K., Lo, L.-M., Hung, T.-H., Liu, C.-Y., & Chiou, W.-K. (2022). Positive intervention effect of mobile health application based on mindfulness and social support theory on postpartum depression symptoms of puerperae. *BMC Women's Health*, *22*(1), 413. Advance online publication. DOI: 10.1186/s12905-022-01996-4 PMID: 36217135

Liu, Y., & Wang, X. (2021). Application of Smart Mobile Medical Services in Maternal Health Care Management. *Contrast Media & Molecular Imaging*, *2021*, 1–6. DOI: 10.1155/2021/6249736 PMID: 34949971

Li, Z., Wang, L., Wu, X., Jiang, J., Qiang, W., Xie, H., Zhou, H., Wu, S., Shao, Y., & Chen, W. (2023). Artificial intelligence in ophthalmology: The path to the real-world clinic. *Cell Reports Medicine*, *4*(7), 101095–101095. DOI: 10.1016/j.xcrm.2023.101095 PMID: 37385253

Llave, C. L., Uy, M. E. V., Lam, H. Y., Aldaba, J. G., Yacapin, C. C., Miranda, M. B., Valverde, H. A., Silva, W. T., Nawaz, S., Slavkovsky, R. C., Mooney, J., & Vodicka, E. L. (2022). The cost-effectiveness of human papillomavirus vaccination in the Philippines. *Vaccine*, *40*(27), 3802–3811. DOI: 10.1016/j.vaccine.2022.05.025 PMID: 35606237

Long, H., Li, S., & Chen, Y. (2023). Digital health in chronic obstructive pulmonary disease. *Chronic Diseases and Translational Medicine*, *9*(2), 1–12. DOI: 10.1002/cdt3.68 PMID: 37305103

Lopes, H., Baptista-Leite, R., Hermenegildo, C., & Atun, R. (2024). Digital Gamification Tool (Let's Control Flu) to Increase Vaccination Coverage Rates: Proposal for Algorithm Development. *JMIR Research Protocols*, *13*, e55613. DOI: 10.2196/55613 PMID: 39255031

Love, R. P., Hardy, B.-J., Heffernan, C., Heyd, A., Cardinal-Grant, M., Sparling, L., Healy, B., Smylie, J., & Long, R. (2022). Developing data governance agreements with Indigenous communities in Canada: Toward equitable tuberculosis programming, research, and reconciliation. *Health and Human Rights*, *24*(1), 21. PMID: 35747272

Luna, D., Almerares, A., Mayan, J. C.III, González Bernaldo de Quirós, F., & Otero, C. (2014). Health Informatics in Developing Countries: Going beyond Pilot Practices to Sustainable Implementations: A Review of the Current Challenges. *Healthcare Informatics Research*, *20*(1), 3. DOI: 10.4258/hir.2014.20.1.3 PMID: 24627813

Luvsan, M.-E., Vodicka, E., Jugder, U., Tudev, U., Clark, A., Groman, D., Otgonbayar, D., Demberelsuren, S., LaMongtagne, D. S., & Pecenka, C. (2022). The potential cost-effectiveness of HPV vaccination among girls in Mongolia. *Vaccine: X*, *11*, 100161. DOI: 10.1016/j.jvacx.2022.100161 PMID: 35509519

Macnaughton, G. (2016). Advancing global health and human rights in the neoliberal era. *Health and Human Rights*, *18*(2), 255.

Mahmood, H., Mckinstry, B., Luz, S., Fairhurst, K., Nasim, S., & Hazir, T. (2020). Community health worker-based mobile health (mHealth) approaches for improving management and caregiver knowledge of common childhood infections: A systematic review. *Journal of Global Health*, *10*(2), 020438. Advance online publication. DOI: 10.7189/jogh.10.020438 PMID: 33437462

Mahoney, R. T., & Maynard, J. E. (1999). The introduction of new vaccines into developing countries. *Vaccine*, *17*(7), 646–652. DOI: 10.1016/S0264-410X(98)00246-1 PMID: 10067669

Malik, N., Arya, N., & Gupta, S. (2024). The metaverse in healthcare: The emerging future of the next generation. In *The Metaverse for the Healthcare Industry* (pp. 33–58). Springer., DOI: 10.1007/978-3-031-60073-9_3

Malvolti, S., Soble, A., Bloem, P., LaMontagne, D. S., Aggarwal, R., Pitisuttithum, P., Rees, H., & Cernuschi, T. (2023). The Global Demand and Supply Balance of the Human Papillomavirus Vaccine: Implications for the Global Strategy for the Elimination of Cervical Cancer. *Vaccines*, *12*(1), 4. DOI: 10.3390/vaccines12010004 PMID: 38276663

Mark Gurman. (2023). *Apple plans AI-powered health coaching service, mood tracker, and iPad health app*. Available at: https://techxplore.com/news/2023-04-apple-ai-powered-health-mood-tracker.html (Accessed: July 30th 2024).

Marko, J. G. O., Neagu, C. D., & Anand, P. B. (2025). Examining inclusivity: The use of AI and diverse populations in health and social care. *BMC Medical Informatics and Decision Making*, *25*(1), 57. Advance online publication. DOI: 10.1186/s12911-025-02884-1 PMID: 39910518

Marmot, M., Allen, J., Bell, R., Bloomer, E., & Goldblatt, P. (2012). WHO European review of social determinants of health and the health divide. *Lancet*, *380*(9846), 1011–1029. DOI: 10.1016/S0140-6736(12)61228-8 PMID: 22964159

Marshall, G. (2025, February 26). Case study: Vsee breaks down telehealth language barriers with Languageline integration. LanguageLine Solutions. https://www.languageline.com/blog/case-study-vsee-breaks-down-telehealth-languag e-barriers-with-languageline-integration

Matthew Dennis. (2019, November 28). *China adds 70 new medicines to National Reimbursement Drug List, with average price cuts of 61%*. First Word Pharma.

Maulana, N., Soewondo, P., Adani, N., Limasalle, P., & Pattnaik, A. (2022). How Jaminan Kesehatan Nasional (JKN) coverage influences out-of-pocket (OOP) payments by vulnerable populations in Indonesia. *PLOS Global Public Health*, *2*(7), e0000203. DOI: 10.1371/journal.pgph.0000203 PMID: 36962301

Mazzuca, D., Borselli, M., Gratteri, S., Zampogna, G., Feola, A., Della Corte, M., Guarna, F., Scorcia, V., & Giannaccare, G. (2022). Applications and Current Medico-Legal Challenges of Telemedicine in Ophthalmology. *International Journal of Environmental Research and Public Health*, *19*(9), 5614. DOI: 10.3390/ijerph19095614 PMID: 35565003

Mbunge, E., & Sibiya, M. N. (2024). Mobile Health Interventions for Improving Maternal and Child Health Outcomes in South Africa: A Systematic Review. *Global Health Journal (Amsterdam, Netherlands)*, *8*(3), 103–112. Advance online publication. DOI: 10.1016/j.glohj.2024.08.002

Mbuthia, F., Reid, M., & Fichardt, A. (2019). mHealth communication to strengthen postnatal care in rural areas: A systematic review. *BMC Pregnancy and Childbirth*, *19*(1), 406. Advance online publication. DOI: 10.1186/s12884-019-2531-0 PMID: 31694578

McCoy, D., Kapilashrami, A., Kumar, R., Rhule, E., & Khosla, R. (2024). Developing an agenda for the decolonization of global health. *Bulletin of the World Health Organization*, *102*(2), 130–136. DOI: 10.2471/BLT.23.289949 PMID: 38313156

McKinney, S. M., Sieniek, M., Godbole, V., Godwin, J., Antropova, N., Ashrafian, H., & Suleyman, M. (2020). International evaluation of an AI system for breast cancer screening. *Nature*, *577*(7788), 89–94. DOI: 10.1038/s41586-019-1799-6 PMID: 31894144

McKinsey & Company. (2021, October). *The dawn of China's biopharma innovation.* McKinsey Global Institute. https://www.mckinsey.com/industries/life-sciences/our-insights/the-dawn-of-chinas-biopharma-innovation

McKinsey & Company. (2024). *2024 BioCentury China Healthcare Summit: McKinsey biopharma report*. https://www.scribd.com/document/854593184/2024-BioCentury-China-Healthcare-Summit-McKinsey-Biopharma-report

McMillan, K. D. (2024, November 14). How patients are hacking healthcare with open source technology. Digital Health Insights. https://dhinsights.org/news/how-patients-are-hacking-healthcare-with-open-source-technology

MedAccess. (2024). *MedAccess Impact case studies 2024* (October 2024, pp. 1-9). https://medaccess.org/wp-content/uploads/2024/11/MedAccess-Impact-Case-Studies-2024.pdf

Mededge. (2024). Healing at home: Why virtual wards are the future of healthcare. https://mededgemea.com/healing-at-home-why-virtual-wards-are-the-future-of-healthcare/

Mediavilla, J., & Garcia-Arias, J. (2019). Philanthrocapitalism as a neoliberal (development agenda) artefact: Philanthropic discourse and hegemony in (financing for) international development. *Globalizations*, *16*(6), 857–875. DOI: 10.1080/14747731.2018.1560187

Meessen, B., Akhnif, E., Kiendrebeogo, J. A., & Zeng, W. (2019). Health financing reforms in Africa. *Health Systems and Reform*, *5*(3), 176–188.

Mendelson, D., & Mendelson, D. (2017). Legal protections for personal health information in the age of big data – A proposal for regulatory framework. Ethics, Public [Article number or page range] [if available]. *Health & Medicine*, •••, 4.

Mendoza, B. (2020). Decolonial theories in comparison. *Journal of World Philosophies*, *5*(1), 43–60.

Mercuri, M., Hackett, K., Barnabas, R. V., & Emerson, C. I. (2024). Evaluation of a single-dose HPV vaccine strategy for promoting vaccine, health, and gender equity. *The Lancet. Infectious Diseases*, *24*(10), e654–e658. DOI: 10.1016/S1473-3099(24)00227-5 PMID: 38734009

Michigan Institute for Healthcare Policy and Innovation. (2018). OSA in older adults: Often present, seldom investigated. https://ihpi.umich.edu/news/osa-older-adults-often-present-seldom-investigated

Michigan Medicine. (2025). Clinical trial opens to study groundbreaking 3D printed device for babies with rare respiratory disease. https://www.michiganmedicine.org/news-release/clinical-trial-opens-study-groundbreaking-3d-printed-device-babies-rare-respiratory-disease

Micolo, G. (2025, April 24). *Angolans spread the word: Cervical cancer is vaccine-preventable*. Gavi. https://www.gavi.org/vaccineswork/angolans-spread-word-cervical-cancer-vaccine-preventable

Mihaila, S. (2023, February). *Mamahood launches femtech app to support women in the Middle East and North Africa*. FemTech World. https://www.femtechworld.co.uk/news/mamahood-launches-femtech-app-to-support-women-in-the-middle-east-and-north-africa/

Mildon, A., & Sellen, D. (2019). Use of mobile phones for behavior change communication to improve maternal, newborn and child health: A scoping review. *Journal of Global Health, 9*(2), 020425. Advance online publication. DOI: 10.7189/jogh.09.020425 PMID: 31893032

Miller, L. E., Buzi, A., Williams, A., Rogers, R. S., Ortiz, A. G., Jones-Ho, K. O., & Elden, L. M. (2020). Reliability and accuracy of remote fiberoptic nasopharyngolaryngoscopy in the pediatric population. *Ear, Nose, & Throat Journal, 100*(8), 604–609. DOI: 10.1177/0145561320919109 PMID: 32283977

Ministry of Education. (2021). The Council of Ministers approves the establishment of the "Research, Development and Innovation Development Authority". Ministry of Education, 4 June. https://www.moe.gov.sa/ar/mediacenter/MOEnews/Pages/REC1442-892.aspx (Accessed: 14 June 2024).

Ministry of Health and Family Welfare, Government of India. (2018). *Comprehensive primary health care through health and wellness centers*. https://mohfw.gov.in/documents/policy-documents (Accessed June 30, 2024)

Ministry of Health. (2023). *Protocol for the Prevention of Cognitive Impairment*, 24. https://www.moh.gov.sa/en/Ministry/MediaCenter/Publications/Documents/Ministry_of_Health_Protocol_for_the_Prevention_of_Cognitive_Impairment.pdf

Mitchell, R. J., & Bates, P. (2011). Measuring health-related productivity loss. *Population Health Management, 14*(2), 93–98. DOI: 10.1089/pop.2010.0014 PMID: 21091370

Mittelstadt, B. D. (2019). Principles alone cannot guarantee ethical AI. *Nature Machine Intelligence*, *1*(11), 501–507. DOI: 10.1038/s42256-019-0114-4

Mohamad, R. M., Alsaeed, M. S. A., Merdad, A. H., Alghaith, D. M., Binnshwan, F. M., Albusaad, R. A., Almuslem, M. Y., Alamri, R. A., Awaji, H. H. H., Alqahtani, M. N., & Alamrani, A. A. (2023). Evaluating the general population of Saudi Arabia for their knowledge, attitudes, and practices towards dementia. *Cureus*, *15*(12), e49865–e49865. DOI: 10.7759/cureus.49865 PMID: 38170079

Mohammed-Rajput, N. A., Smith, D. C., Mamlin, B., Biondich, P., & Doebbeling, B. N. (2011). OpenMRS, a global medical records system collaborative: Factors influencing successful implementation. *AMIA ... Annual Symposium Proceedings - AMIA Symposium. AMIA Symposium*, *2011*, 960. PMID: 22195155

Mohammed, Y., & Malhotra, A. (2025). AI-enabled diagnostics and equity in healthcare access. *Digital Health*, *5*, 100086. https://www.sciencedirect.com/science/article/pii/S2772485925000286

Montagni, I., Mabchour, I., & Tzourio, C. (2019). Digital Gamification to Enhance Vaccine Knowledge and Uptake: Scoping Review (Preprint). *JMIR Serious Games*, *8*(2), e16983. Advance online publication. DOI: 10.2196/16983 PMID: 32348271

Mori, N., & Mlambiti, R. (2020). Determinants of customers' adoption of mobile banking in Tanzania: Further evidence from a diffusion of innovation theory. Journal of Entrepreneurship. *Management and Innovation*, *16*(2), 203–230. DOI: 10.7341/20201627

Moulaei, K., Akhlaghpour, S., & Fatehi, F. (2025). Patient consent for the secondary use of health data in artificial intelligence (AI) models: A scoping review. *International Journal of Medical Informatics*, *198*, 105872. DOI: 10.1016/j.ijmedinf.2025.105872 PMID: 40107041

Mphahlele, M., & Mash, R. (2019). Barriers and facilitators of mobile health in Africa. *PLoS One*, *14*(4), e0214870. Advance online publication. DOI: 10.1371/journal.pone.0214870 PMID: 30943250

Mugambi, M. M., & Matula, P. D. (2025). "Application of Kotter's 8-step change management model and administrative strategies for effective curriculum change in universities". A systematic literature review. *International Journal of Research and Innovation in Social Science*, *9*(01), 3490–3501. DOI: 10.47772/IJRISS.2025.9010277

Mullard, A. (2016). Parsing clinical success rates. *Nature Reviews. Drug Discovery*, *15*(7), 447–447. DOI: 10.1038/nrd.2016.136 PMID: 27357012

Mulumba, M., Ruano, A. L., Perehudoff, K., & Ooms, G. (2021). *Decolonizing health governance: A Uganda case study on the influence of political history on community participation*. Health and Human Rights Journal.

Mumtaz, Z., Salway, S., Bhatti, A., Shanner, L., Zaman, S., Laing, L., & Ellison, G. T. H. (2014). Improving Maternal Health in Pakistan: Toward a Deeper Understanding of the Social Determinants of Poor Women's Access to Maternal Health Services. *American Journal of Public Health, 104*(S1), S17–S24. DOI: 10.2105/AJPH.2013.301377 PMID: 24354817

Mundial, B. (2014).. . *World Development Indicators*, •••, 2014.

Muraskin, W. (2005). *Crusade to Immunize the World's Children* (1st ed.). USC Marshall Global BioBusiness Initiative.

Murewanhema, G., Moyo, E., Dzobo, M., Mandishora-Dube, R. S., & Dzinamarira, T. (2024). Human papilloma virus vaccination in the resource-limited settings of sub-Saharan Africa: Challenges and recommendations. *Vaccine: X, 20*, 100549. DOI: 10.1016/j.jvacx.2024.100549 PMID: 39263366

Murphy, A., Palafox, B., Walli-Attaei, M., Powell-Jackson, T., Rangarajan, S., Alhabib, K. F., Avezum, A. J., Calik, K. B. T., Chifamba, J., Choudhury, T., Dagenais, G., Dans, A. L., Gupta, R., Iqbal, R., Kaur, M., Kelishadi, R., Khatib, R., Kruger, I. M., Kutty, V. R., & McKee, M. (2020). The household economic burden of noncommunicable diseases in 18 countries. *BMJ Global Health, 5*(2), e002040. DOI: 10.1136/bmjgh-2019-002040 PMID: 32133191

Murphy, R. L. (1972). Accuracy of dermatologic diagnosis by television. *Archives of Dermatology, 105*(6), 833. DOI: 10.1001/archderm.1972.01620090005001 PMID: 5030231

Murray, C. J., Ikuta, K. S., Sharara, F., Swetschinski, L., Aguilar, G. R., Gray, A., Han, C., Bisignano, C., Rao, P., Wool, E., Johnson, S. C., Browne, A. J., Chipeta, M. G., Fell, F., Hackett, S., Haines-Woodhouse, G., Hamadani, B. H. K., Kumaran, E. A. P., McManigal, B., & Hay, S. I. (2022). Global burden of bacterial antimicrobial resistance in 2019: A systematic analysis. *Lancet, 399*(10325), 629–655. DOI: 10.1016/S0140-6736(21)02724-0 PMID: 35065702

Muyombo, T. (2024, May). Advanced air mobility: ICAO's approach and global collaboration [Conference presentation]. ICAO AAM 2024 Symposium. https://www.icao.int/Meetings/AAM2024/Presentations/DAY1/1.1.B%20-%20Thomas%20Muyombo.pdf

Mwenda, V., Jalang'o, R., Miano, C., Bor, J.-P., Nyangasi, M., Mecca, L., Were, V., Kariithi, E., Pecenka, C., Schuind, A., Abbas, K., & Clark, A. (2023). Impact, cost-effectiveness, and budget implications of HPV vaccination in Kenya: A modelling study. *Vaccine, 41*(29), 4228–4238. DOI: 10.1016/j.vaccine.2023.05.019 PMID: 37296015

Najati, I. (2025). Exploring the failure factors of blockchain adopting projects: A case study of TradeLens through the lens of commons theory. *Frontiers in Blockchain, 8*, 1503595. Advance online publication. DOI: 10.3389/fbloc.2025.1503595

Nanda, M., & Sharma, R. (2023a). A comprehensive examination of the economic impact of out-of-pocket health expenditures in India. *Health Policy and Planning, 38*(8), 926–938. DOI: 10.1093/heapol/czad050 PMID: 37409740

Nanda, M., & Sharma, R. (2023b). Assessing the impact of anaesthetic and surgical task-shifting globally: A systematic literature review. *Health Policy and Planning, 38*(8), 960–994. DOI: 10.1093/heapol/czad059 PMID: 37506040

Nasdaq. (2016, February 3). *Chinese cancer biotech BeiGene prices IPO at $24, high end of range.* https://www.nasdaq.com/articles/chinese-cancer-biotech-beigene-prices-ipo-24-high-end-range-2016-02-03

National Academies of Sciences, Engineering, and Medicine, Health and Medicine Division, Board on Global Health, & Forum on Microbial Threats. (2018). Urbanization and slums: Infectious diseases in the built environment: Proceedings of a workshop. National Academies Press. https://www.ncbi.nlm.nih.gov/books/NBK507339/

National Health Authority, Government of India. (2025). *About PM-JAY.* https://nha.gov.in/PM-JAY (Accessed August 24, 2025)

National Health Commission of the PRC. (2020, June 28). *News.* https://en.nhc.gov.cn/2020-06/28/c_80923.htm

National Medical Products Administration. (2018). *Announcement on adjusting the review and approval procedures for drug clinical trials* (No. 50 of 2018). Center for Drug Evaluation.

National Medical Products Administration. (2020). *Procedures for the review and approval of priority review and approval of drug marketing authorizations (Interim).* Center for Drug Evaluation.

National Medical Products Administration. (2024). *2023 drug review annual report.* Center for Drug Evaluation.

National People's Congress. (2020). *Patent law of the People's Republic of China (Fourth Amendment)*. Adopted October 17, 2020; Effective June 1, 2021. https://www.wipo.int/wipolex/en/legislation/details/21027

National Research Council (US) Committee on Future Directions for Behavioral and Social Sciences Research at the National Institutes of Health. Singer, B. H., & Ryff, C. D. (Eds.). (2001). New horizons in health: An integrative approach. National Academies Press. https://www.ncbi.nlm.nih.gov/books/NBK43780/

National Sample Survey Office. (2016). *Employment-unemployment survey*. http://mospi.nic.in (Accessed June 28, 2024)

National Statistical Office. (2020). *Periodic labour force survey*. http://mospi.nic.in (Accessed June 28, 2024)

NCMH. (2020). 3MDR study – A new treatment for PTSD: Final report. National Centre for Mental Health. https://www.ncmh.info/2020/05/22/3mdr-study-a-new-treatment-for-ptsd-final-report/

Ndembi, N., Rammer, B., Fokam, J., Dinodia, U., Tessema, S. K., Nsengimana, J. P., Mwangi, S., Adzogenu, E., Dongmo, L. T., Rees, B., O'Connor, B., Crowell, T. A., Wilmot, J., Colizzi, V., Ngongo, N., & Kaseya, J. (2025). Integrating artificial intelligence into African health systems and emergency response: Need for an ethical framework and guidelines. *Journal of Public Health in Africa, 16*(1). Advance online publication. DOI: 10.4102/jphia.v16i1.876 PMID: 40182750

Ndiaye, C. (2024, November 10). *Dose Of Hope: How Updated Vaccine Policy Can Protect More Women Against Cervical Cancer—Health Policy Watch. Health Policy Watch*. https://healthpolicy-watch.news/dose-of-hope-how-updated-vaccine-policy-can-protect-more-women-against-cervical-cancer

Ndlovu, K., Scott, R. E., & Mars, M. (2021). Interoperability opportunities and challenges in linking mhealth applications and eRecord systems: Botswana as an exemplar. *BMC Medical Informatics and Decision Making, 21*(1), 246. Advance online publication. DOI: 10.1186/s12911-021-01606-7 PMID: 34419020

Nelson, J., Joshua, B., & Matthew, F. (2025). Personalized medicine: Tailoring treatment plans using AI insights. ResearchGate. https://www.researchgate.net/publication/391950621_Personalized_Medicine_Tailoring_Treatment_Plans_Using_AI_Insights

Ng, B. P., Park, C., Silverman, C. L., Eckhoff, D. O., Guest, J. C., & Díaz, D. A. (2022). Accessibility and utilisation of telehealth services among older adults during COVID-19 pandemic in the United States. *Health & Social Care in the Community, 30*(5). Advance online publication. DOI: 10.1111/hsc.13709 PMID: 34994028

NHS Confederation. (2023, May 23). Realising the potential of virtual wards.

NHS Digital. (2021). *NHS statistics*. Available at: https://digital.nhs.uk/ (Accessed: July 29th 2024).

Nkwo, M., Orji, R., & Ajah, I. (2021). A Health Belief Model Approach to Evaluating Maternal Health Behaviors among Africans - Design Implications for Personalized Persuasive Technologies. *Adjunct Proceedings of the 29th ACM Conference on User Modeling, Adaptation and Personalization*. DOI: 10.1145/3450614.3464624

NMPA & CNIPA. (2021). *Measures for the implementation of the mechanism for early settlement of drug patent disputes (Trial Implementation)* [Announcement No. 89 of 2021]. https://english.nmpa.gov.cn/2021-07/04/c_661004.htm

Noor Eddin, A., Hamsho, K., Adi, G., Al-Rimawi, M., Alfuwais, M., Abdul Rab, S., Alkattan, K., & Yaqinuddin, A. (2023). Cerebrospinal fluid microRNAs as potential biomarkers in Alzheimer's disease. *Frontiers in Aging Neuroscience, 15*, 1210191–1210191. DOI: 10.3389/fnagi.2023.1210191 PMID: 37476007

Nordic Council of Ministers. (2021). *Healthcare innovation in Northern Europe*. Available at: https://www.norden.org/en (Accessed: July 30th 2024).

Norori, N., Hu, Q., Aellen, F. M., Faraci, F. D., & Tzovara, A. (2021). Addressing bias in big data and AI for health care: A call for open science. *Patterns (New York, N.Y.), 2*(10), 100347. Advance online publication. DOI: 10.1016/j.patter.2021.100347 PMID: 34693373

Norris, P. (2001). *Digital divide: Civic engagement, information poverty, and the Internet worldwide*. Cambridge University Press., DOI: 10.1017/CBO9781139164887

Not Impossible Labs. (2013). Project Daniel. https://www.notimpossible.com/projects/project-daniel

Nuijten, M. (2021). Pricing Zolgensma – the world's most expensive drug. *Journal of Market Access & Health Policy, 10*(1), 2022353. Advance online publication. DOI: 10.1080/20016689.2021.2022353 PMID: 34992762

O'Brien, G. L., Sinnott, S. J., Walshe, V., Mulcahy, M., & Byrne, S. (2020). Health policy triangle framework: Narrative review of the recent literature. *Health Policy OPEN, 1*, 100016. DOI: 10.1016/j.hpopen.2020.100016 PMID: 37383316

O'Hare, B. A.-M. (2019). International corporate tax avoidance and domestic government health expenditure. *Bulletin of the World Health Organization*, *97*(11), 746–753. DOI: 10.2471/BLT.18.220897 PMID: 31673190

O'Shea, A. M., Gibson, M., Merchant, J., Rewerts, K., Miell, K., Kaboli, P. J., & Shimada, S. L. (2023). Understanding rural–urban differences in veterans' internet access, use and patient preferences for telemedicine. *The Journal of Rural Health : Official Journal of the American Rural Health Association and the National Rural Health Care Association*, *40*(3), 438–445. DOI: 10.1111/jrh.12805 PMID: 37935649

Obermeyer, Z., Powers, B., Vogeli, C., & Mullainathan, S. (2019). Dissecting racial bias in an algorithm used to manage the health of populations. *Science*, *366*(6464), 447–453. DOI: 10.1126/science.aax2342 PMID: 31649194

Obrist, B., Dillip, A., Kalolo, A., Mayumana, I. M., Rutishauser, M., & Simon, V. T. (2022). Savings groups for social health protection: A social resilience study in rural Tanzania. *Diseases (Basel, Switzerland)*, *10*(3), 63. Advance online publication. DOI: 10.3390/diseases10030063 PMID: 36135219

OECD. (2018). *Private philanthropy for development*. OECD Publishing.

OECD. (2021). *Health at a Glance: Europe 2021*: Organisation for Economic Co-operation and Development Available at: https://www.oecd.org/en/topics/health.html (Accessed: July 30th 2024).

Office for Civil Rights. (2023, October 17). Telehealth privacy and security tips for patients. https://www.hhs.gov/hipaa/for-professionals/privacy/guidance/telehealth-privacy-security/index.html

Office for National Statistics. (2024). *Deflators and how we use them in economic estimates*. https://www.ons.gov.uk/economy/inflationandpriceindices/methodologies/deflatorsandhowweusethemineconomicestimates#:~:text=The%20deflator%20and%20its%20source,use%20an%20import%20price%20index (Accessed June 28, 2024)

Office for National Statistics. (2025). National life tables – Life expectancy in the UK: 2021 to 2023. https://www.ons.gov.uk/peoplepopulationandcommunity/birthsdeathsandmarriages/lifeexpectancies/bulletins/nationallifetablesunitedkingdom/2021to2023additionaldata

Office for National Statistics. (n.d.). Life expectancy for local areas of Great Britain: Between 2001 to 2003 and 2021 to 2023. https://www.ons.gov.uk/peoplepopulationandcommunity/healthandsocialcare/healthandlifeexpectancies/bulletins/lifeexpectancyforlocalareasoftheuk/between2001to2003and2021to2023/previous/

Oh, D., To, D., Corso, M., Murnaghan, K., Yu, H., & Cancelliere, C. (2024). Agreement and concurrent validity between telehealth and in-person diagnosis of musculoskeletal conditions: A systematic review. *Chiropractic & Manual Therapies*, *32*(1), 21. Advance online publication. DOI: 10.1186/s12998-024-00542-3 PMID: 38872176

Okonofua, F. E., Ntoimo, L., Johnson, E., Sombié, I., Ojuolape, S., Igboin, B., Imongan, W., Ekwo, C., Udenigwe, O., Yaya, S., Wallis, A. B., & Adeniran, J. (2023). Texting for life: A mobile phone application to connect pregnant women with emergency transport and obstetric care in rural Nigeria. *BMC Pregnancy and Childbirth*, *23*(1), 139. Advance online publication. DOI: 10.1186/s12884-023-05424-9 PMID: 36882709

Olaniran, A., Briggs, J., Pradhan, A., Bogue, E., Schreiber, B., Dini, H. S., Hurkchand, H., & Ballard, M. (2022). Stock-outs of essential medicines among community health workers in low- and middle-income countries: A systematic literature review. *Human Resources for Health*, *20*, 58. DOI: 10.1186/s12960-022-00755-8 PMID: 35840965

Olivari, B. S., French, M. E., & McGuire, L. C. (2020). The Public Health Road Map to respond to the growing dementia crisis. *Innovation in Aging*, *4*(1), igz043. Advance online publication. DOI: 10.1093/geroni/igz043 PMID: 32405541

Ollio, J., Gyan, A., & Gyan, E. (2022). Using telehealth to provide behavioral healthcare to young adults and college students. Perspectives in Health Information Management. https://pmc.ncbi.nlm.nih.gov/articles/PMC9013217/

Ononge, S., Magunda, A., Balaba, D., Waiswa, P., Okello, D., Kaula, H., Zalwango, S., Bua, D. A., Ayebare, A., Kaharuza, F., Bennett, C., Sulzbach, S., Keller, B., & Mugerwa, Y. (2023). Strengthening Kampala's Urban Referral System for Maternal and Newborn Care Through Establishment of an Emergency Call and Dispatch Center. *Global Health, Science and Practice*, *11*(3), e2200332. Advance online publication. DOI: 10.9745/GHSP-D-22-00332 PMID: 37348939

Onwujekwe, O., Hanson, K., & Uzochukwu, B. (2019). Examining inequalities in incidence of catastrophic health expenditures on different healthcare services and health facilities in Nigeria. *PLoS One*, *7*(7), e40811. DOI: 10.1371/journal.pone.0040811 PMID: 22815828

Ortega, B., Sanjuán, J., & Casquero, A. (2020). Illicit financial flows and the provision of child and maternal health services in low- and middle-income countries. *BMC International Health and Human Rights*, *20*(1), 15. Advance online publication. DOI: 10.1186/s12914-020-00236-w PMID: 32653039

Oxfam. (2009). Blind optimism: Challenging the myths about private health care in poor countries (Oxfam Briefing Paper).

Oyebode, O., Fowles, J., Steeves, D., & Orji, R. (2022). Machine learning techniques in adaptive and personalized systems for health and wellness. *International Journal of Human-Computer Interaction, 38*(9), 1–25. DOI: 10.1080/10447318.2022.2031352

Oyler, J. V. (2025, October 29). *From vision to global transformation – The journey of 15 years of BeOne Medicines*. OncoDaily. https://oncodaily.com/voices/beone-medicines-400325

Pae, C. U. (2015). Why systematic review rather than narrative review? *Psychiatry Investigation, 12*(3), 417–419. DOI: 10.4306/pi.2015.12.3.417 PMID: 26207140

Park, J., Shin, H., Choi, H. J., Heo, J., & Kim, W.-H. (2021). A rapid review of the use of appropriate technology in global health. *Academic Society for Appropriate Technology, 8*(4), 1–12. DOI: 10.37675/jat.2021.7.2.235

Patel, G., Brosnan, C., & Taylor, A. (2023). Understanding the role of context in health policy implementation: A qualitative study of factors influencing traditional medicine integration in the Indian public healthcare system. *Health Sociology Review : The Journal of the Health Section of the Australian Sociological Association, 32*(3), 294–310. DOI: 10.1080/14461242.2023.2210550 PMID: 37222411

PATH. (2011). *Implementing HPV Vaccination Programs, practical experience from PATH* (pp. 1–36). PATH. https://media.path.org/documents/RH_ccp_hpv_vaccination.pdf

PATH. (2012). *Evaluating HPV vaccination pilots, practical experience from PATH* (pp. 1–46). https://media.path.org/documents/RH_ccp_hpv_pilots.pdf

Paul, M., Maglaras, L., Ferrag, M. A., & Almomani, I. (2023). Digitization of healthcare sector: A study on privacy and security concerns. *ICT Express, 9*(4), 571–588. https://www.sciencedirect.com/science/article/pii/S2405959523000243. DOI: 10.1016/j.icte.2023.02.007

Pedersen, M., & Dunne, S. (2020). Dewey's broad account of habit and its relevance for change management: A conceptual clarification with pragmatic illustrations. *Journal of Change Management, 20*(3), 247–263. DOI: 10.1080/14697017.2020.1755342

Perehudoff, K., 't Hoen, E., & Boulet, P. (2021). Overriding drug and medical technology patents for pandemic recovery: A legitimate move for high-income countries, too. *BMJ Global Health, 6*(4), e005518. Advance online publication. DOI: 10.1136/bmjgh-2021-005518 PMID: 33827793

Peters, D. H., Garg, A., Bloom, G., Walker, D. G., Brieger, W. R., & Hafizur Rahman, M. (2008). Poverty and Access to Health Care in Developing Countries. *Annals of the New York Academy of Sciences, 1136*(1), 161–171. DOI: 10.1196/annals.1425.011 PMID: 17954679

Petretto, D. R., Carrogu, G. P., Gaviano, L., Berti, R., Pinna, M., Petretto, A. D., & Pili, R. (2024). Telemedicine, e-health, and digital health equity: A scoping review. *Clinical Practice and Epidemiology in Mental Health, 20*(1), e17450179279732. DOI: 10.2174/0117450179279732231211110248 PMID: 38660571

Pharma Board Room. (2026, January 27). *The sea turtles: China's top pharma talent comes home.* https://pharmaboardroom.com/articles/the-sea-turtles-chinas-top-pharma-talent-comes-home/

PharmaCube News. (2024). *China's pharmaceutical sector marks a 'breakthrough era': A decade-long commercialization review (2015-2024).* PharmaCube Global. https://global.pharmcube.com/

Pike, J., Melnick, A., Gastañaduy, P. A., Kay, M., Harbison, J., Leidner, A. J., Rice, S., Asato, K., Schwartz, L., & DeBolt, C. (2021). Societal Costs of a Measles Outbreak. *Pediatrics, 147*(4), e2020027037. DOI: 10.1542/peds.2020-027037 PMID: 33712549

Pillai, K., & Obasanjo, I. (2023). Assessing the implementation of India's new health reform program, Ayushman Bharat, in two Southern states: Kerala and Tamil Nadu. *World Medical & Health Policy, 15*(1), 6–20. DOI: 10.1002/wmh3.535

Pisani, E., Olivier Kok, M., & Nugroho, K. (2017). Indonesia's road to universal health coverage: A political journey. *Health Policy and Planning, 32*(2), 267–276. DOI: 10.1093/heapol/czw120 PMID: 28207049

Plotkin, S., Robinson, J. M., Cunningham, G., Iqbal, R., & Larsen, S. (2017). The complexity and cost of vaccine manufacturing – An overview. *Vaccine, 35*(33), 4064–4071. DOI: 10.1016/j.vaccine.2017.06.003 PMID: 28647170

Pollack, J., & Pollack, R. (2015). Using Kotter's eight stage process to manage an organizational change program: Presentation and practice. *Systemic Practice and Action Research, 28*(1), 51–66. DOI: 10.1007/s11213-014-9317-0

Porter, T. (2025, January 16). Digital transformation in healthcare (2025 guide). VisualSP. https://www.visualsp.com/blog/digital-transformation-in-healthcare/

Porter, M. E. (2010). What Is Value in Health Care? *The New England Journal of Medicine, 363*(26), 2477–2481. DOI: 10.1056/NEJMp1011024 PMID: 21142528

Porter, M. E., & Kaplan, R. S. (2016). How to Pay for Health Care. *Harvard Business Review, 94*(7-8), 88–134. PMID: 27526565

Porter, M. E., & Lee, T. H. (2013). The strategy that will fix health care. *Harvard Business Review, 91*(10), 50.

Prabhakaran, S., Dutta, A., Fagan, T., & Ginivan, M. (2019). *Financial sustainability of Indonesia's Jaminan Kesehatan Nasional: Performance, prospects and policy options*. Palladium, Health Policy Plus and Tim Nasional Percepatan Penanggulangan Kemiskinan (TNP2K).

Prasad, S. S. V., Singh, C., Naik, B. N., Pandey, S., & Rao, R. (2023). Awareness of the Ayushman Bharat–Pradhan Mantri Jan Arogya Yojana in the rural community: A cross-sectional study in Eastern India. *Cureus, 15*(3), e35901. DOI: 10.7759/cureus.35901 PMID: 37033537

Prata, N., Passano, P., Sreenivas, A., & Gerdts, C. E. (2010). Maternal Mortality in Developing Countries: Challenges in Scaling-Up Priority Interventions. *Women's Health (London, England), 6*(2), 311–327. DOI: 10.2217/WHE.10.8 PMID: 20187734

Prem, K., Choi, Y. H., Bénard, É., Burger, E. A., Hadley, L., Laprise, J.-F., Regan, M. C., Drolet, M., Sy, S., Abbas, K., Portnoy, A., Kim, J. J., Brisson, M., & Jit, M. (2023). Global impact and cost-effectiveness of one-dose versus two-dose human papillomavirus vaccination schedules: A comparative modelling analysis. *BMC Medicine, 21*(1), 313. DOI: 10.1186/s12916-023-02988-3 PMID: 37635227

Prince, M., Wimo, A., Guerchet, M., Ali, G. C., Wu, Y. T., & Prina, M. (2015). *World Alzheimer report 2015. The global impact of dementia: an analysis of prevalence, incidence, cost and trends*. https://www.alzint.org/resource/world-alzheimer-report-2015/ (Accessed 24 October 2023).

Prinja, S., Nimesh, R., Gupta, A., Bahuguna, P., Thakur, J. S., Gupta, M., & Singh, T. (2016). Impact assessment and cost-effectiveness of m-health application used by community health workers for maternal, newborn and child health care services in rural Uttar Pradesh, India: A study protocol. *Global Health Action, 9*(1), 31473. DOI: 10.3402/gha.v9.31473 PMID: 27189200

PRNewswire. (2020, August 17). *Innovent and Lilly announce expansion of TYVYT® (sintilimab injection) licensing agreement*. https://www.prnewswire.com/news-releases/innovent-and-lilly-announce-expansion-of-tyvyt-sintilimab-injection-licensing-agreement-301113764.html

Program, H. S. T. (2021). *Health Sector Transformation Program Delivery Plan.* https://www.vision2030.gov.sa/media/0wop2tds/hstp_eng.pdf (2021, accessed May 31, 2024).

Pronker, E. S., Weenen, T. C., Commandeur, H., Claassen, E. H. J. H. M., & Osterhaus, A. D. M. E. (2013). Risk in Vaccine Research and Development Quantified. *PLoS One*, *8*(3), e57755. DOI: 10.1371/journal.pone.0057755 PMID: 23526951

Public Relations of BKPK. (2025). *National health accounts 2020.* International Labour Organization.

Qassem, T., Itani, L., Nasr, W., Al-Ayyat, D., Javaid, S. F., & Al-Sinawi, H. (2023). Prevalence and economic burden of dementia in the Arab world. *BJPsych Open*, *9*(4), e126. DOI: 10.1192/bjo.2023.517 PMID: 37439065

Qiu, S., Miller, M. I., Joshi, P. S., Lee, J. C., Xue, C., Ni, Y., Wang, Y., De Anda-Duran, I., Hwang, P. H., Cramer, J. A., Dwyer, B. C., Hao, H., Kaku, M. C., Kedar, S., Lee, P. H., Mian, A. Z., Murman, D. L., O'Shea, S., Paul, A. B., & Kolachalama, V. B. (2022). Multimodal deep learning for Alzheimer's disease dementia assessment. *Nature Communications*, *13*(1), 3404. DOI: 10.1038/s41467-022-31037-5 PMID: 35725739

Quintana, Y., & McWhirter, J. (2017). Culturally Appropriate Behavioral Change in Maternal Health: Role of Mobile and Online Technologies Over Time. *Computers in Healthcare*, •••, 217–233. DOI: 10.1007/978-3-319-51732-2_10

Radanliev, P. (2025). AI ethics: Integrating transparency, fairness, and privacy in AI development. [tandfonline.com]. *Applied Artificial Intelligence*, *39*(1), e2463722. DOI: 10.1080/08839514.2025.2463722

Rahman, R. (2020). The privatization of health care system in Saudi Arabia. *Health Services Insights*, *13*, 117863292093449. DOI: 10.1177/1178632920934497 PMID: 32636636

Rakheja, S., Mehta, D., Aggarwal, I., Goel, H., Joseph, D., Jain, J., Deep, G., Grover, M., Verma, P., & Singh, B. (2025). Knowledge, Attitude and Awareness of HPV Vaccination among College-Going Girls (18–26 years) in Delhi NCR. *Asian Pacific Journal of Cancer Nursing*, 20250806–20250806. https://doi.org/DOI: 10.31557/apjcn.1967.20250806

Ramakrishnan, R., Rao, S., & He, J.-R. (2021). Perinatal health predictors using artificial intelligence: A review. *Women's Health (London, England)*, *17*, 174550652110461. DOI: 10.1177/17455065211046132 PMID: 34519596

Ratner, L., Sridhar, S., Rosman, S. L., Junior, J., Gyan-Kesse, L., Edwards, J., & Russ, C. M. (2022). Learner milestones to guide decolonial global health education. *Annals of Global Health*, *88*(1), 99. Advance online publication. DOI: 10.5334/aogh.3866 PMID: 36380745

Raymond, D., Sheikh, K., & Gourshettiwar, P. (2024). Blockchain technology in healthcare: A revolution in data security, interoperability, and patient privacy. *AIP Conference Proceedings*, *3188*(1), 100054. DOI: 10.1063/5.0240159

RDi. (n.d.). The real cost of paper in a digital hospital. Inicio UK. https://inicio.uk/the-real-cost-of-paper-in-a-digital-hospital/

Regan, K. (2024, March 14). *Is HPV vaccination cost effective?* https://www.path.org/our-impact/articles/is-hpv-vaccination-cost-effective/

Remy, C., Agarwal, S. K., Kumar, A., & Srivastava, S. (2013). Supporting Voice Content Sharing among Underprivileged People in Urban India. *Lecture Notes in Computer Science*, *8120*, 489–506. DOI: 10.1007/978-3-642-40498-6_38

REPPARE. (2025, June 8). Innovative Health Financing Mechanisms for Advancing Pandemic Preparedness: 'Huge Untapped Potential' or False Advertising? ★ Brownstone Institute. *Brownstone Institute.* https://brownstone.org/articles/innovative-health-financing-mechanisms-for-advancing-pandemic-preparedness-huge-untapped-potential-or-false-advertising/

Results for Development. (2017). *Immunization Financing, a resource guide for advocates, policymakers, and program managers* (pp. 1–128). R4D. https://www.r4d.org/wp-content/uploads/Immunization_Financing_Resource_Guide_2017_FULL.pdf

Reuters. (2018, October 30). *China's Innovent Biologics raises $421 million in HK IPO: sources.* https://www.reuters.com/article/innovent-biologics-ipo-idUSL3N1X921G/

Rezaei, M., Jafari-Sadeghi, V., Cao, D., & Mahdiraji, H. A. (2021). Key indicators of ethical challenges in digital healthcare: A combined Delphi exploration and confirmative factor analysis approach with evidence from Khorasan province in Iran. *Technological Forecasting and Social Change*, *167*, 120724. DOI: 10.1016/j.techfore.2021.120724

Romanello, M., McGushin, A., Di Napoli, C., Drummond, P., Hughes, N., Jamart, L., & Costello, A. (2021). The 2021 report of the Lancet Countdown on health and climate change: Code red for a healthy future. *Lancet*, *398*(10311), 1619–1662. DOI: 10.1016/S0140-6736(21)01787-6 PMID: 34687662

Romero, M. J., & Ravenscroft, J. (2022). *History repeated II: Why public-private partnerships are not the solution*. EURODAD.

Rosenblatt, M., Boutin, M. M., & Nussbaum, S. R. (2016). Innovation in medicine and device development, regulatory review, and use of clinical advances. *Journal of the American Medical Association, 316*(16), 1671. DOI: 10.1001/jama.2016.12486 PMID: 27669080

Rother, E. T. (2007). Systematic literature review X narrative review. *Acta Paulista de Enfermagem, 20*, v–vi. DOI: 10.1590/S0103-21002007000200001

Saatchi, A. G., Pallotti, F., & Sullivan, P. (2023). Network approaches and interventions in healthcare settings: A systematic scoping review. *PLoS One, 18*(2), e0282050. DOI: 10.1371/journal.pone.0282050 PMID: 36821554

Sabermahani, A., Sirizi, M. J., Zolala, F., & Nazari, S. (2021). Out-of-pocket costs and importance of nonmedical and indirect costs of inpatients. *Value in Health Regional Issues, 24*, 141–147. DOI: 10.1016/j.vhri.2020.05.004 PMID: 33578362

Sabreena Basheer, K. C. (2023). *Apple to launch AI-powered health app with emotion tracking*: Analytics Vidhya. Available at: https://www.analyticsvidhya.com/blog/2023/05/apple-to-launch-ai-powered-health-app-with-emotion-tracking-and-more/ (Accessed: July 29th 2024).

Saeed, A., Bin Saeed, A., & AlAhmri, F. A. (2023). Saudi Arabia health systems: Challenging and future transformations with artificial intelligence. *Cureus, 15*(4), e37826–e37826. DOI: 10.7759/cureus.37826 PMID: 37214025

Sahoo, P. M., Rout, H. S., & Jakovljevic, M. (2023). Contemporary universal health coverage in India: The case of federal state of Odisha (Orissa). *Risk Management and Healthcare Policy, 16*, 1131–1143. DOI: 10.2147/RMHP.S406491 PMID: 37384257

Saionz, A. (2025, November 12). *Inside Hengrui: The making of China's top pharma innovator*. Pharma Boardroom. https://pharmaboardroom.com/articles/inside-hengrui-the-making-of-chinas-top-pharma-innovator/

Sakamoto, J. L., Carandang, R. R., Kharel, M., Shibanuma, A., Yarotskaya, E., Basargina, M., & Jimba, M. (2022). Effects of mHealth on the psychosocial health of pregnant women and mothers: A systematic review. *BMJ Open, 12*(2), e056807. DOI: 10.1136/bmjopen-2021-056807 PMID: 35168981

Saleem, S. M., Pasquale, L. R., Sidoti, P. A., & Tsai, J. C. (2020). Virtual Ophthalmology: Telemedicine in a COVID-19 Era. *American Journal of Ophthalmology, 216*, 237–242. DOI: 10.1016/j.ajo.2020.04.029 PMID: 32360862

Samarasekera, U. (2024). African vaccine manufacturing scheme to boost production. *Lancet, 403*(10444), 2579–2580. DOI: 10.1016/S0140-6736(24)01239-X PMID: 38880099

Santos Ivo, R., Rodrigues, T., Couto, S., & Cossito, M. (2025). The art of bridge building: A look at the European-level cooperation in HTA (EU-HTA). *Journal of Market Access & Health Policy, 13*(2), 26. DOI: 10.3390/jmahp13020026 PMID: 40568381

Sardi, L., Idri, A., Redman, L. M., Alami, H., Bezad, R., & Alemán, J. L. F. (2020). Mobile health applications for postnatal care: Review and analysis of functionalities and technical features. *Computer Methods and Programs in Biomedicine, 184*, 105114. DOI: 10.1016/j.cmpb.2019.105114 PMID: 31655305

Saudi Ministry of Health. (2017). *New Model of Care.* https://www.moh.gov.sa/en/Ministry/vro/Documents/Healthcare-Transformation-Strategy.pdf (Accessed: 26 May 2024).

Saudi Ministry of Health. (2023). *Health Days 2023 - World Alzheimer's Day.* https://www.moh.gov.sa/en/HealthAwareness/healthDay/2023/Pages/default.aspx (Accessed 15 September 2023).

Saxena, A., Trivedi, M., Shroff, Z. C., & Sharma, M. (2022). Improving hospital-based processes for effective implementation of government funded health insurance schemes: Evidence from early implementation of PM-JAY in India. *BMC Health Services Research, 22*(1), 73. DOI: 10.1186/s12913-021-07448-3 PMID: 35031024

Schein, E. H. (2010). *Organizational Culture and Leadership.* John Wiley & Sons.

Schmidt, A., Vassil, K., & Tamm, K. (2024). Blockchain-enabled e-health systems: Lessons from Estonia. *Health Informatics Journal, 30*(2), 145–160. DOI: 10.1177/1460458224123456

Schmidt, J., Schutte, N. M., Buttigieg, S., Novillo-Ortiz, D., Sutherland, E., Anderson, M., & van Kessel, R. (2024). Mapping the regulatory landscape for artificial intelligence in health within the European Union. npj. *Digital Medicine, 7*(8), 1–14. DOI: 10.1038/s41746-023-00985-7

Schuind, A. E., Balaji, K. A., Du, A., Yuan, Y., & Dull, P. (2024). Human papillomavirus prophylactic vaccines: Update on new vaccine development and implications for single-dose policy. *Journal of the National Cancer Institute. Monographs, 2024*(67), 410–416. DOI: 10.1093/jncimonographs/lgae026 PMID: 39529522

Seeley, E., & Kesselheim, A. S. (2020). *Outcomes-based pharmaceutical contracts: An answer to high U.S. drug spending?* The Commonwealth Fund. https://www.commonwealthfund.org/publications/issue-briefs/2020/sep/outcomes-based-pharmaceutical-contracts-answer-high-drug-spending

Seidl, T. (2023). Investing in the knowledge economy: The comparative political economy of public investments in knowledge-based capital. *European Journal of Political Research, 62*(3), 924–944. DOI: 10.1111/1475-6765.12546

Sekalala, S., & Chatikobo, T. (2024). Colonialism in the new digital health agenda. *BMJ Global Health, 9*(2), e014131. Advance online publication. DOI: 10.1136/bmjgh-2023-014131 PMID: 38413105

Serper, M., & Volk, M. L. (2018). Current and future applications of telemedicine to optimise the delivery of care in chronic liver disease. *Clinical Gastroenterology and Hepatology : The Official Clinical Practice Journal of the American Gastroenterological Association, 16*(2), 157–161.e8. DOI: 10.1016/j.cgh.2017.10.004 PMID: 29389489

Seyyedi, N., Rahimi, B., Farrokh Eslamlou, H. R., Timpka, T., & Lotfnezhad Afshar, H. (2019). Mobile phone applications to overcome malnutrition among preschoolers: A systematic review. *BMC Medical Informatics and Decision Making, 19*(1), 83. Advance online publication. DOI: 10.1186/s12911-019-0803-2 PMID: 30953497

Shah, S. R., Munhall, C. C., Nguyen, S. A., O'Rourke, A. K., Miccichi, K., & Meyer, T. A. (2023). Diagnostic accuracy and management concordance of otorhinolaryngological diseases through telehealth or remote visits: A systematic review & meta-analysis. *Journal of Telemedicine and Telecare, 30*(9), 1386–1397. DOI: 10.1177/1357633X231156207 PMID: 36916306

Shamanna, P., Joshi, S., Thajudeen, M., Shah, L., Poon, T., Mohamed, M., & Mohammed, J. (2024). Personalized nutrition in type 2 diabetes remission: Application of digital twin technology for predictive glycemic control. *Frontiers in Endocrinology, 15*, 1485464. Advance online publication. DOI: 10.3389/fendo.2024.1485464 PMID: 39634180

Sharda, S., Kshtriya, P., Agrawal, P. K., Singh, P., Trakroo, A., Joshi, A., Agarwal, A., Goyal, A., D'Aquino, L., Singh, S., Singh, R., & Prinja, S. (2024). Digital supportive supervision (DiSS) of maternal health, child health and nutrition (MCHN) service delivery in Rajasthan, India: Study protocol for impact evaluation and cost-effectiveness analysis. *BMJ Open, 14*(12), e086956–e086956. DOI: 10.1136/bmjopen-2024-086956 PMID: 39740940

Shattock, A. J., Johnson, H. C., Sim, S. Y., Carter, A., Lambach, P., Hutubessy, R. C. W., Thompson, K. M., Badizadegan, K., Lambert, B., Ferrari, M. J., Jit, M., Fu, H., Silal, S. P., Hounsell, R. A., White, R. G., Mosser, J. F., Gaythorpe, K. A. M., Trotter, C. L., Lindstrand, A., & Bar-Zeev, N. (2024). Contribution of vaccination to improved survival and health: Modelling 50 years of the Expanded Programme on Immunization. *Lancet*, *403*(10441), 2307–2316. DOI: 10.1016/S0140-6736(24)00850-X PMID: 38705159

Shaver, J. (2022). The state of telehealth before and after the COVID-19 pandemic. *Primary Care*, *49*(4), 517–530. DOI: 10.1016/j.pop.2022.04.002 PMID: 36357058

Shaw, J. A., & Donia, J. (2021). The Sociotechnical Ethics of Digital Health: A Critique and Extension of Approaches From Bioethics. *Frontiers in Digital Health*, *3*, 725088. Advance online publication. DOI: 10.3389/fdgth.2021.725088 PMID: 34713196

Shawwa, L. (2023). The use of telemedicine in medical education and patient care. *Cureus*. Advance online publication. DOI: 10.7759/cureus.37766 PMID: 37213963

Shin, J., Tampi, R., Joshi, P., Jester, D. J., & Jeste, D. V. (2025). Social determinants of health associated with neuropsychiatric symptoms of dementia and mild cognitive impairment: A narrative review. *International Psychogeriatrics*, *100152*, 100152. Advance online publication. DOI: 10.1016/j.inpsyc.2025.100152 PMID: 41102089

Shruddha, K., Deepshika, R., Rakesh, M., & Shewethashree, M. (2025). Knowledge, utilisation and perception regarding Ayushman Bharat Pradhan Mantri Jan Arogya Yojana among Mysuru residents: Insights from a cross-sectional analysis. *International Journal of Community Medicine and Public Health*. https://www.ijcmph.com/index.php/ijcmph/article/download/14176/8536/69304

Siemens Healthineers. (2023, September 2). *Patient twin: Why Sophia is no longer afraid of cancer*. Siemens Healthineers Perspectives. https://www.siemens-healthineers.com/perspectives/digital-patient-twin-cancer-care

Silver, F. H., Mesica, A., Gonzalez-Mercedes, M., & Deshmukh, T. (2022). Identification of cancerous skin lesions using vibrational optical coherence tomography (VOCT): Use of VOCT in conjunction with machine learning to diagnose skin cancer remotely using telemedicine. *Cancers (Basel)*, *15*(1), 156. Advance online publication. DOI: 10.3390/cancers15010156 PMID: 36612151

Sim, S. Y., Watts, E., Constenla, D., Brenzel, L., & Patenaude, B. N. (2020). Return On Investment From Immunization Against 10 Pathogens In 94 Low- And Middle-Income Countries, 2011–30. *Health Affairs (Project Hope)*, *39*(8), 1343–1353. DOI: 10.1377/hlthaff.2020.00103 PMID: 32744930

Singh, L., Siddhanta, A., Singh, A. K., Prinja, S., Sharma, A., Sikka, H., & Goswami, L. (2023). Potential impact of the insurance on catastrophic health expenditures among the urban poor population in India. *Journal of Health Management, 25*(4), 996–1008. DOI: 10.1177/09720634221088425

Sittrop, D., & Crosthwaite, C. (2021). Minimising risk: The application of Kotter's change management model on customer relationship management systems. A case study. *Journal of Risk and Financial Management, 14*(10), 1–20. DOI: 10.3390/jrfm14100496

Solar, O., & Irwin, A. (2010). A conceptual framework for action on the social determinants of health. World Health Organization. https://www.who.int/publications/i/item/9789241500852

Sowon, K., & Chigona, W. (2020). *Trust in mHealth: How do Maternal Health Clients Accept and Use mHealth Interventions?* DOI: 10.1145/3410886.3410895

Soyege, D., Alabi, M. O., & Yusuf, T. A. (2024). Health informatics in developing countries: Challenges and opportunities. ResearchGate. https://www.researchgate.net/publication/390109885

Sreelatha, O. K., & Ramesh, S. V. S. (2016). Teleophthalmology: Improving patient outcomes? *Clinical Ophthalmology (Auckland, N.Z.), 10*(1), 285–295. DOI: 10.2147/OPTH.S80487 PMID: 26929592

Srivastava, A., Avan, B. I., Rajbangshi, P., & Bhattacharyya, S. (2015). Determinants of women's satisfaction with maternal health care: A review of literature from developing countries. *BMC Pregnancy and Childbirth, 15*(1), 97. Advance online publication. DOI: 10.1186/s12884-015-0525-0 PMID: 25928085

Stefaniak, I., & Aleksandrowicz, A. (2024). Application of a virtual reality-based cognitive-behavioural therapy of social phobia in the treatment of inpatients diagnosed with schizophrenia and social anxiety – a feasibility study. *Frontiers in Psychiatry, 15*, 1379541. Advance online publication. DOI: 10.3389/fpsyt.2024.1379541 PMID: 39659550

Stein, F., & Sridhar, D. (2018). *The financialisation of global health.* University of Edinburgh. DOI: 10.12688/wellcomeopenres.13885.1

Stein, J. D., Brown, M. M., Brown, G. C., Hollands, H., & Sharma, S. (2003). Quality of life with macular degeneration: Perceptions of patients, clinicians, and community members. *The British Journal of Ophthalmology*, *87*(1), 8–12. DOI: 10.1136/bjo.87.1.8 PMID: 12488253

Stephen, R., & Frank, J. (2024). The role of electronic health records in transforming healthcare delivery and financial gains. ResearchGate. https://www.researchgate.net/publication/377407661

Stephen, R., Frank, J., & Miller, T. (2024). The impact of electronic health records on healthcare delivery transformation and economic benefits. ResearchGate. https://www.researchgate.net/publication/377407747

Storeng, K. T., & Béhague, D. P. (2017). "Guilty until proven innocent": The contested use of maternal mortality indicators in global health. [tandfonline.com]. *Critical Public Health*, *27*(2), 163–176. DOI: 10.1080/09581596.2016.1259459 PMID: 28392630

Subedi, D., Paudel, M., Poudel, S., & Koirala, N. (2024). Food Safety in Developing Countries: Common Foodborne and Waterborne Illnesses, Regulations, Organizational Structure, and Challenges of Food Safety in the Context of Nepal. *Food Frontiers*. Advance online publication. DOI: 10.1002/fft2.517

Succar, T. M. P., Grigg, J. M. M. D. F., Beaver, H. A. M. D., & Lee, A. G. M. D. (2016). A systematic review of best practices in teaching ophthalmology to medical students. *Survey of Ophthalmology*, *61*(1), 83–94. DOI: 10.1016/j.survophthal.2015.09.001 PMID: 26363187

Suri, T., & Jack, W. (2016). The long-run poverty and gender impacts of mobile money. *Science*, *354*(6317), 1288–1292. DOI: 10.1126/science.aah5309 PMID: 27940873

Sylverken, A. A., Owusu, M., Agbavor, B., Kwarteng, A., Ayisi-Boateng, N. K., Ofori, P., El-Duah, P., Yeboah, R., Aryeetey, S., Addo Asamoah, J., Ekekpi, R. Z., Oppong, M., Gorman, R., Brempong, K. A., Nyarko-Afriyie, E., Owusu Bonsu, F., Larsen-Reindorf, R., Rockson Adjei, M., Boateng, G., & Phillips, R. O. (2022). Using drones to transport suspected COVID-19 samples: Experiences from the second largest testing centre in Ghana, West Africa. *PLoS One*, *17*(11), e0277057. DOI: 10.1371/journal.pone.0277057 PMID: 36318579

Tacheva, B., Brown, G. W., Bell, D., & von Agris, J. (2025). The devil's in the detail: An appraisal of the use of innovative financing mechanisms for pandemic prevention, preparedness and response. *Globalization and Health*, *21*(1), 13. DOI: 10.1186/s12992-025-01103-w PMID: 40148959

Tamrat, T., & Kachnowski, S. (2011). Special Delivery: An Analysis of mHealth in Maternal and Newborn Health Programs and Their Outcomes Around the World. *Maternal and Child Health Journal*, *16*(5), 1092–1101. DOI: 10.1007/s10995-011-0836-3 PMID: 21688111

Tan, J. C. K., Ferdi, A. C., Gillies, M. C., & Watson, S. L. (2019). Clinical Registries in Ophthalmology. *Ophthalmology, 126*(5), 655–662. DOI: 10.1016/j.ophtha.2018.12.030 PMID: 30572076

Tarun Singh Sodha, Grønbæk, A., Bhandari, A., B. Daly Mary, Ajit Kisanrao Sudke, & Smith, L. (2022). mHealth learning tool for skilled birth attendants: scaling the Safe Delivery App in India. *BMJ Open Quality, 11*(Suppl 1), e001928–e001928. DOI: 10.1136/bmjoq-2022-001928

Taslakian, E. N., Garber, K., & Shekherdimian, S. (2021). Diaspora engagement: A scoping review of diaspora involvement with strengthening health systems of their origin country. *Global Health Action, 15*(1), 2009165. Advance online publication. DOI: 10.1080/16549716.2021.2009165 PMID: 34904934

Tate, E. B., Spruijt-Metz, D., O'Reilly, G., Jordan-Marsh, M., Gotsis, M., Pentz, M. A., & Dunton, G. F. (2013). mHealth approaches to child obesity prevention: Successes, unique challenges, and next directions. *Translational Behavioral Medicine, 3*(4), 406–415. DOI: 10.1007/s13142-013-0222-3 PMID: 24294329

Tayeb, H. O., Khallaf, R. A., Muayqil, T. A., Alkeridy, W. A., Alibrahim, F. S., Alfaify, O. A., Qadi, N., & Tarazi, F. I. (2023). The future of Alzheimer disease immunotherapies in Saudi Arabia: Consensus statement of the Saudi Chapter of Cognitive and Behavioral Neurology. *Neurosciences, 28*(2), 77–84. DOI: 10.17712/nsj.2023.2.20220133 PMID: 37045461

Tenni, B., Moir, H. V. J., Townsend, B., Kilic, B., Farrell, A.-M., Keegel, T., & Gleeson, D. (2022). What is the impact of intellectual property rules on access to medicines? A systematic review. *Globalization and Health, 18*(1), 40. Advance online publication. DOI: 10.1186/s12992-022-00826-4 PMID: 35428250

Terrell, E. A., Aftab, S., Babitz, A., Butler, L., Hernandez, N. G., Hornik, B., Lee, K., Perez, J., Sotolongo, E., & Thomas, J. (2021). The evolution of telehealth from pre-COVID-19 pandemic through a hybrid virtual care delivery model: A pediatric hospital's journey. *International Journal ofTelerehabilitation, 13*(2), e6432. Advance online publication. DOI: 10.5195/ijt.2021.6432 PMID: 35646232

Thakkar, V. (2024, March 12). Modernising traditional maternal care in Guatemala. Think Global Health. https://www.thinkglobalhealth.org/article/modernizing-traditional-maternal-care-guatemala

Thakur, R., & Faizan, M. A. (2024). Magnitude of health expenditure induced removable poverty in India: Some reflections of Ayushman Bharat. *Heliyon, 10*(1), e25212. DOI: 10.1016/j.heliyon.2023.e23464 PMID: 38187230

Thaler, R. H., & Sunstein, C. R. (2021). *Nudge: The final edition*. Penguin Books.

The Global Fund. (2025, July 9). *Global Fund secures access to breakthrough HIV prevention drug lenacapavir for low- and middle-income countries*. https://www.theglobalfund.org/en/news/2025/2025-07-09-global-fund-secures-access-breakthrough-hiv-prevention-drug-lenacapavir/

The King's Fund. (n.d.). Health inequalities in a nutshell. https://www.kingsfund.org.uk/insight-and-analysis/data-and-charts/health-inequalities-nutshell

The Pharma Letter. (2020, January 21). *China's national generics procurement cuts prices up to 93%*. https://www.thepharmaletter.com/generics-news/china-s-national-generics-procurement-cuts-prices-up-to-93

ThinkWell. (2020). *Innovative Financing Mechanisms for Health*. https://thinkwell.global/resources/innovative-financing-mechanisms-for-health/ (Accessed 2 July 2024)

Thobias, J., & Kiwanuka, A. (2018). Design and implementation of an m-health data model for improving health information access for reproductive and child health services in low resource settings using a participatory action research approach. *BMC Medical Informatics and Decision Making*, *18*(1), 45. Advance online publication. DOI: 10.1186/s12911-018-0622-x PMID: 29941008

Thomson, M., Kentikelenis, A., & Stubbs, T. (2017). Structural adjustment programmes adversely affect vulnerable populations: A systematic-narrative review of their effect on child and maternal health. *Public Health Reviews*, *38*(1), 13. Advance online publication. DOI: 10.1186/s40985-017-0059-2 PMID: 29450085

Tilahun, B., Gashu, K. D., Mekonnen, Z. A., Endehabtu, B. F., & Angaw, D. A. (2021). Mapping the role of digital health technologies in prevention and control of COVID-19 pandemic: Review of the literature. *Yearbook of Medical Informatics*, *30*(1), 1–12. DOI: 10.1055/s-0041-1726505 PMID: 34479378

Ting, D. S. W., Pasquale, L. R., Peng, L., Campbell, J. P., Lee, A. Y., Raman, R., Tan, G. S. W., Schmetterer, L., Keane, P. A., & Wong, T. Y. (2019). Artificial intelligence and deep learning in ophthalmology. *The British Journal of Ophthalmology*, *103*(2), 167–175. DOI: 10.1136/bjophthalmol-2018-313173 PMID: 30361278

Today Online. (2016, June 17). *China's biotech revolution ushered in by 'sea turtles'*. https://www.todayonline.com/world/chinas-beotech-revolution-ushered-sea-turtles

Todnem, R. (2005). Organisational change management: A critical review. *Journal of Change Management*, *5*(4), 369–380. DOI: 10.1080/14697010500359250

Torab-Miandoab, A., Samad-Soltani, T., Jodati, A., & Rezaei-Hachesu, P. (2023, January 24). Interoperability of heterogeneous health information systems: A systematic literature review. *BMC Medical Informatics and Decision Making*, *23*(1), 18. Advance online publication. DOI: 10.1186/s12911-023-02115-5 PMID: 36694161

Tornimbene, B., Leiva Rioja, Z. B., Brownstein, J., Dunn, A., Faye, S., Kong, J., Malou, N., Nordon, C., Rader, B., & Morgan, O. (2025). Harnessing the power of artificial intelligence for disease-surveillance purposes. *BMC Proceedings*, *19*(S4, Suppl 4), 7. Advance online publication. DOI: 10.1186/s12919-025-00320-w PMID: 40050981

Toure, A. (2025). Ethical AI in public health: A global path to reduce inequalities. *Global Society*. https://www.globalsociety.earth/post/ethical-ai-in-public-health-a-global-path-to-reduce-inequalities

Tricco, A. C., Lillie, E., Zarin, W., O'Brien, K. K., Colquhoun, H., Levac, D., Moher, D., Peters, M. D. J., Horsley, T., Weeks, L., Hempel, S., Akl, E. A., Chang, C., McGowan, J., Stewart, L., Hartling, L., Aldcroft, A., Wilson, M. G., Garritty, C., & Straus, S. E. (2018). PRISMA extension for scoping reviews (PRISMA-ScR): Checklist and explanation. *Annals of Internal Medicine*, *169*(7), 467–473. DOI: 10.7326/M18-0850 PMID: 30178033

Tripp, N., Hainey, K., Liu, A., Poulton, A., Peek, M., Kim, J., & Nanan, R. (2014). An emerging model of maternity care: Smartphone, midwife, doctor? *Women and Birth : Journal of the Australian College of Midwives*, *27*(1), 64–67. DOI: 10.1016/j.wombi.2013.11.001 PMID: 24295598

Trude, A. C. B., Martins, R. C., Martins-Silva, T., Blumenberg, C., Carpena, M. X., Del-Ponte, B., & Loret de Mola, C. (2021). A WhatsApp-Based Intervention to Improve Maternal Social Support and Maternal–Child Health in Southern Brazil: The Text-Message Intervention to Enhance Social Support (TIES) Feasibility Study. *Inquiry : a Journal of Medical Care Organization, Provision and Financing*, *58*, 00469580211048701. DOI: 10.1177/00469580211048701 PMID: 34619999

Tulchinsky, T. H., Varavikova, E. A., & Cohen, M. J. (2023). Family health and primary prevention. *Elsevier EBooks*, 467–549. DOI: 10.1016/B978-0-12-822957-6.00007-7

Ud Din, M. A., Dar, M. H., & Haseen, S. (2023). Inter-state disparities in government health expenditure in India: A study of national rural health mission. *International Journal of Health Governance*, *28*(1), 82–94. DOI: 10.1108/IJHG-12-2022-0108

UK Government. (2023, September 13). What are community diagnostic centres?https://www.gov.uk/government/news/what-are-community-diagnostic-centres

Ullah, A. K. M., & Chattoraj, D. (2025). Traveling across global divides: Freedom or barriers to move? *World Affairs*, *188*(1), e12062. Advance online publication. DOI: 10.1002/waf2.12062

UNICEF. (2019). *Human Papillomavirus Vaccine: Supply and Demand Update* (pp. 1–12). https://www.unicef.org/supply/sites/unicef.org.supply/files/2020-03/human-papillomavirus-vaccine-HPV-supply-and-demand-update.pdf

UNICEF. (2020). *Health technology and innovations in Africa*. UNICEF.

UNICEF. (2025). *Human Papilloma Virus (HPV) vaccine price data | UNICEF Supply Division*. https://www.unicef.org/supply/documents/human-papilloma-virus-hpv-vaccine-price-data

United Nations Development Programme. (2023). Bridge the digital divide – Digital standards. https://www.undp.org/digital/standards/2-bridge-digital-divide

United Nations. (2012). *World population prospects: The 2012 revision*. https://www.un.org/en/development/desa/publications/world-population-prospectsthe-2012-revision.html (Accessed: 13 June 2024).

Urias, E., & Ramani, S. V. (2020). Access to medicines after TRIPS: Is compulsory licensing an effective mechanism to lower drug prices? A review of the existing evidence. *Journal of International Business Policy*, *3*(4), 367–384. Advance online publication. DOI: 10.1057/s42214-020-00068-4

USC Schaeffer Center. (2019, July 2). *Using the drug pricing Netflix model to help states tackle the Hep C crisis*. https://schaeffer.usc.edu/research/using-the-drug-pricing-netflix-model-to-help-states-tackle-the-hep-c-crisis/

Usmani, M. T. (2002). *An introduction to Islamic finance*. Kluwer Law International.

Vaidya, A. (2022, December 29). Understanding telehealth barriers for limited English proficiency patients. TechTarget. https://www.techtarget.com/virtualhealthcare/feature/Understanding-Telehealth-Barriers-for-Limited-English-Proficiency-Patients

Varnosfaderani, S. R., Ahmadi, M., & Jebraeily, M. (2024). The role of mHealth in managing chronic diseases. *BMC Medical Informatics and Decision Making*, *24*, 99. https://pmc.ncbi.nlm.nih.gov/articles/PMC11047988/

Vilhelmsson, A. (2024). Navigating the climate-health nexus: Linking health data with climate data to advance public health interventions. *BMC Global and Public Health*, *2*(1), 73. Advance online publication. DOI: 10.1186/s44263-024-00109-7 PMID: 39681937

Vinze, S., Chodosh, J., Lee, M., Wright, J., & Borson, S. (2023). The national public health response to Alzheimer's disease and related dementias: Origins, evolution, and recommendations to improve early detection. *Alzheimer's & Dementia : The Journal of the Alzheimer's Association*, *19*(9), 4276–4286. DOI: 10.1002/alz.13376 PMID: 37435983

Vo, D.-K., & Trinh, K. T. L. (2024). Advances in wearable biosensors for healthcare: Current trends, applications, and future perspectives. *Biosensors (Basel)*, *14*(11), 301. Advance online publication. DOI: 10.3390/bios14110560 PMID: 39590019

Volk, J., Palanker, D., O'Brien, M., & Goe, C. (2021, June 23). States' actions to expand telemedicine access during COVID-19 and future policy considerations. The Commonwealth Fund. https://www.commonwealthfund.org/publications/issue-briefs/2021/jun/states-actions-expand-telemedicine-access-covid-19

Voto, T. P., Voto, B. E., & Ngepah, N. (2025). The impact of out-of-pocket health expenditure and public health expenditure on poverty in sub-Saharan Africa. *Economies (Basel)*, *13*(5), 134. DOI: 10.3390/economies13050134

Wagstaff, A., Eozenou, P., & Smitz, M. (2019). Out-of-pocket expenditures on health: A global stocktake (No. 8808). World Bank. https://openknowledge.worldbank.org/entities/publication/b1d12b58-634a-5fdf-b678-d7182b81633b

Wagstaff, A., Flores, G., Hsu, J., Smitz, M. F., Chepynoga, K., Eozenou, P., & Buisman, L. R. (2018). Progress on catastrophic health spending in 133 countries: A retrospective observational study. *The Lancet. Global Health*, *6*(2), e169–e179. DOI: 10.1016/S2214-109X(17)30429-1 PMID: 29248367

Walter, Y. (2024). Managing the race to the moon: Global policy and governance in artificial intelligence regulation—A contemporary overview and an analysis of socioeconomic consequences. *Discover Artificial Intelligence*, *4*(1), 14. Advance online publication. DOI: 10.1007/s44163-024-00109-4

Walt, G., & Gilson, L. (1994). Reforming the health sector in developing countries: The central role of policy analysis. *Health Policy and Planning*, *9*(4), 353–370. DOI: 10.1093/heapol/9.4.353 PMID: 10139469

Washington, G. (2022, June 8). Ensuring accessible telehealth for Deaf & Hard of Hearing patients. American Telemedicine Association. https://www.americantelemed.org/uncategorized/ensuring-accessible-telehealth-for-deaf-hard-of-hearing-patients/

Wehrwein, P. (2023, November 28). They cost millions. How payers might manage those astronomical gene therapy bills. *Managed Healthcare Executive*. https://www.managedhealthcareexecutive.com/view/they-cost-millions-how-payers-might-manage-their-gene-therapy-bills

Weiner, J. P., Yeh, S., & Bai, G. (2024). Adoption of digital health tools in hospital systems. *Journal of Medical Internet Research*, *26*, e12345. https://pmc.ncbi.nlm.nih.gov/articles/PMC11977975/

Weinstein, R. S., Lopez, A. M., Joseph, B. A., Erps, K. A., Holcomb, M., Barker, G. P., & Krupinski, E. A. (2014). Telemedicine, telehealth, and mobile health applications that work: Opportunities and barriers. *The American Journal of Medicine*, *127*(3), 183–187. DOI: 10.1016/j.amjmed.2013.09.032 PMID: 24384059

Wen, D., Khan, S. M., Xu, A. J., Ibrahim, H., Smith, L., Caballero, J., Zepeda, L., de Blas Perez, C., Denniston, A. K., Liu, X., & Matin, R. N. (2022). Characteristics of publicly available skin cancer image datasets: A systematic review. *The Lancet. Digital Health*, *4*(1), e64–e74. DOI: 10.1016/S2589-7500(21)00252-1 PMID: 34772649

WHO. (2015). Human papillomavirus vaccines: WHO position paper, October 2014-Recommendations. *Vaccine*, *33*(36), 4383–4384. DOI: 10.1016/j.vaccine.2014.12.002 PMID: 25510390

WHO. (2020). *World Health Statistics*: World Health Organization. Available at: https://www.who.int/data/gho/publications/world-health-statistics (Accessed: July 30th 2024).

WHO. (2022). *Child mortality and causes of death*. Www.who.int. https://www.who.int/data/gho/data/themes/topics/topic-details/GHO/child-mortality-and-causes-of-death

WHO. (2024). *Considerations for human papillomavirus (HPV) vaccine product choice* (2nd ed.). https://www.who.int/publications/i/item/9789240089167

WHO. (2025). *WHO Immunization Data portal—Detail Page*. Immunization Data. https://immunizationdata.who.int/global/wiise-detail-page

Whyle, E., & Olivier, J. (2020). Social values and health systems in health policy and systems research: A mixed-method systematic review and evidence map. *Health Policy and Planning*, *35*(6), 735–751. DOI: 10.1093/heapol/czaa038 PMID: 32374881

Wigley, A. S., Tejedor-Garavito, N., Alegana, V., Carioli, A., Ruktanonchai, C. W., Pezzulo, C., Matthews, Z., Tatem, A. J., & Nilsen, K. (2020). Measuring the availability and geographical accessibility of maternal health services across sub-Saharan Africa. *BMC Medicine*, *18*(1), 237. Advance online publication. DOI: 10.1186/s12916-020-01707-6 PMID: 32895051

Williams, O. D., Ooms, G., & Hill, P. S. (2015). Cautionary notes on a global tiered pricing framework for medicines. *American Journal of Public Health*, *105*(7), 1290–1293. DOI: 10.2105/AJPH.2015.302554 PMID: 25973806

Wilson, L. S., & Maeder, A. J. (2015). Recent directions in telemedicine: Review of trends in research and practice. *Healthcare Informatics Research*, *21*(4), 213–222. DOI: 10.4258/hir.2015.21.4.213 PMID: 26618026

Wispelwey, B., Osuagwu, C., Mills, D., Goronga, T., & Morse, M. (2023). Towards a bidirectional decoloniality in academic global health: Insights from settler colonialism and racial capitalism. *The Lancet. Global Health*, *11*(9), e1469–e1474. DOI: 10.1016/S2214-109X(23)00307-8 PMID: 37591594

Wong, G. (2008). Developing China's homegrown biotechnology workforce. *Nature Biotechnology*, *26*(3), 353–354. DOI: 10.1038/nbt0308-353 PMID: 18327247

World Bank Group. (2025, December 6). *Gavi and World Bank Group deepen collaboration to boost health system resilience and regional vaccine manufacturing*. https://www.worldbank.org/en/news/press-release/2025/12/06/gavi-wbg-collaboration-boosts-health-system-resilience-regional-vaccine-manufacturing

World Bank. (1980). Health sector policy paper.

World Bank. (2015). *Access to electricity (% of population)*. https://databank.worldbank.org/metadataglossary/world-development-indicators/series/EG.ELC.ACCS.ZS (Accessed June 29, 2024)

World Bank. (2019, April 8). Record high remittances sent globally in 2018. https://www.worldbank.org/en/news/press-release/2019/04/08/record-high-remittances-sent-globally-in-2018

World Bank. (2020). World Bank COVID-19 response. https://www.worldbank.org/en/news/factsheet/2020/10/14/world-bank-covid-19-response

World Bank. (2021). *Health expenditure (% of GDP) – India*. https://data.worldbank.org (Accessed June 30, 2024)

World Bank. (2022). *Africa health overview*. World Bank.

World Bank. (2023). *Tracking universal health coverage 2023 global monitoring report.*

World Bank. (2023). Universal health coverage as a sustainable development goal. https://datatopics.worldbank.org/world-development-indicators/stories/universal-health-coverage-as-a-sustainable-development-goal.html

World Bank. (2024a). *World Bank open data.* https://data.worldbank.org (Accessed June 29, 2024)

World Bank. (2024b). *Inflation, consumer prices (annual %) – India.* https://data.worldbank.org/indicator/FP.CPI.TOTL.ZG?locations=IN (Accessed June 29, 2024)

World Economic Forum. (2021). Innovating in health financing in Africa. World Economic Forum.

World Economic Forum. (2025). *7 ways AI is transforming healthcare.* https://www.weforum.org/stories/2025/08/ai-transforming-global-health/

World Economic Forum. (2025, April 28). *A new era in global aid: Why locally led, market-based solutions are the best route to resilience.* World Economic Forum. https://www.weforum.org/stories/2025/04/global-aid-new-era-resilience/

World Health Organization & World Bank. (2017). Tracking universal health coverage: 2017 global monitoring report. https://www.who.int/news/item/13-12-2017-world-bank-and-who-half-the-world-lacks-access-to-essential-health-services-100-million-still-pushed-into-extreme-poverty-because-of-health-expenses

World Health Organization. (1978). Declaration of Alma-Ata.

World Health Organization. (2014). *Household air pollution.* https://www.who.int/data/gho/data/themes/topics/topic-details/GHO/household-air-pollution (Accessed June 15, 2024)

World Health Organization. (2019). *Primary health care on the road to universal health coverage: 2019 global monitoring report.* WHO.

World Health Organization. (2019). Risk reduction of cognitive decline and dementia: WHO guidelines. In *Risk reduction of cognitive decline and dementia: WHO guidelines* (pp. 96-96). https://pesquisa.bvsalud.org/portal/resource/pt/biblio-1015308

World Health Organization. (2020a). *Global spending on health: Weathering the storm.* https://www.who.int/publications/i/item/9789240017788 (Accessed June 29, 2024)

World Health Organization. (2020a). Global strategy on human resources for health: Workforce 2030. World Health Organization. https://www.who.int/publications/i/item/9789241511131

World Health Organization. (2020b). *World health statistics 2020: Monitoring health for the SDGs, sustainable development goals.* https://www.who.int/publications/i/item/9789240005105 (Accessed June 29, 2024)

World Health Organization. (2021). *Global Status Report on the Public Health Response to Dementia.* https://iris.who.int/bitstream/handle/10665/344701/9789240033245-eng.pdf?sequence=1 (Accessed: 29 May 2024).

World Health Organization. (2021). *Global strategy on digital health 2020-2025.* WHO.

World Health Organization. (2021). Global strategy on digital health 2020–2025. World Health Organization. https://www.who.int/publications/i/item/9789240020924

World Health Organization. (2021b). *Global monitoring report on financial protection in health 2021.* https://www.who.int/publications/i/item/9789240040953 (Accessed June 29, 2024)

World Health Organization. (2021c). *India: Ayushman Bharat for a new India – 2022.* https://www.who.int/india/news/detail/26-09-2021-ayushman-bharat-for-a-new-india-2022 (Accessed June 29, 2024)

World Health Organization. (2022).. . *World Malaria Report, 2022,* •••. https://www.who.int/teams/global-malaria-programme/reports/world-malaria-report-2022

World Health Organization. (2023). *Health financing in Africa.* WHO.

World Health Organization. (2023). *Maternal Mental Health.* World Health Organization. https://www.who.int/teams/mental-health-and-substance-use/promotion-prevention/maternal-mental-health

World Health Organization. (2023a, April 20). WHO releases the largest global collection of health inequality data. https://www.who.int/news/item/20-04-2023-who-releases-the-largest-global-collection-of-health-inequality-data

World Health Organization. (2023b). Noncommunicable diseases. https://www.who.int/health-topics/noncommunicable-diseases

World Health Organization. (2023c). World health statistics 2023: Monitoring health for the SDGs. World Health Organization. https://www.who.int/publications/i/item/9789240074323

World Health Organization. (2024). *Domestic general government health expenditure (GGHE-D) as percentage of general government expenditure (GGE) (%).* https://www.who.int/data/gho/indicator-metadata-registry/imr-details/4956 (Accessed June 29, 2024)

World Health Organization. (2024, May 7). WHO Results Report 2023 https://www.who.int/news/item/07-05-2024-who-results-report-2023-shows-notable-health-achievements-and-calls-for-concerted-drive-toward-sustainable-development-goals

World Health Organization. (2025). *Indonesia's success in achieving 90 percent coverage and minimizing out-of-pocket expenses through national health insurance expansion.* https://www.who.int/about/accountability/results/who-results-report-2020-mtr/country-story/2023/indonesia-s-success-in-achieving-90-percent-coverage-and-minimizing-out-of-pocket-expenses-through-national-health-insurance-expansion (Accessed August 24, 2025)

World Health Organization. (2025, April 4). Current health expenditure (% of GDP). https://data.worldbank.org/indicator/SH.XPD.CHEX.GD.ZS

World Health Organization. (2025, April 7). *Maternal Mortality.* World Health Organization. https://www.who.int/news-room/fact-sheets/detail/maternal-mortality

World Health Organization. (2025, June 27). *Pandemic prevention, preparedness and response agreement.* https://www.who.int/news-room/questions-and-answers/item/pandemic-prevention-preparedness-and-response-agreement

World Health Organization. (2025a, June 24). Public notice and comments on the Technical Advisory Group on the use of digital technologies to enhance access to assistive technology. https://www.who.int/news-room/articles-detail/public-notice-and-comments-on-the-technical-advisory-group-on-the-use-of-digital-technologies-to-enhance-access-to-assistive-technology

World Health Organization. (2025b). More than 30-year difference in life expectancy highlights health inequities. United Nations News. https://news.un.org/en/story/2025/05/1162931

Writer, A. S. (2025, April 29). Implementing white-box AI for enhanced transparency in enterprise systems. AiThority. https://aithority.com/machine-learning/implementing-white-box-ai-for-enhanced-transparency-in-enterprise-systems/

Xu, K., Soucat, A., & Kutzin, J. (2019). *Public spending on health: A closer look at global trends.* World Health Organization.

Xu, M. A., Choi, J., Capasso, A., & DiClemente, R. J. (2024). Improving HPV Vaccination Uptake Among Adolescents in Low Resource Settings: Sociocultural and Socioeconomic Barriers and Facilitators. *Adolescent Health, Medicine and Therapeutics*, *15*, 73–82. DOI: 10.2147/AHMT.S394119 PMID: 39100520

Xu, T., Yang, X., He, X., & Wu, J. (2022). The Study on Cervical Cancer Burden in 127 Countries and Its Socioeconomic Influence Factors. *Journal of Epidemiology and Global Health*, *13*(1), 154–161. DOI: 10.1007/s44197-022-00081-1 PMID: 36542301

Yan, C. H., Lin, K. X., Zheng, X. Y., & Meng, X. H. (2025). Interrupted time series analysis of the impact of DIP reform on hospitalization costs in different types of hospitals. *Frontiers in Public Health*, *13*, 1644476. DOI: 10.3389/fpubh.2025.1644476 PMID: 41179796

Yang, J., & Yang, Y. (2022). Regulatory lessons from China's COVID-19 vaccines development and approval policies. *Acta Materia Medica*, *1*(1), 16–25. DOI: 10.15212/AMM-2021-0008

Yates, R. (2009). Universal health care and the removal of user fees. *Lancet*, *373*(9680), 2078–2081. DOI: 10.1016/S0140-6736(09)60258-0 PMID: 19362359

Yaya, S., & Ghose, B. (2019). Global Inequality in Maternal Health Care Service Utilization: Implications for Sustainable Development Goals. *Health Equity*, *3*(1), 145–154. DOI: 10.1089/heq.2018.0082 PMID: 31289773

Yeung, A. W. K., Torkamani, A., Butte, A. J., Glicksberg, B. S., Schuller, B., Rodriguez, B., Ting, D. S. W., Bates, D., Schaden, E., Peng, H., Willschke, H., van der Laak, J., Car, J., Rahimi, K., Celi, L. A., Banach, M., Kletecka-Pulker, M., Kimberger, O., Eils, R., & Atanasov, A. G. (2023). The promise of digital healthcare technologies. *Frontiers in Public Health*, *11*, 1196596. Advance online publication. DOI: 10.3389/fpubh.2023.1196596 PMID: 37822534

Yin, L., Ng, F., Rutherford-Rojas, M., Williams, M., Cornes, S., Fernandez, A., Garcia, M. E., Khoong, E. C., & Khoong, C. A. C. (2022). Assessing medical student readiness to navigate language barriers in telehealth: Cross-sectional survey study. *JMIR Medical Education*, *8*(3), e36096. https://mededu.jmir.org/2022/3/e36096. DOI: 10.2196/36096 PMID: 35969421

Younus, A., & Zaenuri, M. (2024). Public-private collaboration to overcome the digital divide in government digital transformation. ResearchGate. https://www.researchgate.net/publication/381006838

Younus, M., & Zaenuri, M. (2024). Public-private collaboration to overcome the digital divide in digital transformation of government. Digital Zone: Jurnal Teknologi Informasi dan Komunikasi, 15(1), 28–41.

Zadey, S., & Sharma, D. (2025). From decolonizing global health to neo-colonization by local elites: From the frying pan into the fire. *PLOS Global Public Health*, *5*(2), e0004196. Advance online publication. DOI: 10.1371/journal.pgph.0004196 PMID: 39908326

Zagorski, N. (2005). Profile of Xiaodong Wang. *Proceedings of the National Academy of Sciences of the United States of America*, *103*(1), 7–9. DOI: 10.1073/pnas.0509187103 PMID: 16380419

Zahariadis, N. (2019). The multiple streams framework: Structure, limitations, prospects. In *Theories of the policy process* (2nd ed., pp. 65–92). Routledge. DOI: 10.4324/9780367274689-3

Zajko, M. (2022). Artificial intelligence, algorithms, and social inequality: Sociological contributions to contemporary debates. *Sociology Compass*, *16*(3), e12962. Advance online publication. DOI: 10.1111/soc4.12962

Zhai, S., Wang, Q., Zhu, Z., Han, R., Lv, Y., Zhu, C., Zhang, R., Zhang, L., & Yang, L. (2025). Impact of Market Authorization Holder (MAH) system on pharmaceutical innovation in China. *Journal of Pharmaceutical Policy and Practice*, *18*(1), 2551794. DOI: 10.1080/20523211.2025.2551794 PMID: 40918402

Zhang, X., Chen, S., & Tang, S. (2025). *Comparative analysis of the national immunization programmes in select ASEAN and SAARC countries: Progress and challenges.* https://iris.who.int/bitstream/handle/10665/380387/9789290620785-eng.pdf

Zhang, H., Fu, X., Wu, Y., Tang, Y., Jin, H., & Xie, B. (2025). The impact of DRG-based payment reform on inpatient healthcare utilization: Evidence from a natural experiment in China. *Health Care*, *13*(19), 2424. DOI: 10.3390/healthcare13192424 PMID: 41095510

Zhang, H., Patenaude, B., Zhang, H., Jit, M., & Fang, H. (2024). Global vaccine coverage and childhood survival estimates: 1990–2019. *Bulletin of the World Health Organization*, *102*(4), 276–287. DOI: 10.2471/BLT.23.290129 PMID: 38562199

Zhang, J., & Li, X. (2025). Technological and industrial trends in China's pharmaceutical sector. *Frontiers in Pharmacology*, *16*, 1579037. DOI: 10.3389/fphar.2025.1579037 PMID: 41035909

Zhang, J., Tang, S., & Sun, P. (2025). From command-control to lifecycle regulation: Balancing innovation and safety in China's pharmaceutical legislation. *Health Care, 13*(6), 588. Advance online publication. DOI: 10.3390/healthcare13060588 PMID: 40150438

Zhang, P., Dong, L., Chen, H., Chai, Y., & Liu, J. (2018). The Rise and Need for Mobile Apps for Maternal and Child Health Care in China: Survey Based on App Markets. *JMIR mHealth and uHealth, 6*(6), e140. DOI: 10.2196/mhealth.9302 PMID: 29884601

Zhao, B., & Wu, J. (2023). Impact of China's national volume-based procurement on drug procurement price, volume, and expenditure: An interrupted time series analysis in Tianjin. *International Journal of Health Policy and Management, 12*, 7724. DOI: 10.34172/ijhpm.2023.7724 PMID: 38618801

Zhao, F. (Ed.). (2006). *Maximize business profits through e-partnerships*. IRM Press. DOI: 10.4018/978-1-59140-788-1

Zilka, N., & Novak, M. (2006). The tangled story of Alois Alzheimer. *Bratislavské Lekárske Listy, 107*(9-10), 343–345. PMID: 17262985

Zulman, D. M., Wong, E. P., Slightam, C., Gregory, A., Jacobs, J. C., Kimerling, R., Blonigen, D. M., Peters, J., & Heyworth, L. (2019). Making connections: Nationwide implementation of video telehealth tablets to address access barriers in veterans. *JAMIA Open, 2*(3), 323–329. DOI: 10.1093/jamiaopen/ooz024 PMID: 32766533

Zwetsloot, R. (2020, April). *China's approach to tech talent competition: Policies, results, and the developing global response*. Brookings Institution. https://www.brookings.edu/articles/chinas-approach-to-tech-talent-competition/

About the Contributors

Cong Sui is a HealthTech innovator and consultant with dual PhDs and an MBA. He is currently working in West Midlands Health Tech Innovation Accelerator supported by West Midlands Combined Authority. He devotes himself to the whole innovation journey, including the initial innovation, commercialising innovations, investing innovations and the final adoption into global health system. He aims to accelerate innovations and apply entrepreneurial skills to deliver quality healthcare services and address the global health challenges, e.g. sustainability, health equity, universal health coverage, etc. He was invited as an Investment Mentor at the Asian Financial Forum (AFF). He participated in a consulting project aimed at developing an innovative national health system for the Saudi Arabia Ministry of Health. Additionally, he acts as a contributor to establish the Global Health & Digital Innovation Foundation. Dr Sui is also a research fellow in the Healthcare Technologies Institute based at the University of Birmingham. As a biomaterial scientist and chemical engineer, his extensive research backgrounds encompass orthopedic wound, biomaterial, nanotechnology, imaging and microencapsulation. Dr. Sui has published 12 papers and has filed 2 patents. One of his patented technology has addressed a critical challenge in the FMCG sector, garnering attention from more than 20 national and international companies. This work has been published in Chemical Engineering Science, invited by an executive editor of the journal. In addition, he conducted several industrial R&D projects for FMCG companies, including Unilever, Firmenich and Philips UK. Dr Sui was awarded an MBA in Global Health (with distinction) from the Global Business School for Health at University College London in 2024. He completed his first PhD in Biomaterials at Hefei National Laboratory for Physical Sciences at the Microscale, University of Science and Technology of China in 2017, followed by a second PhD in Chemical Engineering from the University of Birmingham in 2018. In addition to his academic achievements, Dr Sui also attended executive courses in Venture Capital Fundamentals at London Business School, Leading Digital Transformation in Health

Care at Harvard University and Business, International Relations and the Political Economy at London School of Economics and Political Science.

Poshan (Sam) Yu is a Chinese-Australian professional with an astonishingly diverse background and an extensive collection of remarkable accomplishments. In the academic sphere, he currently teaches at the University of Victoria Program at Soochow University. Previously, he held the position of an external professor of financial technology and finance at SKEMA Business School. He also serves as a visiting researcher at the Australian Studies Centre of Shanghai University, a guest professor at emlyon business school China, and an adjunct faculty member at George Washington University's master (finance) program at Renmin University of China. As a visiting professor at Krirk University in Thailand and an EU-Asia research coordinator at the European Business Institute in Luxembourg, he brings a truly global perspective to his teaching and research activities. He is a member of the IP & Innovation Researchers of Asia (IPIRA) Network and the Global South Dialogue on Economic Crime (GSDEC), further enriching his academic engagement. His prior role as a casual academic at the University of South Australia Business School has significantly enhanced and diversified his academic portfolio. From September 2020 to February 2021, he held the position of visiting scholar at The Chinese University of Hong Kong on two occasions. His scholarly pursuits are extensive and multifaceted. As an editor for the European Academic Journal (Special Issue) - European Business Institute in Luxembourg, an editor for Humanities & Social Sciences Communications (an SSCI-indexed journal), and an associate editor for the International Journal of Interdisciplinary Research in Social Science, he plays a crucial role in the dissemination of knowledge. He is an ad hoc reviewer for a number of prestigious journals and academic presses, including Applied Economics, Applied Artificial Intelligence, Cogent Economics & Finance, Humanities and Social Sciences Communications, Journal of Chinese Economic and Business Studies, Journal of Digital Learning and Education, The Singapore Economic Review, ILMA Journal of Social Sciences & Economics, Journal of Environmental Issues and Climate Change, Advances in Global Economic and Business Journal, The Interdisciplinary Social Sciences Journal Collection, Common Ground Research Networks, Imprint - Xi'an Jiaotong-Liverpool University, Innovative Teaching and Learning, IBT Journal of Business Studies, Journal of Infrastructure Policy and Development, and Innovative Informatics and Artificial Intelligence Research. Moreover, he is an international editorial advisory board member for several edited books such as Advancing STEM Education and Innovation in a Time of Distance Learning (Scopus-indexed), Multidisciplinary Perspectives Towards Building a Digitally Competent Society (Scopus-indexed), Handbook of Research on SDGs for Economic Development, Social Development, and Environmental Protection, and Implications for Entrepreneurship and Enterprise Development in the Blue Economy. He has released more than 12 journal articles, among which 6 are listed as ABDC: B/SSCI. He has also contributed over 70 peer-reviewed book chapters imprinted by renowned publishers like IGI Global, Routledge, and Springer. He has edited 22 books, with 14 English-edited books indexed by Scopus and 6 Chinese-edited books. Notably, the book about Innovation & Exploration: The Development of FinTech in Jiangsu China has received the 14th Outstanding Achievement Award of Philosophy and Social Sciences in Suzhou and the 3rd prize of the 2018 Jiangsu Provincial Education Science Research Achievement Award by Jiangsu Provincial Department of Education. His receipt of four Xi'an Jiaotong-Liverpool University (XJTLU) National University Teaching Innovation Awards from 2016 to 2020 and being recognized as a top contender in the same national competition in 2016 led to his appointment as the Institute of Leadership and Education Advanced Development (ILEAD) Research Fellow by XJTLU. In 2021, he received The Outstanding Contribution Award for Industrial Research Development in China, CIE100 issued by Wisdom China Magazine: Beijing. Beyond academia, he is actively involved in various industries. He is an entrepreneur and venture capitalist, collaborating with alumni and senior faculty members from Cambridge University. Additionally, he is a guest financial news commentator on over 30 media platforms in China. In the business world, he holds significant positions. He is a regional partner in China for FasterCapital based in Dubai, United Arab Emirates. He also serves as vice president at Tinbowah Investment in Beijing and as an honorary vice president of the Belt and Road Blockchain Association. Furthermore, he mentors businesses for AIC RAISE in Coimbatore, India, the Griffith Industry Mentoring Program in Australia, and University College London Innovation & Enterprise. In 2023, he was invited to act as a venture capital panel judge and mentor at 'Y&Archer A Stream 2023' conference in Jeju, South Korea. His research interests are broad and encompass financial technology, regulatory technology, blockchain, web 3.0 in financial services, generative AI, public-private partnerships, mergers and acquisitions, private equity, venture capital, startups, family offices, IoTs, supply chain finance, intellectual property, art finance, wine, back-door listing, intangible cultural heritage, and Chinese economy & policy. His extensive experience in international fintech, edtech, startup, social media, and cleantech companies across India, the UK, Australia, Hong Kong, and China is truly remarkable. His three-year tenure in significant leadership positions within the Chinese-Australian media marketing and public relations sector, along with his role as an OzAsia Festival Ambassador in Australia, has exerted a profound influence on his current modus operandi as an academic and business consultant. Additionally, it has considerably broadened his perspective within the international multicultural arts community and enlarged his business network. This multifaceted experience has furnished him with a more comprehensive and inclusive outlook on academia, industry, and research. He is fully dedicated to making substantial contributions in these areas and is keen on furthering his development in the future. Incidentally, Sam has an inclination towards wine, arts, and reading.

Sam Agbo was born in the town of Minna, now in Niger State, Nigeria 68 years ago. He is the firstborn to his wonderful parents, John and Janet Agbo. His father served as a policeman, while his mother was a dedicated housewife and entrepreneur who invested wholeheartedly in his primary and secondary education. From a young age, Dr. Agbo's potential was evident. As a school librarian in primary school, he developed a deep love for reading, writing, and listening to short stories on the radio—a pastime that nurtured his creativity and imagination. In 1973, he became the Senior Prefect (Head boy) of St. Paul's College, Zaria. During this time, he balanced his responsibilities as a leader, a goalkeeper for the school's football team, and a dedicated student, achieving academic excellence. In 1975, Dr. Agbo embarked on his university education at the University of Lagos, where he graduated as a medical doctor. Over the past four decades, he has committed his life to serving others, focusing on saving mothers, children, and those affected by conflict and disasters. His work has spanned multiple countries, where he has provided technical leadership to help rebuild and strengthen he

***

Bàbá Ayé is the senior policy officer responsible for the Health and Social Services Sector of Public Services International (PSI), the global union federation of 30 million women and men delivering public services in 155 countries across the world. Bàbá is also Co-President of the Geneva Global Health Hub (G2H2) and a contributing editor of the Review of African Political Economy (ROAPE). He has served on several World Health Organization (WHO) guideline development & technical advisory groups, including the WHO COVID-19 Infection Prevention and Control Guideline Development Group, the WHO guidelines development group on policy and support for community-based health worker programmes, and the WHO Technical Advisory Group on Integrated Health and Care Workforce. Before joining PSI, Bàbá worked with the Medical and Health Workers' Union of Nigeria (MHWUN), leaving the union as Deputy Secretary General, after twenty-five years of service. He also served at different times in Nigeria as spokesperson of the National Association of Nigerian Students (NANS) during a period of military dictatorship; National Convener of the United Action for Democracy (UAD) and Deputy National Secretary of the Labour Party (LP). Bàbá helped form the West

African Health Sector Unions' Network (WAHSUN) in the 2000s and served as its pioneering General Secretary.

Benny Godwin J. Davidson is a seasoned academic and experienced Management Consultant with over 12 years of expertise in teaching, research, and industry. He currently serves as an Assistant Professor at the University of the Fraser Valley and is a Sessional Faculty member at University Canada West and Acsenda School of Management. Through his ongoing research, Dr. Davidson continues to contribute to knowledge advancement, bringing fresh perspectives to both his consulting and teaching practices. His research interests include consumer behavior, marketing strategy, and real estate purchase decisions. Additionally, Dr. Davidson serves as a member of the Research Ethics Board, ensuring the integrity of research practices at his institutions.

Julie Davies is Professor of Healthcare Management and Leadership Development and Head of Business School Accreditations, Rankings and Reputation, including UN PRME, at Brunel Business School. She is an editorial board member of Long Range Planning and chairs the EDI subcommittee of Kirkwood Hospice. Julie has designed and delivered executive education programmes in Australia, China, India, Kuwait, Mozambique, Russia, Saudi Arabia, Singapore,Vietnam, at London Business School, and globally for an international business school deans' programme. Previously, she was inaugural Director of the MBA Health programme and a professor at University College London, Deputy Director of the Chartered Association of Business Schools, and managed award winning postgraduate distance learning programmes in finance and economics at the School of Oriental and African Studies. She is a law graduate and has a PhD in strategic leadership from Warwick University. Professor Davies' research interests include hybrid and responsible leadership, strategic management, societal impact and qualitative research.

Jossy P. George is a distinguished academic and leader, currently serving as the Director of CHRIST (Deemed to be University) at the BGR Campus in Bangalore. With a unique combination of qualifications in both Computer Science and Human Resources, he holds dual master's degrees in these fields. His educational journey includes completing the Faculty Development Programme (FDPM) from the prestigious Indian Institute of Management (IIM), Ahmedabad, and obtaining a Doctorate in Computer Science from Christ University. His career is marked by extensive research, particularly in the area of "Technology in Higher Education," where he has led numerous significant projects. His contributions to the academic world extend beyond research, as he has authored several research papers that have been published in both national and international journals.

Nabeel Goheer joined Central Superior Services of the Government of Pakistan in 1994. He started with the Foreign Economic Affairs division and later served as the Manager of Prime Minister's Program 2010, Special Assistant to the Minister for Planning and Development and General Manager of Small and Medium Enterprise Development Authority before moving to the United Kingdom in 2004. After completing Ph.D. from the Judge Business School of the University of Cambridge, he became a multilateral diplomat in 2007 and worked with the United Nations and Commonwealth systems for fifteen years in progressively responsible positions until 2021- last served as an Assistant Secretary-General. Presently he is the Vice President of PATH – a social enterprise in global health advancing equity, innovation and partnerships. He is the Chief of Asia, Middle East and Europe operations and the High Representative for China. In the last four years, he has spearheaded several strategic initiatives including the G-20 engagement, innovative financing, and the Climate-Health program. In addition to his executive role, Nabeel is on the Governing Boards of Middlesex University, the Royal Overseas League, UK, and the Foundation of Appropriate Technologies in Health, Switzerland. Furthermore, he is a Health Executive in Residence at the UCL Global Business School for Health; a member of the World Economic Forum's Ai Resilient Governance and Regulation group; and a leadership resource for the UN System Staff College in Italy. Nabeel is married, lives in London, and is passionate about leadership development for responsible global governance, systemic societal transformation and harmonious coexistence.

Adrien Lucci is a healthcare leader with a strong academic and clinical background. He holds a Master of Business Administration with Distinction from University College London's Global Business School for Health. He also earned an MSc in Sports Medicine, Exercise and Health from UCL and a Master's in Physiotherapy from Université Libre de Bruxelles. Currently serving as Regional Manager for Colosseum Dental UK, Adrien focuses on driving operational excellence, sustainable growth, and innovation across dental practices nationwide.

Marwan Madkhali is a healthcare bossines analyst and digital health consultant with an MBA from UCL, specializing in emerging technologies in healthcare and transformation strategy across the GCC.

Peter Varghese Muttungal is Professor of Social Sciences and the Campus Administrator & Director of Student Affairs at CHRIST (Deemed to be University) Delhi NCR. He has a Ph.D in Educational Psychology from Bharathiar University, Coimbatore. He also completed an EdLEAP Executive Leadership Program from Indian Institute of Management (IIM), Kolkata and is a UB Fellow for 2022-23 from Singapore Management University. His research interest is in the areas of Educational Leadership in Higher Education.

Emeka Nwankwo possesses hands-on field experience in Result-Based Monitoring & Evaluation (RBME) and Digital Health policy & program management. He currently works in the M&E division of Nigeria's Federal Ministry of Health (Department of Health Planning, Research and Statistics). In his current role, he has conducted impact evaluation of health system components within various health institutions and national programs. He has also facilitated sessions across the various building blocks of Digital Health. He is currently conducting global health research at Nagasaki University, Japan.

Nishi Priya is a research scholar at Christ University, Delhi NCR. She holds a Master's in Counseling Psychology, where she graduated with the first rank in her class. Her academic and research interests lie at the intersection of applied psychology, organizational behavior, and artificial intelligence.

Ameneh Ghazal Saatchi is the Founder and CEO of the Global Policy Network (GPN), an independent policy institute committed to advancing equitable and locally relevant policies in health, education, and sustainability. Through GPN, Ameneh bridges the gap between innovation and implementation by connecting policymakers, academia, and industry leaders. The organisation drives impact through evidence-based research, policy advocacy, strategic convening, and cross-sector collaboration. A recognised health policy leader with extensive UK and international experience, Ameneh works at the intersection of research, policy, and practice. Her mission is to empower organisations to move beyond service delivery and embrace evidence-based advocacy, shaping policies that influence the future of healthcare systems globally. Ameneh is an ACE-certified coach and PRINCE2-qualified project leader, with her work having been presented at major conferences and published in top academic journals. Passionate about innovation, equity, and collaboration, she is dedicated to driving sustainable transformation in healthcare worldwide.

Melanie Stanton is a graduate student in pursuit of her Master of Public Health in Epidemiology at the UT Health Houston School of Public Health. Ms. Stanton is passionate about public health and health equity, with particular interest in maternal and child health, chronic, and autoimmune diseases.

Jiawei Tang is the Co-founder and COO of Global Biopharma Partnerships. She holds a Master's degree in Digital Transformation in Healthcare Management and brings over 15 years of extensive experience in the healthcare and life sciences industry, with a proven track record in sales, corporate strategy, and marketing.

Her professional background includes 12 years in management roles at Pfizer, a global pharmaceutical leader, and one year as Commercial Strategy Director at Resolian, a renowned contract research organization (CRO). She has successfully led and implemented numerous brand transformation, corporate strategy, integrated marketing communications, and business innovation projects across major markets, including the United States, the United Kingdom, Australia, and China. In addition to her professional work, Jiawei serves in volunteer leadership roles at several nonprofit healthcare organizations, including as a Geographic Expansion Leadership Member at the Healthcare Business Association,as an Advisory Borad member of One Patient One cure and as Vice President of the Chinese Biopharmaceutical Association Greater Philadelphia.

Shai Wen is a University College London (UCL) MBA graduate with cross-sector experience spanning investment management and consulting, with a focus on healthcare transformation, digital health innovation, and cross-border healthcare applications. She has also gained experience in the pharmaceutical industry through roles at Viatris and Fosun Pharma. Her work focuses on the intersection of artificial intelligence, diagnostic innovation, and healthcare systems transformation, particularly in the translation of AI-enabled tools into real-world clinical and primary care settings.

Yuan Yuan is country representative in the PATH China representative office in Shanghai. She manages the relationships with partners in China and oversees management and business development for PATH China office. Ms. Yuan joined PATH in January 2007 and has been in multiple roles including Finance & Administration Officer, Project Manager and Alliance Manager. In her 18 years at PATH, her projects include Japanese Encephalitis vaccine WHO prequalification, Rotavirus vaccine development, Pneumococcal conjugate vaccine development, Oral Polio Vaccine international clinical trial, Sabin IPV D antigen international standardization and HPV vaccine prequalification. She is familiar with the life cycle of vaccines including manufacturing, quality, clinical, regulatory, pharmacovigilance, biosafety and biosecurity. In January 2023, Ms. Yuan was elected as the Secretary General of the Council for the Promotion of International Vaccine Cooperation (CPIVC) under the Chinese Association for Vaccines (CAV). Prior to joining PATH, she worked as a project manager with Integrity Metals in Singapore and Indonesia. Ms. Yuan obtained her B.A., MBA, and MPH from Peking University.

Index

A

B

C

D

E

F

G

H

I

L

M

O

P

R

S

T

U

V

W

www.ingramcontent.com/pod-product-compliance
Lightning Source LLC
LaVergne TN
LVHW062333300926
849161LV00007B/1671